Scotland

FOR

DUMMIES

6TH EDITION

Scotland

FOR

DUMMIES®

6TH EDITION

by Barry Shelby

FOR

DUMMIES®

A Wiley Brand

Scotland For Dummies®, 6th Edition

Published by
John Wiley & Sons, Inc.
111 River St.
Hoboken, NJ 07030-5774
www.wiley.com

For general information on our other products and services, please contact our Customer Care Department within the U.S. at 877-762-2974, outside the U.S. at 317-572-3993, or fax 317-572-4002.

For technical support, please visit www.wiley.com/techsupport.

Wiley publishes in a variety of print and electronic formats and by print-on-demand. Some material included with standard print versions of this book may not be included in e-books or in print-on-demand. If this book refers to media such as a CD or DVD that is not included in the version you purchased, you may download this material at http://booksupport.wiley.com. For more information about Wiley products, visit www.wiley.com.

ISBN 978-0-470-38514-2 (pbk); ISBN 978-1-118-05849-7 (ebk); ISBN 978-1-118-05850-3 (ebk); ISBN 978-1-118-05851-0 (ebk)

Manufactured in the United States of America

10 9 8 7 6 5 4 3 2

WILEY

About the Author

Barry Shelby was born in 1960 in Berkeley, California, where he graduated from the University of California in 1982. He later received a master's degree in journalism from Northwestern University in Illinois. For 13 years, he was an editor at *World Press Review* magazine in Manhattan. Since moving to Scotland in 1997, Shelby has been a castle caretaker on the Clyde Coast, a "temp" with the national railway company, and a freelance contributor to various newspapers and magazines, including *FreeRange, The Guardian, The Glasgow Herald,* and *The List* magazine, among others. The author of *Frommer's Edinburgh & Glasow* and *Frommer's Edinburgh & Glasgow Day by Day,* he is married to a Scot and currently lives on a croft in the Outer Hebrides.

Publisher's Acknowledgments

Some of the people who helped bring this book to market include the following:

Editorial

Editors: Ian Skinnari,
Development Editor;
Katie Robinson, Production Editor

Copy Editor: Faren Bachelis

Cartographer: Guy Ruggiero

Editorial Assistant: Andrea Kahn

Senior Photo Editor: Richard Fox

Cover Photos:
Front: ©Deco / Alamy Images
Back: ©Blaine Harrington III
Photography

Cartoons: Rich Tennant
(www.the5thwave.com)

Composition Services

Project Coordinator:
Sheree Montgomery

Layout and Graphics: Joyce Haughey,
SDJumper, Heather Pope,
Julie Trippetti

Proofreaders: Laura Albert,
Cara L. Buitron

Indexer: Estalita Slivoskey

Publishing and Editorial for Consumer Dummies

Kathleen Nebenhaus, Vice President and Executive Publisher

David Palmer, Associate Publisher

Kristin Ferguson-Wagstaffe, Product Development Director

Publishing for Technology Dummies

Andy Cummings, Vice President and Publisher

Composition Services

Debbie Stailey, Director of Composition Services

Contents at a Glance

Maps at a Glance

Table of Contents

Introduction

● ●

*T*his guide is a departure from conventional travel guidebooks and you're no dummy for choosing it. Rather than just throwing out dizzying reams of information for you to plod through until you're too exhausted to distinguish Edinburgh from Inverness, *Scotland For Dummies,* 6th Edition, sifts for you the proverbial golden wheat from the disposable chaff.

I will take you through the whole process of putting together your trip to Scotland, from the ins and outs of a manageable itinerary to advice on choosing the right places to stay or how much time to allot for attractions and activities. Each and every recommendation may not be perfect for you. The goal is to show what may interest you (whether it's castles, museums, pubs, or open countryside) and what, on the other hand, may not float your boat. Your time is valuable, so this book strives to get right to the point. *Scotland For Dummies,* 6th Edition, is designed to give you a clear picture of what you need to know and what your options are, so that you can make informed decisions easily and efficiently.

About This Book

Some parts of Scotland are bound to interest you more than others, so don't feel as if you have to read this book cover to cover. If you want to focus on metropolitan life, for example, then simply concentrate on Part III's chapters, devoted to Edinburgh and Glasgow. If the lore of the Loch Ness monster or the lure of the Hebridean Islands intrigues you, then you can find valuable information in Part VI. And if you're drawn to picturesque settings that are less touristy than the famous attractions, then *Scotland For Dummies,* 6th Edition, can point you in the right direction as well.

Of course this guide has up-to-date information and recommendations on the best hotels and restaurants in Scotland's major cities and regions. It also has information on shopping and nightlife, attractions, walking tours, helpful historical asides, and details on what makes Scotland unique — whether that's golf courses or the tallest mountains and most pristine seas in the entire United Kingdom.

Please be advised that travel information is subject to change at any time, and this is especially true of prices. It never hurts to check the Internet or write or call ahead for confirmation of the current situation when making your travel plans. The author, his editors, and publisher can't be held responsible for the experiences of readers while traveling. Your safety is important to us, however, so we encourage you to stay alert and be aware of your surroundings. Keep a close eye on cameras, purses, and wallets, all favorite targets of thieves and pickpockets.

Conventions Used in This Book

Scotland For Dummies, 6th Edition, is designed to be a quick read (in whatever order you choose), so the listings for hotels, restaurants, and sights are standardized throughout the chapters. Each listing offers you an idea of what a place is like and then gives you details about specific addresses, prices, and hours of operation.

Other conventions include:

- ✔ Abbreviations for commonly accepted credit cards used throughout this book.
  - AE: American Express
  - DC: Diners Club
  - MC: MasterCard
  - V: Visa

- ✔ An alphabetical listing of hotels, restaurants, and attractions in each chapter.

- ✔ Page references for maps, given whenever possible, to help you locate hotels, restaurants, attractions, and the like. If a hotel, restaurant, or attraction is in an out-of-the-way area, however, it may not appear on a map. In chapters on the major cities, information about bus routes, and, in Glasgow, subway stops, is given as well.

- ✔ Prices are listed in British pounds sterling (£). At the time of writing, a pound was equal to about $1.50–$1.60 in U.S. money, but there have been quite large variations in exchange rates over the past decade. Before the financial/banking crisis of 2008–09, the pound was equal to more than £2. If you're concerned about the current exchange rates, check with your bank.

Price is often a factor when choosing hotels and restaurants, and Scotland is not a particularly cheap place to visit. The relative costs of accommodations and meals are indicated with dollar signs. Specific prices are given, too, but the dollar signs are a quick way for you to see if a place is in your budget. My scale for accommodations and restaurants ranges from one dollar sign ($) to four ($$$$). Most hotel prices are per night for double rooms (rather than per person per night). The cost of a meal generally means dinner with at least two courses and a drink per person. The following table helps you decipher what the dollar signs mean.

Cost	Hotel	Restaurant
$	Less than £75	About £15
$$	£75–£150	£15–£30
$$$	£151–£200	£31–£50
$$$$	More than £200	More than £50

Due to the range of accommodations in Edinburgh and Glasgow, the hotels and guesthouses in Chapters 11 and 12 (on Edinburgh and Glasgow, respectively) are divided into two categories — favorites and those that don't quite make my preferred list but still get a seal of approval. Don't hesitate to consider the "runner-up" hotels — the amenities and the services they offer make them all reasonable choices as you decide where to rest your head at night.

Foolish Assumptions?

This book makes some assumptions about you and what your needs may be as a traveler. Here's what *Dummies* guides generally think may apply to you.

- ✔ You're an experienced traveler who hasn't had much time to explore Scotland but wants expert advice when you finally do get a chance to enjoy any part of the country.

- ✔ You're an inexperienced traveler looking for guidance when determining whether to take a trip to Scotland and how to plan for it.

- ✔ You're not looking for a book that provides all the information available about Scotland or that lists every hotel, restaurant, or attraction available to you. Instead, you want a book that focuses on the places that will give you the best, unique experiences in Scotland.

If you fit any of these criteria, then *Scotland For Dummies,* 6th Edition, is the book for you.

How This Book Is Organized

Scotland For Dummies, 6th Edition, consists of five parts. The chapters within each part cover specific components in detail.

Part 1: Introducing Scotland

This part directs you to the very best Scotland has to offer and touches on issues you need to consider before actually getting down to the nitty-gritty of trip planning. Chapter 3 gives you a rundown of the various regions covered in *Scotland for Dummies*. Part I includes a brief history of Scotland as well as recommended reading, when and where to go, and detailed itineraries to consider.

Part II: Planning Your Trip to Scotland

This part gets down to the nuts and bolts of trip planning, including information on managing your money, options on getting to Scotland, getting around the country, and reserving hotel rooms. It also addresses special considerations for families, seniors, travelers with disabilities, and students, as well as gay, lesbian, and transgender travelers.

Part III: Edinburgh and Glasgow

You may only have time to see Scotland's two major cities, so I devote a chapter to each, with details on hotels, restaurants, top attractions, shopping, walking tours, and nightlife. Plus, you can find information on how to get around, how much time you need to see things, suggested itineraries, and recommended side trips.

Part IV: The Major Regions

This part contains chapters on Scotland's major regions: from Southern Scotland to the Highlands, from Ayrshire and Argyll to the Hebridean Islands. Each chapter has suggestions on accommodations, places to dine out, and attractions, not to mention some useful information on shopping and nightlife. For a quick overview of Scotland, including descriptions of these regions, flip to Chapter 3.

Part V: The Part of Tens

Every *For Dummies* book has a Part of Tens. These breezy chapters have down-and-dirty lists that highlight the best: whether golf courses, castles, or natural attractions.

In the back of the book, I've included an appendix — the *Dummies*'s "Quick Concierge" printed on yellow paper— containing lots of handy information you may need when traveling in Scotland, such as phone numbers and addresses of emergency personnel or area hospitals and pharmacies, lists of local newspapers and magazines, protocol for sending mail or finding taxis, and more. Check out this appendix when you're faced with the little questions that may come up as you travel.

Icons Used in This Book

Watch out for the icons sprinkled throughout the margins of this book. They are signposts that highlight special tips, draw your attention to things you don't want to miss, and give you a heads-up on a variety of topics.

Indicates money-saving tips and/or great deals.

 Highlights the best each destination has to offer in all categories — hotels, restaurants, attractions, activities, shopping, and nightlife.

 Identifies annoying or potentially dangerous situations such as tourist traps, unsafe neighborhoods, budgetary rip-offs, and other things to beware.

 Advice on things to do and ways to schedule your time.

 Attractions, hotels, restaurants, and activities that are particularly hospitable to children or people traveling with kids.

 This icon points out secret little finds or useful resources that are worth the extra bit of effort to get to or find.

Where to Go from Here

As I've already mentioned, this travel guide isn't designed to be read from beginning to end (although you're certainly welcome to do so). Instead, it provides detailed and well-organized information on loads of topics — from getting around Scotland to finding the best restaurants. So choose your own adventure and look for the topics or destinations you want to explore by using the Table of Contents or the Index.

As you start to prepare for your visit to Scotland, remember that planning is half the fun. Choosing your destinations and solidifying the details shouldn't be a chore. Make the homebound part of the process a voyage of discovery, and you'll end up with a vacation that's much more rewarding and enriching. See you in Scotland!

Part I
Introducing Scotland

The 5th Wave   By Rich Tennant

"It's the room next door. They suggest you deflate your souvenir bagpipes before trying to pack them in your luggage."

In this part . . .

Scotland, with its rich and evocative past, has much to offer the traveler. But visitors don't come here just for the history: The country's vibrant cities, natural beauty, indigenous culture, and friendly people are all additional draws.

This part brings you Scotland's best, from hotels and restaurants to castles and art galleries. You'll find useful itineraries to help you decide what to see if your time is limited. This part also contains a condensed history, a glossary of the Scots' language, a list of suggested books and films to help get you in the mood, and lots more. When's the best season to visit? Are discounts available for seniors or children? What, for heaven's sake, is haggis? Look no further; the answers are here.

Chapter 1

Discovering the Best of Scotland

* *

In This Chapter

▶ Staying in the top hotels and dining in the best restaurants
▶ Discovering the best castles and museums
▶ Drinking in the best pubs and bars

* *

*T*o start things off, let's begin with the highlights: some of the best that Scotland has to offer travelers, from unforgettable experiences and attractions to excellent hotels and top-rated restaurants; from first-class castles and museums to a selection of world-renowned golf courses, friendly pubs, and more. Entries in this chapter — as well as listings later in the book — are ordered alphabetically, under each main heading, not by preference. Keep your eyes open for the "Best of the Best" icons throughout *Scotland For Dummies.*

The Best Travel Experiences

✔ **Ardnamurchan Peninsula:** One of the more easily reached but seemingly remote areas of the Western Highlands, and isolated enough to feel like an island, this forested and mountainous neck of land stretching toward the Inner Hebridean Islands ends at the most westerly point of the entire British mainland. See Chapter 18.

✔ **Edinburgh's Old Town:** This district of the capital is probably the most visited location in all of Scotland — and not without good reason. Running along the spine of a hill and extending from the ancient castle to the history-filled Palace of Holyroodhouse, Edinburgh's Old Town is a delight to wander through. Make sure you take time to explore the alleyways. See Chapter 11.

✔ **Glasgow's City Centre:** The thriving heart of a modern European city, the core of Glasgow — Scotland's largest metropolis — offers some of the finest examples of monumental Victorian architecture in the world. The streets here follow a strict grid pattern, so you don't need to worry about getting lost. See Chapter 12.

✔ **Glen Coe:** Glen Coe is such a spectacular valley that it's hard to reconcile such natural beauty with its bloody history. The visitor center near Glencoe village is an award-winner, with details on hiking, geology, and the clan battles that occurred here. See Chapter 18.

✔ **Loch Lomond:** Located so near Glasgow, this loch is the largest inland body of water in all of Great Britain. It's only about a 30- to 45-minute drive or train ride from the Glasgow city limits. When you reach the loch, you can hike, canoe, or just relax. See Chapter 16.

✔ **Loch Ness:** This loch is mysterious and legendary — if somewhat overrated in my mind. In addition to looking out for Nessie, the elusive and mythical monster, you should seek out other local attractions, such as Urquhart (pronounced *ir*-ket) Castle, and travel around the surrounding countryside. See Chapter 18.

✔ **Mull** or **Skye:** These two islands of the Inner Hebrides are among the easiest and most impressive ones to reach from the mainland. However accessible, they still provide some amazing scenery and a true taste of life on the many isles that cover the western shores of Scotland. See Chapter 19.

✔ **Outer Hebrides:** From Lewis in the north — with its standing stones, desolate moors, and windswept cliffs — to Harris and its blue seas lapping on white, shell-sand beaches, and then farther south to more rocky hills, innumerable tidal inlets, and dune-lined beaches, the Outer Hebrides (aka Western Isles) are unequaled in Scotland for a maritime and island experience. See Chapter 19.

✔ **Sands of Morar:** North of the quiet port of Arisaig in the Western Highlands, the Sands of Morar offer beautiful bleached beaches set against postcard-pretty seas. You can almost reach out and touch the islands of Rhum and Eigg from here; or catch a ferry to mountainous Skye from nearby Mallaig. See Chapter 18.

✔ **Sandwood Bay:** An environmentally protected area near Blairmore in the Northwest Highlands has a beach that, by most accounts, is the most beautiful and unsullied in all of Great Britain's mainland sandy shorelines. See Chapter 18.

The Best Accommodations in Edinburgh and Glasgow

Edinburgh

✔ **Best Boutique Hotel: The Bonham.** In an upscale, western New Town neighborhood of the Scottish capital, the Bonham offers some of the most alluring accommodations in a city filled with fine hotels. See Chapter 11.

✔ **Best Traditional Hotel: Balmoral Hotel.** With a Michelin-star restaurant, attentive doormen dressed in kilts, and a romantic pile to rival any others, the Balmoral is legendary, and it's located smack in the heart of the capital. See Chapter 11.

✔ **Best Rooms near the Castle: The Witchery by the Castle.** As its list of celebrity guests testifies, The Witchery offers opulence and individuality in a manner not seen anywhere else in Old Town. See Chapter 11.

✔ **Best Hotel in Leith: Malmaison.** At the port of Leith, Malmaison is about a 15-minute ride north of Edinburgh's center. Named after Joséphine's mansion outside Paris, the hotel celebrates the Auld Alliance of France and Scotland, and occupies a Victorian building built in 1900. See Chapter 11.

✔ **Best Hotel Health Spa: Sheraton Grand Hotel.** Near the city's conference center, the Sheraton Grand has wonderful facilities in an adjoining building. Especially noteworthy is the roof-top indoor/outdoor pool. See Chapter 11.

Glasgow

✔ **Best Boutique Hotel: Hotel du Vin at One Devonshire Gardens.** In a West End neighborhood filled with sandstone-fronted town houses, this hotel at the well-known address stands out. It's a recreation of a high-bourgeois, very proper Scottish home from the early 1900s, boasting antique furnishings and discreetly concealed modern comforts. See Chapter 12.

✔ **Best Hip Hotel: Brunswick Hotel.** With only 18 rooms, the Brunswick exudes cool in the city's hip Merchant City district of the City Centre. The design is modern and minimalist, but is executed with character and class. See Chapter 12.

✔ **Best in the Commercial Centre: Blythswood Square.** Linked to the Bonham (see listing in previous section), this hotel and spa, which opened in 2009–10, is the most remarked-upon newcomer in over a decade. See Chapter 12.

The Best Small and Country House Hotels

✔ **Ardanaiseig Hotel,** Kilchrenan, Argyll: This stone Scottish baronial mansion, built in the 1830s, offers a good bit of luxury in an out-of-the-way corner of Argyllshire, on the way toward the Western Highlands. See Chapter 15.

✔ **Argyll Hotel,** Iona, the Hebrides: This charming, traditional hotel, in the village of Iona, is comfortable and environmentally conscious, with its own organic vegetable garden and an ethos of not disturbing the fragile island ecology. See Chapter 19.

✔ **Darroch Learg,** Ballater, the Northeast: This hotel is one of the more highly regarded inns in the Royal Deeside region, near the Queen's estate at Balmoral, several historic castles, and the Speyside whisky trail. See Chapter 17.

✔ **Glenapp Castle,** Ballantrae, South Ayrshire: Glenapp is a beautifully decorated pile close to Stranraer, with Victorian baronial splendor and antiques, oil paintings, and elegant touches. See Chapter 14.

✔ **Knockinaam Lodge,** near Portpatrick, Dumfries, and Galloway: With a Michelin-star restaurant, Knockinaam combines exquisite meals with a secluded seaside setting on the Rhinns of Galloway. See Chapter 14.

✔ **Prestonfield,** Edinburgh: Although it's within the city, this hotel rises from the meadows in Jacobean splendor, amid gardens, pastures, and woodlands, below Arthur's Seat on the south side of the Scottish capital. See Chapter 11.

The Best Dining in Edinburgh and Glasgow

Edinburgh

✔ **Best Cafe: Spoon.** Spoon forks out some of the best soups, salads, sandwiches, and bistro style main courses in Edinburgh — and the freshly made cakes and other sweet stuff are perhaps even better. See Chapter 11.

✔ **Best Fine-Dining Restaurant: Restaurant Martin Wishart.** With one of the city's precious Michelin stars and its most talented chef/owner, Restaurant Martin Wishart is where the leading out-of-town chefs dine when they visit Edinburgh. See Chapter 11.

✔ **Best Italian Restaurant: Santini.** Although many of the more established Italian restaurants in town don't like hearing it, Santini usually gets the rave reviews and sets the highest standards. See Chapter 11.

✔ **Best Modern Scottish Restaurant: Forth Floor.** Combining excellent contemporary Scottish cooking with some commanding vistas over Edinburgh's New Town. See Chapter 11.

✔ **Best Restaurant Views: Oloroso.** This category is almost a dead heat between Oloroso and Forth Floor (see above). The nod just goes to Oloroso. See Chapter 11.

Glasgow

✔ **Best Bistro: Cafe Gandolfi.** This landmark in the Merchant City district offers straightforward and delicious dishes, whether you choose a bowl of Cullen skink (smoked haddock chowder) or a sirloin steak sandwich. See Chapter 12.

✔ **Best Seafood Restaurant: Gamba.** This Commercial Centre basement restaurant celebrated its tenth year in 2008. Over the preceding decade, it proved to be the most consistent place for excellent fish and shellfish meals. See Chapter 12.

✔ **Best Indian Restaurants: The Dhabba** or **Mother India.** Glasgow loves its Indian cuisine, but these two restaurants offer something better than the norm, favoring dishes that are more subtle, in surroundings that are less clichéd than the typical curry houses. See Chapter 12.

✔ **Best Pub Food: Stravaigin Café Bar.** With an award-winning restaurant in the basement, the ground-floor pub Stravaigin offers similarly top-notch quality food — at a fraction of the restaurant price. See Chapter 12.

✔ **Best on a Budget: Wee Curry Shop.** A brief stroll from the shopping precincts of Sauchiehall Street, the Wee Curry Shop is a tiny gem of a restaurant, serving freshly prepared Indian cuisine at bargain prices. See Chapter 12.

The Best Rural Restaurants

✔ **Applecross Inn,** Applecross, the Western Highlands: The inn may not be the easiest place in Scotland to reach, but many visitors agree that the twists and turns of the road to Applecross are well worth the journey for a meal here. See Chapter 18.

✔ **Braidwoods,** Dalry, North Ayrshire: One of the standout restaurants in Ayrshire and holder of a Michelin star and other accolades, Braidwoods is expensive but worth the price. See Chapter 15.

✔ **Creagan House,** Strathyre, the Trossachs: Run by Cherry and Gordon Gunn, the restaurant is part of an unassuming but charming inn in a 17th-century farmhouse. See Chapter 16.

✔ **Mhor,** near Balquhidder, the Trossachs: Just up the road a bit from the Creagan, this loch-side restaurant is a perennial favorite of travelers who love food and are passing through the Trossach mountains. See Chapter 16.

✔ **Restaurant Andrew Fairlie,** Gleneagles Hotel, Auchterarder, Perthshire: It may be the finest dining experience in the country, and Chef Fairlie is arguably the most talented cook in Scotland. See Chapter 16.

✔ **Seafood Cabin,** Skipness, Argyll: Not a restaurant, but I love this place on a sunny summer day, when you can nosh at picnic benches and tables on fresh seafood and take in the view of a castle, the sea, and Isle of Arran. See Chapter 15.

✔ **Three Chimneys Restaurant,** Colbost, Isle of Skye: Probably the most popular and most famous restaurant in the Hebridean Islands, the Three Chimneys serves superb Scottish cuisine paired with produce from Skye, its island home. See Chapter 19.

The Best Castles

✔ **Blair Castle,** Blair, Perthshire: Blair is chock-full o' stuff: art, armor, flags, stag horns, and more goodies not typically found on the standard furniture-and-portrait castle tour. See Chapter 17.

✔ **Caerlaverock Castle,** near Dumfries, Dumfries and Galloway: Once a target of English armies, the impressive ruins of Caerlaverock (pronounced ka-*liver*-ick) are what remain of one of Scotland's more classic medieval castles, and its magnificent moat is still intact. See Chapter 14.

✔ **Castle Tioram,** Blain, Ardnamurchan: The ruins of this small fortress sit along the picturesque shores of Loch Moidart. You can enjoy some good hiking trails near the castle, too. See Chapter 18.

✔ **Doune Castle,** near Stirling: Fans of the film *Monty Python and the Holy Grail* may recognize Doune. Thanks to its limited restoration, visitors get a good idea of what living here in the 14th century was like. See Chapter 16.

✔ **Duart Castle,** Craignure, Isle of Mull: Duart was abandoned in 1751, but thanks to the efforts of Fitzroy Maclean, it was restored from ruins in 1911. It's worth making your way up the narrow, twisting stairs, because you can walk outside on the parapet at the top of the castle. See Chapter 19.

✔ **Eilean Donan Castle,** Dornie, the Highlands: This is probably the most photographed stone pile in Scotland (after Edinburgh Castle, that is). On an islet in Loch Duich, Eilean Donan is a quintessential castle. See Chapter 18.

✔ **Stirling Castle,** Stirling: This castle was the residence of Mary, Queen of Scots, her son James VI of Scotland (and later James I of England), and other Stuart monarchs. One section, the Great Hall, stands out for miles thanks to the creamy, almost yellow exterior that apparently replicates its original color. See Chapter 16.

The Best Cathedrals, Churches, and Abbeys

✔ **Dunfermline Abbey and Palace,** Dunfermline, Fife: This abbey is on the site of a Celtic church and an 11th-century house of worship dedicated to the Holy Trinity; traces of this history are visible beneath gratings in the floor of the old nave. See Chapter 16.

✔ **Glasgow Cathedral,** Glasgow: This cathedral is also known as the Cathedral of St. Kentigern or St. Mungo's, and it dates from the 13th century. The edifice is mainland Scotland's only complete medieval cathedral. See Chapter 12.

✔ **High Kirk of St. Giles,** Edinburgh: Just a brief walk downhill from Edinburgh Castle, this church, sometimes called St. Giles Cathedral —its steeple, in particular — is one of the most important architectural landmarks along the Royal Mile. See Chapter 11.

✔ **Iona Abbey and Nunnery,** Iona, the Hebrides: This spiritual landmark is a significant shrine to the earliest days of Christianity in Scotland. See Chapter 19.

✔ **Jedburgh Abbey,** Jedburgh, the Borders: This abbey is one of four Borders abbeys commissioned by Scots King David I in the 12th century. See Chapter 14.

✔ **Melrose Abbey,** Melrose, the Borders: The heart of Scots King Robert the Bruce is rumored to be buried somewhere on the grounds of this abbey, which sits amid spectacular ruins. See Chapter 14.

✔ **St. Vincent Street Church,** Glasgow: This church offers limited access to visitors, but it's the most visible landmark attributed to the city's great architect, Alexander "Greek" Thomson. See Chapter 12.

The Best Art Galleries

✔ **The Burrell Collection,** Glasgow: This gallery houses the treasures left to Glasgow by Sir William Burrell, a wealthy ship owner and industrialist who had a lifelong passion for art. He started collecting at age 14 and only ceased when he died, at the age of 96, in 1958. See Chapter 12.

✔ **Hunterian Art Gallery,** Glasgow: The Hunterian holds the artistic estate of James McNeill Whistler, with some 60 of his paintings as well as some by the Scottish Colourists. It also boasts a collection of Charles Rennie Mackintosh–designed furnishings. See Chapter 12.

✔ **Kelvingrove Art Gallery and Museum,** Glasgow: This is the remarkable flagship of the city's well-regarded municipal art collection, housed in the recently restored masterpiece of Victorian architecture. See Chapter 12.

✔ **Kirkcaldy Museum and Art Gallery,** Kirkcaldy, Fife: I have a particular soft spot for this modest provincial gallery and museum because I think it has one of the single best collections of Scottish Colourist paintings and other Scottish works from the 19th and 20th centuries. See Chapter 16.

✔ **National Gallery of Scotland,** Edinburgh: The National Gallery offers a collection that has been chosen with great care and expanded by bequests, gifts, loans, and purchases. See Chapter 11.

✔ **Scottish National Gallery of Modern Art,** Edinburgh: This gallery houses Scotland's national collection of 20th-century art in a converted 1828 school that's set on 4.8 hectares (12 acres) of grounds. See Chapter 11.

✔ **Scottish National Portrait Gallery,** Edinburgh: Designed by Rowand Anderson, the gallery gives you a chance to stand before the faces of many famous people from Scottish history. See Chapter 11.

The Best Museums and Historic Attractions

✔ **Burns Cottage and Museum,** Alloway, Ayrshire: This attraction may be basic, but it remains a must-see for even casual fans of Scotland greatest poet, Robert Burns. See Chapter 15.

✔ **Calanais Standing Stones,** Callanish, Isle of Lewis, the Hebrides: This ancient circle and cross-shaped formation of large upright stones is known as the "Scottish Stonehenge" and is one of the most significant prehistoric sites in Scotland. See Chapter 19.

✔ **Calton Hill,** Edinburgh: This landmark mound of rock and earth rises about 105m (350 ft.) above the city and is crowned with monuments. It's the main reason that Edinburgh is called the "Athens of the North." See Chapter 11.

✔ **Culloden Moor Battlefield,** near Inverness, the Highlands: This boggy moorland in the Highlands is where the hopes of Bonnie Prince Charlie's Jacobite uprising of 1745 (begun at Glenfinnan) ended in complete defeat in 1746. See Chapter 18.

✔ **Gladstone's Land,** Edinburgh: This 17th-century merchant's house, looking suitably weathered and aged, is decorated in period-style furnishings. It features colorful, if faded, paintings of flowers and fruit on a sensitively restored timber ceiling. See Chapter 11.

✔ **Glasgow School of Art,** Glasgow: This building was designed by Scotland's great architect, Charles Rennie Mackintosh, whose global reputation comes largely from this magnificent example on Garnethill above Sauchiehall Street. See Chapter 12.

✔ **Glenfinnan Monument,** Glenfinnan, the Highlands: This monument marks the hopeful start of the 1745 Jacobite rebellion, led by Bonnie Prince Charlie, who was trying to reclaim the English and Scottish crowns for his Stuart family lineage. See Chapter 18.

✔ **Museum of Scotland,** Edinburgh: A most impressive modern sandstone building not far from the Royal Mile, the museum is home to exhibits that follow the story of Scotland, including archaeology, technology and science, the decorative arts, royalty, and geology. See Chapter 11.

✔ **The Palace and Abbey of Holyroodhouse,** Edinburgh: The palace was first built in the 16th century adjacent to an Augustinian abbey that David I established in the 12th century. Today, the royal family stays here whenever they occasionally visit Edinburgh. When they're not in residence, the palace is open to visitors. See Chapter 11.

✔ **Skara Brae,** Orkney: This is the best-preserved prehistoric beach-side village in northern Europe. For an idea of what you'll see here, think Pompeii-meets-the-Neolithic. See Chapter 20.

The Best Historic Houses and Gardens

✔ **Abbotsford,** near Galashiels, the Borders: Abbotsford is the mansion that Scotland's best-known novelist, Sir Walter Scott, built and lived in from 1817 until his death. You can visit extensive gardens and grounds on the property, plus the private chapel added after Scott's death. See Chapter 14.

✔ **Culzean Castle,** South Ayrshire: This castle overlooking the Firth of Clyde is a fine example of Robert Adam's "castellated" style (built with turrets and ramparts). It replaced an earlier castle kept as the family seat of the powerful Kennedy clan. See Chapter 15.

✔ **Hill House,** Helensburgh, West Dumbartonshire: The design of this house was inspired by Scottish Baronial style, but it's still pure Charles Rennie Mackintosh, from the asymmetrical juxtaposition of windows and clean lines that blend sharp geometry and gentle curves to the sumptuous but uncluttered interior. See Chapter 13.

✔ **Holmwood House,** Glasgow: This 1858 villa designed by Alexander "Greek" Thomson is probably the best example of his innovative style as applied to stately Victorian homes. See Chapter 12.

✔ **Inverewe Garden,** Poolewe: On the south-facing shores of Loch Ewe, in the Northwest Highlands, Inverewe has an amazing collection of plants in this sprawling garden considering how far north it's situated. See Chapter 18.

✔ **Little Sparta,** Dunsyre: This garden was devised by one of Scotland's most intriguing artists of the 20th and 21st centuries, Ian Hamilton Finlay. See Chapter 14.

✔ **Logan Botanic Garden,** Port Logan: This garden has palms, tree ferns, and other exotic plants that you wouldn't expect to see in Scotland, such as towering flowering columns of echium pininanas, native to the Canary Islands. See Chapter 14.

✔ **Mount Stuart,** Isle of Bute: This neo-Gothic red sandstone mansion belongs to the Marquess of Bute's family, but it's open to the public for much of the year. See Chapter 15.

✔ **Royal Botanic Garden,** Edinburgh: Royal Botanic, with its acres of land to explore, is one of the grandest gardens in all of Great Britain, which is certainly saying something. See Chapter 11.

✔ **Traquair House,** Innerleithen: This house dates from the 10th century and is perhaps Scotland's most romantic house, rich in its association with Mary, Queen of Scots and the Jacobite uprisings. See Chapter 14.

The Best Small Towns

✔ **Culross:** Thanks largely to the National Trust for Scotland, Culross, in Fife, shows what a Scottish village in the 16th to 18th centuries was like, with its cobbled streets lined by stout cottages featuring crow-stepped gables. See Chapter 16.

✔ **Dirleton:** Midway between North Berwick and Gullane, and east of Edinburgh, Dirleton is cited by many as the prettiest village in Scotland. It's picture-postcard perfect, not like a real town at all, but rather one that appears to have been created for a movie set. See Chapter 13.

✔ **Kirkcudbright:** On the southern coast of the Scottish mainland, near the Solway Firth, this quaint village of charming cottages, many with colorful pastel paint jobs, was once a leading artists' colony. See Chapter 14.

✔ **Plockton:** Located not far from Eilean Donan Castle, Plockton is probably the prettiest village in the Highlands. It sits on the shores of Loch Carron, and you'll be amazed to find palm trees. See Chapter 18.

✔ **Tobermory:** Made famous by a BBC children's TV program (in which it was called Balamory), this port on the Isle of Mull has a crescent full of pastel painted buildings facing the popular West Coast harbor. See Chapter 19.

✔ **Ullapool:** This town has the busiest fishing harbor in the northwest of Scotland, and it's also a popular resort — the last outpost before the sparsely populated Northern Highlands. See Chapter 18.

The Best Distilleries

✔ **Caol Ila Distillery,** Port Askaig, Islay Argyll: I've not seen a distillery with a more impressive view, in this case across a narrow sound to the hilly Isle of Jura. See Chapter 15.

✔ **Edradour Distillery,** Pitlochry, Perthshire: Visitors get a good primer on the whisky-making process at this mini-distillery. See Chapter 17.

✔ **Glenfiddich Distillery,** Dufftown, the Northeast: In contrast to Edradour, this is one of Scotland's largest whisky factories, set amid the rolling wooded hills of the famous Speyside region. See Chapter 17.

✔ **Laphroaig Distillery,** Islay, Argyll: With more than a half-dozen distilleries, Islay (pronounced *eye*-la) is Scotland's whisky island. Laphroaig has a distinctive peaty flavor with a whiff of sea air (some say they can even taste a little seaweed). See Chapter 15.

The Best Golf Courses

✔ **Muirfield Golf Course,** Gullane, East Lothian: Muirfield is ranked among the world's great golf courses. It's the home course of the Honorable Company of Edinburgh Golfers — the world's oldest club. See Chapter 13.

✔ **Royal Troon Golf Club,** South Ayrshire: The city and its environs offer several sandy links courses, most prominently the Royal Troon Golf Club. But try the municipal courses for a bargain round as well. See Chapter 15.

✔ **St. Andrews,** Fife: Surely Scotland's most famous golf mecca, St. Andrews offers five 18-hole courses as well as one 9-hole course for beginners and children, all owned by a trust and open to the public. See Chapter 16.

✔ **Turnberry Hotel Golf Courses,** South Ayrshire: Like the Royal Troon, Turnberry has been the scene of Open tournaments and other professional golfing events over the years. Guests of the Westin Turnberry hotel get priority here. See Chapter 15.

The Best Pubs and Bars

✔ **Café Royal Circle Bar,** Edinburgh: This New Town pub stands out as a longtime favorite, boasting lots of atmosphere and Victorian trappings. It attracts a sea of drinkers, locals as well as visitors. See Chapter 11.

✔ **Claichaig Inn,** Glencoe, the Highlands: This hotel has a rustic pub with a wood-burning stove, although it's really the staff's sunny dispositions that warm the woody lounge and bar. Claichaig Inn is especially popular with hikers. See Chapter 18.

✔ **Drover's Inn,** Inverarnan, Loch Lomond: This hotel has an atmospheric pub, with an open fire burning, barmen in kilts, and plenty of foot and car travelers nursing their drinks at the north end of Loch Lomond. See Chapter 16.

✔ **The Horse Shoe,** Glasgow: With its long, horseshoe-shaped bar and central location, this pub is a throwback to the days of so-called Palace Pubs in Scotland. See Chapter 12.

✔ **Mishnish,** Tobermory, Isle of Mull: This pub on the Isle of Mull is a rather big quayside bar for such a diminutive town. See Chapter 19.

✔ **The Pot Still,** Glasgow: This pub gets the nod because of its selection of single malts, which easily numbers into the hundreds. See Chapter 12.

✔ **The Prince of Wales,** Aberdeen: With the longest bar in town and a convivial atmosphere, this pub is possibly the best place to grab a pint in Aberdeen. See Chapter 17.

✔ **The Shore,** Edinburgh: This pub in Leith fits seamlessly into its seaside port surroundings without resorting to a lot of the usual decorations of cork and netting. It has excellent food, too. See Chapter 11.

Chapter 2

Digging Deeper into Scotland

In This Chapter

▶ Brushing up (briefly) on Scottish history

▶ Talking (a wee bit) like a Scot

▶ Understanding what's best to eat and drink

▶ Getting a grip on key books and movies about Scotland

*I*n this chapter, I give you a concise bit of history to elevate your knowledge of a country with national origins that are among the oldest in Europe. We'll also take a look at the Scottish dialect, vernacular expressions, and a bit of the Gaelic. I also cover the basics of Scottish food, which can be as misunderstood as the locals' accents. Interested in the Scottish folk-music scene? This chapter will offer some hints on where to enjoy it, plus it has my list of highly recommended films about — or at least set in — Scotland and books about the country and its people.

Scotland 101: The Main Events

Geographically, Scotland is tiny compared with the United States or Australia, and small by most European standards, too: The country occupies the northern one-third or so of the United Kingdom, covering about 78,725 sq. km (30,410 sq. miles). That makes it a bit bigger than the combined size of Massachusetts, Vermont, and New Hampshire — or not quite the size of Austria. It is about 440km (275 miles) long and only 248km (154 miles) wide at its broadest point. Most of the land is less than about 64km (40 miles) from the sea, and Scotland has more than 750 islands, although only about 10 percent of them are inhabited. Scotland's population has hovered around five million for the past 50 years; so while the country may be geographically small, it is not very densely populated. A majority of its residents live in the Central Belt, in and around Glasgow and Edinburgh, the country's two largest cities. They have a combined population of more than 1.5 million, and probably as many again live in the suburbs, towns, and villages near to them.

The key to comprehending — and, in part, enjoying — Scotland is to know at least a bit of the country's long and sometimes complex history. For much of its existence, Scotland had full (if disputed) autonomy from England, its larger, more populous, and sometimes pushy neighbor to the south. Although the Scottish and English crowns were joined (1603) and the countries were unified into Great Britain (1707), they remain distinct nations.

Early history

Standing stones, burial chambers, and *brochs* (circular stone towers) are the remaining signs of Scotland's earliest residents, but little is known about these first Neolithic tribes that were living in parts of the country thousands of years before Romans arrived. When the Romans invaded in about a.d. 82, much of the land was occupied by a people they called the **Picts** (the Painted Ones). Despite some spectacular bloodletting, the Romans never really conquered the indigenous people in Scotland, and the building of Hadrian's Wall (well south of the current border with England) effectively marked the northern limits of Rome's influence. Sometime before a.d. 500, however, the Irish Celtic tribes, called (however confusingly) "Scots," began to successfully colonize the land, beginning with western coastal areas nearest Northern Ireland, creating the kingdom **Dalriada.**

The Dark and Middle Ages

The Celtic Scots and the Picts were united around 843, while pressures of invasion from the south and Scandinavia helped mold Scotland into a relatively cohesive unit. Under Malcolm II (1005–34), tribes that occupied the southwest and southeast parts of the Scottish mainland were merged with the Scots and the Picts.

Scotland's terrain is full of lochs (not lakes; see "Braving the Burr: Scottish English" for more local terminology), hills, rivers, and mountains; and they divide the territory very effectively. It can take a long time to cover a small distance by foot, on horseback, or even in a modern car. Extended families or clans once dominated regions, and the country was often preoccupied with the territorial battles of clan allegiances.

Some of Scotland's most legendary heroes lived in the late 13th century, particularly **William Wallace** (1270–1305), who drove the English out of Perth and Stirling. Later, **Robert the Bruce** (1274–1329), crowned at Scone in 1306, decisively defeated Edward II of England in 1314 at the battle of Bannockburn, near Stirling.

In 1320, after decades of war against English invaders and occupiers, barons loyal to Scottish King Robert the Bruce put their names on a letter to the Pope, the **Declaration of Arbroath.** The letter not only clearly affirmed the nation's independence but also addressed notions of freedom and liberty — abstract ideals that most countries didn't contemplate for hundreds of years. In the 15th and 16th centuries, the royal **Stuart** line was established, providing a succession of kings (and one notable queen).

Scots identity

Scots are sometimes mistaken to be English by foreigners. Any visitors should avoid that faux pas. Think of it as calling a Canadian a U.S. citizen or mistaking a New Zealander for an Australian. Scotland's union with England effectively relegated Scotland in 1707 to little more than an administrative region within Great Britain. Devolution in 1999 has helped improve that situation. Even though Edinburgh — called the Athens of the North — has long been an intellectual center and Glasgow was the "Second City" of the British Empire, many written histories of "Britain" tend to focus on English royalty over the ages and sometimes completely ignore developments in Scotland. In some cases, Scots are treated with condescension by the English, which helps to explain why Scots, at times, can act as if they have chips on their shoulders.

The Reformation

The passions of the Protestant Reformation arrived on an already turbulent Scottish scene in the 16th century. The main protagonist was undoubtedly **John Knox,** a devout disciple of the Geneva firebrand John Calvin. Knox had a particular mixture of piety, conservatism, strict morality, stubbornness, and intellectual independence that some see as a pronounced feature of the Scottish character today.

Knox helped shape the democratic form of the Scottish Church: Most important among his tenets were provisions for a self-governing congregation, including schools and schooling. Thus, Knox effectively encouraged literacy.

Knox vehemently opposed the reign of one of Scotland's most famous (and tragic) monarchs: **Mary, Queen of Scots** (1542–1587). A Roman Catholic Scot of French upbringing, Mary attempted to govern a land (about which she knew little) in the throes of the Reformation.

Following some disastrous political and romantic alliances, Mary fled Scotland and went to England, where she was jailed and eventually executed on orders of her cousin Elizabeth I. Ironically, Mary's son — **James VI of Scotland** — succeeded the childless Elizabeth and became king of England (James I) in 1603, thus uniting the Scottish and English crowns (Wales had long since been absorbed by England) and creating a United Kingdom. Scotland continued to have a Parliament of earls, barons, and the like.

A few famous Scots in history

✔ Robert Burns (1759–1796): Scotland's plowman poet, known in many languages and countries

✔ Sir Alexander Fleming (1881–1955): Nobel Prize winner who discovered penicillin

✔ David Hume (1711–1776): Laid the foundation for intellectual and philosophical pursuits using the concept of secular morality

✔ David Livingstone (1813–1873): Medical missionary and African explorer who named Victoria Falls on the Zambezi River

✔ Flora MacDonald (1725–1790): Key person in rescuing Bonnie Prince Charlie from British troops after his defeat at Culloden

✔ John Muir (1834–1914): Pioneering conservationist who discovered California's Yosemite Valley and founded the Sierra Club

✔ Sir Walter Scott (1771–1832): Romantic novelist and poet who occupies a position of preeminence in English literature

✔ Adam Smith (1723–1790): Author of *The Wealth of Nations,* which underpins the modern science of economics

Union and the Jacobites

In the 17th century, Scotland's sovereignty diminished, as Scottish royalty spent most of its time in London. In 1689, the final Stuart monarch, the staunchly Catholic James VII (and II of England) fled to France, ending the rule of Scottish kings. In 1707, Scotland had little choice but to merge with England in a constitutionally united Great Britain. This union abolished the Scottish Parliament, and anyone loyal to the Stuarts (known as the "Jacobites," from the Latin for James) could only vainly attempt to restore the Stuart line of royalty. But despite defeat in 1715, the Jacobites didn't give up.

Thirty years later, Charles Edward Stuart (the Young Pretender), better known as **Bonnie Prince Charlie,** picked up the gauntlet. He was the central figure in a 1745 revolt that nearly worked. Initially successful, starting from the Highlands, Stuart and his supporters easily reached Derby, only about 200km (125 miles) from London. The British capital was reportedly in a panic. But Charlie and the Jacobites made an ill-conceived tactical retreat to Scotland, where they were eventually crushed at the **Battle of Culloden,** near Inverness. Charlie went on an infamous run, avoiding capture and eventually returning to France. His followers, left behind in Scotland, weren't so lucky, and a brutal crackdown ensued.

The Scottish Enlightenment and economic growth

During the 18th century, rapid progress in the emerging industrial age produced prominent Scots who made broad and sweeping contributions to practically all fields. The Scottish Enlightenment brought forward important philosophers such as **David Hume** and **Adam Smith.** Many industrial inventions that altered the history of the developing world, such as the steam engine, were either invented or perfected by Scottish genius and industry.

Scotland's union with England and Wales began to reap dividends, and the Scottish economy underwent a radical transformation. As trade with British overseas colonies increased, the port of Glasgow, in particular, flourished. Its merchants grew rich on the tobacco trade with Virginia and the Carolinas.

But life wasn't good for everyone. The infamous **Highland Clearances** (1750–1850) expelled tenant farmers, or *crofters,* from their ancestral lands to make way primarily for sheep grazing, which brought higher returns to the landowning class. Similarly, people in the Scottish Lowlands were forcibly moved off the land. Increased industrialization and migration into urban centers changed the national demographic forever, while a massive wave of emigration created a global **Scottish Diaspora.**

Edinburgh's **New Town** was begun in the mid-1700s and today is a World Heritage site recognized by the United Nations. Later, Victorian builders turned Glasgow into a showcase of 19th-century architecture.

The 20th and 21st centuries

By the 1960s and 1970s, Scotland found that its industrial plants couldn't compete with the emerging manufacturing powerhouses of Asia and elsewhere. A glimmer of light appeared on the Scottish economic horizon in the 1970s: The discovery of **North Sea oil** lifted the British economy considerably and became a source of irritation for independence-minded Scots who saw most of the profits going south into England.

In 1997, under a newly elected Labour government in London, the Scottish electorate was given a chance to vote on **devolution** — a fancy word for limited sovereignty. The referendum passed, allowing Scotland to have its own government and legislature for the first time since the 1707 union with England. The new **Scottish Parliament,** based in Edinburgh, has limited taxing powers and can enact laws regarding health, education, transportation, and public housing — but it has no authority over matters of finance, defense, immigration, and foreign policy. In 2007, the Scottish National Party, which strongly backs independence for the nation, won the general election and formed the government in Edinburgh — much to the dismay of partisan unionists in the Labour, Conservative, and Liberal Democratic parties, who oppose full Scottish sovereignty.

Scotland timeline

✔ 6000 b.c.: The earliest known residents of Scotland establish settlements on the Argyll peninsulas.

✔ 3000 b.c.: Neolithic people begin constructing enduring monuments and burial chambers, such as the standing stones on the Isle of Lewis or tombs on Orkney.

✔ a.d. 90: Romans abandon the hope of conquering Scotland, retreating to England and the relative safety of Hadrian's Wall.

✔ 400–600: Celtic Scots from Ireland bring Christianity and establish the Dalriadic kingdom in western Scotland.

✔ 1270: William Wallace, key patriot in deflecting the forces of Edward I of England (who wishes to conquer Scotland), is born.

✔ 1306–1328: Robert the Bruce leads an open rebellion against English hegemony, and England eventually recognizes Scotland's sovereignty.

✔ 1424: James I is crowned, establishing the Stuart royal line and succession, when his son is made king in 1437.

✔ 1587: Mary, Queen of Scots is executed on orders of her cousin Queen Elizabeth.

✔ 1603: Mary's son, James VI of Scotland, accedes to the throne of England as James I, thus unifying the crown.

✔ 1707: The union of England and Scotland takes place, and the Scottish Parliament is dissolved.

✔ 1750–1850: Britain experiences rapid industrialization. The Clearances strip many *crofters* of their farms, creating epic bitterness and forcing new patterns of Scottish migration.

✔ Late 19th century: Astonishing success in the sciences propels Scotland into a source of industrial know-how around the globe.

✔ Mid–20th century: The decline of traditional industries, especially shipbuilding, painfully redefines the nature of Scottish industry.

✔ 1970: The discovery of oil deposits in the North Sea brings new vitality to Scotland.

✔ 1997: Scotland passes a referendum on "devolution" within Great Britain.

✔ 1999: Elections for the Scottish Parliament are held, and, soon after, Queen Elizabeth opens the first Scottish Parliament in almost 300 years.

✔ 2004: The controversially expensive and much delayed Parliament building opens in Edinburgh.

✔ 2007: The Scottish National Party wins the Scottish election and forms the first nationalist government, hoping to deliver independence within ten years.

Taste of Scotland: Not just Haggis or Haddock

For too many years, a lot of restaurants in Scotland (and most of the U.K.) were known for boiled meats and watery, overcooked vegetables. But in the past 25 years or so, independent restaurants have displayed significant improvements in culinary Scotland, where the best ingredients that the country produces have been married with other styles and influences.

Let's begin with traditional Scottish cooking, which is hearty. Staples include **fish** (such as haddock, a fish similar to cod, which is often smoked); **potatoes** (called tatties); **swedes** (called neeps); **oatcakes; porridge oats;** local game, such as **grouse** or **venison;** and **haggis,** which remains Scotland's national dish — though it's perhaps more symbolic than gustatory.

Modern Scottish cuisine is diverse and innovative, borrowing from French and even Far Eastern techniques and using local produce such as scallops or lamb. One of Scotland's best-known food exports is **Aberdeen Angus** beef, but equally fine is Scottish hill **lamb,** known for its tender, tasty meat. Ranging from pheasant and grouse to rabbit and venison, game also has a key spot in the Scottish natural larder.

Fish, in this land of seas, rivers, and lochs, is a mainstay, from wild halibut to the herring that's transformed into the elegant **kipper** (see the "Culinary lingo" sidebar, below). Scottish smoked salmon is, of course, a delicacy known around the globe. Scottish shellfish is world-class, whether clams, mussels, scallops, crabs, or lobsters and their smaller relative, **langoustines.**

Scottish **raspberries** are among the finest in the world. You definitely need to try some of Scotland's excellent **cheeses** as well. One of the best is Criffel, from the south of the country: a creamy and rich semisoft cheese made from the milk of Shorthorn cows that graze only in organic pastures. Delicious.

At many hotels or B&Bs, one hearty meal you should enjoy is a **Scottish breakfast,** or the **full fry-up.** Expect most or all of the following: eggs, bacon, sausage, black pudding, cooked tomatoes and mushrooms, fried bread or potato scones, baked beans, toast, marmalade or jam, juice, and coffee or tea.

These days, the word "eclectic" describes Scotland's metropolitan **restaurant scene,** particularly in Edinburgh and Glasgow. Indian restaurants abound, as do French, Italian, Chinese, and Thai options. In the rural areas, the selection can be hit or miss; stick to my recommendations and you should do just fine. Scots today can eat better than ever before. Nevertheless, much of the population seems to subsist on takeout fish and chips or, rather, **fish suppers.**

Culinary lingo

Here are a few foods that you're likely to come across in Scotland.

- ✔ **black pudding or marag dubh:** savory sausage of oats, blood, and spices
- ✔ **bridie:** meat and potato pie
- ✔ **cullen skink:** creamy smoked haddock chowder
- ✔ **haggis:** plump sausage of finely diced sheep offal (heart, liver, lungs, and so on), oatmeal, and spices
- ✔ **kippers:** smoked herrings
- ✔ **neep:** swede or large turnip
- ✔ **tattie:** potato
- ✔ **toastie:** toasted sandwich

Braving the Burr: Scottish English

English is the principal language in Scotland, but considering local expressions, regional vernacular, and Scottish accent (the burr — roughly equivalent to the Irish brogue), it can occasionally sound like a different tongue. The standard joke about England and Scotland being "two countries divided by a common language" is not far wrong. Don't worry; at times even Scots from one region of the nation don't know what someone from another area is precisely saying.

Gaelic and Scots

In early history, the prevailing tongue across western and northern Scotland was a Celtic language, **Gaelic.** In certain areas of the Highlands and Islands, it is still common to hear conversations in Gaelic (which rhymes with garlic, rather that the Irish *gay*-lick). Northumbrian English was introduced from the south, and the language known as Lowland Scottish, or **Scots,** then developed; Scots borrowed from Gaelic, Scandinavian dialects, Dutch, and French.

After the royal court moved to England in 1603, Scottish people who didn't still speak Gaelic mostly used a vernacular English, the language of their beloved Bible. Meanwhile, traditional Scots speech was looked upon as an awkward, coarse tongue. In the 18th century, English also became the language of university instruction. By the end of the 20th century, TV and radio had begun to further dilute the more pronounced burrs and lilts of the Scottish accent. However, the dialect and speech patterns of the people in Scotland remain rich. In Aberdeen, the standard salutation is "Fit like?" In Stornoway on the Isle of Lewis, the exchange begins, "What's fresh?"

Gaelic, while not widely spoken, is certainly far from dead — particularly in such places as the Western Isles, where about 60 percent of the population can speak it. Even public-affairs TV in Scotland airs a few programs in the language (with subtitles for those completely befuddled by Gaelic).

To save you from having to maintain one of those polite but puzzled smiles on your face while talking to locals, review this handy glossary of some common words from both Gaelic and Scots as well as some standard British English substitutions for North American English.

auld	old	**lift**	elevator
aye	yes	**loch**	freshwater lake or large sea inlet
bonnie	pretty		
boot	car trunk	**messages**	groceries or the shopping
burn	creek	**pavement**	sidewalk
cairn	stone landmark	**petrol**	gasoline
ceilidh	social dance	**quid**	pound sterling
cheers	thanks	**stramash**	disturbance
dinnae	don't or didn't	**stushie**	fuss
glen	valley	**take-away**	to go
hen	woman	**till**	cash register
howff	meeting place or pub	**tins**	canned goods
ken	know or known	**torch**	flashlight
lad	boy·	**wee**	little
lassie	girl		

Pub Life in Scotland

Much of the socializing in Scotland centers on the local pub. The pub's more than a watering hole. It can be the gathering place for an entire community, the key place where the locals go to share news and exchange gossip. At certain pubs, pickup sessions of traditional and folk music are common.

Even if you're not a big drinker, going out for a pint of lager, a dram of whisky, or even just a bite to eat at a Scottish *howff* can be a memorable part of your trip, as you're almost guaranteed to meet real Scots.

Don't tip the bar staff: You'll immediately be identified as an outsider, and your generosity won't get you a free round of drinks, either. On the issue of rounds, it's quite common for individuals in groups to buy a round for everyone at the table during any drinking session. It's considered bad manners if you never take your turn to buy a round but get a drink at every other round. Alternatively, you can beg out when anyone asks if you want another drink before they order the round, drink at your own pace, and buy only your own.

Join 'em for a pint of beer

The most widely available, mass-produced Scottish beers are Tennents lager and McEwens ale, but from region to region, you may find a number of local breweries, making anything from light-colored lagers to dark ales. Among them, Deuchars IPA, Black Isle Organic Blonde, and Orkney's Dark Island are standouts. The most popular stout remains Guinness, from neighboring Ireland, while the potent Stella Artois, from the Continent, is the best-selling premium lager.

Traditionally, the strength of Scottish ale (as distinct from lager) is labeled by shillings (for example, Belhaven 80/–). The higher the number, the stronger the beer. Today, with cask-conditioned ales, the bar can tell you the alcohol content, ABV: Four is standard, six is strong.

Remember, practically all beer in Scotland has higher alcohol content than any sold in North America. And that even goes for familiar American brands such as Budweiser. So, take it easy.

Whisky galore

If you're in Scotland (or almost anywhere in Europe), you don't need to identify it as *Scotch* whisky. Most connoisseurs prefer varieties of single malt whisky, the taste of which depends largely on where it's distilled: sweet Lowland, peaty Island, or smooth and balanced Highland. Single malts are seen as sipping whiskies and are rarely served with anything other than a few drops of tap water. If you want a cocktail made with whisky, expect it to be a well-known blend, such as Famous Grouse or Bell's, and not single malt, such as Glemorangie or Laphroaig. If you want a North American bourbon, rye, or sour-mash whiskey, you need to name the brand: for example, Jack Daniel's or Maker's Mark.

A bit of whisky terminology

Scotland is home to a host of whisky experts, and, in case you meet some, here are a few helpful terms to keep in mind.

- **dram:** A shot of spirits (usually whisky), roughly 35 milliliters or about an ounce
- **neat:** Whisky served without ice or water
- **nip:** A whisky chaser to a pint of beer
- **usige beatha** (ooshka *bay*): Water of life; the Gaelic for the word whisky

If you're ordering a whisky, simply ask for a dram of your desired brand. Again, the established way to drink the spirit is neat — that is, nothing added. But some say a few drops of tap water bring out the aroma and flavor.

Tuning Your Ear to Scottish Music

Scottish music is considerably more than "Scotland the Brave" played on bagpipes, although you may well hear that during your stay. Bagpipes and the rousing, indeed ear-shattering, sounds they can create are entrenched in the national identity and culture of Scotland.

Every summer, Glasgow hosts an international piping competition that draws thousands of pipers (many of whom also perform as part of Edinburgh's Military Tattoo, a show featuring music, marching, and military exercises). At annual Burns Suppers, the meal is brought into the dining room with a bagpipe accompaniment. Pipers are common at wedding receptions and at social dances or *ceilidhs* (*kay*-lees).

But a lone piper may pop up anytime, anywhere. Once on a misty late-summer's day at the Highland Monument to Bonnie Prince Charlie in Glenfinnan, I saw one suddenly begin blowing on a nearby hillside. No kidding.

But the pipes are just part of it. The Gaelic-influenced songs and sounds of the Hebridean Islands and the Highlands have been around for centuries. The fiddle, accordion, flute, guitar, and Celtic drum are all part of the musical tradition. The best chance to hear the real deal is at a jam session in a pub or a local gig.

The Scottish folk or Celtic music scene is going strong, with annual music festivals from Orkney and Lewis to Glasgow and Ayrshire, often featuring English and Irish folk players, too. Many young musicians, after a turn or two with rock bands, have returned to Scottish roots music, too.

Visiting Golf's Hallowed Ground

Golf may have originated in mainland Europe (or China, according to some accounts), but Scotland at least gets full credit for developing the sport and codifying its rules. Golf has been played here for more than 500 years. In places such as eastern Fife or North Ayrshire, you're likely to see someone knocking a golf ball around a park — or signs saying such activity is prohibited.

If you're at an established club and need a caddy, don't be surprised if he isn't young — the average age of a golf caddy here is about 50. Most courses don't provide motorized carts (although they're popping up more and more). Finally, please *do not* play a championship course if you're a beginner or even an intermediate.

Visitors (men and women) can play on all public and most private-members courses (Chapter 21 lists ten of the best), but at the exclusive clubs, members receive priority for tee times. Many courses have dress codes, so play it safe and wear a shirt with a collar, long pants, and proper golf shoes if you're heading to the links.

Exploring Scotland's Great Outdoors

Scotland has long had world-class fishing, while its sailing, hill-walking, and hiking are first rate, too.

Outdoor walks in Scotland can take you through wooded glens, beach dunes, or windswept mountains. Trail markings range from clear to non-existent. It never hurts to have a detailed map and compass. If you're going someplace extreme, tell someone where you'll be hiking and when you expect to be back.

 If you're hiking on the hills and mountains of the Highlands and Islands, you must take all the precautions that you would if you were climbing in much higher Alpine conditions. The weather can change dramatically in a short period of time.

If you're an angler, Scotland doesn't require a national license to fish. Instead, you buy permits locally at bait-and-tackle shops and post offices, or request permission from landowners. Areas for anglers are often marked and say where you can obtain a license or permission. Local tourism offices can usually provide you with more information.

As for the wildlife, in the right seasons, the marshes of Scotland teem with migratory birds, the seas offer whale-watching, and the Highlands and Islands boast eagle-nesting sites. This side of the tourism business is just beginning to catch on, as is "green tourism." The tourist board now gives out recommendations for those hotels that it considers environmentally friendly.

Background Check: Recommended Movies and Books

If you're looking to find out more about Scotland than just what's in this book, you have a variety of films and books at your disposal. The following sections list some suggestions.

Movies

The ten films listed below are among the best and/or most popular movies made about Scotland and its people.

✔ *Braveheart* (1995): This movie — hardly historically accurate but often moving nonetheless — probably did more to stir overseas interest in Scotland than any promotional campaign ever cooked up by the tourist board. Mel Gibson stars as the 13th-century patriot William Wallace in this sweeping Academy Award–winning epic.

✔ *Gregory's Girl* (1981): A simple comedy about an awkward high school student (played by gawky John Gordon-Sinclair) in a modern (and mostly hideous) 20th-century New Town near Glasgow. Quirky but loveable.

✔ *I Know Where I'm Going!* (1945): This is a charming, funny WWII-era black-and-white film from the great British team of Powell and Pressburger. It takes a young English fiancée on a suspenseful, romantic adventure to the Isle of Mull.

✔ *Local Hero* (1983): In this sweetly eclectic comedy, villagers on a gorgeous stretch of Scottish coastline (mostly filmed near Mallaig) expect to cash in big time because of Texan oil-industry interest. But events conspire against greed.

✔ *My Name Is Joe* (1998): Although not entirely lacking humor and romance, this film paints a rather grim, if generally accurate, picture of Glaswegians struggling with their addictions and inner demons.

✔ *Orphans* (1997): Actor Peter Mullan (star of *My Name Is Joe*) wrote and directed this outlandish and very, very dark comedy with lots of foul language about the day the Flynn family in Glasgow tried to bury their recently deceased mother.

✔ *The 39 Steps* (1935): Director Alfred Hitchcock and scriptwriter Charles Bennett almost completely reset John Buchan's tale of spies and intrigue. Instead of sticking to the Borders, the film transports the hero to the Highlands. Good idea.

✔ *Trainspotting* (1996): Based one of the most popular contemporary books by Scottish author Irvine Welsh, *Trainspotting* is the gritty and often hilarious account of a group of unrepentant drug-addled characters in Edinburgh in the 1980s.

✔ *Whisky Galore* (1949): Retitled *Tight Little Island* in America, this classic movie is based on a true story. The residents of a small and remote Scottish island get an intoxicating windfall when a ship carrying 50,000 cases of whisky crashes off their coast during WWII.

✔ *The Wicker Man* (1973): A cult classic of cinema about a strange New Age community on a picturesque Scottish isle — and the secrets they keep from a mainland constable of the law. Occasionally silly, but the climax is spectacular.

Books

There are too many books about Scotland to mention them all, so I've chosen to highlight my favorites in three main categories: biography, fiction, and history.

Biography

- ✔ *Bonnie Prince Charlie* (Canongate, 1989), by Fitzroy Maclean, tells the tale of one of the most romantic royal characters in Scottish history.

- ✔ *The Life of Robert Burns* (Canongate Classics, 1998), by Catherine Carswell, is the groundbreaking look at the life of Scotland's national poet. First published in the 1930s, Carswell's assessment was so frank — particularly regarding the poet's romantic and sexual liaisons — that many took offense.

- ✔ *Robert Louis Stevenson: A Biography* (HarperCollins, 2005), by Claire Harman, follows the trail of the frail adventurer and world-famous author, from his Edinburgh birthplace to Europe and finally to his last home in the South Pacific.

- ✔ *The Sound of Sleat: A Painter's Life* (Picador, 1999), by Jon Schueler, is a remarkable autobiography by American-born abstract impressionist Schueler, who found his muse in the land and especially the sky of Scotland. He even made a second home near the Western Highland port of Mallaig.

Fiction

- ✔ *Black & Blue* (Orion) by Ian Rankin is one of the crime writer's best efforts in the much celebrate Inspector Rebus detective series of novels.

- ✔ *The Heart of Midlothian* (Penguin Classics), by Sir Walter Scott, was declared a masterpiece in 1818 and remains Scott's seminal piece of fiction, influencing the later works of such authors as Balzac, Hawthorne, and Dickens.

- ✔ *Kidnapped* (Penguin Classics), by Robert Louis Stevenson, follows the adventures of young David Balfour after he's spirited out of Edinburgh and ends up on the wrong side of the law in the Western Highlands. The story is as entertaining today as it was upon publication in 1886.

- ✔ *Lanark: A Life in Four Books* (Pub Group West, 2003), by Alasdair Gray, is perhaps the most important contemporary novel published in Scotland in the last 100 years. Gray is an eccentric of the first order, but this work of fiction (first published in 1981 and illustrated by the author, too), despite some fantastical detours, gets to the core of urban Scotland.

✔ *The Prime of Miss Jean Brodie* (Perennial Classics, 1999), by Muriel Spark, and *Trainspotting* (W. W. Norton & Company, 1996), by Irvine Welsh, are both better known for their cinematic adaptations, but in their own very different ways, both novels manage to capture elements of Edinburgh life.

History

✔ *Scotland: A New History* (Pimlico, 1992), by Michael Lynch, is a good take on Scottish history from ancient times up to the 1990s.

✔ *The Scottish Enlightenment: The Scots' Invention of the Modern World* (Crown, 2001), by American historian Arthur Herman, offers a clear and extremely readable explanation of the impact that Scottish thinkers had on the world.

✔ *The Scottish Nation: 1700–2000* (Penguin, 2001), by academic Tom Devine, is a good, recently published historical overview of Scotland. Devine is one of the few historians to examine how people were driven from the Scottish Lowlands, as well as more famous and lamentable clearances from the Highlands.

✔ *Stone Voices: The Search for Scotland* (Hill & Wang, 2003), by Neal Ascherson, is a quest for the national character of Scotland. In a series of anecdotes and reflections, journalist Ascherson helps readers understand the worthy sentiments behind Scottish independence and begins to redress the imbalance of Scottish histories so often written by the English.

Chapter 3

Deciding Where and When to Go

In This Chapter

▶ Looking at Scotland's terrain, main cities, and major regions
▶ Evaluating when to go, season by season
▶ Anticipating Scotland's changeable weather
▶ Planning for festivals and events

*T*he next time you meet someone who's recently been to Scotland, ask what the place is like; you might get a wistful, faraway look as an initial answer. That is because the country has the potential for magical experiences. With the history and contemporary culture of Edinburgh and Glasgow, the breathtakingly scenery of Highlands and Islands, and some of the friendliest English-speaking people in the world, Scotland is bound to leave fond memories. From urban chic to ancient castles and abbeys, from misty glens to craggy coastlines, Scotland is a dream (as well as dreamy) destination.

But the success of a Scottish vacation can depend on where and when you go. This chapter has my advice and insight (as someone who has lived in and traveled across Scotland for more than a dozen years) so that you can more easily determine the best way to spend your Scottish vacation.

Let's start with a geographic breakdown of the country, in order to give you a better idea of what the various regions have to offer and how long you may want to stay in each area — especially given your particular interests and travel budget. Then I'll address the weather. Finally, check out the calendar of events at the end of the chapter. Remember: Good planning should ensure that certain factors — whether short winter days or not giving yourself enough time to see the big attractions — don't prevent you from having a satisfying experience.

Going Everywhere You Want to Be

The first thing to understand about Scotland is this: It may be a small country geographically, but the terrain is frequently divided by mountains, rivers, and lochs — especially north of the Central Belt. Many roads don't travel in straight lines; a few of them only have one lane. So, although the distance of the proverbial crow's flight may seem short, your travels across the country may — and possibly will — take longer than you expect. But slow down and enjoy the ride.

Scotland's biggest topographical feature is the Highlands. Its boundary runs roughly diagonally across the country, from the southwest to the northeast. If you draw a straight line, west to east (say from the Isle of Mull to the River Tay), you will go from rocky islands and distinctive mountain terrain to gentle moorland and rolling hills of the upper Lowlands.

Any division of Scotland into distinct regions is bound to be a bit arbitrary: There's often no clean line to divide one area from another. I've done my best to present the regions accurately and logically.

But sometimes that means my geographic breakdown of the country doesn't match what you'll get from, say, local governments or the Scottish tourist board. For example, I group the Isle of Mull with the other islands of the Hebrides (Chapter 19). VisitScotland — the national tourist board — lumps the Isle of Mull into a broad region stretching well across the country to the east (which I think is a mistake). I will highlight locations where there are similar discrepancies and possible confusion for you.

For more information on the country's cities and regions, check out Part III, which discusses Scotland's two major cities of Edinburgh and Glasgow, and Part IV, which has the lowdown on major regions in the country. The areas in Part IV are introduced from south to north, starting with the Borders and southwest regions and finishing with the Scottish Highlands and Islands.

Edinburgh and Glasgow

Let's face it: Many, and possibly most, visitors to Scotland never get any farther than the country's two principal cities. And that's okay. They're excellent destinations in their own right; and, from them, travelers can take side trips to get at least a sampling of Scotland's other charms (see Chapter 13).

Although only a 50-minute train ride apart, **Edinburgh** (see Chapter 11) and **Glasgow** (see Chapter 12) are notably different but equally fascinating and culturally rich. Think of them as the McCartney and Lennon of Scotland, making their own unique contributions and creating a dynamic duo.

Edinburgh (*eddin*-burra, with a short "e" as in "Edward") is the capital of Scotland. It has a historic Old Town and a New Town — albeit one whose beginnings are actually older than the founding of the United States. As the second most popular tourist destination in the whole of Great Britain (London is the first, of course) Edinburgh and its charms are internationally recognized, as is the city's annual summer arts festival. In addition, it boasts a striking cityscape — a castle on a hill being just one of several noteworthy landmarks — as well as the royal Palace of Holyroodhouse.

Glasgow (*glazz*-go) is older than Edinburgh but appears more modern these days. Traditionally viewed as a working-class industrial metropolis, Glasgow thrived as the "Second City" of the British Empire in the 18th and 19th centuries, and today it offers the best concentration of Victorian architecture in the U.K. After an economic decline in the 20th century and a reputation (deservedly or not) of crime, grime, and gangsters, Glasgow emerged in the 1980s and 1990s as the cultural hot spot of Scotland, boasting leading artists and best-selling indie rock bands.

Southern Scotland

The southernmost regions of Scotland are the **Borders,** aptly named because it borders Northumberland in northern England, and **Dumfries and Galloway,** which stretches southwest along the Solway Firth (which clearly divides England and Scotland) to the Irish Sea. These regions certainly have their own allure and attractions, whether Abbotsford — Sir Walter Scott's mansion — or the Logan Botanic Gardens, with its subtropical plants. The town of Dumfries (dum-*freece*) was the final home of the national poet Robert Burns (1759–1796). In the village of Melrose, the ruins of an ancient abbey commissioned by Scotland's King David I in the 12th century can be found. If you have time for an extended stay, both regions merit a few days of exploring.

 Alternatively, some of southern Scotland's highlights can be seen on side trips from either Edinburgh or Glasgow. (See Chapter 14 for more information on both the Borders and Dumfries and Galloway.)

Ayrshire and Argyll

Ayrshire (*air*-shyer) is the long and primarily coastal region southwest of Glasgow, best known for golf and its associations with Robert Burns. The region certainly offers most of the landmarks and attractions associated with Burn, the great plowman poet. Ayrshire is also home to some of the best links-style golf courses in Scotland, if not the world. **Argyll** (ar-*guile*) encompasses the central west coast of Scotland, its remote peninsulas, and the southernmost islands, such as **Gigha** or **Islay,** where much of the country's famous whisky is made. This is the heart of the ancient Kingdom of Dalriada, where the first Celtic people settled in the 5th century and also a region where Norse colonies were established until the 13th century.

If you have time, the scenic **Kintyre Peninsula** and the isle of **Arran** (sometimes described as Scotland in miniature) can be worth including on your itinerary, as well as the port of **Oban** (*oh*-bin), the gateway to the Inner Hebrides, and **Inveraray,** on the shores of Loch Fyne. But even if you don't have time to explore the region fully, you would be remiss to skip such places as **Culzean Castle,** which is close enough to Glasgow for an easy, satisfying day-long side trip. (See Chapter 15 for more information on both Ayrshire and Argyll.)

Fife and the Trossachs

North of Edinburgh, across the Firth of Forth, is the ancient Kingdom of **Fife;** moving west across the country takes in the historic city of **Stirling** and the **Trossach** mountains — rather like the Highlands only smaller, less dramatic, and more wooded. Fife is a reasonably compact area and is perhaps best known for the town of **St. Andrews.** Golfers make the pilgrimage here from all over the world, but it is also a pretty great little east-coast college town, with Scotland's first university (and the third oldest in Great Britain after Oxford and Cambridge). Another golf mecca lies inland: the famous Gleneagles resort, with its first-class hotel and perhaps the best restaurant in Scotland, Restaurant Andrew Fairlie (p. 312).

History buffs will enjoy a visit to the town of Stirling, with its excellent castle, Old Town wall, and picturesque monument to William Wallace (of *Braveheart* fame). The **Trossachs** are the old stamping grounds of the legendary Rob Roy and provided the setting for Walter Scott's romantic poetry.

Like some landmarks in the Borders and in Ayrshire, highlights of Fife, Stirling, and the Trossachs — including the famously bonnie, bonnie banks of **Loch Lomond** — can be covered in day trips from Edinburgh or Glasgow. (All of this is discussed in more detail in Chapter 16.)

Tayside and Northeast Scotland

North of Fife and east of the Highlands are the **River Tay** and the city of **Dundee.** A bit farther north, on the eastern side of Scotland, are the **Grampian Mountains, Royal Deeside** (home of the monarchy's retreat at Balmoral castle), and the oil-prosperous city of **Aberdeen.** I have put them all together in my chapter on **Tayside** and the **Northeast.** The region offers castles, whisky distilleries, and handsome countryside. (For details on this area, flip to Chapter 17.)

The Highlands

The Scottish **Highlands** is a huge and justifiable tourist magnet. For better or for worse, however, the region's best-known attraction is still a mythical creature swimming in the waters of **Loch Ness.** Yes, the loch is a big, dark, and brooding body of water.

Glossary of place names

So you're passing through quaint Highland and Island settlements with some essentially unpronounceable names, such as Bunavoneadar, Altnacraig, or Invercharan. Wonder what they mean? Many towns and hamlets incorporate the Gaelic words (or their English transliterations) for geographical and topographical features. Use this glossary to get closer to their meanings.

- ✔ **alt:** stream
- ✔ **ben:** mountain
- ✔ **cnoc:** hill
- ✔ **craig:** rock
- ✔ **drum:** ridge
- ✔ **dun:** hill fort
- ✔ **eilean:** island

- ✔ **glen:** valley
- ✔ **inver:** river mouth
- ✔ **loch:** fresh-water lake or large salt-water inlet
- ✔ **mor:** great
- ✔ **ness:** cape
- ✔ **tarbert:** isthmus

But it's not the best thing about the Highlands. You're not likely to see any monster and may feel that the place has elements of a tourist trap. So see it and move on. The official capital of the Highlands is the small city of **Inverness.** Although it's not particularly exciting, it has some good guesthouses, a lively music scene, excellent restaurants, and a first-rate live performance/theater/cinema complex, Eden Court. Plus the city provides a good jumping-off spot for exploring the Black Isle or other parts of the nearby Highlands.

But for my money, the craggy **Western Highlands** is the real attraction, and perhaps even the proverbial soul of Scotland. Steeped in proud lore and sad tragedy, from the Jacobite uprising to the massacre of **Glen Coe,** the scenery is ultimately what will leave an indelible mark on your memory.

The mountains are ancient and rise from the sea with utter majesty; the beach sands on the "Road to the Isles," west of Fort William, near Mallaig, are brilliantly white and unspoiled. Villages, such as **Plockton,** look like picture postcards, set near the sea in the shadow of nearby peaks. North of the port of **Ullapool,** the country is beautifully desolate and sparsely populated, and **Cape Wrath** feels like the end of the Earth. This is the place to go if you enjoy wide open spaces. (The Highlands are discussed at length in Chapter 18.)

The Hebridean Islands

And it only gets better. If you have time to conquer part of the Highlands, you should also make a point to visit at least one of the country's islands off the west and northwest coastline of Scotland. The **Hebrides** (*heb*-rid-eez) is a vast archipelago of some 600 islands, including large inhabited islands and lots of small, uninhabited ones. Worth the ferry trip — and possibly an overnight stay or two — are such islands as **Mull** and its little sister, **Iona,** an ancient landmark of Celtic Christianity in Scotland. North of there, the **Isle of Skye** is the biggest island of the **Inner Hebrides;** it's the most accessible (thanks to a land bridge as well as ferry service), and it's debatably the most scenic (though you'll get into arguments over that claim).

If you're feeling more adventurous and want more room to yourself, then head out to the wind-swept, 225km-long (140-mile) chain of islands known as the **Western Isles** or **Outer Hebrides:** islands such as **Barra, Harris, Lewis** (my home), or the **Uists.** Here, at the most northwesterly part of Europe, you'll find windswept wild moors, rocky coastlines, amazing white-sand beaches with grassy dunes, impossibly cerulean seas, and prehistoric standing stones — and a lot of the time you'll have them pretty much to yourself. Fantastic.

Alternatively, the time-strapped traveler can make a day trip to Inner Hebridean isle of **Eigg** from the mainland port village of **Arisaig.** (Turn to Chapter 19 for more details on the Hebrides.)

Shetland and Orkney islands

The far northern island chains of **Shetland** and **Orkney** are remote and rural. Unless you specifically have the time and inclination, they may not be worth the trouble to visit. On the other hand, they feature some nearly unparalleled archaeological sites, while their very remoteness makes them a welcome reprieve from the more trodden tourist trail. (They're discussed briefly in Chapter 20.)

Not quite ready for prime time

Alas, this book doesn't have room to cover each and every part of Scotland. The northernmost areas of the mainland, and towns such as Tongue, Wick, and Scrabster, aren't addressed at all. My apologies for that, especially to any surfers among the readership: The north coast is a mecca for those seeking new breakers. Most of the Scottish islands are uninhabited, and only 60 are larger than about 8 sq. km (3 sq. miles). Unfortunately, I don't have adequate space for isles such as Jura or Tiree. Sorry. I've also kept the chapter on Shetland and Orkney concise, and I don't go into too many specifics about Aberdeenshire and Moray. I believe these are destinations for long-term visitors — or for travelers with a specific interest in them. If you want to visit an uninhabited island or spend time in a location not adequately dealt with in *Scotland For Dummies,* please visit a tourist information center.

Scheduling Your Time

Many tourists are tempted to try and see everything — especially the curious and ambitious ones. Good luck. Alas, in the frantic effort to do it all, you can miss as much as you catch. Plus, you might be exhausted at the end of it. What's the point?

This book covers most of Scotland and gives you itineraries that take you from one side of the country to the other and back again. But if your time is limited, you should consider simply staying in Edinburgh and Glasgow, which have plenty to offer, and using them as bases for any excursions. Chapter 13 and the first chapters of Part IV are full of attractions within striking distance of the region's two biggest cities.

Of course, the Highlands and Islands are spectacular. But if you don't fancy the idea of sleeping in a different bed every night, find a location that offers a variety of sights to see and things to do in the vicinity of other places you want to visit. For example, from the pretty seaside village of Arisaig, you can easily get to Skye, see Glenfinnan and Fort William to the east, or go south to Movern and Ardnamurchan.

If you don't see it all in one go, then you'll just have to plan a return trip — or use this book to vicariously experience the bits you missed.

Mild (if damp) weather, thanks to the Gulf Stream

You've probably heard about Scottish weather. The Scots like to joke about getting "four seasons in one day." That means rain, wind, and sunshine in one day — sometimes all at the same time.

In contrast to continental Europe, Scotland is spared extremes in weather, largely thanks to the effects of the Gulf Stream (sometimes known as the North Atlantic Drift), which sweeps up from the Caribbean. No matter what time of year you choose to visit Scotland, however, chances are slim that you'll make it back home *without* some Scottish raindrops falling on your head. Always have a waterproof coat handy. While the weather is occasionally wet, temperatures in most areas rarely fall below freezing (particularly in these days of climate change), except on mountain tops or in the depth of winter.

A few places in Scotland certainly get more rain than others. For example, the Isle of Mull in the west is notoriously prone to precipitation, while the Moray coast in the northeast is probably the most consistently sunny spot. After living here more than ten years, I can assure you that you never know: A recent summer was a washout in Glasgow and Edinburgh, while on the Western Isles it was one of the driest in memory.

Scotland is reasonably cool year-round (see Table 3-1). However, global warming is causing average temperatures to rise slowly. While a few summer weeks can see temperatures rise above 27°C (80°F), it is usually between about 16°C and 21°C (the 60s°F). In the colder months, there is not much risk of getting frostbite, except on mountaintops and during occasional cold snaps.

Table 3-1		Average Monthly Temperatures in Scotland									
	Jan	**Feb**	**Mar**	**Apr**	**May**	**June**	**July**	**Aug**	**Sep**	**Oct**	**Nov**	**Dec**
F°	33–48	34–49	35–51	39–52	42–58	49–63	52–67	51–67	47–61	42–55	35–50	34–49
°C	1–8	2–9	3–11	4–12	6–14	9–18	12–20	11–20	8–17	6–13	3–10	2–9

Here comes the sun

The amount of daylight varies greatly in Scotland's northern latitudes. The price paid for long, languorous days in the summer is lengthy, dark nights during winter. If you depend upon natural light to see the sights that you're most interested in, visiting from May through September allows you to take advantage of the longer days.

Before you leave home, get up-to-date weather forecasts on the Internet. The Web site www.metoffice.gov.uk/weather/ — run by the U.K. Meteorological Office — is a good source for the latest information on current conditions and has reasonably accurate forecasts.

Revealing the Secrets of the Seasons

Weather isn't the only consideration when planning your trip. The high summer season brings crowds and traveling families, while the low season carries the possibility of some attractions and hotels being closed. Each season boasts certain advantages and drawbacks, which I share in this section.

Summer

The most popular and possibly best time to tour Scotland is summer, when the country is geared to receive tourists and the weather's usually (though not always) drier and warmer than at other times of the year. For the unsure traveler, traveling in the summer is your best bet; you'll have lots of company and plenty of leads to follow.

The upside

In the summer, all attractions, hotels, and restaurants — no matter how remote — are open. All tourist information centers are open, too; some seven days a week, and a few don't close until well into the evening.

Summer's the busiest tourist season, but crowds aren't always a bad thing. Streets teeming with people may actually enhance your trip.

Scotland's a friendly place, so throwing a ton of visitors into the mix can create a spirited atmosphere. Plus, the Edinburgh International Festival and Edinburgh Festival Fringe combine to create one of the biggest annual cultural events in Europe every August.

The days are long during this time of year. In fact, if you're in the far north, the sun never really appears to set. Even down in Edinburgh, sunlight lasts well into the night; and, on the west coast, you can discern a glimmer of fading light as late as 11:30 p.m. Of course, the sun rises about 4:30 a.m., too.

The weather? Well, if you've got your heart set on fine and dry weather; if you're allergic (either physically or emotionally) to drizzle, fog, or rain; or if it's your tan that you want to work on, then don't go to Scotland. The place is rarely sweltering. Instead, summer conditions can be comfortably warm and breezy during the day and drop to light-sweater temperature at night. You will likely get caught in some rain, especially on the islands, in June, July, and August.

The downside

During the summer, tourists can overwhelm many popular attractions and towns. The influx of visitors, especially in Edinburgh from late July to early September, may mean that hotels don't have any available rooms for last-minute travelers. Plus, normally quiet villages, such as Pitlochry or Plockton, start to resemble Fifth Avenue, with crowds pouring off tour buses. If you're craving a break from the masses, summer may not be the time to come to Scotland, unless you plan to travel to the country's extremities.

Seasonal rates are another downside to visiting in the summer: Accommodations can be more expensive than in other seasons. For many travelers, the worst thing about summer in the Western Highlands and Islands is the *midges* (*mid*-gees) — flying, blood-sucking no-see-um bugs that can drive you to serious distraction and leave a plethora of tiny but itchy bites. There are also biting horseflies called *cleggs*. Make sure you have netting and some effective bug spray if you're heading to the western costal regions in the summer.

 Summers on the western islands can be quite rainy because they take the brunt of the prevailing trade winds off the Atlantic Ocean. The consistently best times to visit this region are usually May to mid-June or September into early October, when dry periods are more prevalent, although the temperatures, especially at night, will be a tad cooler.

Fall

Autumn is probably the most underrated time to visit Scotland. The weather can be quite good, with a strong possibility of sunny, dry stretches. Even when it's stormy, the weather fronts often move through quickly. Mild days without too much rain, and daylight extending to at

least 8 p.m. (until the clocks go back), are great for marathon sightseeing. Summer crowds have diminished and hotel rates are easing, too.

The upside

Beginning in mid-September, the high season has run its course and
room prices begin to fall. Everything is less crowded. The pubs and restaurants belong to the locals again as they reclaim their turf from the
tourist hordes. In autumn, you're more likely to find bars — especially in
Edinburgh — filled with locals rather than tourists.

Days remain reasonably long, and if you're traveling in the west, the
midges usually get knocked back by the first cool nights (what a relief).
In rural inland areas, trees may begin to change color toward the end of
fall, and with the sun lower in the sky, the natural light can be magical.

The downside

The more seasonal and far-flung attractions, as well as some tourist
offices, begin to shut down or at least restrict their hours in the fall.
Winterlike weather can set in quickly at the end of autumn.

Autumn may mean fewer tourists, but plenty of people still travel this
time of year. Autumn nights in Scotland can start to be surprisingly cool.
In the Highlands, you may even experience a light frost or snow flurry.

Winter

Conditions aren't ideal, but Scottish winters are quite a bit less severe
than you might assume. Anyone visiting from Idaho, Illinois, or
Pennsylvania will find them mild, in fact. From November through
March, the main cities function normally, and golf along the southwest
coast remains a lure. Days can be very short, however, and some tourist
attractions, as well as inns in the countryside, may be closed until
springtime.

The upside

Prices are at their lowest all across the country in the winter, and you're
likely to find the cheapest airfares of the year. Because it's the least popular time to travel, more special rates and package deals are offered.
Places like the Outer Hebrides offer a real escape from "civilization" and
people, if that's what you're after.

If you dislike crowds, winter's best time for you to see Scotland. It's
also a good time to visit city museums, galleries, and year-round attractions. And the landscape is almost as beautiful as during the full swing of
summer.

For snowboarding and skiing, a few resorts offer adequate facilities in
the Highlands. But lots of winter snow is not guaranteed anymore. For
snow, 2009–10 was a good year; the best in probably 25 years. If golf is

your bag, then head for the links courses in Ayrshire. They're sandy and drain well, allowing play through the season.

The downside

The winter weather can be *driech* (gloomy and wet). It's predictably cool, rainy, and windy from January through March. The temperature rarely dips to extreme lows and snowfalls aren't as heavy as they used to be, but blizzards can still hit on occasion. The sun usually doesn't rise until 9:30 a.m., and then it's gone by 4 p.m.

Attractions, especially outside the cities and most run by the National Trust of Scotland, can be shuttered in winter, and lots of places have shorter hours. Many rural hotels, B&Bs, and restaurants close for the season as well. If you're a broadminded and independent traveler, you still can find plenty of things to do. But you'll have fewer established tourist highlights than in the other seasons.

The exceptions to general winter travel bargains are the weeks of Christmas and New Year's, when accommodations rates equal those of the high summer season.

Spring

Spring can start slowly in Scotland, and even in May, the weather can still feel rather wintry some days. But they are quickly lengthening, and some people consider this to be the ideal time to travel in Scotland.

The upside

Warming temperatures (however gradually) and longer days combine to make for promising conditions for touring the countryside. The ground is carpeted in spring greenery, and the plants are beginning their displays (the rhododendrons, in particular, are breathtaking Mar–May). Rain showers are often isolated, and they may last only part of the day.

By the time spring rolls around, the tourist industry has had its break and is ready to resume playing host. Country inns and travel information offices reopen, but because the high season hasn't hit yet, crowds are manageable.

The downside

Scotland can remain pretty rainy from March through June, and a snowy outbreak or two isn't unusual in March or April. Nights remain cool even if days are warming up, so packing for the weather can be a chore.

Easter, wherever it falls, traditionally marks the beginning of the high season, so prices start to go up at that point. But these days, foreign visitors start flooding in (especially to Edinburgh) before that magic date, so it looks as if the tourist season is stretching beyond its normal boundaries.

Perusing a Calendar of Events

Scotland certainly has its share of annual festivals and special events throughout the year, with the centerpiece being Edinburgh, which holds several simultaneous festivals in August. Highland games are held in most regions from summer to early autumn. Where possible, I include telephone contacts and Web sites. Log on to www.visitscotland.com for information on the events highlighted below and more.

January

The best attended annual festival in Glasgow, and the largest of its kind in the world, **Celtic Connections** kicks off the year every January. The two main venues for performances are the Royal Concert Hall, which produces the event, and the recently renovated City Halls. Contemporary and traditional folk music, world music, and dance are all represented. For details, call Glasgow Royal Concert Hall, Sauchiehall Street. Call ☎ **0141-353-8080**, or visit www.celticconnections.com. Mid-January to the end of January.

On **Burns Night,** the anniversary of poet Robert Burns's birth, special suppers are held across the country and particularly in Ayrshire. It's an evening of storytelling, whisky, and traditional Scottish dishes such as haggis. January 25.

In Shetland's capital, Lerwick, **Up Helly Aa** is a fire festival with a torch-lit parade that celebrates the Nordic and Viking influences in this remote part of Scotland. For details, call the local tourist board at ☎ **08701-999-440**. January 31.

February

New Territories is Glasgow's annual international festival of cutting-edge performance art, dance, and drama. Log on to www.newmoves.co.uk for more details. Early February to mid-March.

March

In Lanark, south of Glasgow, the **Whuppity Scourie Festival** aims to beat the winter blahs. The town sponsors dancing, singing, music, and storytelling activities. March 1.

In the Highlands' capital, the annual **Inverness Music Festival** is a competition of amateur artists from across the country, including solo singers, choirs, and ensembles of musicians. There are also classes conducted throughout the festival. Call ☎ **01463-716-616**, or visit www.invernessmusicfestival.org. Early to mid-March.

For the better part of two weeks, the **Fort William Mountain Festival** brings international cinema devoted to the great outdoors to the town of Fort William in the Western Highlands. The event also includes lectures and workshops. Call ☎ **01397-700-001,** or visit www.mountainfilm festival.co.uk. Early to mid-March.

The **Glasgow International Comedy Festival** was inaugurated in 2003, bringing a diverse range of some of the funniest men and women to stages around the city. Call ☎ **0141-552-2070,** or visit www.glasgow comedyfestival.com. Mid-March to the end of the month.

April

For two weeks during the **Edinburgh International Science Festival,** adults and kids can enjoy some 250 shows, workshops, exhibitions, and lectures that are lots of fun and quite interesting. Call ☎ **0131-557-5588,** or visit www.sciencefestival.co.uk. Early to mid-April.

The **Melrose Sevens,** held in Melrose, south of Edinburgh, is a world-famous international rugby event that features seven high-octane players on each side. Call ☎ **01896-822-993,** or visit www.melrose7s.com. Mid-April.

For one long weekend in April, under a big-top tent in Glasgow's George Square, galleries from across the U.K. set up stalls and sell artwork during the **Glasgow Art Fair** (www.glasgowartfair.com). That four-day event is complemented every second year by a contemporary art festival, **Glasgow International,** with exhibits at local galleries (www.glasgowinternational.org). Last two weeks of April.

Contemporary and avant-garde music events at various venues in three cities — Aberdeen, Edinburgh, and Glasgow — are the hooks of the annual **Triptych** festival (www.triptychfestival.com). Last weekend of April.

The **Beltane Fire Festival** on Calton Hill, Edinburgh, celebrates pre-Christian tradition and the arrival of spring blossoms with primal drums and dancing. A bit of nudity is almost guaranteed. Call ☎ **131-228-5353,** or visit www.beltane.org. April 30.

For some 30 years, Shetland has hosted the annual **Shetland Folk Festival,** with concerts and spontaneous sessions where local and visiting musicians get together and jam. Call ☎ **01595-694-757,** or visit www.shetlandfolkfestival.com. Late April to early May.

May

Football fans flock to Glasgow for the **Scottish Cup Final.** This game is the deciding match after months of a single-elimination soccer tournament, where teams from the lower semiprofessional and amateur divisions of Scottish football get a chance to compete with the Scottish giants of the sport. Hamden Park. Call ☎ **0141-616-6000,** or visit www.scottishfa.co.uk. Early May.

Not to be outdone by Shetland, its northern island neighbors, Orkney has its own **Orkney Folk Festival.** For more than 25 years, it's brought in musicians from the mainland and Scandinavia for a set of concerts over four days. Call ☎ **01856-851-331,** or visit www.orkneyfolkfestival.com. Penultimate week in May.

The **Perth Festival of the Arts,** the city's annual festival of music, art, and drama, features local and international talent. Call ☎ **0845-612-6330,** or visit www.perthfestival.co.uk. Last ten days of May.

In Ayr, south of Glasgow, **Burns an' a' That!** celebrates the life of Robert Burns, with contemporary artists and performers — mainly in music. Call ☎ **01292-290-300,** or visit www.burnsfestival.com. Late May.

June

During the **Common Riding Festivals,** hundreds of horse riders parade around Selkirk, Hawick, and other towns in the Borders, commemorating the ancient practice of marking a town's territory. Throughout June.

Glasgow's **West End Festival** is the city's most vibrant community-based event, in its most happening neighborhood. The party includes live music concerts, a street parade, and other events. Call ☎ **0141-341-0844,** or visit www.westendfestival.co.uk. Throughout most of June.

Once held in August, the **Edinburgh International Film Festival** moved in 2008 to a less-crowded slot in the Scottish capital's cultural calendar. This is the longest-running annual celebration of cinema in Europe. Call ☎ **0131-228-4051,** or visit www.edfilmfest.org.uk. Mid- to late June.

The **St Magnus Festival,** on Orkney, showcases new singing, composing, and acting talents, mixing modern and classical sounds with drama and dance. It culminates on the longest day of the year, which, in Orkney, means almost 24 hours of daylight. Call ☎ **01856-871-445,** or visit www.stmagnusfestival.com. Third week in June.

The Royal Highland Show, in Ingliston, near Edinburgh, is Scotland's premier agriculture and rural-life fair. It features pedigreed livestock, flowers, show jumping, crafts, and more. Call ☎ **0131-335-6200,** or visit www.royalhighlandshow.org. Third weekend in June.

At the **Glasgow International Jazz Festival,** improvising musicians from all over the world come together to perform at various venues around the city. Call ☎ **0141-552-3552,** or visit www.jazzfest.co.uk. End of June.

July

In Stornoway, the capital of the Outer Hebrides, the annual **Hebridean Celtic Festival** combines outdoor folk-oriented concerts with more intimate shows at the An Lanntair Arts Centre. Call ☎ **01851-621-234,** or visit www.hebceltfest.com. Mid-July.

T in the Park, in Balado, is Scotland's largest annual two-day outdoor pop and rock festival. Many major (and a few minor) bands from the U.S. and the U.K. play on multiple stages. Visit www.tinthepark.com. Mid-July.

Barclays Scottish Open, at the Loch Lomond Golf Club, northwest of Glasgow, is held on the weekend before the Open, Great Britain's most important golfing event, drawing many of the sport's international stars. Visit www.barclaysscottishopen.co.uk. Mid-July.

The **Glasgow River Festival** is a two-day family oriented event with exhibitions, sailing, and other festivities on the River Clyde. Visit www.glasgowriverfestival.co.uk. Mid-July.

The longest-running jazz festival in the U.K. is the **Edinburgh Jazz & Blues Festival.** The whole city opens its doors to host the best jazz and blues performances. Call ☎ 0131-667-7776, or visit www.edinburgh jazzfestival.co.uk. Last week of July.

August

The cultural highlight of Edinburgh's year comes every August during what is collectively called the **Edinburgh Festival.** It is actually a few concurrent festivals. Since it began in 1947, the flagship **Edinburgh International Festival** has attracted artists and performance companies of the highest caliber in classical music, opera, ballet, or theater. Running simultaneously is the now much bigger **Edinburgh Festival Fringe,** and it alone encompasses some 1,800 performances in a cultural bonanza, drawing major talent — especially comics — from around the world. Edinburgh also hosts the **Edinburgh International Book Festival** and the Edinburgh **Jazz & Blues Festival** (see events listing for June), at about the same time. For information on all the Edinburgh festivals, visit www.edinburghfestivals.co.uk. Throughout August.

One of the season's most popular traditional spectacles is the **Edinburgh Military Tattoo,** featuring music, marching, and military exercises on the floodlit esplanade of Edinburgh Castle every evening. Call ☎ 0131-225-1188, or visit www.edintattoo.co.uk. Throughout August.

Piping Live! brings bagpipe players and ensembles from around the world to Glasgow. The weeklong festival culminates with the **World Pipe Championships,** pitting some 200 pipe bands from around the world for the highest honors. Call ☎ 0141-241-4400, or visit www.piping festival.co.uk. Mid-August.

The largest of Scotland's many Highland games — the **Cowal Highland Gathering** — is not actually held in the Highlands but rather in the Cowal peninsular town of Dunoon, west of Glasgow. The events usually attract up to 3,000 or more competitors from as far away as British Columbia and New Zealand. Call ☎ 01369-703-206, or visit www.cowalgathering.co.uk. End of August.

September

The Braemar Gathering is probably the best known of the annual Highland Games, regularly attended by members of the Royal family, whose Balmoral Castle is nearby. Spectators take in piping, dancing, and strength competitions. Call ☎ **01339-755-377,** or visit www.braemar gathering.org. First weekend in September.

For a couple of weekends every September, **Doors Open Days** ensures that important buildings, typically closed to the public, are opened for visitors. It's a rare opportunity to see the interiors of historic and architecturally significant edifices all over Scotland. Visit www.doorsopen days.org.uk. Throughout September.

The **Taste of Mull & Iona Food Festival** is a weeklong celebration of local produce, from wild seafood to farmed oysters to homemade cheeses. It includes farm tours, wildlife walks, boat trips, and special feasts. Visit www.mi-food.co.uk. Early to mid-September.

Literary types should consider the **Wigtown Book Festival,** where the southwestern village of Wigtown, with its numerous secondhand and antiquary bookshops, hosts readings and other events. Call ☎ **01988-402-036,** or visit www.wigtownbookfestival.com. End of September to early October.

The **Darvel Music Festival,** in the village of Darvel in Ayrshire, south of Glasgow, is a recent addition to the Strathclyde cultural calendar. It features an eclectic array of musicians, primarily folk and up-and-coming talent. Visit www.darvelmusicfestival.org. Last weekend in September or early October.

October

Glasgay! brings one of the U.K.'s largest festivals of gay, lesbian, bisexual, and transgender culture to Glasgow, with club nights, music, and performance art. Visit www.glasgay.com. October to early November.

Scotland's largest celebration of the Gaelic language, Celtic heritage, and traditional Highlands and Islands music, the **Royal National Mod** moves from one place to the next every year. In 2010, for example, it was in Caithness. In 2011 it's scheduled to be in the Western Isles, and then Dunoon in 2012. If the Gaels' culture interests you, check to see whether the festival fits your itinerary. Call ☎ **01463-709-705,** or visit www. the-mod.co.uk. Mid-October.

November

The capital gets an early start on the holiday season with **Edinburgh's Christmas,** featuring outdoor markets and fairground rides. Visit www. edinburghschristmas.com. From late November to Christmas Eve.

St. Andrew's Day celebrates Scotland's patron saint, and events surrounding November 30 include exhibits, concerts, and fireworks — particularly in St. Andrews, where there are weeklong celebrations, as well as other locations. Some Scots would like to see St. Andrew's Day be as big a celebration as the Irish St. Patrick's Day. End of November.

December

In Scotland, New Year's Eve is called **Hogmanay,** and events take place across the country. But Edinburgh marks the holiday with a weeklong extravaganza of events (many free), culminating with a December 31 street party, rock concert, and fireworks display (www.edinburghs hogmanay.org). Glasgow has celebrations on Hogmanay that include outdoor concerts (www.winterfestglasgow.com). Last week in December.

If you're in the country and looking for something different on New Year's Eve, perhaps the **Stonehaven Fireball Festival** is the ticket for you. In this northeastern port town, locals parade down the main street literally swinging huge fireballs to ward off darkness and welcome the new year. Visit www.stonehavenfireballs.co.uk. December 31.

Chapter 4

Following an Itinerary: Five Fine Options

In This Chapter

▶ Following a one-week tour of Edinburgh and Glasgow
▶ Taking time for a two-week tour of most of Scotland
▶ Finding places that should please the children
▶ Discovering Scotland's great outdoors in the Highlands and Western Islands

*H*owever willing we are to leave a few things to chance, most of us want to have a bit of structure when we travel. With that in mind, this chapter suggests some practical itineraries. The first two are appropriate if you have one or two weeks to explore Scotland. Then I suggest a seven-day route designed particularly for traveling families. Finally, for those who want to focus on the big, beautiful rural, coastal, and mountainous countryside, I've put together a pair of one-week itineraries: one that focuses on the wonderful Highlands, the other on the singular Scottish Islands. These are just some suggestions, and alas they leave out a few areas, such as the Kintyre Peninsula and the Isle of Islay, famous for its whisky.

In each itinerary, I direct you to the proper chapters to find in-depth information on the sights and attractions listed. Alternatively, consult the Index at the back of the book, which directs you to the appropriate city and region chapters in Parts III and IV.

 You may be planning to rent a car for your stay in Scotland. If you want to see just Edinburgh and Glasgow, however, you're probably better off without one.

Some side trips are more difficult to make without an automobile, but regions such as Fife and Ayrshire (and cities such as Stirling) can be visited by train or by bus. Even the shores of Loch Lomond can be reached by train, so don't feel obliged to use a smog-spewing gas guzzler unless you need the utter freedom to explore and take all sorts of back roads.

Seeing Many Highlights in One Week

If you have seven days to explore, you're not going to see everything that Scotland has to offer. Worry not: With a bit of enterprise, you can see quite a lot despite the time limitations.

I strongly suggest that you principally visit Edinburgh and Glasgow, using them as bases for excursions into the surrounding countryside. The one-week itinerary in this section offers the option of one overnight stay on the fringes of the Highlands or south of the principal cities. You may prefer to try and cover more of the country by staying in different places every night. If that's the case, then you may want to combine part of this section with parts of the next section on a two-week trip to Scotland.

Day 1

Start in the capital, **Edinburgh.** In your first 24 hours, familiarize yourself with the city by taking one of the hop-on, hop-off **tour buses,** which are open-air. Then stick to the city's famous **Old Town** and stroll the **Royal Mile,** taking in attractions such as **Edinburgh Castle, Gladstone's Land, St. Giles Cathedral,** and the **Palace of Holyroodhouse.** Later **pop into a pub** for a drink and dine at one of the city's fine restaurants. You can find complete information on Old Town and its major attractions, pubs, and restaurants in Chapter 11.

Day 2

Your priority today is Edinburgh's museums and galleries. If you're a history buff, the **Museum of Scotland** should top your list. For art, hit as many national galleries as possible, whether Old Masters at the flagship **National Gallery of Scotland** on the Mound (between Old and New Town), more recent works at the **Scottish National Gallery of Modern Art,** or luminaries depicted in the **Scottish National Portrait Gallery.** For details on all these (and more), see Chapter 11.

Day 3

Take your first day trip outside the city today. I offer three distinct choices here, not because I can't decide but because I want you to know your options. Pick between the **Kingdom of Fife,** which is just across the Forth River from Edinburgh (see Chapter 16); the ancient city and castle of **Stirling** (see Chapter 16); or **East Lothian** and the **Borders** (see Chapters 13 and 14). Each option provides a break from the city and exposes you to the readily available countryside.

Day 4

It's a travel day, but you're only going some 72km (45 miles) west to Scotland's biggest city, **Glasgow.** The trip takes less than an hour by train. Once there, first take one of the hop-on, hop-off **tour bus** rides that leave frequently from George Square in the heart of the city. Return to the commercial center after your tour, and explore some of the city's **free museums,** visit the medieval **Glasgow Cathedral,** or follow my walking tour (in Chapter 12) to admire the famous **Victorian architecture** or the work of **Charles Rennie Mackintosh.** Flip to Chapter 12 for more information on Glasgow, including hints on the city's top pubs and restaurants.

Day 5

Explore the leafy environs of Glasgow's most desirable district, the **West End,** which is home to the city's 500-plus-year-old university and an excellent municipal art collection in the recently refurbished, the spiffing **Kelvingrove Art Museum and Gallery.** Shop, drink, and dine on the West End's main street, **Byres Road.** Another of Glasgow's art-centric priorities is the unique **Burrell Collection,** which requires a trip to the Pollok Country Park on the city's south side. You'll find more information on all Glasgow has to offer in Chapter 12, where you can also take note of my suggested one-, two-, and three-day (or more) itineraries of the city.

Day 6

Alas, time is running short, so another day trip with the option of an overnight stay is my suggestion. Go west/southwest by train or auto to Wemyss Bay and take the ferry to the **Isle of Bute** to get a taste of island life. Or perhaps head toward the Highlands, stopping along the bonnie banks of **Loch Lomond.** You can make it back to Glasgow, but you may prefer to stay in the country this evening. See Chapters 15 or 16 for details.

Day 7

Unbelievably, your time is almost up. You may want to go south of Glasgow into **"Burns Country,"** in Ayrshire, an excursion that can include visits to the birthplace of 18th century poet Robert Burns as well as stops at golfing hotspots, such as **Turnberry,** and a tour of historic properties, such as **Culzean Castle,** with its magnificent seaside prospect, gardens, and parkland. (See Chapter 15 for more information on these and other attractions in the area.) If you passed on Stirling earlier in your visit, you can get there just as easily from Glasgow. Chapter 16 has all the details.

The Best You Can See in Two Weeks

In two weeks, you can see bits of the major regions of Scotland and a fair number of the major attractions, too.

Days 1, 2, and 3

Obviously, I don't want to exclude **Edinburgh** and **Glasgow** from this itinerary, so you can spend your first two days in Edinburgh, following the itinerary outlined in the previous section. But give the capital an extra 24 hours so that on the third day you can pick up some additional quality time in this fabulous city, or take an additional day trip as outlined above. (After a detour south, this itinerary takes you to Glasgow, too, on days 6 and 7.)

Day 4

Now's your chance to see some of **southern Scotland.** Head for **Melrose** and its historic 12th Century abbey and also see **Abbotsford,** the mansion of writer Sir Walter Scott. Then journey west to Dumfries and Galloway. **Dumfries** is a pleasant southern Scottish town, sometimes referred to as the "Queen of the South," with national bard Robert Burns's final home, which is now a museum. If you have the inclination, head to the lovely harbor town of **Portpatrick** on the Rhinns of Galloway, a picturesque coastal settlement boasting a natural harbor with excellent seaside views. See Chapter 14.

Day 5

Travel north toward Glasgow, stopping to take in **Culzean Castle** and **"Burns Country,"** which are outlined in Day 7 of "Seeing Many Highlights in One Week."

Days 6 and 7

These are your days to spend in **Glasgow.** Follow my earlier suggestions for what to see and do in "Seeing Many Highlights in One Week," outlined above.

Day 8

Head north of the city toward the **Highlands,** via **Loch Lomond.** Depending on your ambitions, this journey can include a detour to Loch Fyne and Loch Awe, but it's probably best to head for **Oban** (see Chapter 15) and then on the Calmac ferry to the **Isle of Mull.**

Day 9

Spend today touring the isle of **Mull** and the ancient Christian settlement of **Iona.** From Oban you can join a guided tour if you prefer. If you want to spend the night, you may wish to consider the wee, historic Isle of Iona or some place in **Tobermory,** Mull's principal port town on the north side of the island. See Chapter 19 for more information.

Day 10

From the port of Tobermory, you can take a ferry (in summer) to the remote peninsula of **Ardnamurchan,** which is the westernmost point of the British mainland. Along the way, you can stop to take in the handsome ruins of **Castle Tioram,** the small port of **Arisaig,** majestic **Sands of Morar,** and the working harbor of **Mallaig.** From the last point, another Calmac ferry departs to the **Isle of Skye.** Just north of the Armadale ferry terminal on Skye is the **Clan Donald** visitor center. You have time to visit the center and drive up to **Portree,** Skye's main port, before heading back to the mainland via the bridge at the **Kyle of Lochalsh.** From Uig on Skye another ferry sails to the Outer Hebrides (but that is part of another itinerary later in this chapter). See Chapters 18 and 19 for details on the areas and attractions of Day 10.

Day 11

Stop at **Eilean Donan** (possibly the most photographed Highland castle) and the picturesque seaside town of **Plockton** before you start the lovely drive to **Inverness** and the northern shores of **Loch Ness.** If you're hungry for more of this kind of scenery, see the Highland itinerary later in this chapter. For details on the area, flip to Chapters 18 and 19.

Day 12

Here's your chance to see Nessie, the Loch Ness Monster. Don't spend too much time at Loch Ness, however, because you need to get across the mountains to Highland Perthshire. Here, it's worth your time to have a gander at a few castles, such as **Braemar** or **Blair Atholl,** and perhaps make a stop at a whisky distillery. See Chapter 17 for more on the area.

Day 13

As you head back toward the center of Scotland, take in **Perth** as well as the golfing mecca and ancient settlement of **St. Andrews** in Fife (see Chapter 16).

Day 14

On the last day of your tour, visit **Stirling** if you haven't already done so, or alternatively, see more of coastal **Fife** on your way back to Edinburgh, where this itinerary began a fortnight ago.

Discovering Scotland with Kids

Touring history-heavy castles or art-laden museums with children in tow doesn't have to be a big headache or a battle of patience and wills. Plenty of attractions appeal to all ages. If you're traveling with little ones, following the loose itinerary in this section can be the path of least resistance. When you're in Edinburgh and Glasgow, you don't need a car; public transportation and an occasional taxi should suffice. However, upon leaving those two cities, a car becomes necessary to complete this tour.

 As you follow the cross-references in this section and jump to other chapters in this book, look for the Kid Friendly icon, which points out the best attractions, restaurants, and so on to visit with children.

Begin in **Edinburgh,** and make sure to visit **Edinburgh Castle.** The self-guided audio tour may confuse little kids, but the castle is interesting and fun to explore even without any commentary. Nearby, the **Camera Obscura** usually fascinates children. You can make a trip to the **Edinburgh Zoo** to see the penguin parade; and, while in town, visit the toy-filled **Museum of Childhood.** See Chapter 11 for more information on Edinburgh's attractions.

Next it's on to **Glasgow,** where you can break up your other sightseeing with kiddie favorites such as the aforementioned **Kelvingrove Art Gallery and Museum;** interactive exhibits at the **Science Centre;** and the fun, hands-on **People's Palace.** For a breath of fresh air (and to burn off any excess energy), take a romp around **Glasgow Green.**

A couple of side trips from Glasgow can take two entire days. You can head south along the coast, where the kids can comb beaches, see the cottage where poet Robert Burns was born, and romp about the adventure playground at **Culzean Castle.** In the other direction is Stirling, offering a bit of history and education at **Bannockburn,** good exploring in **Stirling Castle,** and some entertainment (and frights) in the tour of Stirling's **Old Town Jail.**

From Glasgow, you may want to head north through spectacular **Glen Coe** and perhaps spend a day exploring the area around Fort William, hiking or mountain biking around **Ben Nevis,** the highest peak in Great Britain. Next comes the **Loch Ness** region, which is generally a load of fun for children. Check out one of the Loch Ness exhibitions and one of the sonar-scoping monster-hunting cruises.

On the road back to Edinburgh, you can stop at **J. M. Barrie's Birthplace** in Kirriemuir (Barrie wrote *Peter Pan*) and visit **Deep Sea World,** just north of Edinburgh in North Queensferry.

Touring Scotland's Great Western Highlands

Scotland has no shortage of things to see, and most regions have their own unique attractions. But among the best regions is the open terrain of the **Highlands.** Why not go to the top of the Scottish — and for that matter, the U.K. — mainland and see some of the unspoiled spaces? For this seven-day itinerary (I don't break it down into exact days, so you can adjust the plans as you like), you can take the train from Glasgow, Edinburgh, or even London up to Inverness and rent a car there. For more details on Highlands attractions, and for lists of accommodations and restaurants in this area, see Chapter 18.

From **Inverness,** head north across the Black Isle, through **Tain,** and across the Dornoch Firth. Make a brief stop to see the cathedral in **Dornoch,** and then head up through Lairg to the northern shore.

At Tongue, you may want to stop to see the Highland cattle that roam the beaches here, and then go west to **Durness,** a settlement that John Lennon visited as a child (which is why a small monument stands in his memory). One natural curiosity is **Smoo Cave,** although what's really spectacular is the craggy shoreline, which leads to remote **Cape Wrath.** For some excellent crafts, visit **Balnakeil** — an artists' colony in an abandoned military base that's a throwback to the 1960s if there ever was one.

From Durness, head south along more beautiful, pristine seashore toward **Scourie.** But before you get there, you really must detour out to Blairmore, park the car, and hike into the one of the best beaches in Great Britain at **Sandwood Bay.** You can also hike to Cape Wrath from Sandwood, if you're ambitious.

To appreciate just how wild, beautiful, and unpopulated the Western Highlands region of Scotland truly is, detour at Kylesku to the peninsula with the stone monument known as the **Old Man of Stoer,** or simply carry on through the mountains to the active fishing port of **Ullapool.** It's hardly a big town, but it seems like the height of civilization after you've spent time farther north.

Inverewe Garden is the next highlight, although your drive south provides ample opportunities to stop and sightsee, like at **Gruinard Bay,** where you may just spot some sea otters splashing in the surf.

The road south twists and turns past Gairloch, Loch Torridon, and the road to **Applecross** (where the inn serves famously delicious meals) before arriving in aforementioned **Plockton,** perhaps the most picturesque village in the Highlands. Kick back, relax, and toast your Highland excursion on your final night of this tour.

Beware of the midge

I love the western extremities of Scotland, but for many, the region is home to the nastiest beast in the nation. The *midge* (*mid*-gee) is a tiny flying insect (a no-see-um) that arrives in swarms on moist, still days and leaves a terrifically itchy bite. If you can't resist the call of the west, arm yourself with some effective bug repellant.

Touring the Highlands and the Hebrides

If you want to combine mountainous terrain with sea ferries and scenic island life, then the itinerary in this section is the one for you. It's only slightly less ambitious than the previous Highland tour, showing you a bit of the Highlands and Hebridean islands, too. For more details on the places mentioned in this section, see Chapters 18 and 19.

This tour begins in **Fort William.** Not a spectacular place, this is the spot to satisfy your shopping urges, before heading north by car. Start off on the "Road to the Isles," which takes past the **Glenfinnan Monument** and its visitors center at the tip of Loch Shiel. This is where Bonnie Prince Charlie rallied Highlanders in 1745. There is another landmark here, one of Victorian engineering: the soaring arched train viaduct made more famous by the Harry Potter film.

Past here, the highway has been improved to decrease travel times, but I suggest taking the old shore road from **Arisaig,** a quaint harbor village where you can catch a boat to the small Isle of Eigg. Up the coast is another of the best stretches of beach in Scotland — the **Sands of Morar** — and the deepest, darkest loch in the country: **Loch Morar.**

At **Mallaig,** catch the short ferry crossing across the **Sound of Sleat** to Armadale and the craggy, mountainous **Isle of Skye.** The largest of the Inner Hebrides, Skye has plenty of attractions from the **Cuillin Hills** to the **Museum of Island Life** to **Dunvegan Castle.**

You don't need to buy round-trip (return) tickets for ferry crossings. The boat operator, Caledonian MacBrayne, also has a host of "island hopscotch" tickets so that you can leave from one mainland port and return to another.

From Uig, Skye, another ferry (about two hours) can take you across to the **Outer Hebrides,** the famous Western Isles of Scotland. You can go either to Lochmaddy on **North Uist** or Tarbert on **Harris.** Either way, explore both mountains and amazing beaches whose seas on sunny days are as clear and blue as you will ever see. On stormy days, it is as rough as any you will ever see.

Finally, head north to the **Isle of Lewis,** the northwestern outpost of Europe and the largest of the Outer Hebrides. Although many think of Lewis as only vast stretches of treeless peat bog (a wet desert), in fact, it is the most diverse of the Western Isles. Among the attractions: more remarkable sands (whether Uig or North Tolsta), hill walking, prehistoric monuments, such as the standing **Callanish Stones,** and a lot more.

To complete your tour, visit **Stornoway,** the only town in the Outer Hebrides, where you can catch a Calmac ferry back to the mainland or a flight to Inverness, Edinburgh, and Glasgow.

Planning Your Trip: Mileage Chart

Use Table 4-1 to help you plan your travel itinerary in Scotland, but remember: Roads can be narrow and winding, so allot extra time to get from point A to point B.

It's important to be realistic about the amount of time you'll spend in the car or bus burning up precious daylight hours. If you try to hit Ullapool and Inverness in one full (and tiring) day, then you spend most of your day driving the distance between the two cities and see only a few big sights. Try to get up and out early — that means breakfast at 8:30 a.m. instead of 11 a.m. And don't try to cram too much into each day. If you're constantly rushing from one place to the next, then you won't enjoy anything you see. That said, you know your limits and I have known people to travel from Oxford, England, to Port Charlotte on Isle of Islay in one day. Impressive.

Table 4-1 Distances (in Miles) between Some of Scotland's Towns and Cities

Aberdeen								
179	Ayr							
129	79	Edinburgh						
157	141	131	Fort William					
146	33	45	116	Glasgow				
105	207	154	64	175	Inverness			
84	95	45	106	62	117	Perth		
119	64	36	96	27	143	35	Stirling	
158	258	208	109	222	56	165	193	Ullapool

Part II
Planning Your Trip to Scotland

The 5th Wave   By Rich Tennant

"They said they offered a very inexpensive package tour."

In this part . . .

*T*he chapters in Part II are designed to get down to the nitty-gritty of planning your trip: I offer advice and guidance on determining how much your trip to Scotland might cost and how to make a sensible budget; finding out which airlines go where (and finding the smartest value in airfares); deciding the best ways to get around Scotland when you're there; figuring out how to drive on Scotland's roads; finding the right accommodations for your needs; and managing passports. And that's not all.

In this part, you can find advice on what to do if you get sick in Scotland and whether you should invest in travel insurance. If you're a traveler with special needs and interests, issues important to you are covered here, as well. In short, the following pages are filled with all the info you need to plan your trip to Scotland.

Chapter 5

Managing Your Money

In This Chapter
▶ Creating a realistic budget for your trip to Scotland
▶ Reviewing money-saving tips
▶ Understanding the local currency and how best to get it
▶ Carrying money conveniently and safely

*A*n important consideration for any vacation is your budget, of course. How much will the trip cost and where will the money be best spent? You don't want to waste good money, but you probably don't want to be tied down to a bare-bones budget that restricts you from seeing the highlights of Scotland.

The smartest way to travel is to plan your spending in advance: In large part, this means understanding ahead of time what things will cost. But keep in mind that sometimes you get what you pay for.

This chapter covers what you can expect to pay for transportation, accommodations, dining, and sightseeing while in Scotland. Plus, I include some money-saving tips. As a hands-on bonus, the Dummies budget worksheet (Table 5-2) will help you plot out your expenses.

Keep in mind that **exchange rates** are constantly fluctuating. As I write, after watching the dollar gain quite a lot of value against the pound, owing to stresses in the financial markets, it has fallen again as the Fed has been expanding money supply. Because of the recent oscillation and uncertainty about the economic situations to come, it is impossible for me to give you a precise conversion when you read this. Throughout the book, I have thought of £1 equal to about $1.50 to $1.60.

If you want to play it safe: overestimate. Essentially double all pound amounts and that will give you a generous dollar equivalent: For example, a £10 meal is virtually $20. Alternatively, visit www.xe.com/ucc to see the most current pound-to-dollar conversion rate. But remember, the consumer rates may not equal the official dollar–pound rate.

Alas, goods in Scotland often carry a similar numerical price in pounds as they would in dollars back in the U.S. For example, a digital camera that costs $250 in New York might be priced at, say, £230 in Edinburgh. But, of course, that means it's more expensive in Scotland.

I suspect that you want to enjoy your stay and don't want to be constantly converting pounds to dollars before making every purchase. But if your desire is to keep costs down, be wary, and make sure you're getting a bargain or at least spending your money wisely.

Planning Your Budget

As you have probably already guessed, Scotland is not the cheapest European destination. But it's not the most expensive place to visit, either. Can you do Scotland on $10 a day? No, quite honestly — unless you sleep at the roadside and mainly eat cans of baked beans. On $25 a day? Possibly, if you don't mind camping or bunking in a youth hostel and eating very basic meals over a campfire. Being realistic, however, you can bet on a figure more like $125 to $200 per person per day — more if you factor in full-time car rental and gasoline (petrol) costs. And that figure doesn't include the cost of actually getting to Scotland.

But sometimes you do get what you pay for. In this case, Scotland usually compensates for the proverbial price of admission.

Transportation

Car rental (or *car hire*) isn't especially exorbitant, but visitors will likely find the cost of vehicle fuel (diesel or *petrol)* to be staggeringly high. Remember, here it's is priced in liters, not gallons. It costs about 3.5 times more than the average in the United States. On the plus side, however, your rental car will probably get exceptional miles per gallon (which, oddly, is how that figure is still measured here), and the driving distances across Scotland are generally miniscule compared to cross-country travel in the United States, Canada, and Australia. Usually the car-rental rates include unlimited mileage. Check with your auto insurance company to see if you need to buy extra coverage for when you're in Scotland. (I discuss insurance coverage for travelers in Chapter 10.)

Although it may limit your mobility, using public transportation can help cut your costs, particularly if you buy tickets in advance. If you're only planning to visit Edinburgh, Glasgow, and some side-trip destinations, you don't really need to rent a car.

Lodging

Hotel rooms in Scotland aren't cheap, but prices over the past five years have remained steady. If, however, you do your homework and scour accommodations Web sites, you *will* find rates considerably lower than the standard "tariff" that may be quoted by each hotel. If you want luxury or a spectacular view, you will have to pay a premium. If you just need a leak-proof roof over your head, a place to wash, and a clean bed, then you can easily save money on your lodging.

Better too much than not enough

Make sure you have access to emergency money in case you need it. If you golf, add up greens fees and the price of renting clubs (assuming you're not lugging your own around the country). Do you plan to buy clothes, jewelry, crystal, and antiques, or just pick up a few postcards, a snow globe, and a couple of cheap souvenirs? A modest piece of crystal can set you back $80; a nice Edinburgh sweatshirt, about $50. So gauge your impulse-buying tendencies and factor that into your budget as well.

Generally speaking, a double room at a hotel runs about $150 at the low end to about $250 per night; double rooms at smaller, more modest guesthouses or B&Bs may be around $80 to $125. At the high end of the scale you can spend $350 or quite a bit more. Self-catering cottages rented by the week ($450–$1,200 per week) and country B&Bs are almost always less expensive (a bit under $50 per person). Rooms with their own bathrooms (en suite) cost more than those without. Places that remain open year-round often charge less during the low season, October through March.

Dining

American visitors with their calculators at the ready will find out that most food is typically more expensive in Scotland than in most of the U.S. But you can cut your dining expenses by not choosing the ritziest restaurant in town every night. Keep an eye out for lunch specials and early bird or pre-theater menus — they offer considerable savings. On the Web, investigate www.5pm.co.uk, which offers reductions on early evening dining options, particularly in Edinburgh and Glasgow. If you stay in self-catering accommodations, you'll spend less on food by cooking at your rental cottage or apartment. Some groceries, particularly premium items, such as organic chicken, cost about the same as in the U.S. metropolitan market.

A good per-person allowance for a sit-in lunch is $12 (soup/sandwich) to $25 (nice two-course meal), and for dinner between $30 and $60, on average, but much higher at the best restaurants. Many hotels and lodges include a big cooked breakfast in the room rate, so at least you often don't have to figure that meal into your daily food budget.

Sightseeing

The price of admission to many tourist attractions in Scotland is slightly more modest than what you may expect to find in other western European countries. In Edinburgh, the permanent exhibitions of the Scottish national galleries are priced just right: absolutely free. And similarly, in Glasgow, the city-run museums don't charge admission. All the natural beauty of the countryside, from the Ayrshire coastline to the Highlands, doesn't cost you a thing and, indeed, is priceless. Historic sites run by Historic Scotland and the National Trust for Scotland are a bit pricey, but if you plan to see several, consider a membership or joint-entrance tickets.

Even if you see two or three attractions each day, a fair amount to budget for sights is $20 per person per day.

Shopping

Jump back up to the introduction to this chapter and recall what I have already said about consumer retail goods and their U.K. prices. A pair of Calvin Kleins may have about the same sticker price as its counterpart in the U.S., but they will actually cost a lot more, given the exchange rate. Still, you can find "homegrown" commodities in Scotland that are less expensive when purchased here: woolen goods and cashmere, local crafts and arts, and more. Be selective in your purchases, and your bank balance will be better off.

Nightlife

As with sightseeing, you may find that things are cheaper than you anticipated, particularly the theater, dance, and even opera. In pubs and bars, prices of alcohol are at the higher end but not ridiculously so. In general, expect the equivalent of big-city (Toronto, San Francisco, Melbourne) prices for nightlife in Scotland. A pint of lager or ale will cost between $4 and $6. A dram of whisky is sometimes as little as $3, but cocktails are at least $6 and typically more.

In Table 5-1, I take the daily estimates laid out in this section and add them up for a projection of how much it typically costs to accommodate and entertain one person for one week in Scotland.

Table 5-1   Per-Person Expenses for a Week in Scotland

Expense	Cost
Airfare (round-trip New York City–London–Glasgow/ Edinburgh)	$500–$700
Rental car	$200–$400
Two to three tanks of gas	$150–$250
Seven nights in modest hotels ($75 per person)	$525
Seven lunches ($15 each average)	$105
Seven dinners ($28 each average)	$196
Sightseeing admissions ($20 per day average)	$140
Souvenirs and miscellaneous ($10 per day average)	$70
Grand Total	$1,886–$2,386

Cutting Costs without Cutting the Fun

If worries about travel costs mean you're hesitant to go to Scotland, you have two options: Simply stay home and miss out — or get over it. Sure, Scotland isn't the cheapest European country to visit, but it *can* be made more affordable. Make sensible decisions, look for those bargains that don't cheapen the experience, and you should be fine.

Some tourists demand to be pampered in five-star hotels, but those places are exceptionally expensive in Scotland. If you're flexible when it comes to the pampering, you should seek out the smaller lodges and guesthouses that are priced to fit tighter travel budgets. A nice perk of most Scottish accommodations is that breakfast is included in the price of the room. Sometimes it's even hearty enough to keep you full until dinner.

Also, some visitor attractions are free. Even if you stick to seeing things that cost nothing (although you shouldn't skip the other sights just because of the cost), you'll still experience a vast amount of the country.

You can find plenty of ways, some little and some big, to cut down on costs. Here are some smart ways to save on your trip to Scotland.

- ✓ **Go midseason or in the off season.** Traveling between mid-September and mid-April should save you money on your airfare and accommodations. The days leading up to and just after Christmas, New Year's Eve, and Easter are the exceptions, and prices jump up during those periods. (See Chapter 3 for more info on Scotland's seasons.)

- ✓ **Travel midweek.** Most everybody wants to travel on the weekends, but those willing to travel on a Tuesday, Wednesday, or Thursday can usually find cheaper flights. When inquiring about airfares, ask if you get a cheaper rate if you fly on a different day. Also remember that staying over a Saturday night can occasionally cut airfares by half.

- ✓ **Remember that group rates can save money.** And you don't necessarily have to be one of a busload to get them. Sometimes a party as small as three people qualifies for group rates.

- ✓ **Get the Explorer Pass.** Historic Scotland, which operates some 75 historic attractions across Scotland, offers an Explorer Pass that allows multiple entries to all of their sites, from Iona Abbey to St. Andrews Cathedral to Edinburgh Castle. The pass is sold at most of the sites run by the organization. For more information, call ☎ 0131-668-8831, or visit www.historic-scotland.gov.uk.

- ✓ **Try a package deal.** Many people believe that planning a trip entirely on their own is less expensive, but they're not necessarily correct. Travel packages can save not only money but time. A single phone call to a travel agent or package tour operator can take care of your flight, accommodations, transportation within the country, and sightseeing arrangements. Even if you're not up for a complete package — if you'd prefer to pay for your plane tickets with frequent-flier miles, say, or if you don't like some of the things the package tour operators offer — you can book room-car deals (which include a free rental car) or other combo packages directly through many hotels. Chapter 6 contains more details on package deals.

✓ **Always ask about discounts.** Membership in AAA, frequent-flier plans, trade unions, AARP, university alumni associations, or other groups often qualifies you for discounted rates on plane tickets, hotel rooms, and (mainly with U.S.-based companies) car rentals. Some car-rental companies give discounts to employees of companies that have corporate accounts. With valid identification, students, teachers, youths, and seniors may be entitled to discounts. Many attractions have discounted family prices. Ask about everything — you may be pleasantly surprised.

✓ **Book your rental car at weekly rates, when possible.** Weekly rentals are most often offered at a discounted rate.

✓ **Know where to buy gasoline (petrol).** The United Kingdom has some of the highest gasoline prices in Europe, and parts of rural Scotland have the highest prices in the U.K. For the most part, the smaller the town, the higher the price of gas. One way to ease the burden of these exorbitant rates is to fill your tank in cities and larger towns. Also, you may find lower gas prices at petrol stations at large supermarkets, such as Tesco or Asda.

✓ **Don't rent a gas guzzler.** Renting a smaller car is cheaper, and you save money on gas to boot. Unless you're traveling with kids and need lots of space, don't go beyond the economy size. For more on car rentals, see Chapter 7.

✓ **Walk.** All cities in the country are easy to explore on foot, even Glasgow and Edinburgh. Hoofing it can save you a few extra pounds (and even burn off a few from your waistline). As a bonus, you'll get to know your destination more intimately as you explore at a slower pace.

✓ **Skimp on souvenirs.** As a general rule, souvenirs specially created for the tourist market are poorly made and overpriced. If you're concerned about money, you can definitely do without the T-shirts, key chains, and other trinkets.

✓ **Use ATMs to get money.** The exchange rate of most banks' ATM machines — or *cash points* — is surprisingly competitive. Yes, your bank back home may charge a small fee, but it won't charge a percentage commission on the money you withdraw. And yes, it comes out in the local currency, not dollars.

✓ **Use libraries for Internet access.** Because of Western tourists' growing use of the Internet, online access is popping up all over Scotland. Most town libraries have access, and they usually don't

charge or require you to be a member. This policy may change in
the coming years, but for now, libraries are a good, cheap option
for surfing the Web.

✔ **Pick up free, coupon-packed visitor pamphlets and magazines.**
Detailed maps, feature articles, dining and shopping directories,
and discount and freebie coupons make these pocket-size give-
aways a smart pickup. You'll find these types of materials in tourist
board offices and perhaps in the lobby of your hotel.

✔ **Skip the fantabulous hotel-room views.** Rooms with great views
are the most expensive in any hotel. Unless you're planning to hang
out in your room all day, why hand over the extra dough?

✔ **Get out of town.** In many places, hotels located just outside popular tourist areas may be a great bargain and require only a little
more driving — and they may even offer free parking. Sure, you
may not get all the fancy amenities, and you'll probably have to
carry your own bags, but the rooms may be just as comfortable
and a whole lot cheaper.

✔ **Ask whether your children can stay in your room for free.**
Although many accommodations in Scotland charge by the head,
some may allow your little ones to stay for free. Even if you have
to pay $10 or $15 for a rollaway bed, you'll save hundreds by not
having to pay for two rooms.

✔ **Avoid making phone calls from a hotel room.** The inflated fees
that hotels charge for phone calls are scandalous. Walk to the nearest coin- or card-operated phone to make calls within and out of
the country.

✔ **Consider rooms that aren't en suite.** Rooms without a bathroom
are cheaper, although they're increasingly hard to find. Sharing a
bathroom may be a small sacrifice when it comes to saving money,
and it doesn't really detract from your trip. Group hostel rooms are
even cheaper if you're willing to rough it a bit more.

✔ **Check out accommodations with kitchens.** By renting self-catering
apartments or cottages for a week or more, you can save money
overall on accommodations (especially if you're traveling with a
group), and on food, because you can prepare your own meals in
the kitchen. By avoiding big-ticket restaurant meals, you'll save a
heck of a lot of money.

✔ **Have the same meal for less money.** If you enjoy a late lunch (or an
early evening meal) at a nice restaurant and settle for a snack later,
your wallet will thank you. Lunch and pretheater menus often offer the
same food as dinner menus, but the prices are much less expensive.

✔ **Before you leave home, check prices on items you think you may
want to buy.** This way, you'll know whether you're really getting a
bargain by buying items abroad. Spending a little time surfing the
Web is an easy way to find the information you need.

✔ **Look before you tip.** Some restaurants include a service fee or gratuity on the bill, especially if you're with a group. Study your bill: You could be paying a double tip by mistake. And don't tip bartenders for drinks — they don't expect it.

Table 5-2	Your Scotland Budget Worksheet
Expense	*Amount*
Airfare (multiplied by number of people traveling)	
Car rental (if you expect to rent one)	
Gas (expect to need one tank, at about $60, for every four to five days of driving)	
Lodging (multiplied by the number of nights you'll be in the country)	
Breakfast (your room rate likely includes it)	
Lunch (multiplied by the number of days in the country)	
Dinner (multiplied by the number of days in the country)	
Attractions (admission charges to museums, gardens, tours, theaters, nightclubs, and so on)	
Souvenirs (T-shirts, postcards, and that antique you just gotta have)	
Tips (think 10 percent–15 percent of your meal total, plus $1 a bag every time a bellhop moves your luggage)	
Incidentals (whisky, snacks, and so on)	
Getting from your hometown to the airport, plus long-term parking (if applicable)	
Grand Total	

Handling Money

After you settle on a budget for your trip, you can start figuring out the nuts and bolts of carrying money abroad. How much money do you want to bring along? Do you want to carry cold, hard cash, credit cards, traveler's checks, or all three? How can you get more money after you're in Scotland? What's the best way to exchange dollars for pounds? And how can you ensure that your money will be safe and secure while you're vacationing?

You're the best judge of how much cash you feel comfortable carrying or what currency alternative is your favorite. That's not going to change much just because you're on vacation. True, you'll probably be moving around more and incurring more expenses than you generally do (unless you happen to eat out every meal when you're at home), and you may let your mind slip into vacation mode and not be as vigilant about your safety as when you're in work mode, but, those factors aside, the only type of payment that won't be available to you away from home is your personal checkbook (or, as it's spelled in Scotland, *chequebook*). This section offers nearly everything you need to know about money matters in Scotland.

The local currency: What it's worth to you

The currency in Scotland, *British pence* and *pounds sterling,* is quite similar to American cents and dollars. The denominations of your loose change (though not the sizes) are almost the same: The few anomalies include 2-pence coins, the 20-pence coin (there's no equivalent to the U.S. quarter), and the 1- and 2-pound coins. Pence are often just referred to as "p," such as in "Do you have 30p for the pay phone?" A pound is also known colloquially as a quid. Some people may refer to a "bob" — this is equivalent to 5p, which used to be known as a "shilling" before the decimal system was imposed in 1971.

Although the U.K.'s official central bank, called the Bank of England, controls monetary matters across Great Britain and Northern Ireland, a couple of banks in Scotland, such as the Clydesdale Bank, have permission to print Scottish bills in 5-, 10-, and 20-pound denominations. They feature Scottish historical figures such as Sir Walter Scott or William Wallace (rather than the queen). There's no value difference between these pound notes and those printed in England, and both are accepted throughout Scotland.

 Be careful if you travel to England with Scottish bank notes: They're often not accepted by shops and restaurants, where employees are unaccustomed to seeing Scottish bank names on the folding money. Err on the side of caution and go to a bank and exchange any Scottish bills for Bank of England notes before heading south of the border.

As I've said throughout this chapter, goods and services are often more expensive in Scotland than they would be in the U.S. or in other English-speaking countries. Many items sold in Scotland are priced with the same numerical amount as they would be in the U.S. — for instance, if a soda costs a dollar in the U.S., it's often priced at a pound in Scotland. This increase isn't true of all items, but it gives you a general idea of how far your new cash and weighty coins will go.

Remember, the exchange rate fluctuates minute by minute. The best source for up-to-date currency exchange information is online at www. xe.com/ucc. The average rates are shown in Table 5-3.

Table 5-3	Typical Currency Exchange Rates
One Dollar	*Equals*
$1 U.S.	About 61p
$1 Canadian	About 61p
$1 Australian	About 62p
$1 New Zealand	About 48p
One British Pound	*Equals*
£1	$1.62 U.S.
£1	About $1.63 Canadian
£1	About $1.60 Australian
£1	About $2.04 New Zealand

You can exchange money anywhere you see the **Bureau de Change** sign. You will often see it at travel agencies, banks, post offices, and tourist information offices. Generally, you'll get the best rates at banks; the local tourist office can tell you the location of the bank branch nearest you.

Using ATMs and carrying cash

The easiest and best way to get cash away from home is from an ATM (automated teller machine), sometimes referred to as a "cash machine," or "cash point." The **Cirrus** (☎ 800-424-7787; www.mastercard.com) and **PLUS** (☎ 800-843-7587; www.visa.com) networks span the globe; look at the back of your bank card to see which network you're on, then call or check online for ATM locations at your destination. For example, the PLUS ATM locator (visa.via.infonow.net/locator/global) indicates that there are 100 machines in and around Edinburgh. Even up north in Inverness, it lists 84.

Be sure you know your personal identification number (PIN) before you leave home. Also remember that many banks impose a fee every time your card is used at a different bank's ATM, and that fee can be higher for international transactions (up to $5 or more) than for domestic ones (where they're rarely more than $1.50). On top of this, the bank from which you withdraw cash may charge its own fee. To compare banks' ATM fees within the U.S., use www.bankrate.com. For international withdrawal fees, ask your bank.

In many international destinations, ATMs offer the best exchange rates, even taking into account the extra withdrawal fees you may be charged. Avoid exchanging money at commercial exchange bureaus and hotels, which often have the highest transaction fees.

Not all ATMs in Scotland are connected to the global banking networks. This is especially true in rural areas and in small banks. It's best to not depend solely on ATMs for cash when you're traveling. Also, the security risks are the same here as at home. If someone steals your card and knows your personal identification number (PIN), the crook will try to drain your bank account. Recently, machines have been rigged to "swallow" cards, which are later extracted and used illegally. All this is rare in Scotland, but, nevertheless, you should exercise caution and avoid using ATMs late at night or in poorly lit urban areas.

Be sure to check your daily withdrawal limit with your bank before you set off on your trip. Remember, if your limit is $250, you'll be able to withdraw only about £150.

If you lose your ATM card, contact your bank at home and report the loss immediately. You don't want your bank account depleted in the event that the card (and, in a worst-case scenario, personal identification number) falls into the wrong hands.

Charging ahead with credit cards

Credit cards are a safe way to carry money: They also provide a convenient record of all your expenses, and they generally offer relatively good exchange rates. You can also withdraw cash advances from your credit cards at banks or ATMs, provided you know your PIN. If you've forgotten yours, or didn't even know you had one, call the number on the back of your credit card and ask the bank to send it to you. It usually takes five to seven business days, though some banks will provide the number over the phone if you tell them your mother's maiden name or some other personal information.

Remember that when you use your credit card abroad, many banks now assess a 1 percent to 3 percent **"transaction fee"** on all charges you incur abroad (whether you're using the local currency or your native currency). But credit cards still may be the smart way to go when you factor in such things as exorbitant ATM fees and higher traveler's check exchange rates (and service fees).

Some credit-card companies recommend that you notify them of any upcoming trip abroad; that way they won't become suspicious when the card is used in a foreign destination (and they won't block your charges). Even if you don't call your credit-card company in advance, you can always call the card's toll-free emergency number if a charge is refused — a good reason to carry the phone number with you. But perhaps the most important lesson here is to carry more than one card with you on your trip; a card might not work for any number of reasons, so having a backup is the smart way to go.

Visa and MasterCard are both widely used in Scotland. American Express is accepted by most major businesses, but Diners Club is less frequently accepted.

All credit cards issued in Scotland have a computer chip in them and users must know their PIN in order to make purchases. No signatures are required. Cards without chips can still be used, however.

Toting traveler's checks

You can buy traveler's checks at most banks. They are offered in denominations of $20, $50, $100, $500, and sometimes $1,000. Generally, you'll pay a service charge ranging from 1 percent to 4 percent. The most popular traveler's checks are offered by **American Express** (☎ 800-807-6233, or ☎ 800-221-7282 for cardholders — the latter number accepts collect calls, offers service in several foreign languages, and exempts Amex gold and platinum cardholders from the 1 percent fee); **Visa** (☎ 800-732-1322); and **MasterCard** (☎ 800-223-9920).

If you choose to carry traveler's checks, be sure to keep a record of their serial numbers separate from your checks, in the event that they are stolen or lost. You'll get a refund faster if you know the numbers.

American Express, Thomas Cook, Visa, and **MasterCard** offer **foreign-currency traveler's checks,** useful if you're traveling to one country or to the euro zone; they're accepted at locations where dollar checks may not be.

Taking Taxes into Account

All goods and services in Scotland have a tax or tariff roughly similar to the local sales taxes in the U.S., although it is always included in the sticker price rather than later at the cash register. It's called a value-added tax (VAT) and in January 2011 it was raised to a rather whopping 20 percent (up from 17.5 percent). The good news is that any tourists who live outside the European Union are entitled to get a refund on any VAT paid for goods that they take out of the E.U. — as long as they make those purchases at shops that are part of the Retail Export Scheme (look for signs saying "Tax Free Shopping"). The tax-back scheme is great for tourists who spend large sums of money on books, jewelry, gifts, clothes — you name it (except, alas, for services such as hotels, restaurants, and car rental).

But many tourists come to Scotland, spend lots of money, and never find out how to get their VAT back or don't bother because they don't fully understand how it works. To ensure that you don't make the same mistake, here's your quick guide to the VAT.

When you make your purchase, show your passport and ask for a tax refund form. Fill out the form and keep any receipts. When you leave the U.K., submit the form to Customs for approval. Once Customs has stamped it, there are a variety of ways to recover the tax. You can mail the form back to the shop and arrange repayment by post. Some shops are part of networks run by commercial refund companies, which you later contact for a refund, although an administration fee may be charged. Some London airport terminals may have refund booths where immediate repayments can be received.

If you are traveling on to another E.U. country, you won't be able to get your VAT refund. Also, U.K. Customs advises that you should arrange the method of tax reimbursement with the retailer when you purchase the product. For more information, log on to www.visitbritain.com and do a site search for "VAT refunds." For more information on a commercial refund company, try logging on to www.globalrefund.com or www.premiertaxfree.com.

 Remember not all VATs are refundable. Those added to services aren't refundable. Hotels, restaurants, and car rentals, for example, charge VAT that you can't get back.

Protecting Yourself and Your Money

Rest easy: You're going to a safe country. The occurrence of violent crime is reasonably low in Scotland, although it's higher in some city districts, of course. Handguns are banned across the entire U.K., and Scotland has so few pistols on the streets that, as a rule, police don't even carry them. In 2006, a report found that cops in the entire country had only shot firearms 34 times in seven years.

Theft is not a major problem — especially if you use common sense and guard yourself against it. Pickpockets look for people who seem to have the most money on them and know the least about where they are. Getting money from an ATM late at night on a deserted street in Glasgow or Edinburgh is not particularly wise. Also, don't leave large sums of money lying around your hotel in the city, unless it is one with good security.

Crime is a fact of modern city life. In many rural areas of Scotland, however, people don't even bother locking their house doors at night.

Dealing with a lost or stolen wallet

If your wallet is lost or stolen, don't panic. Be sure to tell all of your credit-card companies the minute you discover your wallet is missing, and file a report at the nearest police precinct. Contact the police by going to a station, stopping a passing cop, or dialing ☎ **999** on any telephone. Your credit-card company or insurer may require a police report number or record of the loss. Most credit-card companies have an emergency toll-free number to call if your card is lost or stolen; they may be able to wire you a cash advance immediately or deliver an emergency credit card in a day or two. **Visa**'s U.S. emergency number is ☎ **800-847-2911** or 410-581-9994. **American Express** cardholders and traveler's check holders should call ☎ **800-221-7282. MasterCard** holders should call ☎ **800-307-7309** or 636-722-7111. For other credit cards, call the toll-free-number directory at ☎ **800-555-1212.**

The phone numbers to report lost or stolen credit cards while you're in Scotland are:

- ✔ **American Express** (☎ **01273-696-933**)
- ✔ **Diners Club** (☎ **0870-190-0011**)
- ✔ **MasterCard** (☎ **0800-964-767**)
- ✔ **Visa** (☎ **0800-891-725**)

If you need emergency cash over the weekend, when all banks and American Express offices are closed, you can have money wired to you via **Western Union** (☎ **800-325-6000;** www.westernunion.com).

Identity theft and fraud are potential complications of losing your wallet, especially if you've lost your driver's license along with your cash and credit cards. Notify the major credit-reporting bureaus immediately; placing a fraud alert on your records may protect you against liability for criminal activity. The three major U.S. credit-reporting agencies are **Equifax** (☎ **800-766-0008;** www.equifax.com), **Experian** (☎ **888-397-3742;** www.experian.com), and **TransUnion** (☎ **800-680-7289;** www.transunion.com).

If you lose your passport, contact the U.S. consulate in Edinburgh by calling ☎ **0131-556-8315;** you will need to travel to London and appear in person at the U.S. Embassy to get a new passport. Finally, if you've lost all forms of photo ID, call your airline and explain the situation; they might allow you to board the plane if you have a copy of your passport or birth certificate and a copy of the police report you've filed.

Chapter 6

Getting to Scotland

. . . .

In This Chapter

▶ Flying to Scotland with the fewest layovers
▶ Taking the train up from England to Scotland
▶ Weighing the pros and cons of escorted tours

. . . .

Whether visiting castles, making new acquaintances in local pubs, or exploring the Highlands and Islands: each activity is just one part of your trip to Scotland. Unless, you already live there, the first task is getting yourself to the country. Several resources, however, make planning your travel to Scotland virtually painless. This chapter discusses how to find those resources in addition to helpful hints on things from bargain airfares to the lowdown on love-'em-or-hate-'em package tours.

Flying to Scotland

You're most likely to fly into the United Kingdom, arriving in Scotland directly (which is possible from the eastern U.S. or Europe) or via one of England's many airports, from Manchester to London Heathrow.

Identifying your airline options

The few carriers that fly to Scotland directly from the U.S. have changed over recent years. Often the service is seasonal (May–Sept). But certainly, flights from the North American eastern seaboard remain, whether Continental, US Airways, American Airlines, or British Airways.

On the other hand, almost every airline in the world seems to fly into one of London's airports, so getting north from there to Scotland will entail only a short flight (about one hour, unless you're headed to the Highlands) or a five-hour train ride to Scotland's main cities, Glasgow and Edinburgh.

 If you're traveling from Down Under, no airlines currently fly directly from Australia or New Zealand to Scotland. All flights on international airlines from these two countries go through London.

The major airlines listed below offer U.K. flights, including a few direct to Scotland. Be sure to call more than one airline to compare prices.

- ✔ **Air Canada** (☎ **888-247-2262;** www.aircanada.ca)
- ✔ **American Airlines** (☎ **800-433-7300;** www.aa.com)
- ✔ **British Airways** (☎ **800-247-9297;** www.britishairways.com)
- ✔ **Continental Airlines** (☎ **800-231-0856;** www.continental.com)
- ✔ **Delta Airlines** (☎ **800-241-4141;** www.delta.com)
- ✔ **Northwest Airlines** (☎ **800-447-4747;** www.nwa.com)
- ✔ **United Airlines** (☎ **800-538-2929;** www.united.com)
- ✔ **US Airways** (☎ **800-428-4322;** www.usairways.com)
- ✔ **Virgin Atlantic** (☎ **800-862-8621;** www.virgin-atlantic.com)

If you travel via London, you can opt for a short flight to Scotland. British Airways (☎ **0844-493-0787;** www.britishairways.com) has several per day. **Flybe** (☎ **0871-700-2000,** or 44-1392-268-500 from outside the U.K.; www.flybe.com) is a discount airline that crisscrosses the U.K., and recently took over routes to the Western Isles.

Regardless of whether you're coming to Scotland directly or from a transfer point, you'll most likely fly into Glasgow or Edinburgh. Both airports are easy to get in and out of and offer easy transportation into the cities. Because of the frequency of flights into these airports, you're more likely to find a cheap fare to them than to smaller Scottish cities, such as Inverness, Aberdeen, or Dundee. Both Edinburgh and Glasgow offer perfectly fine airports, and neither option outweighs the other in terms of proximity to a city.

In terms of air traffic volumes, **Edinburgh International Airport** (☎ **0870-040-0007;** www.edinburghairport.com) recently took over from Glasgow. It is about 10km (6 miles) west of the city center and has become a growing hub for flights both within the British Isles and to and from Continental Europe. **Glasgow International Airport** (☎ **0870-040-0008;** www.glasgowairport.com) is at Abbotsinch, near Paisley, only about 16km (10 miles) west of the city via M8. South of Glasgow is **Prestwick International Airport** (☎ **0871-223-0700;** www.gpia.co.uk), which is favored by some of the low-budget airlines such as **RyanAir** (☎ **0871-246-0000;** www.ryanair.com). Prestwick is on the railway line to Ayr, about a 45-minute ride from Glasgow's Central Station. (For pointers on planning your itinerary, and help on deciding your arrival and departure points, see Chapter 4; for details on getting to Edinburgh or Glasgow, see Chapters 11 and 12.)

Getting the best deal on your airfare

U.S. airlines arguably operate unlike any other industry. Every one offers virtually the same product (one economy seat is like any other), but prices for that basic service can vary widely, depending upon when and how you book your fare.

Business travelers who require the flexibility to buy their tickets at a moments notice and also need to get to specific places will pay (or at least their companies pay) the full fare. But if you can book your ticket well in advance, stay over Saturday night, and are willing to travel mid-week (Tues–Thurs), you might bag a significantly less expensive ticket. It pays to plan ahead, most of the time.

 Search **the Internet** for cheap fares. The most popular online travel agencies are **Travelocity** (www.travelocity.com), **Expedia** (www.expedia.com), and **Orbitz** (www.orbitz.com). In the U.K., go to **Travelsupermarket** (☎ 0845-345-5708; www.travelsupermarket.com), a flight search engine that offers comparisons for the budget airlines whose seats often end up in bucket-shop sales. Other Web sites for booking airline tickets online include www.cheapflights.com, www.smartertravel.com, www.priceline.com, and www.opodo.com. Meta search sites (which find and then direct you to airline and hotel Web sites for booking) include **SideStep** (www.sidestep.com) and **Kayak.com** (www.kayak.com), the latter of which includes fares for budget carriers as well as the major airlines. In addition, most **airlines** offer online-only fares that even their phone agents know nothing about.

Watch local newspapers for **promotional specials** or **fare wars,** when airlines lower prices on their most popular routes. Also keep an eye on price fluctuations and deals at Web sites such as **Airfarewatchdog** (www.airfarewatchdog.com) and **Farecast** (www.farecast.com).

Frequent-flier membership doesn't cost a cent, but membership may entitle you to prompter service if your luggage is stolen or your flight is canceled or delayed, and if you want to change your seat (especially once you've racked up some miles), it becomes easier. And you don't always have to fly to earn points; **frequent-flier credit cards** can earn you thousands of miles for doing your everyday shopping. With more than 70 mileage awards programs on the market, consumers have never had more options. Investigate the program details of your favorite airlines before you sink points into any one. Consider which airlines have hubs in the airport nearest you, and, of those carriers, which have the most advantageous alliances, given your most common routes. To play the frequent-flier game to your best advantage, consult the community bulletin boards on **FlyerTalk** (www.flyertalk.com), or go to Randy Petersen's **Inside Flyer** (www.insideflyer.com). Petersen and friends review all the programs in detail and post regular updates on changes in policies and trends.

Taking the Train

Taking a train to Scotland from London or from other cities in the U.K. has been subject to improvements over the past decade, even if it doesn't yet match the quality and quantity of railway service on the continent. It isn't as fast as flying, but you get to admire the countryside, arrive right in the heart of town, and reduce the carbon footprint of your trip. For the approximately five hour journey from London to Edinburgh or Glasgow, you might inquire about sleeper compartments on overnight trains.

The trains that link London to Edinburgh (via Newcastle) on the East Coast Main Line are reasonably fast, efficient, and generally relaxing, with restaurant and bar service as well as air-conditioning. Trains depart throughout the day from London's King's Cross Station (call National Railway Enquiries at ☎ 08457-48-49-50 for rail info; from outside the U.K., call ☎ 44-207-278-5240) and arrive in Edinburgh at **Waverley Station** in the heart of the city. The trip generally takes four and a half hours. Off-peak fares bought in advance can range widely, from around £25 to £100, and governments often suggest they should be less variable (while doing very little to regulate them). A fully flexible "buy anytime, travel anytime" standard, open single fare is upwards of £140. The Caledonian Sleeper service for overnight travel can cost about £100, but online bargains booked well in advance can mean the trip may cost as little at £40. You can easily make taxi and bus connections at Waverley Station, which also serves Glasgow with a **First ScotRail** (www.first group.com/scotrail) shuttle service every 15 minutes during the day and every 30 minutes in the evenings until about 11:30 p.m.

Trains to Glasgow terminate at **Central Station** in the heart of the city (call National Railway Enquiries at ☎ 08457-48-49-50 for rail info; from outside the U.K. call ☎ 44-207-278-5240). The trains that directly link London's Euston Station to Glasgow (via Preston and Carlisle) use the West Coast Main Line. The service (operated by Virgin; ☎ 08457-222-333; www.virgin.com/trains) departs London every hour or so. The company in charge of the track, Network Rail, has done a lot of work to upgrade the West Coast Main Line, and travel times are coming down. Virgin Rail prices, similar to other U.K. train operators, are diverse and complicated. In general, you might get a one-way ticket for as little as £35, although the standard advance-purchase ticket is more likely to be between £90 and £130.

Glasgow's Central Station is also the terminus for trains arriving from the southwest of Scotland, and a hub for numerous trains to city suburbs in most directions. A ten-minute walk away (or via shuttle bus 398) is **Queen Street Station.** From here, First ScotRail shuttle service (see above) is available to and from Edinburgh.

Joining an Escorted Tour

You may be one of the many people who love escorted tours. (I personally don't abide them.) They certainly have their luxuries: the tour company takes care of all the details and tells you what to expect on each leg of your journey. You know most of your costs up front and you don't get many surprises. An advantage to escorted tours is that they can take you to the maximum number of sights in the minimum amount of time with the least amount of hassle.

 If you decide to go with an escorted tour, purchasing travel insurance is strongly recommended, especially if the tour operator asks to you pay your trip costs up front. But don't buy insurance from the tour operator. If the operator can't fulfill its obligation to provide you with the tour you paid for, there's no reason to think that it will fulfill its insurance duty, either. Get travel insurance through an independent agency. (You can find out more about the ins and outs of travel insurance in Chapter 10.)

When choosing an escorted tour, along with finding out whether you have to put down a deposit and when final payment is due, ask a few simple questions before you buy:

✔ **What is the cancellation policy?** Can the operator cancel the trip if it doesn't get enough people? How late can you cancel if you're unable to go? Do you get a refund if you cancel? If the operator cancels?

✔ **How jam-packed is the schedule?** Does the tour schedule try to fit 25 hours' worth of activity into a 24-hour day, or does it give you ample time to relax by the pool or shop? If getting up at 7 a.m. every day and not returning to your hotel until 6 or 7 p.m. sounds like a grind, certain escorted tours may not be for you. Like me, you may prefer more free time.

✔ **How large is the group?** The smaller the group, the less time you spend waiting for people to get on and off the bus. Tour operators may give you an evasive answer to this question because they may not know the exact size of the group until everybody has made reservations, but they should be able to give you a rough estimate. Also, get an idea of the general age range of the group; whether the tour's geared to seniors, students, families, or some other demographic may affect your decision to sign up.

✔ **Is there a minimum group size?** Some tours have a minimum group size and may cancel the tour if it doesn't book enough people. Find out if a quota exists and how close the operator is to reaching it. Again, tour operators may be evasive in their answers, but it may help you select a tour that's sure to happen.

✔ **What exactly is included?** Don't assume anything. You may have
to pay to get yourself to and from the airport. A box lunch may be
included in an excursion, but drinks may be extra. How much flexibility do you have? Can you opt out of certain activities, or does
the bus leave once a day with no exceptions? Are all your meals
planned in advance? Can you choose your main course at dinner?

Depending on your recreational passions, one of the following escorted
tour companies may suit you:

✔ **CIE Tours International** (☎ 800-CIE-TOUR; www.cietours.com)
does tours of the United Kingdom and offers a five-day, four-night
escorted tour of Scotland, among other tours. The Web site features a helpful tour index with package prices, descriptions, and
itineraries. Expect to pay around $700 (not counting airfare) per
person.

✔ **Cosmos** (☎ 800-276-1241; www.cosmosvacations.com) is the
budget arm of Globus (http://globusjourneys.com) and offers
scaled-down versions of the Globus trips (although you don't see a
great price difference), with a tour guide and RV on hand at all
times. Prices (including airfare) run from $1,400 to $1,900 per
person.

✔ **Scottish Tours** (☎ 0131-557-8008; www.scottishtours.co.uk)
offers six mini-tours in air-conditioned buses departing from
Edinburgh. The most elaborate is a three-day, two-night excursion
that goes from the Scottish capital to Inverness on day one and
then visits the northeastern tip of the country. Per-person rates
start at around £10 for one-day trips and go up to £225 for two
nights (including breakfast and accommodations).

For more information on bus tours within Scotland, please see Seeing
Scotland by Bus in Chapter 6.

Choosing a Package Tour

For some destinations, package tours may be a smart way to go.
Occasionally a package tour that includes airfare, hotel, and transportation to and from the airport can cost little more the price of a hotel stay
that you book yourself. That's because packages are sold in bulk to tour
operators, who then resell them to the public. If golf is your primary
interest for going to Scotland, then a packaged golf tour might be just
the thing.

Package tours can vary widely. Some offer a better class of hotels than
others; some provide the same hotels for lower prices. Some book
flights on scheduled airlines; others sell charters. In certain packages,

your choice of accommodations and travel days may be limited. Some tours let you choose between escorted vacations and independent vacations; others allow you to add on just a few excursions or escorted day trips (also at discounted prices) without booking an entirely escorted tour.

Depending on your interests, one of the following packaged tour companies may suit you.

- ✔ **Brian Moore International Tours** (☎ 800-982-2299; www.bmit.com) offers "Air Inclusive" vacations to Edinburgh from around $500 during the low season.

- ✔ **CIE Tours International** (☎ 800-CIE-TOUR; www.cietours.com): Details can be found in the section "Joining an Escorted Tour," earlier in this chapter.

- ✔ **Thistle Golf (Scotland) Limited** (☎ 0141-248-4554; www.thistlegolf.co.uk) offers various golfing tours, such as one that covers both Ayrshire in the southwest and St. Andrews northeast of Edinburgh. Prices depend on the touring region and the length of your stay, so contact the company for details.

Chapter 7

Getting Around Scotland

In This Chapter

▶ Renting cars and navigating "single track" road in Scotland
▶ Catching the breathtaking views by train or bus
▶ Getting to the beautiful islands by ferry

*Y*ou do have choices when it comes to getting around Scotland: **train, car, bus, ferry, bicycle,** or **by foot.** Some visitors to Scotland rent cars for the duration of their visits because automobiles provide a sense of mobility that travelers appreciate — and are accustomed to. Certainly, in remote areas such as the Highlands, some form of personal transportation is almost essential because villages are few and far between; plus, public transportation can be limited.

Still, if your budget restraints, length of stay, or specific destinations don't make driving mandatory, a variety of public transportation options can get you where you need to go. I have been from Glasgow to the isles of Mull and Iona, and even farther afield to the Outer Hebrides, depending solely on trains, buses, and ferries (plus my own two feet and a rented bicycle or taxi). It imposed some limitations, for sure, but it also liberated me from the burden of driving, either in traffic or on bendy, one-lane roads. If your trip is primarily to Edinburgh and/or Glasgow, you don't really need a car at all.

But I have also toured the very northern parts of the country in a rented camper-van, taking my time, stopping frequently to have a better look at the majestic scenery, and taking detours whenever I liked. Just remember, if you are traveling throughout Scotland by road, the country is a virtual archipelago. Settlements are separated by deep valleys, ragged mountains, and especially long lochs; you may have to travel 100 miles to cover 50 miles as the proverbial crow would fly. Plus, remote areas often have only single-track — that means one-lane — roads, which will keep your speed down.

This all means that some journeys, which don't seem terribly far on the map, may take longer than anticipated, as narrow roads wind up and over mountains — or snake around the shores of lochs.

Getting Around by Car

For certain, seeing Scotland by car has its advantages, most notably the lack of timetables to keep in mind and greater control over where you want to go and when you want to go there. But you need to be aware of some driving-related issues that you will encounter while exploring Scotland by car.

To drive a car in Scotland for a limited period (up to 12 months), be certain that you have a valid driver's license issued by local authorities where you live permanently; you don't need any special license.

Getting along with fewer road signs

One of the biggest complaints that tourists have about driving around Scotland is the relative paucity of road signs. Most major attractions are well marked, but the motorways around cities can be confusing, freeway access roads within the city are sometimes tricky to navigate, and country highways often seem to lack the necessary signage. Having a good map close at hand (as well as a navigator who can read it) to help track your progress is always helpful. When in doubt, however, simply stop and ask for directions.

Keeping up with changing street names

You're in a city, you're driving along such-and-such road, then suddenly it has a new name, and two minutes later it changes again. This curious phenomenon may come up as you ply Scotland's city streets. For example, the famous Royal Mile in Edinburgh, between the castle and Palace of Holyroodhouse, actually takes four different names along the way, from Castlehill to Canongate. Now that's royally confusing. Again, keep a map handy and refer to it often.

Driving on the left, roundabouts, and other differences

If you're used to driving on the right-hand side of the road, driving on the left-hand side is a shock initially. Perhaps what feels the strangest is the fact that the driver's seat and wheel are on the right-hand side of the car while the gearshift is on the left (although the relative positions of the clutch, brake pedal, and accelerator are the same).

Like in the rest of Europe, most cars in Scotland have manual-transmission stick shifts. If you need an automatic, make sure to request one specifically when reserving your rental car or van.

You merge to the right to get on highways, and you pass cars on the right while slower traffic stays in the left lanes. Don't pass cars (*overtake* in local parlance) by using a left-hand lane designed for slower traffic. I know you may use the slower traffic lanes all the time at home for passing cars, but it's rarely seen here. Overtake slower traffic only by using right-hand lanes meant for faster traffic. And after you've safely passed someone, the courtesy to other drivers who may want to pass you is to return to a center or left-hand lane.

Roundabouts (traffic circles) can be slightly tricky, but you will get the hang of them. First, traffic moves in a clockwise direction through roundabouts. As you near one, remember that any traffic approaching you from the right, either in the roundabout or entering the roundabout, has the right of way. You must always yield to traffic approaching from the right, and only drive into the roundabout when traffic clears from the right. Once in, use your left turn signal to indicate which exit you intend to take from a roundabout. If you find yourself driving in a right-hand lane toward the core of a roundabout and can't get safely to your desired exit (on the left), don't barge across. Simply go around the circle again and prepare to exit the next time you approach your exit.

Staying safe on "single-track" roads

When you're driving through the rural countryside or in small villages, it's quite common to find only one-lane, or *single-track,* roads carrying two-way traffic. Don't panic. These roads will always have passing places, marked with a square- or sometimes diamond-shaped sign. If you see a vehicle approaching in the opposite direction, pull into the passing place, if it's on your left, giving the other person room to pass. You can confirm your intentions by putting on your left turn signal (and you may find that some drivers will flash their headlights in recognition).

If, however, the passing place is to the right on the single-track road, *do not* pull into it. Stop where you are and just stay put (put on your left turn signal if you like) and allow the oncoming vehicle to use the pull-over space in order to slide by you.

In general, the driver who gets to a passing place first is meant to use it, but don't get involved in games of "chicken" to see who pulls off first. Play it safe and be the one to give way. Also, on hills, the vehicle going uphill has the right of way, as it is safer to reverse up a slope than down one.

It's a simple courtesy to acknowledge the other driver (who's passing you or whom you're passing) with a small wave, sometimes as simple as a raised finger (not the middle one) from the steering wheel.

Planning your gasoline expenditures

Gas, called *petrol* in Scotland, is costly. Like everywhere, the cost of gasoline in Scotland has risen this decade. Remember that the prices posted here are per *liter,* not per gallon. You may find yourself paying more than $3 for a liter — and there are nearly four of them in a gallon. (Does public transportation sound a bit more appealing now?) Obviously, to get the best gas mileage, rent the smallest vehicle you can. A small car also helps you more easily navigate narrow roads.

Laying down the law on parking

In cities and towns, you will find some parking garages and outdoor car lots. Street parking is also fine, but don't assume that the absence of American-style meters means that parking on the street is free. Check the signs. You may have to buy a ticket from a nearby machine that indicates how long you can stay. Purchase a ticket and use the sticky backing paper to affix it to your window. This system is used in some parking lots, too. Some residential neighborhoods in the cities are very restrictive and allow only local residents to park in available places. Also, you can never park where there is a double yellow line running along the curb, nor where you see a zigzag white line.

Safety tips to know before you get behind the wheel

Here are some important traffic rules and laws to help you get around safely and legally.

✔ At intersections marked with an inverted triangle (with the point facing you) or at roundabouts, yield to traffic.

✔ You should not make left-hand turns (the equivalent of right-hand turns in America) when the traffic light is red.

✔ The general speed limit on the open road is 96kmph (60 mph) unless otherwise posted. Standard 96kmph (60 mph) signs bear only a black circle with a slash mark through it. When the speed limit is other than 96kmph (60 mph), you see a sign with a red circle and the limit written inside in black. You often see these signs when entering small towns, where you should reduce your speed to 48kmph (30 mph), which is also the limit in cities, unless otherwise marked. On motorways, the speed limit is generally 113kmph (70 mph), although plenty of drivers go faster.

✔ At *zebra* cross walks with a flashing yellow globe light, you yield to pedestrian traffic but proceed with caution when clear.

✔ A sign with a red circle and a red x through the middle means no stopping or parking during posted hours. A zigzag white line along the curb also means no parking or stopping unless it's due to traffic signals or congestion.

✔ Drivers and front-seat passengers must wear seat belts. If your car has back-seat seat belts, passengers seated there should wear them also.

Renting a Car

Rates for car rental (or car *hire,* in local parlance) can vary. The price depends on the size of the car, the length of time you keep it, where and when you pick it up and drop it off, where you take it, and other factors. Asking a few key questions may save you money.

✔ Companies add a drop-off charge if you don't return the car to the same rental location.

✔ Ask if the rate is cheaper if you pick up the car at a location in town rather than at the airport (which sometimes adds a tax).

✔ Find out whether age is an issue. Some car-rental companies add a fee for drivers under 25 — and some don't rent to them at all.

✔ If you see an advertised price, be sure to ask for that specific rate; otherwise you may be charged the standard (higher) rate. Don't forget to mention membership in AAA, AARP, trade unions, and other associations, such as university alumni groups, when making a reservation. These memberships may entitle you to discounts.

✔ Check your frequent-flier accounts for special deals.

✔ Weekend rates may be lower than weekday rates. If you're keeping the car five or more days, a weekly rate may be cheaper than the daily rate. Ask if the rate is the same for pickup on Friday morning as it is on Thursday night.

✔ As with other aspects of planning your trip, using the Internet can make comparison shopping for a car rental much easier. You can check rates at most of the major rental agencies' Web sites. Plus, all the major travel sites — such as **Travelocity** (www.travelocity. com) or **Expedia** (www.expedia.com), for example — have search engines that can dig up discounted car-rental rates. Just enter the car size you want and the pickup and return dates and locations, and the server returns a price. You can even make the reservation through any of these sites.

In addition to the standard rental prices, some optional charges might apply to car rentals (and some not-so-optional charges, such as taxes). In Scotland, you can pay a bit more to reduce the amount you would be obligated to shell out if you have an accident. For example, an additional $8 or so per day for a weekly rental will reduce your deductible (or *excess* in the U.K.) considerably. Regardless, the car is fully insured against damage you incur to your vehicle or someone else's.

Some companies have a habit of giving you a vehicle with a partially full tank and you must return it with just that amount. If it is less, they will charge you a premium to get it back to the right level. Make sure you are clear how much is in the tank before you leave with your rental.

Because the driver's side is on the right in Scotland, your left arm, not your right, controls the stick shift. Rental companies have few vehicles with automatic transmissions, so request one specifically if you don't know how to operate a manual transmission — or don't think your left arm is up to it. Minivans, or *people movers,* are more likely to offer the option of automatic transmissions.

As for the class of car available, you can expect a variety of levels: **budget** or **small** (generally two-door run-arounds), **compact** (small but might have four doors), **medium** or **midsize** (four doors, more head room, and larger trunk), and **large** or **family** (bigger still). Companies often offer upgrades. You may think you want a larger vehicle, but remember that roads can be narrow. Get the smallest car you can, taking into consideration your driving comfort, the comfort of your fellow travelers, and the amount of luggage you're carrying. **Air-conditioning** and **unlimited mileage** are standard, but always confirm that there are no mileage charges.

The following are a couple of issues you need to address when arranging for your rental car.

- ✔ **Where and when to pick up the car:** If you fly into Edinburgh or Glasgow and plan to stay in the city for two or more days, wait to get the car until you're just about to head out to the countryside. In the city, you don't need a car. Some companies have pickup locations in or near the city. If you're planning to leave town immediately or early the next morning, however, getting the car upon arrival is a good idea. You can set out according to plan, and you save the time and hassle of having to go back to the airport or locate the rental agency the next day.

- ✔ **How to pay for the car:** Some companies require a deposit, generally on a credit card, when you make your reservation. If you book by phone, the clerk may ask for the card number then; otherwise, you use your credit card at the rental desk.

If you're not sure how long you need a car (if, maybe, you're thinking about coming back to Glasgow early to see more city sights), book your rental for the shorter amount of time and extend it from the road with a simple phone call rather than bringing the car back early. If you've booked a car for a week but bring it back after only four days, the company will post the refund to your credit card.

Rental-car companies in Scotland

All the major rental agencies are represented at the country's two primary airports. In addition, in Glasgow, you can find

- ✔ **Arnold Clark:** multiple locations (☎ **0845-607-4500;** www.arnold clarkrental.com)
- ✔ **Avis:** 70 Lancefield St. (☎ **0870-608-6339;** www.avis.co.uk)
- ✔ **Budget:** 101 Waterloo St. (☎ **0800-212-636;** www.budget.co.uk)

In Edinburgh, try

- ✔ **Avis:** 5 West Park Place (☎ **0870-153-9103;** www.avis.co.uk)
- ✔ **Hertz:** 10 Picardy Place (☎ **0870-846-0013;** www.hertz.co.uk)
- ✔ **Thrifty:** 42 Haymarket Terrace (☎ **0131-337-1319;** www.thrifty.co.uk)

Does your boot go in your luggage or your luggage in your boot?

To spare you the confusion of car-related words and phrases in Scotland, here's a list of the most commonly used (and most commonly confused) terms you may come across.

- **boot:** trunk
- **bonnet:** hood
- **motorways:** freeways
- **pavement:** sidewalk
- **petrol:** gasoline
- **roundabouts:** traffic circles (or "rotaries" if you're a New Englander); make sure you go left and yield to the right

---

Taking the Train

First ScotRail runs the trains in Scotland. It's not a publicly owned company, but rather a private firm that has a contract to operate the trains. To confuse matters, the railway lines are owned by a different, pseudo-private company called Network Rail (formerly Railtrack). Privatization of the railways has proved to be a poor decision for most of Great Britain, which once led the way in the development of the railroad.

The advantage of train travel is that you can generally sit back, relax, and enjoy the scenery in a way that is often difficult when traveling by road. With some exceptions, the trains in Scotland are reasonably efficient and comfortable. On the downside, trains are more expensive than in most European countries, and they travel to fewer destinations than would be ideal. Curiously, some of the long-haul routes (for example, Glasgow to Inverness) use carriages that don't have sufficient space for luggage. Nevertheless, when the trains run on time, railway travel is a good way to get from one part of the country to another.

Edinburgh Waverley has trains going southeast toward Berwick, west to Glasgow, northwest toward Stirling, and north through Fife, Tayside, and the Northeast. In a few years, it should also have trains going south into the Borders. Glasgow's Central Station is the terminus for trains coming from the southwest through Ayrshire and west from Clyde Coasts towns such as Greenock. Glasgow's Queen Street Station offers service to the west (Helenburgh, for example), northwest into Argyll and the Highlands, and north through Stirling and on into Tayside and Northeast. For journey planning, contact **Traveline Scotland** at ☎ **0870-608-2608,** or log on to www.travelinescotland.com.

Generally speaking, you should have no problem buying **tickets** a half-hour before departure. But to save money and ensure you have seats on the longer trips, it never hurts to reserve in advance. For 24-hour rail and fare information, call **National Rail Enquiries** ☎ **08457-484-950,** or log on to www.firstscotrail.com. For general inquires, call **First ScotRail** at ☎ **0845-601-5929.**

Seeing Scotland by Bus

Buses are an adequate way to see Scotland. They often make more stops than the trains and are thus slower. But they cost less. The usual downsides apply to bus travel: You're not free to stop wherever and whenever you want, you're stuck with the same people for hours at a time, and there's not much space to move. Regardless, the seating is normally comfortable and bus travel can be a good way to meet people. For journey planning, contact **Traveline Scotland** at ☎ **0870-608-2608,** or log on to www.travelinescotland.com.

Scottish Citylink is Scotland's largest cross-country bus company. It offers services to 200 towns and cities across Scotland, including Glasgow, Edinburgh, Dundee, Aberdeen, Stirling, Perth, Inverness, Aviemore, Thurso, Ullapool, Oban, Campbeltown, Lochgilphead, Fort William, Portree, Glencoe, Dunfermline, and Dumfries. Information, prices, times, and routes can be obtained by calling ☎ **0870-550-5050** or by visiting www.citylink.co.uk. **Stagecoach** is another major operator, running buses to northeast Scotland, the Highlands, and through central and southern areas. The company can be reached by calling ☎ **01292-613-500** or by visiting www.stagecoachbus.com.

Sightseeing bus tours can give a taste of the often-stunning countryside on one-, two-, and three-day excursions. If this is your kind of travel, consider the following tour companies.

- ✔ **Heart of Scotland Tours** (☎ **0131-558-8855;** www.heartofscotlandtours.co.uk) offers one- to three-day minibus tours that depart from Edinburgh's Waterloo Place near Calton Hill at 8 and 9 a.m. One-day tours return to Edinburgh between 6 and 8 p.m. that evening. Three-day tours include the Highlands and the Isle of Skye. Prices range from £25 to £35 for one-day trips and upwards of £100 per person (exclusive of accommodations) for the multiday tours.

- ✔ **MacBackpackers** (☎ **0131-558-9900;** www.macbackpackers.com), a company that runs youth hostels, offers tours of Scotland stopping at places such as Pitlochry, Inverness, Skye, Fort William, Oban, and Edinburgh. And I'm sure I have even seen them on the Isle of Lewis. A five-day tour is about £130. Accommodations are not included, but they are guaranteed at hostels, which can cost upwards of £15 per night.

✔ **Scottish Tours** (☎ **800-890-7375** in the U.S., or 0141-880-3399; www. scottishtours.co.uk) offers one- to six-day sightseeing tours of the country in air-conditioned buses. The most elaborate is the "Highland Explorer" package, which departs from either Edinburgh or Glasgow, taking passengers to Inverness, the jumping-off point for minibus excursions with a local guide to the Isle of Skye, John O'Groats, and more. For £20 you can "tour Scotland," while prices for multiday excursions can run £550 and up for a single tourist (including breakfast and hotel accommodations).

✔ **Timberbush Tours** (☎ **0131-226-6066;** www.timberbush-tours. co.uk) uses minibuses to take small groups to various locations, from Edinburgh (from half-day to three-day) and Glasgow (one-day only). One half-day tour is called "Kings, Queens & Heroes," and operates off season, stopping at Linlithgow, Bannockburn, and Stirling. Prices for the three-day tour to Skye, the Highlands, and Loch Ness range from £90 in low season to £120 at the height of summer. Prices cover only transportation and guide.

By Plane

Internal Scottish flights may be the way to go if you need to get quickly from Glasgow or Edinburgh to Inverness in the Highlands, Stornoway on the Isle of Lewis, or Kirkwall on the Orkney Islands. I have heard about rich Americans determined to "see" the entire country in one week, jumping on flights from Edinburgh, Aberdeen, Inverness, Dundee, and Stornoway. Most internal Scotland services were recently transferred to a "discount" airline, **Flybe** (☎ **0871-700-2000,** or 44-1392-268-500 from outside the U.K.; www.flybe.com). Flybe now operates flights for **LoganAir** (☎ **0141-848-7594;** www.loganair.co.uk). No matter what the carrier, the flights are not cheap. You may pay up to $300 for a short trip. Go to the airport Web sites for latest details on flights, times, and carriers: www.edinburghairport.com or www.glasgowairport. com.

Finally, by Ferry

The preferable way (if you ask me) to get to the Scottish Islands or from one island to the next in the Hebrides (see Chapter 19) is by ferry. Few trips are more sublime than those that include a boat ride on Scotland's picturesque seas. One company, **Caledonian MacBrayne,** or **CalMac** for short, runs the major routes between islands. You can take your car on most of the ferries, but a few islands are vehicle-free and want to stay that way. Remember to call the day before you hope to go out, because heavy seas can cancel ferry travel.

If you plan to see more than one island, you might look into CalMac's "Island Hopscotch" fares, which offer island-hopping tickets to selected destinations and are valid for one month. For example you can rove from the mainland ferry terminal at Mallaig to Skye, Skye to Harris, Harris to Uist, and Uist back to the mainland port of Oban.

- ✔ **Caledonian MacBrayne** (☎ **01475-650-100;** www.calmac.co.uk), or CalMac, as it's more colloquially known, serves 22 islands and four peninsulas over the western coast of Scotland.

- ✔ **NorthLink Ferries** (☎ **0845-600-0449;** www.northlinkferries. co.uk) sails to Shetland and Orkney.

Chapter 8

Booking Your Accommodations

- -

In This Chapter

▶ Knowing what to expect from Scotland's accommodations

▶ Estimating how much you'll pay to stay

▶ Determining your lodging needs

▶ Finding the best rates and reserving the best rooms

- -

*I*n this chapter, I provide an overview of the types of accommodations available in Scotland, helping you choose what feels right in terms of style, comfort, and your budget. Rooms are not cheap, but discounts can be found. Lists of individual hotels, B&Bs, hostels, and so on appear in the city (Part III) and regional (Part IV) chapters later in this book.

Getting to Know Your Options

VisitScotland has instituted a **grading system** that ranks all types of accommodations on the basis of their available amenities, as well as more subjective criteria such as hospitality, ambience, food, and the condition of the property. This ranking system can be useful, but it can also be misleading. The ranking may be lower than the place actually deserves simply because a room lacks a telephone or doesn't include a television. Alternatively, it could have all modern conveniences but is run by a tyrant. Decide if certain amenities, such as a minibar or trouser press in your room, are important to you, think about whether small family run operations are best for you, and then find out what's being offered by hotels or B&Bs.

 Accommodations involved in the tourist board's grading system display a blue plaque or sticker (usually on or by the door) showing the number of stars earned, whether a hotel, guest house, or vacation cottage. If you don't see the plaque and the lodging isn't in the grading system, it's not necessarily a bad place to stay, but if you have a bad experience, VisitScotland has no authority to reprimand the establishment.

The tourist board's grading system doesn't rate the size, location, or price of the place. And remember, it also only rates those establishments that pay to join VisitScotland, which means that some worthy accommodations are conspicuously absent.

Knowing What You'll Pay

I've tried to include some options for the budget-minded, but you should anticipate that accommodations will eat up a good chunk of your traveling expenses. In all my listings, the cost of a **double room** — one room for you and a guest to stay in together — is given. I often give you a price range for a double room, which might reflect different room sizes, rooms with views compared to those with none, or the off-season rate compared to the high-season rate. In no instance will I give the price per person per night, although many B&Bs or smaller hotels do price their accommodations in that manner. Most places offer a **full breakfast** — or at least a light continental breakfast — as part of the rate.

Each hotel listing is prefaced with a number of dollar signs, ranging from one ($) to four ($$$$), corresponding to price per room per night. Use Table 8-1 as a pricing scale for quick reference; it shows you what to expect for room size and standard amenities in each of these price categories.

Table 8-1	Key to Hotel Dollar Signs	
Dollar Sign(s)	**Price Range**	**What to Expect**
$	Under £60 (approximately less than $100)	These places are relatively simple and basic. There may be no bar or restaurant. Rooms could be small, and such amenities as televisions are not necessarily provided. But the welcome you get may be terrific.
$$	£61–£150	These midrange accommodations offer more room and amenities, such as guest lounges, nicer toiletries, bars, restaurants, and perhaps even room service.
$$$	£151–£225	Higher-class still, these accommodations begin to look plush. Think chocolates on your pillow, a spotless restaurant, sharp bar, maybe even invaluable views.
$$$$	£225 and up	These top-rated accommodations come with luxury amenities, fine-dining restaurants, multiple bars and lounges, gyms and spas, and iPod docks, but you may pay handsomely for 'em.

Determining Your Accommodations Needs

It's likely that you'll be staying in **hotels, B&Bs,** or **guesthouses,** so that is the focus my listings. Wherever you stay, all my recommendations mean you can expect generally friendly service, clean rooms, and a decent breakfast. Smaller hotels with dining rooms, however, can be quite restrictive about when food is available.

The quality of food offered can vary from inn to inn. You may be frustrated to find that although you're staying in a hotel at the edge of a plentiful loch, the fish on the menu is frozen and deep-fried. If cuisine is important to you, do a bit of homework before you decide where you're going to stay, especially if dinners are included in the room price.

Unless you are going to focus exclusively on one region, you probably won't be interested in week-long stays, although you may run across a posh castle for rent or a basic self-catering flat or cottage while planning your trip to Scotland. Check the Internet or local tourism boards for just the right mansion or quaint cozy cabin amid the heather. A final budget-minded option is youth **hostels,** though age is often no consideration.

You can find out much about the country's different types of accommodations and available package deals at the tourist board's Web site, www.visitscotland.com. The site lists a range of lodging choices, including hotels, guesthouses, bed-and-breakfasts, trailer and camping parks, and self-catering cottages.

Hotels

In practically every hotel room, you will find tea- and instant-coffee-making equipment (electric kettles and cups). Bellhops (porters) aren't so common, however, except at the expensive places. Smaller hotels may not have a 24-hour reception desk staff. As a practice and courtesy in such establishments, try to let a member of hotel staff know if you plan to be out late and make sure you can get back in.

Hotels are used to catering to tourists, and many will be helpful even if they lack dedicated concierges. Larger hotels have gyms, room service, and an in-house restaurant and pub. Because you're a resident, hotels are required to keep the bar open until you retire for the night (but don't abuse the privilege).

Hotel chains can be found in Scotland's cities and larger towns. In some cases, taverns or restaurants have overnight rooms, too. If you choose to take a room in a pub, just be certain you're not going to be troubled if the Saturday night karaoke goes on until midnight.

Calling the auld country

If you want to book your room over the phone, or if the place where you want to stay doesn't take Internet reservations, you will need to know **how to call Scotland.** To call Scotland from anywhere in the world, dial the international access code (for example, 011 from the U.S.), then the country code (44 for the U.K.), then the city or local code (for example, Glasgow is 141), and then the number. (**Note:** When you're calling from within Great Britain, you need to add a zero before the city code.)

For example, if you're in the States and you want to call a favorite watering hole in Glasgow, the Babbity Bowster, just to make sure they'll have enough wine ready when you get there, you dial:

International		Country		City		Number
011	+	44	+	141	+	552-5055

Remember, Scotland is five hours ahead of Eastern Time in the U.S. (eight hours ahead of the West Coast). If it's 1 p.m. in Philadelphia, it's 6 p.m. in Peterhead. If its 6 a.m. in Berkeley, it is 2 p.m. in Brechin. If you're trying to call a business in Scotland, call before noon Eastern Time to be safe (before 9 a.m. in San Francisco).

Bed-and-breakfasts (B&Bs)

Many Scottish B&Bs and guesthouses take their hospitality seriously. You usually get to know the owners (likely the same folks who cook and serve your breakfast) — and you may come away feeling that you've made a new acquaintance or two. A guesthouse is, for the most part, the same thing as a B&B, although generally a little larger.

Some B&Bs offer just a spare and comfortable bedroom (usually with a bathroom attached) in someone's private residence. Some B&B rooms will not have en suite facilities, but a toilet and bathroom shared by other residents. It that's a problem for you, make sure you ask for a room with its own bathroom (which may cost a bit more).

Bed-and-breakfasts aren't large — most are lucky to have four guest rooms. The better-known B&Bs tend to fill up quickly during the high season, so make your reservations as early as possible. Some B&Bs don't accept credit cards, so be prepared to pay in cash.

One advantage of choosing B&Bs over hotels is the price: They are usually less expensive, but you don't get the extra amenities of a hotel.

Self-catering cottages

Properties offered as *self-catering* run the gamut from modern apartments to rooms within castles to mountain cabins. I list a few but not many. Taking a self-catering cottage or chalet is similar to renting a condo. It's a place to settle into and do things like you might at home. At self-catering properties, you can cook your own meals and make your own beds (or not).

Be certain you know what is provided in a self-catering facility — for example, the provision of towels and bed linens may cost extra.

With self-catering properties, the price isn't calculated per person and is generally set for the week (although some also rent by the weekend, for two to three days). When you take into account the amount of money you would pay for hotels and B&Bs, staying in a self-catering lodging can cut costs considerably. Food costs also decrease when you're buying your own and cooking it yourself. If you're budget-minded, self-catering is an option worth checking out.

A good place to begin researching self-catering properties is the **Association of Scotland's Self-Caterers** (www.assc.co.uk), whose members include owners and operators of a wide range of self-catering properties, from cottages to chalets to lodges to castles.

Hostels

Hostels have a reputation of being the accommodations of choice for students and frugal travelers. If the image you have of hostels is a place full of young, perky travelers who can go for long stretches without showers or food, you're partly correct (though only to a degree). Hostels are best for independent travelers who don't spend much time in their rooms and want to stick to a frugal accommodations budget. And although these accommodations are called "youth hostels," they take guests of any age, even if most of the people you encounter are in their 20s. They're also usually really great places to meet fellow travelers.

Hostels sometimes don't allow guests to remain in the building during the day. You may have to get out and about from 11 a.m. to 4 p.m., whether you like it or not.

Quality and service vary from one hostel to the next throughout Scotland. Some hostels offer communal kitchens for you to bring in and cook your own food. Some even have private rooms with en-suite bathrooms. Families can also stay in hostels, renting a room with four bunks. The majority of hostels, though, are places where people sleep dorm-style — anywhere from four to dozens of people to a room, usually in bunk beds.

Hostels provide a blanket and pillow and sometimes sheets, but to be safe, you should bring your own sleeping bag or sleep sack (or expect to rent sheets from the hostel).

You can get a hostel bed for £10 a night and you will rarely pay more than £25. I only list a few, and these are ones that have "private" rooms as well as bunk-house-style accommodations.

One general resource to check out is www.hostels.com. And if you know you'll be taking the backpacking route through Scotland, you may want to contact the Scottish Youth Hostel Association (☎ **0870-155-3255** for reservations, or 01786-891-400 for general inquiries; www.syha.org.uk).

 Security isn't a major problem in Scotland's hostels, but it's something to consider. Any time you're sleeping in a room full of strangers, take precautions to ensure the safety of yourself and your personal belongings.

Finding the Best Room at the Best Rate

The **rack rate** is the standard — and that typically means maximum — price a hotel charges for a room. You sometimes see these rates printed on the fire/emergency exit diagrams posted on the back of your door.

Hotels are happy to charge you the rack rate, but you can almost always do better. Perhaps the best way to avoid paying the rack rate is quite simple: Just ask for a cheaper or discounted rate. You may be pleasantly surprised.

In all but the smallest accommodations, the rate you pay for a room depends on many factors — chiefly how you make your reservation. A travel agent may be able to negotiate a better price with certain hotels than you can get by yourself. (That's because the hotel often gives the agent a discount in exchange for steering business toward that hotel.)

 Reserving a room through the hotel's toll-free reservation number may result in a lower rate than calling the hotel directly. On the other hand, the central reservations number may not know about discount rates at specific locations. For example, local franchises may offer a special group rate for a wedding or family reunion, but they may neglect to tell the central booking line. Your best bet is to call both the local number and the toll-free number and see which one gives you a better deal.

Room rates (even rack rates) can change with the season, as occupancy rates rise and fall. But even within a given season, room prices are subject to change without notice, so the rates quoted in this book may be different from the actual rate you receive when you make your reservation.

 Remember, in Scotland, lodging rates fall from about the beginning of October until Christmas and New Year's (when they jump up to high-season prices for a couple of weeks), and then they stay more affordable until mid-March or Easter.

Some of the nicer country-house hotels close entirely in January. See Chapter 3 for a discussion of Scotland's high- and low-travel seasons. If you think you want a package tour that includes accommodations, flip to Chapter 6.

Surfing the Web for hotel deals

Independent Internet hotel-booking agencies representing hotels and guesthouses in Scotland have multiplied in mind-boggling numbers, and they're the best way to get a reduced price for a room. Shopping online for hotels is generally done one of two ways: by booking through the hotel's own Web site or through an independent booking agency (or a fare-service agency such as Priceline). Keep in mind that prices can vary considerably from site to site, and be aware that hotels at the top of a site's listing may be there for no other reason than that they paid money to get the placement.

In addition to the general multipurpose online travel booking sites **Travelocity, Expedia,** or **Orbitz,** you can book hotels through other more dedicated sites such as **Hotels.com** or **Quikbook.com.**

 I find **TripAdvisor.com** possibly the most useful of Web sites thanks to its independent consumer reviews.

 But always look for balanced views and don't discount a hotel because of a couple of poor comments. Some people can only moan and will find every fault under the sky. I look for places with multiple reviews (with many recently posted) and then for a generally positive set of reports. Often you can't go wrong.

For online hotel-reservations services in Scotland, try www.visit scotland.com. If you're looking for something more unusual, you may want to consider a farm stay; you can find information at www.scot farmhols.co.uk.

It's a good idea to **get a confirmation number** and **make a printout** of any online booking transaction.

Reserving the Best Room

 After you make your reservation, asking one or two more pointed questions can go a long way toward making sure you get the best room in the house. Always ask for a corner room. They're usually larger, quieter, and have more windows and light than standard rooms, and they don't always cost more. Also ask if the hotel is renovating; if it is, request a room away from the renovation work. Inquire, too, about the location of the restaurants, bars, and discos in the hotel — all sources of annoying noise. If you want a view, ask specifically for a room that offers one. And if you aren't happy with your room when you arrive, talk to the front desk. If they have another room, they should be happy to re-accommodate you, within reason.

Chapter 9

Catering to Special Travel Needs or Interests

Scotland's population is generally a friendly one that welcomes visitors of all stripes. No matter where you are, however, some aspects of travel can be challenging for people with special needs. This chapter provides basic advice to help make your trip successful for everyone involved.

Traveling with the Brood: Advice for Families

Scotland may not top the list of countries that ease the burden of traveling with children, but it *is* getting better. Throughout this book, I flag (with the kid-friendly icon) those spots that are particularly appealing prospects for families. But remember that a few hotels still actively discourage families with children and/or prohibit toddlers from the dining room at night, so it pays to double check.

You can find good family oriented vacation advice on the Internet at

- ✔ **Family Travel Files** (www.thefamilytravelfiles.com): A site that offers an online magazine and a directory of off-the-beaten-path tours and tour operators for families

- ✔ **Family Travel Forum** (www.familytravelforum.com): A comprehensive site that offers customized trip planning

✔ **Family Travel Network** (www.familytravelnetwork.com): An award-winning site that offers travel features, deals, and tips

✔ **Traveling Internationally with Your Kids** (www.travelwith yourkids.com): Another comprehensive site that offers customized trip planning

To help ensure a peaceful trip with children in tow, take care of a few preliminaries before lift-off.

✔ Check what your children have packed. You want to make sure that they have the clothes necessary for any changes in the weather and make sure they haven't overpacked.

✔ Bring a few toys for younger children, but nothing that can't be replaced if it's lost along the way.

✔ Music and even books on tape or CD are great diversions. Small games work well for those times when the scenery isn't sufficiently engaging. Having a deck of cards handy is a good idea for restaurant visits.

Getting to Scotland and exploring with kids

Remember, each child, regardless of age, is expected to have a passport. Some airlines offer child-companion fares and have a children's menu upon request.

Car-rental companies in Scotland will provide necessary car seats, and all vehicles have rear seat belts. The law requires that children be buckled in regardless of whether they're in the front or back seats.

Keep in mind that most attractions and some public-transportation options offer reduced prices for children. And most attractions, even places that don't seem particularly family oriented, offer family group prices (usually for two adults and two or three children).

To locate accommodations, restaurants, and attractions that are particularly kid-friendly, refer to the "Kids" icon throughout this guide.

Finding a family friendly hotel

Contact your hotel, guesthouse, or B&B before you go to find out about potential cost-cutting accommodations for families with children. Many times, an extra cot for a child is free or just a small additional cost. Also, some places have a baby-sitter list.

Making Age Work for You: Advice for Seniors

Most of the paid attractions in Scotland offer discounts (tickets that are called, as you probably know, "concessions") to senior citizens (aka *pensioners* or *OAPs — old age pensioners*). People older than age 60 usually qualify for reduced admission to theaters, museums, and other attractions. Hotels may offer discounts for seniors. Most public transportation is less costly for older people, although local service may require a special ID that's too much of a bother to obtain if you're only in town for a day or two. Scots over the age of 60 ride buses for free, but that perk is not given to visitors.

Members of **AARP,** 601 E St. NW, Washington, DC 20049 (☎ **888-687-2277** or 202-434-2277; www.aarp.org), are eligible for discounts on hotels, airfares, and car rentals.

Elderhostel (☎ **800-454-5768;** www.roadscholar.org) arranges study programs in more than 80 countries around the world for those ages 55 and older (and a companion of any age). Most courses last for two to four weeks abroad; and many include airfare, modest accommodations, meals, and tuition.

Recommended publications offering travel resources and discounts for seniors include: the quarterly magazine *Travel 50 & Beyond* (www.travel50andbeyond.com); *Travel Unlimited: Uncommon Adventures for the Mature Traveler* (Avalon); *101 Tips for Mature Travelers,* available from Grand Circle Travel (☎ **800-221-2610** or 617-350-7500; www.gct.com); *The 50+ Traveler's Guidebook* (St. Martin's Press); and *Unbelievably Good Deals and Great Adventures That You Absolutely Can't Get Unless You're Over 50,* by Joann Rattner Heilman (McGraw-Hill).

Many senior-targeted tours of Scotland are of the tour-bus variety, with free trips thrown in for those who organize groups of 20 or more. If you're seeking more independent travel, you should probably consult a regular travel agent to make your travel plans (see Chapter 6).

Accessing Scotland: Advice for Travelers with Disabilities

Most disabilities shouldn't stop anyone from traveling. Scotland's cities are reasonably well equipped to accommodate those with disabilities. However, not everything in Scotland will be easy. Some train stations are barely accessible. Historical attractions, such as castles, by their very nature, with cobblestone paths and narrow stairs, are difficult for even some able-bodied visitors to navigate. Some B&Bs and small hotels with lots of stairs and no elevators aren't suitable, either. In the last few years, Scotland has toughened its rules on access for those with disabilities, so matters are improving.

Call ahead to attractions and B&Bs to check their facilities, but you can feel fairly confident that newer restaurants and modern hotels will be entirely accessible.

The "Information for Visitors with Disabilities" guide, published by the National Trust of Scotland, is available at most tourist offices. It lists attractions in Scotland and details the accessibility of each portion of the attraction (for example, the castle may be accessible but the gardens and toilets may not be). The publication even details access points and views that are accessible from a wheelchair.

Travel agencies and organizations

Many travel agencies offer customized tours and itineraries for travelers with disabilities.

- **Access-Able Travel Source** (☎ 303-232-2979; www.access-able. com) offers extensive information on accessibility and advice for traveling around the world with disabilities.

- **Accessible Journeys** (☎ 800-846-4537 or 610-521-0339; www. disabilitytravel.com) offers travel planning and information for mature travelers, slow walkers, wheelchair travelers, and their families and friends.

- **Flying Wheels Travel** (☎ 507-451-5005; www.flyingwheels travel.com) offers escorted tours and cruises that emphasize sports and private tours in minivans with lifts.

Organizations that offer assistance to travelers with disabilities include

- **American Foundation for the Blind** (AFB; ☎ 800-232-5463; www. afb.org): A referral resource for the blind or visually impaired that includes information on traveling with Seeing Eye dogs.

- **MossRehab ResourceNet** (www.mossresourcenet.org): Provides a library of accessible-travel resources online.

- **Society for Accessible Travel & Hospitality** (SATH; ☎ 212-447-7284; www.sath.org): Offers a wealth of travel resources for people with all types of disabilities and recommendations on destinations, access guides, travel agents, tour operators, vehicle rentals, and companion services.

Transportation

Avis Rent A Car has a program called "Avis Access" (☎ **888-879-4273;** www.avis.com) that offers special car features such as swivel seats, spinner knobs, and hand controls.

Following the Rainbow: Advice for Gay and Lesbian Travelers

Although perhaps not considered the most liberally minded country in Europe, Scotland is safe for gay and lesbian travelers. Glasgow and Edinburgh are progressive cities that are home to substantial (though possibly subdued, depending on what you're used to) gay populations. Smaller towns and villages may be less tolerant, and open displays of affection may feel more conspicuous. Hotels should not discriminate against same-sex couples, and a few B&Bs that have recently made it an issue also made the news for discriminating.

For more information and support, contact the **Gay and Lesbian Switchboard** (☎ **0141-847-0447**) in Glasgow, which also operates the LGBT Centre (☎ **0141-221-7203**). The line offers health advice, workshops, and cultural events in the community.

The International Gay and Lesbian Travel Association (IGLTA; ☎ 800-448-8550 or 954-776-2626; www.iglta.org) offers an online directory of gay- and lesbian-friendly travel businesses; on the organization's Web site, click "Members" for a detailed list.

Many agencies offer tours and travel itineraries developed specifically for gay and lesbian travelers.

  ✔ **Now, Voyager** (☎ **800-255-6951;** www.nowvoyager.com) is a well-known San Francisco–based gay-owned and -operated travel service.

The following travel guides are available at most travel bookstores and gay and lesbian bookstores, or you can order them from **Giovanni's Room Bookstore** (☎ **215-923-2960;** www.giovannisroom.com):

  ✔ The *Damron* guides (www.damron.com) include annual books for gay men and lesbians.

  ✔ *Gay Travel A to Z: The World of Gay & Lesbian Travel Options at Your Fingertips,* by Marianne Ferrari (Ferrari International; Box 35575, Phoenix, AZ 85069), is a very good gay and lesbian guidebook series.

> ✔ *Out and About* (☎ **800-929-2268** or 415-644-8044; www.outand
> about.com) offers guidebooks and a newsletter ($20 per year; ten
> issues) packed with solid information on the global gay and lesbian
> scene.

Uncovering Your Scottish Roots

If you have a surname beginning with Mac (which simply means "son
of") or one of the common lowland Scottish monikers from Burns to
Armstrong, you're probably a descendant of Scotland and may have ties
to a clan — people with common ancestry.

Clans and clan societies maintain their own museums throughout
Scotland, and local tourist offices can give you details about where to
locate them. Bookstores here also sell clan histories and maps.

Genealogical records are kept at the **General Register Office for
Scotland,** New Register House, 3 W. Register St., Edinburgh (☎ **0131-
334-0380;** www.gro-scotland.gov.uk), where you can search for a
fee. The system is strictly self-service, and the office gets very crowded
in summer.

The official government source for genealogical data has also been
added to the Web. Log on to www.scotlandspeople.gov.uk. The
Web site's census data go back more than 100 years.

Chapter 10

Taking Care of the Remaining Details

*B*efore heading off to Scotland, you need to take care of some important business. The information I provide in this chapter should help you get all your ducks in a row.

Getting a Passport

A valid passport is the only legal form of identification accepted around the world. You can't cross an international border without one. Getting a passport is easy, but the process takes some time.

Applying for a U.S. passport

The Web sites listed provide downloadable passport applications as well as the current fees for processing applications. For an up-to-date, country-by-country listing of passport requirements around the world, go to the "International Travel" tab of the U.S. State Department Web site at http://travel.state.gov. *Note:* Children are required to present a passport when entering the United States at airports. More information on obtaining a passport for a minor can be found at the State Department Web site.

Allow plenty of time before your trip to apply for a passport; processing normally takes four to six weeks (three weeks for expedited service), but can take longer during busy periods (especially spring). And remember that if you need a passport in a hurry, you pay a higher processing fee.

Applying for other passports

The following list offers more information for citizens of Australia, Canada, Ireland, and New Zealand.

- ✔ **Australians** can pick up an application from your local post office or any branch of Passports Australia, but you must schedule an interview at the passport office to present your application materials. Call the **Australian Passport Information Service** at ☎ 131-232, or visit the government Web site at www.passports.gov.au.

- ✔ **Canadians** can pick up applications at travel agencies throughout Canada or from the central **Passport Office,** Department of Foreign Affairs and International Trade, Ottawa, ON K1A 0G3 (☎ **800-567-6868;** www.ppt.gc.ca). *Note:* Canadian children who travel must have their own passport. However, if you hold a valid Canadian passport issued before December 11, 2001, that bears the name of your child, the passport remains valid for you and your child until it expires.

- ✔ Residents of **Ireland** can apply for a ten-year passport at the **Passport Office,** Setanta Centre, Molesworth Street, Dublin 2 (☎ **01-671-1633;** www.irlgov.ie/iveagh). Those under age 18 or over 65 must apply for a three-year passport. You can also apply at 1A South Mall, Cork (☎ **21-494-4700**) or at most main post offices.

- ✔ **New Zealanders** can pick up a passport application at any New Zealand Passports Office or download it from their Web site (☎ **0800-225-050** in New Zealand, or 04-474-8100; www.passports.govt.nz).

Playing It Safe with Travel and Medical Insurance

Three kinds of travel insurance are available to you: trip-cancellation insurance, medical insurance, and lost-luggage insurance. The cost of travel insurance varies widely depending on the cost and length of your trip, your age and health, and the type of trip you're taking, but expect to pay between 5 percent and 8 percent of the cost of the vacation itself.

Trip-cancellation insurance

Trip-cancellation insurance will help retrieve your money if you have to back out of a trip or depart early, or if your travel supplier goes bankrupt. Trip cancellation traditionally covers such events as sickness, natural disasters, and State Department advisories. The latest news in trip-cancellation insurance is the availability of **expanded hurricane coverage** and the **"any-reason"** cancellation coverage — which costs more but covers cancellations made for any reason. You won't get back 100 percent of your prepaid trip cost, but you'll be refunded a substantial portion. **TravelSafe** (☎ **888-885-7233;** www.travelsafe. com) offers both types of coverage. Expedia also offers any-reason cancellation coverage for its air-hotel packages.

Other recommended insurers include **AccessAmerica** (☎ 866-807-3982; www.accessamerica.com), **Travel Guard** (☎ 800-826-4919; www. travelguard.com), **Travel Insured International** (☎ 800-243-3174; www.travelinsured.com); and **Travelex Insurance Services** (☎ 888-457-4602; www.travelex-insurance.com).

You can get estimates from various providers through the Web site www.InsureMyTrip.com. Enter your trip cost and dates, your age, and other information, for prices from more than a dozen companies.

Medical insurance

For travel overseas, you may want to look into **medical insurance.** Most U.S. health plans (including Medicare and Medicaid) do not provide coverage, and the ones that do often require you to pay for services up front and reimburse you only after you return home.

If you require additional medical insurance, try **MEDEX Assistance** (☎ **410-453-6300;** www.medexassist.com) or **Travel Assistance International** (☎ **800-821-2828;** www.travelassistance.com; for general information on services, call the company's **Worldwide Assistance Services, Inc.,** at ☎ **800-777-8710**).

Canadians should check with their provincial health plan offices or call **Health Canada** (☎ **866-225-0709;** www.hc-sc.gc.ca) to find out the extent of their coverage and what documentation and receipts they must take home in case they are treated overseas.

Lost luggage insurance

On international flights (including U.S. portions of international trips), baggage coverage is limited to approximately $9.07 per pound, up to approximately $635 per checked bag. If you plan to check items more valuable than what's covered by the standard liability, see if your homeowner's policy covers your valuables, get baggage insurance as part of your comprehensive travel-insurance package, or buy Travel Guard's "BagTrak" product. I would not suggest buying insurance at the airport — it's usually overpriced.

Be sure to take any valuables or irreplaceable items with you in your carry-on luggage, because many valuables (including books, money, and electronics) aren't covered by airline policies.

If your luggage is lost, immediately file a lost-luggage claim at the airport, detailing the luggage contents. For most airlines, you must report delayed, damaged, or lost baggage within four hours of arrival. Airlines are required to deliver found luggage directly to your house or destination free of charge.

Staying Healthy When You Travel

You don't need any special vaccinations or shots to travel in Scotland. The threat of bird flu will continue to be debated, but any risks to you from either live poultry or wild bird populations will be miniscule.

If you have a serious and/or chronic illness, talk to your doctor before leaving on a trip. For conditions such as epilepsy, diabetes, or heart problems, wear a **MedicAlert identification tag** (☎ **888-633-4298;** www. medicalert.org), which immediately alerts doctors to your condition and gives them access to your records through MedicAlert's 24-hour hot line. Contact the **International Association for Medical Assistance to Travelers (IAMAT;** ☎ **716-754-4883,** or 416-652-0137 in Canada; www. iamat.org) for tips on travel and health concerns in Scotland and lists of local doctors. Also, the United States **Centers for Disease Control and Prevention** (☎ **800-311-3435;** www.cdc.gov) provides up-to-date information on health hazards by region or country and offers tips on food safety. The Web site www.tripprep.com, sponsored by a consortium of travel-medicine practitioners, may also offer helpful advice on traveling abroad. You can find listings of reliable clinics overseas at the **International Society of Travel Medicine** (www.istm.org).

In Scotland, health care is nationalized and free. Hospital emergency rooms will treat anyone, regardless of whether they're local residents or tourists.

Staying Connected by Cellphone and E-mail

Staying in touch while traveling is easier than ever, thanks to cellphones and the Internet. Of course, if what you're interested in is an escape, you may want to skip the section below. Otherwise, read on.

Using a cellphone outside the U.S.

First of all, they're called "mobiles" (*moe*-biles) in Scotland. The three letters that define much of the world's wireless capabilities are GSM (Global System for Mobiles), a big, seamless network that makes for easy cross-border cellphone use throughout Europe and dozens of other countries worldwide. In the U.S., T-Mobile, AT&T Wireless, and Cingular use this quasi-universal system; in Canada, Microcell, and some Rogers customers are GSM, and all Europeans and most Australians use GSM.

If your cellphone is on a GSM system and you have a world-capable multiband phone, such as many Sony Ericsson, Motorola, or Samsung models, you can make and receive calls across much of the globe, from Andorra to Uganda. Just call your wireless operator and ask for international roaming to be activated on your account. Unfortunately, per-minute charges on the network can be high.

Avoiding "economy-class syndrome"

Deep vein thrombosis, or as it's know in the world of flying, "economy-class syndrome," is a blood clot that develops in a deep vein. It's a potentially deadly condition that can be caused by sitting in cramped conditions, such as an airplane cabin, for too long. During a flight (especially a long-haul flight), get up, walk around, and stretch your legs every 60 to 90 minutes to keep your blood flowing. Other preventative measures include frequent flexing of the legs while sitting, drinking lots of water, and avoiding alcohol and sleeping pills. If you have a history of deep vein thrombosis, heart disease, or other condition that puts you at high risk, some experts recommend wearing compression stockings or taking anticoagulants when you fly; always ask your physician about the best course for you. Symptoms of deep vein thrombosis include leg pain or swelling, or even shortness of breath.

If you have an unlocked phone — one that allows you to install removable computer memory phone chips (called SIM cards) — you can switch over to a cheap, prepaid SIM card (found at a local retailer) in Scotland. (Show your phone to the salesperson when you go to buy a SIM card; not all phones work on all networks.) With the new card, you get a local phone number and much, much lower calling rates. If your phone is locked, you may be able to have it unlocked. Just call your cellular operator and say you'll be going abroad and want to use the phone with a local provider.

If you don't have a cellphone, or if your phone is locked, then renting a phone is another possibility. Although you can rent a phone from any number of overseas sites, including kiosks at airports and at car-rental agencies, I suggest renting the phone before you leave home. That way you can give loved ones and business associates your new number, make sure the phone works, and take the phone wherever you go. Getting the phone before you leave is especially helpful if you're planning to visit Scotland and then go through several other countries, where local phone-rental agencies often bill in local currency and may not let you take the phone to another country.

Phone rental isn't cheap. You usually pay $40 to $50 per week, plus airtime fees of at least $1 per minute. If you're traveling to the U.K. or Europe, though, local rental companies often offer free incoming calls within their home country, which can save you big bucks. Shop around.

Two good wireless rental companies in the States are **InTouch Global** (☎ **800-872-7626;** www.intouchglobal.com) and **RoadPost** (☎ **888-290-1606** or 905-272-5665; www.roadpost.com). Give the company your itinerary, and someone will tell you what wireless products you need. For no charge, InTouch also advises you on whether your existing phone will work overseas; simply call ☎ **703-222-7161** between 9 a.m. and 4 p.m. EST, or go to www.intouchglobal.com/travel.htm.

In the U.K., you can rent (or "hire") phones from

- **Adam Phones** (☎ **0800-123-000** within the U.K., 44-20-8742-0101 outside the U.K., or ☎ 866-GSM-HIRE [476-4473] within the U.S.; www.adamphones.com)

- **Cellhire UK** (☎ **0800-610-610** within the U.K., 44-1904-610-610 outside the U.K., or 866-246-6546 within the U.S.; www.cellhire.co.uk)

Accessing the Internet

Travelers have any number of ways to check e-mail and access the Internet on the road. Of course, using your own laptop — or even a smartphone — provides the most flexibility. But even if you don't have a computer, you can access e-mail and even your office computer from cybercafes, many hotels, and libraries.

It's hard nowadays to find a city that *doesn't* have a few cybercafes. Although no definitive directory for cybercafes exists — these are independent businesses, after all — two places to start looking are at www.cybercaptive.com and www.cybercafe.com.

Aside from cybercafes, most youth hostels and an increasing number of hotels and B&Bs have at least one computer you can use to access the Internet. Essentially all **public libraries** in Scotland offer Internet access free or for a small charge. Major airports have Internet kiosks scattered throughout their terminals, too. These give you Web access for a per-minute fee that's usually higher than cybercafe prices. Avoid hotel business centers unless you're willing to pay exorbitant rates.

If you need to access files on your office computer while you're away, look into a service called **GoToMyPC** (www.gotomypc.com). The service provides a Web-based interface for you to access and manipulate a distant PC from anywhere — even from a cybercafe — provided your "target" PC is on and has an always-on connection to the Internet.

Using your own computer

If you're bringing your own computer with you, more and more hotels, cafes, and retailers are signing on as Wi-Fi "hotspots." **Boingo** (www.boingo.com) and **Wayport** (www.wayport.com) have set up networks in airports and high-class hotel lobbies. Users of iPass have access to a few hundred wireless hotel lobby setups. To locate other hotspots that provide free wireless networks in cities around the world, go to www.personaltelco.net/index.cgi/WirelessCommunities.

For dial-up access, most business-class hotels throughout the world offer dataports for laptop modems. In addition, major Internet service providers (ISPs) have **local access numbers** around the world, allowing you to go online by placing a local call. The **iPass** network also has dial-up numbers around the world. You have to sign up with an iPass provider, which will then tell you how to set up your computer for your destination(s). For a list of iPass providers, go to www.ipass.com and click on "Individuals Buy Now." One solid provider is **i2roam** (☎ **866-811-6209** or 920-235-0475; www.i2roam.com).

Scotland Unplugged: Getting Your Electric Stuff to Work

The plugs in Scotland are different from those in the U.S. and Canada. You can buy a cheap adapter, but it won't address the problem of different voltages. In the U.S. and Canada, the current is 120 volts. In Scotland, it's officially 230 volts, although 240 volts are common. If you plug in your hair dryer, even with an adapter, you're likely to blow a fuse or burn out the appliance. You can buy a voltage transformer (check out www.walkabouttravelgear.com), but they can be expensive and not worth the cost if you're planning a short stay.

Some travel appliances, such as shavers and irons, have a nice feature called dual voltage that adapts to the change, but unless your appliance gives a voltage range (such as 110v–220v), don't chance it. Bring a battery-operated alarm clock (for when you can't get a wake-up call) and shaver (if you're averse to disposables) as well as a battery-powered personal stereo (if you can't bear to be without your tunes).

Keeping Up with Airline Security Measures

Security procedures at U.S. airports are stable and consistent. Generally, you'll be fine if you arrive at the airport **two hours** before an international flight; if you show up late, tell an airline employee and you might be whisked to the front of the line.

Keep your passport at the ready to show at check-in, the security checkpoint, and sometimes even the gate.

Passengers with e-tickets can beat the ticket-counter lines by using airport **electronic kiosks** or even **online check-in** from their home computer. Online check-in involves logging on to your airline's Web site, accessing your reservation, and printing out your boarding pass — and the airline may even offer you bonus miles to do so! If you're using a kiosk at the airport, **bring the credit card** you used to book the ticket or your frequent-flier card. Print out your boarding pass from the kiosk and simply proceed to the security checkpoint with your pass and a photo ID. **Curbside check-in** is also a good way to avoid lines, although a few airlines still ban curbside check-in; call before you go.

Speed up security by **not wearing metal objects** such as big belt buckles. If you've got metallic body parts, a note from your doctor can prevent a long chat with the security screeners. Remember that only **ticketed passengers** are allowed past security, except for folks escorting passengers with disabilities or children.

On the matter of **what you can carry on** and **what you can't:** Travelers in the U.S. are allowed one carry-on bag, plus a "personal item" such as a purse, briefcase, or laptop bag. Carry-on hoarders can stuff all sorts of things into a laptop bag; as long as it has a laptop in it, it's still considered a personal item. The Transportation Security Administration (TSA) has issued a list of restricted items; check its Web site (www.tsa.gov/travelers/airtravel/prohibited/permitted-prohibited-items.shtm) for details.

Airport screeners may decide that your checked luggage needs to be searched by hand. You can now purchase luggage locks that allow screeners to open and relock a checked bag if hand-searching is necessary. Look for Travel Sentry–certified locks at luggage or travel shops and Brookstone stores (you can buy them online at www.brookstone.com). For more information on the locks, visit www.travelsentry.org.

Part III

Edinburgh and Glasgow

The 5th Wave

By Rich Tennant

"We were in Edinburgh this summer. I loved the
New Town section, but Edward preferred the
medieval feel of Old Town."

In this part . . .

You find out about the charms and attractions of
Scotland's two major cities: Edinburgh and Glasgow.
There is also information about some of the sights that are
within easy striking distance of each or both of the cities.
Though noticeably different from one another, each city is
worth a visit, and you'll find plenty of suggestions here of
what to do and see. Edinburgh, Scotland's capital, is most
famous for its castle and picturesque setting, while Glasgow,
once among the greatest shipbuilding centers of the world, is
a more modern and bustling big city (though not too big).

The chapters in Part III offer everything from advice on getting there to getting around — as well as hints on how to discover the best places to stay and dine. You also get the
lowdown on the cities' finest sights and attractions, insider
tips on quintessential Scottish pubs and cafes, and a walking
tour in each city.

Chapter 11

Edinburgh

. . . .

In This Chapter

▶ Getting around Edinburgh's compact environs

▶ Discovering the best places to stay and eat

▶ Exploring the city's historic, artistic, and cultural sights

▶ Shopping for quintessential Edinburgh gifts and souvenirs

▶ Finding the best spots for a pint and live music

. . . .

*E*dinburgh has been called one of Europe's fairest cities and "Athens of the North." And many experienced travelers to the U.K. say: If you can visit *only* two cities in all of Great Britain, it should be London first and Edinburgh second. That is essentially correct. But which one first?

Edinburgh is built on extinct volcanoes at a large inlet from the North Sea (the Firth of Forth) and the modern city is enveloped by rolling hills, lakes, and forests. The Scottish capital began as a small, fortified settlement on its craggiest hill, known today as Castle Hill. Indeed, because of its defensive attributes, Edinburgh (remember "burgh" is pronounced *burra* in Scotland) became an important, protected place for the country's rulers. Defensive walls long since dismantled, in the main, Edinburgh is a virtual crossroad of Scotland: Most visitors stop in or pass through the city while in Scotland.

Edinburgh is filled with historic, intellectual, and literary associations. Names such as Mary, Queen of Scots and her nemesis, the Protestant reformer John Knox; pioneer economic theorist Adam Smith and philosopher David Hume; authors Sir Walter Scott, Robert Louis Stevenson, and Sir Arthur Conan Doyle; as well as inventor Alexander Graham Bell: They are all part of Edinburgh's past.

Today the city is famous for its annual world-class cultural event, the summer's **Edinburgh Festival.** It is actually several festivals at once: books, comedy, drama, classical music, dance, and more. But this ancient seat of Scottish royalty has year-round attractions. When the festival-goers have returned home, the city's pace is more relaxed, the price of accommodations drops, and the inhabitants — though not especially celebrated for their bonhomie — are under less pressure and offer a hospitable welcome.

Edinburgh is a city that lends itself to walking. Its **Old Town** and **New Town** are full of moody cobbled alleys, elegant streetscapes, handsome squares, and placid parks. From several hilltops, panoramic views across the city can be enjoyed.

In addition to being Scotland's political center, Edinburgh has also been its cultural locus, even if that particular distinction — especially in terms of the contemporary arts — has been lost to Glasgow (see Chapter 12) over the last few decades. Edinburgh is home to the country's several **national galleries.** And its location provides the perfect point for excursions. Notable nearby attractions include Linlithgow Palace, where Mary, Queen of Scots was born, and attractive seaside villages, such as North Berwick, east of Edinburgh. (Turn to Chapter 13 for more information on day-trip options.) Any visitor to Scotland should try to give Edinburgh at least two or three days — and, if you have the time, you won't regret staying longer.

Getting to Edinburgh

Although there are a few direct flights to Edinburgh from North America, a stopover in London's Heathrow airport (or some other European hub) is probably more common. If you're coming north from London, your options include taking the train. If you're coming from elsewhere in Scotland, major bus and railway routes serve Edinburgh. Having a car within the city of Edinburgh isn't necessary (nor even preferable), but the city is easily reached via freeways and highways, if you choose to drive.

By air

Edinburgh is only about an hour's flying time from London, which is 633km (393 miles) south. **Edinburgh International Airport (☎ 0131-333-1000)** is about 10km (6 miles) west of the city's center, and has become a growing hub for flights both within the British Isles and to and from Continental Europe.

Remember, however, that Glasgow International Airport is only about 90km (55 miles) away and shouldn't be discounted even if your eventual destination is Edinburgh. (For information on arriving in Glasgow by air, see Chapter 12.)

Orienting yourself

Edinburgh's airport terminal is compact, so there's little possibility of getting lost. Immigration control and Customs agents are vigilant, but the security scene is less tense than at a giant air terminal such as London's Heathrow. Usually you find just one line (or *queue,* in local parlance) at passport checks for visitors arriving from outside the European Union. Before heading into town, you may want to stop at the airport's **VisitScotland** information and accommodations desk (☎ **0131-473-3600;** www.visitscotland.org), which is generally open Monday

through Saturday from 6:15 a.m. to 7:45 p.m. and Sunday from 9 a.m. to
4:30 p.m.

Getting into town

From Edinburgh airport, the Airlink bus makes the trip to the city center
about every ten minutes during peak times, terminating at Waverley
Bridge near the central railway station. The fare is £3.50 one-way. The
trip from the airport into town takes about 25 minutes (sometimes
longer during rush hour). Overnight service is provided by the Night
Bus: N22. Visit www.flybybus.com for details of Airlink bus service.

A taxi into the city costs about £15 or more, depending on traffic, and
the ride takes about the same amount of time as the bus. Look for the
taxi stand when exiting the airport.

By train

The trains that link London to Edinburgh (via Newcastle) on the so-
called East Coast Main Line are reasonably fast, efficient, and generally
relaxing, with a restaurant and bar service as well as air-conditioning.
Trains depart every hour or so from London's King's Cross Station and
arrive in Edinburgh at **Waverley Station** in the heart of the city (contact
National Railway Enquiries at ☎ **0845-748-4950** for rail info; www.
nationalrail.co.uk). The trip generally takes four and a half hours.

Off-peak fares bought in advance can range widely, from around £25 to
£100. Off-peak first-class tickets purchased in advance also range widely,
from about £30 to £120, although the cheapest fares seem to be rarely
available. A fully flexible "buy anytime, travel anytime" standard open
single fare is upwards of £150. The Caledonian Sleeper service for overnight travel can cost about £100, but online bargains booked well in
advance can mean the trip may cost as little as £25. Taxi and bus connections are easily made at Waverley Station, which also serves
Glasgow's Queen Street Station with an efficient railway **shuttle service**
every 15 minutes during the day and every 30 minutes in the evening
until about 11:30 p.m.

By bus

National Express (☎ **0870-580-8080;** www.nationalexpress.com)
runs buses daily (typically 9:30 a.m., noon, and 11 p.m. for direct service) from London's Victoria Coach Station to Edinburgh. Standard
round-trip fare is about £45. Without stopovers, the trip should take less
than ten hours. Edinburgh's **bus station** is near St. Andrew Square
(☎ **0870-550-5050** for information).

By car

Edinburgh is 74km (46 miles) east of Glasgow and 169km (105 miles)
north of Newcastle-upon-Tyne in England. No express motorway links
London directly to Edinburgh. The M1 from London takes you most of

the way north, but you have to come into Edinburgh via secondary roads — either the coastal A1 or inland A68. Alternatively, you can travel the well-used motorways in the west of the U.K. From London, take the M1 to the M6 (near Coventry), which links to the M74 at Carlisle. Then travel to the M8 southeast of Glasgow, which takes you Edinburgh's ring road or beltway. Allow eight hours or more for the drive north from London.

Orienting Yourself in Edinburgh

Central Edinburgh is divided into two distinct historic districts: An **Old Town** and the larger **New Town.** (Note that the locals generally drop the definite article "the" when referring to these two districts; so shall I.) Old Town is where the city began: Once called "Auld Reekie," because of its smoky atmosphere, it is today chock-a-block with tourist attractions and shops, its sidewalks often full of out-of-town visitors from Easter until autumn. By contrast, New Town is a product of a golden age of enlightenment in Edinburgh, displaying mid–to-late-18th-century modernism in town planning.

The **Royal Mile** is the main thoroughfare in Old Town, running from Edinburgh Castle in the west to the Palace of Holyroodhouse in the east. Both British **royalty** and Scotland's **Parliament** (revived in 1999) are based in Old Town, as are municipal government and the country's legal elite. Another famous area, at the southern base of the castle, is the **Grassmarket,** both a street and a district, where convicted criminals were once hanged on the gallows. Today the place is home to several restaurants, pubs, and hotels.

New Town is actually fairly old, older than the U.S. North of Edinburgh's original settlement, across what is today the park called Princes Street Gardens, New Town was first settled in the 18th century — about one decade before the American Declaration of Independence was signed. By the beginning of the 1800s, classic squares, streets, and town houses were complete, and the original district was soon expanded with more Georgian designs. **Princes Street** is the area's primary shopping precinct, with broad sidewalks and Princes Street Gardens running its entire length — all with panoramic views across the valley of Old Town and Edinburgh Castle.

North of, and running parallel to, Princes Street is New Town's second great boulevard, **George Street.** It begins at St. Andrew Square and runs west to Charlotte Square. Directly north of George Street is another impressive thoroughfare, **Queen Street,** which opens onto Queen Street Gardens on its north side and features views of the Firth of Forth. You may also hear a lot about **Rose Street,** between Princes Street and George Street, and its many pubs, shops, and restaurants.

Edinburgh's **Southside** and **West End** are primarily residential, and affluent. The Southside is home to both the well-regarded Edinburgh

University (which makes parts of the area quite lively) and a sprawling park known as the Meadows. The West End includes the last of New Town developments, begun at the beginning of the 19th century. In addition to desirable town house residences, it has theaters, several small B&Bs, and swank boutique hotels.

Leith is north of the city center and is Edinburgh's historic port where the Water of Leith (a small river that meanders through the city) meets the wide Firth of Forth.

Leith briefly served as the Scottish capital in the middle of the 16th century, and so strategic was its location that Oliver Cromwell's invading forces built a citadel there in the 17th century. Leith remained an independent burgh until the 20th century. Fans of Irvine Welsh (author of *Trainspotting*) probably know that the area has a rough-and-tumble reputation. But today, the sailors and most of its shipping have gone, and lots of luxury apartments are being built instead. Still, Leith carries reminders of its evocative maritime past and offers a good selection of seafood restaurants and nautical-themed pubs. It's also now the home of the royal yacht *Britannia*.

 Despite its steep hills, often linked by bridges, Edinburgh is a walkable city. Little alleys *(wynds)* and passageways *(closes)* are accessible only by foot. So bring a pair of comfortable shoes and start strolling — you get a great feel for what the city has to offer.

Introducing the neighborhoods

Edinburgh has a host of districts, some of which appear to include only a few streets and many that can be folded into the broader areas of Old and New Towns.

Old Town

Old Town is where Edinburgh began. Its spine is the **Royal Mile,** a medieval thoroughfare stretching for about 1.6km (1 mile) from Edinburgh Castle downhill to the Palace of Holyroodhouse. The Royal Mile is one boulevard with four segments bearing different names: Castlehill, Lawnmarket, High Street, and Canongate. English author Daniel Defoe wrote of the Royal Mile: "This is perhaps the largest, longest, and finest street for buildings and number of inhabitants in the world." Old Town also includes the areas of Grassmarket and Cowgate.

New Town

Lying predominantly north of Old Town, the first New Town bloomed between 1766 and 1840 as one of the largest Georgian developments in the world. It grew to encompass the northern half of the heart of the city. New Town is the largest historic conservation area in Great Britain and has at least 25,000 residents. It is made up of a network of squares, streets, terraces, and circuses, reaching from Haymarket in the west to

Leith Walk in the east. The neighborhood also extends from Canonmills in the north to Princes Street, its most famous artery, in the south.

Stockbridge

Today part of the greater New Town area, Stockbridge is a one-time village that still feels rather like a small town because of its tight-knit community. Northwest of the castle and straddling the Water of Leith, it's a good place for visitors to the city to relax, especially in the friendly cafes, pubs, restaurants, and shops.

Haymarket and Dalry

West of the city center by about 1.5km (1 mile), these two districts may be off the beaten path for most visitors. Haymarket centers on the Haymarket railway station (an alternative to Waverley for travelers to and from Glasgow and the west, or places much farther north). Dalry is slowly opening some interesting, though largely neighborhood-oriented, restaurants. Just a bit farther out of town from Haymarket is Murrayfield, the Scottish national rugby stadium.

Tollcross and West End

Edinburgh's theater district and Conference Center are in the area west of the castle. The West End neighborhoods near Shandwick Place are rather exclusive. Although the district of Tollcross appears a bit rough, it's rapidly changing and becoming more visitor-friendly.

Southside: Marchmont and Bruntsfield

About 1.5km (1 mile) south of High Street, Marchmont was constructed between 1869 and 1914 to offer new housing to people who could no longer afford to live in New Town. Its northern border is the Meadows. Sometimes visitors go south to this neighborhood, seeking a more affordable B&B in one of the little homes that receive guests.

Bruntsfield is west of the Meadows and is named for Bruntsfield Links (a short-hole public golf course). Now a largely residential district, the area was the ground on which James IV apparently gathered the Scottish army that he marched to defeat at Flodden in 1513. You can find moderately priced accommodations in this vicinity.

Calton

Encompassing Calton Hill, with its Regent and Royal terraces (streets), this district borders the so-called Pink Triangle, Edinburgh's version of a gay-friendly district. Edinburgh has a lively LGBT population, which focuses socially on an area from the top of Leith Walk to Broughton Street. The area is not, however, a dedicated gay district, such as San Francisco's Castro or Christopher Street in Manhattan's Greenwich Village; it's just part and parcel of lively Calton, with its bars, nightclubs, and restaurants.

Leith Walk and the Port of Leith

Leith Walk isn't technically a neighborhood but is instead the main artery that connects Edinburgh's city center to the port of Leith. Off of it are Easter Road (home of Hibernian football club) and the districts of Pilrig and South Leith. A venture along Leith Walk presents you with a true cross-section of Edinburgh.

Leith lies only a few kilometers north of Princes Street and is the city's major harbor, opening onto the Firth of Forth. In terms of maritime might, the port isn't what it used to be; its glory days were back when stevedores unloaded cargos by hand. The area is currently experiencing urban renewal, however, and visitors come here for the pubs and restaurants, many of which specialize in seafood.

Finding information after you arrive

Edinburgh Information Centre, atop the Princes Mall, near Waverley Station (**VisitScotland; ☎ 0131-473-3600** or 0845-225-5121; fax: 0131-473-3881; www.edinburgh.org; Bus: 3, 8, 22, 25, or 31), can give you sightseeing information and also arrange lodgings. The center sells bus tours, theater tickets, and souvenirs of Edinburgh. It also has racks and racks of free brochures. It's open year-round; typically the hours are Monday through Saturday from 9 a.m. to 7 p.m. and Sunday from 10 a.m. to 7 p.m., though it is open later during the Festival and closes earlier in the winter months.

Getting Around Edinburgh

Because of its narrow lanes, wynds, and closes, you can only honestly explore Old Town in any depth on foot. Edinburgh is fairly convenient for the visitor who likes to walk (see the section "Taking a walking tour," later in this chapter), because most of the major attractions are located along the Royal Mile, Princes Street, or one of the major streets of New Town.

The city doesn't have a subway or underground, although a tram system began to be built in 2008. Initially, it will take passengers up or down Princes Street and Leith Walk. Eventually, it may cross Leith into Newhaven and Granton, circling back to Haymarket, with a spur running west to the airport. None of this is expected to be operational until 2011, and until then bus service on routes that use the streets where tram track is being laid will be disrupted.

By bus

Because there is no underground or subway in Edinburgh, and only limited commuter-train service, the city's rather numerous buses provide the chief method of public transportation. There are lots of them, and most seem to go down Princes Street as some point on their route.

Edinburgh Orientation

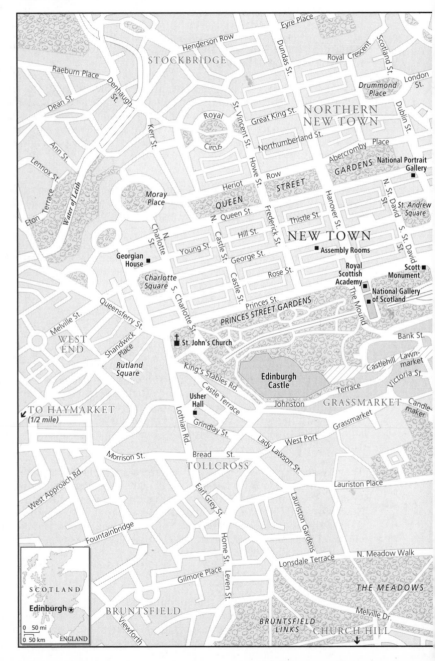

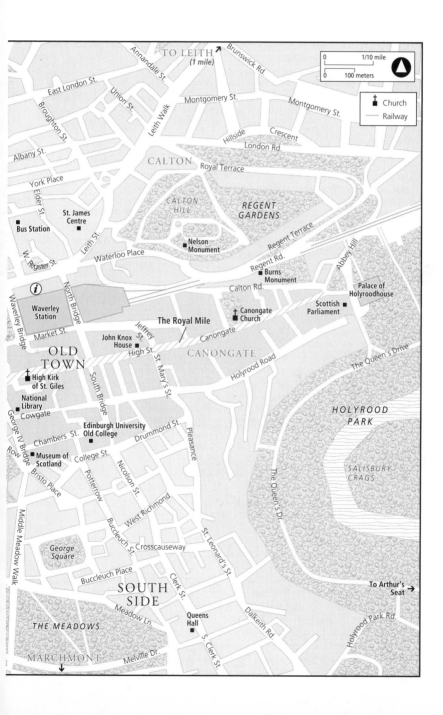

TO LEITH ↗
(1 mile)

Annandale St.
Brunswick Rd.
East London St.
Union St.
Leith Walk
Montgomery St.
Montgomery St.
Broughton St.
Hillside
Crescent
London Rd.
Albany St.
CALTON
Royal Terrace
York Place
Elder St.
CALTON HILL
REGENT GARDENS
St. James Centre
W. Register St.
Bus Station
Leith St.
Waterloo Place
Nelson Monument
Regent Terrace
Regent Rd.
Abbey Hill
Burns Monument
Calton Rd.
Palace of Holyroodhouse
Waverley Station
North Bridge
The Royal Mile
Canongate Church
Scottish Parliament
Waverley Bridge
Market St.
OLD TOWN
John Knox House
Jeffrey St.
High St.
Canongate
CANONGATE
The Queen's Drive
High Kirk of St. Giles
South Bridge
St. Mary's St.
Holyrood Road
National Library
Cowgate
HOLYROOD PARK
George IV Bridge
Chambers St.
Edinburgh University Old College
Drummond St.
Pleasance
Row
Museum of Scotland
College St.
Nicolson St.
SALISBURY CRAGS
Bristo Place
Potterrow
West Richmond
St. Leonard's St.
The Queen's Dr.
Middle Meadow Walk
George Square
Buccleuch St.
Crosscauseway
Buccleuch Place
SOUTH SIDE
Clerk St.
To Arthur's Seat →
THE MEADOWS
Meadow Ln.
Queens Hall
S. Clerk St.
Dalkeith Rd.
Holyrood Park Rd.
MARCHMONT ↓
Melville Dr.

0 ——— 1/10 mile
0 ——— 100 meters

✝ Church
—— Railway

Fares depend on the distance traveled, with the adult one-way (single) **minimum fare** £1.20 covering the central Edinburgh districts. Bus drivers, by the way, will not make change, so carry the correct amount in coins, or expect to pay more.

If you plan multiple trips in one day, purchase a **Dayticket** that allows unlimited travel on city buses for one day at a cost of £3 for adults and £2.40 for children. At Travelshops, one-week **RideaCard** passes, which allow unlimited travel on buses, can be purchased for £13 adults, £11 students, and £9 children.

Also the tourist tour buses, which begin and terminate at Waverley Bridge, offer hop-on, hop-off service at any of their stops on the set circuit of primarily Old and New Towns.

You can get advance tickets and further information in the city center at the **Waverley Bridge Travelshop,** Waverley Bridge, open Monday to Saturday 8:15 a.m. to 6 p.m., and Sunday 9:30 a.m. to 5:15 p.m.; or at 27 Hanover Street Travelshop, open Monday to Saturday 8:15 a.m. to 6 p.m. For details on fares and timetables, call ☎ **0131-555-6363,** or log on to www.lothianbuses.co.uk.

By taxi

One way to get around the city is to hail a taxi or pick one up at a taxi stand. Meters begin at £2, and a typical trek across town costs about £7. Taxi stands (ranks) are at High Street near South Bridge, Waverley and Haymarket stations, Hanover Street, North St. Andrew Street, and Lauriston Place. Fares are displayed on the front of the taxi, and charges are posted, including extra fees for night drivers or destinations outside the city limits. You can also call a taxi ahead of time. Try **City Cabs,** at ☎ **0131-228-1211,** or **Central Radio Taxis,** at ☎ **0131-229-2468.**

By car

Unless you absolutely can't avoid it, I would strongly advise that you simply don't drive in Edinburgh — it's a tricky and frustrating business, even for natives. Speed bumps, one-way streets, dedicated bus lanes, and tram construction are all good reasons to forego the private automobile.

Parking is expensive and also can be difficult to find. Metered parking is available, but you need the right change and have to watch out for traffic wardens who issue tickets. Some zones are marked permit holders only — and they mean it. Your vehicle will likely be towed if you don't have a permit. A double yellow line along the curb indicates no parking at any time. A single yellow line along the curb may allow you to park; check for posted restrictions, or you may incur a ticket there as well. Major parking lots (car parks) are at Castle Terrace (near Edinburgh Castle), Waverley Station, and St. James Centre (close to the east end of Princes Street).

Famous Edinburghers

Famous Edinburgh residents include *Harry Potter* author J. K. Rowling, who has become one of the best-selling writers in history and wrote her first book in one of the city's coffee shops. David Hume lived at James Court in Old Town in the 18th century. James Boswell, Robert Louis Stevenson, Sir Walter Scott, and Flora MacDonald also made their homes here. One of the city's most famous former residents, Sean Connery, grew up in the Fenton Bridge tenements, and Queen Elizabeth knighted him in 2000 at the Palace of Holyroodhouse. The actor, most widely known for his many James Bond films, had previously dismissed the idea of knighthood as long as Scotland was denied independent rule. (See Chapter 2 for more on the political history of Scotland.)

You may want a rental car for touring the countryside or heading onward. Many agencies grant discounts to those who reserve cars in advance (see Chapter 7 for more information). Most rental agencies will accept your foreign driver's license, provided you've held it for more than a year and are older than 21. Most of the major car-rental companies maintain offices at the Edinburgh airport, in case you want to rent a car on the spot. In the city, try **Avis** on West Park Place (☎ **0870-153-9103**), **Hertz** on Picardy Place (☎ **0870-864-0013**), or **Thrifty** on Haymarket Terrace (☎ **0131-337-1319**).

By bicycle

Bicycles are a more common mode of transportation in Edinburgh than in Glasgow. Nevertheless, biking is probably a good idea only for visitors in good shape, given that the city is set on a series of ridges and the streets are often cobbled. If you're determined to bike your way through Edinburgh, try **Rent-a-Bike Edinburgh,** 29 Blackfriars St., near High Street (☎ **0131-556-5560;** www.cyclescotland.co.uk; Bus: 35). Depending on the type of bike you rent, charges average around £15 per day or £70 for the week, but partial-day rentals are also possible. A credit-card imprint will be taken as security. The same company that operates Rent-a-Bike Edinburgh also runs **Scottish Cycle Safaris,** which organizes tours in the city and across Scotland. They can equip you for excursions; and because they have branches in places such as Oban, Inverness, and Skye, you can drop off your bike and equipment there at the end of your trip, if it's more convenient.

On foot

Walking Edinburgh is definitely the best way to see the city center and most of the town. (But I also recommend using buses or taxis, if the distances seem too great.)

Staying in Style

Edinburgh offers many options for accommodations, from the super posh and fabulously pricey five-star hotels to youth hostels. It's a city that anticipates bundles of tourists and travelers, whether seasonal backpackers, school groups, and families—or professional types in the Scottish capital on commercial and governmental matters. Also, note that in compliance with Scottish law, all premises are nonsmoking (though some will have designated outdoor smoking areas).

Be warned, however: During the period of the Edinburgh Festival — from late July through to early September — the hotels, guesthouses, hostels, and B&Bs fill up. If you're planning a visit at that time, be sure to reserve your accommodations as far in advance as possible. Otherwise you may end up in a town or village as many as 40km (55 miles) from the city center. And don't be surprised if the standard rates for accommodations in Edinburgh are higher — in isolated cases twice as high — during August, particularly at smaller hotels.

The **Edinburgh Information Centre** is near Waverley Station, atop the Princes Mall shopping center, at 3 Princes St. (☎ **0131-473-3800,** 0845-225-5121, or 44-1506-832-121 from overseas; fax: 0131-473-3881; www.edinburgh.org; Bus: 3, 8, 22, 25, or 31).

The Information Centre, in conjunction with the Scottish tourist board, compiles a lengthy list of small hotels, guesthouses, and private homes providing B&B-type lodging for as little as £30 per person. A £4 booking fee is charged and a 10 percent deposit is expected if you book through the center. For the best availability, make your reservation about four weeks in advance, especially during summer. The center is open year-round; typically the hours are Monday through Saturday from 9 a.m. to 7 p.m. and Sunday from 10 a.m. to 7 p.m., although it's open later during the Festival and closes earlier in the winter months.

VisitScotland also provides ratings of accommodations, which are based largely on amenities. Due to the ratings system, the stars can be limited for smaller operations that may not offer all the modern conveniences but are still perfectly good places to stay. References to stars in the information below are those bestowed by the tourist board, and I have more to say about what they mean in Chapter 8.

The Internet can be a treasure trove of discounted rates, if you have the time and inclination to dig around a bit. In some cases, bargains are only available when you use Web-based booking services. Some of these special prices and promotions are noted below. See Chapter 8 for more details on booking your hotel.

Among hostels with private rooms, the **Edinburgh Central,** 9 Haddington Place (☎ **0845-293-7373**), is a good bet, with single rooms starting at

£34. If you have an early flight out and need a hotel that's convenient to the airport, consider the 244-unit **Edinburgh Marriott,** 111 Glasgow Rd. (☎ **0131-334-9191**), off A8 on Edinburgh's western outskirts. It offers doubles from about £150, including breakfast. Facilities include an indoor pool, gym, sauna, and restaurant.

The top hotels

Here's a list of my recommended places to stay in Edinburgh. Rack rates are the standard full prices that a hotel charges for a room. You may not have to pay the full amount of the published rates, however, except in high season, and even then there may be reductions. Last minute and Internet bookings may also offer less expensive tariffs (but may also carry penalties for cancellation). Unless otherwise indicated, the rates I give include breakfast.

Balmoral Hotel
$$$$ New Town

Almost directly above Waverley Rail Station, the Balmoral's soaring clock tower is a city landmark, famously set five minutes fast for the benefit of those on the way to the train. The best accommodations — such as room 520, the Dee Suite — are sumptuously furnished, with an ample sitting room and a huge, well-appointed bathroom, not to mention fabulous views towards the castle. Dining options at the Balmoral include the elegant and Michelin-star-earning **Number One** (p. 148). Kilted doormen supply the Scottish atmosphere from the start, and afternoon tea is served in the high-ceilinged Palm Court.

See map p. 133. 1 Princes St. ☎ **800-223-6800** *in the U.S., or 0131-556-2414. Fax: 0131-557-3747.* www.thebalmoralhotel.com. *Bus: 3, 8, 22, 25, 30. Rack rates: £220–£290 double; £250–£350 superior double; from £465 suite. AE, DC, MC, V.*

The Bonham
$$$$ New Town

One of Edinburgh's most stylish hotels, the Bonham is actually three West End town houses now linked internally. Perhaps the jewel in the crown of the Townhouse group of hotels in Edinburgh (which also includes the Edinburgh Residence, Howard, and Channings; see reviews below), the Bonham's rooms have individual themes and plush upholsteries. Each offers a hip blend of old and new. Bathrooms are state-of-the-art, with expensive toiletries. The **Restaurant** at the Bonham provides elegant yet modern dining rooms. In addition to the standard rates, mid- and off-season special discounts, including breakfast, are available for two people staying at least two nights.

See map p. 133. 35 Drumsheugh Gardens. ☎ **0131-226-6050.** *Fax: 0131-226-6080.* www.thebonham.com. *Bus: 19, 37. Rack rates: £100–£25 small double; £195–£240 standard double; £340 suite. AE, DC, MC, V.*

Edinburgh Accommodations

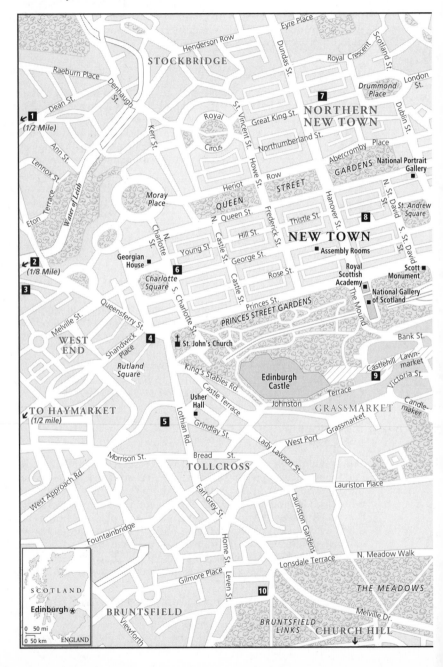

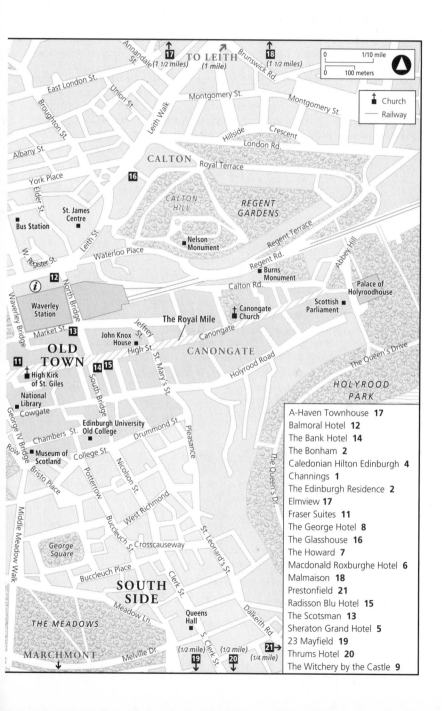

TO LEITH

A-Haven Townhouse **17**
Balmoral Hotel **12**
The Bank Hotel **14**
The Bonham **2**
Caledonian Hilton Edinburgh **4**
Channings **1**
The Edinburgh Residence **2**
Elmview **17**
Fraser Suites **11**
The George Hotel **8**
The Glasshouse **16**
The Howard **7**
Macdonald Roxburghe Hotel **6**
Malmaison **18**
Prestonfield **21**
Radisson Blu Hotel **15**
The Scotsman **13**
Sheraton Grand Hotel **5**
23 Mayfield **19**
Thrums Hotel **20**
The Witchery by the Castle **9**

Caledonian Hilton Edinburgh
$$$$ New Town

This hotel is another of the city's landmarks and offers commanding views toward the nearby Edinburgh Castle and over Princes Street Gardens. The public rooms are reminiscent of Edwardian splendor, and the guest rooms (some exceptionally spacious and others quite small) are rather conservatively styled with reproduction furniture. Bathrooms come with tub/shower combinations. Fine-dining meals are served in the **Pompadour Restaurant.** A traditional tea is featured in the high-ceilinged lounge. On the Internet, advance booking means savings.

See map p. 133. Princes Street. ☎ **0131-222-8888.** *Fax: 0131-222-8889.* www.caledonian.hilton.com. *Bus: 12, 25, 33. Rack rates: £180–£380 double; from £340 suite. Children 15 and under stay free in parent's room with a second room for children discounted. AE, DC, MC, V.*

Channings
$$$ Near New Town

Five Edwardian terrace houses were combined to create this hotel with nearly 50 rooms, located in a tranquil residential area near Stockbridge. Channings maintains the atmosphere of a Scottish country house, with oak paneling, ornate fireplaces, molded ceilings, and antiques. The guest rooms are outfitted in a modern style; the front units get the views, but the rear ones offer more seclusion. Even if you're not a guest, consider a meal here; **Channings Restaurant** offers fine fare.

See map p. 133. 15 S. Learmonth Gardens. ☎ **0131-315-2226.** *Fax: 0131-332-9631.* www.channings.co.uk. *Bus: 37. Rack rates: £100–£150 double. AE, DC, MC, V.*

The Edinburgh Residence
$$$$ West End

Part of the Townhouse group (which includes the Bonham, Howard, and Channings), this is one of the finest luxury hotels in Scotland, a series of elegant suites installed in a trio of architecturally beautiful and sensitively restored Georgian buildings in the West End. As you enter, grand staircases and classic wood paneling greet you, but the units have all the modern conveniences that befit five-star accommodations. The rooms are the ultimate in comfort, with a trio of suites having their own private entrances. All units are spacious. If you are traveling off season, it is worth checking the Web site promotions that offer savings.

See map p. 133. 7 Rothesay Terrace. ☎ **0131-226-3380.** *Fax: 0131-226-3381.* www.theedinburghresidence.com. *Bus: 36. Rack rates: £125–£400 suite. AE, MC, V.*

The Howard
$$$$ New Town

Dubbed one of the most exclusive five-star hotels in the city, this lovely hotel is made up of a set of linked Georgian town houses in the northern

New Town, just down the hill from the Queen Street Gardens. Some of the aura of a private home remains. Accommodations are midsize to spacious; units are individually and elegantly decorated, with some of the best bathrooms in town — featuring power and double showers and, in some, Jacuzzis. The décor is traditional and modern, incorporating antiques and reproductions alike. Service is a hallmark of the Howard, with a team of butlers who tend to individual needs — even unpacking your luggage, should you so desire.

See map p. 133. 34 Great King St. ☎ **0131-557-3500.** *Fax: 0131-557-6515.* www.the howard.com. *Bus: 23, 27. Rack rates: £190–£275 double. AE, DC, MC, V.*

Malmaison
$$$ Leith

This is Leith's stylish boutique hotel, located in the old harbor district, only a few steps from the Water of Leith. Malmaison was converted from an 1883 seamen's mission/dorm and is capped by a stately stone clock tower. Overall, it's a hip, unpretentious place with a minimalist décor. Rooms are average in size but well equipped. The leisure facilities are limited to an exercise room, but you find the brasserie and wine bar favored by locals. Even during summertime, at least before the festival begins, Malmaison's online reservations offer good discounts.

See map p. 133. 1 Tower Place. ☎ **0131-468-5000.** *Fax: 0131-468-5002.* www. malmaison-edinburgh.com. *Bus: 16, 35. Rack rates: £125–£200 double. AE, DC, MC, V.*

Prestonfield
$$$$ Southside

Prestonfield underwent a £3-million refurbishment in 2003 under the guidance of James Thomson, who owns The Witchery by the Castle (see listing later in this section). Rising in Jacobean splendor amid 5.3 hectares (13 acres) of gardens, pastures, and woodlands, the pile was built in the 17th century, serving first as the home of the city's Lord Provost (ceremonial mayor). It has entertained a varied group of luminaries over the years, from David Hume and Benjamin Franklin to pop stars and actors such as Sean Connery and Minnie Driver. Guests appreciate the traditional atmosphere and 1680s architecture as well as the peacocks and Highland cattle that strut and stroll across the grounds. The spacious bedrooms (bestowed five stars by the tourist board) hide all mod conveniences (such as Bose sound systems, DVD players, and flatscreen TVs) behind velvet-lined walls. The restaurant, **Rhubarb,** is as theatrical as they come, with plush furnishings and décor to match the mansion. Reduced midweek rates are sometimes available.

See map p. 133. Priestfield Road. ☎ **0131-225-7800.** *Fax: 0131-668-3976.* www. prestonfield.com. *Bus: 2, 14, 30. Rack rates: £285 double. AE, MC, V.*

The Scotsman
$$$–$$$$ **Old Town**

Only minutes from the Royal Mile or Princes Street, this is one of the brightest and most stylish hotels in Old Town. Its name honors the newspaper that was published on these premises for nearly a century. Traditional styling and cutting-edge design are wed in the 1904 baronial limestone pile, a city landmark since it was first constructed. The 68 units, from the Study Room to the Baron Suite, vary in size (from 28 sq. m/300 sq. ft. to a whopping 103 sq. m/1,110 sq. ft.) and aspect, such as views of the castle or toward Calton Hill and Firth of Forth. They include state-of-the-art bathrooms and such extras as two-way service closets, which means someone may pick up your laundry virtually unnoticed. The two-floor penthouse suite is in a category of its own, with a private elevator and balcony with barbecue. The in-house dining option is the smart **North Bridge Brasserie** (restored in 2008).

See map p. 133. 20 N. Bridge St. ☎ **0131-556-5565.** *Fax: 0131-652-3652.* www.theeton collection.com. *Bus: 3, 8, 14, 29. Rack rates: £300–£375 double. AE, DC, MC, V.*

Sheraton Grand Hotel
$$$$ **West End**

On the grounds of a former railway siding near Edinburgh's Usher Hall, Traverse, and Royal Lyceum theaters, this six-story postmodern structure houses a glamorous hotel and office complex. The Sheraton is elegant, with soaring public rooms and rich carpeting. Boasting a state-of-the-art spa and leisure facilities (including a roof-top indoor/outdoor pool), the hotel pretty much has it all. The spacious, well-furnished units have double-glazed windows; glamorous suites are available, as are rooms for travelers with disabilities. The castle-view rooms on the top floors are best (and most expensive). The main restaurant, with views of the wind-swept Festival Square, presents well-prepared meals and a lavish Sunday buffet, while an annex houses the Italian restaurant **Santini** (p. 150) below the spa.

See map p. 133. 1 Festival Sq. ☎ **800-325-3535** *in the U.S. and Canada, or 0131-229-9131. Fax: 0131-228-4510.* www.sheratonedinburgh.co.uk. *Bus: 10, 22, 30. Rack rates: £180–£360 double. AE, DC, MC, V.*

The Witchery by the Castle
$$$$ **Old Town**

Part of the famous Edinburgh restaurant (p. 152), the overnight accommodations in the Witchery offer romantic, sumptuous, and theatrically decorated rooms with Gothic antiques and elaborate tapestries. Most of the hype about the suites is true: "the perfect lust-den," "Scotland's most romantic hotel," or "a jewel-box setting." *Cosmopolitan* magazine among others has hailed this place as one of the world's "most wonderful" places to stay. Each lavishly decorated suite (named the Library, Vestry, Armoury, and the like) features splendid furnishings — "fit for a lord and his lady" — and such extras as books, chocolates, a Bose sound system, and a complimentary bottle of champagne. Each suite has its own individual character. Sempill features an oak four-poster bed in a red-velvet-lined bedroom. The buildings near the castle date from the 17th century, filled with open fires, opulent beds, and luxurious sitting areas. The list of celebrity guests includes Michael Douglas and Catherine Zeta Jones, *Simpsons* creator Matt Groening, and Jack Nicholson.

See map p. 133. Castlehill, The Royal Mile. ☎ **0131-225-5613.** *Fax: 0131-220-4392.* www.thewitchery.com. *Bus: 28. Rack rates: from £300 suite. AE, DC, MC, V.*

Runner-up hotels and B&Bs

A-Haven Townhouse

$–$$ **Leith** The A-Haven is a classy ivy-covered Victorian, with rooms outfitted in mostly traditional furnishings. Some units overlook the Firth of Forth, while the opposite side of the building opens onto views of Arthur's Seat. Some rooms are large enough and supply cots to accommodate families. *See map p. 133. 180 Ferry Rd.* ☎ *0131-554-6559.* www.a-haven.co.uk.

The Bank Hotel

$$ **Old Town** This hotel offers better value than many of its competitors in this busy part of the Royal Mile. From the 1920s to the 1990s, it was a branch of the Bank of Scotland, and the past is still evident in its Greek-influenced architecture. Inside you discover high ceilings, well-chosen furnishings, and king-size beds. *See map p. 133. 1 S. Bridge St.* ☎ *0131-622-6800.* www.festival-inns.co.uk.

Elmview

$$ **Southside** This luxurious bed-and-breakfast, in a row of Victorian town houses, is on the edge of Bruntsfield Links, at the northwest corner of the Meadows. Each of the rooms is well furnished with en-suite bathrooms. The only possible hang-up is that immediate street parking is reserved for permanent residents. *See map p. 133. 15 Glengyle Terrace.* ☎ *0131-0228-1973.* www.elmview.co.uk.

The George Hotel

$$$ **New Town** The buildings that house this inn were first erected in the 1780s, transformed with alterations of Corinthian and neo-Renaissance style during the next 150 years or so before becoming the posh George Hotel in 1950. In 2006, a £12-million renovation took place. A stylish new restaurant and bar, Tempus, was introduced then. *See map p. 133. 19–21 George St.* ☎ *0131-225-1251.* www.principal-hayley.com.

The Glasshouse

$$$ **New Town (Calton)** Among the top so-called "boutique" hotels of Edinburgh, the Glasshouse combines old and new, with an impressive stone church facade harmonizing with a modern glass structure. Many of

the sleek bedrooms offer panoramic views of the city. A special feature of the Glasshouse is the rooftop bar and garden for hotel guests. *See map p. 133. 2 Greenside Place.* ☎ **0131-525-8200.** www.theetoncollection.com/hotels/glasshouse.

Macdonald Roxburghe Hotel

$$$ **New Town** Housed in Georgian buildings designed by Robert Adam, the Roxburghe provides classy atmosphere, reflected in the elegant drawing room with its ornate ceiling and woodwork, antique furnishings, and tall arched windows. The largest rooms have traditional features such as imposing fireplaces. *See map p. 133. 38 Charlotte St. (at George Street).* ☎ **0131-240-5500.** www.macdonaldhotels.co.uk.

Radisson Blu Hotel

$$$ **Old Town** Formerly the Crowne Plaza, this is for many the preferred big hotel in Old Town, halfway between Edinburgh Castle and Holyroodhouse, on the Royal Mile. The hotel offers first-class facilities and a jet-stream pool. *See map p. 133. 80 High St.* ☎ **0131-473-6590.** www.radisson blu.co.uk/hotel-edinburgh.

Thrums Hotel

$–$$ **Southside** This small 15-unit hotel has high-ceilinged guest rooms with some antique furnishings. Children are particularly welcomed here: Some accommodations are set aside as family rooms, while the garden offers an outdoor play area. Six units come with a shower-only bathroom; the rest are equipped with tub/shower combinations. *See map p. 133. 14–15 Minto St.* ☎ **0131-667-5545.** www.thrumshotel.com.

23 Mayfield

$–$$ **Southside** Run since June 2008 by the former owners of the well-regarded Aonach Mor, this handsome three-story sandstone guesthouse is about 1.6km (1 mile) from the center of the city. Not all of the units are large, but they tend toward the plush side. Family rooms have one double and two single beds; the deluxe four-poster rooms have mahogany furniture. *See map p. 133. 23 Mayfield Gardens.* ☎ **0131-667-5806.** www.23mayfield.co.uk.

Fraser Suites Edinburgh

$$$ **Old Town** Opened in February 2010, this boutique hotel is just off the Royal Mile near St. Giles Cathedral. The worst it seems one can say is that some of the rooms have quite restricted views (which means they are the least expensive). All have designer furniture, plush carpeting, and the latest in bathroom attractions: a "rainfall shower." There are also suites with full kitchens and dining space. Its restaurant — Glasshouse Off the Mile — offers contemporary Scottish cuisine, such as rump of Pershire lamb rubbed in cumin rock salt. *See map p. 133. 12–26 St. Giles St.* ☎ **0131-221-7200.** www.edinburgh.frasershospitality.com.

Dining Out

Too many people still think that cuisine in Scotland begins and ends with haggis, the stuffed sheep's stomach. Believe me, there's a lot more to the country's food.

Thankfully, Scotland's reputation for excellent fresh produce is growing. Look out for the following delights in season: shellfish such as oysters, mussels, scallops, or langoustines (aka Dublin Bay prawns); locally landed finned fish (such as sole, megrim, halibut, or sea bass); and, finally, meats such as venison, Borders lamb and Hebridean mutton, or Aberdeen Angus and Highland beef. Fresh fruits and vegetables include asparagus, garlic (yes, garlic), purple-sprouting broccoli, world-class raspberries, and, of course, potatoes. Of the latter, some claim that the spuds grown in sandy soils of Ayrshire are unparalleled for their fluffy texture and rich taste.

The city of Edinburgh boasts many of the best restaurants in Scotland, indeed a few of the best in the U.K., and the choices the capital has to offer are more diverse today than ever before. You will find an array of contemporary Scottish and modern British restaurants as well as French, fish, and brasserie-style eateries along with cuisines from around the world, particularly Indian and Thai. Plus, several restaurants exclusively cater to vegetarians.

Many, probably most, restaurants close in the afternoon, so if you're looking for lunch, don't leave it 'til too late in the day. The hours I provide in the listings that follow reflect when food may be ordered, but bars on the premises may keep longer hours. Many restaurants also close for business on either Sunday or Monday — and sometimes both. But during the annual Edinburgh Festival from late July to the beginning of September, many restaurants also offer extended hours. Given the crowds during this time, you should always reserve a table in advance, and at the best restaurants, booking a table is mandatory.

For more ideas on dining options, buy *The List* magazine's (www.list.co.uk) annual **Eating & Drinking Guide,** a publication that reviews hundreds of restaurants, bars, and cafes in Edinburgh (and Glasgow).

Scotland is getting better at welcoming families, but it's still a far cry from the family-friendliness of, say, Italy or France. That said, give the local restaurants a try, and resist the temptation to resort to well-known international chains or fast-food outlets.

Prices

Prices may well seem expensive if you convert the cost of meals into American dollars. Still, you can find a range of choices for most budgets. The prices I list here already include the 17.5 percent VAT, so there're no hidden surprises when the bill comes. If you're looking for bargains, inquire about pretheater special menus, which can sometimes be almost half the

Edinburgh Dining

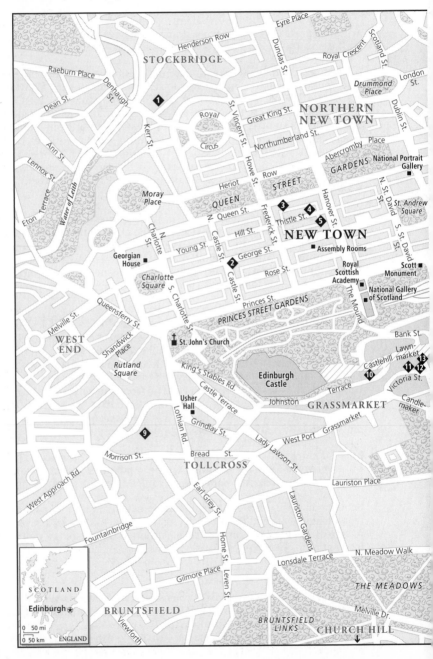

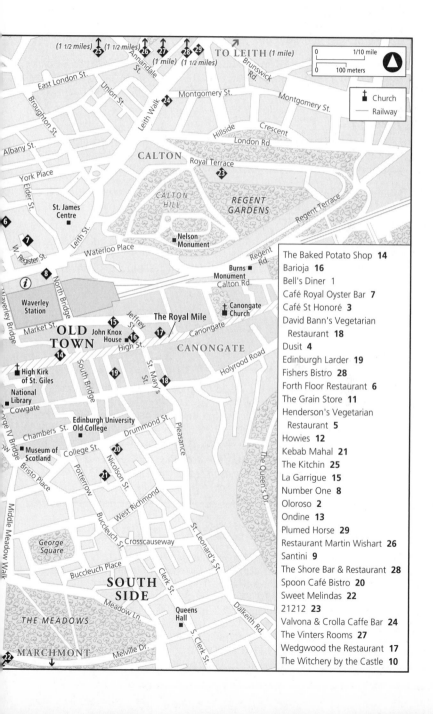

(1 1/2 miles) **25** (1 1/2 miles) **26** **27** **28** **29**
(1 mile) (1 1/2 miles)
↗ TO LEITH (1 mile)

East London St.

Union St.

Annandale St.

Leith Walk

Montgomery St.

Montgomery St.

Brunswick Rd.

Broughton St.

Albany St.

York Place

Elder St.

St. James Centre

Leith St.

24

Hillside Crescent

London Rd.

CALTON Royal Terrace

23

CALTON HILL

REGENT GARDENS

Regent Terrace

Nelson Monument

6

7

W. Register St.

North Bridge

Waterloo Place

Regent Rd.

Burns Monument

Calton Rd.

8

Waverley Station

Waverley Bridge

Market St.

Jeffrey St.

OLD TOWN

John Knox House

15

16

17

The Royal Mile

High St.

Canongate

† Canongate Church

CANONGATE

Holyrood Road

14

High Kirk of St. Giles

National Library

Cowgate

South Bridge

19

St. Mary's

18

The Queen's Dr.

George IV Bridge

Bristo Place

Chambers St.

Museum of Scotland

College St.

Edinburgh University Old College

Drummond St.

Pleasance

20

21

Potterrow

Nicolson St.

West Richmond

George Square

Buccleuch St.

Crosscauseway

Buccleuch Place

SOUTH SIDE

Middle Meadow Walk

THE MEADOWS

Meadow Ln.

MARCHMONT

Melville Dr.

Clerk St.

Queens Hall

St. Leonard's St.

Dalkeith Rd.

S. Clerk St.

0   1/10 mile
0   100 meters

† Church
— Railway

The Baked Potato Shop **14**
Barioja **16**
Bell's Diner **1**
Café Royal Oyster Bar **7**
Café St Honoré **3**
David Bann's Vegetarian Restaurant **18**
Dusit **4**
Edinburgh Larder **19**
Fishers Bistro **28**
Forth Floor Restaurant **6**
The Grain Store **11**
Henderson's Vegetarian Restaurant **5**
Howies **12**
Kebab Mahal **21**
The Kitchin **25**
La Garrigue **15**
Number One **8**
Oloroso **2**
Ondine **13**
Plumed Horse **29**
Restaurant Martin Wishart **26**
Santini **9**
The Shore Bar & Restaurant **28**
Spoon Café Bistro **20**
Sweet Melindas **22**
21212 **23**
Valvona & Crolla Caffe Bar **24**
The Vinters Rooms **27**
Wedgwood the Restaurant **17**
The Witchery by the Castle **10**

price of the regular dinner menu — or at least two courses for the price of the normal dinner entree. If you have Internet access, log on to www.5pm.co.uk for a list of restaurants offering early evening dining discounts.

Lunch and pretheater menus in Edinburgh often offer the same food as the full dinner menus but at a much better price. If you're trying to save money on your food bills, have a big late lunch or early evening meal.

Tipping

A 10 percent gratuity is standard for service, although you shouldn't hesitate to leave nothing if you were badly treated. On the other hand, if you were truly impressed, consider leaving 15 percent to 20 percent.

In a few restaurants, 10 percent service charge is included in the bill automatically, so add another tip on top of it. The automatic gratuity can be deleted if the service was genuinely dreadful.

Smoking

In 2006, Scotland adopted a complete ban on smoking in all enclosed public spaces, including bars and restaurants, some of which have set up outdoor smoking areas.

The top restaurants and cafes

Barioja
$-$$ Old Town   SPANISH

Just off the Royal Mile (near the World's End Close), with views north to Calton Hill and the Royal High School, this casual tapas bar is relaxed and usually staffed by natives of Spanish-speaking countries. The kitchen's tapas come in reasonably substantial portions: whether deep-fried squid, garlicky king prawns, or spicy chorizo sausages. Desserts are posted on the blackboard.

See map p. 141. 19 Jeffrey St. ☎ 0131-557-3622. Bus: 36. Tapas: £4–£10. AE, MC, V. Open: Mon–Sat 11 a.m.–11 p.m.; Sun noon to 10 p.m.

Award Winning Dining in Leith

Ten years ago, Edinburgh dining was good, but today it is on the way to becoming nationally recognized as among the best in the UK. There are five restaurants that boast a Michelin Red Guide star, one of the top honors, and three of these are in Leith. Best among them is **Restaurant Martin Wishart,** whose chef/owner Martin Wishart is one of the most talented in Europe. **The Kitchin** restaurant features the cooking of 30-something Tom Kitchin, a certain rising star in Britain, who is becoming something of a TV celebrity. Finally, but not necessarily least, the **Plumed Horse** is the most recent restaurant in Edinburgh to join the top ranks (although at his previous restaurant in southern Scotland, chef/owner Tony Borthwick once hit the heights).

Bell's Diner
$–$$ **Stockbridge   AMERICAN**

If you're a connoisseur of the chargrilled patty of real ground beef, consider unassuming Bell's Diner in Stockbridge. Open for some 30-odd years, it is a proverbial institution in Edinburgh. The diner's burgers (available in three different weights) are handmade and cooked to order with a variety of toppings (cheese to garlic butter). They are served with fries, salad, and a full array of condiments. The operation's only drawback, aside from its rather limited space, is the limited hours of operation. Lunch only on a Saturday, which seems a shame.

See map p. 141. 17 St. Stephen St. ☎ **0131-225-8116.** *Reservations recommended. Bus: 24, 29, or 42. Main courses: £6.50–£9. Open: Sun–Fri 6–10:15 p.m.; Sat noon to 10:15 p.m.*

Café Royal Oyster Bar
$$–$$$ **New Town   FISH/SEAFOOD**

The Café Royal has been here for some 140 years, and thankfully, its many splendid Victorian touches remain intact. The main menu offers more than just oysters: Salmon, venison, langoustines, lobster, beef, and rabbit are often featured menu selections. The restaurant closes after lunch and reopens for dinner, but the adjacent **Café Royal Circle Bar** is open throughout the day. The menu there is more limited but also less pricey. A highlight of this stylish room is the tile pictures of notable inventors.

See map p. 141. 17a W. Register St. ☎ **0131-556-4124.** *Reservations recommended. Bus: 8 or 29. Main courses: £14–£22. AE, MC, V. Open: Restaurant Mon–Sun noon to 2 p.m. and 6–10 p.m.; bar Mon–Wed 11 a.m.–11 p.m.; Thurs 11 a.m. to midnight; Fri–Sat 11 a.m.–1 a.m.*

Cafe St Honoré
$$ **New Town   FRENCH BISTRO**

A New Town favorite, this Parisian-style brasserie with a classic black-and-white-checkered floor is deliberately rapidly paced at lunch and more sedate in the evening. An upbeat and usually enthusiastic staff serves French cuisine with Scottish influences, such as Borders beef with Dauphinoise potatoes and bonbons made of Stornoway black pudding from the Outer Hebrides.

See map p. 141. 34 NW Thistle Street Lane. ☎ **0131-226-2211.** www.cafe sthonore.com. *Reservations recommended. Bus: 24, 29, or 42. Fixed-price two-course lunch: £17. Main courses: £8–£20. AE, MC, V. Open: Daily noon to 2 p.m. and 6–10 p.m.*

Picnic fare

The Edinburgh weather doesn't always lend itself to outdoor dining on an expanse of lawn, but there are certainly days when the sun shines warmly enough to enjoy a picnic at Princes Street Gardens, the Meadows, Holyrood Park, or along the Water of Leith or in the Botanic Gardens.

If you're in the central area of town, the best place to pick up some deli goods is undoubtedly **Valvona & Crolla,** 19 Elm Row (at the top of Leith Walk; ☎ **0131-556-6066**). This Italian shop has an excellent reputation throughout the U.K. and offers a wonderful range of cheeses, cured meats, and fresh fruit and vegetables, plus baked goods from rolls to sourdough loaves, all the condiments you may need, and wine. Another option in New Town is the food hall at the top of **Harvey Nichols** department store, 30–34 St. Andrew Sq. (☎ **0131-524-8388**). Freshly prepared salads, lots of dried goods, and fresh fruit and vegetables are all stocked here.

In Stockbridge, **IJ Mellis Cheesemongers,** on Bakers Place (☎ **0131-225-6566**), sells award-winning British and Irish cheeses. The Mellis staff really know their stuff, and you can find the shop in Old Town, on Victoria Street, and south of the city center, on Morningside Road.

If you're on the south side of the city near the Meadows, **Peckham's,** on Bruntsfield Place (☎ **0131-229-7054**), is a solid choice for filling a picnic basket. But if you like Mexican food — Monterey Jack cheese, real tortillas, and the like — visit **Lupe Pintos** in Tollcross, at 24 Leven St. (near the King's Theatre; ☎ **0131-228-6241**). The shop also stocks some American goods, such as beef jerky, dill pickles, and peanut butter.

Heading toward the Botanic Gardens on the other side of town in Canonmills, at the roundabout, is a nice Spanish deli called **Dionika** (☎ **0131-652-3993**).

David Bann
$$ Old Town   VEGETARIAN

Chef David Bann has been at the forefront of meat-free cooking in Edinburgh for two decades. He comes from the school of thought that says vegetarian meals can be both tasty *and* healthy. The menu at his eponymous restaurant (located just a short stroll south of Royal Mile) is eclectic: Dishes have international influences, from Mexico to Thailand. The dining room is as stylish as the cooking, and to top it off, the prices are very reasonable.

See map p. 141. 56–58 St. Mary's St. ☎ **0131-556-5888.** *www.davidbann.com. Reservations recommended. Bus: 36. Main courses: £7.50–£12. AE, MC, V. Open: Daily noon to 10 p.m.*

Dusit
$$–$$$ New Town   THAI

Thistle Street — little more than a slender lane with narrow sidewalks — has become a hotbed for dining out, and this unassuming restaurant has quickly developed a reputation for being one of the best in the city for Thai cuisine. The menu is not typical and has a tendency toward modern dishes such as chargrilled duck with nuts, mango, and shallots. Some of the main courses incorporate Scottish produce, such as venison, and the seafood options are plentiful.

See map p. 141. 49a Thistle St. ☎ **0131-220-6846.** www.dusit.co.uk. *Reservations recommended. Bus: 24, 29, or 42. Fixed-price two-course lunch £11. Main courses: £12–£18. AE, MC, V. Open: Mon–Sat noon to 3 p.m. and 6–11 p.m.; Sun noon to 11 p.m.*

Fishers Bistro
$$–$$$ Leith   FISH/SEAFOOD

This place is a favorite for its seafood and view of the harbor at Leith. The Miller family founded the restaurant in the early 1990s, and their chefs offer such enticing dishes as fresh Loch Fyne oysters, acclaimed as among Great Britain's finest; mussels in white wine sauce; or breaded and crispy fish cakes. Of course the fresh fish depends on what's been landed: It might be sea trout or turbot. If you can't make it to Leith, you can also find a branch of the restaurant in New Town, **Fishers in the City** (☎ **0131-225-5109**), at 58 Thistle St.

See map p. 141. 1 The Shore. ☎ **0131-554-5666.** www.fishersbistros.co.uk. *Reservations recommended. Bus: 16, 22, 35, or 36. Main courses: £12–£18. AE, MC, V. Open: Daily noon to 10:30 p.m.*

Forth Floor Restaurant
$$$ New Town   MODERN SCOTTISH

No, that's not a misspelling of the name: This restaurant at the top of the Harvey Nichols boutique department store has excellent views of the Firth of Forth from the fourth floor of the building. It combines excellent contemporary Scottish cooking with those commanding vistas. While you do feel like you're dining in a department store annex (despite the slick, minimalist decor), the food can be phenomenal, whether roast monkfish with chorizo and red-wine butter or a light salad with endive and seasonal truffles. The produce used by the kitchen is notably well sourced and fresh, such as West Coast langoustines in an amuse-bouche to start your meal, or beef certified by the Scottish Beef Club. The brasserie menu, while less extensive than the restaurant's selections, offers good value with a fixed-price £15 lunch and serves an "afternoon menu" between lunch and dinner. The bar mixes some wonderful cocktails.

See map p. 141. Harvey Nichols, 30–34 St. Andrew Sq. ☎ **0131-524-8350.** www.harvey nichols.com. *Reservations recommended. Bus: 8, 10, 12, or 45. Main courses: £16–£22. AE, DC, MC, V. Open: Tues–Sat noon to 10 p.m.; Sun–Mon lunches only.*

The Grain Store
$$$ Old Town   SCOTTISH/MODERN BRITISH

With its dining room up some unassuming stairs and wooden tables set amid raw stone walls, the Grain Store capably captures some Old Town essence and atmosphere. The cooking of owner Carlo Coxon is ambitious and innovative: For example, the menu might include dishes such as a saddle of Highland venison with a beetroot fondant, or Pithivier (that is a French tart) of brown hare with a puff pastry shell. While the evening à la carte menu is not cheap, the fixed-price lunches are moderately priced.

See map p. 141. 30 Victoria St. ☎ **0131-225-7635.** www.grainstore-restaurant. co.uk. *Reservations recommended. Bus: 2, 41, or 42. Fixed-price two-course lunch: £13. Main courses: £17–£25. AE, MC, V. Open: Daily noon to 2 p.m. and 6–10 p.m. (to 11 p.m. Fri–Sat).*

Henderson's Vegetarian Restaurant
$ New Town   VEGETARIAN

Right in the heart of New Town, Henderson's is another bona fide institution in the Scottish capital. Once called the "Salad Table," the business (which includes Henderson's Bistro around the corner and another outlet on Lothian Road) recently went for a more formal title, and added an art gallery, too. Regardless, Henderson's is a long-standing stalwart of healthy, relatively inexpensive meat-free food. Dishes, such as vegetable stroganoff or mushroom and spinach crepe, complement a choice of one dozen different salads: whether Greek or spicy bean. Wines include organic options.

See map p. 141. 94 Hanover St. ☎ **0131-225-2131.** www.hendersonsof edinburgh.co.uk. *Bus: 13, 23, or 27. Fixed-price two-course lunch: £9.50. Main courses: £6–£8. MC, V. Open: Mon–Sat 8 a.m.–10:30 p.m.*

Howies
$$ Old Town   SCOTTISH/CONTINENTAL

David Howie Scott opened his first restaurant with modest ambitions (for example, guests brought their own wine), and then he created a minor empire in Edinburgh, with a couple of branches elsewhere in Scotland as well. In the capital city, there are four. The one on Victoria Street in Old Town is probably the most convenient. The minichain's motto is "fine food without the faff" — and I might add "sold at reasonable prices" as well. Typical dishes include pan-seared supreme of chicken, honey-cured Scottish salmon, or gnocchi with fresh basil pesto. You can still bring your own bottle, but the wine list at Howies is as reasonably priced as its menu.

See map p. 141. 10–14 Victoria St. ☎ 0131-225-1721. www.howies.uk.com. Reservations recommended. Bus: 2, 41, or 42. Fixed-price two-course meal: Lunch £10. Main courses: £10–£16. AE, MC, V. Open: Daily noon to 2:30 p.m. and 6–10 p.m.

Kebab Mahal
$ Southside   INDIAN

The kebab is usually a late-night meal wolfed down by students standing in the streets after they have danced their heads off in the clubs. And while the late weekend hours of this simple diner means they do indeed attract students, Kebab Mahal is much more. Drawing a cross-section of the city, from dusty construction workers on a break to tweed-clad professors grading papers, this basic Indian restaurant — where you may have to share your table with others — has become a landmark. Although the counter is full of hot food, most of the main courses are prepared separately in a kitchen to the rear. True to its Islamic owner's faith, Kebab Mahal doesn't have a license to serve alcohol, and doesn't allow diners to bring their own, either. It also closes every Friday from 1 to 2 p.m. for prayers.

See map p. 141. 7 Nicolson Sq. ☎ 0131-667-5214. Bus: 3, 5, 29, 31, or 35. Main courses: £4–£6. No credit cards. Open: Sun–Thurs noon to midnight; Fri–Sat noon to 2 a.m.

The Kitchin
$$$$ Leith   FRENCH/MODERN SCOTTISH

After opening this contemporary restaurant in 2006, the appropriately named chef/owner Tom Kitchin quickly garnered a Michelin star, among other awards. Now he is among the catering business's professional elite, appearing on national TV. The chef's motto is "from nature to plate" and his French-inspired recipes capture attention. He likes to use top seasonal and daring Scottish ingredients, whether fricasseed lamb's sweetbreads or wild halibut carpaccio. Terrine of pig's head meat might be served with mustard dressing and root vegetable rémoulade. Less challenging but no less appealing is hake filet atop pasta with braised fennel. Kitchin combines youth, talent, and ambition — one to watch.

See map p. 141. 78 Commercial Quay. ☎ 0131-555-1755. www.thekitchin.com. Bus: 16, 22, 35, or 36. Reservations required. Fixed-price lunch: £25. Main courses: £30. MC, V. Open: Tues–Sat 12:30–2 p.m. and 7–10 p.m.

La Garrigue
$$–$$$ Old Town   FRENCH

The chef and proprietor of La Garrigue, Jean Michel Gauffre, hails from the southern French region of Languedoc, and he attempts to re-create the fresh and rustic cooking of his home here in Edinburgh. The feeling of the dining room is casual but smart, with some stylish handmade furniture and almost naive paintings on the wall. The menu might feature a hearty roast or cassoulet (stew) with beans and meat, as well as a more delicate pan-fried filet of bream. The wines are from southern France, too. Often, Chef Gauffre will come in the dining room to see how things are going and have a friendly chat. He knows the small touches can go a long way.

See map p. 141. 31 Jeffrey St. ☎ 0131-557-3032. www.lagarrigue.co.uk. Reservations recommended. Bus: 36. Fixed-price two-course meal: lunch £14. Fixed-price dinner £26. AE, MC, V. Open: Mon–Sat noon to 2:30 p.m. and 6:30–10:30 p.m.

Number One
$$$$ **New Town** SCOTTISH/CONTINENTAL

This is the premier restaurant in the city's centrally sited premier hotel, with a Michelin Red Guide star for superior cuisine. You can sample the likes of scallop and cauliflower risotto, or perhaps venison loin with juniper jus. Dessert brings some rather exotic choices, such as mulled wine parfait with a cinnamon sauce, a variety of sorbets, or a selection of mature cheeses. Wines are excellent if pricey, but then so is the meal — a special treat while you're in Edinburgh.

See map p. 141. Balmoral Hotel, 1 Princes St. ☎ 0131-557-6727. www.thebalmoral hotel.com. Reservations recommended. Bus: 3, 8, 19, or 30. Fixed-price three-course dinner: £60. AE, DC, MC, V. Open: Daily 7–10 p.m.

Ondine
$$–$$$ **New Town** SEAFOOD/FISH

This newcomer to the Edinburgh dining scene has perhaps made the biggest, pardon the pun, splash with its fresh seafood and fish dishes, using sustainably caught produce. Chef Roy Brett moves comfortably from fish soup to clam linguine with garlic and red chilies to lemon sole (filet or whole), served with shrimp and capers. Housed in the same building with the new Hotel Missoni, Ondine offers diners an informal atmosphere that seafood restaurants should have but plenty of class, as well

See map p. 141. 2 George IV Bridge. ☎ 0131-226-1888. www.ondinerestaurant. co.uk. Reservations recommended. Bus: 2, 41, or 42. Fixed-price lunch £15. Main courses £15–£22. MC, V. Daily noon to 10 p.m. (Sun till 4 p.m.).

Oloroso
$$$ **New Town** SCOTTISH/INTERNATIONAL

Oloroso's chef and owner, Tony Singh, is a Scottish-born Sikh with a cheerful demeanor and an imaginative approach to cooking Scottish produce. Here in his rooftop restaurant, with an ample veranda (open in summer) and excellent panoramic views, the feel is contemporary and swanky. Intentionally, there is little decoration, as the vistas provide enough interest. Frequently changing menus include dishes such as veal T-bones or fresh fish from the grill menu to pan-fried breast of duck with

Puy lentils and black pudding (from the main menu). The bar, which mixes some mean cocktails, is usually open until 1 a.m.

See map p. 141. 33 Castle St. ☎ **0131-226-7614.** *www.oloroso.co.uk. Reservations recommended. Bus: 24, 29, or 42. Fixed-price lunch £19. Main courses: £15–£25. MC, V. Open: Daily noon to 2:30 p.m. and 7–10 p.m.*

Plumed Horse
$$$$ Leith MODERN SCOTTISH/FRENCH

This restaurant came to Edinburgh in 2006 from southern Scotland, where it held a Michelin star. That distinction was lost for a year or so, but chef/owner Tony Borthwick has regained the accolade and hasn't looked back. Although the dining space is both more cramped and more traditional in feel than his Leith competition, Borthwick cooking is as contemporary as his rivals (and just a little bit less expensive, too). Dishes such as rose of veal with mushrooms and Madeira cream sauce are elegantly and attractively presented.

See map p. 141. 50–54 Henderson St. ☎ **0131-554-5556.** *www.plumedhorse. co.uk. Bus: 22 or 36. Reservations required Fixed-price lunch £25. Fixed-price dinner £45. MC, V. Open: Tues–Sat noon to 1:30 p.m. and 7–9 p.m.*

Restaurant Martin Wishart
$$$$ Leith MODERN FRENCH

Despite a vaunted Michelin star and many local awards, chef/owner Martin Wishart is the antithesis of the high-profile prima donna or loud-mouthed TV chef. One of Scotland's leading kitchen masters, he takes his accolades in stride and strives to improve the quality of his high-price establishment in this now fashionable part of the Leith docklands. The décor is minimalist, featuring modern art. His menu, which changes frequently, is kept short and sweet, taking advantage of the best of the season; think John Dory with leeks, salsify, and mussel and almond gratin. Flavors are notoriously intense; sometimes almost unfathomable — but always imaginative and completely memorable. Celeriac puree and crispy pumpkinseed treats might accompany braised ox cheek or a seared scallop might arrive with Bellota ham and Parmesan velouté. Staff is everywhere and completely understands both the food and the wine they serve. If you're not on a budget, push the boat out and go for the tasting menu. If money is tight, try the set lunches. Make your reservation well in advance: Getting a table can be tricky.

See map p. 141. 54 The Shore. ☎ **0131-553-3557.** *www.martin-wishart. co.uk. Reservations required. Bus: 22 or 36. Fixed-price lunch £28. Main courses: £40. Fixed price six-course tasting menu: £65. AE, MC, V. Open: Tues–Fri noon to 2 p.m. and 6:45–9:30 p.m.; Sat noon to 1:30 p.m. and 6:45–9:30 p.m.*

Family-friendly fare

The Baked Potato Shop (56 Cockburn St.; ☎ 0131-225-7572): Children generally delight in being taken to this favorite lunch spot, just off the High Street in Old Town, where they can order fluffy baked potatoes, with a choice of half a dozen hot fillings, along with all sorts of other dishes, including chili and a variety of salads. It's cheap, too.

Valvona & Crolla Caffe Bar (19 Elm Row; ☎ 0131-556-6066): Also at the top of Leith Walk, this place is best known as one of the U.K.'s finest Italian delis. But if you can get past the tempting salamis, cheeses, and other delicacies, V&C offers a cafe that welcomes children in that way that Italians seem to do best.

Santini
$$–$$$ West End   ITALIAN

This modern restaurant in a building adjacent to the Sheraton Grand Hotel in the West End offers some of the capital's classiest Italian cooking. This small international chain, with other branches in Milan and London, serves dishes such as fish antipasti with seared whitefish and chargrilled prawns, or venison and pork belly. For lunch, in addition to a well-priced two-course meal, it has introduced an Italian version of the Japanese bento box.

See map p. 141. 8 Conference St. ☎ 0131-221-7788. *Bus: 1, 2, 10, 24, or 34. Fixed-price two-course lunch: £9.50. Main courses: £15–£22. AE, MC, V. Open: Mon–Fri noon to 2:30 p.m. and 6:30–9:30 p.m.; Sat 6:30–10:30 p.m.*

The Shore Bar & Restaurant
$$ Leith   SCOTTISH/FISH

Whether diners eat in the unassuming pub or in the only slightly more formal dining room to one side, they should appreciate the simplicity and ease of this operation. The menu moved away from its dedication to fish in 2008, and now includes steaks, lamb shanks, and roast duck. The bar is still one of the best in Leith. It often has live music in the evenings, good ale on tap, and a sincere seaport ambience all the time.

See map p. 141. 3 Shore. ☎ 0131-553-5080. *Bus: 16, 22, 35, or 36. Main courses: £10–£15. AE, MC, V. Open: Daily noon to 10 p.m.*

Spoon Café Bistro
$ Old Town/Southside   CAFE

This particular "spoon" is far from greasy. The contemporary cafe moved into new premises in 2009, thus fulfilling the long-standing ambitions of an operation that originally lacked the facilities at its first location on Blackfriars Street. Owner Richard Alexander could cook at the best restaurants in town. Instead, he has opted for his own operation that combines a relaxed ambience, first-rate espresso-based coffees, and the assured hand of a classically trained chef. The soups are always superb, whether meat-free options—such as lentil and red onion or a roast pepper and eggplant—or Italian ham and pea soup. Sandwiches are prepared freshly, and now you can get more elaborate dishes such as crispy pan-seared trout fillet with cider vinegar dressing or braised beef with baby potatoes. Alternatively, you can still simply drop in for a piece of home-made cake: moist carrot or rich chocolate.

See map p. 141. 6a Nicolson St. ☎ 0131-556-6922. www.spooncafe.co.uk. Bus: 3, 5, 29, 31, or 35. Soups from £3; sandwiches and salads from £4.50. Main courses: £10. MC, V. Open: Mon–Sat 10 a.m.–10 p.m.; Sun noon to 6 p.m.

Sweet Melindas
$$ Marchmont (Southside)   SCOTTISH/FISH

The capital's Marchmont neighborhood, although just south of the Meadows, is far enough from the well-trod traveler's trail to seem kilometers away from touristy Edinburgh. This locally owned and operated restaurant is a neighborhood favorite and merits a visit from those outsiders who admire simple and amiable surroundings. The cooking tends to emphasize fish (which the chefs purchase from the shop next door) in dishes such as crispy squid salad or roast cod with a sesame and ginger sauce. But the menu is not limited to the fruits of the sea. Often there is seasonal game, such as pigeon or venison, and a reasonable selection of vegetarian options as well.

See map p. 141. 11 Roseneath St. ☎ 0131-229-7953. Reservations recommended. Bus: 24 or 41. Fixed-price lunch: £13. Fixed-price dinner: £23. AE, MC, V. Open: Mon 6–10 p.m.; Tues–Sat noon to 2 p.m. and 6–10 p.m.

21212
$$$$ New Town   FRENCH

A decade or so ago, Edinburgh had no restaurants with a Michelin star. Hard to imagine these day. This was the fifth in the city to gain such notoriety in 2010. Chef Paul Kitching left a vaunted restaurant in Manchester to set up his own operation with partner Katie O'Brien in the Scottish capital. Although Kitching has dismissed with some of his more extravagant habits, such as a 45-course meal, he is still astounding food critics. The choices here are five: two options for the opener, one for the first intermediate, two choices for a middle course . . . and if you see a pattern emerging, the name of the restaurant confirms it. Gentle, slow cooking is a signature, as is seemingly odd but successful combinations of ingredients, such as beef with tart lemon curd or a bread and butter pudding with cucumber, dried cherries, and sunflower seeds.

See map p. 141. 3 Royal Terrace, Calton Hill ☎ 0845-22-21212. Bus: 1, 15, 19, 26, 34, or 44. Reservations required. Bus: 1, 15, 19, 26, or 34. Fixed-price lunch: £25. Fixed-priced dinner: £65. AE, MC, V. Open: Tues–Sat noon to 1:45 p.m. and 6:45–9:30 p.m.

Tea for two?

A new choice in town is **The Edinburgh Larder,** 15 Blackfriars St. (☎ **0131-556-6922**), for specially sourced teas (and coffees) as well as rich cakes such as dark chocolate and beet. If you want a formal venue, try the Palm Court at the **Balmoral Hotel,** 1 Princes St. (☎ **0131-556-2414**).

The Vintners Rooms
$$$–$$$$ Leith   FRENCH

This impressive stone building was constructed in the 17th century as a warehouse for the barrels and barrels of Bordeaux (claret) and port wine that came to Scotland from France. And that Auld Alliance carries on with this restaurant, one of the most romantic in Edinburgh. After a change in management a few years ago, its reputation has never been higher. The French-born chef uses Scottish produce in a host of confidently Gallic dishes. The menu might feature roast stuffed fig with goat cheese and Parma ham, steamed halibut with a classic artichoke Barigoule, or roast *côte de boeuf* (rib steak) for two with béarnaise sauce.

See map p. 141. The Vaults, 87 Giles St. ☎ *0131-554-6767.* www.thevintners rooms.com. *Bus: 22 or 36. Reservations recommended. Main courses: £18–£23. AE, MC, V. Open: Tues–Sat noon to 2 p.m. and 7–10 p.m.*

Wedgwood the Restaurant
$$–$$$ Old Town   SCOTTISH/MODERN BRITISH

Perhaps the next place to earn an internationally recognized accolade is this small restaurant run by Chef Paul Wedgwood (no connections with the famous bone china producers). The menus change with the seasons, and recipes combine Scottish ingredients with some Asian influences here and there. A popular signature dish has been salmon done three ways: poached, smoked, and cured, each with different accompaniments. Expect a glass of sparkling wine and appetizing amuse-bouche to start the evening, with intermediate palate cleansers such as a bubbly raspberry and ginger beer concoction. Given the restaurant's cozy confines, booking is effectively mandatory.

See map p. 141. 267 Canongate. ☎ *0131-558-8737.* www.wedgwoodtherestaurant. co.uk. *Bus: 35 or 36. Reservations recommended. Fixed-price lunch: £10. Main courses: £15–£20. MC, V. Daily noon to 3 p.m. and 6–10 p.m.*

The Witchery by the Castle
$$$–$$$$ Old Town   SCOTTISH

This restaurant, so named because of historical connections to medieval executions nearby and lingering ghosts, serves classy Scottish food in classy surroundings, with dishes that feature ingredients such as Angus beef, Scottish lobster, or Loch Fyne oysters. Well-prepared, old-time British favorites, such as an omelet Arnold Bennett (made with cream and smoked fish), contrast with specials such as pan-roasted monkfish with a thyme and lemon risotto. Atmospheric and good for special occasions, it is also ideal for a sumptuous late meal. In addition to the dining room nearest the street, there is also the "Secret Garden" farther down the narrow close.

See map p. 141. Boswell Court, Castlehill, Royal Mile. ☎ *0131-225-5613.* www.the witchery.com. *Reservations required. Bus: 28. Fixed-price two-course lunch or pre-/post-theater dinner: £13. Main courses: £18–£25. AE, DC, MC, V. Open: Daily noon to 4 p.m. and 5:30–11:30 p.m.*

Exploring Edinburgh

Edinburgh's reputation is enormous, and the city lives up to most of the hype. The second-most-popular destination after London for visitors to Great Britain, the Scottish capital is one of the most picturesque cities in Europe. Built on a set of hills, it's unarguably dramatic.

Edinburgh's **Old Town** is at the city's heart, featuring the dramatic Edinburgh Castle at the top end of the **Royal Mile,** a street that follows the spine of a hill down to the Palace of Holyroodhouse. For many visitors, this *is* Edinburgh, with its mews, closes, and alleyways.

But across the valley to the north, a valley now filled by the verdant Princes Street Gardens, is the city's **New Town,** which dates from the 1770s. Here you can find tidy streets and broad avenues, with shops, squares, and attractions such as the **National Portrait Gallery.** New Town reaches out to the villagelike setting of Stockbridge, from which one can walk along the city's narrow meandering river, the Water of Leith, to Dean Village (another district that feels almost rural in nature), home of the **National Gallery of Modern Art** and its sister art venue, the **Dean Gallery.**

South of Old Town is the sprawling **Meadows,** with its acres of grass, the precincts of Edinburgh University, and suburbs such as Marchmont. To the north are the port of **Leith** and the **Firth of Forth,** which empties into the North Sea.

The only problem with Edinburgh's many attractions is deciding what you have time to see. You would need at least a few days to visit every place listed in this section, so you need to make some decisions depending on how long you're planning to be in the city. If you have children in tow, fewer galleries and more family attractions would probably be best; if you like art, more museums and fewer wanders may be in store.

Edinburgh's famous annual cultural celebration — the **Edinburgh Festival** — brings in tourists and lovers of all forms of art from around the world. But if you prefer a bit more space and smaller crowds, avoid the month of August in Edinburgh.

During the Edinburgh Festival, many museums that are normally closed on Sunday are open, and hours are generally extended. Some museums that open only in summer are also open on public holidays.

The top attractions

Calton Hill
New Town

Rising some 106m (350 ft.) above sea level, this bluff full of monuments is partially responsible for Edinburgh's being called the "Athens of the North." People scale the hill not only to see the landmarks up close but also to enjoy the panoramic views of the Firth of Forth and the city. The unfinished colonnades at the summit are part of the so-called **National Monument,** which was meant to honor the Scottish soldiers killed during the Napoleonic wars. However, money for the project ran out in 1829, and the William H. Playfair–designed structure (once referred to as "Edinburgh Disgrace") was never finished. It remains, nevertheless, an impressive folly.

The **Nelson Monument,** containing mementos of the hero of Trafalgar, dates from 1815 and rises more than 30m (100 ft.) above the hill. A time ball at the top of the monument falls at 1 p.m. Monday through Saturday, and historically it helped sailors in Leith set their timepieces. From April through September, the monument is open Monday 1 to 6 p.m. and Tuesday through Saturday 10 a.m. to 6 p.m.; from October through March, it's open Monday through Saturday from 10 a.m. to 3 p.m. Admission is £3.

The old **City Observatory** along the western summit of Calton Hill was designed in 1818 by Playfair, whose uncle was the president of the Astronomical Institute. Nearby, the circular **Dougal Stewart's Monument** of 1831 (by Playfair as well) is not dissimilar to colonnades of the nearby 1830 **Burns Monument.** Designed by Thomas Hamilton on the southern slopes of Calton Hill, the latter replicates the Choragic Monument of Lysicrates in Athens, which was also the inspiration for Hamilton's earlier monument to honor the poet in Alloway (see Chapter 15).

Down the hill toward Princes Street, the Old Calton Burial Grounds offers a curiosity of special interest to United States history buffs. The **Emancipation Monument** (or **Lincoln Monument**), erected in 1893, was dedicated to soldiers of Scottish descent who lost their lives in America's Civil War. It has a statue of President Abraham Lincoln with a freed slave at his feet. Some famous Scots are buried in this cemetery, too, with elaborate tombs honoring their memory (notably the Robert Adam–designed tomb for philosopher David Hume).

Take at least one hour to explore all of Calton Hill and its monuments.

See map p. 156. Walk up Calton Hill from the north end of Princes Street or from Leith Street. You can also drive up and park. Admission: Free. Open: Year-round dawn to dusk.

Edinburgh Castle
Old Town

Few locations in Scotland have lore equal to that of Edinburgh Castle. The very early history is somewhat vague, but in the 11th century, Malcolm III and his Saxon queen, later venerated as St. Margaret, founded a building on this spot. There's only a fragment of what is believed to be their original pile; it is part of St. Margaret's Chapel, which dates principally to the 12th century. After centuries of destruction, demolitions, and upheavals, the buildings that stand today are basically those that resulted from the castle's role as a military garrison over the past 300-odd years. Remarkably, the castle still has barracks for soldiers. Many of the displays are devoted to military history, which might limit the place's appeal for some (including me). The castle vaults served as prisons for foreign soldiers in the 18th century, and these great storerooms held hundreds of Napoleonic soldiers in the early 19th century. Some prisoners made wall carvings that are still visible today.

However, it is not all about war. Visitors can see where Mary, Queen of Scots gave birth to James VI of Scotland (later James I of England) in 1566. Scottish Parliaments used to convene in the Great Hall of the castle. Another highlight for visitors is the Scottish Crown Jewels, used at the coronations, along with the scepter and sword of state of Scotland and the infamous Stone of Scone. Note that last entry is 45 minutes before closing; and buying tickets online in advance will save time during busy times. Allow about two hours.

See map p. 156. Castlehill. ☎ **0131-225-9846.** www.edinburghcastle.gov.uk. *Bus: 23, 27, 41, or 45. Admission: £14 adults, £12 students and seniors, and £7.50 children. Open: Daily Apr–Sept 9:30 a.m.–6 p.m.; Oct–Mar 9:30 a.m.–5 p.m.*

Gladstone's Land
Old Town

This is one of my favorite historical attractions in Old Town. Run by the National Trust for Scotland, which rescued the property from demolition in the 1930s, this 17th-century merchant's house is decorated in period-style furnishings. It's not very large and is perhaps worth a visit if only to get an impression of the confined living conditions some 400 years ago, even for the well off. The merchant Gladstone (then spelled Gledstane) expanded the original 16th-century structure he purchased in 1617 both upward and toward the street. In the front room, added to the second floor, you still can see the original facade with its friezes of classical columns and arches. I particularly admire the sensitively restored timber ceiling, suitably weathered and aged but with colorful paintings of flowers and fruit. Allow about one hour.

See map p. 156. 477B Lawnmarket. ☎ **0131-226-5856.** www.nts.org.uk. *Bus: 23, 27, 41, or 45. Admission: £5.50 adults, £4.50 children, and £15 family. Open: Daily Apr–June and Sept–Oct 10 a.m.–5 p.m.; July–Aug 9:30 a.m.–7:30 p.m.; and Nov–Mar 10 a.m.–5 p.m.*

Edinburgh Attractions

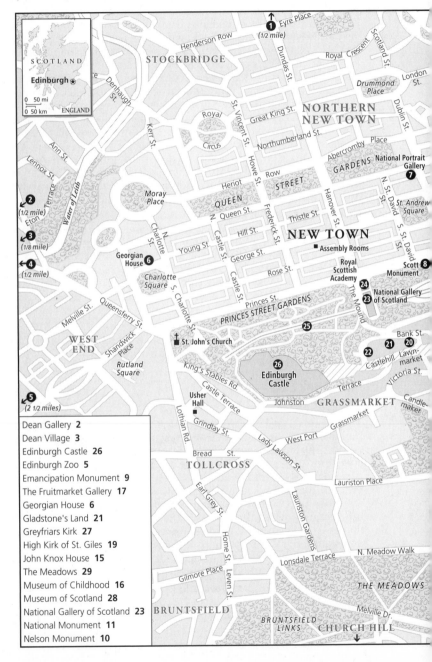

Dean Gallery **2**
Dean Village **3**
Edinburgh Castle **26**
Edinburgh Zoo **5**
Emancipation Monument **9**
The Fruitmarket Gallery **17**
Georgian House **6**
Gladstone's Land **21**
Greyfriars Kirk **27**
High Kirk of St. Giles **19**
John Knox House **15**
The Meadows **29**
Museum of Childhood **16**
Museum of Scotland **28**
National Gallery of Scotland **23**
National Monument **11**
Nelson Monument **10**

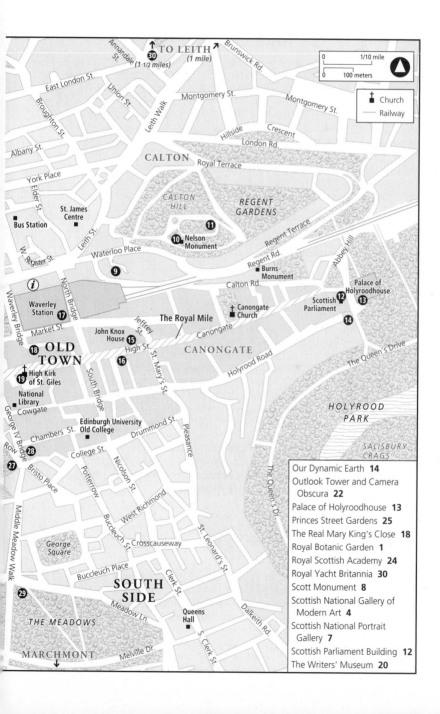

TO LEITH (1 mile)
30 (1 1/2 miles)

0   1/10 mile
0   100 meters

† Church
— Railway

Annandale St.
Union St.
East London St.
Brunswick Rd.
Montgomery St.
Leith Walk
Montgomery St.
Broughton St.
Hillside
Crescent
London Rd.
Albany St.
York Place
Elder St.
CALTON
Royal Terrace
St. James Centre
CALTON HILL
REGENT GARDENS
Bus Station
Leith St.
11
10 Nelson Monument
Waterloo Place
Regent Terrace
9
Regent Rd.
W. Register St.
Burns Monument
(i)
North Bridge
Calton Rd.
Abbey Hill
Palace of Holyroodhouse
Waverley Station **17**
Market St.
Scottish Parliament **12**
13
Jeffrey St.
† Canongate Church
14
The Royal Mile
Waverley Bridge
18 **OLD TOWN**
John Knox House **15**
High St.
Canongate
CANONGATE
16
St. Mary's St.
The Queen's Drive
19 High Kirk of St. Giles
South Bridge
Holyrood Road
National Library
Cowgate
HOLYROOD PARK
George IV Bridge
Edinburgh University Old College
Drummond St.
Chambers St.
Pleasance
SALISBURY CRAGS
28
College St.
27
Bristo Place
Potterrow
Nicolson St.
West Richmond
Buccleuch St.
Crosscauseway
St. Leonard's St.
The Queen's Dr.
Middle Meadow Walk
George Square
Buccleuch Place
Clerk St.
SOUTH SIDE
29
Meadow Ln.
Queens Hall
Dalkeith Rd.
THE MEADOWS
MARCHMONT
Melville Dr.
S. Clerk St.

Our Dynamic Earth **14**
Outlook Tower and Camera Obscura **22**
Palace of Holyroodhouse **13**
Princes Street Gardens **25**
The Real Mary King's Close **18**
Royal Botanic Garden **1**
Royal Scottish Academy **24**
Royal Yacht Britannia **30**
Scott Monument **8**
Scottish National Gallery of Modern Art **4**
Scottish National Portrait Gallery **7**
Scottish Parliament Building **12**
The Writers' Museum **20**

For fans of Mr. Hyde

Not far from Gladstone's Land is **Brodie's Close,** a stone-floored alley off the Lawnmarket. It was named after the well-respected cabinet-making father of the notorious William Brodie, who was a reputable councilor and deacon of trades by day — but a notorious thief and ne'er-do-well by night. Brodie's apparent split personality (actually he was simply calculating and devious) was possibly the inspiration for *The Strange Case of Dr. Jekyll and Mr. Hyde,* by Robert Louis Stevenson. Brodie was finally caught and hanged for his crimes in 1788. In a final irony, the mechanism used in the hangman's scaffold was perfected by none other than Brodie himself — and he tried to defy its action by secretly wearing a steel collar under his shirt. It didn't work. Across the street from Brodie's Close is one of the more famous pubs along the Royal Mile: **Deacon Brodie's Tavern,** 435 Lawnmarket (☎ **0131-225-6531**).

Museum of Scotland
Old Town

Opened in 1998, this impressive museum housed in an modern sandstone building not far from the Royal Mile follows the story of Scotland with exhibits on archaeology, technology, science, the decorative arts, royalty, and geology. Hundreds of millions of years of Scottish history are distilled on each of the museum's floors. There's a total of some 12,000 items, ranging from 2.9-billion-year-old rocks found on the island of South Uist to a cute Hillman Imp, one of the last of 500 automobiles manufactured in Scotland. One gallery is devoted to Scotland's centuries as an independent nation before it merged with England and Wales to form Great Britain. Another gallery, devoted to industry and empire from 1707 to 1914, includes exhibits on shipbuilding, whisky distilling, railways, and such textiles as the tartan and paisley. The roof garden has excellent views, the **Tower Restaurant** offers superb lunches (☎ **0131-225-3003**), and the adjacent **Royal Museum** (whose three-year upgrade ends sometime in 2011) includes a well-preserved and airy Victorian-era Main Hall and some 36 more galleries.

See map p. 156. Chambers Street. ☎ 0131-247-4422. www.nms.ac.uk. *Bus: 2, 7, 23, 31, 35, 41, or 42. Admission: Free. Open: Daily year-round 10 a.m.–5 p.m.*

National Gallery of Scotland
New Town

Although the quantity of fine art held by Scotland may appear small compared to collections of larger European countries, it has been chosen with great care and expanded by bequests, gifts, loans, and purchases. These rooms have only enough space to display part of the entire body of works. One major acquisition in last decade was Botticelli's *The Virgin Adoring the Sleeping Christ Child.* The gallery also has works by El Greco and Velázquez, and Dutch art by Rembrandt and Van Dyck. Impressionism and post-Impressionism are represented by Cézanne, Degas, van Gogh, Monet,

Renoir, Gauguin, and Seurat. In the basement wing (opened in 1978), Scottish art is highlighted, including late-19th-century work by the "Glasgow Boys," represented by artists such as Sir James Guthrie. Another favorite is the whimsical portrait of *The Rev. Robert Walker Skating on Duddingston Loch,* by (although some dispute this) Sir Henry Raeburn, in the late 18th century.

Next door is the **Royal Scottish Academy** (☎ **0131-624-6200**), connected by the modern-designed Weston Link. The RSA was renovated and now hosts blockbuster exhibitions, such as paintings by Monet, Titian, or the 20th century virtuoso Joan Eardley. Allow about one and a half hours.

A convenient way to see the Scottish National Galleries is by catching the courtesy gallery bus that stops at each branch.

See map p. 156. 2 The Mound. ☎ *0131-624-6200.* www.nationalgalleries. org. *Bus: 23, 27, 41, 42, 45, or National Galleries shuttle. Admission: Free to permanent collections, admission prices vary for special exhibitions. Open: Fri–Wed 10 a.m.–5 p.m.; Thurs 10 a.m.–7 p.m. Closed Dec 25–26.*

The Palace of Holyroodhouse
Old Town

King James IV, at the beginning of the 16th century, established this palace adjacent to an abbey that King David I founded in 1128. The **abbey** is a ruin now and what you see today of the palace was mostly built for Charles II in the 1670s. But Mary, Queen of Scots used the palace regularly.

The northwest tower is the earliest piece of the original pile still intact, and this wing provides the most intriguing element of any tour inside. It was the scene of Holyroodhouse's most dramatic incident. Mary Stuart's closest courtier and advisor, David Rizzio, was stabbed repeatedly (allegedly in front of the pregnant queen) on March 9, 1566, by accomplices of her jealous husband, Lord Darnley. Display cases in Mary's Outer Chamber have several diverting Stuart relics, curios, and bits of history. One of the more curious exhibits is a piece of needlework done by Mary depicting a cat-and-mouse scene. (Her cousin, Elizabeth I, is the cat.)

The palace suffered long periods of neglect, but it basked in brief glory during a ball thrown by Bonnie Prince Charlie in the mid–18th century, during the peak of his feverish (and doomed) rebellion to restore the Stuart line to monarchy. Today the royal family stays here whenever they visit Edinburgh. When they're not in residence, the palace is open to visitors, and you see the various reception rooms where the queen dines, entertains, and meets Scottish government leaders. Some of the rich tapestries, paneling, massive fireplaces, and antiques from the 1700s are still in place. The Great Gallery boasts portraits of all Scottish monarchs. More recently, the modern **Queen's Gallery** (additional admission charged) opened to display works from the royal collection, whether Mughal art or Dutch paintings. Even if the original Abbey is roofless and in ruins, you can possibly imagine its grandeur, as well as seeing the vault where the remains of King James V were kept. On the path behind the nave, remnants of the foundations of other ecclesiastical buildings are apparent.

Hume in Nor' Loch

When the area of Princes Street Gardens was still a bog, the distinguished philosopher and renowned agnostic David Hume fell in, couldn't get out, and called for help from a passing woman. She recognized him, denounced his lack of faith, and refused to offer her umbrella to pull him out of the mire until he recited the Lord's Prayer. Presumably, he obliged.

Adjacent to Holyroodhouse is **Holyrood Park,** Edinburgh's largest outdoor public space. With rocky crags, a loch, sweeping meadows, and the ruins of a chapel, it's a wee bit of the Scottish countryside in the city, and a great place for a picnic. If you're fit and ambitious, climb up to the summit of 250m-high (823-ft.) **Arthur's Seat,** from which the panorama is breathtaking. The name doesn't refer to King Arthur, as many people assume, but perhaps is a reference to Prince Arthur of Strathclyde or a corruption of *Ard Thor,* Gaelic for "height of Thor." Allow about two or three hours.

See map p. 157. Canongate, at the eastern end of the Royal Mile. ☎ **0131-556-5100.** *www.royalcollection.org.uk. Bus: 35, 36, or open-top tours. Admission (includes audio tour): £10 adults, £9.30 seniors and students, £6.20 children 5–16, £27 family. Open: Daily Apr–Oct 9:30 a.m.–6 p.m.; Nov–Mar 9:30 a.m.–3:45 p.m. Closed when royal family in residence, often mid-May to late June and at Christmas.*

Princes Street Gardens
New Town

By draining the then-fetid Nor' Loch below the Royal Mile, between Old and New Towns, the city created its most magnificent outdoor public space: the Princes Street Gardens. The banks are steep but grassy and great for a quick bit of sun, should it shine. In wintertime, there is usually an ice rink set up and often part of the park is used for various food and gift markets. With Edinburgh Castle above, this has to be one of the most photographed parks in Europe. If you want a little exercise, climb the 287 steps to the top of the 60m (200-ft.) **Scott Monument** (£3 admission charged) in the East Gardens for a better view. Resembling a church spire on a continental European cathedral, the Gothic-inspired monument is one of Edinburgh's most recognizable landmarks. In the center of the tall spire is a large seated statue of Sir Walter Scott and his dog, Maida, with Scott's heroes carved as small figures in the monument. Allow about one hour.

See map p. 157. Princes Street. ☎ **0131-529-4068.** *www.cac.org.uk. Bus: 3, 10, 12, 17, 25, or 44. Admission: Garden free; Scott monument £3. Open: Gardens daily dawn to dusk; monument Apr–Sept Mon–Sat 9 a.m.–6 p.m. and Sun 10 a.m.–6 p.m.; Oct–Mar Mon–Sat 9 a.m.–3 p.m. and Sun 10 a.m.–3 p.m.*

Royal Botanic Garden
New Town

This is one of the grandest parks in all of Great Britain, which is certainly saying something. Sprawling across 28 hectares (70 acres), it dates from the late 17th century, when it was originally used for medical studies. In spring, the various rhododendrons, from ground cover to gigantic shrubs, are almost reason alone to visit, but the variety of plants in various areas assures year-round interest, whether in the rock garden or along the deep "herbaceous" borders elsewhere. When it comes to research, only Kew Gardens in London does more. The grounds include numerous glass houses, the Palm House (Great Britain's tallest) being foremost among them. Inverleith House is a venue for art exhibitions and has the **Terrace Cafe,** too. Allow about one and a half hours.

See map p. 157. Inverleith Row. ☎ *0131-552-7171.* www.rbge.org.uk. *Bus: 8, 17, 23, or 27. Admission: Donations accepted. Open: Daily Apr–Sept 10 a.m.–7 p.m.; Mar and Oct–Dec 10 a.m.–6 p.m.; Jan–Feb 10 a.m.–4 p.m.*

Scottish National Gallery of Modern Art
New Town/West End

Scotland's national collection of 20th-century art occupies a gallery converted from an 1828 school set on 4.8 hectares (12 acres) of grounds, about a 20-minute walk from the Haymarket railway station. The collection is international in scope and quality despite its modest size, with works ranging from Matisse, Braque, Miró, and Picasso to Balthus, Lichtenstein, and Hockney. The grounds in front of the museum have been dramatically landscaped, with a swirl of grassy terraces and a pond: A piece of art itself called *Landform,* by Baltimore-born Charles Jencks. A cafe sells light refreshments and salads. Allow about one and a half hours.

See map p. 157. 75 Belford Rd. ☎ *0131-624-6200.* www.nationalgalleries.org. *Bus: 13 or National Galleries shuttle. Admission: Free, except for some temporary exhibits. Open: Fri–Wed 10 a.m.–5 p.m.; Thurs 10 a.m.–7 p.m. Closed Dec 25–26.*

Scottish National Portrait Gallery
New Town

Housed in a red-stone, Victorian, neo-Gothic pile designed by Robert Rowand Anderson at the east end of Queen Street, this is the first purpose-built portrait gallery in the world. Until late 2011, it's closed for its first major refurbishment. Meanwhile follow its progress on a blog or see some of the country's portrait collection — such as Mary, Queen of Scots; Flora Macdonald; enlightenment thinkers; Sean Connery; and comedian Billy Connolly — at one of the other National Gallery outlets. Allow about one and a half hours.

See map p. 157. 1 Queen St. ☎ *0131-624-6200.* www.nationalgalleries.org. *Bus: 4, 10, 12, 16, 26, or National Galleries shuttle. Admission: Free, except for some temporary exhibits. Open: Fri–Wed 10 a.m.–5 p.m.; Thurs 10 a.m.–7 p.m. Closed Dec 25–26.*

Scottish Parliament Building
Old Town

After much controversy over its cost — the better part of £500 million — and over the time it took to construct, the new Scottish Parliament opened in autumn of 2004. Designed by the late Barcelona-based architect Enric Miralles, it's a remarkable bit of modern design and probably worth the expense and delays. The abstract motif repeated on the facade was apparently inspired by Raeburn's painting *The Rev. Robert Walker Skating on Duddingston Loch,* which hangs in the National Gallery of Scotland (see listing earlier). The public can make a free visit and get tickets to seats in the main debating chamber or take a guided tour, which goes into the bowels of Scottish political life. Allow about one hour.

See map p. 157. Holyrood Road. ☎ **0131-348-5000.** www.scottish.parliament. uk. *Bus: 35. Admission: Free. Open: Business days (when Parliament is in session) Tues–Thurs 9 a.m.–7 p.m.; all nonbusiness days (when Parliament is in recess and all Mon and Fri) Apr–Oct 10 a.m.–6 p.m., Nov–Mar 10 a.m.–4 p.m.; year-round Sat–Sun 10 a.m.–4 p.m. Last admission 45 min. before closing. Closed Dec 25–26 and Jan 1–2.*

More cool things to see and do

Dean Gallery
New Town/West End

Opening in 1999 across the road from the Scottish Gallery of Modern Art, the Dean Gallery provides a home for surrealist art and includes a replica studio of Leith-born pop-art pioneer Eduardo Paolozzi. He gave an extensive body of his private collection to the National Galleries of Scotland, including prints, drawings, plaster maquettes, and molds. The artist's mammoth composition of the robotic Vulcan dominates the entrance hall. Elsewhere works by Salvador Dalí, Max Ernst, and Joan Miró are displayed, while the Dean also hosts traveling and special exhibitions of modern art. Allow about one hour.

See map p. 156. 73 Belford Rd. ☎ **0131-624-6200.** www.nationalgalleries.org. *Bus 13 or National Galleries shuttle. Admission: Free to permanent collection; prices vary for special exhibitions. Open: Daily year-round 10 a.m.–5 p.m. Closed Dec 25–26.*

Edinburgh Zoo
Corstorphine, west of Murrayfield

Scotland's largest animal collection is 4.5km (3 miles) west of Edinburgh's city center on 32 hectares (80 acres) of hillside parkland, offering unrivaled views from the Pentlands to the Firth of Forth. Run by the Royal Zoological Society of Scotland, the zoo emphasizes its role in the conservation of wildlife and contains more than 1,500 animals, including a few endangered species: snow leopards, white rhinos, pygmy hippos, and others. The zoo has the largest penguin colony in Europe, housed in the world's largest penguin enclosure. From April to September, a penguin parade is held daily at 2:15 p.m. Allow at least two hours.

See map p. 156. 134 Corstorphine Rd. ☎ 0131-334-9171. www.edinburghzoo. org.uk. Bus: 12, 26, 31, or 100 (Airlink). Admission: £16 adults, £11 children, and £48 family. Open: Daily Apr–Sept 9 a.m.–6 p.m.; Oct and Mar 9 a.m.–5 p.m.; Nov–Feb 9 a.m.–4:30 p.m.

The Fruitmarket Gallery
New Town

Near Waverley Station, this is one of the city's leading independent, contemporary art gallery, housed in an old covered market that was dramatically updated and modernized by architect Richard Murphy in the early 1990s. It hosts exhibits of internationally renowned modern and conceptual artists, including Louise Bourgeois, Cindy Sherman, and Yoko Ono — and local champions, such as Chad McCail and Nathan Coley. The Fruitmarket's bookshop and cafe are equally appealing. Across the street is the less innovative but still worthy city-run Edinburgh **City Art Centre** (2 Market St.; ☎ 0131-529-3993). Allow about one hour.

See map p. 156. 45 Market St. ☎ 0131-225-2383. www.fruitmarket.co.uk. Bus: 36. Admission: Free. Open: Mon–Sat 11 a.m.–6 p.m.; Sun noon to 5 p.m. Closed Dec 25–27.

Georgian House
New Town

Charlotte Square, designed by the great Robert Adam, was the final piece of the city's first New Town development. The National Trust for Scotland has two bits of property here: No. 28, on the south side of the square (its headquarters with a small gallery); and, on the northern side, this town house, which has been refurbished and opened to the public. The furniture is mainly Hepplewhite, Chippendale, and Sheraton, all from the 18th century. A sturdy old four-poster bed with an original 18th-century canopy occupies a ground-floor bedroom. The nearby dining room has a table set with fine Wedgwood china as well as the "piss pot" that was passed around after the womenfolk had retired. Allow about one hour.

See map p. 156. 7 Charlotte Sq. ☎ 0131-226-3318. www.nts.org.uk. Bus: 10, 19, or 41. Admission: £5.50 adults; £4.50 children, students, and seniors; £15 family. Open: Daily July–Aug 10 a.m.–7 p.m.; Apr–June and Sept–Oct 10 a.m.–5 p.m.; Nov and Mar 11 a.m.–3 p.m. Closed Dec–Feb.

Greyfriars Kirk
Old Town

Although the churches of Scotland are not generally on the same scale as the cathedrals of the European Continent, they do have their own slightly austere allure. Dedicated in 1620, this kirk was the first "reformed" church in Edinburgh and became the center of a good bit of history. It was built amid a cemetery that Queen Mary proposed in 1562 because there was no more burial space at St. Giles Cathedral on the Royal Mile. In 1638, the National Covenant, favoring Scottish Presbyterianism to the English

Episcopacy, was signed here and an original copy is displayed. Among the many restorations, one in the 1930s brought in California redwood to create the current ceiling. The kirkyard's collection of 17th-century monuments and gravestones is impressive. The most celebrated grave, however, contains a 19th-century policeman whose faithful dog, Bobby, reputedly stood watch for years. The tenacious terrier's first portrait (painted in 1867) hangs here, while a statue of the wee dog — made famous by Hollywood — is nearby at the top of Candlemaker Row, just outside the pub named in his honor. Allow about one hour.

See map p. 156. Greyfriars Place. ☎ **0131-225-1900.** `www.greyfriarskirk.com`. *Bus: 2, 23, 27, 41, 42, or 45. Admission: Free. Open: Apr–Oct Mon–Fri 10:30 a.m.–4:30 p.m., Sat 10:30 a.m.–2:30 p.m.; Nov–Mar Thurs 1:30–3:30 p.m., or by special arrangement.*

High Kirk of St. Giles (St. Giles Cathedral)
Old Town

A short walk from Edinburgh Castle, this church and its steeple in particular are among of the most important architectural landmarks along the Royal Mile. It has historical significance, too. Here is where John Knox, Scotland's Martin Luther, preached his sermons on the Reformation. Often called St. Giles Cathedral, the building combines a dark and brooding stone exterior (the result of a Victorian-era restoration) with surprisingly graceful buttresses. Only the tower represents the medieval era of the church. One of its outstanding internal features is Thistle Chapel, housing beautiful stalls and notable heraldic stained-glass windows. Allow about one hour.

See map p. 156. High Street. ☎ **0131-225-9442.** *Bus: 23, 27, 28, 35, 41, or 42. Admission: Free, but £3 donation suggested. Open: May–Sept Mon–Fri 9 a.m.–7 p.m., Sat 9 a.m.–5 p.m., Sun 1–5 p.m.; Oct–Apr Mon–Sat 9 a.m.–5 p.m., Sun 1–5 p.m.*

John Knox House
Old Town

This is arguably the most picturesque dwelling house in Edinburgh. It's characteristic of the "lands" that used to flank the Royal Mile, and the interiors are noteworthy for the painted ceiling. John Knox is acknowledged as the father of the Presbyterian Church of Scotland, the Protestant tenets of which he established in 1560. While some regard him as a prototypical Puritan, he actually proposed progressive changes in the ruling of the church and in education. But Knox lived at a time of great religious and political upheaval; he spent two years as a galley slave and later lived in exile in Geneva. Upon his return, he became minister of St. Giles and worked to ensure the Reformation's success in Scotland.

Even if you're not overly interested in the firebrand reformer (who may have never lived here anyway), this late-15th-century house still merits a visit. Before Knox allegedly moved in, it was the home of James Mosman, goldsmith to the Catholic Mary, Queen of Scots (no friend of Knox, therefore). The house is now integrated into the completely modernized **Scottish Storytelling Centre.** Allow about one hour.

See map p. 156. 43–45 High St. ☎ **0131-556-9579.** *Bus: 35 or 36. Admission: £4 adults, £1 children 8 and older. Open: Mon–Sat 10 a.m.–6 p.m. (July–Aug also open Sun noon to 6 p.m.)*

The Meadows
Southside

South of Old Town, this expansive public park separates the city center from the now leafy neighborhoods that popped up in the 18th and 19th centuries. The Meadows dates to the 1700s, when a loch on the location was drained. Tree-lined paths crisscross the soccer, rugby, and cricket fields, and you can find plenty of space for having a picnic or flying a kite. At the far western end of the Meadows is Bruntsfield Links, a short-hole course that has a role in golf history as one of the places where the sport was first played — and it still can be during the summer. Allow one to four hours.

See map p. 156. Melville Drive. Admission: Free. Open: Dawn to dusk. Bus: 24 or 41.

Museum of Childhood
Old Town

Allegedly the world's first museum devoted solely to the history of childhood, this popular and free museum is just past the intersection of High and Blackfriars streets. The contents of its four floors range from antique toys to games to exhibits on health, education, and costumes; plus there are video presentations and an activity area. Not surprisingly, this is often the noisiest museum in town, although some argue that adults enjoy it more than kids do. Allow about one hour.

See map p. 156. 42 High St. ☎ **0131-529-4142.** www.cac.org.uk. *Bus: 35. Admission: Free. Open: Mon–Sat 10 a.m.–5 p.m.; Sun noon to 5 p.m.*

Our Dynamic Earth
Old Town

Under a futuristic tentlike canopy near the new Scottish Parliament, Our Dynamic Earth celebrates the evolution and diversity of the planet, with emphasis on the seismological and biological processes that led from the Big Bang to the world we know today. The presentation has been called "physical evolution as interpreted by Disney" — audio and video clips, buttons you can push to simulate earthquakes, meteor showers, and views of outer space. There is the slimy green primordial soup where life began and a series of specialized aquariums, some with replicas of early life forms, others with actual living sharks, dolphins, and coral. A simulated tropical rain forest darkens skies at 15-minute intervals, offering torrents of rainfall. On the premises are a restaurant, a cafe, a children's play area, and a gift shop. Last entry is 70 minutes before closing. Allow about one and a half hours.

See map p. 157. Holyrood Road. ☎ **0131-550-7800.** www.dynamicearth.co.uk. *Bus 35 or 36. Admission: £11 adults, £9 seniors and students, £7 children 3–15. Open: Daily Sept–May 10 a.m.–6 p.m.; June–Aug 9:30 a.m.–6:30 p.m.*

The creator of *Treasure Island*

Robert Louis Stevenson (1850–94) was a restless character. Raised in Edinburgh, he found the place unsuitable for his frail constitution. This, combined with wanderlust, meant that he spent much of his life traveling and living outside his native Scotland. The author has been alternately hailed as Scotland's greatest writer and dismissed as nothing more than the creator of tall tales for children, though surely the former is more accurate.

He was the son of Margaret and Thomas Stevenson, born into a family famed for its Scottish civil-engineering projects, especially lighthouses. Robert was a sickly child and, as a young adult, something of disappointment to his father. After he allowed his son to bow out of engineering and the lucrative family business, Thomas made Robert attend law school, vowing that "the devious and barren paths of literature" were not suitable. Undaunted, Stevenson became a writer and a bit of a rogue. One of his favorite bars still stands today: Rutherford's, on Drummond Street near South Bridge Street.

Determined to roam ("I shall be a nomad") and write, he went to France where he met and later married an American, Fanny Osborne, with whom he traveled to California. Following the success of *The Sea-Cook* (1881), which became the ever-popular *Treasure Island,* Stevenson produced *The Strange Case of Dr. Jekyll and Mr. Hyde,* an instant bestseller and his most famous work — thanks in no small part to later Hollywood adaptations. That was quickly followed by the classic *Kidnapped* (1886), his most evocative book. It reflects the troubled political times in Scotland after the failed 1745 rebellion of Bonnie Prince Charlie. The book takes its 16-year-old hero on an adventure across the Western Highlands.

Eventually Stevenson and Fanny settled in Samoa, hoping to find a climate that would suit his scarred lungs. While there, Stevenson worked on the unfinished classic, *Weir of Hermiston* (published posthumously in 1896). On December 3, 1894, only 43 years old, he collapsed and died.

Outlook Tower and Camera Obscura
Old Town

The 150-year-old periscope-like lens at the top of the Outlook Tower throws an image of nearby streets and buildings onto a circular table, which can be almost magically magnified with just a bit of cardboard. Guides reveal this trick and help to identify landmarks and discuss highlights of Edinburgh's history. In addition, the observation deck offers free telescopes, and there are several exhibits in the "World of Illusions" with an optical theme that will keep some children occupied. What is disappointing, however, is the dearth of information on the man responsible for the Camera Obscura, Sir Patrick Geddes, a polymath who worked tirelessly to improve the fortunes of the Old Town in the 19th and 20th centuries and kept it from being torn down. The last camera presentation begins one hour before closing. Allow about one hour.

See map p. 157. Castlehill. ☎ **0131-226-3709.** *Bus: 23, 27, 41, or 45. Admission: £9 adults, £7.25 seniors and students, £6.50 children. Open: Daily Apr–June and Sept–Oct daily 9:30 a.m.–6 p.m.; July–Aug 9:30 a.m.–7:30 p.m.; Nov–Mar 10 a.m.–5 p.m.*

The Real Mary King's Close
Old Town

Beneath Edinburgh's City Chambers lies a warren of now hidden alleys where once people lived and worked. When the Royal Exchange (now the City Chambers) was constructed in 1753, the top floors of the existing buildings were torn down and the lower sections were left standing to be used as the foundations. This left a number of dark, mysterious passages largely intact. These underground "closes," originally very narrow walkways with houses on either side, date back centuries. Led by guides dressed up as characters from the past, you can revisit the turbulent and plague-ridden days of the 17th century. Dim lighting and an audio track are intended to add to the experience. But of course in their day, these lanes weren't covered by a massive building. Still, this is a popular attraction so booking in advance is recommended. The tour takes about one hour.

See map p. 157. 2 Warriston Close, High Street. ☎ **0870-243-0160.** www.real marykingsclose.com. *Bus: 23, 27, 28, 35, 41, or 42. Admission: £11 adults, £6 students and children 5–15 years old (under 5 not allowed). Reservations requested. Open: Apr–July and Sept–Oct daily 10 a.m.–9 p.m.; Nov–Mar Sun–Thurs 10 a.m.–5 p.m. and Fri–Sat 10 a.m.–9 p.m. Closed Dec 25.*

Royal Yacht Britannia
Leith

The royal yacht *Britannia* launched on April 16, 1953, and traveled more than one million miles before it was decommissioned in December 1997. Several cities then competed to permanently harbor the ship as a tourist attraction. The port of Leith won, and today the ship is moored next to the Ocean Terminal shopping mall some 3km (2 miles) from Edinburgh's center. Once you're aboard, a 90-minute audio tour will guide you about the vessel. You can see where Prince Charles and Princess Diana strolled the deck on their honeymoon; visit the drawing room and the Royal apartments; and explore the engine room, galleys, and captain's cabin. Allow about one and a half hours.

See map p. 157. Ocean Terminal, Ocean Dr., Leith. ☎ **0131-555-5566.** www.royal yachtbritannia.co.uk. *Bus: 22, 34, 35, or Majestic Tour Bus. Reservations recommended. Admission: £11 adults, £9 seniors, £6.75 children 5–17 (under 5 free), £31 family. Tours: Daily Apr–May and June–Oct daily 10 a.m.–4 p.m.; July–Sept 9:30 a.m.–4:30 p.m.; Nov–Mar daily 10 a.m.–3:30 p.m. Closed Dec 25 and Jan 1.*

The Writers' Museum
Old Town

This restored 17th-century house contains a trove of portraits, relics, and manuscripts relating to Scotland's greatest men of letters: Robert Burns

(1759–96), Sir Walter Scott (1771–1832), and Robert Louis Stevenson (1850–94). The Writers' Museum is often a surprisingly uncrowded space. The basement is my personal favorite, with a good deal of items from the life of Stevenson (including his fishing rod and riding boots), as well as a gallery of black-and-white photographs taken when he lived in the South Pacific. The main floor is devoted to Scott with his dining-room table from his home at 39 Castle St., his pipe, chess set, and original manuscripts. Another set of rooms gives details of Burns's life (note his page-one death notice in a copy of London's *Herald*, dated July 27, 1796) along with his writing desk, a few rare manuscripts, portraits, and other items. The premises, Lady Stair's House, with its narrow passages and low clearances, were originally built in 1622 for Edinburgh merchant Sir William Gray. Outside in the Markars' Close, flagstones have been engraved with the words of Scotland's best writers. Allow about one hour.

See map p. 157. In Lady Stair's House, off Lawnmarket. ☎ **0131-529-4901.** www. cac.org.uk. *Bus: 23, 27, 41, or 45. Admission: Free. Open: Mon–Sat 10 a.m.–5 p.m. (in Aug also Sun noon to 5 p.m.).*

Guided tours

For an entertaining, one-hour overview and introduction to the principal attractions of Edinburgh, consider the **Edinburgh Bus Tours** that leave every 20 minutes or so from Waverley Bridge from April to late October. You can see most of the major sights along the Royal Mile, the Grassmarket, Princes Street, George Street, and more from the double-decker open-top motor coaches. Three tours — Edinburgh Tour (green buses), City Sightseeing (red buses), and Mac Tours (vintage buses) — all cover roughly the same ground in Old Town and New Town. The Majestic Tour buses, however, make short work of the city center, as they go down to Leith as well. Tickets are valid for 24 hours, and you can hop on and hop off the bus at designated stops as you choose. The first tour is at 9:30 a.m., and the last is usually around 5:40 p.m. (slightly later July–Sept). For more information on Edinburgh Bus Tours, call ☎ **0131-220-0770** (www.edinburghtour.com). Tickets are £13 adults, £11 seniors and students, £5 children (free for children under 5), and £31 for a family.

The **Edinburgh Literary Pub Tour** traces the footsteps of such literary greats as Robert Burns, Robert Louis Stevenson, and Sir Walter Scott, going into the city's taverns and highlighting the tales of *The Strange Case of Dr. Jekyll and Mr. Hyde* or the erotic love poetry of Burns. They leave nightly at 7:30 p.m. from the Beehive Inn, a popular pub on the Grassmarket, from May to September; Thursday to Sunday in March, April, and October; and only on Friday from November to March. For more information, call ☎ **0131-226-6665** (www.edinburghliterary pubtour.co.uk). Reservations are recommended for groups during the high season. You can purchase tickets at the Beehive; prices are £8.50.

Edinburgh's history is filled with tales of ghosts, gore, and witchcraft, and the **Witchery Tours** are enlivened by characters who leap out of seemingly nowhere when you least expect it. Two tours — the 90-minute

"Ghost & Gore" and the 78-minute "Murder & Mystery" — overlap in parts. Scenes of horrific torture, murder, and supernatural occurrence in Old Town are visited under the cloak of darkness. The ghost tour (which runs May–Aug) departs nightly at 7 and 7:30 p.m., with the Murder tour (year-round) leaving at 9 and 9:30 p.m. All tours depart from outside the Witchery Restaurant on Castlehill. For tickets — £7.50 adults, £5 children — visit the tour office at 84 West Bow (☎ 0131-225-6745; www. witcherytours.com). Reservations are required.

Mercat Tours is a well-established company that conducts popular walking tours of the city, covering a range of interests from "Secrets of the Royal Mile" to "Ghosts & Ghouls," which only takes place in the evening. The tours leave from the Mercat Cross, outside St. Giles Cathedral, on the Royal Mile. Contact Mercat Tours (☎ 0131-255-5443; www.mercat tours.co.uk) for reservations. Tickets cost £8.50 adults, £5 for children.

Edinburgh's big summer events

The cultural highlight of Edinburgh's year comes every August during the **Edinburgh International Festival** and **Edinburgh Festival Fringe.** Since 1947, the International Festival has attracted artists and companies of the highest rank, whether in classical music, opera, ballet, or theater. Running almost simultaneously is the Fringe, an opportunity for anybody — professionals or nonprofessionals, individuals, groups of friends, or a whole company — to put on a show wherever they can find an empty stage or street corner. For many people today the Fringe *is* the festival, with its late-night revues, world-class comedy, contemporary drama, university theater presentations, and even full-length opera. Over the years, the Fringe has become increasingly established (and sponsored), though hardly less experimental and unexpected.

As if the International Festival and the Fringe weren't enough, Edinburgh also hosts, at about the same time, a variety of other festivals. In Charlotte Square, the **Book Festival** has become a huge annual event, drawing authors such as J.K. Rowling and Toni Morrison. You may also stumble upon a **Jazz Festival** or **Television Festival.** One of the season's more popular spectacles is the **Military Tattoo** on the floodlit esplanade of Edinburgh Castle. The show features precision marching of not only Scottish regiments but also soldiers and performers (including bands, drill teams, and gymnasts) from dozens of countries.

Ticket prices for festivals, the Fringe, and other shows or events vary from £1 to £50. The headquarters for the International Festival is The Hub, Castle Hill (☎ 0131-473-2000). The Fringe is based at 180 High St. (☎ 0131-226-0000). General information on festivals and most events can be found on the Web at www.edinburghfestivals. co.uk.

Suggested one-, two-, and three-day itineraries

You may just want to wander around Edinburgh, which is easy enough — it's a small place and many of the tourist attractions are within the central part of the city. However, if your time in the capital is limited to a few days, here are some suggested itineraries that highlight some of the very best things to do and see.

If you have one day

If you're unfortunate enough to only have one day in Edinburgh, I suggest that you stick to the city's famous **Royal Mile** and **Old Town.** It is every bit a day's worth of activity, with plenty of history and attractions from Edinburgh Castle to the Palace of Holyroodhouse, shops, restaurants, and pubs. Wander down some of the alleys off the Royal Mile, too.

If you have two days

Follow my one-day itinerary for your first day, and on your second day take the hop-on, hop-off bus tour that emphasizes **New Town.** Your ticket is good for 24 hours (although the buses stop running in the late afternoon/ early evening). Get off on Calton Hill for the views, which Robert Louis Stevenson said were the best in the city. Amble down Princes Street for a bit of shopping, and afterwards take a break in Princes Street Gardens. Admire some art at one of the branches of the National Gallery.

If you have three days

Your first two days should be filled with the activities I suggest above. On your third day, take in **Leith,** Edinburgh's once rough-and-tumble port. A seaside village that is now part of Edinburgh, Leith has a rich history of its own. Today it also offers some good restaurants and lively pubs. On your way back into the city center, also worth a visit, is the **Botanic Gardens.** It's one of the best in Great Britain — and that's saying a lot. If you have any time to spare, visit Stockbridge or the Meadows, which have an off-the-main-tourist-tracks feel to them.

If you (are lucky and) have four days or more

Start with my recommendations from the previous sections and then on your fourth day climb **Arthur's Seat** for views of the city and the sea, or if you have children, take the family to the **Edinburgh Zoo.** Explore the regions around the city, heading east to the coast near North Berwick or west to nearby historic Linlithgow.

Taking a walking tour

Given that Edinburgh is a relatively compact city, walking is one of the best ways to see it. This fact is especially true in Old Town, where passages and alleys — or closes (pronounced *cloz*-es) and vennels, as the locals prefer to call them — run off both sides of the main street like ribs from a spine. You really owe it to yourself to wander down a few of them to appreciate the medieval core of the Scottish capital.

If you want to leave the tourist trail, however, I have devised the following walk south of the Royal Mile, which will give you a notion of what "real" Edinburgh is like — and it will also take you past some historical and architectural highlights. The route is only about 1.2km (2 miles) long and shouldn't take you more than an hour or so to complete (if you don't go into buildings or get distracted, that is).

Start the walk at:

1. **West Bow**

   Initially this street zigzagged right up the steep slope from the Grassmarket to Castlehill. With the 19th-century addition of Victoria Street, however, West Bow links more easily with the Royal Mile via George IV Bridge. The combination of Victoria Street and West Bow creates a charming and winding road of unpretentious shops, bars, and restaurants. At the base of the street is the West Bow Well, which was built in 1674. To the west is the Grassmarket.

   Go southeast from Cowgate. Head up Candlemaker Row to:

2. **Greyfriars Kirk**

   This isn't the church you see while ascending Candlemaker Row, but instead it lies to the right at the top. Greyfriars Kirk was completed in 1620 (for some history, flip back to the church's listing in the section "More cool things to see and do," earlier in this chapter).

   Cross George IV Bridge to Chambers Street and the:

3. **Museum of Scotland**

   Directly in front of you, as you leave Greyfriars, is the impressive and modern Museum of Scotland. It was designed by architects Benson and Forsyth and constructed mostly with sandstone from the northeast of Scotland. (Next door on Chambers Street is the Royal Museum, a bonus if you have free time.) Chambers Street is named after a 19th-century lord provost (the equivalent of a mayor) whose statue stands in front of the museum's Victorian Great Hall. Farther down off Chambers Street, on what is today Guthrie Street, you can find Sir Walter Scott's birthplace.

   Continue east on Chambers Street to South Bridge, turning right (south). At this corner is the:

4. **Old College**

   The 1781 exteriors of the University of Edinburgh Old College have been called the greatest public work of Robert Adam. The university was established in 1583 by James VI (later James I of England), and this "Old College" actually replaced an earlier campus. In the southwest corner is the entrance to the Talbot Rice gallery (www.trg.ed.ac.uk), which displays contemporary art. One of Robert Louis Stevenson's favorite saloons — Rutherford's Bar — is on nearby Drummond Street, and a plaque commemorating his admiration for it is posted. The neighborhood also offers more recent literary history: A cafe here is reputedly where J. K. Rowling began writing the Harry Potter series. The establishment has since become a Chinese restaurant.

At Drummond Street, South Bridge becomes Nicolson Street. Continue south on it to:

5. **Nicolson Square**

The impressive building you passed on the left (across from the modern Festival Theatre) before arriving at this square was the Surgeons' Hall, designed by William Playfair in the 1830s. Nicolson Square dates to 1756, and the buildings along its north fringe apparently were the first to be built here. In the square's park you can see the Brassfounders' Column, created by James Gowans in 1886.

Leave the square at the west on Marshall Street, turn left (south) onto Potterrow, and turn right (west) at the parking lot entrance and Crichton Street to:

6. **George Square**

Almost entirely redeveloped by the University of Edinburgh in the 20th century, George Square originally had uniform, if less than startling, mid-18th-century town houses. The square predates the city's New Town developments, and some of the early buildings are still standing on the western side of the square. The park provides a quiet daytime retreat. Sir Walter Scott played in this park as a child. (A little trivia: The square was named after the brother of the designer James Brown, not a king.)

Exit the square at the southwest corner, turning right (west) into:

7. **The Meadows**

This sweeping park separates central Edinburgh from the southern suburbs, such as Marchmont, which were largely developed in the 19th century. At the Western end is Bruntsfield Links, which some speculate entertained golfers in the 17th century and still has a short course with many holes available for play today.

Turn right a short distance later (at the black cycle network marker) and follow the bike/pedestrian path, Meadow Walk, north to:

8. **Teviot Place**

The triangle of land formed by Teviot Place, Forrest Road, and Bristo Place is a hotbed of university life today, with its cafes and bars. To the right (east) is the Medical School. To the left (west) on Lauriston Place is the Royal Infirmary of Edinburgh. George Watson's Hospital on the grounds dates to the 1740s, but Scots baronial (a type of architecture) buildings superseded it in the 19th century, adopting the open-plan dictates of Florence Nightingale.

Hogmanay party

Hogmanay is New Year's Eve and Edinburgh hosts one of the biggest New Year's Eve parties on the planet. In Scotland, the festivities traditionally don't really even begin until the clock strikes midnight, and then they continue until daybreak or later. In 1993, the Edinburgh City Council began a three-day Hogmanay festival featuring rock bands, street theater, and a lively procession. By 1997, the event had become so big that participation is now reserved for ticket holders. For information, visit www. edinburghshogmanay.org.

Walk west on Lauriston Place to:

9. **George Heriot's School**

   Heriot was nicknamed "the Jinglin' Geordie," and as jeweler to James VI, he exemplified the courtiers and royal hangers-on who left Scotland and made their fortunes in London after the unification of the crowns at the beginning of the 17th century. Heriot, at least, decided to pay Edinburgh back by leaving more than £20,000 ($37,000) to build a facility for disadvantaged boys. Of the 200-odd windows in the Renaissance pile, only two are exactly alike. Today, the building is a private school for boys and girls.

   Continue on Lauriston Place to the edge of the campus and turn right on Heriot Place. Continue down the steps and take the path, called the Vennel, to the:

10. **Grassmarket**

    Located just at the top of the steep steps of the Vennel is another piece of the Flodden Wall, the southwest bastion, indicating how the Grassmarket was enclosed in the city by the 16th century. Now home to loads of bars and restaurants, the Grassmarket — in the shadow of the castle — hosted a weekly market for more than 400 years. Until the 1780s, the Grassmarket also was the site of public gallows and a place where zealous Protestants — known as the Covenators — were hung, as was Maggie Dickson, who, according to legend, came back to life. She at least has a pub named after her today. At the nearby White Hart Inn, Burns and Wordsworth both are said to have lodged.

Shopping in Edinburgh

Edinburgh may lack all of the shopping options available in Glasgow, but it has a combination of newfangled boutiques, souvenir shops, and traditional department stores, such as the classic John Lewis. With the addition a few years ago of the fashionista's favorite, Harvey Nichols, Edinburgh is certainly challenging the more style-conscious city to the west.

Goods are not inexpensive, however. Many items carry the same numerical price in pounds as they would in American dollars. So, a pair of hiking shoes that cost $100 in New York might well be priced £100 in Edinburgh, making them significantly more expensive.

Best shopping areas

New Town's **Princes Street** is a primary shopping artery in the Scottish capital; it's home to leading department stores, including the home-grown Jenners and the British staple Marks & Spencer. But for the posher shops, such as Cruise or Laura Ashley, **George Street** tops the lot. In between is **Rose Street,** a narrow pedestrian lane that's best known for its pubs but is actually full of more shops.

For tourists on the hunt for more traditional souvenirs, the **Royal Mile** in Old Town presents the Mother Lode, whether it's tartan or trinkets you seek. For small boutiques, try **William Street** in the West End.

Shopping hours in Edinburgh are generally only from 9 or 10 a.m. to 6 p.m., Monday through Wednesday and Friday and Saturday. Thursday is the so-called late shopping day, with many shops opening at 9 or 10 a.m. and remaining open to 7 or 8 p.m. Shops open Sunday from 11 a.m. or noon and close at around 5 p.m., although smaller operations may remain closed on Sunday.

Shopping complexes

In addition to the primary shopping districts in New Town and Old Town, a few shopping malls with a concentration of shops are scattered around. The newest is in Leith: **Ocean Terminal** (☎ **0131-555-8888;** www.oceanterminal.com). Debenhams, French Connection, Gap, and other stores have set out their stalls in this retail cathedral, which gets a lot of foot traffic from tourists because the royal yacht *Britannia* is moored here as well.

Above Waverley train station and beneath the city's main tourist information center, **Princes Mall** (☎ **0131-557-3759;** www.princesmall-edinburgh.co.uk) appears to have something for everyone — except a leading department store. About 80 shops sell fashions, accessories, gifts, books, jewelry, and beauty products, and a food court offers the typical fast-food outlets.

St James Centre (☎ **0131-557-0050;** www.stjamesshopping.com) is slightly more upscale than Princes Mall. At the top of Leith Walk near Calton Hill, this shopping center is anchored by John Lewis's department store, giving the place a nice touch of respectability.

What to look for and where to find it

If your shopping intentions are less of the browsing variety, here are some of Edinburgh's specialized shopping options.

Antiques

✔ **Carson Clark Gallery,** a specialist in antique sea charts and maps, is the place for a unique souvenir. One of my favorite prints is an early-19th-century graphic depiction the headwaters, topography, and length of Scotland's major rivers. In addition to fascinating old maps, there are also smart reproductions of historic etchings and prints. 181 Canongate (☎ **0131-556-4710**).

Books

✔ **McNaughtan's Bookshop** is one of the city's best antiquarian and secondhand book purveyors. Consider it a must-stop for book lovers. 3a–4a Haddington Place, at the top of Leith Walk, near Gayfield Square (☎ **0131-556-5897;** www.mcnaughtansbookshop.com).

✔ **Waterstone's** is a giant Barnes & Noble–like operation, with plenty of stock and a lot of soft seats. It's the most prominent book retailer in the city center and has a good Scottish section on the ground floor. Other branches in New Town are at the western end of Princes Street and on George Street. 128 Princes St. (☎ **0131-226-2666**).

Clothing/fashion

✔ **Arkangel** is in the city's affluent West End, which offers a host of boutique shops. This one specializes in women's designers and sells brands that no other store in Scotland does. U.K. designer duds sold here include Clara Collins and Ginka. 4 William St., West End (☎ **0131-226-4466**).

✔ **Corniche** is one of the more sophisticated boutiques in Edinburgh; if it's the latest in Scottish fashion, expect to find it here. Offerings have included "Anglomania kilts," created by that controversial lady of clothing design, Vivienne Westwood, as well as fashions by Gautier, Katherine Hamnett, and Yamamoto. 2 Jeffrey St., near the Royal Mile (☎ **0131-556-3707**).

✔ **Cruise** is commonly associated with Glasgow, but this home-grown fashion outlet began in Edinburgh's Old Town — not generally considered fertile ground for the avant-garde. You can still find a shop off the Royal Mile, but this New Town outlet is the focus for couture. 94 George St. (☎ **0131-226-3524**).

✔ **Walker Slater** is a handsome shop full of well-made and contemporary (if understated) men's clothes, which are usually made of cotton and dyed in rich, earthy hues. It also carries Mackintosh overcoats and accessories for the smart gentleman about town. 20 Victoria St. (☎ **0131-220-2636**).

Crafts and jewelry

✔ **Alistir Wood Tait** is a jewelry store with a reputation for Scottish gems and precious metals such as agates, Scottish gold, garnets, and sapphires. Ask to see the artful depictions of Luckenbooths — two entwined hearts capped by a royal crest, usually fashioned as pendants. 116A Rose St. (☎ **0131-225-4105;** www.alistirtait gem.co.uk).

✔ **Hamilton & Inches** has sold gold and silver jewelry, porcelain and silver, and gift items, including quaichs, since 1866. Folkloric *quaichs* (drinking vessels now mostly used to give as gifts) originated in the West Highlands as whisky measures crafted from wood or horn. They were later gentrified into something resembling silver chafing dishes, each with a pair of lugs (ears) fashioned into Celtic or thistle patterns. 87 George St. (☎ **0131-225-4898;** www.hamilton andinches.com).

✔ **Ness Scotland** has two shops filled with whimsical accessories scoured from around the country — from the Orkney Islands to the Borders. Ness offers hand-loomed cardigans and tasteful scarves, amid much more. 336 Lawnmarket. (☎ **0131-225-8155**).

Department stores

✔ **Harvey Nichols** opened in 2002 with much celebration but was a tad slow to catch on. Perhaps traditional shoppers were not quite prepared for floors of expensive labels and designers such as Jimmy Choo or Alexander McQueen. But they're learning. 30–34 St. Andrew Sq. (☎ **0131-524-8388;** www.harveynichols.com).

✔ **Jenners** opened in 1838, and the shop's neo-Gothic facade is almost as much an Edinburgh landmark as the Scott Monument just across Princes Street. Although controversially sold in 2005 to House of Fraser, the store's array of local and international merchandise hasn't changed much. It also has a food hall with a wide array of gift-oriented Scottish products, including heather honey, Dundee marmalade, and a vast selection of shortbreads. 48 Princes St. (☎ **0870-607-2841**).

✔ **John Lewis** is the largest department store in Scotland, and this branch is many people's first choice when it comes to shopping for clothes, appliances, furniture, toys, and more. St. James Centre, near Picardy Place, at the top of Leith Walk (☎ **0131-556-9121**).

Edibles

See the sidebar "Picnic fare," earlier in this chapter, for select food markets with Scottish specialties.

Gifts

✔ **Geraldine's of Edinburgh** is also known as the "Doll Hospital." Each of the heirloom-quality dolls here requires days of labor to create, and has a hand-painted porcelain head and sometimes an elaborate coiffure. Also available are fully jointed, all-mohair teddy bears. 133–135 Canongate (☎ **0131-556-4295**).

✔ **Tartan Gift Shops** has a chart indicating the place of origin (in Scotland) of family names, accompanied by a bewildering array of hunt and dress tartans for men and women, all sold by the yard. The shop also carries a line of lambs-wool and cashmere sweaters. 54 High St. (☎ **0131-558-3187**).

Hats, knits, and woolens

✔ **Bill Baber** is a workshop/store that turns out artfully modernized adaptations of traditional Scottish patterns for men and women alike. Expect to find traditional knits spiced up with strands of Caribbean-inspired turquoise or aqua or rugged-looking blazers or sweaters suitable for treks or bike rides through the moors. 66 Grassmarket (☎ **0131-225-3249**; www.billbaber.com).

✔ **Fabhatrix** has hundreds of handmade felt hats and caps, many practical as well as attractive and some downright frivolous but extremely fun. Remember: Keep your head warm and your whole body stays warm. 13 Cowgatehead, near Grassmarket (☎ **0131-225-9222**).

✔ **Ragamuffin** sells what's termed "wearable art," created by some 150 designers from all over the U.K. The apparel here is one-of-a-kind. Well, not exactly — Ragamuffin also has a shop way up north on the Isle of Skye. 276 Canongate, Royal Mile (☎ **0131-557-6007**; www.ragamuffinonline.co.uk).

Music

✔ **Avalanche** usually has a bunch of harmless goth kids hanging out in front of it. You can find this branch of the excellent CD shop where the steep steps of the Fleshmarket close meet Cockburn Street. It's best for new releases of indie bands. Another Avalanche shop is on West Nicolson Street. 60 Cockburn St., near the Royal Mile (☎ **0131-225-3939**).

Tartans and kilts

✔ **Anta** sells some of the most stylish tartans. Woolen blankets with hand-purled fringe are woven here on old-style looms. Crocket's Land, 91–93 West Bow (☎ **0131-225-4616**).

✔ **Geoffrey (Tailor) Kiltmakers** has a list of customers that includes Sean Connery, Dr. Ruth Westheimer, members of Scotland's rugby teams, and Mel Gibson. It stocks 200 of Scotland's best-known tartan patterns and is revolutionizing the kilt by establishing a subsidiary called 21st-Century Kilts, which makes them in fabrics ranging from denim to leather. 57–59 High St. (☎ **0131-557-0256**).

✔ **Hector Russell,** a well-known kilt-makers shop on the Royal Mile, creates bespoke — that's made-to-order — clothes made from tartans. Another branch is located on Princes Street. 137–141 High St. (☎ **0131-558-1254**).

✔ **James Pringle Weavers** produces a large variety of wool items, including cashmere sweaters, tartan and tweed ties, travel rugs, tweed hats, and tam o' shanters. In addition, it boasts a clan ancestry center with a database containing more than 50,000 family names. 70–74 Bangor Rd., Leith (☎ **0131-553-5161**).

Whisky

✔ **Royal Mile Whiskies** stock some 1,000 different whiskies from Scotland and other nations. Prices range from around £20 to £900. Staff know their stuff, so tell them what you prefer (for example, smoky, peaty, sweet, and so on) and they find a bottle to please you. 379 High St. (☎ **0131-622-6255**).

Living It Up after Dark

Every August, Edinburgh becomes the cultural capital of Europe and the envy of every other tourist board in the U.K. when it hosts the **International Festival, Festival Fringe, Book Festival,** and **Jazz Festival.** Together these festivals bring in thousands of visitors to see hundreds of world-class acts — in drama, dance, music, comedy, and more. In August, the Scottish capital becomes a proverbial "city that never sleeps."

Although the yearly festivals (www.edinburghfestivals.co.uk) are no doubt the peak of Edinburgh's social calendar, the city offers a pretty good selection of entertainment choices throughout the year. Visitors can busy themselves with the cinema, clubs, theater, opera, ballet, and other diversions such as a night at the pub.

For a complete rundown of what's happening in Edinburgh, pick up a copy of *The List,* a biweekly magazine available at all major newsstands and bookshops. It previews, reviews, and gives the full details of arts events here — and in Glasgow.

The performing arts

The West End is the cradle of theater and music, home to the legendary and innovative **Traverse Theatre** as well as the **Royal Lyceum Theatre** and the classic **Usher Hall** for concerts.

✔ **Edinburgh Festival Theatre** reopened in 1994, after serious renovations, in time for the Edinburgh Festival (hence the name). Located on the south side of the city, about a ten-minute walk from the Royal Mile and right near the University of Edinburgh's Old Campus, the 1,900-seat theater hosts the national opera and ballet, touring companies, and orchestras. Tickets are £5 to £45. 13–29 Nicolson St. (☎ **0131-529-6000** box office, or 0131-662-1112 administration; www.eft.co.uk; Bus: 5, 7, 8, or 29).

✔ **Edinburgh Playhouse** is best known for hosting popular plays or musicals and other mainstream acts when they come to town, whether it's *Miss Saigon* or *Lord of the Dance*. Formerly a cinema, the playhouse is the largest theater in Great Britain, with more than 3,000 seats. Tickets are £8 to £35. 18–22 Greenside Place (☎ 0131-524-3333; www.edinburgh-playhouse.co.uk; Bus: 5 or 22).

✔ **Kings Theatre** is a 1,300-seat late-Victorian-era venue with a dome ceiling and rather Glasgow-style stained-glass doors and red-stone frontage. Located on the edge of Tollcross, southwest of the castle, it offers a wide repertoire, especially traveling West End productions, productions of the Scottish National Theatre, and other classical entertainment, ballet, and opera. During December and January, it's the premier theater for popular pantomime productions in Edinburgh. Tickets range from £5 to £20. 2 Leven St. (☎ 0131-529-6000; www.eft.co.uk; Bus: 11, 15, or 17).

✔ **Royal Lyceum Theatre** (built in 1883) has a most enviable reputation, with presentations that range from the most famous works of Shakespeare to new Scottish playwrights. It's home to the leading theater production company in the city, often hiring the best Scottish actors, such as Brian Cox, Billy Boyd *(Lord of the Rings)*, and Siobhan Redmond — when they're not preoccupied with Hollywood, that is. Grindlay Street (☎ 0131-248-4848 box office, or 0131-238-4800 general inquiries; www.lyceum.org; Bus: 1, 10, 15, or 34).

✔ **Traverse Theatre** is just around the corner from the Royal Lyceum and is something of a local legend. Beginning in the 1960s as an experimental theater company that doubled as a bohemian social club, it still produces the height of contemporary drama in Scotland. This custom-made subterranean complex actually contains two theaters, seating 100 and 250, respectively, on the benches. Upstairs, the Traverse Bar is where you find the hippest dramatists, actors, and their courtiers. Tickets are £5 to £15. 10 Cambridge St. (☎ 0131-228-1404; www.traverse.co.uk; Bus: 11 or 15).

✔ **Usher Hall** is unbeatable when it comes to concerts. Built in the 1890s, thanks to the bequest of distiller Andrew Usher, this Beaux Arts building is Edinburgh's equivalent of Carnegie Hall. During the International Festival, it hosts such ensembles as the Cleveland or London Philharmonic orchestras. But Usher Hall isn't only a venue for classical music: Top touring jazz, world music, and pop acts play here throughout the year. Tickets are £8 to £50. Lothian Road (☎ 0131-228-1155; www.usherhall.co.uk; Bus: 1, 10, 15, or 34).

Comedy

Given the importance of the Edinburgh Festival Fringe, where the vaunted Perrier Award for comedy can launch a career, the stand-up comedian is, er, taken very seriously in the Scottish capital.

✔ **Jongleurs Comedy Club** is a corporate-owned entity from down south with more than a dozen venues across the U.K. Jongleurs came to Scotland a few years back, dragging along its own cadre of house funny men (and funny women) as well as some touring comedians from overseas. Tickets are £4 to £15. Omni Centre, Greenside Place (☎ **0870-787-0707;** www.jongleurs.com; Bus: 7 or 22).

✔ **The Stand,** just down the hill from St. Andrew Square, is the premier local comedy venue. Big acts are reserved for weekend nights, while local talent try their jokes and tales during the week. On Sundays, no admission is charged for brunch performances. Tickets range from £1 to £8. 5 York Place (☎ **0131-558-7272;** www.thestand.co.uk; Bus: 8 or 17).

Dance clubs

Clubbing isn't quite as popular now as it was in the 1980s and 1990s, but it probably still draws more people than the folk, jazz, and classical music scenes combined. Below is just a sampling of clubs in Edinburgh.

✔ **Bongo Club** offers a varied music policy throughout the week — funk, dub, and experimental. This venue has more reasonably priced drinks than many others. The cover charge can be up to £8. The club is open daily from 10 p.m. to 3 a.m. Moray House, 37 Holyrood Rd. (☎ **0131-558-7604;** www.thebongoclub.co.uk; Bus: 35).

✔ **Po Na Na** is a branch of a successful chain of clubs in Great Britain. The theme is a Moroccan Casbah with décor to match, thanks to wall mosaics, brass lanterns, and artifacts shipped in from Marrakech. The dance mix varies from hip-hop and funk to disco and sounds of the '80s. The cover can be up to £5. Po Na Na is open daily until 3 a.m. 43B Frederick St. (☎ **0131-226-2224;** www.ponana.co.uk; Bus: 80).

Folk music

Although touring folk acts — American performers, such as Gillian Welch, are pretty huge in Scotland — get booked into the larger music halls, the day-to-day folk scene in Edinburgh takes place in unassuming public houses.

✔ **The Royal Oak** is where Old Town meets the Southside, just a few minutes' walk from the Royal Mile off South Bridge. The pub is the home of live Scottish folk music. On Sundays, from 8:30 p.m. on, various guests play at the "Wee Folk Club." Tickets are £3. The Royal Oak is open daily until 2 a.m. 1 Infirmary St. (☎ **0131-557-2967;** Bus: 3, 5, 8, or 29).

✔ **Sandy Bell's** offers live folk or traditional music virtually every night from about 9 p.m. and all day Saturday and Sunday. This small pub near the Museum of Scotland is a landmark for Scottish and Gaelic culture. Sandy Bell's is open Monday through Saturday from 11:30 a.m. to 1 a.m. and Sunday from 12:30 to 11 p.m. 25 Forrest Rd. (☎ **0131-225-2751;** Bus: 2 or 42).

Late-night eats

Okay, okay, it's Friday or Saturday night. You've been out to a play, the pub, or dance club, and now you're utterly starving, but it's somewhere between 11 p.m. and 1 a.m. You're not exactly sure because your watch seems to be keeping Australian time at the moment. Food will help. The area around Edinburgh University is your best bet. Try **Negociants** (45 Lothian St.; ☎ 0131-225-6313). It serves food until midnight during the week and until 2 a.m. on Friday and Saturday nights (that is, Sat–Sun mornings). My favorite is **Kebab Mahal** (see p. 147).

Rock, pop, and jazz

Although it's not listed here, the very big acts — whether Bob Dylan, R.E.M., or the Rolling Stones, for example — are likely to play outdoors at the national rugby facility, **Murrayfield Stadium.**

✔ **Corn Exchange** is a bit of a haul out of the city center. But this venue was meant to compete with the likes of Glasgow's infamous Barrowland ballroom, where touring groups absolutely love to appear. The comparison isn't really fair, but the Corn Exchange isn't a bad medium-to-small-size hall (capacity 3,000) to see rock acts. 11 New Market Rd. (☎ **0131-477-3500;** www.ece.uk.com; Bus: 4 or 28).

✔ **The Liquid Room** has space for fewer than 1,000 people. This is Edinburgh's best venue for catching the sweat off the brows of groups; it's also a busy dance club when not hosting such groups. 9c Victoria St. (☎ **0131-225-2564;** www.liquidroom.com; Bus: 35).

Bars and pubs

In a city with no shortage of drinking spots, the most active areas for pubs and clubs are the **Cowgate** and **Grassmarket** in Old Town and **Broughton Street** in New Town, although the university precincts on the Southside are lively, as are the pubs near **The Shore** in the Port of Leith. Unless otherwise noted, the bars and pubs listed below are generally open Sunday through Thursday from 11 a.m. or noon until 11 p.m. or midnight, often closing at 1 or 2 a.m. on Friday and Saturday nights. They are all nonsmoking indoors.

✔ **The Abbotsford**'s bartenders have been pouring pints since around 1900. The gaslight era is still alive here thanks to the preservation of the dark paneling and ornate plaster ceiling. The ales on tap change about once a week, and you can find a good selection of single-malt whiskies, too. Platters of food are dispensed from the bar Monday through Saturday from noon to 3 p.m. and 5:30 to 10 p.m. 3 Rose St. (☎ **0131-225-5276;** Bus: 3, 28, or 45).

✔ **Black Bo's** is a stone's throw from the Royal Mile. Many visitors may find its dark walls and mix-and-match furniture downright plain, but it has a rather unforced hipness. And due to its proximity to the hostels of Blackfriars Street, Black Bo's often hosts chatty groups of young foreigners enjoying a pint or two. DJs play from Wednesday to Saturday; downstairs is a pool room with a jukebox. The bar doesn't serve food, but its mostly vegetarian restaurant next door does. 57 Blackfriars St. (☎ **0131-557-6136;** Bus: 35).

✔ **Bow Bar,** located just below Edinburgh Castle, is a classic Edinburgh pub that appears little changed by time or tampered with by foolish trends. Surprise: It's only a few more than a dozen years old. Never mind that, though. The pub looks the part of a classic and features some eight cask-conditioned ales, which change regularly. The Scottish brewed options may include the dark and smooth Lia Fail (Gaelic for "Stone of Destiny," the rock on which Scottish kings were enthroned), from the Perthshire-based Inveralmond Brewery. No food is served. 80 West Bow (☎ **0131-226-7667;** Bus: 2 or 35).

✔ **Café Royal Circle Bar** is a well-preserved Victorian-era pub. Spacious booths, combined with plenty of room around the island bar, create a comfortable and stylish place to drink. Above-average food from the same kitchen as the neighboring oyster bar/restaurant is served daily. 17 W. Register St. (☎ **0131-556-1884;** Bus: 8 or 13).

✔ **Opal Lounge,** in New Town, is an excellent example of the so-called modern-style bar. After opening in 2001, it became the haunt of Prince William when the heir to the British throne attended St. Andrew's University. Opal Lounge draws a predominantly young, well-dressed, and affluent crowd, combining a long list of cocktails with a cavernous underground space. Drinks are served daily from noon to 3 a.m.; food of an Asian-fusion nature is served daily from noon to 10 p.m. 51a George St. (☎ **0131-226-2275;** Bus: 24, 29, or 42).

✔ **The Outhouse** is one of the more contemporary outfits on or near busy Broughton Street. The bar was renovated in 2003 with rich brown hues. During good weather spells, a beer garden out back offers an excellent open-air retreat; and some outdoor heaters help take the chill off the night. 14 Broughton Street Lane (☎ **0131-557-6688;** Bus: 8 or 17).

✔ **The Shore,** down in Leith, fits seamlessly into the seaside port ambience without resorting to a lot of the usual decorations of cork and netting. The place is small, but on nice days they put a few seats out front to soak in the afternoon sun. On three nights of the week, you can find live folk and jazz music. Food is served from noon to 2:30 p.m. and 6:30 to 10 p.m. 3–4 The Shore (☎ **0131-553-5080;** Bus: 16 or 36).

Going to the cinema

✔ **Cameo** cinema gets occasionally threatened with redevelopment but it remains one of the best independent film houses in Scotland, showing arts, indie, foreign, and classic cinema. 38 Home St. (☎ **0871-704-2052.** Bus: 10, 11, 16, or 24.)

✔ **The Filmhouse,** the capital's most important cinema, is the focus of the Edinburgh Film Festival — one of the oldest annual film festivals in the world. The movies shown here are foreign and art house, classic and experimental, documentary and shorts. Plus, the Filmhouse hosts discussions and lectures with directors during the festival and at other points throughout the year. The cafe/bar does drinks, serves light meals, and remains open late. Consider this a must-stop for any visiting film buffs. 88 Lothian Rd. (☎ **0131-228-2688;** www.filmhousecinema.com; Bus: 10, 22, or 30).

✔ **Vue Edinburgh** is a big glass-fronted multiplex below Calton Hill, at the roundabout near the top of Leith Walk. It offers first-run, big commercial releases. Omni Centre, Greenside Place (☎ **0871-224-0240;** www.myvue.com; Bus: 7 or 22).

Fast Facts: Edinburgh

American Express

The office is at 69 George St., at Frederick Street (☎ 0131-718-2501; Bus: 13, 19, or 41). It's open Monday to Friday from 9 a.m. to 5:30 p.m. and on Saturday 9 a.m. to 5 p.m.

Business Hours

In Edinburgh, banks are usually open Monday through Friday from 9 or 9:30 a.m. to 4 or 5 p.m., with some branches sometimes shutting early one day a week and opening late on another. Shops are generally open Monday through Saturday from 9 or 10 a.m. to 6 p.m.; on Thursday, retail stores are open late, usually until about 8 p.m. Many shops are now open on Sunday as well. In general, business hours are Monday through Friday from 9 a.m. to 5 p.m., although some offices will close early on Friday. Food supermarkets generally keep later hours.

Currency Exchange

Many banks in Old Town and New Town exchange currency. Post offices run Bureaux de Change, as does the Edinburgh Information Office (☎ 0131-473-3800). Major hotels also exchange currency but charge a premium for the service. ATMs in the city center are linked to major banking systems such as Cirrus and Plus, so you are almost definitely able to draw money directly from your bank account at home.

Dentists

If you have a dental emergency, go to the Edinburgh Dental Institute, 39 Lauriston Place (☎ 0131-536-4900; Bus: 35), open Monday through Friday from 9 a.m. to 3 p.m. Alternatively, call the National Health Service Helpline (☎ 0800-224-488).

Doctors

You can seek help from the Edinburgh Royal Infirmary, 1 Lauriston Place (☎ 0131-536-1000; Bus: 35). The emergency department is open 24 hours.

Emergencies

Call ☎ **999** in an emergency to summon the police, an ambulance, or firefighters. This is a free call.

Hot Lines

Edinburgh and Lothian Woman's Aid is available by calling ☎ 0131-229-1419. Lothian Gay and Lesbian Switchboard (☎ 0131-556-4049) offers advice from 7:30 to 10 p.m. daily; the Lesbian Line is ☎ 0131-557-0751.

Internet Access

EasyEverything, at 58 Rose St., between Frederick and Hanover streets (www.easyeverything.com; Bus: 42), is open daily from 7:30 a.m. to 10:30 p.m. It has 448 terminals. Edinburgh public libraries will have computers with internet connections. Many cafes and hotels now have Wi-Fi.

Laundry/Dry Cleaning

For your dry-cleaning needs, the most central service is probably at Johnson's Cleaners, 23 Frederick St. (☎ 0131-225-8095; Bus: 13, 19, or 42), which is open Monday through Friday from 8 a.m. to 5:30 p.m. and Saturday from 8:30 a.m. to 4 p.m.

Luggage Storage/Lockers

Generally speaking, you can store luggage in lockers at Waverley Station or with your hotel.

Newspapers

Published since 1817, the *Scotsman* is a quality daily newspaper with a national and international perspective, while its sister publication, the *Evening News,* concentrates more on local affairs. For comprehensive arts and entertainment listings and reviews of local shows, buy *The List* magazine, which is published every other Thursday and weekly during the Festival. *Metro,* a free daily (Mon–Fri) available on buses and in train stations, also gives listings of daily events.

Pharmacies

Boots the Chemist has various outlets, including one at 48 Shandwick Place, west of Princes Street (☎ 0131-225-6757; Bus: 12 or 25). It's open Monday through Friday from 8 a.m. to 8 p.m., Saturday from 8 a.m. to 6 p.m., and Sunday from 10:30 a.m. to 4:30 p.m.

Post Office

The Edinburgh Branch Post Office, St. James Centre, is open Monday through Saturday from 9 a.m. to 5:30 p.m. For general postal information and customer service, call ☎ 0845-722-3344.

Restrooms

These are found at rail stations, terminals, restaurants, hotels, pubs, and department stores. A system of public toilets, often marked wc, is in place at strategic corners and squares throughout the city. They're safe and clean but likely to be closed late in the evening.

Safety

Edinburgh is generally one of Europe's safest capitals. But that doesn't mean crimes, especially muggings, don't occur. They do, largely because of Edinburgh's problems with drug abuse.

Weather

For online weather forecasts, check www.metoffice.gov.uk.

Chapter 12

Glasgow

- -

In This Chapter

▶ Getting into town and getting around the city of Glasgow

▶ Discovering the best places to stay and the hottest eateries

▶ Exploring Glasgow, from the Merchant City to the West End

▶ Seeing art treasures at the Kelvingrove and Burrell galleries

▶ Following the Mackintosh and "Greek" Thomson architecture trails

- -

*G*lasgow is only about 74km (46 miles) west of Scotland's capital, Edinburgh, but there's a noticeable contrast between the two cities. Glasgow (*glaaz*-go) doesn't offer the fairy-tale setting of the Scottish capital, but compensates with a lively culture, big-city feel, and gregarious locals.

Glasgow's origins are actually quite ancient, making Edinburgh seem comparatively young. In the 6th century, some 500 years before the first foundations of Edinburgh Castle were set, St. Kentigern (or St. Mungo) is believed to have begun a monastery at the site of **Glasgow Cathedral,** on a hillside along a creek, the Molendiner Burn, that feeds into the mighty River Clyde. Glasgow is a logical site for settlement because it had one of the best places to ford the Clyde before it widens on its way to the sea, which is some 32km (20 miles) away to the west.

However, aside from the Cathedral itself, practically none of this medieval ecclesiastical center (which included a university) remains, and much of Glasgow's historical records (kept at the Cathedral) were lost during the Protestant Reformation. The city became the country's economic powerhouse in the 18th century. Glasgow quickly grew into Scotland's largest city (it is the fourth most populous in the entire U.K.). The boom began in earnest with the tobacco trade to the New World, in which Glasgow outpaced rivals such as London and Bristol largely due to faster sailing times to the New World.

The city then became famous worldwide for shipbuilding, with docks that produced the *Queen Mary, Queen Elizabeth,* and other fabled ocean liners. It was, for a while, the Second City of the Empire. But postindustrial decline gave Glasgow a poor reputation as a city of slums, particularly in contrast to the enduring charms of Edinburgh. Internationally, the city may even now struggle to convince those who last saw Glasgow in the 1970s or early '80s that it's a safe, vibrant, and cosmopolitan city. But it is, indeed, one of the best cities in the U.K.

Throughout the 1980s, Glasgow reversed its fortune by becoming Scotland's contemporary cultural capital, drawing talent from across the U.K., whether in visual art or rock 'n' roll. Decades of grime were sandblasted away from its monumental Victorian buildings and visitors began to recognize that the city had one of Europe's best municipally owned collections of art in the **Burrell Collection** and **Kelvingrove Art Gallery.** In 1990, the city was deemed the European Capital of Culture (a prestigious honor awarded by the European Council of Ministers), thus certifying the changes that had occurred.

Glasgow is not a city without flaws, however. Pockets of poverty remain in its peripheral housing projects (called *estates* or *schemes*). A major motorway cuts a scar through the center of town (and another intrusive freeway is being finished in 2011). Although the splendor of what architectural critics have hailed as "the greatest surviving example of a Victorian city" remains, occasionally Glasgow officials still seem too willing to allow historic buildings to be knocked down.

Glasgow is a good gateway for exploring **Burns Country,** in Ayrshire to the southwest. From the city, you can also tour **Loch Lomond** and see some of the **Highlands,** and you're less than an hour away from **Stirling** and the **Trossach** mountains. Also on Glasgow's doorstep is the scenic estuary of the Firth of Clyde, with islands only a short ride and ferry sailing away. For details on those regions within striking distance from Glasgow, see the chapters in Part IV, "The Major Regions."

Getting to Glasgow

Most flights into Glasgow International Airport from North America connect via London, but some airlines offer direct service. If you're traveling up from London, you can easily take the train to Glasgow. If you're coming from elsewhere in Scotland, highway, train, and bus routes arrive from all directions. The city's two central railway stations (Central and Queen Street) are a couple of blocks from George Square, in the heart of the town, thus within walking distance of each other. Figuring out the best way to come into Glasgow is easy — it all depends on the time you have and the flexibility you desire.

By air

Glasgow International Airport (☎ **0870-040-0008** or 0141-887-1111; www.glasgowairport.com) is located at Abbotsinch, near Paisley, only about 16km (10 miles) west of Glasgow via M8. Monday through Friday, **British Airways (BA)** runs a frequent shuttle service between London's Heathrow Airport and Glasgow. The first flight departs London at around 7 a.m. and the last flight leaves at about 9 p.m.; service is reduced on weekends, depending on volume. Of course, BA offers dozens of international flights into Heathrow. For flight schedules and fares, call BA in London at ☎ **0870-551-1155,** or log on to www.ba.com, which offers a slight discount on ticket prices.

The schedule of direct flights from North America to Glasgow is subject to change. In recent years, **Continental** (☎ **800-523-3273** in the U.S.; www.continental.com) has offered direct service out of Newark International, while **US Airways** (☎ **800-622-1015;** www.usairways.com) has operated flights between Glasgow and Philadelphia for at least half of the year.

BMI (formerly British Midland; ☎ **0870-607-0555;** www.flybmi.com) is another internal U.K. carrier and has flights to European hubs, too. **Aer Lingus** (☎ **800-223-6537,** or 0845-084-4444 at Dublin Airport; www.aerlingus.ie) flies daily from Dublin to Glasgow.

South of Glasgow is **Prestwick International Airport** (☎ **0871-223-0700**), which is favored by some of the low-budget airlines, such as **RyanAir** (☎ **0871-246-0000;** www.ryanair.com). Prestwick is on the main ScotRail line to Ayr, about a 45-minute ride from Glasgow's Central Station. Remember also that **Edinburgh International Airport** is less than 74km (46 miles) away.

Orienting yourself

Glasgow airport is fairly small and therefore presents scant opportunities for getting lost. Immigration control and customs agents are vigilant, but the scene is quite a bit more relaxed than at giant air terminals such as London's Heathrow. Usually there is just one line *(queue)* for visitors from outside the European Union. Arrivals with E.U. passports can generally breeze right through.

Getting into town from the airport

Regular **GlasgowFlyer** bus service (route no. 500; www.glasgowflyer.co.uk) runs frequently between the airport and the city center, terminating at the Buchanan Street Bus Station. The ride takes only about 20 minutes (though it can be much longer during rush hour) and it costs £4.50 for a one-way (single) ticket or £7 for an open return. A taxi to the city center costs about £17.

By train

Trains from London arrive in Glasgow at **Central Station** in the heart of the city (for rail and fare information, contact **National Rail Enquiries;** ☎ **08457-48-49-50;** www.nationalrail.co.uk). The trains that directly link London and Glasgow (via Preston and Carlisle) run on the so-called West Coast Main Line, which had billions of pounds spent on it to create a faster service.

 Alas, in 2010, the newly elected Conservative/Liberal Democratic coalition government announced big cuts to the transportation budget, which could and almost certainly will mean massive increases in train fares in the following five to ten years.

The trains (operated by **Virgin; ☎ 08457-222-333;** www.virgin.com/trains) on the West Coast Main Line depart from London's Euston Station every hour or so and the trip to Glasgow generally takes five and a half hours.

Virgin prices, similar to all the U.K.'s train-operating companies, are varied and complicated. In general, you might get a one-way ticket for as little as £25, although the standard advance-purchase ticket is more likely to be between £90 and £100.

You may prefer trains from London's Kings Cross station, up the East Coast Main Line via Newcastle to Edinburgh; then via Motherwell to Glasgow. The trip takes about the same amount of time as one on the West Coast Main Line. Glasgow's Central Station is also the terminus for trains from the southwest of Scotland and a hub for numerous trains to city suburbs in most directions.

A ten-minute walk away from Central Station (or via bus no. 398) is **Queen Street Station.** From here, the **ScotRail shuttle service** to and from Edinburgh runs every 15 minutes during the day and every 30 minutes in the evenings, until about 11:30 p.m. The round-trip fare during off-peak times (travel from 9:15 a.m.–4:30 p.m. and after 6:30 p.m.) is about £10, and the trip takes about 50 minutes.

Trains to the north (Stirling, Aberdeen, and such Highland destinations as Oban, Inverness, and Fort William), as well as to Glasgow's suburbs, also run frequently through Queen Street Station. By the way, after London, Glasgow has the biggest commuter rail network in Great Britain.

By bus

The journey from London to Glasgow by bus can take at least eight hours. The operators of the buses seem to exchange routes every couple of years, and so it can be confusing. As of this writing, a new service run by **Megabus** (www.megabus.com) is offering the best deal, with one-way fares as low as £15. Buses depart London's Victoria Coach Station to Glasgow's **Buchanan Street Bus Station (☎ 0870-608-2608),** about 2 blocks north of the Queen Street Station on North Hanover Street. Scottish **CityLink (☎ 0870-550-5050;** www.citylink.co.uk) also has frequent bus service to and from Edinburgh.

By car

Glasgow is about 347km (216 miles) north of Manchester, and some 650km (405 miles) north of London. Motorways link London to Glasgow. From England and the south, Glasgow is reached by the M1 or M5 to the M6 in the Midlands, which becomes the M74 at Carlisle. The M74 runs north to Glasgow.

Other routes into the city are the M8 from Edinburgh, the M77 (A77) from Ayr, and the A8 from the west (this becomes the M8 around the town of Port Glasgow). The A82 comes into the city from the northwest (the Western Highlands) on the north bank of the Clyde, and the A80 also goes into the city. (This route is the southwestern section of the M80 and the M9 from Stirling.)

Orienting Yourself in Glasgow

Glasgow is a vibrant modern city with offices, shops, art galleries, theaters, multiplex cinemas, and music halls — not to mention hundreds of bars and restaurants. The monumental heart of Glasgow lies north of the **River Clyde.** This central area is divided between the larger and mostly **Victorian Commercial Centre** and the more compact district now designated the **Merchant City** (in honor of the tobacco and cotton "lords" who lived and ran businesses there from the 1700s). The Merchant City is (roughly) to Glasgow as SoHo is to Manhattan: full of warehouses converted to condos, stylish bars, and trendy restaurants. The **City Centre** offers loads of shopping opportunities on the predominantly pedestrian-only stretches of Argyle, Buchanan, and Sauchiehall streets. If the river creates a southern boundary for "downtown" Glasgow, then the M8 motorway creates both its western and northern limits. The eastern boundary is set by **High Street;** while now on the fringes of the city center, this boulevard was historically at the core of old Glasgow.

Virtually all evidence of Glasgow's medieval existence was demolished by the well-meaning — if history-destroying — urban-renewal schemes of late Georgian and Victorian Glasgow. Practically nothing remains to give any idea of how the city looked before the 18th-century boom, which is a shame because, by some accounts, it was once one of Europe's most attractive medieval burghs. Still standing on the hill at the top of the High Street, however, is **Glasgow Cathedral,** an excellent example of pre-Reformation Gothic architecture that dates in part to the 12th century. Across the square is Provand's Lordship, the city's oldest surviving house, built in the 1470s. Down High Street you find the Tolbooth Steeple (circa 1626) at Glasgow Cross, and nearer the River Clyde is **Glasgow Green,** one of Britain's first large-scale public parks. Glasgow reputedly has more green space per resident than any other European city.

Across town, the city's salubrious and leafy **West End** is home to the University of Glasgow, Kelvingrove Park, and the terraces of Woodlands Hill, rising to Park Circus, which afford excellent views. In the park is a red sandstone palace, the city's **Kelvingrove Art Gallery and Museum** (refurbished and re-opened to mass popular appeal in 2006). Nearby, the tower of Glasgow University dominates Gilmorehill. The district's main street is **Byres Road,** the social and entertainment destination in the West End, full of restaurants, cafes, bars, and shops.

The city's **Southside** sprawls from the River Clyde and is largely residential. A little more than 5km (3 miles) southwest of Glasgow's center in wooded Pollok Country Park is the vaunted **Burrell Collection.** This museum of antiquity and art has become one of the city's top tourist attractions. The commercial heart of the Southside is **Shawlands,** which offers an increasing number of good restaurants; nearby Queens Park is a hilly classic of Victorian planning.

Glasgow's **East End** is only slowly redeveloping after its industrial heyday when tons and tons of steel were manufactured. It's the least affluent district in Glasgow and, according to surveys, is one of the poorest and least healthy areas in all of Europe. But statistics don't tell the entire story. Visitors to the East End's **Gallowgate** on the weekend should see the flea-market stalls of the **Barras.** And East End neighborhoods such as **Dennistoun** are gradually drawing young, creative types who can no longer afford apartments in the West End or the Southside — a renaissance is simmering.

Introducing the neighborhoods

Glasgow is composed of a variety of neighborhoods and districts, from the compact urban area of the Merchant City to the inner-suburban and University of Glasgow–dominated area called Hillhead.

City Centre

Cathedral (Townhead)

St. Mungo apparently arrived here in a.d. 543 and built his little church in what's now the northeastern part of the city's center. **Glasgow Cathedral** (aka St. Kentigern's or St. Mungo's) was at one time surrounded by a variety of buildings: prebendal manses and the long-destroyed Bishops Castle, which stood between the cathedral's west facade and the Provand's Lordship, which still exists in largely its original form. East of the cathedral is one of Britain's largest Victorian cemeteries, Glasgow's Central Necropolis.

Merchant City

The city's first New Town development lies southeast of the city's modern core. The so-called Merchant City extends from Trongate and Argyle Street in the south to George Street in the north. Because the medieval closes off the High Street were regarded as festering sores, the affluent moved to newly developed areas to the west. Now, Merchant City is one of few inner-city areas of Glasgow in which people reside.

Gallowgate

One of the streets that prosperous city businessmen once strolled, the Gallowgate is today the beginning of the city's East End. The Saracen's Head Inn stood here and took in such distinguished guests as Dr. Samuel Johnson and James Boswell in 1774 after the duo's famous tour of the Hebrides. Today, the Gallowgate is best known for the **Barras Market** and **Barrowland,** a one-time ballroom that's now a popular live-music venue.

Saltmarket

The first settlements in Glasgow were on the hill by the Cathedral, but existing almost as early were dwellings in this area at the opposite end of High Street, along the banks of the Clyde. The Saltmarket served as the trading post where the river could be forded. The street named the Bridgegate (*brig*-it) leads to the first crossing erected over the Clyde. Today **Victoria Bridge** crosses the river at the same spot. Constructed in the 1850s, it is the oldest bridge in Glasgow.

Commercial Centre

The biggest of the central districts of Glasgow, the city's Commercial Centre includes areas of 19th-century development, such as Blythswood and Charing Cross (although the latter was severed from the city by the M8 freeway). This area offers Victorian architecture at its finest. Luckily, even though the city had a mind to tear it all to the ground in the mid- to late 1960s, city leaders realized that it had something of real international interest and preserved the area instead.

Broomielaw

It has been said that "the Clyde made Glasgow." From docks here in Broomielaw, Glasgow imported tobacco, cotton, and rum and shipped its manufactured goods around the world. After becoming a rather lost and neglected part of the city, Broomielaw today is targeted for renewal, with luxury flats planned along the riverbank.

Garnethill

Up the steep slopes north of Sauchiehall Street, this neighborhood is best known for the Charles Rennie Mackintosh–designed **Glasgow School of Art.** Developed in the late 1800s, Garnethill offers good views of the city and is also home to the first proper synagogue built in Scotland.

West End

Woodlands

Centering on Park Circus at the crown of Woodlands Hill, this neighborhood is the first one just west of the M8 freeway. It is a mix of residential tenements and retail stretches, particularly on Woodland and Great Western roads. South to the river lies the district of **Finnieston,** and its most visible landmark is the old shipbuilding crane that stands like some giant dinosaur. Along the Clyde is the Scottish Exhibition Centre. West of Woodlands is **Kelvingrove,** with its art gallery, museum, and impressive park.

Hillhead

With the Gilmorehill campus of the University of Glasgow, Hillhead is rather dominated by academia. Its main boulevard is Byres Road, which is the High Street of the West End. In addition to the university, two other major institutions reside in Hillhead: BBC Scotland, on Queen Margaret Drive, and NHS Western Infirmary, next to the University.

Partick

The railway station at Partick is one of the few in the city to translate the stop's name into Gaelic: Partaig. Indeed, the neighborhood has a bit of Highland pride, although there's no particular evidence that Highland people have settled here in great masses. Partick is one of the less pretentious districts of the central West End. To the north are leafy and affluent **Hyndland** and **Dowanhill.**

Southside

Gorbals

If one area seems to represent the slums of early-20th-century Glasgow, it's Gorbals. This neighborhood, just across the Clyde from the city's center, developed a rather notorious reputation for mean streets and unsanitary tenements. As such, the city demolished Gorbals in the early 1960s and erected sets of modern, high apartment towers, which in turn developed a reputation for unsavory and unpleasant conditions. I personally wish that some of the old Gorbals still stood. Today, the towers are coming down and the New Gorbals has been developed on a more human scale, although the fabric of the place still seems torn and frayed. One good thing is that it's home to the **Citizens' Theatre,** one of the most innovative and democratic in the U.K.

Govan

Govan was settled as early as the 10th century, making it another ecclesiastical focal point along with the medieval cathedral north of the river. Until 1912, it was an independent burgh and was one of the key shipbuilding districts on the south banks of the Clyde. One of the first major shipyards in the neighborhood, Mackie & Thomson, opened in 1840. But with the demise of shipbuilding, the fortunes of Govan fell, too. Today, there is hope that the **Science Centre** and other developments in the area (such as a planned new Transport Museum) will revive Govan's fortunes.

Pollokshaws

Along with **Pollokshields** and **Crosshill,** these neighborhoods form the heart of the city's more modern Southside suburbs. **Pollok Park** and the **Burrell Collection** are the key tourist attractions. Queens Park is perhaps better and more verdant than Kelvingrove Park, even if it lacks the monuments and statues of its West End counterpart.

Finding information after you arrive

The **Greater Glasgow and Clyde Valley Tourist Board,** 11 George Sq. (☎ **0141-204-4400;** www.seeglasgow.com; Underground: Buchanan Street), is possibly the country's most helpful office. In addition to piles of brochures, you can find a small bookshop, a Bureau de Change, and a hotel reservation service that charges a booking fee of £3 for local accommodations. During peak season, the office is open Monday through Saturday from 9 a.m. to 7 p.m. and Sunday from 10 a.m. to 6 p.m. Hours are more limited during winter months.

Information about travel can be a bit more frustrating. Start with **Traveline Scotland** (☎ **0871-200-2233;** www.travelinescotland. com), which offers timetable information and advice on routes, but can't quote ticket prices. It will give out the telephone numbers of private bus companies or rail operators, and you will then have to call them for information on ticket prices.

Getting Around Glasgow

One of the best ways to explore Glasgow is on foot, but then I like walking. The center of town is laid out in a grid, which makes map reading relatively easy. However, some of the city's significant attractions, such as the Burrell Collection, are in surrounding districts and to visit those you need to rely on public transportation or a car.

By subway (underground)

The underground, which the city prefers to call officially "the subway," offers a basic 15-stop circular system linking the City Centre, West End, and a bit of the near Southside. Generally, the wait for trains is no more than five to eight minutes, but trains run at longer intervals on Sunday and at night. The one-way fare is $1.10, or you can buy a 20-trip ticket for $19. Another option is the all-day Discovery Ticket for $3.50. The underground runs Monday through Saturday from 6:30 a.m. to about 11:30 p.m.; but, on Sunday, it's only from 11 a.m. to about 6 p.m.

The **Transcentre** (local ticket sales only) at St. Enoch subway station, 2 blocks from the Central Station, is generally open Monday through Saturday from 8:30 a.m. to 5:30 p.m., but it closes early on Wednesday. On Sunday, the hours are 10 a.m. to 5 p.m.

Glasgow and the surrounding region have the largest urban and commuter rail network in Great Britain, after London, and these trains are useful for visitors. Like the subway, the system is managed by the **Strathclyde Partnership for Transport (SPT),** and service runs through both Central and Queen Street stations. During the day, trains run as frequently as every ten minutes or so to destinations in the West End and on the Southside. Service is less frequent after the evening rush hour and terminates around midnight. The trains aren't cheap by European standards: A typical round-trip (return) fare is $3 to $5.50.

For families on an excursion, the SPT **Daytripper** ticket can offer excellent value. For about $18, two adults and up to four children (5–15 years old) can travel anywhere in the system (including broad swaths of Ayrshire) by train, the underground, most buses, and even a few ferries. For one adult and two children the fare is $9.80.

For information on **SPT tickets,** call ☎ **0141-332-6811** Monday through Saturday from 9 a.m. to 5 p.m., or log on to www.spt.co.uk.

Glasgow Orientation

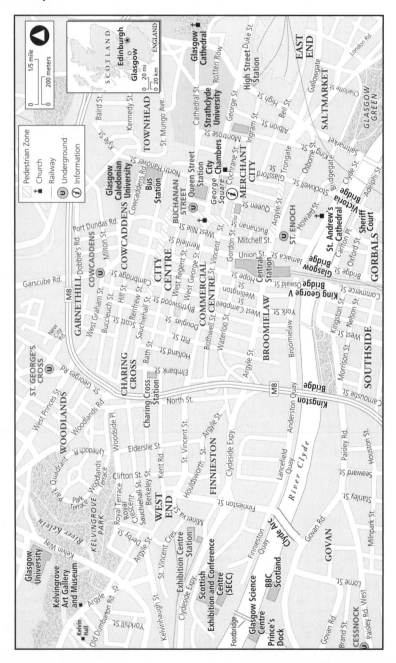

By bus

Glasgow has an extensive (though somewhat confusing) bus service run primarily by the privately owned **First Group** company (www.first group.com). Routes tend to go between east and west or north and south points, with almost all buses coming through the center of Glasgow. Service should be frequent during the day, although, irritatingly, buses seem to arrive at the same time. After 11 p.m., service is curtailed on most routes, but some (for example, the 40 and 62) run all night (at least on weekends), but there is a premium put on tickets. Typically, one-way (single) fares cost no more than $1.80. An all-day ticket is about $4. A weeklong bus pass costs $16. The city bus station is the **Buchanan Street Bus Station.**

By taxi

Metered taxis are the same excellent ones found in Edinburgh or London — the so-called Fast Black, which you can hail or pick up at taxi ranks in the central city. Alternatively, you can call **TOA Taxis** at ☎ 0141-429-7070. No matter the company, fares are displayed on a meter next to the driver. When a taxi is available on the street, a sign on the roof is lit. Most taxi trips within the city cost $6 to $16. A surcharge is imposed for late-night/early-morning runs. **Private hire** cars, run by various companies, are also available, but they can't be hailed. Call ☎ 0141-774-3000.

By car

Glasgow, in reality, goes a long way toward encouraging car use, with several multistory parking lots offering parking prices cheaper than public transit tickets. But traffic, at times, is absolute murder. Metered street parking is available, but expensive. Some zones in residential areas are marked permit holders only — your vehicle may be towed if you lack a permit. A double yellow line along the curb indicates no parking at any time. A single yellow line along the curb indicates restrictions, too, so be sure and read the signs on what the limitations are.

If you want to rent a car, it's best to arrange the rental in advance. If you rent a car locally, most companies will accept your foreign driver's license. All the major rental agencies are represented at the airport. In addition, in the city, try **Avis** at 70 Lancefield St. (☎ 0870-608-6339), **Budget** at 101 Waterloo St. (☎ 0800-212-636), or **Arnold Clark** at multiple locations (☎ 0845-607-4500).

By bicycle

Although bikes aren't as widely used in Glasgow as in Edinburgh, most parts of the city are fine for biking. For rentals, go to a well-recommended shop just off Byres Road: **West End Cycles,** 16–18 Chancellor St. (☎ 0141-357-1344; Underground: Hillhead or Kelvinhall, or Bus: 9 or 18). The shop is close to the National Cycle Trail that leads to Loch Lomond, and you can hire a bike well suited to the hilly terrain of Glasgow and surrounding areas. Bikes cost about $15 per day and a cash deposit or the imprint of a valid credit card will be necessary as security. Closer to the city center, **Alpine Bikes,** in the TISO Outdoor Centre, 50 Couper St. (☎ **0141-552-8575**), near Buchanan Bus Station, offers limited cycle rental. Prices start at £8.

On foot

I contend that walking is the best way to see the Glasgow city center and most of the town (using trains, buses, or taxis if the distances seem too great or the weather is really foul). Some boulevards (such as Buchanan or Sauchiehall streets) have even been made into pedestrian malls.

 But as in any bustling metropolis that's now rather over-dependent on the use of cars, pedestrians should always exercise caution at intersections and other crossing points. Glasgow drivers (including those behind the wheels of city buses) can be a tad aggressive at times. Remember: Cars drive on the left, so when you cross a street, make certain to look both ways.

Staying in Style

The tourist trade in Glasgow is less seasonal than in Edinburgh, with visitors arriving in a steady (but smaller) stream to Scotland's largest city. However, Glasgow is a popular spot for business conferences, and the increase in budget-airline flights from the European continent has clearly increased the overall number of visitors. So if, for example, an international association of astrologists is in town, finding accommodations may be difficult.

Whenever you decide to visit, I recommend that you reserve a room in advance. Some lodging is predictably expensive (though, of course, that partially depends on the relative strength of the dollar to the pound), but many business-oriented hotels offer bargains on weekends, and the number of budget options is increasing. Plus, the Internet can be a real treasure trove of reduced room rates. The Glasgow and Clyde Valley Tourism Office (www.visitscotland.com) offers a **National Booking & Information Service** (☎ **0845-225-5121** from within the U.K., 44-1506-832-121 from outside the U.K.). Lines are open (local time) Monday through Friday from 8 a.m. to 8 p.m. (until 5:30 p.m. in the off season), Saturday from 9 a.m. to 5:30 p.m., and Sunday (during the high season) from 10 a.m. to 4 p.m. The fee for this booking service is £4. All rates quoted below include breakfast, unless otherwise noted.

The top hotels and B&Bs

ABode
$$$ **Commercial Centre**

Formerly the Arthouse hotel, this handsome Edwardian building, only a few blocks from both Central and Queen Street train stations, was originally built to house school board offices. Today, it is a 65-room boutique hotel smack in the heart of the city center. The eponymous fine-dining restaurant, **Michael Caines @ ABode** (p. 212), is under the overall direction of a Michelin-starred chef from England, while a more casual cafe bistro is located in the basement.

See map p. 198. 129 Bath St. ☎ **0141-221-6789.** *Fax: 0141-221-6777.* www.abode hotels.co.uk/glasgow. *Underground: Buchanan St. Rack rates: From £100–£170 double. AE, DC, MC, V.*

Alamo Guest House
$–$$ West End

This highly regarded small hotel faces Kelvingrove Park, the Art Gallery, and Glasgow University. The period furniture and Victorian interior-design details (especially in the entrance hallway) are particularly impressive for the price. Most of the 12 bedrooms, however, share bathroom facilities. Breakfast is buffet style. Still, hard to beat the price.

See map p. 198. 46 Gray St., Glasgow, G3 7SE. ☎ **0141-339-2395.** www.alamo guesthouse.com. *Underground: Kelvinhall. Rack rates: £66 double. MC, V.*

Blythswood Square
$$$–$$$$ Commercial Centre

This most recent addition to the upper end of the market comes from Edinburgh's vaunted Townhouse Group. Extensive renovations have turned the one-time Royal Scottish Automobile Club into a luxury spa hotel. The smart, symmetrical Georgian-style building itself dates to the 1820s: It was originally a block full of town houses facing the square that the auto club knocked together 100 years later. Opening in progression, the much-promoted spa (free allocated time slots excluding treatments for all guests) was still under construction in autumn 2010, although the hotel overnight rooms and well-received restaurant and bar were accepting visitors.

See map p. 198. 11 Blythswood Sq., Glasgow, G2 4AD ☎ **0141-208-2458.** www. townhousecompany.com/blythswoodsquare. *Underground: Buchanan St. Rack rates: £120–£245 double. AE, MC, V.*

Babbity Bowster
$–$$ Merchant City

Housed in a reconstructed late-18th-century house, the Babbity Bowster is a small inn with fairly large character, due in part to the classic design by brothers James and Robert Adam; the rest comes courtesy of the acerbic wit of owner Fraser Laurie (he with the eye patch). The units are well appointed, if modest. But the Babbity Bowster is for travelers who don't spend much time in their rooms. The location is convenient to the many local pubs and restaurants in the nightlife hotbed of the Merchant City, and you only have a five- to ten-minute walk to the heart of central Glasgow. The Babbity's ground-level pub (see later in this chapter) is

Glasgow Accommodations

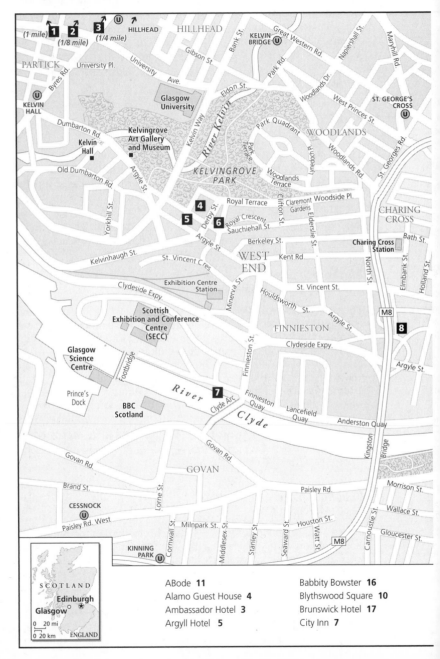

ABode **11**
Alamo Guest House **4**
Ambassador Hotel **3**
Argyll Hotel **5**

Babbity Bowster **16**
Blythswood Square **10**
Brunswick Hotel **17**
City Inn **7**

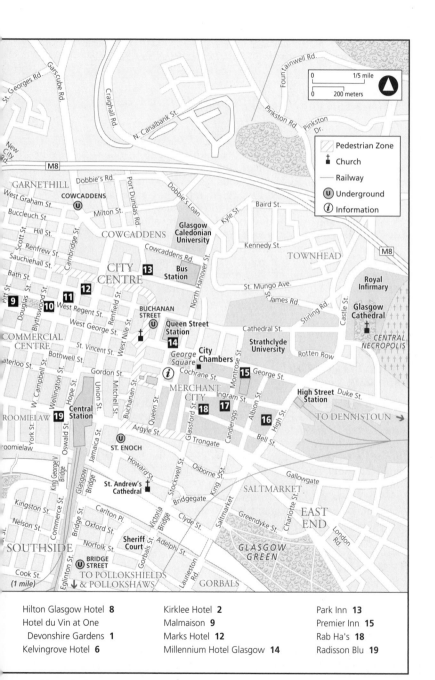

Hilton Glasgow Hotel **8**	Kirklee Hotel **2**	Park Inn **13**
Hotel du Vin at One	Malmaison **9**	Premier Inn **15**
Devonshire Gardens **1**	Marks Hotel **12**	Rab Ha's **18**
Kelvingrove Hotel **6**	Millennium Hotel Glasgow **14**	Radisson Blu **19**

convivial and a second-floor restaurant, **Schottische,** offers French-influenced cooking in the evenings only.

See map p. 198. 16–18 Blackfriars St. (off High Street). ☎ **0141-552-5055.** *Fax: 0141-552-7774. Underground: Buchanan St. Train: High St. Rack rates: £80 double. AE, MC, V.*

Brunswick Hotel
$$ Merchant City

In the Merchant City, the Brunswick Hotel is one of the hippest places to stay in Glasgow. The modern, minimalist design — from the popular cafe/bar Brutti Ma Buoni to the bedrooms with their sleek look — has aged well since the Brunswick's opening in the 1990s. It remains one of a relatively few independently and locally run hotels in town. Some of the 18 units may be on the small side (indeed they're advertised as "compact"), but they are soothing and inviting, with neutral tones, comfortable mattresses, and adequate bathrooms (several with both tubs and showers). For all its trendiness, however, the Brunswick is far from pretentiously run. The owners, Michael and Stephen, are fun-loving cosmopolitans. Indeed, its cafe's name literally means "ugly but good," which may accurately describe the misshapen pizzas that the kitchen churns out, but actually says more about the place's sense of humor. Breakfast is continental style.

See map p. 198. 106–108 Brunswick St. ☎ **0141-552-0001.** *Fax: 0141-552-1551.* www. brunswickhotel.co.uk. *Underground: Buchanan St. Rack rates: £50–£100 double; £400 penthouse suite. AE, DC, MC, V.*

Hilton Glasgow Hotel
$$$–$$$$ Commercial Centre

Glasgow's first-class Hilton is centrally located but oddly situated over the stretch of M8 freeway that slashes through the city of Glasgow. Perhaps the caliber of guests ensures that they all take taxis or have private cars because actually trying to get to and from the place on foot is hardly salubrious amid motorway access roads. Still, the hotel is a dignified and modern hotel, one that has a good deal of class and shine. The 20-story building's numerous units — plush and conservative — offer fine city views. Those staying on the executive floors enjoy the enhanced facilities of a semiprivate club. Dining options include a casual New York deli–style buffet called **Minsky's,** as well as the posh **Camerons,** with first-rate and expensive modern Scottish cuisine.

See map p. 198. 1 William St. ☎ **800-445-8667** *in the U.S. and Canada, or 0141-204-5555. Fax: 0141-204-5004.* www.hilton.co.uk/glasgow. *Train: Charing Cross. Rack rates: £140–£230 double. AE, DC, MC, V.*

Hotel du Vin at One Devonshire Gardens
$$$–$$$$ West End

This hotel (which most still call simply One Devonshire) has been the most glamorous the city has to offer for more than a decade. It's the place where the great and good traditionally stay. Of the guest rooms, the "Balfour" (aka the luxury town house) is the most impressive, with a sitting room, sauna, dining space, exercise room, and so on. Hush Heath, fashioned after a Kentish Manor House, is not far behind in luxury. The Vettriano Suite (in honor of the popular Scottish artist, whose works hang there) has a luxury bathtub in the bedroom (although there are separate toilet/bathing facilities down the stairs, too). I'm not sure there is a poor room in the place. The hotel has an excellent fine-dining, modern restaurant, **Bistro du Vin** (see later in this chapter); and, for all the obvious sumptuousness, it is also family friendly.

See map p. 198. 1 Devonshire Gardens. ☎ **0141-339-2001.** *Fax: 0141-337-1663. www. onedevonshiregardens.com. Underground: Hillhead. Rack rates: From £145 double. AE, DC, MC, V.*

Kelvingrove Hotel
$$ West End

Three generations of women in the Somerville family have made a difference to this guesthouse since buying it in October 2002. They are welcoming hoteliers with 30 years' experience running small lodges in Edinburgh, Inverness, and the Isle of Arran. Staff is helpful, orienting new arrivals, answering questions, booking cabs, or just generally conversing with visitors. The rooms are comfortable with mainly modern furnishings, set within the converted flats on the ground and garden levels. Number 24 is a particularly bright and reasonably spacious family room with kitchenette.

See map p. 198. 944 Sauchiehall St. ☎ **0141-339-5011.** *Fax: 0141-339-6566. www. kelvingrove-hotel.co.uk. Underground: Kelvinhall. Bus: 18, 62, or city sightseeing bus. Rack rates: £60. MC, V.*

Malmaison
$$$ Charing Cross   Commercial Centre

Today there are hip and sophisticated Malmaisons across the U.K., but it all began in Scotland. This converted church, with its fine Greek-styled exterior (though not Eastern Orthodox but rather Episcopal in origin), offers only a few of the original details on the inside — the décor is sleek and modern. In 1997, an annex designed to complement the architectural character of the facade was added to provide additional guest rooms. The 72 units are chic and well appointed with special extras such as CD players, some specially commissioned art, and top-of-the-line toiletries. Rooms vary in dimensions — and, if size matters for you, those in the original church conversion are bigger, with high ceilings — although there is no elevator to the older part of the hotel. In the vaulted spaces below reception is the popular brasserie and champagne bar.

See map p. 198. 278 W. George St. ☎ **0141-572-1000.** *Fax: 0141-572-1002. www. malmaison-glasgow.com. Train: Charing Cross. Bus: 62. Rack rates: £140 double. AE, DC, MC, V.*

Millennium Hotel Glasgow
$$$–$$$$ **George Square** **Commercial Centre**

Following a $5-million upgrade at the turn of the millennium, this land-mark hotel (once called the Copthorne and erected at the beginning of the 19th century) has most of the amenities and services you'd expect of a highly rated hotel. Adjacent to Queen Street Station, the hotel faces the city's central plaza, George Square, and offers views of the opulent Glasgow city chambers, with a conservatory space for dining and drinks. The best units are at the front of the building. The ground-floor restaurant, **Brasserie on George Square,** offers an elegant, neocolonial — but not stuffy — dining experience, while the hotel's Georgics Bar has an excellent selection of wines, many served by the glass.

See map p. 198. George Square. ☎ **0141-332-6711.** *Fax: 0141-332-4264.* www.millenniumhotels.com. *Underground: Buchanan St. Train: Queen St. Rack rates: From £145 double. AE, DC, MC, V.*

Radisson Blu
$$$–$$$$ **Commercial Centre**

Still shiny and new since its November 2002 opening, the Radisson has set architectural standards for hotels in Glasgow. Its dramatic and curving facade is just a stone's throw from Central Station, but it's in a slightly iffy location on the fringe of a portion of the City Centre that's still being rede-veloped. Contemporary units, with blonde-wood details and Scandinavian cool, have all the modern conveniences. The 13,935-sq.-m (15,000-sq.-ft.) club-and-fitness facility includes a 15m (49-ft.) pool and state-of-the-art gym. Its restaurants, **Collage** and **TaPaell'ya,** offer two distinct dining options.

See map p. 198. 301 Argyle St. ☎ **0141-204-3333.** *Fax: 0141-204-3344.* www.radissonsas.com. *Underground: St. Enoch. Rack rates: From £150 double. AE, DC, MC, V.*

Runner-up hotels and B&Bs

Ambassador Hotel
$$ **West End**

Across from the Botanic Gardens, this small 16-unit hotel/guesthouse in an early-20th-century Edwardian mansion overlooks the Kelvin River. Each of the individually decorated and attractively furnished bedrooms has a bathroom with tub and/or shower. The hotel is well situated for exploring the West End, with many good restaurants or brasseries nearby on Byres Road. Suites are spacious enough to accommodate five to seven guests. *See map p. 198. 7 Kelvin Dr.* ☎ **0141-946-1018.** *Fax: 0141-945-5377.* www.glasgowhotelsandapartments.co.uk.

Argyll Hotel
$$ **West End**

The Argyll lives up to its Scottish name: It's full of tartan and kilts. You almost expect this traditional feel to be part of a Highland lodge rather than an urban inn. The hotel has a clutch of spacious family rooms, and one double has a firm four-poster bed and corner-filling bathtub. *See map p. 198. 969–973 Sauchiehall St.* ☎ *0141-337-3313. Fax: 0141-337-3283.* www.argyllhotelglasgow.co.uk.

City Inn
$$ West End

This smart hotel near the conference center, with its waterside terrace, isn't exactly in the heart of the action — but neither is it very far away. Part of a small chain with other hotels in London, Birmingham, Bristol, and Manchester, the City Inn is modern and contemporary with good facilities. *See map p. 198. Finnieston Quay.* ☎ *0141-240-1002. Fax: 0141-248-2754.* www.cityinn.com.

Kirklee Hotel
$$ West End

A red-sandstone Edwardian terraced house, with elegant bay windows near the West End's diverse nightlife, the Kirklee is often recommended by locals. It's graced with a rose garden that has won several awards. Most of the high-ceilinged guest rooms are average size, but some are large enough to accommodate families. *See map p. 198. 11 Kensington Gate.* ☎ *0141-334-5555. Fax: 0141-339-3828.* www.kirkleehotel.co.uk.

Marks Hotel
$$ Commercial Centre

Location, location, location: This modern boutique-style inn is centrally located around the corner from the Mackintosh-designed Willow Tea Rooms. It rises impressively from street level, with oddly angled windows that appear to look down on the ground below. *See map p. 198. 110 Bath St.* ☎ *0141-353-0800. Fax: 0141-353-0900.* www.markshotels.com.

Park Inn
$$–$$$ Commercial Centre

Formerly Langs, this modern hotel opposite the Glasgow Royal Concert Hall and adjacent Buchanan Bus Station, is now in the hands of the Park Inn chain of hotels. Bedrooms in various shapes, sizes, and configurations are available, and each attempts to offer a certain flair. However, the Park Inn is in a busy spot, and late-night noise can be a nuisance for some. *See map p. 198. 2 Port Dundas Place.* ☎ *0141-333-1500. Fax: 0141-333-5700.* www.rezidorparkinn.com.

Premier Inn
$–$$ Merchant City

A branch of an inexpensively priced chain of hotels, this hotel is functional, if not particularly full of character. A fair amount of new construction is going on in the area, so the neighborhood can be noisy during the day. Rooms that overlook the old kirkyard and cemetery are preferable to those facing busy George Street and the Strathclyde University parking lot across the road. *See map p. 198. 187 George St.* ☎ *0870-238-3320. Fax: 0141-553-2719.* www.premierinn.com.

Rab Ha's

$$ **Merchant City**

This small boutique hotel has overnight rooms above a popular and urbane pub on the ground level, as well as a modern restaurant in the basement. The units have dark slate flooring in the bathrooms, specially commissioned glass, photographic prints, and flatscreen televisions. *See map p. 198. 83 Hutcheson St.* ☎ *0141-572-0400. Fax: 0141-572-0402.* www.rabhas.com.

Dining in Glasgow

Like Edinburgh, the dining scene in Glasgow is diverse and includes some outstanding places to dine out. The recession of 2008–09 hit the industry rather hard, but the choice remains good, from the Merchant City district right across to the West End. Although the city cannot boast about any Michelin stars (in stark contrast to Edinburgh), that also means that Glasgow's best is less costly, and the city has some seriously stylish dining rooms, budget-minded bistros, and a mix of ethnic eateries.

Today, some of the best fresh Scottish produce is served up here, whether it's shellfish and seafood from the nearby West Coast sea lochs; Ayrshire meat, such as pork and lamb; or Aberdeen Angus steaks. You can also find an ever-increasing number of ethnic restaurants. The immigrant groups who have most influenced Glasgow's cuisine are Italians and families from the Asian subcontinent, mainly the Punjab region. There's a surfeit of Italian and Indian restaurants, not to mention a decent choice of Chinese and Greek restaurants.

 A lot of restaurants close on Sunday or Monday (sometimes both), and many lock up after lunch, reopening again for dinner at around 6 p.m. The hours listed here are for when food is served; bars on the premises may stay open longer.

For ideas on dining options, buy *The List* magazine's annual **Eating & Drinking Guide,** a comprehensive review of hundreds of eateries in Glasgow (and Edinburgh).

Scotland is getting better at welcoming families, but it's still a far cry from the Continental approach of, say, Italy or France. That said, give the local restaurants a try, and resist the temptation to resort to well-known international chains or fast-food outlets.

Prices

Prices in general could seem expensive if you're the type to immediately convert pounds back into dollars. Still, a range of restaurant choices is available for most budgets. The prices listed here include the 20 percent VAT (value-added tax), so you shouldn't see any hidden surprises when the bill comes. If you're looking for bargains, inquire about pretheater special menus, which can be discounted as much as half the price of regular dinner menus.

Lunch menus in Glasgow often offer the same food as the full dinner menus but at a much better price. If you're trying to save money on your food bills, have a big late lunch or early meal in the evening.

Log on to www.5pm.co.uk for a list of restaurants offering early dining deals.

Tipping

A gratuity of 10 percent is the norm for service, although leave nothing if you were badly treated. On the other hand, if you were truly impressed with the service you received, consider leaving 15 percent to 20 percent. In a few restaurants, service is included in the bill automatically, but this charge can be deleted if the service was dreadful.

Smoking

Smoking is prohibited by law from all enclosed public spaces in Scotland, which includes restaurants and bars. Some places, however, may provide outdoor seating where smoking is allowed.

The top restaurants and cafes

Balbir's
$$ **West End** INDIAN

After a break from running restaurants in Glasgow, Balbir Singh Sumal returned in 2005 to open this large place, serving first-class curries and other Indian specialties. Dishes are lighter than the norm, as his chefs eschew ghee in favor of low-cholesterol rapeseed oil. The tandoori oven is used to good effect with dishes, especially a starter of barbecued salmon, served with fresh chutney. Although not looking particularly worn, 2010 saw a renovation of the interiors. If you're on Glasgow's south side, check out his **Saffron Lounge** at 61 Kilmarnock Rd. (☎ 0141-632-8564).

See map p. 206. 7 Church St. ☎ 0141-339-7711. Underground: Kelvinhall. Main courses: £8–£14. AE, MC, V. Open: Daily 5–10 p.m.

Bistro at One Devonshire Gardens
$$$–$$$$ **West End** MODERN SCOTTISH

In the luxurious Hotel du Vin, this restaurant sets the bar nearly as high as the world-class inn (see p. 200). Chef du Cuisine Paul Tamburrini takes care of the food, with dishes such as braised oxtail terrine, shellfish and

Glasgow Dining

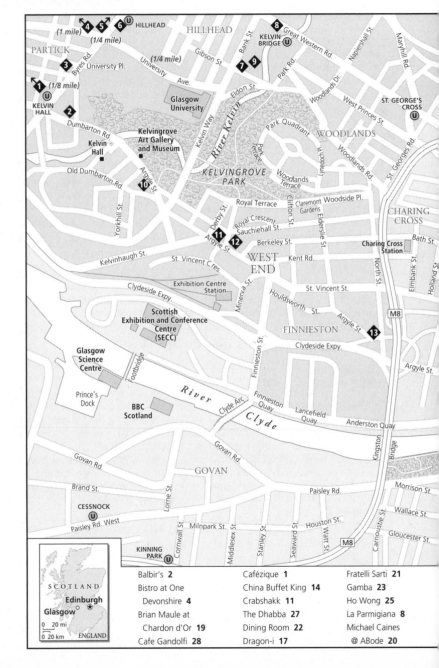

Balbir's **2**	Caféézique **1**	Fratelli Sarti **21**
Bistro at One	China Buffet King **14**	Gamba **23**
Devonshire **4**	Crabshakk **11**	Ho Wong **25**
Brian Maule at	The Dhabba **27**	La Parmigiana **8**
Chardon d'Or **19**	Dining Room **22**	Michael Caines
Cafe Gandolfi **28**	Dragon-i **17**	@ ABode **20**

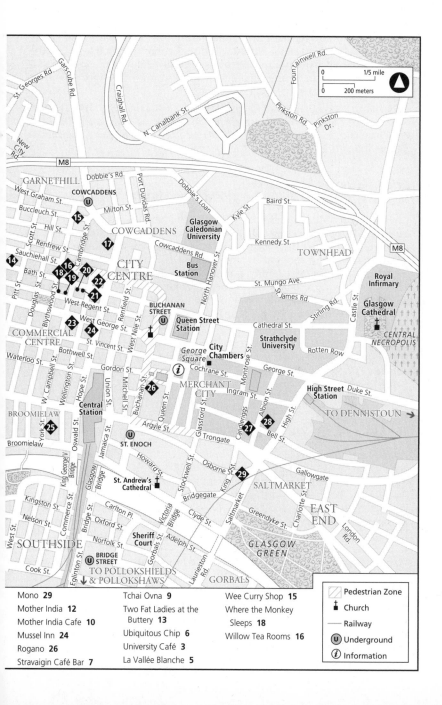

Mono **29**
Mother India **12**
Mother India Cafe **10**
Mussel Inn **24**
Rogano **26**
Stravaigin Café Bar **7**

Tchai Ovna **9**
Two Fat Ladies at the
  Buttery **13**
Ubiquitous Chip **6**
University Café **3**
La Vallée Blanche **5**

Wee Curry Shop **15**
Where the Monkey
  Sleeps **18**
Willow Tea Rooms **16**

☐ Pedestrian Zone
✝ Church
— Railway
Ⓤ Underground
ⓘ Information

smoked haddock soufflé, or butter roasted loin of roe deer. The wine list is large, and the house selections are both diverse and relatively afford-able. Surroundings feel elegant but not stuffy. Staff are relaxed but classy and informed about the foods and wines that come to the table. While the restaurant at this landmark address hasn't quite achieved the heights that it once soared to under the guidance of Michelin star chef Andrew Fairlie, it is certainly flying in the right direction.

Hotel du Vin at One Devonshire Gardens, 1 Devonshire Gardens. ☎ **0141-339-2001.** *www.hotelduvin.com. Reservations required. Fixed-price lunch £15. Main courses: £20–£25. AE, MC, V. Open: Mon–Fri noon to 2:30 p.m. and 6–10 p.m.; Sat 6–10 p.m.; Sun 12:30–3 p.m. and 6–10 p.m.*

Brian Maule at Chardon d'Or
$$$–$$$$ **Commercial Centre   FRENCH/SCOTTISH**

Chef Brian Maule trained with some of the best chefs in France and became part of the team working with the highly respected Roux brothers in London. After rising in rank to head chef at their vaunted Michelin star–winning Gavroche restaurant, he decided to go north and return to Scotland with his young family, opening his own restaurant in Glasgow in 2001. (Maule was born in Ayrshire, near Glasgow.) His place is considered among the finest in the city, with excellent ingredients and an ambience that's classy but not at all stuffy. Fresh fish and lamb dishes are recommended.

See map p. 206. 176 West Regent St. ☎ **0141-248-3801.** *www.brianmaule.com. Reservations required. Underground: Buchanan Street. Fixed-price lunch: £17. Main courses: £20–£26. AE, MC, V. Open: Mon–Fri noon to 2:30 p.m. and 6–10 p.m.; Sat 6–10:30 p.m. Closed Sun (and bank holidays).*

Cafe Gandolfi
$$ **Merchant City   SCOTTISH/CONTINENTAL**

For many local foodies in the Merchant City, this is their favorite: It offers solid cooking at the right price and a friendly ambience. Owner Seumas MacInnes hails from a Hebridean family, so the black pudding comes down from Stornoway on the Isle of Lewis, while the haggis hails from Dingwall in the Highlands. They are both particularly recommended — as is Gandolfi's creamy Cullen skink (smoked haddock chowder) or one of the light pasta dishes. Although if you're hungry, go for the steak sand-wich. The ground-floor room has original, organic, and comfortable wooden furniture created by the Tim Stead workshop in Scotland. Upstairs above the cafe/bistro is **Bar Gandolfi,** which is a bit livelier, while up the street a few doors is **Gandolfi Fish,** the owner's dedicated fish restaurant at 84 Albion St. (☎ **0141-552-9475**).

See map p. 206. 64 Albion St. ☎ **0141-552-6813.** *www.cafegandolfi.com. Reservations recommended. Underground: Buchanan St. Train: High St. Main courses: £8–£12. MC, V. Open: Daily 9 a.m.–11:30 p.m.*

Picnic fare

According to some translations, Glasgow, or *glascau,* means "dear green place." And this "dear green place" has no shortage of picnic spots, whether in sprawling Glasgow Green, along the Clyde near the city center; Kelvingrove Park; or the Botanic Gardens, in the West End — not to mention Pollok Country Park or Queens Park on the Southside.

If you're in the city center, gravitate toward **Pekhams,** in the Merchant City near George Square, 61 Glassford St. (☎ 0141-553-0666), which has a full delicatessen with fresh bread and a wine shop.

In the West End, you are truly spoiled for choice: The options include the wonderful **Heart Buchanan Fine Food and Wine,** 380 Byres Rd. (☎ 0141-334-7626); **Delizique,** 70 Hyndland St. (☎ 0141-339-2000); another branch of **Pekhams,** 124 Byres Rd. (☎ 0141-357-1454); and **Kember & Jones Fine Food Emporium,** 134 Byres Rd. (☎ 0141-337-3851).

For some of the best cheese in the U.K., visit the **IJ Mellis Cheesemonger** branch in Glasgow, at 492 Great Western Rd. (☎ 0141-339-8998). Nearby is the Glasgow branch of **Lupe Pintos,** at 313 Great Western Rd. (☎ 0141-334-5444); it's the perfect stop for Mexican and American foodstuffs. On the Southside in the Shawlands district near Queens Park, the **1901 Deli,** at 11 Skirving St. (☎ 0141-632-1630), has a good supply of goodies for any outdoor feast.

Cafezique
$–$$ West End   CAFE/BISTRO

You're not likely to stumble across Cafezique, but West End locals will know how to find this modern, split level cafe in the Partick neighborhood of the West End. Up the hill from Dumbarton Road and Mansfield Park (which hosts the farmers' markets every fortnight), this busy little space serves up everything from spicy Bloody Marys, cappuccinos, and scones with jam, to knock-out eggs Benedict. Proper main courses are also served up, such as pork chops with mustard mash or grilled Halloumi (cheese) salad, with pickled red onion and pistachio nuts. There's not an inch of unused space, but staff manages to make all feel welcomed. Great wee place.

66 Hyndland St. ☎ *0141-339-7180. Underground: Kelvinhall. Reservations suggested. Main courses £6–£12. MC, V. Open: Daily 9 a.m.–10 p.m.*

Crabshakk
$$–$$$ West End   FISH/SEAFOOD

Established in 2009 by a family with links to Scotland's Western Isles, the only confusing thing about this newcomer is the decision to misspell the name. Not that it seems to be hurting them. Book first. The menu ranges from moderately priced fish dishes, such as smoked mackerel and horseradish or a fish club sandwich with chips, to more pricey whole crab or lobster. And they're only available if found fresh in the market that week.

Crab cakes are a signature dish, and they're wonderfully lacking any potato filler. Langoustines are sold cold or grilled, in small or larger portions. The Finnieston district of Glasgow is a growing foodie destination; but, for visitors, this may feel a bit off the beaten track.

1114 Argyle St. ☎ 0141-334-6127. www.crabshakk.com. Reservations recommended. Underground: Kelvinhall. Bus: 62. Main courses: £7–£17. MC, V. Open: Tues–Sat noon to 10 p.m.; Sun noon to 6 p.m.

The Dhabba
$$–$$$ Merchant City   INDIAN

Glaswegians love their Indian food, as visitors can tell from the sheer number of Indian restaurants in the city. When the Dhabba opened in late 2002, it wasn't your typical Glasgow curry house: It's rather more refined, expensive, and stylish. Others since have followed its lead. In an attempt to be authentic, the restaurant specializes in north Indian dishes and foregoes the bright food coloring that so many other restaurants use. In addition to spicy dishes featuring lamb, chicken, and prawns, the menu also features an excellent selection of vegetarian dishes, which are noticeably less costly than the meat options. Up the street is Dhabba's sister restaurant, **Dakhin** (89 Candleriggs; ☎ **0141-553-2585**), which specializes in lighter south Indian food and serves real, papery rice flour dosas, too.

See map p. 206. 44 Candleriggs. ☎ 0141-553-1249. www.thedhabba.com. Reservations recommended. Underground: St Enoch. Fixed-price lunch: £10. Main courses: £8–£20. AE, MC, V. Open: Mon–Fri noon to 2 p.m. and 5–11 p.m.; Sat–Sun 1–11 p.m.

Dining Room
$$$ Commercial Centre   MODERN SCOTTISH

Formerly Papingo, this is one the best new developments in Glasgow's city center: the return of Chef Jim Kerr after a spell in the hinterlands. Joining with Alan Tomkins (co-owner of Gamba, see below), Kerr has found a partner who should allow him to do what he wants—and some predict that could be Michelin recognition. But even without that, Dining Room is pretty exceptional. Kerr's sashimi starter of delicate slices of uncooked fish is made more memorable with strands of ginger, tomato, chives, soy, and tart citrus yuzu fruit juice. Main courses might include rump of Shetland lamb or roast guinea fowl. Staff is relaxed but totally professional.

See map p. 206. 104 Bath St. ☎ 0141-332-6678. www.diningroomglasgow.com. Underground: Buchanan Street. Reservations recommended. Fixed-price lunch: £14. Main courses £15–£24. AE, MC, V. Open: Mon–Sat noon to 2:30 p.m. and 5–10 p.m., Sun 5–10 p.m.

Dragon-i
$$–$$$ **Commercial Centre**   **CHINESE/FAR EAST**

Convenient for the Theatre Royal, which is virtually across the street, this contemporary Chinese/Far Eastern restaurant is always packed before a show. Expect the unexpected at the elegant Dragon-i, whose cuisine never falls into the bland or typical chow-mein standards. Instead, the menu has dishes such as tiger prawns with asparagus in a garlic chardonnay sauce or chicken with sautéed apples and pineapples. The wine list is also excellent for a Chinese restaurant, and the pretheater menu is good value (just make sure you have a booking if there is a performance across the street).

See map p. 206. 313 Hope St. ☎ *0141-332-7728.* www.dragon-i.co.uk. *Underground: Cowcaddens. Reservations recommended. Main courses: £11–£16. AE, MC, V. Open: Mon–Fri noon to 2 p.m.; daily 5–10 p.m.*

Fratelli Sarti
$–$$ **Commercial Centre**   **ITALIAN**

This dual restaurant and cafe feels like a family run cafe/bistro crossed with a delicatessen. Indeed, you can still buy pasta, grains, beans, canned goods, and wines here, although they stopped carrying deli meats and cheeses a few years ago. The pizzas are excellent, with thin, crispy crusts and modest amounts of sauce, cheese, and toppings, which prevent them from becoming a sloppy mess. Pasta dishes, such as "al forno" with penne, sausage, and spinach, are filling. Come here even if you just want a real Italian espresso and pastry. If you'd like a slightly more formal setting, try the Fratelli Sarti at 21 Renfield St. (☎ **0141-572-7000**).

See map p. 206. 133 Wellington St. ☎ *0141-204-0440.* www.fratellisarti. com. *Underground: Buchanan Street. Reservations recommended. Main courses: £8–£12. AE, MC, V. Open: Mon–Fri 8 a.m.–10 p.m.; Sat 10 a.m.–10 p.m.; Sun noon to 10 p.m.*

Gamba
$$$–$$$$ **Commercial Centre**   **FISH/SEAFOOD**

For many (myself included) this restaurant is Glasgow's best bet on the strength of its fresh fish and seafood dishes prepared by Chef and co-owner Derek Marshall — complemented by the professional and cordial staff. The basement venture is modern and stylish without feeling excessively fancy. Starters include Marshall's signature fish soup or sashimi, with succulent slices of salmon and scallops. Main courses may include whole lemon sole in browned butter or delicate pan-seared sea bream. And desserts are not an afterthought either, whether smooth panna cotta or ice cream infused with Scotch whisky. If you're on a tight budget, however, try the lunch or pretheater fixed-price menu.

See map p. 206. 225a W. George St. ☎ **0141-572-0899**. www.gamba.co.uk. *Reservations required. Underground: Buchanan Street. Fixed-price lunch: £17. Main courses: £20–£26. AE, MC, V. Open: Mon–Sat noon to 2:30 p.m. and 5–10:30 p.m.*

Family-friendly fare

For an all-you-can-eat, buffet-only Chinese restaurant, try the **China Buffet King,** 349 Sauchiehall St. (☎ **0141-333-1788**). It is centrally located, with a good variety of Chinese food and some European dishes, at discount prices for children. Open daily from noon to 11 p.m.

A "Knickerbocker Glory" is an extremely elaborate ice-cream sundae (with fruit, jelly, and more), and few places do it better than the **University Café,** 87 Byres Rd. (☎ **0141-339-5217**). This Art Deco landmark has all its original features, from booths to counter. Open Wednesday through Monday from 9 a.m. to 10 p.m. or so.

Ho Wong
$$$ Broomielaw/Commercial Centre   CHINESE

One of the city's fanciest Chinese restaurants, this classy establishment is on a rather inauspicious block between the river and Argyle Street, just southwest of Glasgow's Central Station (near the Radisson SAS hotel; p. 202). The ambience is refined and even a bit romantic. There are usually several duck dishes on the menu, along with a few types of fresh lobster, plenty of fish options, and some sizzling platters as well. If you have trouble deciding, the buffet makes life a bit easier.

See map p. 206. 82 York St. ☎ *0141-221-3550.* www.ho-wong.com. *Reservations recommended. Underground: St. Enoch. Fixed-price lunch: £11. Main courses: £14–£22. AE, MC, V. Open: Mon–Sat noon to 2 p.m. and 6–11:30 p.m.; Sun 5–10:30 p.m.*

La Parmigiana
$$$ West End   ITALIAN

This remains the favorite fine-dining Italian restaurant in Glasgow, providing a cosmopolitan and Continental atmosphere. A well-established, 25-year-old business of the Giovanazzi family, Parmigiana is often recommended for its fish and meat dishes, whether grilled salmon with honey-roasted vegetables, pan-fried pork cutlet with caramelized apple, or roast breast of guinea fowl stuffed with porcini mushrooms. A highlight of the pasta options is lobster ravioli with basil cream sauce. Service by waiters in smart black vests is usually impeccable.

See map p. 206. 447 Great Western Rd. ☎ *0141-334-0686.* www.laparmigiana. co.uk. *Reservations required. Underground: Kelvinbridge. Fixed-price lunch £15. Main courses: £16–£22. AE, DC, MC, V. Open: Mon–Sat noon to 2:30 p.m. and 5:30–10:30 p.m.*

Michael Caines @ ABode
$$$ Commercial Centre   FRENCH/SCOTTISH

When it opened in 2005, this restaurant had ambitions to be the best in the city. Chef/owner Michael Caines appears on British TV and had already earned Michelin stars in England, but that didn't happen here. Still, it is hard to find fault with cooking and presentation of dishes, such as salmon with spinach ravioli or saddle of venison with "boulangere" (slowly cooked) potatoes, squash puree, and red cabbage. The dining room is modern and stylish, as you would expect in a boutique hotel such as ABode (see p. 196). In addition to this fine-dining restaurant, there is a cafe/bar in the basement.

See map p. 206. 129 Bath St. ☎ **0141-572-6011.** www.michaelcaines.com. *Reservations required. Underground: Buchanan Street. Fixed-price lunch: £13. Fixed-price dinner £19. AE, MC, V. Open: Tues–Sat noon to 2:30 p.m. and 6–10 p.m.*

Mono
$ Saltmarket   VEGAN

In the Saltmarket district near the River Clyde, Mono does basic dairy-free and meat-free meals in laid-back surroundings. Not only a cafe/restaurant with a bar, Mono also houses a CD shop (see "Shopping," later in this chapter) with the latest in indie rock and non-mainstream music. Homemade soups or veggie burgers with fries are typical. The owners also stock a selection of organic wines. Live music, mostly but not exclusively of an acoustic nature, is featured regularly, and the kitchen may close early on gig nights. If this all sounds a tad too "politically correct," relax: It's a welcoming and casual place with a mixed and varied clientele.

See map p. 206. 12 Kings Court. ☎ **0141-553-2400.** *Underground: St. Enoch. Main courses: £5–£9. AE, MC, V. Open: Daily noon to 9 p.m. (bar open until midnight).*

Mother India
$$–$$$ West End   INDIAN

After more than a decade in business, Mother India has established itself as the most respected Indian restaurant in Glasgow: This is the place that people in the know most often recommend. Unlike the norm for Indian restaurants, the menu here isn't overloaded with hundreds of different options. It's short but not simple. Oven-baked fish wrapped in foil is seasoned with aromatic spices, while chicken and zucchini squash are served with a sauce that includes pan-roasted cumin and cardamom. Whether seated on the ground floor or in the dining room above, diners are likely to find the staff courteous and attentive.

Down the road toward the Kelvingrove Gallery, another branch of Mother India with less expensive, small thali-style dishes is worth a stop if you're on a budget: **Mother India's Café** (1355 Argyle St.; ☎ **0141-339-9145**).

See map p. 206. 28 Westminster Terrace (Sauchiehall at Kelvingrove Street). ☎ **0141-221-1663.** www.motherindiaglasgow.co.uk. *Reservations recommended. Underground: Kelvinhall. Fixed-price lunch £9.50. Main courses: £7.50–£12. Open: Mon–Tues 5:30–10 p.m.; Wed–Fri noon to 2:30 p.m. and 5–10:30 p.m.; Sat 1–10:30 p.m.; Sun 4:30–10 p.m.*

Tea for two?

For tea and a snack, join the rest of the tourists in Glasgow and try to secure a table at the landmark **Willow Tea Rooms,** 217 Sauchiehall St. (☎ **0141-332-0521;** Underground: Cowcaddens). When the famed Mrs. Cranston opened the Willow Tea Rooms in 1904, it was something of a sensation due to its unique Charles Rennie Mackintosh design. The building's white facade still stands out from the crowd more than 100 years later. The dining room (one floor above street level) is open Monday to Saturday from 9 a.m. to 5 p.m. and Sunday from noon to 5 p.m. A second branch on Buchanan Street is similarly appointed, if less authentic.

For a more contemporary experience, in the West End overlooking the River Kelvin, **Tchai Ovna,** 42 Otago St. (☎ **0141-357-4524**), has a selection of some 80 teas served in fairly eccentric and bohemian surroundings. In the evenings, you may find live music, poetry, or comedy. Tchai Ovna is open daily from 11 a.m. to 11 p.m.

Mussel Inn

$$–$$$ Commercial Centre   FISH/SEAFOOD

Sister restaurant to the original on Rose Street in Edinburgh, the Mussel Inn has the distinction of being owned by shellfish farmers in the West of Scotland. The kilo pot of mussels you eat here on any given evening may have been harvested only 24 hours earlier. The feel at the Glasgow branch is casual, with an open kitchen, light wood tables, and high ceilings, re-creating the feel you may find if it were located right at the seashore. In addition to the house specialty of steamed mussels served with a choice of broths (from spicy to white wine with garlic), the queen scallop salad is tasty and refreshing, creamy chowders are hearty and filling, and the menu always features a fresh catch of the day.

See map p. 206. 157 Hope St. ☎ *0141-572-1405.* www.mussel-inn.com. *Reservations recommended. Underground: St. Enoch. Main courses: £8–£14. AE, MC, V. Open: Mon–Thurs noon to 2:30 p.m. and 5:30–10 p.m.; Fri–Sat noon to 10 p.m.; Sun 5–10 p.m.*

Rogano

$$$–$$$$ Commercial Centre   FISH/SEAFOOD

A landmark dining establishment, Rogano boasts a well-preserved Art Deco interior, patterned after the *Queen Mary* ocean liner, that dates from the opening of an oyster bar here in 1935. Since then, the space has expanded, and Rogano has hosted virtually every visiting celebrity to the city. Service is attentive and informed. The menu emphasizes seafood, such as halibut or lobster, often in traditional, if possibly old-fashioned, recipes (and alas food doesn't always live up to expectations). A less expensive menu is offered downstairs in **Cafe Rogano,** which serves food straight through the day and where the prices of main courses hover around the £12 mark.

See map p. 206. 11 Exchange Place. ☎ *0141-248-4055.* www.roganoglasgow. com. *Reservations required. Underground: Buchanan Street. Fixed-price lunch: £17. Main courses: £17–£34. AE, DC, MC, V. Open: Daily noon to 2:30 p.m. and 6–10:30 p.m.*

Stravaigin Café Bar
$$ West End   SCOTTISH/GLOBAL

"Think global, eat local" is the motto of Stravaigin, which roughly means "wanderin'" in Scots. While the basement restaurant here is an award-wining enterprise, the ground-level pub/cafe offers less expensive but still memorable food. Scottish produce gets international twists: cheese and herb fritters with sweet chili sauce or roast lamb served with coriander couscous. But you will also find staples such as hearty fish and chips. The atmosphere is always cordial, and prices are lower still during the busy pretheater seating. In the downstairs restaurant, expect concoctions such as Vietnamese-inspired marinated quail served on a candy-smoked egg-plant concasse or mullet served on a bed of Thai noodles with bits of mussels and mushrooms. If you like Stravaigin, you may consider visiting its sister bistro near Byres Road, called, appropriately enough, **Stravaigin 2,** Ruthven Lane (☎ **0141-334-7156**).

See map p. 206. 28 Gibson St. ☎ *0141-334-2665.* www.stravaigin.com. *Underground: Kelvinbridge. Fixed-price lunch: £13. Main courses: £8–£12. AE, MC, V. Open: Daily 11 a.m.–10:30 p.m.*

Two Fat Ladies @ the Buttery
$$$ Commercial Centre/West End   FISH/SCOTTISH

One of the best-known and longest-established dining spaces in Glasgow, though off the beaten track thanks to the manner in which the M8 freeway slashes through the city, the Buttery exudes old-world charm — from its rich, sumptuous bar and lounge to the wood-paneled dining room with white linens. This restaurant and its Victorian tenement home have been standing here since 1870 or so. But in 2007, a new franchise took over the business: Two Fat Ladies, which is a Glasgow operation that best combines moderate prices and excellent fish dishes. In addition to this site, there are branches in the City Centre (118a Blythswood St.; ☎ **0141-847-0088**) and the in West End (88 Dumbarton Rd.; ☎ **0141-339-1944**).

See map p. 206. 652 Argyle St. ☎ *0141-221-8188.* www.twofatladiesrestaurant. com. *Reservations recommended. Train: Anderston. Fixed-price lunch: £16. Main courses: £14–£19. AE, MC, V. Open: Mon–Sat noon to 2:30 p.m. and 5–10 p.m.; Sun 12:30–9 p.m.*

Ubiquitous Chip
$$$$ West End   SCOTTISH

Quite possibly no other restaurant has been more responsible for the culinary renaissance in Scotland than the Ubiquitous Chip. Opening the Chip in 1971, the late Ronnie Clydesdale was ahead of the curve, bringing the best Scottish ingredients into his kitchen — and then to the attention of diners. To this day, the menus state the provenance of the produce, a practice now commonplace in better restaurants. Inside the walls of a former stable, the recently renovated dining room has a roomy interior courtyard with a fountain and masses of climbing vines. The menu may feature Rothesay black pudding, Hebridean Soay lamb, Ardnamurchan venison, Aberdeen Angus filet steak, or Scrabster-landed lythe. Upstairs are a small brasserie, which serves similar quality fare at a fraction of the price, and a friendly pub.

See map p. 206. 12 Ashton Lane, off Byres Road. ☎ **0141-334-5007.** *www.ubiquitous chip.co.uk. Reservations recommended. Underground: Hillhead. Fixed-price meals: Lunch £25; dinner £40. AE, DC, MC, V. Open: Restaurant daily noon to 2:30 p.m. and 5:30–11 p.m. (brasserie daily noon to 11 p.m.).*

La Vallee Blanche
$$$ West End   FRENCH

Opening just before the worst recession on record is awkward timing, but this restaurant, at the top of Byres Road, appears to have ridden out the storm. Named after a glacial gorge, La Vallee Blanche gently mimics Alpine esthetics with wood paneling and lanterns. But the food is not especially rustic. Dishes such as braised pig cheeks, scallops with black pudding and artichoke sauce, or roast guinea fowl are well executed and refined. The set-price lunches emphasize French classics.

360 Byres Rd. ☎ **0141-334-3333.** *www.lavalleeblanche.com. Reservations recommended. Underground: Hillhead. Fixed-price lunch £13. Main courses: £16–£20. MC, V. Open: Tues–Fri noon to 2 p.m. and 5:30–10:30 p.m.; Sat–Sun noon to 10 p.m.*

Wee Curry Shop
$ Commercial Centre   INDIAN

This tiny place is hardly big enough to swing a cat in, but the aptly named Wee Curry Shop offers the best low-cost Indian dishes in the city. Just about five tables are crammed between the front door and the open kitchen, where the chefs prepare everything to order. The menu is concise, with a clutch of opening courses, such as fried pakora, and a half-dozen or so main courses, such as spicy chili garlic chicken. Despite the cheap prices, portions are ample. Although it may feel off the beaten track, the Wee Curry Shop is actually only a short walk from the shopping precincts of Sauchiehall Street.

See map p. 206. 7 Buccleuch St. (near Cambridge Street). ☎ **0141-353-0777.** *Reservations recommended. Underground: Cowcaddens. Fixed-price lunch: £5.25. Main courses: £6.50–£8. Open: Mon–Sat noon to 2 p.m. and 5:30–10 p.m.; Sun 5:30–10 p.m.*

Where the Monkey Sleeps
$ Commercial Centre   CAFE

Downstairs near Blythswood Square, this singular cafe is one of the best daytime places for cappuccinos, soups, and sandwiches in the commercial center of Glasgow. You know you've found it when you see the bikes of messengers who seem to live here when they are not on the streets delivering special letters and business packages. As the name might indicate, this is no ordinary cafe. Sandwich names appear to resemble the hard rock acts so beloved by the owner, and the hit of the mix is probably the "Stoofa," which is a panini with free-range chicken, sage, thyme, red onion, mayo, and balsamic vinegar. Be patient, the place is busy at peak time, but the wait is worth it.

See map p. 206. 182 W. Regent St. ☎ **0141-226-3406.** www.wtms.co.uk. *Underground: Buchanan Street. Soups: £3. Sandwiches: Up to £6. Open: Mon–Fri 8 a.m.–5 p.m.; Sat 10 a.m.–5 p.m.*

Exploring Glasgow

Glasgow for visitors is a reasonably compact and contiguous city— roughly the size of Amsterdam or San Francisco. As its 19th century expansion was inspired in part by such American cities as Chicago, Glasgow's city center is laid out rather U.S.-style on a grid. Not very European, but at least the heart of the city is user friendly. Most visits begin here, amid the rich **Victorian architecture:** 19th-century banks (many of which have been converted to other uses such as restaurants and bars), office buildings, warehouses, and churches. Culturally, the choices in the heart of Glasgow include the **Gallery of Modern Art (GOMA),** the **Lighthouse** (devoted to design and architecture), and the **Centre for Contemporary Art (CCA).** These are all within a fairly short walking distance of one another. Three main boulevards — Argyle, Buchanan, and Sauchiehall streets — form a Z-shape and have been made into predominantly car-free pedestrian zones that offer a wealth of shopping opportunities.

Adjacent to the Commercial Centre is the **Merchant City,** where loft conversions over the past 20 years have created a hip, happening quarter with many lively bars and restaurants. This district skirts the historic heart of Glasgow, but little if anything remains of the medieval city — most of it has been knocked down over the years in various urban renewal schemes. But at either end of the historic High Street, you can see two of the city's more ancient landmarks: **Glasgow Cathedral,** which dates to the 13th century, and the Renaissance **Tolbooth** steeple.

The affluent and urbane **West End** has the city's top university and Kelvingrove Park, as well as some of the city's best restaurants and nightlife. Add in the **Kelvingrove Art Gallery and Museum,** which was fabulously refurbished and reopened in 2006, and the West End is a favorite place for many visitors to explore.

Of course, a river runs through Glasgow, but the city has yet to capitalize fully on the real potential of the **Clyde.** The shipbuilding that made the river famous is long gone, yet there isn't even an active, attractive marina for leisure boats today. Concrete redevelopment of the waterfront, done toward the end of the 20th century, hasn't aged particularly well, although the riverbank, which has a national bicycle path, has a certain run-down, urban charm.

Glasgow Attractions

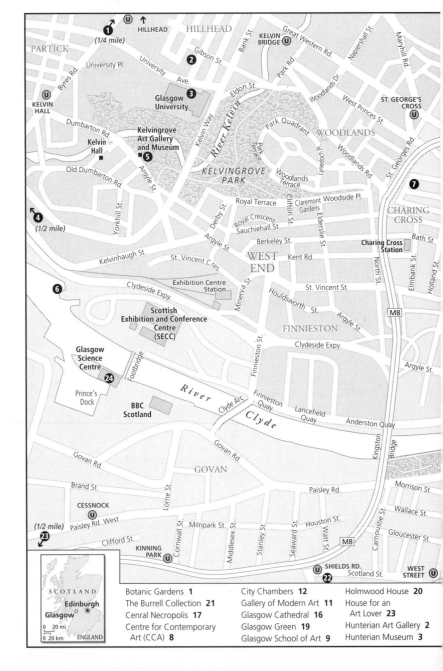

Botanic Gardens **1**
The Burrell Collection **21**
Cenral Necropolis **17**
Centre for Contemporary
   Art (CCA) **8**

City Chambers **12**
Gallery of Modern Art **11**
Glasgow Cathedral **16**
Glasgow Green **19**
Glasgow School of Art **9**

Holmwood House **20**
House for an
   Art Lover **23**
Hunterian Art Gallery **2**
Hunterian Museum **3**

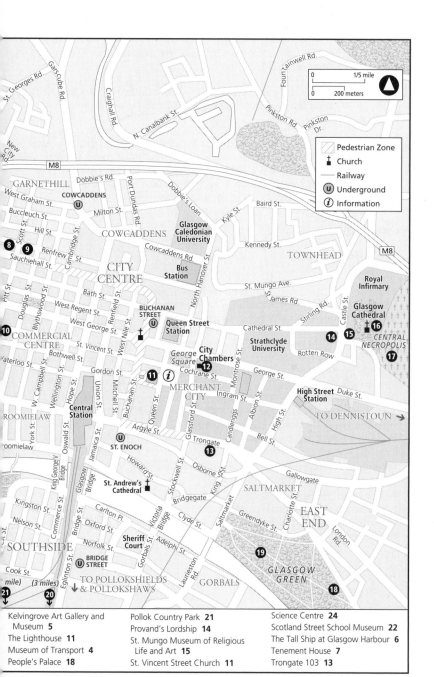

Kelvingrove Art Gallery and Museum **5**
The Lighthouse **11**
Museum of Transport **4**
People's Palace **18**

Pollok Country Park **21**
Provand's Lordship **14**
St. Mungo Museum of Religious Life and Art **15**
St. Vincent Street Church **11**

Science Centre **24**
Scotland Street School Museum **22**
The Tall Ship at Glasgow Harbour **6**
Tenement House **7**
Trongate 103 **13**

On the other side of the River Clyde, the Southside spreads out with mostly residential neighborhoods. Some say this is the "real" Glasgow, and it's home to at least one major, arguably world-class attraction, the **Burrell Collection,** as well as to several other destinations that merit excursions south of the River Clyde.

 At all of Glasgow's city-run museums, from the Gallery of Modern Art to the Burrell Collection, seeing the permanent exhibitions costs you absolutely nothing.

 You'd need at least a few days to visit every place listed in this section, and you'd be more than exhausted by the end of your romp, so you have to make some decisions. If you have children in tow, fewer galleries and more family attractions would be best; if you like art, more museums and fewer wanders may be right up your alley.

The top attractions

 ### *The Burrell Collection*
Southside

This custom-built museum houses many of the 9,000 treasures left to Glasgow by Sir William Burrell, a wealthy ship owner and industrialist who had a lifelong passion for art and artifacts. He started collecting at age 14 and only stopped when he died at the age of 96 in 1958. His tastes were eclectic: Chinese ceramics, French paintings from the 1800s, tapestries, stained-glass windows from churches, even stone doorways from the Middle Ages. Here you can see a vast aggregation of furniture, textiles, ceramics, stained glass, silver, art objects, and pictures. Ancient artifacts, Asian art, and European decorative arts and paintings are featured. It is said that the collector "liked just about everything," and landed one of the very few original bronze casts of Rodin's *The Thinker.* From Sir William's home, Hutton Castle at Berwick-upon-Tweed, the dining room, hall, and drawing room have also been reconstructed and furnished here. A cafe is on site, and you can roam through surrounding Pollok Country Park, some 5km (3 miles) south of the River Clyde.

Nearby **Pollok House (☎ 0141-616-6521)** dates from the 18th century. Now run by the National Trust for Scotland, it features interiors as they were in the Victorian/Edwardian era. Open daily with an admission charge of £8 adults. Allow about two hours.

See map p. 218. Pollok Country Park, 2060 Pollokshaws Rd. ☎ **0141-287-2550.** www. glasgowmuseums.com. *Train: Pollokshaws West. Bus: 45 or 57. Admission: Free. Open: Mon–Thurs and Sat 10 a.m.–5 p.m.; Fri and Sun 11 a.m.–5 p.m. Closed Jan 1 and Dec 25.*

Centre for Contemporary Art (CCA)
Commercial Centre

The CCA is dedicated to the exhibition of cutting-edge art — usually of a conceptual nature — by local artists and those with international reputations. The central and atriumlike space is actually given over to the CCA's popular cafe, but there are other exhibition rooms, plus a small theater, where art-house and foreign films, coordinated by the Glasgow Film Theatre, are screened. Housed in a restored building designed by Alexander "Greek" Thomson, the CCA often hosts art by the nominees for the Beck Futures Awards, which has become one of the leading judges of young talent in Great Britain. Allow about one hour.

See map p. 218. 350 Sauchiehall St. ☎ **0141-352-4900.** http://cca-glasgow. com. *Underground: Cowcaddens. Train: Charing Cross. Bus: 16, 18, 44, or 57. Admission: Free. Open: Tues–Fri 11 a.m.–6 p.m.; Sat 10 a.m.–6 p.m. Closed Sun–Mon, most public holidays, and for two weeks during Christmas and New Year's.*

Gallery of Modern Art (GOMA)
Merchant City

GOMA, as it's usually called, is housed in the former Royal Exchange in Royal Exchange Square, where Ingram Street meets Queen Street. The building — originally surrounded by farmland — was built as a mansion for an 18th-century tobacco magnate. Later it was expanded by one of the city's busy 19th-century architects, David Hamilton, who added a dramatic portico to the front. Now the pile and its square are at the heart of the city, near George Square and Buchanan Street. The galleries, on different floors, are somewhat pretentiously named after earth, fire, air, and water. The permanent collection has works by Stanley Spencer and John Bellany, as well as art from the "new Glasgow Boys," who emerged in the 1980s, such as Peter Howson, Ken Currie, and Steven Campbell. Before controversially becoming the museum in the mid-1990s, the pile was used as a public library; and, recently, the basement was converted to fulfill that function again. Allow about one hour.

See map p. 218. Royal Exchange Square, Queen Street. ☎ **0141-229-1996.** www. glasgowmuseums.com. *Underground: Buchanan Street. Bus: 12, 18, 40, 62, or 66. Admission: Free. Open: Mon–Wed and Sat 10 a.m.–5 p.m.; Thurs 10 a.m.–8 p.m.; Fri and Sun 11 a.m.–5 p.m.*

Glasgow Cathedral
Townhead

Also known as the cathedral of St. Kentigern or St. Mungo's, Glasgow Cathedral dates from the 13th century. The edifice is mainland Scotland's only complete medieval cathedral — the most important ecclesiastical building of that era in the entire country. Unlike other cathedrals across Scotland, this one survived the Reformation practically intact, although 16th-century protestant zeal did purge it of all Roman Catholic relics (as well as destroying plenty of historical documents). Later, misguided architectural "restoration" led to the demolition of its western towers, forever altering the cathedral's appearance.

The lower church is where Gothic design reigns, with an array of pointed arches and piers. The Laigh Kirk (lower church), whose vaulted crypt is said to be one of the finest in Europe, also holds St. Mungo's tomb.

Mungo's death in 612 was recorded, but the annals of his life date only from the 12th century. Other highlights of the interior include the Blackadder aisle and the 15th-century nave with a stone screen (unique in Scotland) showing the seven deadly sins. Allow about one and a half hours.

For one of the best views of the cathedral — and the city, for that matter — I urge you to cross over to the **Central Necropolis,** just east of the cathedral grounds. Built on a proud hill and dominated by a statue of John Knox, this graveyard (modeled in part on the famous Père Lachaise cemetery in Paris) was opened in the 1830s. Coincidentally emblematic of the mixing of ethnic groups in Glasgow, the first person to be buried here was Jewish, as Jews were first to receive permission to use part of the hill as a burial ground. Allow about one hour.

See map p. 218. Glasgow Cathedral, Cathedral Square, Castle Street. ☎ **0141-552-6891.** www.historic-scotland.gov.uk. *Train: High Street. Bus: 11, 36, 37, 38, 42, or 89. Admission: Free. Open: Apr–Sept Mon–Sat 9:30 a.m.–6 p.m., Sun 1–5 p.m.; Oct–Mar Mon–Sat 9:30 a.m.–4 p.m., Sun 1–4 p.m.*

Unappreciated genius: Alexander "Greek" Thomson

Even though architect and designer Charles Rennie Mackintosh (1868–1928) is well known and his worldwide popularity has spurred a cottage industry of "mock-intosh" fakes from jewelry to stationery, a precursor of his was perhaps even more important and innovative. Alexander "Greek" Thomson (1817–75) brought a vision to Victorian Glasgow that was unrivaled by his contemporaries. Although the influence of classical Greek structures — the so-called Greek Revival — was nothing new in the 19th century, Thomson didn't so much replicate Grecian design as hone it to essentials and then mix in Egyptian, Assyrian, and other Eastern-influenced motifs. Similar to Mackintosh's experiences later, Thomson increasingly found himself out of step with the fashions of his day, which architecturally favored Gothic Revival.

An unforgivable number of structures created by the reasonably prolific and successful Thomson have been lost to the wrecker's ball, but some key works remain: terraced houses such as **Moray Place** (where he lived), in the city's Southside, and **Eton Terrace,** in the West End; churches, such as the derelict **Caledonian Road Church** and the still-used **St. Vincent Street Church;** detached homes, such as the **Double Villa** and **Holmwood House;** and commercial structures, such as the **Grecian Buildings** (which today houses the CCA) and **Egyptian Halls.** Just as a Mackintosh trail has been created so that fans can revisit his works, Thomson deserves no less and, in time, may receive his full due.

Ahead of his time: Charles Rennie Mackintosh

Although he's legendary today, architect, designer, and decorator Charles Rennie Mackintosh (1868–1928) was largely forgotten in Scotland at the time of his death. His approach, poised between the Arts and Crafts and Art Nouveau eras, had its fans, however, and history has compensated for any slights he received during his lifetime.

Mackintosh used forms of nature, especially plants, in his interior design motifs, which offered simplicity and harmony that was not the Victorian fashion. Nonetheless, in 1896, Mackintosh's design for the **Glasgow School of Art** won a prestigious competition. Other Mackintosh landmark buildings in the city include the exterior of the old Glasgow Herald building, now the **Lighthouse**; the **Willow Tea Rooms,** on Sauchiehall Street; and the **Scotland Street School.** His West End home from 1906 to 1914 (with wife and collaborator Margaret Macdonald) was itself a work of art, eschewing the fussy clutter of the age for clean, elegant lines. Its interiors have been re-created by the University of Glasgow's Hunterian Gallery (see listing). Forty kilometers (25 miles) west of Glasgow, in Helensburgh, is perhaps his greatest singular achievement: **Hill House,** designed for publisher Walter Blackie in 1902.

Later failures to win commissions locally led Mackintosh to move out of Glasgow, to the southern coast of England and later to Port Vendres, France. In both places, however, his artistic talents were not wasted. He painted watercolors of flowers and landscapes that are as distinctive as his architectural and interior design work.

Glasgow School of Art
Garnethill/Commercial Centre

Architect Charles Rennie Mackintosh's global reputation rests in large part — and deservedly so — on this magnificent building on Garnethill above Sauchiehall Street, a highlight of the Mackintosh trail that legions of his fans from across the world follow through the city. Completed in two stages (1899 and 1909), the building offers a mix of ideas promoted by the Arts and Crafts as well as the Art Nouveau movements. The building is even more amazing because Mackintosh was not yet 30 when he designed the place. It is still a working — and much respected — school whose graduates continue to make their mark in the international art world. Guided tours are the only way to see the entire building, and a highlight of the tour is the library. If you just drop in, the airy landing, one flight up, serves as the school's exhibition space, the Mackintosh Gallery. Around the corner from the main entrance, off Dalhousie Street, you can visit the excellent gift and art supplies shop. Allow at least one hour.

See map p. 218. 167 Renfrew St. ☎ *0141-353-4526.* www.gsa.ac.uk. *Underground: Cowcaddens. Train: Charing Cross. Bus: 16, 18, 44, or 57. Advance reservations recommended for tours. Admission: Tours £8.75 adults, £7 students and seniors, £4 children. Open: Tours Apr–Sept daily 10 a.m., 11 a.m., noon, 2 p.m., 4 p.m. and 5 p.m.; Oct–Mar Mon–Sat 11 a.m. and 3 p.m.; Mackintosh shop open: Daily Apr–Sept 10 a.m.–6 p.m., Oct–Mar 10 a.m.–5 p.m.*

Holmwood House
Southside

This stone villa, designed by Alexander "Greek" Thomson and built in 1858, is probably the best example of his innovative style as applied to stately Victorian homes. Holmwood House is magnificently original, and its restoration (which is ongoing) has revealed that the architect was concerned with almost every element of the house's design, right down to the wallpaper and painted friezes. Visitors have access to most parts of the compact house and surrounding gardens. Most impressive is the overall exterior design as well as the home's parlor, with its circular bay window, the cupola over the staircase, and the detailed cornicing throughout. Allow about one hour.

See map p. 218. 61–63 Netherlee Rd., Cathcart, about 6km (4 miles) south of the city center. ☎ **0141-637-2129.** www.nts.org.uk. *Train: Cathcart. Bus: 44 or 66. Admission: £5.50 adults, £4.50 children, £1 family. Open: Apr–Oct Thurs–Mon noon to 5 p.m. Closed Nov–Mar.*

Hunterian Art Gallery
Hillhead/West End

The University of Glasgow inherited the artistic estate of James McNeill Whistler, with some 60 of his paintings bestowed by his sister-in-law and many hanging in this gallery. The main space exhibits 17th- and 18th-century paintings (Rembrandt to Rubens) and 19th- and 20th-century Scottish works, including some by the so-called Glasgow Boys and the Scottish Colourists, such as Cadell, Hunter, and Fergusson. Temporary exhibits, selected from Scotland's largest collection of prints, are presented in the print gallery. The Hunterian also boasts a collection of Charles Rennie Mackintosh furnishings; and one wing of the building has a re-creation of the architect's Glasgow home from 1906 to 1914 — startling then and no less so today. The **Mackintosh House** covers three levels, decorated in the original style of the famed architect and his artist wife, Margaret Macdonald. All salvageable fittings and fixtures were recovered from the original home before it was demolished in the mid-1960s. The re-creation mimics the original house; the sequence of the rooms is identical. Allow about one and a half hours.

See map p. 218. University of Glasgow, 22 Hillhead St. ☎ **0141-330-5431.** www.hunterian.gla.ac.uk. *Underground: Hillhead. Bus: 44, 59, or city tour. Admission: Gallery free; Mackintosh House £3. Open: Mon–Sat 9:30 a.m.–5 p.m. Closed Sun and public holidays.*

Kelvingrove Art Gallery and Museum
West End

Along with the Burrell Collection (see below), the Kelvingrove Art Gallery and Museum presents the stirring soul of the city's art collection, one of the best amassed by a municipality in Europe. Reopened in 2006 after a three-year and several-million-pound refurbishment, the Kelvingrove can boast that it is the most visited gallery and museum in Scotland — the most popular in the U.K. outside of London. The space features French impressionists and 17th-century Dutch and Flemish paintings. One painting of particular note is *Christ of St. John the Cross* by Spanish surrealist Salvador Dalí. Other highlights include paintings by the Scottish Colourists and the Glasgow Boys, a wing devoted to Mackintosh, as well as more recent art by Anne Redpath and Joan Eardley.

But there is more than art, with exhibits on Scottish and Glasgow history, armory, and war, as well as natural history and nature — often mixing all to good educational effect, such as showing how human armor copied the natural protection of some animals, such as the armadillo. There are plenty of interactive displays and touches of humor, too, such as the creature from which the traditional dish, haggis, is made. The building itself, built for the 1901 Glasgow International Exhibition, is magnificent, as well. In the semi-basement is a new cafe/restaurant. Allow at least two hours, possibly three.

See map p. 218. Argyle Street. ☎ **0141-276-9599.** *www.glasgowmuseums.com. Underground: Kelvinhall. Bus: 9, 16, 18A, 42, or 62. Admission: Free, except for some temporary exhibits. Mon–Thurs and Sat 10 a.m.–5 p.m.; Fri and Sun 11 a.m.–5 p.m.*

People's Palace
East End

This museum covers the social history of Glasgow, with exhibits on how "ordinary people" have lived in the city, especially since the industrial age. It also attempts to explain the Glasgow vernacular — speech patterns and expressions that even Scots from outside the city can have trouble deciphering. Further noteworthy are the murals painted by "new Glasgow Boy" Ken Currie. In front of the museum is the recently restored Doulton Fountain, which was moved here from another spot on Glasgow Green. The spacious **Winter Gardens,** to the rear of the building (along with a cafe), are in a restored Victorian glass house, which offers a nice retreat. Allow about one and a half hours.

See map p. 218. Glasgow Green. ☎ **0141-554-0223.** *www.glasgowmuseums.com. Bus: 16, 18, 40, 61, 62, 64, or 263. Admission: Free. Open: Mon–Thurs and Sat 10 a.m.– 5 p.m.; Fri and Sun 11 a.m.–5 p.m.*

St. Vincent Street-Milton Free Church
Commercial Centre

This should be a four-star, must-see attraction, but public access is limited by the evangelic reformed Free Church of Scotland congregation that worships here. Nevertheless, the church remains the most visible landmark attributed to the city's other great architect, Alexander "Greek" Thomson. Built in 1859, the stone edifice offers two classic Greek porticos facing north and south, aside which a clock tower rises, decorated in all manner of exotic yet curiously sympathetic Egyptian, Assyrian, and even Indian-looking motifs and designs. The interior is surprisingly colorful.

See map p. 218. 265 St. Vincent St. www.greekthomsonchurch.com. Train: Charing Cross. Bus: 62. Admission: Free. Sun services at 11 a.m. and 6:30 p.m. Interiors open only during services.

Science Centre
Govan/Southside

On the banks of the River Clyde and opposite the Scottish Exhibition and Conference Centre, the futuristic-looking buildings of the Science Centre are a focal point to Glasgow's redevelopment of the once rundown former dock lands. The overall theme of the exhibitions is to document 21st-century challenges, as well as Glasgow's contribution to science and technology in the past, present, and future. Families should enjoy the hands-on and interactive activities, whether taking a three-dimensional head scan or starring in their own digital video. The Science Centre also is home to a planetarium and the silver-skinned **IMAX Theatre,** which uses a film with a frame size some ten times larger than the standard 35mm film. The planetarium and theater charge separate admissions. Allow about two hours.

See map p. 218. 50 Pacific Quay. ☎ **0141-420-5010.** *www.glasgowsciencecentre. org. Underground: Cessnock. Train: Exhibition Centre, then walk across the footbridge over the Clyde. Bus: 89 or 90. Admission: £7.95 adults, £5.95 children, students, and seniors. Open: Daily 10 a.m.–6 p.m.*

Tenement House
Garnethill/Commercial Centre

Tenements (or apartment buildings) were what many Glaswegians lived in from the middle of the 19th century, and many still do so today. Run by the National Trust for Scotland, this "museum" is a typical home, preserved with all the fixtures and fittings from the early part of the 20th century: coal fires, box bed in the kitchen, and gas lamps. Indeed, the resident, Miss Agnes Toward, apparently never threw out anything from 1911 to 1965, so there are displays of all sorts of memorabilia, from tickets stubs and letters to ration coupons and photographs from trips down the Clyde. Allow about one hour.

See map p. 218. 145 Buccleuch St., Garnet Hill. ☎ **0141-333-0183.** *www.nts.org. uk. Underground: Cowcaddens. Bus: 11, 20, or 66. Admission: £5.50 adults, £4.50 children, £15 family. Open: Mar–Oct daily 1–5 p.m. Closed Nov–Feb.*

Trongate 103
Merchant City

Opening in 2009, this is an exciting, well-considered artistic development from the City Council. It combines no less than four existing galleries, including the always excellent Glasgow Print Studio, as well as the kinetic sculptures of the Sharmanka Theatre and a Russian Cultural Centre in Café Cossachok. As a locus of creativity, there are also workshops and studios for Glasgow artists. On the first Thursday of the month, the complex opens all the doors and stays open later for the benefit of visitors.

103 Trongate. ☎ **0141-276-8380.** *www.trongate103.com. Admission: Free. Underground: St. Enoch. Bus: 62. Open: Mon–Sat 10 a.m.–5 p.m.; Sun noon to 5 p.m. (though some galleries are closed Mon).*

More cool things to do and see

Botanic Gardens
West End

Glasgow's Botanic Gardens aren't as extensive or as exemplary as the Royal Botanic Gardens in Edinburgh (see p. 161). Nevertheless, they cover some 11 hectares (28 acres). An extensive collection of tropical plants grow in Kibble Palace, the Victorian cast-iron glass house that was recently restored. The plant collection includes some rather acclaimed orchids and begonias. The Botanic Gardens are a good place to unwind and wander, whether through the working vegetable plot or along the banks of the River Kelvin. Allow about one hour.

See map p. 218. Great Western Road. ☎ **0141-334-2422.** *Admission: Free. Underground: Hillhead. Bus: 20, 66, or 90. Open: Gardens daily dawn to dusk; greenhouses daily 10 a.m.–4:45 p.m. (only until 4:15 p.m. in winter).*

City Chambers
Merchant City

Located on George Square, Glasgow's seat of municipal government, the palatial City Chambers, is even more impressive on the inside than on the outside. Even if you don't take the free tour, at least pop your head in to see the cruciform front hall (the only part open to visitors who don't take the tour). Ceiling-tile work and magnificent marble columns appear throughout the building. In fact, the interiors have been used in Hollywood films as a stand-in for both the Vatican and the Kremlin, as well as for an interior shot in *Dr. Zhivago*. The office of the city's Lord Provost (the ceremonial mayor) is here as well. Outside, note a mini Statue of Liberty atop the facade, just below the flag. The tour takes about 45 minutes.

See map p. 218. George Square. ☎ **0141-287-4018.** `www.glasgow.gov.uk`. *Underground: Buchanan Street. Admission: Free. Open: Tours (free) offered Mon–Fri at 10:30 a.m. and 2:30 p.m.*

Glasgow Green
East End

Glasgow Green is the city's oldest park, probably dating back to medieval times. Running along the River Clyde southeast of the Commercial Centre and Merchant City, this huge stretch of green had paths laid and shrubs planted in the middle of the 18th century but didn't formally become a public park until some 100 years later. Its landmarks include the **People's Palace** social history museum and adjoining Winter Garden (see listing earlier in this chapter), the Doulton Fountain, and Nelson's Monument. At the eastern end of the green, the influence of the Doges' Palace in Venice can be easily seen in the colorful facade of the old Templeton Carpet Factory. Near here is a children's large play area. The southern side of Glasgow Green offers dulcet walks along the river. Allow one to four hours.

See map p. 218. Greendyke Street (east of Saltmarket). ☎ **0141-287-5098.** www. glasgow.gov.uk. *Underground: St. Enoch. Bus: 16, 18, 40, 61, 62, or 64. Admission: Free. Open: Daily dawn to dusk.*

House for an Art Lover
Southside

This house, which opened in 1996, was simply based on — or rather inspired by — an incomplete 1901 competition entry of Charles Rennie Mackintosh. Therefore, the building, however elegant, is really just a modern architect's *interpretation* of what Mackintosh had in mind. Crueler minds would call it a pastiche. The tour of the building includes the main hall, the dining room, with its gesso panels, and the music room. Many Mackintosh devotees flock here, but to me it is not the same as the real thing. On the plus side, however, there is the popular **Art Lover's Cafe,** as well as a gift shop, all surrounded by a parkland setting adjacent to Victorian walled gardens. Allow about one hour.

See map p. 218. Bellahouston Park, 10 Dumbreck Rd. ☎ **0141-353-4770.** www. houseforanartlover.co.uk. *Underground: Ibrox. Bus: 9 or 54. Admission: £4.50 adults, £3 students, seniors, children (free for children 9 and under). Open: Apr–Sept Mon–Wed 10 a.m.–4 p.m., Thurs–Sun 10 a.m.–1 p.m.; Oct–Mar Sat–Sun 10 a.m.–1 p.m. Cafe and shop open daily 10 a.m.–5 p.m.*

Hunterian Museum
Hillhead/West End

First opened in 1807, this is Glasgow's oldest museum. It's named after William Hunter, its early benefactor, who donated his private collections in 1783. The original home was a handsome Greek Revival building near High Street, across town on the Old College campus, none of which survives today. Now housed in the main Glasgow University buildings, the collection is wide-ranging: from dinosaur fossils to coins to relics of the Roman occupation and plunder by the Vikings. The story of Captain Cook's voyages is pieced together in ethnographic material from the South Seas. Allow about one hour.

See map p. 218. University of Glasgow, Gilbert-Scott Building. ☎ **0141-330-4221.** www.hunterian.gla.ac.uk. *Underground: Hillhead. Bus: 44, 59, or city tour. Admission: Free. Open: Mon–Sat 9:30 a.m.–5 p.m. Closed Sun and public holidays.*

Museum of Transport
West End

This museum and its collection of many forms of transportation and related technology is closed until summer 2011, when it is expected to reopen in completely new premises as part of the Riverside Museum. For updates on its progress visit the museum's Web site.

www.riversideappeal.org.

Pollok Country Park
Southside

On the Southside, this large, hilly expanse of open space is the home to both the Burrell Collection and Pollok House (see listing earlier in this chapter) but the park merits a visit for its own attributes. Rhododendrons, Japanese maples, and azaleas are part of the formal plantings created at the end of the 19th century by Sir John Stirling Maxwell, whose family were longtime residents of Pollok House. However, the park is best for its glens and pastures, which lend themselves to grazing Highland cattle. Allow one to four hours.

See map p. 218. 2060 Pollokshaws Rd. ☎ **0141-632-9299.** www.glasgow.gov.uk. *Train: Pollokshaws West. Bus: 45 or 57. Admission: Free. Open: Daily dawn to dusk.*

Provand's Lordship
Townhead

Glasgow's oldest house, built in the 1470s, this is the only survivor from what would have been clusters of medieval homes and buildings in this area of the city near Glasgow Cathedral. It is named after a church canon who once resided here. Thanks to the 17th century furniture from the original collection of Sir William Burrell, it shows what the interiors might have been like around 1700. Allow about one hour.

See map p. 218. 3 Castle St. ☎ **0141-552-8819.** www.glasgowmuseums.com. *Train: High St. Bus: 11, 36, 37, 38, 42, or 89. Admission: Free. Open: Mon–Thurs and Sat 10 a.m.–5 p.m.; Fri and Sun 11 a.m.–5 p.m.*

St. Mungo Museum of Religious Life and Art
Townhead

Opened in 1993, this eclectic museum of spirituality is next to Glasgow Cathedral on the site where the Bishop's Castle once stood. It embraces a collection that spans the centuries and highlights various religious groups. It has been hailed as unique in that Buddha, Ganesha, and Shiva, among other spiritual leaders, saints, deities, and historic figures, are treated equally. The grounds include a Zen garden of stone and gravel. Allow about one hour.

See map p. 218. 2 Castle St. ☎ **0141-552-2557.** www.glasgowmuseums.com. *Bus: 11, 36, 38, 42, or 89. Admission: Free. Open: Mon–Thurs and Sat 10 a.m.–5 p.m.; Fri and Sun 11 a.m.–5 p.m.*

Scotland Street School Museum
Southside

Another of Charles Rennie Mackintosh's designs, this building celebrated its centenary in 2005. Given that it is surrounded by light industrial parks and faces the M8 motorway, it seems an odd location for a school. But that's only because all the surrounding apartment buildings were torn down, which is why the school had only about 90 pupils when it shut down in 1979. The museum that occupies this admittedly lesser work from the great architect is devoted to the history of education in Scotland, with reconstructed examples of classrooms from the Victorian, World War II, and 1960s eras. It also has displays of Mackintosh's design for the building. Allow about one hour.

See map p. 218. 225 Scotland St. ☎ **0141-287-0500.** *www.glasgowmuseums.com. Underground: Shields Road. Bus: 89 or 90. Admission: Free. Open: Mon–Thurs and Sat 10 a.m.–5 p.m.; Sun and Fri 11 a.m.–5 p.m.*

The Tall Ship at Glasgow Harbour
West End

Ahoy! Restored in 1999, the SV *Glenlee* is one of only five Clyde-built sailing ships that remain afloat. Built in 1896, it circumnavigated Cape Horn 15 times, and an onboard video shows a black-and-white film illustrating exactly how rough the journey could be. Check out the logbook in the poop cabin. It offers more grim reality, as the captain's diary documents how a sailor is taken ill, recovers, but then dies. You can explore the ship and, while onboard, take in an exhibition detailing cargo-trading history. Allow about one and a half hours.

See map p. 218. 100 Stobcross Rd. ☎ **0141-222-2513.** *www.glenlee.co.uk. Train: Exhibition Centre. Bus: City tour. Admission: £5.95 adults, £4.65 children, seniors, and students. Open: Daily Mar–Oct 10 a.m.–5 p.m.; Nov–Feb 10 a.m.–4 p.m.*

Guided tours

The **City Sightseeing Glasgow** tours circle the town in brightly colored, open-topped buses, departing from George Square about every 15 to 20 minutes between 9:30 a.m. and 5 p.m. You can hop on and off at some 22 designated stops such as Glasgow Green, Glasgow University, or the Royal Concert Hall. Passes are good for two consecutive days. The live commentary can be quite entertaining and informative, too. For more information, contact the office at 153 Queen St. at George Square (☎ **0141-204-0444;** www.scotguide.com). Tickets are £11 adults, £5 children, £25 family.

"The Old Firm"

Glasgow has Scotland's two largest professional soccer teams — Celtic and Rangers — and they are collectively called "the Old Firm." These clubs are among the biggest in the U.K. and both have passionate followers. Alas, given the clubs' histories, fans are also drawn into sectarian (religious/political) disputes that have little to do with modern politics or religion, but can become violent. On some match days, the results are "celebrated" with a few running street battles. The best bet for visitors is to politely avoid discussions regarding the teams, unless you're extremely well versed in Old Firm history and animosities. A safe bet is to declare your allegiance to Partick, Glasgow's small West End club with no sectarian ties.

A festival all its own

There's no doubt that if history could be rewritten, Glasgow would love to be the host of the world-renowned annual Edinburgh Festival. However, the city to the west is not bereft of its own annual happenings. **Celtic Connections** is the best-attended annual festival in Glasgow and the largest of its kind (a folk festival plus more than that description implies) in the world. It kicks off the year every January. The main venue for performances is the Royal Concert Hall, which produces the event. Guests include folk musicians, dancers, and contemporary artists. For more information, contact ☎ **0141-353-8000,** or visit www.celticconnections.com.

If you prefer to keep your feet on the ground and your focus is on the more ghoulish aspects of Glasgow, the guides from **Mercat Glasgow** walking tours are happy to oblige. In season (Easter–Oct), they depart every evening from the Tourist Information Centre at George Square at about 7:30 p.m. Guides re-create macabre Glasgow — a parade of goons including hangmen, ghosts, murderers, and body snatchers. The tours take about one and a half hours. The company also does Historic Glasgow tours on request. For information, contact Mercat at 25 Forth Rd., Bearsden (☎ **0141-586-5378**). Tickets are ₤10.

Waverley Excursions (☎ **0141-221-8152** or 0845-130-4647; www.waverley excursions.co.uk) will take you out on the *Waverley,* considered the world's last "seagoing" paddle steamship, built on the Clyde in 1947. During the summer and depending on weather conditions, it continues to ply the river, with one-day trips beginning at the Glasgow Science Centre. The *Waverley* takes passengers "doon the watter" to historic and scenic places along the Firth of Clyde, sometimes going as far as the Isle of Arran. As you sail along, you can take in what were once vast shipyards turning out more than half the earth's tonnage of oceangoing liners.

Suggested one-, two-, and three-day itineraries

If you feel a bit overwhelmed by all the options of things to do and see in Glasgow, you're not alone. I've laid out a few itineraries in this section to help you focus on your interests and use your time most efficiently, while giving you a good sampling of what Glasgow has to offer. Remember, these are just my ideas — feel free to tailor these itineraries to suit your own schedule and taste.

If you have one day

From George Square (the city's main plaza in front of Glasgow City Chambers and the Queen Street Station), catch one of the open-topped Glasgow **tour buses.** Depending on your guide, the trip can be as entertaining as it is informative. The buses circumnavigate the city from historic **Glasgow Cathedral** and the sprawling riverside park, **Glasgow**

Green in the east, to **Glasgow University** and trendy **Byres Road** in the west. These open tour buses are the best way for visitors to get oriented and understand the city's layout and topography. Tickets are valid for 24 hours, and you can get off and on as much as you desire. Visit at least one of the city-run museums (remember, they're free) and a bona-fide Glasgow pub, such as the **Horse Shoe.**

If you have two days

Spend your first day as I suggest in the one-day itinerary above. Then, try to take in a bit of real **Charles Rennie Mackintosh** architecture by way of an organized tour of the **Art School** on Garnethill, or an unguided visit to the interiors of his family house, reconstructed at Glasgow University's **Hunterian Art Gallery.** Spend more time in the **West End** and check out the renovated **Kelvingrove Art Gallery and Museum.** Or go south and visit the vaunted **Burrell Collection.** Its art and artifacts, from ancient to modern, are the pride of the city, housed in an attractive, contemporary building amid verdant Pollok Country Park.

If you have three days

Follow my one- and two-day itineraries earlier, and on your third day, architecture buffs should discover more about **Alexander "Greek" Thomson,** who preceded Mackintosh by two generations and was equally innovative and important. Try **Holmwood House** on the city's Southside. After London, Glasgow is the second best city for shopping in the entire U.K. But don't be content with the familiar department stores (House of Fraser or John Lewis); seek out the designer labels in Merchant City's **Italian Centre** or some funky shops off Byres Road in the **West End.** Don't miss a visit to the Cathedral; and, if the weather is fine, hike around the nearby **Central Necropolis.** The city's main graveyard occupies a hill, so the views are grand, and the area has also become home to a family of deer.

If you (are lucky and) have four days or more

Having followed my earlier recommendations, those interested in social history may, on their fourth day, want to visit the **People's Palace** museum in **Glasgow Green,** while visitors attuned to contemporary arts have not only the **CCA** but also the **Arches** and **Tramway** to consider. On the weekends, lovers of flea markets owe the **Barras** stalls a visit. You can also take an excursion down the Clyde toward the sea or up the road to **Loch Lomond** and the beginnings of the Highlands. In most directions, it takes a drive of only about 15 to 25 minutes to find open countryside outside Glasgow.

Walking tour: The West End

Because Glasgow is set on fairly gentle hills rising up from a basin created by the River Clyde, the city is amenable to walking. Most perambulations don't involve the scaling of many steep streets, although in order to obtain good vistas, a climb is sometimes obligatory. This stroll takes about two hours (without going inside any buildings) and gives you a sense of Glasgow's salubrious and trendy West End, while hitting some of its landmarks as well. The stroll begins in Charing Cross on Sauchiehall Street, but on the western side of the M8 motorway, which is set in a concrete canyon.

Begin at:

1. **Cameron Fountain**

   From the rusty red-stone fountain, built in 1896 and listing considerably eastward, one can stroll a few blocks south on North Street, which runs parallel to the freeway, to see the Mitchell Library, the largest public reference library in Europe. At the back of the building is the Mitchell Theatre, inscribed with the names of Raphael, Watt, Michelangelo, Newton, and more.

   From the fountain, walk up Woodside Crescent (often abbreviated as "Cres") to:

2. **Woodside Terrace**

   This late Georgian row of homes (designed by George Smith in the 1830s) began an exemplary New Town development. Here you find Greek Doric porticos unlike any in the city. But most of the credit for the overall elegance and charm of Woodlands Hill goes to Charles Wilson, whose designs in the middle of the 19th century are mostly responsible for the terraces up the hillside to Park Circus.

   Continue on Woodside Terrace, turning right (north) on Lynedoch Terrace to Lynedoch Street, and proceed left to:

3. **Trinity College and Park Church Tower**

   The former Trinity College (now Trinity House) is a landmark whose three towers are visible from many approaches to the city. Designed by Charles Wilson, it was constructed in 1857 as the Free Church College. Apparently most of the original interiors were lost when the complex was converted to condos in the 1980s. Across the broad triangular intersection is the cream-colored Park Church Tower. Part of J. T. Rochead's 1856 design, it is the other feature of the neighborhood that is recognizable from some distance. Alas, the church that went with the tower was razed in the late 1960s. Only a steeple remains.

   From here, go left (south) and follow the gentle curve (west) of Woodlands Terrace, turning right (north) at Park Street South to:

4. **Park Circus**

   This oval of handsome and uniform three-story buildings around a small central garden is the heart of Wilson's plans, designed in 1855. No. 22 (now the registration office and site of civil ceremonies) offers the most remarkable interiors, with Corinthian columns and an Art Nouveau billiard room. Attendants are not impressed when uninvited visitors just wander in, however. Luckily, the external door is impressive enough. At the western end of Park Circus is Park Gate, which leads to an entrance to Kelvingrove Park. This promontory offers excellent views towards the University and south to the Clyde.

Enter:

5. **Kelvingrove Park**

Originally West End Park, the development of this hilly and lush open space on the banks of the River Kelvin was commissioned to Sir Joseph Paxton in 1854, although construction apparently began a year before he produced his plans. At this elevated entrance is the statue of Lord Roberts on his steed. Down the hill to the left, the Gothic Stewart Memorial Fountain includes signs of the zodiac and scenes that depict the source of the city's main supply of water: Loch Katrine. Crossing the river below Park Gate at the Highland Light Infantry Memorial is the faded red sandstone Prince of Wales Bridge. Across the bridge, looking back at you, is the head of Thomas Carlyle emerging from the roughly hewn stone.

When facing the bridge at the infantry memorial, go right (north) and follow one of the two paths that run along the river and exit the park at:

6. **Gibson Street**

Leaving the park, turn left (west) and cross the short road bridge that brings you into the Hillhead district, which includes the main campus of the University of Glasgow on Gilmorehill and the Western Infirmary. Gibson Street today offers several eating and drinking options. If you're hungry, stop now.

Continue west on Gibson Street to Bank Street, go right (north) 1 block to Great George Street, then left (west) 1 block to Oakfield Avenue and:

7. **Eton Terrace**

Here, on the corner across from Hillhead High School, the unmistakable work of architect Alexander Thomson is evident in an impressive (if today poorly kept) terrace of eight houses completed in 1864 (following his similarly designed Moray Place). Two temple-like facades serve as bookends, both pushing slightly forward and rising one floor higher than the rest, and have double porches apparently fashioned after the Choragic Monument of Thrassylus in Athens. Ironically, for all his admiration of Eastern design, Thomson never traveled outside the U.K.

Return to the corner of Great George Street and follow Oakfield Avenue south, crossing Gibson Street to University Avenue; then turn right (west) up the hill to the:

8. **University of Glasgow**

Aficionados rightfully bemoan the loss of the original campus east of High Street, which may have offered the best examples of 17th-century architecture in Scotland. The university moved to its current location in the 1860s, and the city could have done worse — a lot worse. The setting high above Kelvingrove Park is befitting of a center of learning. Englishman Sir George Gilbert Scott controversially won the design commission, and his Gothic Revival is punctuated by a tower that rises from the double quadrangle — a virtual beacon on the horizon of the West End. Fragments of the original university can be seen, too, in the facade of Pearce Lodge as well as the salvaged Lion and Unicorn Stair at the chapel.

Cross University Avenue north to Hillhead Street and the:

9. **Hunterian Art Gallery**

Built in the 1980s next to the university library, this gallery houses the school's permanent collection, which includes 18th- and 19th-century Scottish art as well as many works by James McNeill Whistler. Scots-Italian contemporary artist Eduardo Paolozzi designed the chunky cast-aluminum internal doors to the main exhibition space.

Incorporated into the building (past the gift shop) is:

10. **Mackintosh House**

Originally nearby and demolished by the university in the 1960s, the West End home of Charles Rennie Mackintosh and his wife, Margaret Macdonald, is replicated here with furniture and interiors designed by the pair. Visitors enter from the side (the front door is actually several feet above the level of the plaza outside), and see the dining room, sitting room with study, and the couple's bedroom. At the top is a replication of a bedroom Mackintosh designed for a house in England, his final commission.

Return to University Avenue, exit Mackintosh House, turning right to:

11. **University Gardens**

This street features a fine row of houses designed primarily by J. J. Burnet in the 1880s, but it's worth a stop especially to admire no. 12, done by J. Gaff Gillespie in 1900; that house exemplifies Glasgow style and the influences of Mackintosh and Art Nouveau.

Continue down University Gardens, past Queen Margaret Union and other university buildings, going left down the stairs just past the Gregory Building. At the bottom of the stairs, follow the sidewalk and turn right onto:

12. **Ashton Lane**

This cobbled mews is the heart of West End nightlife, although it bustles right through the day, too, with a mix of university students, instructors, and staff, as well as local residents. The host of bars, cafes, and restaurants here include the venerable Ubiquitous Chip, which can be credited for starting (in 1971) the ongoing renaissance of excellent cooking of fresh Scottish produce.

Go left past Ubiquitous Chip down the narrow lane to Byres Road. Just to the right, you can catch the underground (Hillhead station) back to the city center (Buchanan Street station). Or turn right on:

13. **Byres Road**

    Ashton Lane's primary entrance is midway along the proverbial Main Street of this part of Glasgow: Byres Road, which is full of bars, cafes, restaurants, and shops. Rarely less than buzzing, the road exemplifies the West End for many people. If you aren't in a hurry, the streets running west from Byres Road, such as Athole or Huntly Gardens, merit a brief wander to see the proud town houses.

    Proceed north up Byres Road to:

14. **Great Western Road**

    It took an act of Parliament in London in 1836 to create this street, and then a new turnpike road into the city. Today, its four lanes remain one of the main thoroughfares into and out of Glasgow. A stroll west for 5 or 6 blocks from this intersection (Byres and Great Western roads) reveals the opulent terraces (including one by Thomson) along Great Western's southern flank. Going in the opposite direction takes you to more retail and commercial shops.

    Cross Great Western Road to the:

15. **Botanic Gardens**

    Neither as extensive nor as grand as the Royal Botanic Gardens in Edinburgh, this hilly park is pleasant nonetheless. One main attraction, Kibble Palace, is a giant domed cast-iron-and-glass Victorian conservatory with exotic plants. Other greenhouses contain orchid collections, while the outdoor planting includes a working vegetable plot, roses and rhododendrons, and beds with lots of flowering perennials.

Shopping in Glasgow

After London, the capital of Great Britain and a city at least ten times its size, Glasgow apparently has the second most retail space in all of the U.K. It is a shopping mecca for everyone in the west of the country and apparently a reason for people to visit from northern England, too, as it is closer than London and as good as Birmingham.

Among the few retail goods that are high quality *and* priced competitively are fine **wool knits,** particularly cashmere cardigans, sweaters (jumpers), and scarves. Anything produced within the country (with the exception of whisky, which is taxed as heavily as all alcoholic products) should be less expensive than at home: whether **smoked salmon, shortbread,** or **Caithness glass.** Finally, given the number of artists in the country, getting an original piece of **art** to bring home might represent the most value for money.

For visitors from abroad, prices in the U.K. aren't a major selling point. In recent years, the British currency (the pound sterling) has been trading strongly against other major currencies, such as the U.S. dollar and the euro (which most of Great Britain's partners in the European Union use). The good news is that prices for most products in Scotland have been stable since the mid-1990s, and in some cases (for example, clothes) prices have come down in real terms. Nevertheless, many items carry the same numerical price in pounds as they would in American dollars. For example, a digital camera that costs $200 in New York may well be priced almost £200 in Glasgow, making it considerably more expensive in Scotland.

Best shopping areas

The main central area for shopping is defined by the primarily pedestrianized Argyle, Buchanan, and Sauchiehall streets, which join together and form a Z shape right in the heart of the city. But for more unique shops and funkier fashions, it pays to venture into the Merchant City and over to the West End.

And perhaps the city's most unique shopping experience is at the flea market–like stalls at the weekend Barras market, in the East End of Glasgow.

In general, shops in the city are open Monday to Wednesday, Friday, and Saturday from 9 or 10 a.m. until 6 p.m.; and many are open most of the day on Sundays. Only on Thursday do the shops "in town" stay open late — until 8 p.m., at least.

Shopping complexes

Of course, any shopping city worth its salt these days must offer indoor malls. In Glasgow, **Princes Square** (Buchanan Street; ☎ **0141-204-1685;** www.princessquare.co.uk) is the city's most stylish and upmarket shopping center. Housed in a modernized and renovated Victorian building, the mall has many specialty stores, men's and women's fashion outlets, and restaurants, cafes, and bars.

Nearby, between Argyle Street and the River Clyde is the **St. Enoch Shopping Centre** (☎ **0141-204-3900**), whose merchandise is less expensive and a lot less posh than what you find at Princes Square. St. Enoch's resembles a fairly conventional mall, with a couple of major department stores and a food court at one end.

If you're after a fancy wristwatch, silver pendant, or gold ring, go to the historic **Argyll Arcade,** the main entrance to which is at 30 Buchanan St.

Even if the year of its construction (1827) weren't posted above the entrance, you'd still know that this collection of shops beneath a curved glass ceiling is not modern. Purchasing a wedding band here is considered lucky (though some locals beg to differ). The L-shaped arcade contains one of the largest concentrations of retail **jewelers,** both antique and modern, in all of Europe.

The latest contribution to mall shopping in the city center is the **Buchanan Galleries (☎ 0141-333-9898;** www.buchanangalleries. co.uk), found at the top of Buchanan Street. Completed in 1999, this mammoth development is hardly groundbreaking, but it does include the rightfully respected **John Lewis** department store.

On the western outskirts of town, the **Braehead Shopping Centre (☎ 0141-885-1441;** www.braehead.co.uk) opened most recently — and somewhat controversially because it appears to be taking people away from the city center. Braehead's major draw is a sprawling Ikea store and its later hours.

What to look for and where to find it

If your shopping intentions are less of the browsing variety, here are some of Glasgow's specialized shopping options. Unless otherwise indicated, the shops below are in the Commercial Centre of Glasgow and are within walking distance of the Buchanan Street or St. Enoch underground stations.

Antiques

- ✔ **Victorian Village** offers a warren of shops and a pleasantly claustrophobic clutter of goods. Much of the merchandise isn't particularly noteworthy, but you can find some worthwhile pieces if you know what you're after and are willing to go hunting. 93 W. Regent St. (☎ **0141-332-0808**).

Art

- ✔ **Compass Gallery** was opened by Cyril Gerber (see below) to offer affordable pieces of contemporary art by local artists. You can probably find something special for as little as £30 here. The pre-Christmas sale is particularly good. 178 W. Regent St. (☎ **0141-221-6370;** www.compassgallery.co.uk).

- ✔ **Cyril Gerber Fine Art** is one of Glasgow's best small galleries and shops. It veers away from the avant-garde, specializing in British painting of the 19th and 20th centuries. It has good Scottish landscapes and cityscapes, especially works by Colourists and the Glasgow Boys. Gerber has been the city's most respected art authority for several decades, with lots of contacts in art circles throughout Great Britain. 148 W. Regent St. (☎ **0141-221-3095;** www.gerberfineart.co.uk).

- ✔ **Glasgow Print Studio** includes a shop that sells limited-edition etchings, wood blocks, aquatints, and screen prints by members of the prestigious collective as well as other notable artists, such as John Byrne. Now part of the Trongate 103 center (see p. 226), it is better than ever. Prices are good, and there's a framing facility on the premises. 25 King St. (☎ **0141-552-0704;** www.gpsart.co.uk).

Books

✔ **Caledonia Books** is one of the few remaining secondhand and antiquarian shops in the city of Glasgow. It's charming and well run, and the stock here tends to favor quality over quantity. 483 Great Western Rd., West End (☎ **0141-334-9663;** www.caledoniabooks.co.uk).

✔ **Waterstones** is a giant Barnes & Noble–like operation with plenty of stock, a cafe, and a lot of soft seats. The ground floor features a good Scottish section. 174 Sauchiehall St. (☎ **0141-248-4814;** www.waterstones.co.uk).

Clothes

✔ **Che Camille** is the place for bespoke, one-off fashion-led clothing. Run by a young designer, the shop is part clothes shop, design studio, and gallery. The kind of place that can make old-fashioned tweed look cutting edge. Sixth floor, Argyll Chambers, 34 Buchanan St. (☎ **0141-221-9620**).

✔ **Cruise** has the best selection of designer togs in town — better bring your credit cards! Labels include Prada, Armani, D&G, Vivienne Westwood, and more. At the second branch nearby (223 Ingram St.), the Oki-Ni shop-within-the-shop offers limited-edition Adidas and Levi's. 180 Ingram St., Merchant City (☎ **0141-572-3232**).

✔ **Jigsaw** was recently relocated under the glorious dome of the Baroque-style former Savings Bank of Glasgow. This is the fashionable U.K. chain of clothes and accessories for women and juniors. Using its own design team in Kew, West London, Jigsaw opened its first shop in Hampstead some 30 years ago. 177 Ingram St., at Glassford Street (☎ **0141-552-7639**).

✔ **Starry Starry Night** shows just how tiny those Victorians and Edwardians were — although they wore some pretty stunning gowns. This shop (with a branch in the Barras market) normally has a few items worth dusting off. It also stocks secondhand kilts and matching attire. 19 Dowanside Lane, West End (☎ **0141-337-1837**).

✔ **Thomas Pink** is perhaps the closest thing to that temple of preppy sensibilities: Brooks Brothers. This is the place for the finest button-down Oxford shirts that a man could possibly hope for — and a silk tie to match. 1 Royal Bank (☎ **0141-248-9661**).

Department stores

✔ **Debenhams** is a sturdy department store with midrange prices. St. Enoch Shopping Centre, 97 Argyle St. (☎ **0141-221-0088**).

✔ **House of Fraser** is Glasgow's version of Harrods. A Victorian-era glass arcade rises up four stories, and on the various levels you find everything from clothing to Oriental rugs to crystal to hand-made local artifacts of all kinds. 21–45 Buchanan St., at Argyle Street (☎ 0141-221-3880; www.houseoffraser.co.uk).

✔ **John Lewis** is a close equivalent to Macy's, with quality brand names, assured service, and a no-questions-asked return policy on damaged or faulty goods. Buchanan Galleries, 220 Buchanan St. (☎ 0141-353-6677).

✔ **Marks & Spencer** has had its share of problems with shareholders and in board rooms, as anyone who reads international finance pages will know. But the chain carries on with clothing and very good food halls. The two branches in Glasgow are on Argyle and Sauchiehall streets: 2–12 Argyle St. (☎ 0141-552-4546); 172 Sauchiehall St. (☎ 0141-332-6097).

Edibles

See the sidebar "Picnic fare," earlier in this chapter, for a list of select food markets with Scottish specialties.

Gifts and design

✔ **Catherine Shaw** is named after the long-deceased matriarch of the family that still runs this place. It's a somewhat cramped gift shop that has cups, mugs, postcards, jewelry, and souvenirs — a good place for easy-to-pack gifts. 24 Gordon St. (☎ 0141-204-4762). Look for another branch at 31 Argyll Arcade (☎ 0141-221-9038); entrances to the arcade are on both Argyll and Buchanan streets.

✔ **Felix & Oscar** is a wacky and fun shop for offbeat cards and toys, kitsch accessories, fuzzy bags, perfumes and toiletries, and a selection of T-shirts that you're not likely to find anywhere else in Glasgow. (In addition to the flagship, there is another on Cresswell Lane.) 459 Great Western Rd., West End; Underground: Kelvinbridge (☎ 0131-339-8585).

✔ **The Glasgow School of Art Shop** was previously the Mackintosh Shop at the front door of the school, but now it has more space in the basement for art supplies and a stock of bespoke local art — as well as books, cards, stationery, mugs, glassware, and sterling-and-enamel jewelry created from or inspired by the original designs of Charles Rennie Mackintosh. Glasgow School of Art, 11 Dalhousie St. (☎ 0141-353-4500).

Kilts and tartan

✔ **Geoffrey (Tailor) Kiltmakers and Weavers** is both a retailer and a manufacturer of tartans, which means they have all the clans and have also created their own range of 21st-century-style kilts — for better or for worse. 309 Sauchiehall St. (☎ 0141-331-2388; www.geoffreykilts.co.uk).

✔ **Hector Russell** was founded in 1881 and remains Scotland's long-established kilt maker. Crystal and gift items are sold on street level, but the real heart and soul of the place is below, where impeccably crafted and reasonably priced tweed jackets, tartan-patterned accessories, waistcoats, and sweaters of top-quality wool for men and women are displayed. 110 Buchanan St. (☎ **0141-221-0217**).

✔ **James Pringle Weavers** has been in business since 1780. This shop is known for its traditional clothing that includes well-crafted, bulky wool sweaters and a tasteful selection of ties, kilts, and tartans. Some of the merchandise is unique to this shop. Ever slept in a tartan nightshirt? 130 Buchanan St. (☎ **0141-221-3434**).

Music

✔ **Avalanche** is the indie music CD store to beat all others. It's small and cramped (near Queen Street Station), but is the best for the latest releases by everybody from the White Stripes to local stars Belle & Sebastian to up-and-comers. 34 Dundas St. (☎ **0141-332-2099**).

✔ **Fopp** is Glasgow's largest independent outlet. It offers one of the best selections of CDs, ranging from classics to the hottest hits and including music books and vinyl, too. Fopp also stocks a good number of re-releases priced at only £5. 358 Byres Rd., West End (☎ **0141-357-0774**). In addition to the West End flagship, a larger, multistory branch is in the city center on Union Street (☎ **0141-222-2128**).

✔ **Monorail** is located within the vegan restaurant and bar called Mono. This is the most individual of independent CD and record outlets in the city. Glasgow is full of young musicians, and this shop specializes in new music from emerging local acts, as well as the best of cutting-edge bands from elsewhere. 10 King St. (☎ **0141-553-2400**).

Living It Up after Dark

Glasgow — and not Edinburgh — is arguably at the center of contemporary culture in Scotland. There's no doubt that Glasgow has seen the most progress since the middle of the 20th century, when the shipping and industrial boom began to go bust, creating an impression of profound decline. The image was reversed throughout the 1980s. Even during periods of decline, however, Glasgow's local arts scene was always alive, producing musicians, comedians, writers, and visual artists in some abundance.

But ultimately, the truth is this: Both cities contribute mightily — and equally — to the cultural vibrancy of the nation. Their strength as a *pair* of lively cities is considerably more significant than debating which has the most to offer individually. With this idea in mind, the country would do well to improve the public transportation links between the two cities, especially in the wee small hours. Nightlife in both Edinburgh and Glasgow would benefit if officials made it easier to move between the two city centers after dark.

Although the Scottish capital to the east is home to the country's national art galleries and museums, Glasgow is where the national opera and ballet companies, as well as the **Scottish National Orchestra,** are based. It's also the city where young talent is nurtured at the **Royal Scottish Academy of Music and Drama.** Additionally, Glasgow is home to several theaters, including two that rank highly across the U.K. for staging groundbreaking drama: the **Citizens** and the **Tron.** Even more experimental performance can be seen at the **Arches** and **Tramway.**

The performing arts

Although hardly competition for a drama giant such as London, Glasgow's theater scene is the equal of Edinburgh's. Young Scottish playwrights often make their debuts here, and among the classics, you're likely to see anything from Beckett's *Waiting for Godot* to *The Marriage of Figaro.*

- ✔ **The Arches** is located within the vaulted brick arches beneath the railway lines in and out of Central Station. The venue offers a range of inexpensive drama and performances, from edgy new plays to Shakespeare, put on by its own unit as well as visiting companies. But the Arches also has space for a fairly full schedule of live music of all description, regular dance clubs, and visual art exhibits. The cafe/bar at the Arches is, like the one at the Traverse in Edinburgh, a scene unto itself. Tickets are £4 to £10. 253 Argyle St. (☎ 0141-565-1023; www.thearches.co.uk; Underground: St. Enoch).

- ✔ **Citizens Theatre** is perhaps the prime symbol of Glasgow's verve and democratic approach to theater. Located in Gorbals, just across the River Clyde from the Commercial Centre area of Glasgow, the "Citz" is home to a repertory company and has three performance spaces: a main auditorium and two smaller theaters. Ticket prices are always reasonable: £5 to £15. 119 Gorbals St. (☎ 0141-429-0022; www.citz.co.uk; Bus: 5, 12, 20, or 66).

- ✔ **Glasgow Royal Concert Hall** is the home of the **Royal Scottish National Orchestra,** which plays its yearly winter/spring series and pops seasons in the main auditorium. Very little is subtle about this modern music hall, which is the most prestigious performance space in the city for everything from touring ballet companies to pop/rock acts such as Elvis Costello or Jackson Browne. The hall also produces the city's annual Celtic Connections festival every January. Tickets are £10 to £35. 2 Sauchiehall St. (☎ 0141-353-8000; www.grch.com; Underground: Buchanan Street).

- ✔ **The King's Theatre,** an impressive red-sandstone hall, is the place where famous touring Broadway and West End spectacles, such as

Miss Saigon, are likely to appear — as well as locally produced popular and light entertainment, whether comedies, musicals, or family oriented plays. During December and January, the King's is best noted for its over-the-top pantomime presentations, often starring well-known Scottish actors. Tickets are £6 to £26. 297 Bath St. (☎ 0141-240-111; www.theambassadors.com/kings; Train: Charing Cross; Bus: 16 or 18).

✔ **Pavilion Theatre** is, compared to the King's Theatre, an equally historic, if less architecturally distinguished, venue. It specializes in family entertainment, variety shows, light drama, tribute acts, and bands, as well as comedy and occasional modern versions of vaudeville (which, as they assure you around here, is still alive). The Pavilion is a prime location for pantomime around Christmastime. Tickets are £10 to £25. 121 Renfield St. (☎ 0141-332-1846; www.paviliontheatre.co.uk; Underground: Buchanan Street; Bus: 21, 23, or 38).

✔ **The Theatre Royal** is the wonderful home of the ambitious, well-respected **Scottish Opera,** as well as the increasingly acclaimed **Scottish Ballet.** Called by the *Daily Telegraph* "the most beautiful opera theatre in the kingdom," the hall also hosts visiting companies from around the world. Tickets range from £3.50 (standby) to £55. 254 Hope St. (☎ 0141-332-9000; www.theatreroyalglasgow.com; Underground: Cowcaddens; Bus: 20, 40, or 41).

✔ **Tramway** is a postindustrial, huge hangar of an arts venue that famously staged Peter Brook's *The Mahabharata* in the late 1980s. In addition to drama, the former repair shop for the city's trams houses conceptual art exhibits. Tickets for performances range from £4 to £12; exhibit admission is usually free. 25 Albert Dr., Pollokshields, Southside (☎ 0141-330-3050; www.tramway.org; Bus: 38 or 45; Train: Pollokshields East).

✔ **Tron Theatre** is housed in a part of the former Tron Church, which dates from the 15th century. The venue offers one of Scotland's leading stages for new and sometimes experimental dramatic performances. It is often the place where well-acclaimed contemporary local companies, such as Cryptic or Vanishing Point, debut works. In addition to theater, the hall is used for music and dance. The Tron also has a modern bar/cafe as well as a beautifully restored Victorian bar/restaurant serving lunch and dinner, including vegetarian dishes, as well as a fine selection of beer and wine. Tickets are £3 to £20. 63 Trongate (☎ 0141-552-4267; www.tron.co.uk; Underground: St. Enoch).

For a complete rundown of what's happening in the city, pick up a copy of *The List,* a biweekly magazine available at all major newsstands and book shops. *The List* reviews, previews, and gives the details of arts and events in Glasgow and Edinburgh.

Comedy

✔ **Jongleurs Comedy Club** is a corporate-owned entity from down south, with more than a dozen venues across the U.K. The cover charge is £15. UGC Building, Renfield and Renfrew streets (☎ **0870-787-0707;** Underground: Buchanan Street).

✔ **The Stand** opened a second venue in Glasgow after starting and thriving in Edinburgh. Its presence has helped to establish an annual International Comedy Festival every spring in the city. Usually Tuesday night, called "Red Raw," is reserved for amateurs. The cover charge is £2 to £15. 333 Woodlands Rd. (☎ **0870-600-6055;** www.thestand.co.uk; Underground: Kelvinbridge).

Folk music

✔ **Oran Mor** opened in the summer of 2004 as an ambitious center for the performing arts, and includes bars and restaurants as well as different spaces for live music, usually in the folk or Celtic veins. Byres and Great Western roads (☎ **0870-013-2652;** Underground: Hillhead).

✔ **St. Andrew's in the Square** is a sympathetically restored 18th-century church now dedicated to folk and traditional Scottish music. The program also includes chamber orchestra concerts and Scottish country dances in the main hall upstairs. In the basement, **Café Source** serves wholesome Scottish food and hosts regular sessions of jazz and Scottish music, which may be rather reverentially enjoyed by the patrons. Tickets are £5 to £10. 1 St. Andrew's Sq. (☎ **0141-548-6020;** www.standrewsinthesquare.com; Underground: St. Enoch).

✔ **Scotia Bar** is one pub that frequently offers live music that includes, but is not solely, folk. The other place of this sort nearby is the **Clutha Vaults.** No cover charge is required. 112 Stockwell St. (☎ **0141-552-8681**).

Pop, rock, and jazz

✔ **ABC** has room for about 1,250 people in its main hall, making it an excellent place to get a bit closer to the musicians. The building itself dates to 1896 and reportedly screened the first film ever shown in Scotland, although it also housed a permanent circus before reverting to a film house in the 20th century. 300 Sauchiehall St. (☎ **0870-400-0818;** Underground: Cowcaddens.)

✔ **Barrowland** has no seats and may stink of beer, but this former ball-room is the top place in the city to see visiting bands. The hall rocks, and groups generally rank it among the best venues in the U.K. With room for about 2,000 people, Barrowland isn't exactly intimate, but if you can withstand the mosh pit, you feel the sweat of the performers. 244 Gallowgate (☎ **0141-552-4601;** Underground: St. Enoch; Bus: 40, 62, or 262).

✔ **The Academy** is a 2,500-capacity ex–bingo hall that opened as a live music venue in 2003. Not much space to move, but good for bands that favor sit-down audiences. 121 Eglinton Rd. (☎ **0141-418-3000;** Underground: Bridge Street).

✔ **Grand Ole Opry,** a sprawling sandstone building 2.5km (1½ miles) south of the city center, is the largest club in Europe devoted to country and western music. (And they love their country and western music in Glasgow.) The Opry has a bar and dancing (Texas line-style) on two levels and a chuck-wagon eatery that serves affordable steaks and other such fare. Performers are usually from the U.K., but a handful of artists from the States turn up, too. The cover charge is £3 to £10. 2–4 Govan Rd., Paisley Toll Road (☎ **0141-429-5396;** Bus: 9 or 54).

✔ **King Tut's Wah Wah Hut** is a crowded rock bar that has been in business for more than a decade. The upstairs performance space is a good place to check out the Glasgow music and arts crowd as well as local bands and the occasional international act. Successful Scottish acts such as Teenage Fan Club got their starts here. The cover is usually about £5. 272 St. Vincent St. (☎ **0141-221-5279;** Bus: 9 or 62).

✔ **Nice 'n' Sleazy** books live acts to perform in the dark basement space. The cover is quite reasonable, but it can get more expensive if you catch an established act, such as ex-frontman for the Lemonheads, Evan Dando. Holding some 200 patrons, it provides a rare opportunity to catch such musicians in an intimate setting. The cover charge is £5 to £15. 421 Sauchiehall St. (☎ **0141-333-9637;** Bus: 18 or 44; Train: Charing Cross).

✔ **The Scottish Exhibition & Conference Centre,** which incorporates the slightly more intimate Clyde Auditorium (also called the "Armadillo" because of its exterior design), may be somewhat charmless, but it provides Scotland with the only indoor space large enough to host major touring acts, from Ozzy Osbourne to Justin Timberlake. Finnieston Quay (☎ **0141-275-6211;** www.secc.co.uk; Train: Exhibition Centre).

✔ **Stereo** is a vegan cafe with a good basement venue for indie rock acts, such as Cate Le Bon or the Slits, or dance club nights. 28 Renfield St. Lane. (☎ **0141-222-2254;** www.stereocafebar.com; Underground: St. Enoch).

Late-night eats

Famished at four minutes past midnight? Several Indian restaurants are open until 1 a.m., but a couple trump the lot by staying open until 4 a.m. **Charcoals** is in the city center (26 Renfield St.; ☎ 0141-221-9251), while **Spice Gardens** is on the southern bank of the River Clyde (Clyde Place near Bridge Street; ☎ 0141-429-4422).

Dance clubs

✔ **Bamboo** is a stylish basement club with three distinct rooms, one of which is a rather posh cocktail lounge. One room, the Disco Badger club of house and R&B music, gets good notices. Bamboo is open daily from 10 p.m. to 3 a.m. The cover charge is £5 to £10. 51 West Regent St. (☎ 0141-332-1067; Underground: Buchanan Street).

✔ **The Garage** draws a mostly younger crowd for a predominantly Brit pop and indie soundtrack. It's open daily from 11 p.m. to 3 a.m. The cover charge is £2 to £10. 96 Maxwell St. (☎ 0141-221-6511; Underground: Buchanan Street).

Some top bars and pubs

Finally, you have the city's many pubs and bars to consider. Most are friendly places where the locals are likely to strike up a conversation with you. A fine night out trawling the city's many drinking holes is not only entertaining, it can prove to be educational as well.

Pubs and bars are concentrated in the City Centre, Merchant City, and the West End. Hours vary, but most stay open to 11 p.m. or midnight on weeknights, and many have license to remain open until 1 a.m. on the weekends.

✔ **Babbity Bowster** is a civilized place for a pint, with no pounding soundtrack of mindless pop to distract you from conversation. The wine selection is good, and the food is worth sampling as well. Some outdoor seating (although it's rarely in full sun) is also available. Every Saturday from about 4 p.m. on, folk musicians arrive for spontaneous jamming. Drinks are served daily from noon to midnight, food until about 10 p.m. 16 Blackfriars St. (☎ 0141-552-5055; Underground: Buchanan Street).

✔ **Bar 10** is perhaps the granddaddy of the Glasgow-style bar, but, since opening, it has mellowed into a comfortable place for drinking. The groovy design is still apparent, but more important are the good mix of folk and the convenient City Centre location just opposite the Lighthouse architecture center on tiny Mitchell Lane. Comfort food is served from noon to about 5 p.m. Drinks are served Monday through Saturday from noon to midnight and Sunday from 12:30 p.m. to midnight. The place gets even livelier when DJs spin on the weekends. 10 Mitchell Lane (☎ 0141-572-1448; Underground: St. Enoch).

✔ **Blackfriars** has a decent selection of rotating beers, including some from the Continent, even though real ales are less plentiful in Glasgow than in Edinburgh. Jazz is featured in Blackfriars' basement space on Saturdays and Sundays. Drinks are served Monday through Saturday from noon to midnight and Sunday from 12:30 p.m. to midnight. 36 Bell St. (☎ 0141-552-5924; Underground: St. Enoch).

✔ **Bon Accord** is an amiable pub that's the best in the city for hand-pulled cask-conditioned real ale. The pub boasts an array of hand-pumps — a dozen are devoted to real English and Scottish ales, and the rest of the draft and bottled beers and stouts hail from the Czech Republic, Belgium, Germany, Ireland, and Holland. The pub is likely to satisfy your taste in malt whisky as well, and offers affordable pub food. Bon Accord is open Monday through Saturday from noon to midnight and Sunday from noon to 11 p.m. 153 North St. (☎ **0141-248-4427**; Bus: 6, 8, or 16; Train: Charing Cross).

✔ **Brel** is possibly the best of the West End's trendy Ashton Lane's many pubs and bars. Brel has a Belgian theme, with beers and cuisine favoring that country, but it's not overplayed. The music policy is eclectic, with DJs and live acts adding atmosphere to the former stables. The bar is open daily from 10 a.m. to midnight. Food is served Monday through Friday from noon to 3 p.m. and 5 to 10:30 p.m., Saturday and Sunday from noon to 10:30 p.m. 39–43 Ashton Lane (☎ **0141-342-4966**; Underground: Hillhead).

✔ **Heraghty's Free House,** on the city's Southside, is the real McCoy among Glasgow's trendy Irish-themed pubs. It serves up perfect pints of Guinness and Irish *craic* (banter) in almost equal portions. No food, though. Heraghty's is open Monday through Thursday from 11 a.m. to 11 p.m., Friday and Saturday from 11 a.m. to midnight, and Sunday from 12:30 to 11 p.m. 708 Pollokshaws Rd. (☎ **0141-423-0380**; Bus: 38, 45, or 56).

✔ **The Horse Shoe** is the pub you should hit if you can only visit one in Glasgow (though I'm hoping that's not the case). It's one of the last remaining "Palace Pubs" that opened around the turn of the 20th century. The circular, island bar is one of the longest in Europe. Drinks are inexpensive and so is the food from the upstairs buffet. Karaoke draws crowds to the second-floor lounge every night of the week, but conversation and football on the televisions provide the entertainment in the main bar. Drinks are served Monday through Saturday from noon to midnight and Sunday from 12:30 p.m. to midnight. The buffet is open daily until 7:30 p.m., except on Sunday when it closes down at 5 p.m. 17 Drury St. (☎ **0141-229-5711**; Underground: St. Enoch).

✔ **Liquid Ship** is a fairly recent addition to the West End scene. Owned by the same people who run Stravaigin (see p. 215), Liquid Ship is unpretentious and smart but not precisely stylish, with the main bar up a few steps, and a lounge in the basement. Drinks are served Monday through Thursday from noon to 11 p.m., Friday and Saturday from noon to midnight, and Sunday from 12:30 to 11 p.m. Food, platters, and tasty sandwiches on toasted Italian bread are served daily from noon until about 8 p.m. 171 Great Western Rd. (☎ **0141-331-1901**; Underground: St. George's Cross).

- ✔ **Lismore Bar** in Partick is tastefully decorated in a modern manner that still recognizes traditional Highland culture. The whisky selection is good, and the malt of the month is always a bargain. The lounge features live Scottish and Gaelic music Tuesday and Thursday nights. The bar is open Sunday through Thursday from 11 a.m. to 11 p.m. and Friday and Saturday from 11 a.m. to midnight. No food is served. 206 Dumbarton Rd. (☎ **0141-576-0103;** Underground: Kelvinhall).

- ✔ **The Pot Still** is the best place for sampling malt whiskies. You can taste from a selection of hundreds and hundreds of them, in a variety of styles (peaty or sweet), strengths, and maturities (that is, years spent in casks). The Pot Still is open Monday through Thursday from noon to 11 p.m., Friday and Saturday from noon to midnight, and Sunday from 12:30 to 11 p.m. 154 Hope St. (☎ **0141-333-0980;** Underground: Buchanan Street).

- ✔ **Vroni's Wine Bar** is for those who favor the grape over the grain, Bordeaux to brown ale, Sancerre over cider. The feeling of this small bar is Continental, with banquette seating and candlelit tables. It's open Monday through Saturday from 10 a.m. to midnight and Sunday from 12:30 p.m. to midnight, and food is served Monday through Thursday from noon to 7 p.m. and until 3 p.m. on Friday. 47 W. Nile St. (☎ **0141-221-4677;** Underground: Buchanan Street).

- ✔ **WEST** is both a brewery and a bar based on Munich beer halls. In the basement they produce the best, freshest lager in Scotland, following strict German laws for purity and using chemical-free processes. Food leans toward Bavarian dishes, with dumplings, sauerkraut, and meaty mains, with some vegetarian options, too. Drinks are served from noon to midnight; food until about 9 p.m. Binnie Place, Glasgow Green. (☎ **0141-550-0135;** Bus: 16, 43, or 64).

Gay and lesbian Glasgow

Glasgow and its environs are said to have the largest concentration of gays and lesbians in the U.K. outside of London. But there's no identifiable district in the city where the gay and lesbian community is particularly concentrated, although part of the Merchant City has been dubbed the "gay triangle." The **Polo Lounge,** 84 Wilson St., offers a gay but hetero-friendly club often described as a cross between an urbane gentleman's club and a Highland country lodge. It's open daily from 5 p.m. to 1 a.m. (until 3 a.m. Fri–Sat). A £5 cover is charged after 10 p.m. or so. Nearby, **Revolver Bar,** on John Street, is gay owned and operated. The bar has always tried to be a bit more grown-up and to dismiss some of the more cheesy and stereotypical elements of the gay scene, but that doesn't mean that it's not fun or popular. Conversation generally rules, but the jukebox is free. Drinks are served daily from noon to midnight.

Going to the movies

✔ **Cineworld** is the best multiplex in Glasgow. Tickets are £4.50 to £7. 7 Renfrew St. (☎ 0871-200-2000; www.ugccinemas.co.uk; Underground: Buchanan Street).

✔ **Glasgow Film Theatre** has two screens for a well-programmed daily output of independent, foreign, repertory, and art-house films. The building was originally the Cosmo, an Art Deco cinema built in the late 1930s. Within the building, **Café Cosmo** is good for a pre- or post-theater beverage. Tickets are £3 to £5. 12 Rose St. (☎ 0141-332-8128; www.gft.org.uk; Underground: Buchanan Street). The GFT also schedules the films screened at the **Centre for Contemporary Art (CCA),** located at 350 Sauchiehall St.

✔ **The Grosvenor** in the West End was recently refurbished and restored. It has a bar and two downstairs screening rooms with comfy big leather chairs and sofas that you can rent. The cinema screens a mix of mainstream and independent movies. Tickets are £2.50 to £7. Ashton Lane (☎ 0141-339-8444; Underground: Hillhead).

Fast Facts: Glasgow

American Express

The city office has moved to 66 Gordon St. (☎ 0141-225-2905). It is open Monday through Friday from 8:30 a.m. to 5:30 p.m. and Saturday 9 a.m. to noon.

Business Hours

Most offices are open Monday through Friday from 9 a.m. to 5 or 5:30 p.m. Some companies close their doors at 4:30 p.m. on Fridays. Banks are usually open Monday through Friday from 9 or 9:30 a.m. to 4 or 5 p.m., with some branches sometimes closing early on one day a week and opening late on another. Opening times can vary slightly from bank to bank. Shops are generally open Monday through Sunday from 10 a.m. to 6 p.m. On Thursdays, many remain open until 8 p.m.

Currency Exchange

The tourist office at 11 George Sq. (☎ 0141-204-4400) and the American Express office

(see listing earlier) exchange major foreign currencies. Thomas Cook operates a currency exchange at Central Station (generally open until 6 p.m.). Many banks in the city center operate a Bureaux de Change, too, and nearly all banks cash traveler's checks if you have the proper ID. Most ATMs in the city center can also draw money directly from your bank account at home.

Dentists

In an emergency, go to the Accident and Emergency Department of Glasgow Dental Hospital, 378 Sauchiehall St. (☎ 0141-211-9600). Its hours are Monday through Friday from 9:15 a.m. to 3:15 p.m. and Sunday and public holidays from 10:30 a.m. to noon. It's closed on Saturdays. For additional assistance or for emergencies when the hospital is closed, call the National Health Service line (☎ 0800-224-488).

Emergencies

Call ☎ **999** in an emergency to summon the police, an ambulance, or firefighters. This is a free call.

Hospitals

The main hospital for emergency treatment (24 hours) in the city is the Royal Infirmary, 82–86 Castle St. (☎ 0141-211-4000). For additional assistance, call the National Health Service line (☎ 0800-224-488).

Hot lines

The Centre for Women's Health is at Sandyford Place, Sauchiehall Street (☎ 0141-211-6700). Gays and lesbians can call the Strathclyde Gay and Lesbian Switchboard at ☎ 0141-847-0447. The Rape Crisis Centre can be reached at ☎ 0141-331-1990.

Internet Access

You can send or receive e-mail and surf the Net at EasyEverything, 57–61 St. Vincent St. (www.easyeverything.com; Underground: Buchanan Street). This outlet offers more than 350 computers and good rates. It's open Monday through Friday from 7 a.m. to 10 p.m. and Saturday and Sunday from 8 a.m. to 9 p.m. All Glasgow public libraries have Internet access.

Laundry/Dry Cleaning

The most central service is Garnethill Cleaners, 39 Dalhousie St. (☎ 0141-332-2387; Underground: Cowcaddens), which is open Monday through Saturday from about 7:30 a.m. to 6:30 p.m. and Sunday from 8 a.m. to 5 p.m.

Library

The Mitchell Library is on North Street at Kent Road (☎ 0141-287-2999; Train: Charing Cross; Bus: 9 or 16). The 19th-century building is home to one of the largest libraries in Europe. Newspapers and books, as well as kilometers of microfilm, are available. The library is open Monday through Thursday from 9 a.m. to 8 p.m. and Friday and Saturday from 9 a.m. to 5 p.m.

Newspapers and Magazines

Published since 1783, the *Herald* is the major newspaper with national, international, and financial news, sports, and cultural listings. The *Evening Times* offers local news, and the *Daily Record* is for tabloid enthusiasts only. For complete events listings, *The List* magazine is published every other week. On the buses and trains, pick up a free *Metro,* which also has events listings. For international newspapers, go to Borders at 98 Buchanan St. (☎ 0141-222-7700; Underground: Buchanan Street).

Pharmacies

Your best bet is Boots the Chemist at 200 Sauchiehall St. (☎ 0141-332-1925), which is open Monday through Saturday from 8 a.m. to 6 p.m. (until 7 p.m. on Thurs), and Sunday from 11 a.m. to 5 p.m.

Police

In a real emergency, call ☎ **999.** This is a free call. For other inquiries, contact Strathclyde police headquarters on Pitt Street at ☎ 0141-532-2000.

Post Office

The main branch is at 47 St. Vincent's St. (☎ 0141-204-3689; Underground: Buchanan Street). It's open Monday through Friday from 8:30 a.m. to 5:45 p.m. and Saturday from 9 a.m. to 5:30 p.m. For general postal information, call ☎ 0845-722-3344.

Restrooms

Public toilets can be found at rail stations, bus stations, air terminals, restaurants, hotels, pubs, and department stores. Glasgow also has a system of public toilets, often marked wc. Don't hesitate to use them, but they're likely to be closed late in the evening.

Safety

While Glasgow may be the most dangerous city in Scotland, it's relatively safe when compared to cities of its size in the United States. Muggings do occur, and often they're related to Glasgow's drug problem.

The famed razor gangs of Calton, Bridgeton, and the Gorbals are no longer around to earn the city a reputation for violence, but you still should stay alert.

Weather

For weather forecasts check `www.met office.gov.uk`.

Chapter 13

Going Beyond Edinburgh and Glasgow: Day Trips

● ●

In This Chapter

▶ Discovering the coastline and castles of East Lothian

▶ Exploring Linlithgow Palace and Hopetoun House

▶ Seeing New Lanark's groundbreaking workers' village

▶ Visiting the quintessential Mackintosh-designed house

● ●

I don't think that you'll get bored in either Edinburgh or Glasgow, but there are other attractions located near both cities that are worth your consideration, too.

First from Edinburgh: The closest regions are **West Lothian** and **East Lothian,** located on either side of the city. The highlights in these areas include the impressive ruins of **Linlithgow Palace,** a favorite of the Stuart dynasty, and the seaside town of **North Berwick,** with its views of Bass Rock, a seabird sanctuary.

From Glasgow, day-trippers can easily reach Helensburgh on the Firth of Clyde and visit one of architect Charles Rennie Mackintosh's remarkable achievements, **Hill House.** By going inland and up river (that's south, by the way) into the Clyde Valley, you can also visit **New Lanark,** a unique heritage site.

 In addition to the places I mention here, you can see a good deal of the attractions in Chapters 14, 15, and 16 on day trips from Scotland's two major cities. So, if you're staying in one of the cities, your options are diverse.

East Lothian

As the largest town in the area, the royal burgh of **North Berwick** (the "w" is silent) — where the Firth of Forth meets the North Sea — is a good focus for a day trip from Edinburgh. The town dates to the 14th century; in the more modern Victorian and Edwardian times, it was rebuilt to serve as an up-market holiday resort, drawing visitors to its beaches, harbor, and golf courses.

Day Trips from Edinburgh

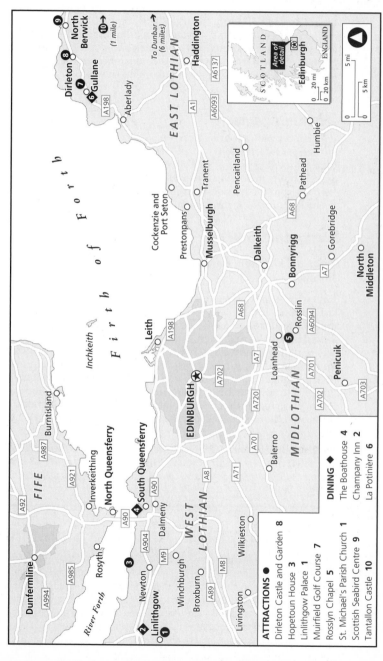

ATTRACTIONS ●

Dirleton Castle and Garden **8**
Hopetoun House **3**
Linlithgow Palace **1**
Muirfield Golf Course **7**
Rosslyn Chapel **5**
St. Michael's Parish Church **1**
Scottish Seabird Centre **9**
Tantallon Castle **10**

DINING ◆

The Boathouse **4**
Champany Inn **2**
La Potinière **6**

Getting there

About 36km (21 miles) east of Edinburgh, North Berwick is on a direct rail line from Edinburgh; the trip takes about 30 minutes. Standard one-way fare is about £5. Bus service from Edinburgh takes a bit over an hour. An all-day ticket to North Berwick and the region around it costs around £6. If you're driving, take the coastal road east from Leith, or use the A1 (marked the south and dunbar), to the A198 (via Gullane) to North Berwick.

Orienting yourself

At North Berwick's tourist office on Quality Street (☎ 01620-892-197), you can get information on boat trips to offshore islands, including Bass Rock, a breeding ground inhabited by about 10,000 gannets (the second largest colony in Scotland) as well as puffins and other birds. You can see the rock from the harbor, but the viewing is even better at Berwick Law, an eroded, once-volcanic lookout point that rises up behind the town.

Seeing the sights

Dirleton Castle and Garden
Dirleton

Run by Historic Scotland today, Dirleton Castle dates from the 13th century. The surrounding gardens — for some visitors, the main attraction — are apparently just as ancient. The ruins are reputed to have been completely sacked in 1650 by Cromwell, but another story holds that the building was only partially destroyed by his army and was further torn down by a local family. Why? Allegedly, the Nisbits desired a romantic ruin on their land after building nearby Archerfield House in the 1660s. Highlights of the self-guided tour include the imposing gate house, vaulted arcades, and a 16th-century dovecot that resembles a beehive. The gardens feature a herbaceous border that Guinness ranks as longest in the world. Allow about one hour.

See map p. 253. On the A198, 5km (2 miles) west of North Berwick. ☎ **01620-850-330.** *www.historic-scotland.gov.uk. Admission: £4.70 adults, £3.80 seniors, £2.80 children 5–15. Open: Apr–Sept daily 9:30 a.m.–5:30 p.m.; Oct–Mar daily 9:30 a.m.–4:30 p.m.*

Dirleton: Prettiest village in Scotland?

Dirleton, midway between North Berwick and Gullane, is one of the prettiest villages in Scotland. In fact, its quaintness and beauty make it seem almost surreal. Undoubtedly high levels of home maintenance make each cottage here look as if it's waiting to be photographed. Because the main road bypasses the village, there's very little traffic. Even the railway station is closed — the last train ran through Dirleton in the mid-1950s. The biggest event for Dirleton occurred in the 1940s, when President Roosevelt and Sir Winston Churchill met here to plan D-Day landings.

Day Trips from Glasgow

ATTRACTIONS
Glenarn Garden **1**
Hill House **2**
Newark Castle **3**
New Lanark **4**

Scottish Seabird Centre
North Berwick

From this popular attraction, situated on a craggy outcropping in North Berwick, you can watch all the bird action out on Bass Rock, whether gannets and puffins, as well as guillemots on the island of Fidra or colonies of seals, thanks to live video links. The Seabird Centre also has a cafe/bistro and activities geared to the family. Allow two hours.

See map p. 253. The Harbour, North Berwick. ☎ *01620-890-202.* www.seabird. org. *Admission: £7.95 adults, £6 seniors and students, £4.50 children. Open: Apr–Sept daily 10 a.m.–6 p.m.; Nov–Jan Mon–Fri 10 a.m.–4 p.m. and Sat–Sun 10 a.m.–5:30 p.m.; Feb–Mar and Oct Mon–Fri 10 a.m.–5 p.m. and Sat–Sun 10 a.m.–5:30 p.m.*

Tantallon Castle
Tantallon

After its construction in the 14th century, on a bluff right above the sea, this became the stronghold of the powerful and somewhat trouble-making Douglas family — the Earls of Angus, who tended to side with England in the wars and disputes with Scotland in the 15th and 16th centuries. Both Stuart kings James IV and James V dispatched troops to Tantallon to try and control the family. Like most castles in the region, it endured a fair number of sieges, but the troops of Oliver Cromwell fully sacked it in the mid-1600s. Nevertheless, the ruins remain formidable, with a square five-story central tower. Allow one hour.

See map p. 253. On the A198, about 3.2km (2 miles) east of North Berwick. ☎ **01620-892-727.** *www.historic-scotland.gov.uk. Admission: £4.70 adults, £3.80 seniors, £2.80 children. Open: Apr–Sept daily 9:30 a.m.–5:30 p.m.; Oct daily 9:30 a.m.–4:30 p.m.; Nov–Mar Sat–Wed 9:30 a.m.–4:30 p.m.*

Dining locally

La Potinière
$$$ Gullane   FRENCH

This legendary and award-winning restaurant, which once had a Michelin star, closed briefly; but, with new owners, Chefs Keith Marley and Mary Runciman, it has been revived. The set-price lunches and dinners offer dishes that are French inspired, using seasonal produce that is usually purchased locally, with everything freshly made on the premises. Décor is unpretentious and charming.

See map p. 253. Main Street, Gullane. ☎ **01620-843-214.** *www.la-potiniere.co.uk. Fixed-price meals: Lunch £19; dinner £40. MC, V. Open: Wed–Sun 12:30–1:30 p.m. and 7–8:30 p.m. Closed Mon–Tues and Sun nights Oct–May.*

Dunbar: Birthplace of John Muir

The man who put the Yosemite Valley of California on the map, founded the Sierra Club, and single-handedly established the national park system in the United States was born April 21, 1838, in the humble harbor town of Dunbar, about 15km (9 miles) southeast of North Berwick. Scots have been rather slow to capitalize on John Muir's international stature and to celebrate the life of the explorer, naturalist, and groundbreaking conservationist. But a trust operating in his name is having an impact on preserving natural habitats across Scotland today. In Dunbar, you can visit his birthplace (126 High St.; ☎ 01368-865-899; www.jmbt.org.uk), which now houses a museum about Muir, his travels, and his work. It is a modest, locally run museum, but if you're a fan of John Muir and appreciate the environmental movement, then a visit here is merited.

Gullane and Muirfield Golf Course

Situated about 8km (5 miles) west of North Berwick and some 28km (16 miles) east of Edinburgh, Gullane (pronounced *gill*-in by many, *gull*-an by others) is another Scottish resort town with a fine beach and a famous golf course. **Gullane Hill** is a nature sanctuary where over 100 species of birds have been spotted. Cross a small wood footbridge from the car park to enter the reserve. Gullane doesn't have any direct rail service; the nearest station is about 4km (2½ miles) south in Drem. Buses depart to Gullane from the Edinburgh bus terminal near St. Andrew's Square (☎ **0800-232-323** for information) and take about one hour.

Muirfield Golf Course (☎ **01620-842-123**) is ranked among the world's great golf courses, and as such, it has hosted the Open Championship in Great Britain. Muirfield is the home course of the Honorable Company of Edinburgh Golfers — the world's oldest golf club — which began at Leith Links in Edinburgh. Developed on a boggy piece of low-lying land in 1891, Muirfield was originally a 16-hole course designed by the legendary Old Tom Morris. Visitors with certified handicaps can play Muirfield on Tuesdays and Thursdays. Greens fees are around£160 for a single round and £200 for the day. Peak times book quickly, but the course usually has availability from mid-October to the end of March.

West Lothian

For tourists, the principal town of this region west of Edinburgh is Linlithgow, where Mary Queen of Scots was born in 1542. Linlithgow's ancient palace is the main attraction. **Falkirk** is a central market town farther west, while South Queensferry sits on the south banks of the Forth River.

Getting there

Linlithgow is only about 26km (16 miles) west of Edinburgh. Trains depart frequently from Edinburgh Waverley Station for the 20-minute ride. A standard round-trip ticket costs about £7. If you're driving from Edinburgh, follow the M8 toward Glasgow, take exit 2 onto the M9, and follow the signs to Linlithgow.

Orienting yourself

The tourist information center is on the road that leads up to the palace. It's open daily from Easter through October.

Rosslyn Chapel: *The Da Vinci Code* connection

Thanks in no small part to Dan Brown's blockbuster novel *The Da Vinci Code,* and the Hollywood film by the same name, the elaborately carved Rosslyn Chapel, south of Edinburgh, is firmly on the trail of those who seek to retrace the historic and mythical path of the Knights Templar. Visitor numbers swelled because of the movie, part of which was filmed here. Sir William St. Clair founded the chapel in 1446, and it has been long noted for its architectural and design idiosyncrasies (though it doesn't have all of those mentioned in Brown's fictional tome). The attraction is easily reached from Edinburgh via the A701, which runs south from Edinburgh. Admission is £7.50 adults, £6 seniors, and £4 students in groups. The chapel is open Monday to Saturday from 9:30 a.m. to 6 p.m. and on Sunday from noon to 4:45 p.m. (with last admissions 30 minutes before closing). For more information and to arrange guided tours call ☎ 0131-440-2159, or log on to www.rosslynchapel.org.uk.

Seeing the sights

Hopetoun House
Near South Queensferry

On the margins of South Queensferry, amid beautifully landscaped grounds, Hopetoun House is one of Scotland's best examples of 18th-century palatial Georgian architecture, featuring design work by Sir William Bruce. It was enlarged and transformed by three members of the architecturally excelled Adam family. You can wander through splendid reception rooms filled with period furniture, Renaissance paintings, statuary, and other artworks. The views of the Firth of Forth are panoramic from the rooftop observation deck. After touring the house, visitors should try to take in the grounds, some 60 hectares (150 acres) of parkland with a walled garden, shorefront trail, and deer park. Last entry is one hour before closing. Allow two hours.

See map p. 253. Off the A904, near South Queensferry, 3km (2 miles) from the Forth Road Bridge. ☎ *0131-331-2451.* www.hopetounhouse.com. *Admission: £8 adults, £7 seniors and students, £4.25 children, £22 family. Open: Easter–Sept daily 10:30 a.m.–5 p.m. Closed Oct–Mar, except for groups with advance reservations.*

Linlithgow Palace
Linlithgow

The birthplace of Mary, Queen of Scots, this was a favorite residence of Scottish royalty in the 15th and 16th centuries — the first building to be called a palace in Scotland. It is now one of the country's most poignant ruins, set on the shores of Linlithgow Loch. Enough of the royal rooms are still intact so that visitors can get an idea of how grand the palace once was. It is a landmark bit of architecture and a romantic touchstone of Scottish history and lore. On this site, the English king, Edward I, occupied a tower house in the 14th century, but Scots who had hidden in a load of hay retook it in 1313. Most of the palace was built by Scotland's King James I between 1425 and 1437. In 1513, Queen Margaret (an English Tudor by birth) waited in vain here for husband James IV to return from the battle of Flodden. When their son James V, also born here, wed Mary of Guise, the palace fountain ran with wine. In 1746, fire gutted the building when government troops who routed Bonnie Prince Charlie at Culloden were barracked in Linlithgow. Last admission 45 minutes before closing. Allow two hours.

See map p. 253. On A706, on the south shore Linlithgow Loch, Linlithgow. ☎ **01506-842-896.** *www.historic-scotland.gov.uk. Admission: £5.20 adults, £4.20 seniors and students, £3.10 children. Open: Apr–Sept daily 9:30 a.m.–5:30 p.m.; Oct–Mar daily 9:30 a.m.–4:30 p.m.*

St. Michael's Parish Church
Linlithgow

Next to Linlithgow Palace stands the medieval kirk of St. Michael, site of worship for many a Scottish monarch after its consecration in 1242. The biggest pre-Reformation parish church in Scotland, it was mostly constructed in the 15th century. In St. Catherine's Aisle, just before the battle of Flodden, King James IV apparently saw an apparition warning him against fighting the English. Perhaps he should have listened. Despite being ravaged by the disciples of John Knox (who actually chided followers for their "excesses") and transformed into a stable by Cromwell's forces, this remains one of Scotland's best examples of a parish church. While providing a dramatic focal point on the landscape, the aluminum spears projecting from the tower were added in the 1960s. Allow one hour.

See map p. 253. Adjacent to Linlithgow Palace, Linlithgow. ☎ **01506-842-188.** *www.stmichaelsparish.org.uk. Admission: Free. Open: May–Sept daily 10:30 a.m.–4 p.m.; Oct–Apr Mon–Fri 10:30 a.m.–1 p.m. (Closed to tourism visits during services, funerals, and weddings.)*

Dining locally

The Boat House
$$ South Queensferry FISH/SEAFOOD

What a vista. This restaurant and wine bar on the main street of South Queensferry positions diners just above the sea — and the views of the Forth rail and suspension road bridges are marvelous. Typical dishes, including grilled herring or monkfish roasted with rosemary, garlic, and olive oil are innovative but not overcomplicated.

See map p. 253. 22 High St., South Queensferry. ☎ **0131-331-5429.** *Fixed-price lunch: £16. Main courses: £12–£18. MC, V. Open: Mon–Sun noon to 2:30 p.m. and 5:30–10 p.m. (Sun last orders at 8 p.m.).*

Spa hotel breaks

If you are looking for bit of pampering out of town, head for **Dalhousie Castle** hotel, in Bonnyrigg. Here they have created an "Aqueous" hydro spa: It combines therapeutic treatments, Jacuzzilike massage pool, Turkish bath, and room for mud cleansing, too. The "total experience" costs about £200. Dalhousie Castle is on the A7 south of Edinburgh (☎ **01875-820-153;** www.dalhousiecastle.co.uk). Another suggested spa is at the **Macdonald Marine Hotel & Spa** in North Berwick, East Lothian. There is an exercise pool, health and fitness program, and "thermal suite". The Spa Day rate (which includes facial, scalp massage, and more) costs about £170. The hotel is on Cromwell Road, North Berwick (☎ **0844-879-9130;** www.macdonaldhotels.co.uk/marine).

Champany Inn
$$$–$$$$ Champany, near Linlithgow   SCOTTISH

You find some of the best steaks in Britain here. The award-winning landmark restaurant also serves oysters, salmon, and lobsters, but beef is the main reason people dine here. Next to the main dining room is the Chop House, offering somewhat less expensive cuts in a more casual atmosphere within the establishment. The wine list — some 2,000 bottles long — has won an award for excellence from *Wine Spectator* magazine. The inn also has 16 handsomely furnished overnight rooms.

See map p. 253. On the A904, 3km (2 miles) northeast of Linlithgow at Champany Corner. ☎ *01506-834-532.* www.champany.com. *Reservations required. Main courses: £25–£50. AE, DC, MC, V. Open: Mon–Fri 12:30–2 p.m. and 7–10 p.m.; Sat 7–10 p.m. Main restaurant closed Sun (Chop House open noon to 10 p.m.).*

The Clyde Valley

From its headwaters well south of Glasgow, the River Clyde meanders north toward the city and then west to the sea. The Clyde Valley south of the city is best known locally for its garden nurseries and their sometimes-quaint tea shops. Near the town of **Lanark,** however, you can find a bona fide bit of history and an attraction that merits a day trip.

Getting there

You can take the train to Lanark from Central Station in Glasgow. Trains depart Glasgow twice an hour, and the trip takes about one hour. Standard same-day round-trip fare is about £9. Buses for Lanark leave Buchanan Bus Station hourly, and the journey takes about 75 minutes. The price of a round-trip ticket is about £6. By car, drive via the M74 motorway, following the signs from exit 9.

Seeing the sights

New Lanark
Near Lanark

Founded first in 1784, New Lanark was a progressive industrial mill and village under the guidance of Robert Owen by the early part of the 19th century. Owen had decided that a content work force would most likely be a productive one. With that philosophy, he set up free education for all employees and their children, a day-care center and social club, and a cooperative store along the banks of the River Clyde in the steep valley below the long-established market town of Lanark. Today, the New Lanark Conservation Trust runs the place as a tourist attraction. (It's also recognized by UNESCO as a World Heritage Site.) Admission includes an educational chair-lift ride that tells the story of what life here was once like, as well as self-guided tours of the principle buildings, such as the factory where cotton was spun and the old school house. A walk upstream brings visitors to the three-tiered Falls of Clyde: well worth the hike if you like waterfalls and walking. Allow two hours.

See map p. 255. Braxfield Road, outside Lanark. ☎ **01555-661-345.** www.new lanark.org. *Admission £6.95 adults, £5.95 children and seniors, £28 family. Open: Daily Apr–Sept 10 a.m.–5 p.m. and Oct–Mar 11 a.m.–5 p.m.*

West of Glasgow

West of Glasgow, the Clyde widens as it empties into the sea. To get to places west, take the train that runs almost every half-hour from Queen Street Station, or head out on the M8 motorway, crossing the river at Erskine and following the northern shoreline. The area doesn't boast a lot of attractions, but the drive can be very pretty, and in **Helensburgh,** the Mackintosh trail leads to the architect and designer's wonderful Hill House.

Glenarn Garden
Rhu (near Helensburgh)

Nestled in a protective hollow, Glenarn is a private garden, established by the Gibson family in the early decades of the 20th century. The rhododendron collection is superb; in early spring, the flowering magnolias can be absolutely stunning. A large rock garden has also been built around an unused quarry. Allow one hour.

See map p. 255. Glenarn Road, off the A814, Rhu. ☎ **01436-820-493.** *Admission: £4. Open: Mid-Mar to Sept dawn to dusk.*

Hill House
Helensburgh

Designed by Charles Rennie Mackintosh for publisher Walter Blackie, this timeless house, set on the hill above the town of Helensburgh (about

48km/30 miles west of Glasgow), has been lovingly restored and opened to the public by the National Trust for Scotland. Inspired by the Scottish Baronial style, Hill House is still pure Mackintosh: from the asymmetrical juxtaposition of windows and clean lines that blend sharp geometry and gentle curves to the sumptuous but uncluttered interior, with custom-made details (such as glass inlays, fireplace tiles, and decorative panels) by both the architect and his artist wife, Margaret Macdonald. Practically the entire house, built at the beginning of the 20th century, is open to the public. The garden, overgrown when the National Trust took over the property in the early 1980s, has been restored to its original state thanks to photographs of the original garden taken in 1905 for a German design magazine. Allow two hours.

See map p. 255. Upper Colquhoun Street, off the B832, Helensburgh. ☎ **01436-673-900.** *www.nts.org.uk. Admission: £8.50 adults, £5.50 children and seniors, £21 family. Open: Apr–Oct daily 1:30–5:30 p.m. Closed Nov–Mar.*

Newark Castle
Port Glasgow

One of the few castles still standing in this part of Scotland, Newark dates to the 15th century. Its most prominent resident was Patrick Maxwell, who made notable additions to the castle but went down in history as a bully who murdered a couple of neighbors and regularly beat his wife. Nice chap, eh? You can see a good deal of this well-preserved castle, from the tower house, built in 1478, to a wood-paneled sleeping chamber and the high ceilings of the main hall, in addition to the old gate house. Allow one hour.

See map p. 255. On the A8, Port Glasgow. ☎ **01475-741-858.** *www.historic-scotland.gov.uk. Admission: £3.70 adults, £3 seniors and students, £2.30 children. Open: Apr–Oct daily 9:30 a.m.–5:30 p.m. (only until 4:30 p.m. in Oct). Closed Nov–Mar.*

Part IV
The Major Regions

The 5th Wave   By Rich Tennant

©RICHTENNANT

SCOTTISH
TOURS

"Looks like our trip into the town of Argyll
will be delayed while we let one of the local
farmers pass with his sheep."

In this part . . .

Some travelers just visit Edinburgh and Glasgow (discussed in Part III) and stop there. That's okay, but if you have more time, you really should get out and about and discover some of the rest of the "real" Scotland — whether the medieval abbeys of southern Scotland, the picturesque ports of Argyll and in the Hebrides, or the sweeping vistas and rugged countryside of the Highlands and Hebridean islands.

Part IV focuses on the major regions of Scotland. In the chapters that follow, you can find out about each region's best attributes — from harbor towns, whisky distilleries, and world-class golf to ancient castles, loch cruises, and largely unspoiled islands. Each chapter has invaluable suggestions on how to get there and get around, which attractions to see, and of course, where to stay and dine.

Chapter 14

Southern Scotland

● ●

In This Chapter
▶ Finding the best places to stay and eat
▶ Discovering the home of Sir Walter Scott
▶ Seeing the famous Borders abbeys
▶ Visiting one of the most picturesque ports in Scotland

● ●

*R*ichly historic southern Scotland is predominantly rural, with vast
open spaces and lots of rolling hills used for grazing livestock. The
area consists of two administrative districts: the Borders, aptly named
as it borders England, and the region known as Dumfries and Galloway
in the southwest. Because most tourists enter Scotland by plane or
train, arriving in either Glasgow or Edinburgh, many tend to travel
through southern Scotland rather than journey *to* the region. But there
are good reasons to visit.

Sure, the area isn't as impressive as the Highlands (see Chapter 18)
when it comes to dramatic natural beauty. Still, the southern part of
Scotland offers attractions that make a trip here worthwhile: stately
homes and the ruins of 12th-century abbeys, quaint towns, meandering
rivers, and a ruggedly scenic peninsula that faces onto the Irish Sea.

Southern Scotland has no regional capital, per se, nor even a bona fide
city. The main towns include Melrose, Peebles, Jedburgh, and Moffat in
the Borders, south of Edinburgh; Dumfries (dum-*freese*), Kirkudbright,
Newton Stewart, and Stranraer are the main hubs south central and
south of Glasgow, respectively.

Ideally, you could take two or three days to cover southern Scotland.
But certain attractions are within striking distance for day trips from
either Edinburgh or Glasgow, depending on how long you allow your
"day" to be. For example, the drive from Glasgow to the town of
Kirkcudbright takes about two hours or so.

Getting There

Buses and (to a much lesser extent) trains run from Edinburgh to southern Scotland. Cutbacks in the 1960s eliminated rail service that used to

penetrate the Borders interior, but one line is to be reopened in 2014 or so. Until then, however, train service to the Borders is limited to the east coast main line that runs from the Scottish capital to Berwick on Tweed, just across the boundary in England.

Buses and trains from Glasgow head south into Dumfries and Galloway, with a western railway line terminating at the sea port Stranraer and the more central route continuing through Dumfries out of Scotland to Carlisle. To plan a trip by public transportation, call Traveline Scotland at ☎ 0871-200-2233, or use its Web site www.travelinescotland.com.

A car is probably the best mode of transportation to cover southern Scotland.

✔ **By car:** From Edinburgh, take the A68 toward Jedburgh, the A1 along the east coast, or, farther west, the A701 to the M74. From Glasgow, the M74 runs south to Moffat, where the A701 continues to the town of Dumfries. You can also get to Dumfries by taking the A76, via Cumnock. If your destination is Galloway, take the A77 south via Ayr and Girvan. If you want to experience the area from England, the M1 to Newcastle links to the A1 or the A68 (via the A69). Coming from northwest England and the Lake District, take the M6 north to the M74 in Carlisle. Cross-country roads from Stranraer to Galashiels are predominantly two-lane routes with a good bit of twists and turns.

✔ **By bus:** Scotland towns are linked by various bus companies that seem to trade routes every couple of years. **National Express** (☎ 08705-808-080; www.nationalexpress.com) has buses that run to southern Scotland from England. Service from Edinburgh south into the Borders is operated by **First Edinburgh** (☎ 08708-727-271; www.firstgroup.com).

✔ **By train: First ScotRail** (☎ 08457-484-950; www.firstscotrail.com) travels to towns in the region, including Berwick on Tweed, Dumfries, and Stranraer. A typical one-way fare from Glasgow to Stranraer is about £20.

✔ **By ferry: Stena Line** (☎ 0870-1129-374; www.stenaline.ferries.org) runs ferry services between Stranraer harbor and Belfast port in Northern Ireland.

Spending the Night

The selections I list below offer some of the best accommodations in the region. All are moderate to expensive, which is typical for southern Scotland, and the hotels offer dinner and full bars for a friendly pint or nightcap. Some have earned star ratings from the tourist board (see Chapter 8 for a description of the rating system). Rates include full breakfast unless otherwise stated. And remember: You may well get a better deal than the advertised rack rates.

Southern Scotland

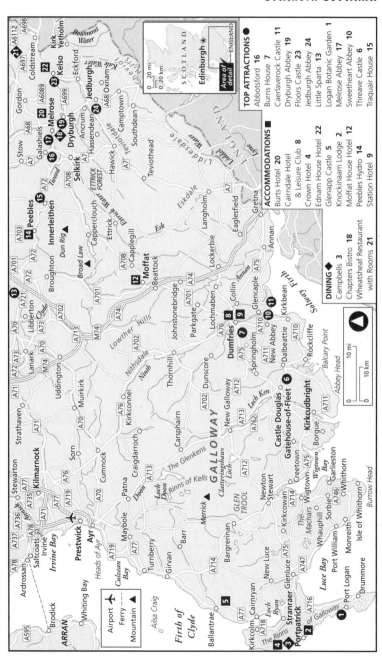

TOP ATTRACTIONS ●

Abbotsford **16**
Burns House **7**
Caerlaverock Castle **11**
Dryburgh Abbey **19**
Floors Castle **23**
Jedburgh Abbey **24**
Little Sparta **13**
Logan Botanic Garden **1**
Melrose Abbey **17**
Sweetheart Abbey **10**
Threave Castle **6**
Traquair House **15**

ACCOMMODATIONS ■

Burts Hotel **20**
Cairndale Hotel
  & Leisure Club **8**
Crown Hotel **4**
Ednam House Hotel **22**
Glenapp Castle **5**
Knockinaam Lodge **2**
Moffat House Hotel **12**
Peebles Hydro **14**
Station Hotel **9**

DINING ◆

Campbells **3**
Chapters Bistro **18**
Wheatsheaf Restaurant
  with Rooms **21**

A lot of accommodations in the region are small bed-and-breakfasts. For more details and rates, contact the **Dumfries & Galloway Tourist Board** (☎ **01387-253-862;** www.visit-dumfries-and-galloway.co.uk), **Scottish Borders Tourist Board** (☎ **0870-608-0404;** www.scot-borders.co.uk), or **VisitScotland** (☎ **0845-22-55-121** within the U.K., or 44-1506-832-121 from outside the U.K.).

Burts Hotel
$$–$$$ Melrose

Within walking distance of Melrose Abbey, this family run inn was built in 1722 to house a local dignitary. The traditional exterior offers a taste of small-town Scotland, although much of the interior décor is modern, with an airy and restful feel. All 20 guest rooms are well furnished and equipped with shower-only bathrooms. The restaurant menu offers such main courses as baked halibut with crab and pea risotto; and, in addition to the more formal dining room, Burt's serves meals in the bistro/bar. Alternative accommodations are offered across the street at the Townhouse Hotel, with double rooms starting at £114.

See map p. 267. Market Square, in the center of town. ☎ **01896-822-285.** *Fax: 01896-822-870.* www.burtshotel.co.uk. *Rack rates: £130 double. AE, DC, MC, V.*

Cairndale Hotel & Leisure Club
$$–$$$ Dumfries

This early-20th-century resort hotel with a stone facade is a good place for a little R&R. The rooms are comfortable, but the best features here are the spa and heated indoor pool. The hotel has 91 units, with 22 suitable for family accommodations. An added conference facility is designed to appeal to a business clientele, but the Cairndale still knows how to treat vacationing guests right.

See map p. 267. 132–136 English St., just off High Street. ☎ **01387-254-111.** *Fax: 01387-250-555.* www.cairndalehotel.co.uk. *Rack rates: £110 double. AE, DC, MC, V.*

Crown Hotel
$$ Portpatrick

It doesn't offer the poshest accommodations in this quaint port town, but the popular and unpretentious Crown is right on the harbor, and the rooms, some of which have big old-fashioned bathtubs, overlook the sea. The hotel has a popular local pub, too, so you may prefer a room in the back to avoid any noise from the bar below.

See map p. 267. 9 North Crescent. ☎ **01766-810-261.** *Fax: 01766-810-551.* www.crownportpatrick.com. *Rack rates: £76 double. AE, MC, V.*

Ednam House Hotel
$$$ Kelso

The Ednam House Hotel occupies an impressive location overlooking the River Tweed. The Georgian mansion, commissioned in 1761, has been owned and operated by the same family since 1928. The rooms and suites are decorated in a traditional manner, which maintains the historic feel of the pile. The hotel also can organize activities and excursions, whether golfing, fishing, hunting, or heritage tours.

See map p. 267. Bridge Street, just off the town square, 1 block north of the Kelso Bridge. ☎ **01573-224-168.** *Fax: 01573-226-319.* www.ednamhouse.com. *Rack rates: £115–£160 double. MC, V.*

Glenapp Castle
$$$$ Ballantrae

Get out your credit cards and be prepared to pay top dollar to stay at this beautifully decorated pile near the cute coastal village of Ballantrae. Glenapp offers guests the royal treatment amid Victorian baronial splendor with antiques, oil paintings, and elegant touches at every turn. The mansion was designed in the 1870s by David Bryce, a celebrated architect of his day, and it overlooks the Irish Sea. Lounges and dining rooms are elegant, and the spacious bedrooms and suites are individually furnished. Tall windows let in the afternoon and long summer evening light, making the rooms bright on many days. The hotel, open seasonally unless by special arrangement, stands on 12 hectares (30 acres) of lovely, secluded grounds that are home to many rare plants.

See map p. 267. Ballantrae, Ayrshire, some 32km (20 miles) south of Ayr. ☎ **01465-831-212.** *Fax: 01465-831-000.* www.glenappcastle.com. *Rack rates: £400–£500 double. Rates include six-course dinner. Closed Jan–Mar. AE, V.*

Knockinaam Lodge
$$$$ Portpatrick

This luxury hotel with well-manicured lawns and gardens, as well as its own private pebble beach on a sheltered cove, is a few miles south of Portpatrick. There are nine rooms; in the country manor house tradition, some of the units feature brass fittings on tubs and tiled fireplaces. In this tranquil and remote setting, Churchill, Eisenhower, and their staffs met during World War II. They're not cheap, but meals (included in the price) are outstanding, the bar excels in its whisky selection, and the kitchen has earned a Michelin star.

See map p. 267. Near Portpatrick. ☎ **01776-810-471.** *Fax: 01776-810-435.* www.knockinaamlodge.com. *Rack rates: £280–£450 double. Rates include dinner. MC, V.*

Moffat House Hotel
$$ Moffat

This 18th-century mansion sits in the center of a garden in the heart of Moffat. The handsome stone building is hard to miss, and lovely trees grace the back garden. Each of the 21 bedrooms is well stocked with amenities, and the restaurant serves fine Scottish cuisine. A literary footnote: It is believed that Poet James MacPherson (thought by some to be the poet Ossian) wrote his disputed works here.

See map p. 267. High Street. ☎ **01683-220-039**. *Fax: 01683-221-288.* www.moffat house.co.uk. *Rack rates: £75–£140 double. AE, MC, V.*

Peebles Hydro
$$$–$$$$ Peebles

Once a Victorian "hydropathic" hotel that claimed to cure whatever ailed you with a hot spring and mineral waters, the Peeble's main features today remain hydrocentric: a pool for the kids and a whirlpool and sauna for the adults. The hotel has some spacious family rooms and 12 hectares (30 acres) of grounds for young ones to explore. Of the more than 125 units, 25 are geared toward families. Other activities at this chateau-style hotel include snooker, pitch-and-putt golf, and badminton.

See map p. 267. Innerleithen Road, on A72 just outside Peebles. ☎ **01721-720-602**. *Fax: 01721-722-999.* www.peebleshydro.co.uk. *Rack rates: £210–£240 double. Rates include dinner. AE, DC, MC, V.*

Station Hotel
$$ Dumfries

The Station's Victorian sandstone building lies near Dumfries's railroad station and the center of town. Part of the Best Western group, the comfortable 100-year-old rooms here have been renovated but still maintain a certain rustic charm. Don't worry about being close to the train tracks; there aren't any late-night trains.

See map p. 267. 49 Lovers Walk, just across from the train station. ☎ **01387-254-316**. *Fax: 01387-250-388.* www.bw-stationhotel.co.uk. *Rack rates: £100 double. AE, DC, MC, V.*

Dining Locally

Campbells
$$ Portpatrick   FISH/SEAFOOD

Facing the crescent-shaped harbor of Portpatrick, this family run restaurant is welcoming and relaxed, a favorite of mine during repeated visits to "the Port." Almost old-fashioned in its unpretentious ways, the décor here mixes rustic seaport with modernity. Fresh fish is the main reason to eat here, and the dishes tend to be unfussy and straightforward in presentation.

See map p. 267. 1 South Crescent. ☎ **01776-810-314.** www.campbells restaurant.co.uk. *Reservations recommended. Main courses: £12–£20. DC, MC, V. Open: Tues–Sun noon to 2:30 p.m. and 6–10 p.m. Closed for 2 weeks in Feb.*

Chapters Bistro
$$ **Near Melrose**   SCOTTISH/GLOBAL

Cross a footbridge over the River Tweed to reach this unassuming bistro near Melrose, run by Kevin and Nicki Winsland. The menu ranges from the house stroganoff to scallops St. Jacques to red snapper to venison with juniper berries.

See map p. 267. Main Street, Gattonside by Melrose. ☎ **01896-823-217.** *Main courses: £10–£16. MC, V. Open: Tues–Sat 6:30–10 p.m.*

The Wheatsheaf @ Swinton
$$–$$$ **Swinton**   MODERN BRITISH

Located between Melrose and Eyemouth, from whose harbor the kitchen secures fresh seafood, the Wheatsheaf is a small hotel and restaurant that pops up on many "best of" lists. You can eat in the pub as well as in the dining room. In addition to fresh fish, Wheatsheaf's menu often offers Borders lamb and organic pork from a local supplier. Accommodations are £112 to £132 for double occupancy.

See map p. 267. Main Street. ☎ **01890-860-257.** www.wheatsheaf-swinton. co.uk. *Reservations recommended. Main courses: £16–£20. MC, V. Open: Daily noon to 2:30 p.m. and 6–9 p.m. Closed on Sun nights Dec–Jan.*

Exploring Southern Scotland

Among the Borders' primary attractions are its stately, historic homes and ancient abbeys. The rolling hills and dense forests of Galloway are attractive and the coastal areas are reasonably dramatic and pictur-esque. The government's historic preservation society, **Historic Scotland,** runs quite a few of the attractions in southern Scotland. I list several below, but for more details, go to the agency's Web site, www. historic-scotland.gov.uk. Don't feel as if you need to visit every abbey and castle in the area; pick some representative ones, enjoy them, and move on.

The top attractions

Abbotsford
Roxburghshire

Abbottsford is the mansion that Sir Walter Scott built and lived in from 1817 until his death. Designed in the Scots baronial style, the house was constructed on land he acquired in 1811. After his literary works, it is considered the author's most enduring monument. Scott was a souvenir hunter, scouring the land for artifacts associated with the historical characters he rendered into fiction. Hence, Abbotsford contains many relics and mementos — whether Rob Roy's sporran or a purse made by Flora MacDonald. One of his other proud possessions is a sword given to the duke of Montrose by Charles I for his cooperation (some say collaboration). The home itself has an entrance that mimics the porch at Linlithgow Palace and a door from Edinburgh's historic Tolbooth. Especially popular is Scott's small study, with writing desk and chair, where he penned some of his most famous works. There are also extensive gardens and grounds to visit, plus the private chapel, added after Scott's death. Allow about two hours.

See map p. 267. Near Galashiels, 3km (2 miles) west of Melrose; just off the A6091 (between the A7 and A68) on the B6360. ☎ **01896-752-043.** www.scotts abbotsford.co.uk. *Admission: House and grounds £7 adults, £3.50 children, £18 family. Open: Late Mar to Oct daily 9:30 a.m.–5 p.m. (only 2–5 p.m. on Sun Mar–May and Oct); Nov–Mar group booking only Mon–Fri.*

Burns House
Dumfries

Most of the Robert Burns Heritage Trail is in Ayrshire (see Chapter 15), but the poet Burns lived the last bit of his short life in this modest cottage, where he died at age 37 in 1796. Burns House has been preserved to look as it did when he resided there for the final few years, and it contains such articles as Burns's writing chair as well as some original manuscripts, letters, and printed editions. A highlight is the author's signature scratched into a windowpane. Allow about one hour.

See map p. 267. Burns Street, between Shakespeare and St. Michael's streets, central Dumfries. ☎ **01387-255-297.** *Admission: Free. Open: Apr–Sept Mon–Sat 10 a.m.–5 p.m., Sun 2–5 p.m.; Oct–Mar Tues–Sat 10 a.m.–1 p.m. and 2–5 p.m.*

Caerlaverock Castle
Near Dumfries

A historic target of English armies in the Wars of Independence, the uniquely triangular shaped Caerlaverock (ka-*liver*-ick) is one of Scotland's classic medieval castles, complete with a water-filled moat and twin-towered gatehouse, as well as some pretty serious battlements — all constructed in distinctive red sandstone. It lies in secured ruins today, but you can still get the sense of what defending this castle may have been like. On the grounds nearby is a replica trebuchet, the device that launched medieval missiles. Among the interior highlights are the Renaissance stone carvings on what is called Nithsdale Lodging, a residence in the courtyard that dates to the 1630s. Walk on the nature trail into the nearby woods to find where an earlier castle stood. Allow about two hours.

See map p. 267. B725, about 13km (8 miles) southeast of Dumfries. ☎ **01387-770-224.** www.historic-scotland.gov.uk. *Admission: £5.20 adults, £4.20 seniors and students, £3.10 children 5–15. Open: Apr–Sept daily 9:30 a.m.–5:30 p.m.; Oct–Mar daily 9:30 a.m.–4:30 p.m.*

Sir Walter Scott: Inventor of historic novels

Today it may be hard to imagine the fame that Walter Scott, poet and novelist, enjoyed as the best-selling author of his day. His works are no longer so widely read, but Scott (1771–1832) was thought to be a master storyteller and today is considered the English language inventor of the historic novel. Before his Waverley series was published in 1814, no modern author writing in English had spun such tales from actual events, examining the lives of individuals who played a role in history — large and small. He created lively characters and realistic pictures of Scottish life in works such as *The Heart of Midlothian.*

Born into a Borders family who then settled in Edinburgh on August 14, 1771, Scott was permanently disabled due to polio he contracted as a child. All his life he was troubled by ill health and later by ailing finances as well. He spent his latter years writing to clear enormous debts incurred when his publishing house and printers collapsed in bankruptcy.

Scott made Scotland and its scenery fashionable across Great Britain, and he played a key role in bringing the Hanoverian George IV to visit Scotland — the first royal visit in a very long time. Although Scott became the most prominent literary figure in Edinburgh, his heart remained in the Borders, where he built his home. Starting with a modest farmhouse, he created Abbotsford, a mansion that became a key tourist destination (p. 271).

Dryburgh Abbey
Near St. Boswells

It's little wonder that Sir Walter Scott chose to be buried here. The abbey ruins, now run under the auspices of Historic Scotland, lie amid giant cedar trees on the banks of the River Tweed. Of the four famed Borders abbeys, Dryburgh was the largest, arguably the most beautiful, and possibly the most attacked by English troops, although it's reasonably well intact today. Scott was interred in the side chapel in 1832. Allow about one hour.

See map p. 267. Off the A68, 3km (2 miles) southeast of Melrose on the B6404 near St. Boswells. ☎ **01835-822-381.** *www.historic-scotland.gov.uk. Admission: £4.70 adults, £3.80 seniors and students, £2.80 children 5–15. Open: Apr–Sept daily 9:30 a.m.–5:30 p.m.; Oct–Mar daily 9:30 a.m.–4:30 p.m.*

Floors Castle
Near Kelso

This mansion was built by William Adam for the first duke of Roxburghe in 1721, and it is today home to the tenth duke and his duchess. More of a sprawling country house than a proper castle, it can nevertheless claim to be the largest inhabited castles in all of Scotland. (It is one of the few fully intact, too.) After viewing the impressive art collection indoors (including paintings by Matisse and Odilon Redon in the Needle Room), venture out and walk one of the nature trails through the woods or along the River Tweed. The walled garden also has an "adventure" playground for the kids. Allow about three hours.

See map p. 267. Hwy. A697, 3km (2 miles) northwest of Kelso. ☎ **01573-223-333.** *www.floorscastle.com. Admission: £7.50 adults, £6.50 seniors and students, £3.50 children 5–16, £19 family. Open: Easter weekend and daily May–Oct 11 a.m.–5 p.m.*

Jedburgh Abbey
Jedburgh

This famous ruined abbey, founded by Scotland's King David I in 1138, is one of the finest. Under the Augustinian canons from Beauvais, France, it achieved abbey status in 1152 and went on to witness much royal pageantry, such as the marriage of Scots King Alexander III to his second wife, Yolande de Dreux in October 1285. The marriage was designed to produce a male heir (alas it did not and this arguably set in motion a succession tussle that latter involved warring with England). Indeed, in 1544 and 1545, the English sacked the abbey during the frequent fighting of the period. After 1560, few efforts were made to repair the abbey. For about 300 years, until 1875, a small section of it served as Jedburgh's parish church, when new premises were found for day-to-day worship. Teams of architects then set to work restoring the abbey to its original medieval design. The abbey remains roofless but is otherwise fairly complete, with most of its exterior stonework now in place.

See map p. 267. In Jedburgh on the A68. ☎ **01835-863-925.** *www.historic-scotland.gov.uk. Admission: £5.20 adults, £4.20 seniors and students, £3.10 children 5–15. Open: Apr–Sept daily 9:30 a.m.–5:30 p.m.; Oct–Mar daily 9:30 a.m.–4:30 p.m.*

Little Sparta
Near Dunsyre

Not highlighted by many guidebooks, this garden was devised by one of Scotland's most intriguing artists, the late Ian Hamilton Finlay, who died on March 27, 2006. It is a surprisingly lush plot of land, given the harsh terrain of the Pentland Hills all around it. Dotted throughout the garden are stone sculptures (many with Finlay's pithy sayings and poems) created in collaboration with master stonemasons and other artists. Little Sparta has been called the "only original garden" created in Great Britain since World War II; in the wake of Finlay's death, a trust has been established to ensure its survival. During the Edinburgh Festival, minibus transport from Edinburgh is usually provided. Allow about one hour.

See map p. 267. Stonypath, near Dunsyre, off the A702 (32km/20 miles southwest of Edinburgh). ☎ **01899-810-252.** *www.littlesparta.co.uk. Admission: £10. Open: June–Sept Wed and Fri–Sun 2:30–5 p.m.*

Historic Scotland's Explorers Pass

If you are planning to see more than a couple of the attractions run by Historic Scotland, then it is worth considering an Explorer's Pass. It provides free admission for either three or seven days. For adults, the three-day pass is £22 and for seven days it is £32; for children it is £12 and £18, respectively; for families the cost is £44 or £63. For up-to-date information, visit www.historic-scotland.gov.uk.

Logan Botanic Garden
Rhinns of Galloway

Run by the Royal Botanic Garden, responsible for the beautiful spread in Edinburgh (see Chapter 11), the gardens on the old Logan estate have charms of their very own. Because of its southwest exposure (which brings mild Gulf Stream air flows) and some protective planting, the gardens have a microclimate that allows the successful cultivation of palms, tree ferns, and other exotic plants such as towering, flowering columns of *echium pininana,* native to the Canary Islands. In addition to the more formal walled garden, Logan also has wilder plantings such as the *gunnera,* with its leaves larger than elephant's ears. Hand-held audio wands can be for used for self-guided tours, and there's an interpretive center with microscopes, too. Allow about two hours.

See map p. 267. B7065, 1.6km (1 mile) outside Port Logan. ☎ **01776-860-231.** *Admission: £5 adults, £4 seniors and students, £1 children, £10 family. Open: Apr–Sept daily 10 a.m.–6 p.m.; Mar and Oct daily 10 a.m.–5 p.m.; Feb Sun only 10 a.m.–4 p.m. Closed Nov–Jan.*

Melrose Abbey
Melrose

These lichen-covered ruins are all that's left of an ecclesiastical community established by Cistercian monks in the 12th century. While the soaring walls you see follow the lines of the original abbey, they were largely constructed in the 15th century. The Gothic design moved Sir Walter Scott to write in the *Lay of the Last Minstrel,* "If thou would'st view fair Melrose aright, go visit in the pale moonlight." The author was also instrumental in ensuring that the decayed remains were preserved in the 19th century. You can still view its sandstone shell, filled with elongated windows and carved capitals, and the finely decorated masonry. It is believed that the heart of Robert the Bruce is interred in the abbey, per his wishes. Allow about one and a half hours.

See map p. 267. Abbey Street, in Melrose. ☎ **01896-822-562.** *www.historic-scotland.gov.uk. Admission: £5.20 adults, £4.20 seniors and students, £3.10 children 5–15. Open: Apr–Sept daily 9:30 a.m.–5:30 p.m.; Oct–Mar daily 9:30 a.m.–4:30 p.m.*

Sweetheart Abbey
New Abbey

The impressive remains of Sweetheart Abbey are worth the short jaunt from Dumfries. An unusual story lies behind the red sandstone structure: Lady Devorgilla of Galloway founded the abbey in 1273 in memory of her husband, John Balliol. She carried his embalmed heart around with her for 22 years, and when she was buried here, in front of the altar, the heart went with her, thus the name Sweetheart Abbey. Allow about one hour.

See map p. 267. Hwy. A710, New Abbey village, 11km (7 miles) south of Dumfries. ☎ *01387-850-397.* www.historic-scotland.gov.uk. *Admission: £3 adults, £2.50 seniors and students, £1.80 children 5–15. Open: Apr–Sept daily 9:30 a.m.– 5:30 p.m.; Oct daily 9:30 a.m.–4:30 p.m.; Nov–Mar Sat–Wed 9:30 a.m.–4:30 p.m.*

Threave Castle
The River Dee

One of the best things about this massive 14th-century tower house (a ruined proper castle) is how you get here. Ring a bell to call a boatman, who ferries you to the island in the River Dee on which the castle sits. Archibald the Grim, the third earl of Douglas, built Threave Castle. It was last used in the 19th century as a prison for Napoleonic War soldiers. Bird-watchers enjoy an opportunity to get up close and personal with the swallows that nest in the ruins from April to September. *Note:* Leave your best shoes at home; the path from the parking area to the boat pickup can get muddy when it rains. And, unlike most Historic Scotland properties in southern Scotland, Threave is closed over the winter. Allow about one hour.

See map p. 267. 5km (3 miles) west of Castle Douglas on A75 (follow signs from the roundabout). ☎ *07711-223-101.* www.historic-scotland.gov.uk. *Admission: £4.20. Open: Apr–Sept daily 9:30 a.m.–5:30 p.m.; Oct 9:30 a.m.–4:30 p.m. Closed Nov–Mar.*

Portpatrick's charming harbor

The site of a natural harbor that has been improved over the years, Portpatrick brought traders from Northern Ireland from the 17th century to the mid–19th century. Although a more sheltered port was established at nearby Stranraer and ferries stopped coming here, Portpatrick remains one of the most picturesque towns in southwest Scotland. Trails lead away from the village, both up and down the coast. Just south of the town, the path goes past the ruins of 15th-century Dunskey Castle, perched on the edge of a cliff above the sea. In the small inlet below is a small beach that seems to capture no end of golf balls hit astray from seaside courses somewhere along the coast. From Portpatrick, the more than 320km-long (200-mile) Southern Upland Way, one of the great long-distance footpaths in Scotland, heads northeast across Scotland from coast to coast. Also worth visiting are the Dunskey Gardens on the eastern outskirts of the town.

Kirkcudbright: The artists' town

Kirkcudbright (kerr-*coo*-bree) became a thriving artists' colony in the late 19th and early 20th century, drawing many notable artists such as leading Glasgow Boy E. A. Hornel, genius graphic artist Jessie M. King, and Scottish Colourist S. J. Peploe. The appeal of this cute village remains, although the colony is more of a heritage spot these days, with galleries keeping the artistic history alive. The center of town is full of small, colorful cottages, many with charming, wee lanes. From April through September, you can visit Hornel's home, Broughton House, a Georgian-era mansion that the artist adapted and expanded to include a studio. The garden is special, too. Call ☎ **01557-330-437**, or log on to the National Trust for Scotland's Web site: www.nts.org.uk. Also of some interest is the city-run Stewartry Museum, which first opened in 1893 and has historical artifacts and art by Jessie King.

Traquair House
Innerleithen

This is perhaps Scotland's most romantic house, little changed since the beginning of the 18th century and dating in part from the 12th century. Traquair House is rich in associations with ancient kings, Mary, Queen of Scots, and the Jacobite uprisings. The Stuarts of Traquair still live in the great mansion, making it, they say, the oldest continuously inhabited house in Scotland. One of the most poignant exhibits is in the King's Room: an ornately carved oak cradle, in which Mary rocked her infant son, who was to become James VI of Scotland and James I of England. Other treasures include embroideries, silver, manuscripts, and paintings. Of particular interest is the brewery, still in operation, producing very fine ales. On the grounds are craft workshops — such as wrought ironwork and woodturning — as well as a maze and woodland walks. There are three sumptuous overnight rooms, too, each going for £180 including full breakfast. Allow about two hours.

See map p. 267. Innerleithen. ☎ *01896-830-323.* www.traquair.co.uk. *Admission: House and grounds £7.50 adults, £6.80 seniors, £4 children, £18 family. Open: Apr, May, and Sept daily noon to 5 p.m.; June–Aug daily 10:30 a.m.–5 p.m.; Oct daily 11 a.m.–3 p.m., Nov Sat–Sun noon to 4 p.m. Closed Dec–Mar.*

More cool things to see and do

✔ **Glen Trool,** 13km (8 miles) north of Newton Stewart (off the A714), is a good place hike for a few hours. The trail that circumnavigates Loch Trool is moderate to easy. On the southern banks, the army of Robert the Bruce is believed to have defeated a much stronger English force in 1307 and across the loch on a high point is Bruce's Stone, which commemorates the victory.

✔ **Mary, Queen of Scots House,** Queen Street, Jedburgh (☎ **01835-863-331**), is where Mary allegedly stayed in 1566, when she was on

a trip to visit her betrothed, the Earl of Bothwell, and became ill
with fever. Now the building is a museum that tells the tragic story
of her life, and features fine tapestries, oil paintings, antique furniture, coats of arms, armor, and some of the queen's possessions.

✔ **Mull of Galloway Nature Reserve,** southern tip of the Rhins of
Galloway, off the A716, is a keen bird-watcher's paradise where the
cliffs rise from the sea by about 85m (280 ft.). This is the southernmost point in all of Scotland.

✔ **The Old Bridge House Museum,** Mill Road, Dumfries (☎ **01387-
256-904**), is a museum that's housed in the oldest building in
Dumfries, a 1660 sandstone structure built into the Devorgilla
Bridge. Today, the museum is devoted to Victorian life. A mid-
19th-century kitchen and antique dental tools are among the
items on display.

✔ The **Robert Burns Centre,** Mill Road, Dumfries (☎ **01387-264-808**),
displays items such as original documents and relics belonging to
Burns, a cast of his skull, and a scale model of 1790s Dumfries;
there's a rather sentimental audiovisual presentation of the poet's
life.

✔ **The Trimontium Exhibition,** Market Square, Melrose (☎ **01896-
822-651**), is a small museum devoted to Trimontium, the legendary
three-peaked Roman hill fort near Melrose. Among the collection
of 1st- and 2nd-century artifacts are a Roman skull and facemask,
tools, weapons, and pottery.

✔ **Wigtown** is Scotland's official book town. Tucked down along the
wide estuary of Wigtown Bay (10km/6 miles south of Newton
Stewart on the A714), the village has virtually back-to-back used
and antiquarian book shops, specializing often in Scottish titles.
At Wigtown, there is also an infamous Covenanters Monument
where one of the female followers of that 17th-century, die-hard
Presbyterian sect was tied to a stake on the shoreline and made to
drown in the rising tide.

Shopping for Local Treasures

The main street in places such as Dumfries or Peebles will usually have
small shops and clothing stores. Almost all the attractions listed in this
chapter have well-stocked gift shops.

The town of Kelso is the home of **Pettigrews** (☎ **01573-224-234;** www.
pettigrews.com), which produces a range of Scottish chutney and
relish at its factory. In the town of Moffat, you can visit the **Woollen Mill**
(☎ **01683-220-134**), which has weaving demonstrations and shops with
tartan, whisky, and more for sale, seven days a week. If you enjoy books,
set aside some time to visit **Wigtown,** of course, which is Scotland's
book town. But if art is more your bag, the seaside village of

Kirkcudbright has developed into an artists community with galleries selling local works.

Here are a couple of other picks worth visiting.

- ✔ **Broughton Gallery,** Broughton Place, Broughton (☎ **01899-830-234**), in a village near Biggar, exhibits contemporary art — paintings, glassware, and ceramics — by Scottish and other British artists. Open during exhibits.

- ✔ **Lighthouse Pottery,** south pier, Portpatrick (☎ **01776-810-284**), is good place to pick up a gift or two, with a selection of jewelry, pottery, and other handmade local crafts. Open 9:30 a.m. to 5 p.m. daily.

Hitting the Local Pubs

Almost every town in southern Scotland has one or two taverns; and, whether unimpressive or not, they often can be a good place to meet the locals. Ask your hotel concierge or guesthouse host to recommend the nearest "local" to your accommodations — walking distance preferred.

Worth special note is the **Globe Inn,** 56 High St., Dumfries (☎ **01387-252-335;** www.globeinndumfries.co.uk). Established at the beginning of the 17th century, the Globe was one of poet Robert Burns's favorite haunts. You can even sit in Burns's favorite seat, just to the left of the fireplace. Other good places for a pint and meal are the **Crown** in Portpatrick and **Burts** in Melrose (see listing information for both in the "Spending the Night" section, earlier in this chapter).

Fast Facts: Southern Scotland

Area Codes

For a small country with less than five million people, Scotland has a bewildering number of local area telephone codes. Those for some of the major towns in southern Scotland: Dumfries is **01387;** Castle Douglas is **01556;** Kelso is **01573;** Melrose is **01896;** Moffat is **01683;** Peebles is **01721;** Selkirk is **01750;** and Stranraer is **01776.** You need to dial the area code only if you're calling from outside the town you want to reach.

ATMs

All the major towns have ATMs at banks (smaller villages may have them in local shops), but these rural cash points may not be linked to international systems.

Emergencies

Dial ☎ **999** for police, fire, or ambulance.

Hospitals

The primary hospital for the region is Dumfries & Galloway Royal Infirmary, Bankend Road, Dumfries (☎ 01387-246-246). Just outside Melrose on the A6091, you'll find Borders General Hospital (☎ 01896-826-000). Garrick Hospital (☎ 01776-703-276) is in Stranraer.

Information

For general information on the region, contact Borders Tourist Information, Shepherd's Mill, Selkirk (☎ 0870-608-0404; www.scot-borders.co.uk) or Dumfries & Galloway Tourist Board, 64 Whitesands, Dumfries (☎ 01387-253-862; www.visit dumfriesandgalloway.co.uk). VisitScotland's main number (☎ 0845-22-55-121) will connect you to local offices, or log on to www.visitscotland.com for more specific information. Or, if you're calling from a country outside the United Kingdom, dial ☎ 44-1506-832-121.

Internet Access

A convenient and affordable place to jump on the Net is Dumfries Internet Centre, 26–28 Brewery St., next to Whitesands, Dumfries (☎ 01387-259-400).

Mail

The main post office in Dumfries is at 34 St. Michael St. (☎ 01387-253-415).

Chapter 15

Ayrshire and Argyll

. . . .

In This Chapter

▶ Getting to and getting to know Ayrshire and Argyll

▶ Seeking out the best places to stay and eat

▶ Discovering the Burns Heritage Trail, Culzean Castle, and more

▶ Hittin' the links in Troon and Turnberry

▶ Exploring central Scotland's picturesque western peninsulas and islands

. . . .

*I*n this chapter, we sweep around the southwest of Scotland and hit the western fringes of central Scotland, too. The region of Ayshire stretches from the southern and western edges of greater Glasgow south to southwest along the Firth of Clyde, bordering Galloway in the south. Argyll, one of my favorite parts of Scotland, covers the western peninsulas of central Scotland and adjacent islands, the heart of the ancient kingdom of Dalriada. While Ayrshire's boundaries are fairly well marked, Argyll is a bit more amorphous, encompassing a region that historically stretches into the Highlands and the inner Hebridean islands.

One of Ayrshire's primary attractions is "Burns Country," because the region was the poet Robert Burns's birthplace as well as his predominant stomping grounds for most of his life. But Ayrshire also has the impressive Culzean Castle and offers golfers some of the best links courses in the world. If you take the train from Glasgow to Ayr, the main town of Ayrshire, you can see one course after another in the sandy dunes along the shoreline.

Argyll, which means the "coast of the Gaels," encompasses such islands as Bute and Gigha as well as the remote Kintyre Peninsula, which is isolated enough that former Beatle Paul McCartney has long owned a ranch there where he retreats from prying eyes. One of the principal cities in northern Argyll is the port of Oban (*oh*-bin), gateway to the Hebrides. Other interesting settlements include Inveraray, on the upper shores of Loch Fyne, and Tarbert midway down the Kintyre Peninsula.

I have included Islay (*eye*-la) in this chapter. While it is one of the inner Hebridean Islands, and might logically seem to belong in Chapter 19, it is reached primarily from ports in Argyll, a region to which is it historically connected. Conversely, information on the Isle of Mull, which geographically could have been included here, is found in Chapter 19 with the other islands of the Hebrides.

If you don't have the time or inclination to give Ayrshire and Argyll several days, remember that visits to places such as the mansion and grounds of Culzean Castle or the quiet roads and beaches on the Isle of Bute can be accomplished as day trips from Glasgow.

Getting There

Your options for getting in and out of the area include scheduled buses and trains that run from Glasgow to a variety of towns, such as Ayr in Ayrshire or Oban in Argyll. If you want to fully explore the Cowal or Kintyre peninsulas or the Clyde coastline, a car is necessary. Of course, ferry services provide the link to the islands (and even between the peninsulas of Cowal and Kintyre). There are also flights to airports near Cambeltown on the Kintyre Peninsula and to the Isle of Islay.

✔ **By car:** From Glasgow, the main road to Ayrshire is the M77 (A77) from the city's Southside. It's the fastest route to towns such as Troon, Ayr, and points farther south, such as Culzean. You can also drive west on the M8, along the Clyde to Greenock or Gourock, connecting to the A78, which goes south along the Firth of Clyde to ports such as Wemyss Bay or Ardrossan. To get to Argyll, take the A82 from the West End of Glasgow north toward Tarbet on the shores of Loch Lomond. From Tarbet, you can take the A83 to Inveraray and down the Kintyre Peninsula or from the A83 to the A815 down to Cowal. The fastest route to Oban is by using the A82 from Tarbet: Go north along Loch Lomond to Crianlarich and Tyndrum, where the A85 goes west to Oban.

✔ **By train: First ScotRail** (☎ 0845-748-4950; www.firstscotrail. com) service overlaps with the greater Glasgow rail service operated by **Strathclyde Partnership for Transport (SPT;** ☎ 0141-333 3708; www.spt.co.uk). Between the two (and they're largely interchangeable, unless you're a dedicated rail fan), you have reasonably frequent service from Glasgow to Ayrshire and more limited trains into Argyll. Remember, however, that trains going southwest toward Ayr — or to Wemyss Bay — depart from Central Station, while those going northwest toward Oban leave from Queen Street Station. A one-way journey to Ayr (55 min.) costs around £7, to Wemyss Bay (50 min.) £6, and to Oban (3 hr.) £19.

✔ **By bus:** From Glasgow, **Scottish Citylink** (☎ 0141-332-9644 or 0870-550-5050; www.citylink.co.uk) runs buses to western Scotland, including towns such as Inveraray and Cambeltown. A standard one-way ticket from Glasgow to Inveraray is about £8 and £15 to Campbeltown. The trip to Inveraray takes about two hours and to Cambeltown about four and a half hours. **Stagecoach Express** (☎ 01292-613-500; www.stagecoachbus.com) also runs buses to Ayr from Glasgow's Buchanan Street bus terminal. The one-way fare to Ayr is about £5 and the trip, using the limited stop X77 service, takes about one hour.

Ayrshire

Benmore Botanic Garden **10**
See "Argyll" map ←
Dunoon
Gourock
Cowal
Greenock
Rothesay
Wemyss Bay
Kelmorlie Castle ⚔
Bute Mount Stuart
Largs
Cumbrae
Millport
Little Cumbrae
West Kilbride
Ardrossan
Saltcoats
← To Arran
Dalry **9**
Kilwinning
Irvine
Troon **8** **7**
6
Prestwick
Firth of Clyde
Ayr
See "Ayr" map ←
A719
Culzean **4**
Turnberry **1** **2**
3
Maybole
Girvan
A77
A714

Loch Lomond National Park
A82
Helensburgh
Loch Lomond
Alexandria
River Clyde
Port Glasgow
A78
Dumbarton
A8
Bridge of Weir
Clyde Muirshiel Regional Park
A737
Johnstone
Lochwinnoch
Stewarton
A735
A736
Dalrymple
A77
A713

Drymen
Stirling ↗
0 — 5 mi
0 — 5 km
Clydebank
Kirkintilloch
M8
Paisley ✈
GLASGOW
M8
Barrhead
A726
East Kilbride
Hamilton
M77
M8
New Lanark →
(9 miles)
Kilmarnock
Galston
A71
A719
A77
Mauchline
A758
A76
Cumnock

SCOTLAND
Area of detail
Edinburgh
Glasgow
0 — 20 mi
0 — 20 km
ENGLAND

Castle ⚔

✔ **By ferry: Caledonian MacBrayne** (☎ **08705-650-000** or 01475-650-100; www.calmac.co.uk) — or CalMac, as it's more colloquially known — serves 22 islands and four peninsulas over the West Coast of Scotland. From Gourock, you can reach Dunoon on the Cowal Peninsula (25-min. crossing). Ferries from Wemyss Bay go to Rothesay on the Isle of Bute (35 min.). The boat for Brodick on Arran departs from Ardrossan (1-hr. crossing). Connections between railway terminals and ferry service are fairly well organized.

There is a five-minute-long crossing from northern Bute to Colintrave on the Cowal Peninsula, and in summer you can also go from Lochranza on Arran to the Kintyre Peninsula near Skipness. A ferry links the Cowal and Kintyre peninsulas from Portvadie to Tarbert (25 min.). From the west coast of Kintyre, ferries to the Isle of Gigha leave from Tayinloan (20-min. crossing), while those to Islay depart from Kennacraig (2 hr., 20 min.).

On a trip across Argyll, you can take advantage of CalMac's "Island Hopscotch" ticket. For example, you may go from Wemyss Bay to Rothesay on Bute, from Bute to the Cowal Peninsula, and then from Cowal to the pretty fishing village of Tarbert on Kintyre. Tickets are around £8 per passenger and £40 for a car. It's fun and sidesteps the much longer, albeit scenic, road routes. Unless you love driving, take the ferries.

CalMac has some competition from another company, **Western Ferry** (☎ **01396-704-452;** www.western-ferries.co.uk), which runs a route to Hunter's Quay in Dunoon from McInroy's Point in Gourock.

✔ **By air: British Airways** (☎ **0870-850-9850;** www.britishairways.com) coordinates direct flights from Glasgow airport to Cambeltown and Islay, but there are only one or two per day, operated by BA's local partner, Loganair. Typically, they cost around £125, and the travel time is 45 minutes.

Spending the Night

When it comes to overnight rooms, you have a variety of options, from luxury country-house hotels to basic B&Bs and self-catering options. Some have received star ratings from the tourist board (VisitScotland), which I occasionally note (please see Chapter 8 for a description of the rating system). In the listings below, room rates generally include full breakfast, unless otherwise stated. And don't forget: You may well get a better deal than the standard rack rates that I quote.

Abbotsford Hotel
$$ Ayr

About 1km (one-half mile) from the center of Ayr, this small hotel with a popular, civilized pub is curiously named after Sir Walter Scott's mansion

Ayr

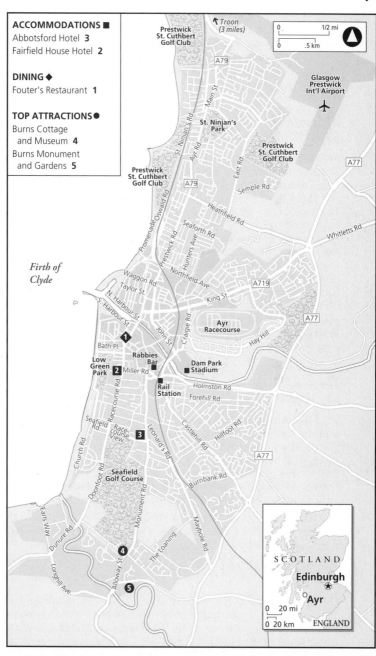

ACCOMMODATIONS ■
Abbotsford Hotel **3**
Fairfield House Hotel **2**

DINING ◆
Fouter's Restaurant **1**

TOP ATTRACTIONS ●
Burns Cottage
and Museum **4**
Burns Monument
and Gardens **5**

↑ *Troon*
(3 miles)

0   1/2 mi
0   .5 km

Prestwick
St. Cuthbert
Golf Club

A79

Glasgow
Prestwick
Int'l Airport

Main St.

St. Ninian's
Park

St. Ninian's Rd.

Ayr Rd.

East Rd.

Prestwick
St. Cuthbert
Golf Club

A77

Prestwick
St. Cuthbert
Golf Club

A79

Semple Rd.

Heathfield Rd.

Promenade

Oswald Rd.

Prestwick Rd.

Seaforth Rd.

Hunters Ave.

Whitletts Rd.

*Firth of
Clyde*

Waggon Rd.

Taylor St.

Northfield Ave.

A719

N. Harbour St.

S. Harbour St.

King St.

A77

John St.

Craigie Rd.

Ayr
Racecourse

Hay Hill

Bath Pl.

Rabbies
Bar

Dam Park
Stadium

Low
Green
Park

Miller Rd.

Rail
Station

Holmston Rd.

Racecourse Rd.

Forehill Rd.

Seafield Rd.

Race-
course
View

Leonard's Rd.

Castlehill Rd.

Hilfoot Rd.

A77

Church Rd.

Seafield
Golf Course

Doonfoot Rd.

Monument Rd.

Burnbank Rd.

Earls Way

Dunure Rd.

Alloway St.

The Loaning

Maybole Rd.

Longhill Ave.

SCOTLAND

Edinburgh ✪

○**Ayr**

0   20 mi
0   20 km

ENGLAND

rather than associating itself with local Ayrshire hero Robert Burns. It is located in a quiet residential neighborhood, less than a ten-minute walk to the shoreline and convenient to the local golf courses, too. Most of the units are smart and comfortable, with flatscreen TVs and modern bathrooms. Family run and friendly, the Abbotsford offers sound, moderately priced accommodations.

See map p. 285. 14 Corsehill Rd., Ayr, Ayrshire. ☎ **01292-261-506.** *Fax: 01292-261-606.* www.abbotsfordhotel.co.uk. *Rack rates: £85 double. MC, V.*

Ardanaiseig Hotel
$$$–$$$$ Kilchrenan

This hotel is arguably the poshest if least accessible place listed in this chapter, so if you seek a bit of luxury in an out-of-the-way corner, read on. The Ardanaiseig (*ard*-na-sag) hotel is a stone Scottish baronial pile built in the 1830s on the shores of Loch Awe; it sits at the end of a curvy single-track road through the woods some 24km (15 miles) from Taynuilt (off the main road to Oban). The gardens are especially colorful in spring when the rhododendrons are in bloom, but they have plenty of year-round interest as well. The public spaces include a large drawing room with views of the hotel's own wee island in the loch. Evening meals, supervised by Chef de Cuisine Gary Goldie, are especially memorable, and every day brings a different four-course menu. The hotel, which prefers not to take small children, has converted the loch-side boat shed into a luxury retreat.

See map p. 287. 5km (3 miles) north of Kilchrenan, off the B845 from Taynuilt, Argyll. ☎ **01866-833-333.** *Fax: 01866-833-222.* www.ardanaiseig.com. *Rack rates: £128–£424 double. AE, MC, V. Closed Jan to mid-Feb.*

The Argyll Hotel
$$ Inveraray

This waterfront hotel overlooks picturesque Loch Fyne. The attractive and stately white building, designed by Robert Adam, was built more than 250 years ago as a coach house to accommodate guests of the third duke of Argyll at nearby Inveraray Castle. Today, the hotel is still welcoming the castle's many tourist visitors, as well as other travelers in Argyll. If you can afford paying a bit more, book a room with a sea view. Advance reservations offer discounts on rack rates.

See map p. 287. Front Street, Argyll. ☎ **01499-302-466.** *Fax: 01499-302-389.* www.the-argyll-hotel.co.uk. *Rack rates: From £65–£105 double. AE, DC, MC, V.*

Fairfield House Hotel
$$$ Ayr

On the seafront at the edge of Ayr's Low Green, Fairfield House is a Victorian mansion/country home that has been restored and converted into a four-star 44-room hotel. The staff is attentive and, like at the Abbotsford (see above), will help you arrange tee times at nearby golf

Argyll

ATTRACTIONS ●

Achamore Gardens **6**
Brodick Castle **9**
Caol Ila Distillery **3**
Inveraray Castle **22**
Kilchurn Castle **19**
Kilmartin House Museum **15**
Laphroaig Distillery **4**
Mount Stuart **14**
Museum of Islay Life **1**
Rothesay Castle **13**
Scottish Sealife Sanctuary **18**

Hunting Lodge Hotel **7**
Kilmichael Country House **8**
Loch Fyne Hotel **21**
Manor House **16**
The Royal an Lochan **11**

ACCOMMODATIONS ■

Ardanaiseig **20**
The Argyll Hotel **21**
Gigha Hotel **5**
Harbour Inn **2**
Hunter's Quay Hotel **24**

DINING ◆

Ee-usk **17**
Loch Fyne Oyster Bar **23**
Russian Tavern at the
    Port Royal Hotel **12**
Seafood Cabin **10**

courses. Rooms in the main building are decorated in a country-house style, while a newer wing offers more modern décor. The units are generally large and luxurious; some of the bathrooms have bidets.

See map p. 285. 12 Fairfield Rd., Ayrshire. ☎ **01292-267-461.** *Fax: 01292-261-456.* www.fairfieldhotel.co.uk. *Rack rates: £130 double. Rates include continental breakfast. AE, DC, MC, V.*

Gigha Hotel
$$ Isle of Gigha

There aren't many options on this lovely, compact island just off the coast of Kintyre; the Gigha Hotel offers the main accommodations, run by the community trust that now owns the isle. Rooms are fairly basic but clean and tidy. Up top, directly facing the sea, are room nos. 1 and 2, which share a bathroom (and you might get a discount if requesting one of them). Otherwise, all units have en-suite facilities. Room no. 7 is spacious, overlooking the rear garden with a bit of sea view. In addition, the hotel operates some self-catering cabins around the island. The restaurant specializes in local, fresh seafood dishes, while the pub is a popular gathering spot for the islanders.

See map p. 287. Ardminish, 1km (½ mile) south of the ferry slip, Argyll. ☎ **01583-505-254.** *Fax: 01583-505-244.* www.gigha.org.uk. *Rack rates: £80 double. MC, V.*

Harbour Inn
$$–$$$ Isle of Islay

Right at the heart of Islay's largest town, Bowmore, and on the shores of Loch Indaal, the four-star Harbour Inn is your best bet for overnight accommodations on the Isle of Islay. It is well positioned for excursions south to Port Ellen and distilleries such as Laphroaig, or around the bay to picturesque towns, such as Portnahaven. Room no. 5 is particularly spacious with a big bathtub (though no shower). The restaurant (see entry later, under "Dining locally") offers assured meals with plenty of local produce, such as scallops from Lagavulin Bay.

See map p. 287. The Square, foot of Main Street, Bowmore, Argyll. ☎ **01496-810-330.** *Fax: 1496-810-990.* www.harbour-inn.com. *Rack rates: From £130 double. MC, V.*

Hunters Quay Hotel
$$ Dunoon

Right on the water, north of the Dunoon town center, this up-to-date and modernized Victorian mansion is very welcoming and comfortable. The ten guest rooms are individually sized and decorated. I'd say this is probably your best option in the immediate vicinity, and they offer friendly service and good food, too.

See map p. 287. Hunters Quay, Marine Parade. ☎ **01369-707-070.** www.hunters quayhotel.co.uk. *Rack rates: £80–£100 double. AE, MC, V.*

Hunting Lodge Hotel
$$ **Kintyre**

While the name led me to expect a 17th-century inn, the Hunting Lodge's 20th-century renovations have, alas, rather masked most of historic charms of this hotel — at least from the outside. But forgive the design of dormers and Mediterranean-style balcony railing and just enjoy the views, especially the languid summer sunsets over the sea. Inside, the whisky bar (with hundreds of single malts) offers the character that the hotel's name promises, and the meals (served daily from noon to 2:30 p.m. and 6:30–9 p.m.) usually feature plenty of local shellfish.

See map p. 287. Just south of Bellchantuy on the A83, Argyll. ☎ **01583-421-323.** *Fax: 01583-421-343.* www.thehuntinglodgehotel.com. *Rack rates: £72–£92 double. MC, V.*

Kilmichael Country House
$$$ **Isle of Arran**

This 300-year-old country house — the oldest on the island — offers some of the most unique accommodations on Arran. The rooms are furnished with antique furniture, fresh flowers, and pleasant pastel upholstery and drapes; two suites have sitting rooms as well as bedrooms. The hotel has pleasant gardens all round with a few exotic plants, while the cuisine in the dining room leans toward Scottish flavors, with dishes such as roasted chestnut soup or rack of lamb. The Kilmichael welcomes children 12 years old and above.

See map p. 287. Glen Coy, near Brodick on a private road off the A841. ☎ **01770-302-219.** *Fax: 01770-302-068.* www.kilmichael.com. *Rack rates: £150–£190 double. MC, V.*

Loch Fyne Hotel
$$$ **Inveraray**

Just north of town, this old stone house is perched on a lovely spot over the loch. The hotel includes a spa with a pool, sauna, and steam room. The bedrooms aren't fancy, but some have beautiful views of the water. Opt for the "superior double" units if you need more space. The food in the restaurant is satisfying and decent value. Occasional staffing problems of late seem to have led to some mixed reviews from recent guests.

See map p. 287. On the A83, just outside Inveraray, Argyll. ☎ **0870-950-6270.** *Fax: 01499-302-348.* www.crerarhotels.com. *Rack rates: £110–£190 double. MC, V.*

Lochgreen House Hotel
$$$ **Troon**

This lovely country-house hotel is set on 12 lush hectares (30 acres) of Ayrshire forest and landscaped gardens. The property opens onto views of the Firth of Clyde and the rocky outcropping island of Ailsa Craig. The interior evokes a more elegant bygone time, with detailed cornices, antique furnishings, and elegant oak and cherry paneling. Guests meet and mingle in two luxurious sitting rooms with log fires or take long walks on the well-landscaped grounds.

See map p. 287. Monktonhill Road, Ayrshire. ☎ **01292-313-343**. *Fax: 01292-318-661.* www.costley-hotels.co.uk. *Rack rates: £150 double. AE, MC, V.*

Malin Court Hotel
$$–$$$ **Maidens**

On one of the more scenic strips of Ayrshire coastline, this well-run hotel fronts the Firth of Clyde. It is a serviceable, welcoming retreat offering a blend of informality and comfort. The 18 bedrooms are mostly medium in size and overlook the famous Turnberry golf course. Staff can arrange hunting, fishing, riding, and sailing, as well as 18 holes on the links. The hotel offers a 20 percent discount for children younger than 16 staying in rooms separate from their parents. Children staying in the same room are only charged for meals.

See map p. 283. On the A719, off the A77, just north of Turnberry, Ayrshire. ☎ **01655-331-457**. *Fax: 01655-331-072.* www.malincourt.co.uk. *Rack rates: £130 double. AE, DC, MC, V.*

The Manor House Hotel
$$$ **Oban**

At one time, the duke of Argyll owned this Georgian residence built in 1780. With its formal exterior, this four-star hotel is warm and inviting inside. The 11 tasteful rooms have not been enlarged from their cozy 18th-century dimensions, but they have views of either Oban Harbour or the garden, plus include fine antiques and floral linens. The Manor House is well known for its fine restaurant, and guests are encouraged to take the full bed, breakfast, and dinner option; rooms with breakfast only are subject to availability.

See map p. 287. Gallanach Road, Argyll. ☎ **01631-562-087**. *Fax: 01631-563-053.* www.manorhouseoban.com. *Rack rates: £177–£265 double including the five-course dinner. AE, MC, V.*

Piersland House Hotel
$$$ **Troon**

William Leiper designed the original lodge of Piersland House in 1899, opposite Royal Troon golf course, for Sir Alexander Walker of the Johnnie Walker whisky family fame. It remained a private residence until 1956. The moderately sized guest rooms at this four-star hotel have traditional country-house styling; for more space and increased privacy, opt for one of the cottages that run along the side of the hotel.

See map p. 283. 15 Craigend Rd., Ayrshire. ☎ **01292-314-747**. *Fax 01292-315-613.* www.piersland.co.uk. *Rack rates: £145 double. AE, MC, V.*

The Royal an Lochan
$$$ Tighnabruaich

The 11-bedroom, four-star Royal an Lochan overlooks the sea in Tighnabruaich, a pleasant sailing and fishing hamlet. The hotel offers plenty of comforts and some luxurious rooms. New owners (whose property search was filmed for a British TV program) have restored part of the inn's original and long-standing name (the Royal Hotel) while not quite jettisoning the more recently adopted Gaelic moniker, which means small loch. Whatever the ownership, the "superior sea view" rooms fit the bill, additionally offering huge king-size beds and ample bathrooms (with tubs and showers), and comfy leather-upholstered furnishings. Meals are served in two conservatory-style dining rooms.

See map p. 287. Tighnabruaich, Argyll. ☎ **01700-811-239.** *Fax: 01700-811-300* `www.hotels-argyll-scotland.co.uk.` *Rack rates: £100–£200 double. AE, MC, V.*

Turnberry
$$$$ Turnberry

The seacoast hotel at Turnberry, built in 1908, is a remarkable and well-known landmark for golfers and other travelers. From afar, you can see the hotel's white facade, red-tile roof, chimneys, and dormers overlooking the practice greens and fairways of the famous course. The public rooms contain Waterford crystal chandeliers, Ionic columns, molded ceilings, and oak paneling. Each of the 220 guest rooms is furnished in a unique, early 1900s style and has a marble-sheathed bathroom. In addition to units in the main hotel, there are cottages and lodges on the grounds. Spa and health facilities are exemplary.

See map p. 283. Maidens Road, off the A77, Ayrshire. ☎ **01655-331-000.** *Fax: 01655-331-706.* `www.turnberry.co.uk.` *Rack rates: £360 double. AE, DC, MC, V.*

Dining Locally

Ayrshire and Argyll are dominated by vast coastline, so some of the finest food you'll find in the region highlights locally landed fish and seafood. Below are some of the best dining options in the region.

Braidwoods
$$$–$$$$ Dalry (Ayrshire)   FRENCH/SCOTTISH

One of the standout and exclusive fine-dining restaurants in Scotland, Braidwoods is housed in a simple cottage (known as a "butt and ben"), which has been converted into a small and not overly formal dining space southwest of Glasgow. Keith and Nicola Braidwood share the cooking chores, and the place gets very busy on weekends. Holder of a Michelin star and other accolades, Braidwoods is fairly expensive but worth the price for dishes such as seared hand-dived Isle of Mull scallops on a fragrant cardamom, lentil, tomato, and coriander sauce.

See map p. 283. Saltcoats Road, off the A737. ☎ **01294-833-544.** www.braidwoods. co.uk. *Reservations required. Fixed-price 3-course dinner: £40 AE, MC, V. Open: Tues 7–9 p.m.; Wed–Sat noon to 2 p.m. and 7–9 p.m.; Sun (mid-Sept to Apr) noon to 2 p.m. Closed in early Jan and early Sept.*

Browns @ Enterkine House
$$$ **Annbank**   **MODERN SCOTTISH**

Dining at this highly rated, five-room country house hotel, done in Art Deco from the 1930s, can be a special treat. East of Ayr, in the village of Annbank, Enterkine's menus emphasize local ingredients, whether seasonal game or fish landed at nearby Troon. The fixed-price dinners are cheaper midweek. There are also some five-star-quality overnight rooms (£210 double occupancy), while the Woodland cottage offers a quirkier retreat.

See map p. 283. Coylton Road, Annbank near Ayr. ☎ **01292-520-580.** www. enterkine.com. *Reservations required. Fixed-price meals: Lunch £19; dinner £30. AE, MC, V. Open: Sun–Fri noon to 2:30 p.m.; daily 7–9 p.m.*

Ee-usk
$$ **Oban**   **FISH/SEAFOOD**

This modern restaurant's name, the phonetic pronunciation of the Gaelic for "fish," sums up the place quite well. It serves a host of simple fish and shellfish dishes, including the creamy delights of smoked haddock soup, Cullen skink, and lightly breaded white fish or fresh shellfish platters. Located at the recently renovated North Pier in Oban, the restaurant has a bayside deck that's perfect for nice days. Ee-usk has a good wine list and some rare Scottish ales, too. No children under 10 allowed after 6 p.m.

See map p. 287. North Pier. ☎ **01631-565-666.** www.eeusk.com. *Main courses: £13–£20. MC, V. Open: Daily noon to 2:30 p.m. and 6–9:30 p.m.*

Fouter's Restaurant
$$–$$$ **Ayr**   **MODERN SCOTTISH**

In the heart of Ayr, Fouter's Restaurant occupies the cellar of an old bank, retaining the original stone floor and a vaulted ceiling. The restaurant's name is derived from the Scottish expression "foutering about," which is equivalent to "fiddling around." But no one's goofing off here: Dishes feature imaginative touches and fresh local produce.

See map p. 285. 2A Academy St. ☎ **01292-261-391.** www.fouters.co.uk. *Reservations recommended. Main courses: £13–£20. AE, DC, MC, V. Open: Tues–Sat noon to 2 p.m. and 6–9 p.m.*

Loch Fyne Restaurant and Oyster Bar
$$–$$$ **Cairndow**   **FISH/SEAFOOD**

On the road to Inveraray near the head of Loch Fyne is the famous Loch Fyne Oyster Bar. The company that owns it farms both oysters and mussels in the clear cool waters of the loch. With a glass of dry white wine at this casual (although almost always busy) restaurant, there are few things finer than a platter of raw oysters or some cooked fish dishes. Be sure to browse the nice gift shop next door.

See map p. 287. At the head of Loch Fyne on the A83. ☎ **01499-600-263.** *Reservations recommended weekdays, required at weekends. Main courses: £11–£20. AE, MC, V. Open: Daily 9 a.m.–8:30 p.m.*

MacCallums of Troon Oyster Bar
$$–$$$ Troon   FISH/SEAFOOD

Near the ferry terminal at the harbor in Troon, this seaside bistro is adjacent to a fresh fish market run by the same company. Oysters, whole sardines, grilled langoustines, sole, and combination platters are usually on the menu here. They also recently added a great little fish-and-chip shop, Wee Hurrie.

See map p. 283. The Harbour, Troon. ☎ **01292-319-339.** *Reservations recommended. Main courses: £12–£22. AE, MC, V. Open: Tues–Sat noon to 2:30 p.m. and 7–9:30 p.m.; Sun noon to 3:30 p.m.*

Russian Tavern at the Port Royal Hotel
$$–$$$ Isle of Bute   RUSSIAN/SEAFOOD

You're not likely find another place like this during your travels in Scotland. In the village of Port Bannatyne, just 3km (2 miles) north of Rothesay on the Isle of Bute, the Port Royal is a family run inn where the house specialties are Russian cuisine (for example, blinis, spicy sausage, and pavlova). Better still is the fresh fish and seafood, provided by a local fisherman. Plus, there are some rarely found Scottish ales served from kegs atop the bar in the small cafe/pub they call the Russian Tavern. Overnight rooms, two with en-suite bathrooms, are basic rather than luxurious.

See map p. 287. Main Street, Port Banatyne, Isle of Bute. ☎ **01700-505-073.** www. butehotel.com. *Main courses: £16–£24. Open: Wed–Mon 12:30–10:30 p.m. Closed Nov–Mar.*

Seafood Cabin
$–$$ Kintyre   FISH/SEAFOOD

Open during the day from June to September, this operation south of Tarbert (also called the Crab Shack) is worth a detour if you fancy sea-food. Food is cooked in a converted 1950s-style minitrailer next to a stone house in the shadow of Skipness Castle, and the meals feature langous-tines, queen scallops, mussels, smoked salmon, and more. It is completely unassuming, with chickens and ducks freely wandering on the grass around the picnic tables. There's no better place on a sunny day to have an organic bottled ale and chow down fresh fruits of the sea. Note that the Seafood Cabin is cash only and closed on Saturday.

See map p. 287. B8001, Skipness, 20km (12 miles) south of Tarbert off the A83. ☎ **01880-760-207.** *Main courses: £8–£16. Open: Sun–Fri 11 a.m.–6 p.m. No credit cards.*

Exploring Ayrshire and Argyll

Just as Sir Walter Scott dominates Lothian and the Borders, the prominence of Robert Burns is felt southwest of Glasgow in Ayrshire. The heart of "Burns Country" is here, although it extends to Dumfries as well (see Chapter 14). Down the Clyde Coast is another popular tourist attraction: **Culzean Castle.** Pronounced "cul-*lane,*" it's more of a mansion than a castle and became a favorite of General Eisenhower, who has a section of the building named after him. This region of Scotland is home to some of the world's great links **golf courses,** including world-famous Royal Troon and Turnberry, with wind-swept coastal views and dunes.

At one time, the royal burgh of **Ayr** was the most popular resort on Scotland's west coast. On the reasonably picturesque Firth of Clyde, it's only some 56km (35 miles) southwest of Glasgow — about an hour by train or by car. For many years it was a busy market town with a more important, and indeed larger, port than Glasgow's until the 18th century. Ayr offers visitors some 4km (2½ miles) of beach.

Argyll is more remote and wilder, a land of peninsulas and islands with lots of seas surrounding it. It is a region with several archaeological sites, because this part of Scotland appears to be the spot where some of the land's earliest human inhabitants settled. Although the heydays of resort towns such as Dunoon on the Cowal Peninsula or Rothesay on the Isle of Bute are past, they are experiencing a mini-revival and remain pleasant places to visit. Argyll-shire landscape ranges from wooded glens to some rather craggy peaks, with plenty of shoreline never far away.

The **Isle of Arran** is sometimes called "Scotland in miniature" because it combines mountains with more pastoral landscapes. Bute and Gigha offer smaller island respites, with quiet country lanes and uncrowded beaches. **Islay** is Scotland's whisky island, with several distilleries, but it is also just a fine place to explore. Parts of Argyll and its towns, such as Oban or Inveraray, can feel as if they have more in common with the Highlands and Western Islands. If you can't fully explore the open spaces in northern Scotland, Argyll can provide a decent substitute.

If you want the freedom to hop around a bit from mainland to island and from island to peninsulas west of Glasgow, then it may be worth buying an "Island Hopscotch" ticket from the ferry operator **Caledonian MacBrayne** (☎ **0870-565-0000;** www.calmac.co.uk). For example, you can hop from Wemyss Bay to the Isle of Bute, from there to Cowal Peninsula, and then onward to the Kintyre Peninsula. In summer, the cost for that excursion is around £10 per passenger and £35 for a car.

The top attractions

Achamore Gardens
Gigha

Toward the southern end of the Isle of Gigha, stately trees begin to dominate the landscape, creating a barrier from the harsher elements of the Atlantic and providing key protection to this memorable garden. Combining both walled and parkland plantings, it was started in 1944 by Sir James Horlick, who then owned the entire island. The best time to visit is spring and early summer to see the exceptional display of the many different species of azalea, camellia, rhododendron, and other subtropical plants. But honestly, there is never a bad time to stroll the many paths. Look out for the blue plumage of the resident peacocks. Allow about two hours.

See map p. 287. 2.5km (1½ miles) south of the ferry. Admission: By donation. Open: Daily 9:30 a.m. to dusk.

Brodick Castle and Country Park
Isle of Arran

The oldest bit of this proud mansion goes way back to the 13th century, but it has had several additions since then, most of them in the Victorian era. The home and stronghold of the dukes of Hamilton for centuries, and more recently a retreat for the duke and duchess of Montrose, the place is full of furnishings and artifacts from both families. The stag heads in the main hall are impressive enough. The immediate grounds offer lots of trails, but from here you can hike (or mountain bike) around an extensive Country Park, as well as follow the paths to Goat Fell and Glen Rosa. Allow about two hours.

See map p. 287. Brodick, Isle of Arran, .6km (4 miles) north of the pier. ☎ **01770-302-202.** www.nts.org.uk. *Admission: £11 adults; £7.50 seniors, students, and children; £26 family. Open: Castle Apr–Oct daily 11 a.m.–4 p.m. (closed Nov–Mar); Country Park daily dawn to dusk.*

Burns Cottage and Museum
Alloway

Although historically underfunded and rather basic, this attraction is now target of major renovation, due to be completed in 2011. Visitors can take a self-guided tour of the cottage that is kept in the fashion of the poet's early childhood, when livestock shared part of the building with humans. The family lived here for about a decade. After that, the cottage was expanded and used as a pub and inn, before the local Burns Society had it restored to the original, more compact size, with original features such as the "box bed" in the kitchen where the poet would have been born. Outside of the cottage is the vegetable plot that the self-sufficient Burns family would have depended on.

The museum has a treasure trove of Burnsiana, keeping the best collection of Burn's manuscripts, first editions of his books — signed in some cases — as well as many letters that Burns wrote and received. Allow about one and a half hours.

See map p. 287. Alloway, 3km (2 miles) south of Ayr on B7024. ☎ **01292-443-700.** *www.burnsheritagepark.com. Admission: £4 adults, £2.50 children and seniors, £10 family. Open: Apr–Sept daily 10 a.m.–5:30 p.m.; Oct–Mar Mon–Sat 10 a.m.–5 p.m.*

Culzean Castle and Country Park
South Ayrshire

This is a fine example of architect Robert Adam's "castellated" style (that is, built with turrets and ramparts), which replaced in the late 1700s an earlier castle keep as the family seat of the powerful Kennedy clan. After World War II, the castle was given to the National Trust for Scotland. Notwithstanding its architectural attributes — whether the celebrated round drawing room or the outstanding oval staircase — the pile is of special interest to many Americans because General Dwight D. Eisenhower was given an apartment for life here. Today, tourists can rent the six-room top-floor flat as vacation accommodations. Fans of the Scottish cult horror film *The Wicker Man* should know that scenes at the home of the devilish character played by Christopher Lee were filmed here as well. Last entry is one hour before closing. Allow about one hour.

See map p. 283. A719, west of Maybole. ☎ **01655-884-455.** *www.nts.org.uk; www.culzeanexperience.org. Admission (including entrance to the Country Park) £13 adults, £9 seniors and children, £32 family. Apr–Oct daily 10:30 a.m.–5 p.m.*

Burns: Humanitarian, poet, skirt-chaser

Robert Burns (1759–96) continues to hold a sentimental spot in the national consciousness of Scotland. In recent years, Ayrshire has begun to host an annual music and cultural festival, "Burns an' a' that" (www.burnsfestival.com), in the spring to celebrate his life. Born in Alloway on a night so gusty that part of the cottage came down, Burns was the son of a simple and pious gardener who encouraged the boy to read and seek an education. Burns was, by trade, a hardworking, though largely unsuccessful, farmer who switched to being a tax collector later in his life.

But the world knows him as the author of poetry, often set to song, such as *Auld Lang Syne,* or narrative masterpieces, such as *Tam O'Shanter.* Other works, such as *A Man's a Man for a' That,* show Burns's humanitarian leanings. In his short life, he wrote hundreds of poems and songs. Burns was also a prodigious pursuer of women who fathered numerous children, legitimate and otherwise. Distinguished but destitute, he died at age 37, of heart disease, in the southern town of Dumfries. Almost immediately, however, contributions to his widow and family were made from across Scotland. Burns was buried with some ceremony on the very day that his wife, Jean, delivered their ninth child.

Arran: Scotland in miniature?

The Isle of Arran, in the Firth of Clyde off the coast of Ayrshire, is often called "Scotland in miniature" because it combines pasture-filled lowlands with mountainous highland scenery. Indeed, the so-called Highland Boundary Fault Line bisects the island diagonally, just as it does the Scottish mainland.

But, increasingly, locals involved in tourism (www.visitarran.com) prefer to call it "Arran, the Island." Whatever, it is a fine place to visit. There are some excellent food producers including the Island Cheese Company, Isle of Arran Brewery, and Creelers, which produces smoked Scottish seafood. There is also some great hiking up to the top of craggy **Goat Fell** (874m/2,867 ft.), in the majestic valley of **Glen Rosa,** or along the rugged southern coastline near **Kildonan,** where you're almost certain to see seals and perhaps even a dolphin or two.

For archery, kayaking, sailing, rock climbing, and more outdoors activities, **Arran Adventure** (☎ **01770-302-244;** www.arranadventure.com) will arrange the works for you. It's based at the Auchrannie Spa Resort in Brodick. If you fancy a unique golfing challenge, then head west across the island from Brodick to Blackwaterfoot and try your luck at the Shiskine course. It has only 12 holes, but between the driving winds and diverting scenery, it has become a legendary challenge. A round costs about £18 ($33). Contact the **Shiskine Golf and Tennis Club** (☎ **01770-860-226;** www.shiskine golf.com).

The primary ferry services (five or six per day) depart from Ardrossan in Ayrshire to the principal town of Brodick (50-min. crossing). There's a seasonal ferry from Claonaig near Skipness (on the Kintyre Peninsula) to Arran's northern port of Lochranza. For ferry information, contact **CalMac** at ☎ **0870-565-0000** (www.calmac.co.uk). Call ☎ **0870-608-2608** for linking public transportation information.

The property surrounding the castle became Scotland's first Country Park in 1969. The expansive grounds contain a formal walled garden, an aviary, a swan pond, a camellia house, an orangery, an adventure playground, and a newly restored 19th-century pagoda. All that, not to mention a deer park, kilometers and kilometers of woodland paths, and a beach, too. Unless you're dead keen on historical houses, the Country Park is arguably the real highlight of a trip to Culzean on a fine Ayrshire day. The views over the sea to the southwest include the rounded rock of an island called Alisa Craig. Some 16km (10 miles) offshore, it's a nesting ground and sanctuary for seabirds. Allow about two hours.

See map p. 283. On the land surrounding Culzean Castle. ☎ **01655-884-400.** *Admission: Included in admission to Culzean Castle; see above. Open: Daily 9 a.m. to dusk.*

Inveraray Castle
Inveraray

This almost picture-perfect pile with fairy-tale spires sits near Loch Fyne, just outside the town of Inveraray. Belonging to the clan Campbell, the castle is still home to the 13th duke and the duchess of Argyll. Highlights in those wings that tourists can visit include the impressive armory hall, a fine collection of French tapestries, and the elaborately decorated state dining room. The grounds are particularly lovely in autumn when the leaves change color and in spring with the rhododendrons in flower. Allow at least one hour.

See map p. 287. On the A83 Trunk Road, 1km (½ mile) northeast of Inveraray on Loch Fyne. ☎ **01499-302-203.** *www.inveraray-castle.com. Admission: £9 adults, £7.50 students and seniors, £6.10 children 15 and under, £25 family. Open: Apr–Oct daily 10 a.m.–5 p.m. Closed Nov–Mar.*

Kilmartin House Museum
Kilmartin

Kilmartin House Museum is located in an area of impressive antiquity. Around here there are some 350 monuments, 150 of which are prehistoric. Settlements in this area of Argyll extend back more than 5,000 years, and it is also noted for being the place where early Celtic people came in the 6th century. The museum is full of fine archaeological artifacts, describing how the Kilmartin Glen has changed over thousands of years. The museum also offers workshops and organizes guided walks to the various local monuments. The museum cafe offers noteworthy food from local suppliers. Allow about two hours.

See map p. 287. Hwy. A816 between Lochgilphead and Oban, Kilmartin, Argyll. ☎ **01546-510-278.** *www.kilmartin.org. Admission: £5 adults, £4 seniors, £2 children, £12 family. Open: Daily Mar–Oct 10 a.m.–5:30 p.m.; Nov–Dec 25 11 a.m.–4 p.m. Closed Jan–Feb.*

Laphroaig Distillery
Islay

There are more than a half-dozen distilleries on the island of Islay (*eye*-la), and Laphroaig (la-*froig*) produce one of Scotland's quintessential island whiskies: smoky, dry, and peaty. Most people either love or loathe it. You don't have to be a fan of Scotch to enjoy a tour of the distillery. To visit and get a tour full of good anecdotes and information, you will need to make an appointment. Tours are usually at 10:15 a.m. or 2:15 p.m. Monday through Friday (and annual maintenance in July–Aug means there is less to see). Allow about one and a half hours.

See map p. 287. Near Port Ellen, on the road to Ardbeg. ☎ **01496-302-418.** *www.laphroaig.com. Admission: Free. Open: By appointment only.*

Bute: The unexplored isle

Officially, Bute considers itself Scotland's unexplored isle but it is perhaps better referred to as the country's underappreciated island. One of the easiest to reach from the mainland, Bute offers obvious attractions (see listing information) such as the Mount Stuart mansion and its great gardens or Rothesay Castle, the circular stronghold at the heart of the island's main port. But explore a bit and you will find the reasonably substantial ruins of an ancient Christian settlement at St. Blane's Church near the southern tip of the island. Walk out to the significantly more meager remains of a chapel dedicated to St. Ninian at St. Ninian's Point on the island's west coast, and you'll still be treated to the company of dozens of seabirds along the windswept shoreline. One thing you'll not have to worry about very much as you explore the rural roads, however, is crowds of tourists.

Mount Stuart
Bute

This neo-Gothic mansion belongs to the Marquess of Bute's family (descendants of the Stuart royal line). Construction of the red sandstone pile was initiated by John Crichton-Stuart, the third marquess (1847–1900), and was still ongoing when he died at the turn of the 20th century. The interiors display certain eccentricities and interests of the man, such as a ceiling in an upstairs room that is covered in stars and constellations to accommodate his interest in astrology. The garden dates back to early decades of the 18th century, when the second earl of Bute moved the family here from the port town of Rothesay. The grounds have a woodlands park, a huge walled area — the so-called wee garden — and a working vegetable plot, too. Allow about two hours.

See map p. 287. A844 near Scoulag, 8km (5 miles) south of Rothesay. ☎ 01700-503-877. www.mountstuart.com. Admission: House and grounds £8 adults, £4 children 5–16; £6.50 seniors; £20 family. Open: House May–Sept Sun–Fri 11 a.m.–5 p.m., Sat 10 a.m.–2:30 p.m.; gardens daily 10 a.m.–6 p.m.

Rothesay Castle
Bute

Located in the heart of Rothesay, only a few minutes' walk from the ferry terminal and harbor, this castle is unusual in Scotland for its circular plan. It dates to the beginning of the 13th century, with a large water-filled moat (with resident water fowl) surrounding the ramparts. Interestingly, the castle plays up the connections that this part of Scotland had with Norse rulers, King Haakon IV in particular (see Chapter 20 for more Norse history on Orkney). It is worth watching a brief video on the Scandinavian influences, battles with native Scots and the latter's eventual victory over the troops from Norway in the 13th century. Although mostly a restored ruin, the castle has an impressive pigeon tower and chapel within the grassy courtyard. If you dare (and you're thin enough), you can descend from the gatehouse into a small dungeon reserved for prisoners. Allow about one and a half hours.

See map p. 287. Rothesay, Isle of Bute. ☎ **01700-502-691.** www.historic-scotland.gov.uk. *Admission £4.20 adults, £3.40 seniors, £2.50 children. Open: Apr–Sept daily 9:30 a.m.–5:30 p.m.; Oct–Mar Sat–Wed daily 9:30 a.m.–4:30 p.m.*

Scottish Sealife Sanctuary
Barcaldine

Formerly called the Oban Seal & Marine Centre, this place offers a hospital and rehab unit for stray, sick, and injured seals. But for human visitors, the marine center has tanks and aquarium that replicate the natural habitats of sea creatures, from crabs to sharks. Other highlights include daily lectures and feedings, as well as a "stud farm" for seahorses as part of a unique breeding program and a sea otter sanctuary. The setting, among tall, shady pine trees by the water's edge, is reminiscent of Northern California. Allow about two hours.

Admission here has essentially doubled in recent years. But you can buy tickets online for discounts on the standard prices given below.

See map p. 287. A828, north of Oban, on the shores of Loch Creran. ☎ **01631-720-386.** www.sealsanctuary.co.uk. *Admission: £13 adults, £12 seniors and students, £10 children 3–14, £33 family. Open: Mar–Oct daily 10 a.m.–5 p.m.; check with center for winter hours.*

Gigha: The good isle

Pronounced *gee*-a with a hard "g" (as in *gear*), this small island off the Kintyre Peninsula gets its name from the ancient Norse ruler King Haakon who once dominated this region of Scotland. It's derived from a Scandinavian word that means "the good isle." And good, indeed, it is. Small (only 10km/6 miles long and about 2km/1¼ mile wide) and placid, Gigha is best known for its Achamore Gardens (see earlier), with their exceptional springtime display of rhododendrons and azaleas. But as a quiet place to escape and relax, it is excellent as well. There are plenty of rural and coastal walks, such as one up the central road. Past an ancient standing stone, it takes you to the Twin Beaches on a narrow isthmus of dunes linking the island to Eilean Garbh, a bulbous peninsula with views across to the isles of Islay and Jura. Gigha is also particularly noteworthy because on March 15, 2002, the residents established a community trust (www.gigha.org.uk) and assumed ownership of the isle.

Islay: Scotland's whisky island

Sometimes called the Queen of the Hebrides, Islay (*eye*-la) is truly Scotland's whisky island, with seven full-scale, world renowned distilleries, such as Ardbeg, Lagavulin, or Bunnahabhain, and also one new boutique "farm distillery" at Kilchoman (www. kilchomandistillery.com), which was established in 2005 — the first built on the island in nearly 125 years.

But there is much more than Scotch to lure you to Islay. Beaches, like the one at Machir Bay, are breathtaking. Villages such as Port Charlotte or Portnahaven are charming and placid. You can take sea cruises and look for seals and whales, or shuck oysters from the farm at Loch Gruinart. On the mull of Oa, the American monument stands in tribute to the loss of more than 250 navel seamen torpedoed offshore in World War I. Both Kilchoman and Kildalton offer masterpieces of medieval stone carving on massive Celtic crosses, befitting the island historical significance at the center of the ancient Gaelic kingdom of Dalriada.

Golfing heavens: Troon and Turnberry

For links-style golf, which emphasizes sandy dunes and rolling golf courses, you can hardly do better than the Ayrshire coastline. While there are a host of options for the avid golfer, the two best-known courses are Troon and Turnberry.

Troon

The resort town of Troon, 11km (7 miles) north of Ayr and 50km (31 miles) southwest of Glasgow, looks out across the Firth of Clyde toward the Isle of Arran. Troon takes its name from the curiously hook-shaped promontory jutting out into the sea: the "trone," or nose.

Troon and its environs offer several sandy links courses, most prominently the **Royal Troon Golf Club,** Craigends Road, Troon, Ayrshire KA10 6EP (☎ **01292-311-555;** www.royaltroon.co.uk). Royal Troon is a 7,150-yard seaside course that hosts the prestigious Open Championship, which was last played here in 2004. Hole 8, the famous "Postage Stamp," may be only 123 yards in distance, but depending upon the wind, pros sometimes need a long iron or wedge to reach the green. A second course, the 6,289-yard Portland is arguably even more challenging. Visitors, with certificate of handicap (20 for men, 30 for women), can play the course from May through October on Monday, Tuesday, and Thursday. The one-day fee to play one round on the Old Course and one on Portland is about £245, which includes morning coffee and a buffet lunch. Two rounds on Portland are about half the cost.

A much less expensive but still gratifying alternative to Royal Troon is to play one of the municipal courses run by the South Ayrshire Council, such as Darnley or Lochgreen, which runs parallel to Royal Troon at spots. Fees during the weekend range from around £20 to £35. Another option is a six-round, seven-day golf pass from the council for less than £100. Log on to www.golfsouthayrshire.com, or call the South Ayrshire Golf hot line at ☎ **01292-616-255.**

Nongolfing visitors will find plenty of room to relax on Troon's 3km (2 miles) of **sandy beaches** stretching along both sides of the harbor; the broad sands and shallow waters make it a safe haven for beach bums. From here you can take boat trips to Arran or the narrow strait north of Bute known as the Kyles of Bute.

Trains from Glasgow's Central Station arrive at the Troon station several times daily (trip time is about 40 min.; cost: £12 for a standard one-day round-trip ticket).

Turnberry

The coastal settlement of Turnberry, 81km (50 miles) south of Glasgow on the A77, was once part of the Culzean Estate. It began to flourish early in the 20th century when rail service (since disbanded) was developed, and a recognized golfing center with a first-class resort hotel was established. However, unlike Troon, which is a reasonably sized port town/village, there isn't much in Turnberry except for the luxury hotel and golf course.

From the original pair of 13-hole golf courses, the complex has developed into the two championship-level courses, Ailsa and Kintyre, known worldwide as the **Turnberry Hotel Golf Courses.** Ailsa's 18 holes have been the scene of Open tournaments and other professional golfing events. Guests of the Westin Turnberry hotel get priority access, especially on the Ailsa course. The fees to play vary. Hotel residents pay between £50 and £150, depending on the course and the season. If you're not staying at Westin Turnberry, rates range from £100 to £220. Log on to www.turnberry.co.uk, or call ☎ **01655-334-032** for details.

Spa breaks

If you want to take it slow, get pampered, and perhaps, when ready, indulge in a bit of exercise, the regions around Glasgow offer several opportunities. On the Isle of Arran, the **Auchranie Spa Resort** (☎ 01770-302-234; www.auchrannie.co.uk) is open year-round now. It offers a range of treatments and therapies, plus a 20m (66-ft.) indoor pool and a games hall for rainy days. It is located on the outskirts of Brodick. Another best bet is **Turnberry** (see below), which has a first-class gym and luxury indoor pool that has views of the sea.

Other cool things to see and do

- **Benmore Botanic Garden,** 11km (7 miles) north of Dunoon on Cowal (☎ **01396-706-261**), is part of the national botanic gardens across Scotland. Rather than formal arrangements and flower beds, this one specializes in forest planting, including an impressive row of Pacific redwoods and a cluster of towering monkey puzzle trees. There is also a good selection of rhododendrons along the miles of interlacing pathways. Open daily March through October.

- **Burns Monument and Gardens,** in Alloway about 1km (one-half mile) from the Burns Cottage, is a Grecian-classical monument, which was replicated in Edinburgh on Calton Hill. It was erected here in 1823 in a ceremony attended by the poet's widow, Jean Armour. The gardens overlook the River Doon and its famous arching bridge.

- **Caol Ila Distillery,** near Port Askaig, Islay (☎ **01496-302-760**), is one of the most distinguished distilleries on Islay, though you may not recognize the name (pronounced cull-*ee*-la). They produce not only their own sublime brand but also the key component of the Johnnie Walker blend. The setting along the narrow straight between Islay and Jura is magical. Open April through October by appointment.

- **Kilchurn Castle,** A85 east of Loch Awe (☎ **01838-200-440**), offers well-maintained ruins that date from the 16th century. They're as much fun to get to as they are to explore — you can either walk up a steep path from the car park or hop on the steamboat ferry for the short ride from the Loch Awe pier.

- **McCaig's Tower,** between Duncraggan and Laurel roads in Oban, was commissioned by a local banker around 1900 in order to employ three stonemasons who were out of work. Though never completed, the arches were intended to house statues of his family. You're free to walk through the monument and enjoy the best view of the town.

- **Museum of Islay Life,** Port Charlotte, Islay (☎ **01496-850-358**). This little museum housed in an old church focuses on the history of the island and life there, as well as the whisky-making process. It may seem a bit thrown together, but it can give context to your visit.

- **Souter Johnnie's Cottage,** in Kirkoswald about 19km (13 miles) south of Ayr, was the home of Burns's pal, the cobbler (or *souter*) named John Davidson. Davidson is name-checked in Burns's tale of Tam O'Shanter, who in real life was another friend named Douglas Graham. The cottage, which dates to 1785, contains Burnsiana, period furniture, and contemporary cobbler's tools. In the nearby kirkyard are the graves of Graham as well as Souter Johnnie and his wife, Ann. Open April through September.

Shopping for Local Treasures

Ayr and Oban are historic market towns, while smaller villages, such as
Tarbert, have some good craft shops. Many of the attractions listed
above have gift shops. The Burns Museum in Alloway (p. 285) is particularly good for souvenirs about the Scottish bard.

- ✓ **The Celtic House,** Shore St. Bowmore, Islay (☎ **01496-810-304**), is
  an excellent all-around shop with crafts, crystal, gifts, clothes, trinkets, and an excellent book selection, too. Open Monday through
  Saturday 10 a.m. to 5 p.m.

- ✓ **Crafty Kitchen,** Ardfern, midway between Oban and Lochgilphead
  (☎ **01852-500-303**), is part craft shop and part cafe. Crafty Kitchen
  features works by Scottish artists and craftspeople. The shop is
  open April through October, Tuesday through Sunday from 10 a.m.
  to 5:30 p.m.

- ✓ **Earra Gael,** the Weighbridge, Tarbert (☎ **01880-820-428**), is a small,
  harbor-side shop specializing in arts and crafts from all corners of
  Argyll, from handmade knitwear to pottery. Open April through
  October, including Sunday in midsummer, from 10 a.m. to 5 p.m.

- ✓ **Islay Woollen Mill,** Bridgeend, Islay (☎ **01496-810-563**), is an arti-
  sanal woolen mill, using fine yarn and making many items, with rich
  and earthy colors, that are a departure from the usual tartans.
  Open Monday through Saturday 9 a.m. to 5 p.m.

- ✓ **Mahailia Jewellery Design,** 150 Barmore Rd., Tarbert (☎ **01880-
  820-331**), is a shop owned by Mahailia Scott, a young jewelry
  designer with an eye for classy, timelessly modern gold and silver
  rings, earrings, bracelets, and more. Her shop is right at the harbor
  in Tarbert. Open Monday through Saturday 10 a.m. to 5 p.m.

Doing the Pub Crawl

Typically, you'll find no shortage of pubs, especially in the larger towns
of Ayrshire and Argyll. In some of the smaller settlements, the local inn
may be the only place to grab a dram of whisky or a pint. Several of the
hotels (and a couple of the dining options) listed earlier in this chapter
have public-house licenses and welcome nonresidents. In addition, consider the following:

- ✓ **Oban Inn,** Stafford Street, Oban (☎ **01631-562-484**). This classic
  whitewashed pub, near the water just off the town's main street,
  has a warm, old-fashioned elegance. It was refurbished in 2008 but
  not to the detriment of its traditional features. Open daily from
  11 a.m. to 1 a.m.

✔ **Rabbie's Bar,** Burns Statue Square, Ayr (☎ **01292-262-112**). The bar has walls covered with the pithy verses of Robert Burns and his portrait. However, don't come here expecting poetry readings in a quiet corner. The crowd, if not particularly literary, is talkative. Open Monday through Saturday from 11 a.m. to 12:30 a.m.; on Sunday, it's open from noon to midnight.

Fast Facts: Ayrshire and Argyll

Area Codes

There are several area codes in Ayrshire and Argyll. Among the main ones: Arran is **01770,** Ayr is **01292,** Bute is **01700,** Campbeltown is **01586,** Gigha is **01583,** Inveraray is **01499,** Islay is **01496,** Oban is **01631,** and Tarbert is **01880.** You need to dial the prefix only if you're calling from outside the area you want to reach.

ATMs

Cash machines at banks in bigger towns are common, but don't expect all to be linked internationally.

Emergencies

Dial ☎ **999** for police, fire, or ambulance.

Hospitals

In Ayrshire, the National Health Service's Ayr Hospital is on Dalmellington Road. (☎ 01292-610-555). The major hospital for emergencies in Argyll is the Lorn and Islands District General Hospital, Glengallan Road, Oban (☎ 01631-567-500). Medical advice is available by calling NHS 24 at ☎ 08454-242-424.

Information

For tourist information online, visit www. visitscotland.com. The Ayr tourist office is at 22 Sandgate, Ayr (☎ 01292-678-100). It's open from Easter to August, Monday through Saturday from 9 a.m. to 6 p.m. (also on Sun 10 a.m.–5 p.m. July–Aug) and September to the day before Easter, Monday through Saturday from 9:15 a.m. to 5 p.m. In Oban, the tourist office is in the Old Church, Argyll Square (☎ 01631-563-122). April to mid-June and mid-September to October, it's open Monday through Friday 9:30 a.m. to 5 p.m. and Saturday and Sunday 10 a.m. to 4 p.m.; mid-June through mid-September, hours are Monday to Saturday 9 a.m. to 8 p.m. and Sunday 9 a.m. to 7 p.m.; and November through March, it's open Monday to Saturday 9:30 a.m. to 5 p.m. and Sunday noon to 4 p.m.

Internet Access

Cafe na Lusan, 9 Craigard Rd., Oban (☎ 01631-567-268), is open Tuesday through Thursday from 11 a.m. to 8 p.m., Friday and Saturday from 11 a.m. to 10 p.m., and Sunday from noon to 7 p.m. The charge is £1 for 15 minutes.

Post Office

The main post offices are Corran Esplanade, Oban (☎ 01631-562-430); Main Street South, Inveraray (☎ 01499-302-062); and 65 Sandgate, Ayr (☎ 0845-722-334).

Chapter 16

The Trossachs to Fife

In This Chapter

▶ Resting your tired feet in cozy hotels

▶ Dining on local lamb

▶ Visiting the stamping grounds of William Wallace and Robert the Bruce

▶ Enjoying a pint at the best local pubs

*T*he area of central Scotland from the Trossachs to Fife teems with attractions — and many are within easy reach of Edinburgh and Glasgow. The region's flagship settlements are the historic city of Stirling in the heart of central Scotland and the east coast port of St. Andrews in Fife. Other key settlements include Dunfermline, Dunblane, and Callander.

Stirling received royal burgh status from King David in 1124 and, for a spell, was the de facto capital of Scotland. Its castle and palace, all largely intact, became a favorite residence for Scottish royalty during the reign of the Stuarts. Many people come to see the historic sites of the surrounding area, which has seen its share of battles between Scottish and the English forces. Both William Wallace, who has a towering monument in Stirling, and King Robert the Bruce led their armies to decisive victories in and around Stirling.

Other things to see and do include visiting **Dunfermline Abbey** in Fife, where early Scottish royalty is buried, and the well-preserved ruins of **Doune Castle** (which Monty Python used in the film *The Holy Grail*) near Dunblane. For natural beauty, the Trossach Mountains begin to approach the majesty of the Highlands, the Queen Elizabeth Forest Park has plenty of wooded glens, and the banks of Loch Lomond are famously bonnie in both song and reality.

The region of **Fife,** north of the Firth of Forth from Edinburgh, still likes to call itself a "kingdom," a distinction dating to Pictish prehistoric times when Abernethy was Fife's capital. Even today, the Kingdom of Fife evokes romantic episodes and the pageantry of Scottish kings. Indeed, some 14 of Scotland's 66 royal burghs lay in this rather self-contained shire on a broad eastern peninsula between the Forth and Tay rivers. If you're at all interested in golf, **St. Andrews** needs no introduction. Home to one of the oldest courses in the world — as well as the association that decides the rules for the sport — St. Andrews, also a college town with cobblestone streets, is the golf mecca of the world. There are many other attractive coastal towns in Fife south and east of St. Andrews in an area known as East Neuk.

Getting to the Trossachs and Fife

You don't necessarily need a car if you're just going to visit St. Andrews or Stirling, because both places are navigable by foot. If your visit is a day trip from Edinburgh or Glasgow, for example, consider taking a train or the bus. Even if you want to see an attraction that lies outside the towns, additional trains and buses are available for short jaunts.

  ✔ **By car:** To get to Stirling from Edinburgh, take the M9; from Glasgow, take the M80. To get to Callander and Trossachs, catch the A84 from Stirling. To get to Loch Lomond, follow the A82 out of Glasgow or the A811 from Stirling. To get to St. Andrews from Edinburgh, cross the Forth Bridge and catch the A92 to the A91. From Glasgow to St. Andrews, take the M80 north toward Stirling, then take the A91. The A91 connects Stirling and St. Andrews.

  ✔ **By train:** To get to Fife from Edinburgh, take the Fife loop, operated by **First ScotRail** (☎ **0845-748-4950;** www.firstscotrail.com) from Haymarket Station. There is no direct train service to St. Andrews, but there's a stop some 13km (8 miles) away at the town of Leuchars. The trip from Edinburgh Haymarket takes about one hour and costs between £14 and £25. After you arrive at Leuchars, you can take a bus to St. Andrews.

  To get to Stirling, trains depart from Edinburgh Waverley and Glasgow Queen Street stations. There are no railway lines into the Trossachs, per se, but you can take the train to Balloch, near Loch Lomond, from Glasgow.

  ✔ **By bus:** For bus timetables, call ☎ **0871-200-2233** or log on to www.travelinescotland.com. The bus ride from Edinburgh to St. Andrews takes about two hours. The ride from Glasgow to Stirling takes about 45 minutes.

Spending the Night

Before you pick your accommodations, it's a good idea to decide what you want to see and in what order so you don't find yourself needlessly crisscrossing the area. For more accommodations choices than those listed below, such as smaller B&Bs, contact the tourism board (☎ **0845-22-55-121;** www.visitscotland.com).

If you don't like what you see below, a few of my "Dining Locally" recommendations — Creagan House and Mhor, for example — also have overnight rooms. Some of the hotels and inns I list have earned star ratings from the tourist board (see Chapter 8 for a description of the rating system). Rates below include full breakfast, unless otherwise stated. And remember: You may well get a better deal than the advertised rack rates.

Cameron House on Loch Lomond
$$$$ Luss

Posh, plush, and perched on the shores of Loch Lomond, the five-star Cameron House hotel offers premier lodgings in 95 units, with four restaurants, a couple of bars, health club, and tennis courts. The midrange deluxe rooms face the water, while the luxury suites are part of the original house and allow guests to have their meals in the sitting rooms. Dinning options include a restaurant under the direction of Edinburgh's Michelin star chef Martin Wishart, with a six-course tasting menu priced at £65.

See map p. 309. A82 north of Balloch, Dumbartonshire. ☎ **01389-755-565.** *www. cameronhouse.co.uk. Rack rates: £180–£210 double. AE, MC, V.*

The Craw's Nest Hotel
$$–$$$ Anstruther

Once a manse (a minister's house if you didn't know), the Craw's Nest traded holiness for hospitality when the building became a hotel. This inn has six suites and two double rooms with four-poster beds amid its 50 units. If you want nice views, ask for a room in the wing overlooking the sea and the Isle of May.

See map p. 319. Bankwell Road, off Pittenweem Road, Fife. ☎ **01333-310-691.** *Fax: 01333-312-216. www.crawsnesthotel.co.uk. Rack rates: From £80 double. AE, DC, MC, V.*

Cromlix House
$$$ Kinbuck

This four-star small hotel is a sportsman's dream, traditionally drawing fishermen and hunters with its 1,200 hectares (2,000 acres) of woodlands that stretch along the Allan Water. But Cromlix House is very romantic as well. The restored three-story Victorian pile captures the elegance of affluence in the 19th century; the sitting rooms and guest rooms are decorated with fine art and period furniture, and common areas such as the library and conservatory have been restored. Online bookings offer substantial savings over standard rates.

See map p. 309. On the B8033 from the A9 north of Stirling. ☎ **01786-822-125.** *Fax 01786-825-450. www.cromlixhouse.com. Rack rates: £200 double. AE, DC, MC, V.*

Drover's Inn
$$ Inverarnan

The stuffed, snarling, and slightly worn animals near the entrance give a pretty good hint about the nature of this rustic tavern with restaurant and

Around Stirling and the Trossachs

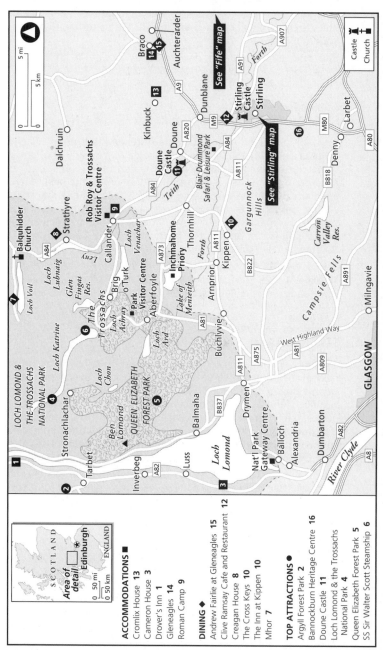

SCOTLAND
Area of detail
Edinburgh
ENGLAND
0   50 mi
0 50 km

ACCOMMODATIONS ■

Cromlix House **13**
Cameron House **3**
Drover's Inn **1**
Gleneagles **14**
Roman Camp **9**

DINING ◆

Andrew Fairlie at Gleneagles **15**
Clive Ramsay Cafe and Restaurant **12**
Creagan House **8**
The Cross Keys **10**
The Inn at Kippen **10**
Mhor **7**

TOP ATTRACTIONS ●

Argyll Forest Park **2**
Bannockburn Heritage Centre **16**
Doune Castle **11**
Loch Lomond & the Trossachs
    National Park **4**
Queen Elizabeth Forest Park **5**
SS Sir Walter Scott Steamship **6**

overnight rooms. The atmospheric pub usually has an open fire going, barmen in kilts, and plenty of travelers nursing their drinks. Main courses are moderately priced as are the accommodations. There are 10 overnight units in the original house, built in 1705, and another 16 rooms have been added in a new building.

See map p. 309. A82 at Inverarnan by Ardlui. ☎ **01301-704-234.** www. droversinn.co.uk. *Rack rates: £58–£78 double. MC, V.*

Gleneagles
$$$$ Auchterarder

Arguably Scotland's most famous hotel-and-golf resort, Gleneagles was built as a swanky inn in 1924 in the style of a French château. Who needs Versailles, when you can have a "Riviera in the Highlands," as the initial acclaim raved? There are more than 250 rooms, the best of which are the specially decorated suites. The Whisky Suites, for example, have separate sitting rooms with dining spaces for sipping single malts or having a relaxed breakfast in your robe. The hotel has its own restaurant, but better still is the one on the premises run by Chef Andrew Fairlie (see "Dining Locally," later in this chapter).

See map p. 309. Auchterarder, off the A823 (19km/12 miles northeast of Stirling). ☎ **866-881-9525** *from the U.S., or 0800-389-3737. Fax: 01764-662-134.* www. gleneagles.com. *Rack rate: £320–£410double. AE, DC, MC, V.*

The Inn at Lathones
$$$ Near Largoward

The Inn at Lathones is set in a picturesque spot just 8km (5 miles) from St. Andrews. It may be 400 years old, but the inn's overnight rooms are thoroughly modern, equipped with Italian furniture, stereos, and roomy bathrooms. Of the 21 units, 6 are considered luxury rooms, which include two suites, one with a 1.8m-plus (6-ft.) four-poster bed. The main house, with a restaurant, offers comfortable public areas with fireplaces and sitting rooms. The bar normally stocks a good selection of Scottish ales and whiskies. Online bookings offer substantial savings over standard rates.

See map p. 319. Off the A915 (8km/5 miles south of St. Andrews on the A915). ☎ **01334-840-494.** *Fax: 01334-840-694.* www.theinn.co.uk. *Rack rates: £180 double. AE, MC, V.*

Keavil House Hotel
$$$ Crossford (near Dunfermline)

This tranquil country hotel, part of the Best Western chain, is set on a dozen acres of forested land and gardens. Many of the 73 bedrooms are generous in size and well appointed, each with a bathroom. Master bedrooms contain four-poster beds. The hotel offers dining in its **Cardoon Restaurant.**

See map p. 319. Main Street, Crossford (3km/2 miles west of Dunfermline). ☎ **01383-736-258.** *Fax: 01383-621-600.* www.keavilhouse.co.uk. *Rack rates: £120 double. AE, DC, MC, V. Closed Dec 31–Jan 1.*

Old Course Hotel
$$$$ St. Andrews

This hotel overlooks the 17th fairway — the infamous "Road Hole" — of its namesake, St. Andrews Old Course (to which the hotel has no formal connection). It is a world-class operation, with price tags to match, boasting 144 bedrooms and 35 suites. It has full spa facilities, of course, as well. The eating and drinking options encompass the contemporary **Sands Grill** seafood bar and restaurant, and fine dining at the **Road Hole Restaurant,** where gentlemen are encouraged to wear jackets to dinner, or the **Jigger Inn,** a whitewashed traditional pub that serves as the unofficial 19th hole for the adjacent golf course. Children younger than 12 can stay in a parent's room at no extra charge.

See map p. 321. Old Station Road, St. Andrews. ☎ **01334-474-371.** *Fax 01334-477-668.* www.oldcoursehotel.co.uk. *Rack rates: £265 double. AE, DC, MC, V.*

The Portcullis
$$ Stirling

This little hotel sits in the shadow of Stirling Castle. The rooms are comfortable but unpretentious, and the staff members are generally friendly. The Portcullis has been around for hundreds of years and has the rustic feel of an old coach inn and tavern. The downstairs bar is a plus or a minus, depending on your point of view — it's perfect for a nightcap, not so perfect if you want to be in bed before 10 p.m. An added touch is the flowers that grow in the lovely walled-in beer garden.

See map p. 317. Next to Stirling Castle. ☎ **01786-472-290.** *Fax: 01786-446-103. Rack rates: £82 double. AE, MC, V.*

Roman Camp
$$$ Callander

This country-house hotel near Roman ruins is one of the more interesting places to stay in the area. Built in 1625 as a hunting lodge, it became a hotel in the 1930s, retaining charming low ceilings, creaking corridors, and snug furniture. The drawing room and conservatory have lovely period furniture and antiques. The River Teith runs along the hotel's beautiful 8 hectares (20 acres) of grounds.

See map p. 309. Off Main Street from the A84. ☎ **01877-330-003.** *Fax: 01877-331-533.* www.romancamphotel.co.uk. *Rack rates: £145 double. AE, DC, MC, V.*

Stirling Highland Hotel
$$$ Stirling

The Barceló Stirling Highland Hotel is housed in a converted Victorian high school in the city's attractive Old Town. This luxury four-star hotel is therefore in easy hoofing distance of the castle and surrounds. There are 46 double rooms and another 20 premium doubles that have seating areas with easy chairs. The health and leisure club is useful, featuring a pool, steam room, gym equipment, and more. Four family rooms include adjoining spaces with bunk beds.

See map p. 317. Spittal Street. ☎ **01786-272-727.** *Fax: 01786-272-829.* www. barcelo-hotels.co.uk. *Rack rates: £150 double. AE, DC, MC, V.*

Dining Locally

Your dining needs may be satisfied by your hotel, between a full breakfast in the morning and a meal in the dining room at night. But if you decide to step outside your hostelry for a bite, this section guides you toward some of the best options — including some of the top dining in all of Scotland. Remember that a few places listed below have overnight rooms, too.

Andrew Fairlie at Gleneagles
$$$$ **Auchterarder   FRENCH**

Andrew Fairlie is probably the most talented chef in Scotland: He not only has prowess in the kitchen but knows how to bring together a talented team. Dinners here are seamless but not particularly stuffy affairs. If you have the money (we're talking £100 per person), go for the six-course tasting, or degustation, menu. The chef's signature dish is smoked lobster, but other highlights may include foie gras terrine with apricot and grapefruit chutney or "twice-cooked" Gressingham duck with Asian watercress salad. In 2006, Fairlie received two Michelin stars — joining an elite group in the U.K.

See map p. 309. Gleneagles Hotel, Auchterarder. ☎ **01764-694-267.** www.andrew fairlie.com. *Reservations required. Fixed-price dinner: £75. AE, MC, V. Open: Mon–Sat 6:30–10 p.m. Closed Sun and most of Jan.*

Barnton Bar & Bistro
$–$$ **Stirling   PUB FOOD**

The city of Stirling isn't exactly rich in dining options, but this casual place is good for a coffee, lunch, or an early evening meal. While there's nothing particularly revelatory on the menu, the Barnton is a friendly and relatively inexpensive place in the middle of Stirling and near the railway station. The premises are a converted pharmacy with a games room to the rear, usually populated with university students.

See map p. 317. 3 Barnton St. ☎ **01786-461-698.** www.thebistro.co.uk. *Main courses: £5–£10. MC, V. Open: Restaurant daily 10:30 a.m.–7:30 p.m.; bar Sun–Thurs noon to midnight, Fri–Sat noon to 1 a.m.*

The Cellar
$$$ **Anstruther   SEAFOOD/SCOTTISH**

The Cellar is among the best restaurants in the region. Located in an ancient fishing village and next door to a fisheries museum, the restaurant is a hot spot for delicacies from the sea. In addition to staples such as crab, scallops, and lobster, the mostly seafood menu includes Scottish beef and dishes such as crayfish-and-mussel bisque and monkfish with herb and garlic sauce. The stone basement dining room is unassuming and comfortable, with candlelight and fireplaces.

See map p. 319. 24 East Green, off the courtyard behind the Fisheries Museum. ☎ **01333-310-378.** _www.cellaranstruther.co.uk. Reservations required. Fixed-price 2-course dinner: £34. AE, DC, MC, V. Open: Mon–Sat 6:30–9 p.m. and Fri–Sat 12:30–2 p.m._

Creagan House
$$$ Strathyre SCOTTISH/FRENCH

Cherry and Gordon Gunn run this charming inn, well situated for country walks, in a 17th-century farmhouse with a few overnight rooms. In the evenings, Gordon repairs to the kitchen where he cooks some sumptuous French-influenced meals using mostly local ingredients. Especially welcome are the vegetables, often grown just up the road, which he prepares to accompany the main courses; these veggies are far from an afterthought. Don't be fooled by the baronial-style splendor of the dining room, however. It's a much, much more recent addition to the historic house. If you're spending the night, the units, including one with a four-poster bed, start at £120, including full breakfast.

See map p. 309. A84, north of Strathyre. ☎ **01877-384-638.** _www.creaganhouse. co.uk. Reservations required. Fixed-price dinner: £30. AE, MC, V. Open: One seating Fri–Tues 7:30–8:30 p.m. Closed Feb._

The Cross Keys
$$–$$$ Kippen MODERN SCOTTISH

One of the oldest inns in the region west of Stirling, the Cross Keys' fortunes have been revived over the past few years thanks to new owners. Deby McGregor and her husband/chef, Brian, provide modern Scottish pub grub from breast of Guinea fowl to Moroccan lamb stew or a simple but always hand-battered fish with real chips. There are three contemporary rooms for overnight stays, each with their own bathroom, for £60 to £80 for double occupancy with breakfast.

Main St., Kippen ☎ **01786-870-293.** _www.kippencrosskeys.com. Main courses £12. AE, M, V. Tues–Fri noon to 3 p.m., 5–9 p.m.; Sat noon to 9 p.m.; Sun noon to 8 p.m._

Hermann's
$$– $$$ Stirling AUSTRIAN/SCOTTISH

This simply decorated restaurant — named after Tyrolean owner Hermann Aschaber — has a unique menu influenced by both Austria and Scotland. So, will it be Jägerschnitzel or roast Barbary duck breast? The aproned staff is excellent and helpful in decoding the menu. And don't even think about skipping the wonderful Austrian desserts. You can't beat the location here, just down the road from Stirling Castle.

See map p. 317. 58 Broad St. ☎ 01786-450-632. www.hermanns.co.uk. Reservations recommended. Fixed-price dinner: £20. AE, DC, MC, V. Open: Daily noon to 2:30 p.m. and 6–10 p.m.

The Inn at Kippen
$$ **Kippen SCOTTISH**

About a 15-minute drive west of Stirling on the A811, Kippen is a typical country village in the rolling hills north of Glasgow. The Inn at Kippen is a modern version of the country pub and restaurant, which specializes in Scottish fare such as lamb cooked two ways: rump roast and mini–shepherds pie. There are also a few overnight rooms at £85.

See map p. 309. Fore Road, Kippen. ☎ 01786-871-010. www.theinnatkippen. co.uk. Main courses: £8–£16. AE, MC, V. Open: Daily noon to 2:30 p.m. and 6–9 p.m.

Mhor
$$$ **Balquhidder MODERN SCOTTISH**

Just up the highway from Creagan House, here is another gem in the heart of the Trossachs serving lunch and dinner at an 18th-century farmhouse that overlooks Loch Voil near the village of Balquhidder. The sunroom dining space is modern and so is the cooking, specializing in seasonal goods. Roast chicken topped with foie gras, belly of pork served with sage and onion jus, or seared fish on a bed of shredded celeriac are just some examples. Dinner is expensive (albeit worth it), though lunches are less costly. The adjoining lodge has 11 attractive rooms starting at £100, which includes breakfast. And in the town of Callander, the same people have an outstanding fish and chips restaurant, Mhor Fish.

See map p. 309. Off the A84 near Balquhidder (9.5km/6 miles west of turnoff). ☎ 01877-384-622. http://mhor.net. Reservations recommended. Fixed-price dinner: £46. AE, MC, V. Open: Daily noon to 1:45 p.m. and 7–8:45 p.m. Closed Jan to mid-Feb.

Ostlers Close
$$–$$$ **Cupar MODERN SCOTTISH**

Fife has a host of good restaurants, and this charming one in a 17th-century building is among the best. Located in the town of Cupar, west of St. Andrews, Ostlers Close emphasizes fresh and local produce. The daily changing menus can feature dishes such as seared Isle of Mull scallops, roast saddle of venison, or roast filet of Pittenweem cod. It's open only for lunch on Saturday.

See map p. 319. 25 Bonnygate, Cupar (11km/7 miles west of St. Andrews). ☎ 01334-655-574. www.ostlersclose.co.uk. Reservations recommended. Main courses: £10–£18. AE, MC, V. Open: Tues–Fri 7–9:30 p.m. and Sat 12:15–1:30 p.m. Closed Sun–Mon.

The Peat Inn
$$$ Near Cupar   MODERN SCOTTISH/FRENCH

The Peat Inn had long had a great reputation, but it came under new ownership in 2006. Luckily, it was taken over by Chef Geoffrey Smeddle, who brought his own awards and accolades — and has since earned a Michelin star for the Peat Inn. The main white-washed building dates to 1760, with eight overnight suites in the adjacent "Residence" (doubles are about £175). Meals highlight local, seasonal ingredients in dishes such as seared scallops with fennel puree, roast filet of beef with chanterelle mushrooms, or tayberry and elderflower tart.

See map p. 319. Peat Inn, at the junction of the B940 and B941. ☎ **01334-840-206**. *Fax 01334-840-530.* www.thepeatinn.co.uk. *Reservations required. Fixed-price lunch: £18. Main courses: £18–£24 Open: Tues–Sat 12:30–1:30 p.m. and 7–9 p.m.*

The Seafood Restaurant
$$$–$$$$ St. Andrews   FISH/SEAFOOD

This St. Andrews restaurant is a second branch for owner Tim Butler and his business partner, Chef Craig Millar, who began their Seafood Restaurant farther down the coast in St. Monans. Here, the location on the seafront is spectacular, and given that the dining room is essentially housed in a glass box, there is no missing the views. Dishes range from crab risotto to pan-seared scallops, with plenty of fancy accompaniments on the side.

See map p. 321. The Scores, St. Andrews. ☎ **01334-479-475**. www.theseafood restaurant.com. *Fixed-price meals: Lunch £22; dinner £45. AE, MC, V. Open: Daily noon to 2:30 p.m. and 6:30–10 p.m.*

Exploring the Trossachs to Fife

There is a lot to cover in this region, which stretches across the country.

North by northwest of Glasgow are the **Trossachs,** a mountain range distinct from the Highlands but appealing for its forests and lochs. One key attraction here is Loch Katrine, popularized by Sir Walter Scott's poem *The Lady of the Lake.* Two villages that provide gateways to the more mountainous northern regions are Callander and Aberfoyle. They're often overrun by the bus tours in the high season because they offer places to rest, eat, and shop during the day.

Historic **Stirling,** with Stirling Castle set dramatically on the hill above the town. During the reign of the Stuart family monarchs in the 16th century, royalty preferred Stirling to Edinburgh, so it became the de facto capital of the country. The coronation of Mary Queen of Scots, only a child at the time, took place in Stirling. High on another hill outside city center stands the prominent Wallace Monument. Nearby, Stirling Bridge is believed to be the crucial site of a 13th-century battle between English invaders and the ragtag band of Scots led by William Wallace (forever immortalized — if fictionalized, as well — in the movie *Braveheart*). On the southern outskirts of the city is another, more famous battleground: Bannockburn. Somewhere around here in 1314, a well-armed English-led force was routed by Scottish troops headed by King Robert the Bruce.

More of a ruin than Stirling Castle, but arguably more evocative, is Doune Castle near the town of Dunblane, which has its own attractive and historic cathedral.

The highlight of Fife for golfers is undoubtedly **St. Andrews,** which many consider the most sacred spot of the sport. But the town itself, named after the country's patron saint, is also of ecclesiastical and scholarly importance. Closer to Edinburgh, **Dunfermline** was once the capital of Scotland; its abbey witnessed the births of royalty and contains the burial grounds of several royals as well.

Want to save a buck or two? At some attractions, you can pay a single discounted price for admission to more than one site: St. Andrews Castle and St. Andrews Cathedral, for example.

The top attractions

Andrew Carnegie Birthplace Museum
Dunfermline

In 1835, future U.S. industrialist and philanthropist Andrew Carnegie (pronounced kar-*ney*-gee in Scotland) was born just down the hill from Dunfermline Abbey. This museum is composed of the 18th-century cottage where he lived as a child and a memorial hall funded by his widow, Louise. Displays tell the story of this weaver's son, who immigrated to America and became one of the richest men in the world. Though a union-busting industrialist, Carnegie gave away hundreds of millions of dollars before his death in 1919. Dunfermline received the first of some 2,810 lending libraries he provided throughout Great Britain and America, and the town was also bequeathed Pittencrieff Park. A statue in the park honors Carnegie, who once worked as a bobbin boy in a cotton factory. Allow about two hours.

See map p. 319. Moodie Street, Dunfermline. ☎ **01383-723-638.** www.carnegie birthplace.com. *Admission: Free. Open: Mar–Nov Mon–Sat 10 a.m.–5 p.m.; Sun 2–5 p.m. Closed Dec–Feb.*

Argyll Forest Park
Near Loch Lomond

Maintained by the Forestry Commission, the Argyll Forest Park offers some 24,000 hectares (60,000 acres) to explore from forest trail strolls to scrambles up the "Arrochar Alps." If you want the latter, try your chances by climbing the Cobbler, whose craggy peak is hard to miss. The trail begins at the head of Loch Long just north of the village of Arrochar on

Stirling

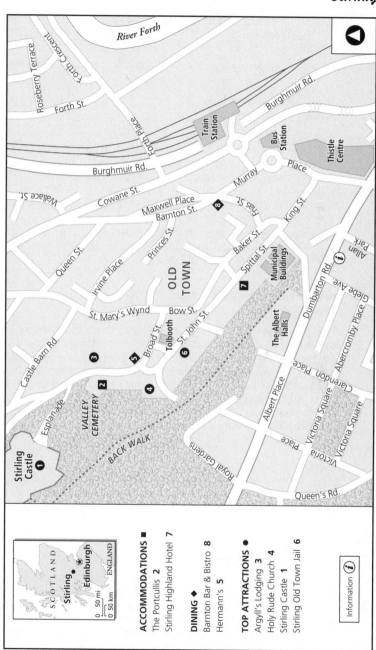

River Forth

Roseberry Terrace

Forth Crescent

Forth St.

Forth Place

Burghmuir Rd.

Train Station

Bus Station

Thistle Centre

Burghmuir Rd.

Wallace St.

Cowane St.

Murray Place

Maxwell Place

Barnton St.

Friars St.

King St.

8

Queen St.

Princes St.

Irvine Place

Baker St.

Spittal St.

OLD TOWN

Municipal Buildings

Allan Park

Dumbarton Rd.

Glebe Ave.

St. Mary's Wynd

Bow St.

7

The Albert Halls

Abercromby Place

Castle Barn Rd.

Broad St.

Tolbooth

St. John St.

Clarendon Place

3

5

6

Albert Place

Victoria Square

Victoria Square

2

4

Esplanade

VALLEY CEMETERY

BACK WALK

Royal Gardens

Victoria Place

Stirling Castle

1

Queen's Rd.

Information **i**

SCOTLAND

Stirling

Edinburgh

ENGLAND

0   50 mi

0   50 km

ACCOMMODATIONS ■
The Portcullis **2**
Stirling Highland Hotel **7**

DINING ◆
Barnton Bar & Bistro **8**
Hermann's **5**

TOP ATTRACTIONS ●
Argyll's Lodging **3**
Holy Rude Church **4**
Stirling Castle **1**
Stirling Old Town Jail **6**

the A83. On a clear day, the view from the summit takes in a good portion of the west coast of Scotland. The area is home to acres of wildflowers, birds, and even seals in the sea lochs. For park information and trail maps, visit the **Ardgartan Visitor Center** (A83, Loch Long; ☎ **01301-702-432**), or log on to www.forestry.gov.uk. Allow two to five hours.

See map p. 309. Arrochar, off the A83. Admission: Free. Open: Daily dawn to dusk.

Argyll's Lodging
Stirling

Sir William Alexander, the founder of Nova Scotia (or "New Scotland"), built this 17th-century town house, one of Scotland's finest surviving Renaissance homes. After being used as a youth hostel in the 20th century, the house is today decorated as it would have been in 1680, when the ninth earl of Argyll lived here, with accurate historic ornaments and period furniture, plus tapestries, paintings, and even clothing from the era. Allow about one hour for tour.

See map p. 317. Castle Wynd. ☎ 01786-431-319. www.historic-scotland. gov.uk. Admission: Included in Stirling Castle ticket (p. 326). Open: Apr–Sept daily 10 a.m.–6 p.m.; Oct–Mar daily 10 a.m.–5 p.m.

Bannockburn Heritage Centre
Near Stirling

The once boggy land along a stream called the Bannock Burn near Stirling was the scene of King Robert the Bruce's victory over the troops of English King Edward II in 1314. The decisive win helped to ensure that Scotland kept its independence from England. The Bannockburn Heritage Centre, run by the National Trust for Scotland, has various exhibits (and gives visitors an opportunity to don some chain mail armor) and also shows an audiovisual presentation re-creating the battle and telling Bruce's story. A short walk through a grassy park (open year-round) takes you to an impressive statue of the Bruce on his steed. Allow about one and a half hours.

See map p. 309. Glasgow Road, off the M80. ☎ 01786-812-664. Admission: £5.50 adults, £4.50 seniors and children, £15 family. Open: Heritage Centre Mar and Oct 10 a.m.–5 p.m.; Apr–Sept daily 10 a.m.–5:30 p.m. Closed Nov–Feb, except for specially reserved group tours.

Deep Sea World
North Queensferry

In the early 1990s, a group of entrepreneurs sealed the edges of an abandoned rock quarry under the Forth Rail Bridge, filled it with sea water, and positioned a 112m (370-ft.) acrylic tunnel on the bottom. Stocked with a menagerie of sea creatures, it is Scotland's most comprehensive aquarium. Now, compared to what you find in cities such as Orlando, this may

Fife

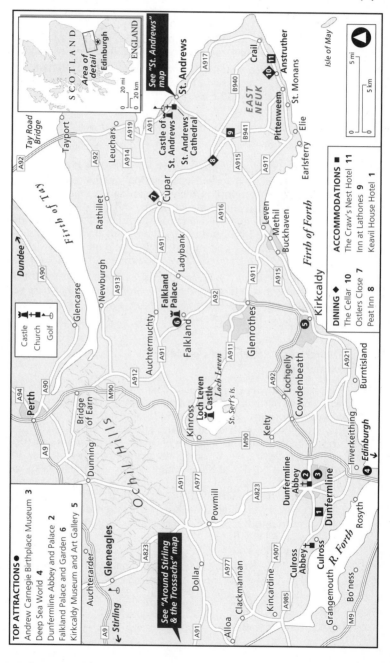

TOP ATTRACTIONS ●
Andrew Carnegie Birthplace Museum **3**
Deep Sea World **4**
Dunfermline Abbey and Palace **2**
Falkland Palace and Garden **6**
Kirkcaldy Museum and Art Gallery **5**

Castle
Church
Golf

DINING ◆
The Cellar **10**
Ostlers Close **7**
Peat Inn **8**

ACCOMMODATIONS ■
The Craw's Nest Hotel **11**
Inn at Lathones **9**
Keavil House Hotel **1**

See "Around Stirling & the Trossachs" map

See "St. Andrews" map

SCOTLAND
Area of detail
Edinburgh
ENGLAND

Isle of May

seem amateurish. But, from the submerged tunnel, you view kelp forests; sandy flats that shelter bottom-dwelling schools of stingray, turbot, and sole; and murky caves favored by conger eels and small sharks. Curiously, the curvature of the tunnel's thick clear plastic makes everything seem about 30 percent smaller than it really is. However, for £155, you can arrange a "shark dive" and see everything full size. Allow about two hours.

See map p. 319. Battery Quarry, North Queensferry. ☎ **01383-411-880.** *www.deep seaworld.com. Admission: £12 adults, £8.25 children, £39 family. Open: Mon–Fri 10 a.m.–5 p.m.; Sat–Sun 10 a.m.–6 p.m.*

Doune Castle
Doune

Fans of the film *Monty Python and the Holy Grail* may recognize the exterior of Doune Castle, as it served as a location for several scenes in the movie. The castle's restoration by Historic Scotland has been mostly limited to making certain the stone structure doesn't fall down, so visitors (especially those with good imaginations) actually get a better idea of what living here in the 14th century may have been like. The castle's low doors, narrow spiral stairs, and overall feeling of damp really drive home the experience of medieval life. Allow about one and a half hours.

See map p. 309. Off the A84 (6.5km/10 miles northwest of Stirling). ☎ **01786-841-742.** *www.historic-scotland.gov.uk. Admission: £4.20 adults, £3.40 seniors, £2.50 children. Open: Apr–Sept daily 9:30 a.m.–5:30 p.m.; Oct–Mar daily 9:30 a.m.– 4:30 p.m. (closed Thurs–Fri Nov–Mar).*

Dunfermline Abbey and Palace
Dunfermline

The ancient town of Dunfermline, 23km (14 miles) northwest of Edinburgh, was a place of royal residence as early as the 11th century. The last British monarch born in Scotland, Charles I, came into the world at Dunfermline. Its abbey was constructed on the site of a Celtic church and a priory church built under the auspices of Queen Margaret around 1070. Some 50 years later, work began on a new priory, which can be visited as the Romanesque "Medieval Nave" today. Abbey status was bestowed in 1150, and thereafter a string of royalty, beginning with David I, was buried at the abbey, including Robert the Bruce (sans heart). The newer sections of the abbey church were built in 1818, and the pulpit was placed over the tomb and memorial to the Bruce. The remains of the royal palace are adjacent to the abbey. Only the southwest wall remains of this once-regal edifice. Allow about two hours.

See map p. 319. St. Margaret's Street, off the M90. ☎ **01383-739-026.** *www.historic-scotland.gov.uk. Admission: £3.70 adults, £3 seniors, £2.20 children 5–15. Open: Apr–Sept daily 9:30 a.m.–5:30 p.m.; Oct daily 9:30 a.m.–4:30 p.m.; Nov–Mar Sat–Wed 9:30 a.m.–4:30 p.m.*

St. Andrews

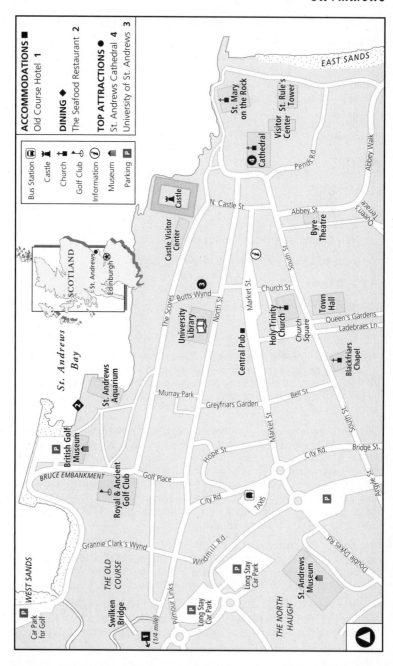

ACCOMMODATIONS ■
Old Course Hotel **1**

DINING ◆
The Seafood Restaurant **2**

TOP ATTRACTIONS ●
St. Andrews Cathedral **4**
University of St. Andrews **3**

Bus Station 🚌
Castle 🏰
Church ✚
Golf Club ⛳
Information ⓘ
Museum 🏛
Parking P

SCOTLAND
St. Andrews
Edinburgh

EAST SANDS

St. Mary on the Rock

St. Rule's Tower
Visitor Center

Cathedral
4

Pends Rd.

Abbey Walk

Queen's Terrace

Castle

Castle Visitor Center

N. Castle St.

Abbey St.

Byre Theatre

ⓘ

South St.

Church St.

Market St.

Town Hall

Queen's Gardens

Ladebraes Ln.

The Scores

Butts Wynd

3

University Library

North St.

Holy Trinity Church

Church Square

Blackfriars Chapel

St. Andrews Bay

St. Andrews Aquarium

2

Murray Park

Central Pub ■

Greyfriars Garden

Bell St.

Market St.

Smith St.

British Golf Museum

P

BRUCE EMBANKMENT

Hope St.

City Rd.

Bridge St.

Royal & Ancient Golf Club

Golf Place

City Rd.

TAXIS

P

Argyle St.

WEST SANDS

Grannie Clark's Wynd

Windmill Rd.

Long Stay Car Park

P

St. Andrews Museum

Double Dykes Rd.

Car Park for Golf
P

THE OLD COURSE

Swilken Bridge

Pilmour Links

1
(1/4 mile)

Long Stay Car Park
P

THE NORTH HAUGH

Hitting the links in St. Andrews

The medieval royal burgh of **St. Andrews,** about 80km (50 miles) from Edinburgh, was once filled with monasteries and ancient buildings, but only a few ruins of its early history survive. Once a revered place of Christian pilgrimage, today the historic town by the sea is best known for golf. It has been played here at least as long ago as the 1600s, though some believe much earlier. The rules of the sport are reviewed, revised, and clarified in St. Andrews by the Royal and Ancient Golf Club, while its Old Course is perhaps the most famous 18 holes in the world. Golfers consider this town to be hallowed ground.

St. Andrews has five 18-hole courses (www.standrews.org.uk) and one course with only 9 holes for beginners and children, all owned by a trust and open to the public. They are:

- ✔ **Old Course:** Where the Open is frequently played; the course possibly dates from the 15th century

- ✔ **New Course:** Designed by Old Tom Morris in 1895

- ✔ **Jubilee Course:** Opened in 1897 in honor of Queen Victoria

- ✔ **Eden Course:** Opened in 1914

- ✔ **Strathyrum Course:** The least difficult 18 holes, designed for those with high or no handicaps

- ✔ **Balgove:** The 9-hole course designed for beginners and hackers; show up and play

For the 18-hole courses, except the Old Course, you should try to reserve your tee time at least one month in advance. You might get onto Jubilee, Eden, or Strathyrum with only 24-hour notice if you're lucky. The reservation office is at ☎ **01334-466-666.** Online bookings for the New Course, Jubilee, Eden, and Strathyrum can be made by logging on to www.linksnet.co.uk.

The Old Course, which frequently hosts the Open (it returned in 2010), is a different kettle of fish: First you need a handicap of 24 for men and 36 for women. You apply in writing one year in advance and, even then, there are no guarantees. There is a daily ballot or lottery, which gives out about 50 percent of the tee times for the following day's play. Apply in person or by telephone before 2 p.m. on the day before play. By post, send applications to Reservations Office, Pilmour House, St. Andrews KY16 9SF, Scotland. Single golfers wishing to play the Old Course should contact the reservations department at reservations@standrews.org.uk.

Greens fees vary from course to course and depending on the time of year. Generally speaking, for the 18-hole courses, expect to pay between £20 and £150. From November to March, it costs around £75 to play the Old Course, using mats that protect the fairways, and between £15 and £40 for the other 18-hole courses.

Facilities for golfers in St. Andrews are legion. Virtually every hotel in town provides assistance to golfers. The **Royal and Ancient Golf Club,** founded in 1754, remains more or less rigidly closed as a private-membership men's club, however. It does traditionally open the doors to the public on St. Andrews Day to view the trophy room. This usually falls on November 30.

If you're looking for more golf-related information, try the **tourist office** in St. Andrews at 70 Market St. (☎ **01334-472-021**). It's open year-round Monday through Saturday and on Sunday, too, during the high season. Call for hours.

Falkland Palace and Garden
Falkland

A rather expensive National Trust attraction to visit, Falkland Palace in Fife was a royal hunting lodge and country home, constructed for the Stuart monarchs between 1450 and 1541. Among the rulers who resided in this impressive specimen of Renaissance architecture were a young Mary, Queen of Scots and her father, James V. The highlights of the palace are the ornate Chapel Royal, King's Bedchamber, and Queen's Room. The gardens were devised after World War II. Also on the grounds is the royal tennis court, only one of two to survive since the 1500s. Allow about two hours.

See map p. 319. High Street, just off the M90, at Junction 8. ☎ **01337-857-397.** www. nts.org.uk. *Admission: £11 adults; £7.50 seniors, students, and children; £26 family. Open: Mar–Oct Mon–Sat 11 a.m.–5 p.m.; Sun 1–5 p.m. Closed Nov–Mar.*

Church of the Holy Rude
Stirling

Among the many interesting aspects of this medieval church — Stirling's second oldest building after the nearby castle — are bullet holes made by Cromwell's troops in the 17th century. Dating in parts from the middle of the 1400s, the Church of the Holy Rude (or Holy Cross) is where Protestant firebrand John Knox preached at the crowning of the one-year-old James VI in 1567. The churchyard and cemetery are worth a walk about for the views and monuments, including a pyramid-shaped one in memory of the Covenanters, who defended the Presbyterian faith. Allow about one hour.

See map p. 317. St. John Street. ☎ **01786-475-275.** www.holyrude.org. *Admission: Donation requested. Open: Easter to Sept daily 11 a.m.–4 p.m. Closed Oct to day before Easter.*

Kirkcaldy Museum and Art Gallery
Kirkcaldy

This place, while modest, is a real find. The artwork in the second-floor galleries is among the best collections by Scottish artists. An entire room is devoted to the brightly hued still-life paintings and landscapes by Scottish Colourist S. J. Peploe. There is more work by Hornel, Hunter, and Fergusson. Another highlight of the collection is a range of paintings by William McTaggart. In addition, you can compare the abstract pure beauty of, say, Joan Eardley's *Breaking Wave* to a recent portrait by Scotland's best-selling, if critically panned, contemporary painter, Jack Vettriano. No comparison. This unassuming and humble attraction is arguably the best small provincial art gallery in Scotland. What's more, all they request are donations from visitors. Allow about one and a half hours.

See map p. 319. War Memorial Gardens, next to the train station. ☎ **01592-412-860.** www.fifedirect.org.uk/museums. *Admission: Free. Open: Mon–Sat 10:30 a.m.–5 p.m.; Sun 2–5 p.m.*

Loch Lomond and the Trossachs National Park
West Dumbartonshire

Loch Lomond, the largest inland body of water in all of Great Britain, is about a 45-minute drive or train ride from the Glasgow city limits. At the loch's southern edge, near the otherwise unremarkable if pleasant town of Balloch, the Lomond Shores development (www.lochlomondshores. com) was opened in 2002. The complex includes a shopping mall, aquarium, and the National Park Gateway Centre, which offers information on the adjacent national park — Scotland's first — that extends up the eastern shores of the loch, comprising some 1,865 sq. km (720 sq. miles).

If you're hiking, the trails up the eastern shoreline are preferable. This is the route that the West Highland Way follows (see sidebar, "Hiking the West Highland Way"). If you are a canoeing or kayaking enthusiast, the Lomond Shores' visitor center has rentals (☎ **01389-602-576;** www.canyou experience.com) for around £15 per hour. Up the western shores, before the notoriously winding road at Tarbet, where the train from Glasgow to Oban stops, visitors can take loch cruises. Golfers will likely be attracted to the Loch Lomond country club, which hosts the annual Scottish Open professional golf championship, near the pleasant resort village of Luss. Allow anywhere from two hours to a full day, depending on your interest.

See map p. 309. National Park Gateway Centre, Lomond Shores, Balloch. ☎ **01389-722-199.** www.lochlomond-trossachs.org. *Admission: Free. Open: Daily 10 a.m.–5 p.m.*

Queen Elizabeth Forest Park
Stirlingshire

East of Loch Lomond, the Queen Elizabeth Forest Park has thousands of acres of unspoiled nature. Many trails wind through the woods and hills of the region, managed by the Forestry Commission. The visitor center (with information and maps), at the David Marshall Lodge near Aberfoyle, is a good base for hiking excursions. If nature walks aren't your thing, however, there are good picnic spots — or you can motor through a part of the park on the scenic Achray Forest Drive (A821). Allow two to four hours.

See map p. 309. David Marshall Lodge, off the A821. ☎ **01877-382-258.** www. forestry.gov.uk. *Admission: Free. Open: Park daily dawn to dusk; visitor center daily 11 a.m.–4 p.m.*

Hiking the West Highland Way

One of Scotland's best-known long-distance footpaths is the **West Highland Way,** established in the 1980s. The trail begins, rather uneventfully, northwest of Glasgow in the affluent suburb of Milngavie (mill-*guy*). But as the trail winds some 153km (95 miles) north along the eastern shore of Loch Lomond, through the desolate and almost prehistoric-looking Rannoch Moor, along the breathtaking and historic Glen Coe, and ending finally in Fort William, it just gets better and better. At the northern terminus, you're at the foot of Ben Nevis, Scotland's highest mountain.

Trains run frequently throughout the day from the Queens Street Station in central Glasgow to Milngavie, the starting point of the walk. The 25-minute trip costs about £3.25 one-way. In Fort William, you can catch the First ScotRail train back to Glasgow. Hikers can backpack and camp along the way or stay at inns conveniently dotted along the trail. Tour companies are available to haul your luggage from stop to stop, too. For details on the West Highland Way, contact the National Park Gateway Centre at ☎ **01389-722-199,** or log on to www.west-highland-way.co.uk.

St. Andrews Cathedral
St. Andrews

Near the Celtic Church of Blessed Mary on the Rock, and by the sea at the east end of town, is St. Andrews Cathedral. Once the largest church in Scotland, it was founded in 1161. The cathedral certified the town as the ecclesiastical capital of the country, but the ruins can only suggest its former beauty and importance. There's a collection of early Christian and medieval monuments, as well as artifacts discovered on the cathedral site. Admission allows entry to nearby **St. Andrews Castle,** where the medieval clergy lived. Allow about two hours.

See map p. 321. A91, off Pends Road. ☎ **01334-472-563.** *www.historic-scotland.gov.uk. Admission: Cathedral and castle £7.20 adults, £5.80 seniors, £4.30 children 5–15. Open: Apr–Sept daily 9:30 a.m.–5:30 p.m.; Oct–Mar daily 9:30 a.m.–4:30 p.m.*

SS Sir Walter Scott Steamship
Loch Katrine

For more than 100 years, this old-fashioned ship has taken passengers out on Loch Katrine to marvel at the beauty of the Trossachs. A bit of floating history, the ship is the last screw-driven steamship regularly sailing with passengers in Scotland (and perhaps age is showing, as the number of trips it makes has been reduced in recent years). It runs between the Trossachs Pier and Stronachlachar and passes an eyeful of stunning views along the way. The ship is named after the renowned author who made Loch Katrine famous in his poem *The Lady of the Lake.* Be warned, however: This popular trip can get overcrowded in the summer, so if you can, go on a weekday. Allow about four hours.

See map p. 309. Loch Katrine, Trossachs. ☎ **01877-332-000.** www.lochkatrine.
com. *Admission: £14 adults, £13 seniors, £9 children. Departures: Apr–Oct (weather
permitting) daily 10:30 a.m., 1:30, and 3 p.m. No sailings Nov–Mar.*

Stirling Castle
Stirling

Once the residence of Scotland's royalty, this striking Renaissance castle
is arguably the finest in the land. It was used by Kings James IV and
James V, as well as by Mary, Queen of Scots (James V's daughter) and her
son, James VI. A natural fortress, the castle on a hill was the region's strategic military point throughout much of the 13th and 14th centuries. Holding
it was a key element leading to the battle of Bannockburn, for example.

Various ongoing renovations are now restoring the castle buildings to a
historically accurate state after years as modern military barracks (the
castle museum explains all). Tapestries are being hand-woven in the
former stable block to hang in the chapel, and on most days you can see
the intricate process. Quite recently restored, the castle's Great Hall
stands out for miles thanks to the creamy, almost yellow exterior that
replicates its original color. From Easter 2011, visitors will be allowed to
enter the royal Renaissance-era palace of James V. It has six apartments,
which have had £12 million worth of work to restore them to their mid–
16th century glory. Even if you don't bother taking a self-guided tour of the
impressive castle (though you probably should), the ramparts and land
surrounding the well-fortified landmark are worth a stroll — particularly
the cemetery and the "Back Walk" along a wall that protected the Old
Town from attack. Last entry inside the castle is 45 minutes before closing. Allow about three hours.

See map p. 317. Castle Wynd. ☎ **01786-450-000.** www.historic-scotland.
gov.uk. *Admission (includes a tour of Argyll's Lodging): £9 adults, £7.20 seniors, £5.40
children 5–15. Open: Apr–Sept daily 10 a.m.–6 p.m.; Oct–Mar daily 10 a.m.–5 p.m.*

Culross: Stepping back in time

Thanks largely to the National Trust for Scotland, this village shows what a Scottish
settlement from the 16th to the 18th century looked like. With its cobbled streets lined
by stout cottages featuring crow-stepped gables, Culross may also have been the birthplace of St. Mungo, who went on to establish the Glasgow Cathedral. James IV made
this port on the Firth of Forth a royal burgh in 1588. The National Trust runs a **visitor
center** (☎ **01383-880-359;** www.nts.org.uk), open daily noon to 5 p.m. from Good
Friday to the end of September, which provides access to the town's palace and other
sites. Adult admission is £8.50.

Stirling Old Town Jail
Stirling

Tour guides don historic garb to take groups through the paces of penal life here, while others role-play as wardens and inmates to help enact the history of the jail. This building is a Victorian replacement for the less humane cells in the old tollbooth across the street. Still, when you see the crank that inmates were made to turn as punishment, one wonders if prison existence had improved all that much. On the top of the building, an observation deck offers good views of the surrounding Old Town. Allow about one and a half hours.

See map p. 317. St. John Street. ☎ **01786-450-050**. *www.oldtownjail.com. Admission: £6.50 adults, £4 children 5–16, £17 family. Open: Daily Apr–Oct 9:30 a.m.–5:30 p.m. (4 p.m. in Oct); Nov–Mar 9:30 a.m.–4:30 p.m.*

University of St Andrews
St. Andrews

This is the oldest university in Scotland and the third oldest in Great Britain, after Oxford and Cambridge. Of its famous students, the most recent graduate was Prince William, heir to the throne after Charles, Prince of Wales (or in Scotland, officially Duke of Rothesay). During terms, you can see packs of students in their characteristic red gowns. The university spreads throughout the town today, but the original site was centered in the districts just west of the cathedral. The gate tower of St. Salvador College, on North Street, dates to the 15th century. Allow one hour.

See map p. 321. www.st-andrews.ac.uk.

More cool things to see and do

- ✔ **British Golf Museum,** Bruce Embankment, St. Andrews (☎ **01334-478-880;** www.britishgolfmuseum.co.uk), is devoted to the history and popularity of the game. Exhibits reveal the evolution of equipment and rules and remarkable facts and feats of the last 500 years.

- ✔ **Byre Theatre,** Abbey Street, St. Andrews (☎ **01334-475-000;** www.byretheatre.com), is the cultural center of St. Andrews; it features dramatic performances ranging from Shakespeare to musical comedies.

- ✔ **Holy Trinity Church,** off South Street, St. Andrews (☎ **01334-474-494**), is a medieval church, re-created at the beginning of the 20th century around the impressive tower, which does actually date to the 1400s. In the original church, John Knox advised the congregation in June 1559 to cleanse the temple and remove all the Catholic monuments to idolatry. In that single day, apparently, the reformation took root in this parish.

- ✔ **The National Wallace Monument,** Alloa Road, Abbey Craig, Stirling (☎ **01786-47-2140;** www.nationalwallacemonument.com), is a 66m (220-ft.) tower set on top of a hill overlooking the surrounding terrain; you're likely to see it if you travel anywhere near Stirling. Built in the 1860s, the monument's popularity soared after the release of *Braveheart,* Mel Gibson's hit 1995 movie depicting William Wallace's life. A shuttle bus runs between a visitor center and the monument.

✔ **Rob Roy and the Trossachs Visitor Centre,** Callander (☎ 01877-330-342; www.robroyvisitorcentre.com), is a museum in the Trossachs region, home of the Clan MacGregor, which offers two versions of Rob Roy MacGregor: the tartan Robin Hood and legendary figure of Sir Walter Scott's novel; and the cattle thief and blackmailer. Whatever the specifics, Rob Roy was certainly a hero to his people and an outlaw in defiance of the English.

Shopping for Local Treasures

Shopping in Stirling and St. Andrews is typical of provincial towns and cities around Scotland, with the former offering the dubious bonus of a shopping mall called the Thistle Centre (near the train station). This area also introduces tourists to another debatable consumer-oriented attraction in Scotland: Highland gateway towns. Both Aberfoyle and Callander fit this bill — one-street burghs cluttered with lots of tartan and woolen shops that attract coach tours, causing the sidewalks to occasionally overflow with tourists on summer days. The road that runs along Loch Lomond, the A82, has a few galleries with art. Remember, as I say in previous chapters, most attractions have decent shops for gifts, souvenirs, and even local crafts, on occasion. Below are a few suggestions for shops that are a cut above.

✔ **The Fotheringham Gallery,** 78 Henderson St., Bridge of Allan (☎ 01786-832-861; www.fotheringhamgallery.co.uk), is a contemporary art gallery and shop with handmade designer jewelry, glass works, sculpture, and paintings — all by contemporary Scottish artists and craftsmen. Open Monday through Saturday 10 a.m. to 5:30 p.m.

✔ **The Green Gallery,** Ballmenoch, Buchlyvie (☎ 01360-850-180; www.greengallery.com), was once a standout in the Highland gateway town of Aberfoyle. Its eclectic collection of contemporary arts and crafts is now in this neighboring village. Friday through Wednesday from 11 a.m. to 5 p.m.

✔ **Jim Farmer Golf Shop,** 1 St. Mary's Place, Market Street, St. Andrews (☎ 01334-476-796), should take care of golfers and maybe even help trim a stroke or two off your handicap (though Jim himself sold the place to new owners in 2007). Shirts, hats, T-shirts, shoes, and more are on hand. Call for hours.

✔ **The Scottish Wool Centre,** off Main Street, Aberfoyle (☎ 01877-382-850; www.scottishwoolcentre.co.uk), is an attraction as well as a shop; this is one store where the kids shouldn't get bored.

Besides exhibits that show everything you want to know about Scottish wool and more, the Spinner's Cottage gives you a chance to make your own wool. There are sheepdog demonstrations and a children's farm (admission charged). Open daily 10 a.m. to 5 p.m.

Doing the Pub Crawl

If you're staying in St. Andrews, check out the watering hole below, which is a notch or two above the norm. Otherwise, practically every village and town in the region has a pub, or stick to the local hotels and inns.

✔ **Central Bar,** 77 Market St. (at College Street), St. Andrews (☎ **01334-478-296**). If you're looking for a quintessential pub, this is a fine one, popular with students and offering a good selection of draft beers, including "guest" ales. Open Monday through Saturday 11 a.m. to 11:45 p.m., and Sunday from 12:30 p.m.

Fast Facts: Trossachs to Fife

Area Code

The area code for Stirling is **01786**; St. Andrews is **01334**; and Aberfoyle and Callander (in the Trossachs) are **01877**. You need to dial the area code only if you're calling from outside the city you want to reach.

Emergencies

Dial ☎ **999** for police, fire, or ambulance.

ATMs

ATMs are readily available at banks in Stirling and St. Andrews.

Hospitals

The hospitals in the area are Stirling Royal Infirmary, Livilands Road, south of the town center (☎ 01786-434-000) and St. Andrews Memorial Hospital, Abbey Walk, south of Abbey Street (☎ 01334-472-327).

Information

You can find tourist offices at 41 Dumbarton Rd., Stirling (☎ 01786-475-019), and 70 Market St., St. Andrews (☎ 01334-472-021). In Callander, the office is at 10 Ancaster Sq.; in Dunfermline, 1 High St.

Internet Access

The best place to surf the Web in this area is at CommsPort, 83 Market St., St. Andrews (☎ 01334-475-181; www.commsport.com). The shop's hours are Monday through Saturday from 8 a.m. until 5:30 p.m., and Sunday from 10:30 a.m. until 6 p.m. The cost is £6 per hour.

Mail

Post offices are at 127 South St., St. Andrews (☎ 01334-472-321), and 4 Broad St., Stirling (☎ 01786-474-537).

Chapter 17

Tayside and the Northeast

*T*his concise chapter covers a fairly large chunk of eastern and north-eastern Scotland: from Dundee and Perth on the River Tay up to the petrochemical-boom city of Aberdeen, and the eastern Moray (pronounced like the name Murray) coast. Among the highlights for visitors: Several castles still stand on the eastern fringes of the Grampian Mountains — including Balmoral (the official royal family retreat) — and a host of whisky distilleries offer tours, too. The ride up (on the A93) to **Braemar** offers quite spectacular visits. But, in my view, compared to the Highlands (see Chapter 18), which encroaches on this region from the west, I can't get as excited about the countryside stretching from Tayside to the Northeast.

So, to repeat, I've kept this chapter succinct, and I suggest that if you head in this direction, you should concentrate briefly on a couple of towns, such as **Perth** and **Pitlochry;** or quaint coastal harbors such as **Stonehaven** and **Pennan** (the latter made famous by the film *Local Hero*). You should visit a few castles, trek through Royal Deeside, and finally, hit a distillery or two near the River Spey.

There are two bona fide cities in this region: **Dundee** and **Aberdeen.** The latter is known as the Granite City, because many of the city center buildings are made from the same sturdy (if somewhat dull) gray stone. Aberdeen is also Scotland's natural-gas capital, the place where the oil industry, tapping reserves way out in the North Sea, has its principal mainland operations. The city has plenty of bars and restaurants but is rather short on attractions, if you ask me.

Perth is an attractive town situated on the River Tay between two large parks, North and South Inch. A royal burgh since the 1200s, Perth has a couple of fine restaurants and lies near one of Scotland's most historic attractions: **Scone Palace** (see p. 339). Pitlochry is one of the most visited inland resort towns in Scotland, mainly because it's just off a main artery (the A9 highway) leading up to Inverness and the Highlands.

Getting There

Getting to and around this part of Scotland isn't quite as easy as it is in other parts of the country. Trains run to Perth, Dundee, and Aberdeen, but the branch system isn't well developed. Bus service to the larger towns is reasonable, but in the end, you're likely to want a car to see the main attractions.

✔ **By car:** From Edinburgh, take the M90 north to Perth, where you have the option of using the A90 along the east coast to Aberdeen, the A9 inland through Pitlochry, or the narrower A93 via Braemar. From Glasgow, use the M80 (A80) to the M9 (A9), which takes you to Perth.

✔ The scenic route is A93, which goes past Braemar, Ballater, and Banchory on its way to Aberdeen.

✔ **By bus: Scottish Citylink** (☎ 0870-550-5050; www.citylink. co.uk) routes cover the two cities and major towns. A typical round-trip bus fare from Edinburgh to Aberdeen is about £30 and the journey takes about four hours. A trip from Glasgow to Perth costs more like £15 and takes approximately one and a half hours.

✔ **By train: First ScotRail** (☎ 08457-48-49-50; www.firstscotrail. com) travels to cities and major towns in the region, including Perth, Pitlochry, Dundee, Arbroath, and Aberdeen. You then have to rely on buses or local taxis to venture farther after you arrive in these towns. ScotRail service dovetails with long-distance trains from England. You can also call National Railway Enquiries at the First ScotRail phone number above for details. Just to give you an idea of prices: A one-way (single) ticket from Glasgow to Aberdeen costs between £12 and £80, depending upon how early you buy it and whether you opt for a "fully flexible" ticket. The trip takes just over two and a half hours.

✔ **By ferry: NorthLink Orkney & Shetland Ferries Ltd.** (☎ 01855-851-144) runs services between Aberdeen and Lerwick.

✔ **By plane: Aberdeen Airport** (☎ 01224-722-331; www.aberdeen airport.com) is 9.5km (6 miles) north of town. Planes connect Aberdeen to London, Glasgow, Edinburgh, and Dundee, as well as the Shetland and Orkney islands. A typical flight from London Heathrow to Aberdeen might cost about £100 to £170. Use the airport Web site for the latest timetables and prices. **Dundee Airport** (☎ 01382-643-242) is on Riverside Drive; it is small and has limited service to Aberdeen and Edinburgh.

Spending the Night

Try to choose accommodations nearest to the key attractions you want to see. Some of the hotels and guesthouses listed here have earned star ratings from the tourist board; see Chapter 8 for a description of VisitScotland's rating system. You may be encouraged to spend more than one night in order to get a better deal. And many of the accommodations are more expensive during the high season. Rates listed below include full breakfast, unless otherwise stated. And remember: You may well get a better deal than the standard, full-fare rack rates.

Braemar Lodge
$$ **Braemar**

This homey, granite-built country house — a renovated Victorian hunting lodge — offers unpretentious, comfortable accommodations. If the hotel is small, the rooms are reasonably spacious and most have views of the mountains. At the oak-paneled bar, guests can sip a whisky nightcap in front of an open fire. Log-style cabins with kitchens are also available for rent by the week and there is also a "bunkhouse"-style hostel on the grounds.

See map p. 333. 6 Glenshee Rd. ☎ **01339-741-627.** *www.braemarlodge.co.uk. Rack rates: £70–£120 double. MC, V.*

Craigellachie Hotel
$$$ **Speyside**

Close to a clutch of whisky distilleries, including Glenfiddich, this charming and hospitable 26-unit hotel is perhaps best known for its Quaich Bar, a virtual library of single-malt whiskies, with some 550 bottles lining the shelves around the entire room. Find the one you prefer and a bartender will pour you a dram. Since 1893, the hotel has served as a welcome retreat in the heart of rural Speyside. By the way, the hotel's name is pronounced, roughly, kray-*gell*-ah-key.

See map p. 333. Off the A93, Craigellachie, Speyside. (3km/2 miles northwest of Dufftown). ☎ **01340-881-204.** *Fax: 01340-881-253. www.oxfordhotelsand inns.com. Rack rates: From £84 double. AE, DC, MC, V.*

Darroch Learg
$$$ **Ballater**

Set on a wooded hillside overlooking the road and the River Dee beyond, this is one of the more highly regarded hotels in the entire region. Stately but friendly, with a reputation for good food, Darroch Learg is my choice to spend a night near the royal spread at Balmoral. A dozen overnight rooms in the main lodge are complemented with five more in a nearby annex. All are well appointed and comfortable.

See map p. 333. Braemar Road (off the A93), on the west side of town. ☎ **01339-755-443.** *Fax: 01339-755-252. www.darrochlearg.co.uk. Rack rates: £130–£230 double (depending on season). AE, DC, MC, V. Closed Jan.*

Tayside and the Northeast

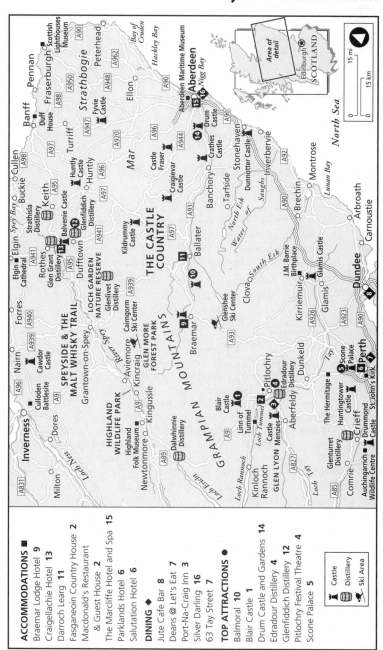

ACCOMMODATIONS ■
Braemar Lodge Hotel **9**
Craigellachie Hotel **13**
Darroch Learg **11**
Fasganeoin Country House **2**
Macdonald's Restaurant
  & Guest House **2**
The Marcliffe Hotel and Spa **15**
Parklands Hotel **6**
Salutation Hotel **6**

DINING ◆
Jute Cafe Bar **8**
Deans @ Let's Eat **7**
Port-Na-Craig Inn **3**
Silver Darling **16**
63 Tay Street **7**

TOP ATTRACTIONS ●
Balmoral **10**
Blair Castle **1**
Drum Castle and Gardens **14**
Edradour Distillery **4**
Glenfiddich Distillery **12**
Pitlochry Festival Theatre **4**
Scone Palace **5**

🏰 Castle
🛢 Distillery
⛷ Ski Area

Fasganeoin Country House
$$ Pitlochry

Just off the main road, this three-star eight-bedroom guesthouse is a few minutes' walk from Pitlochry's town center, or a riverside stroll to the Festival Theatre. The rooms (not all have en suite facilities) are generally comfy and cute, featuring flower and antique motifs. The peaceful grounds offer a lovely respite. Fasganeoin (faze-*gan*-non) means "place for the birds" in Gaelic.

See map p. 333. Perth Road, opposite the Blair Atholl Distillery. ☎ **01796-472-387.** *Fax: 01796-474-285.* www.fasganeoincountryhouse.co.uk. *Rack rates: £72–£84 double with private bathroom. MC, V. Open mid-Mar to late Oct.*

Macdonald's Restaurant & Guest House
$ Pitlochry

This popular inn and dining room in Pitlochry has a loyal following. And why not? The ten bedrooms (seven doubles and two family size) are nicely decorated and the hospitality is generous. But more important, you would be very hard-pressed to beat the price these days. In addition to the restaurant, the premises also have a well-regarded fish-and-chips cafe.

See map p. 333. 140 Atholl Rd. ☎ **01796-472-170.** *Fax: 01796-474-221.* www.macdonalds-pitlochry.co.uk. *Rack rates: £60 double. AE, MC, V.*

The Marcliffe
$$$–$$$$ Aberdeen

This hotel and spa, once known as Marcliffe at Pitfodels, is probably the best place to stay in Aberdeen. If bigwigs from business or government are in town, this is where they meet and sleep. It's often recommended, probably because it combines high-class five-star accommodations with intimate attention. The three-story hotel sits among trees and has a country feel despite its proximity to the city. All of the 35 individually decorated rooms (plus seven suites) are comfortable and spacious, the beds huge, and the antique furniture done in good taste. Spa treatments include aromatherapy. As it's business oriented, weekend rates can be less expensive.

See map p. 333. North Deeside Road, off the A92 (4.8km/3 miles from Aberdeen city center). ☎ **01224-861-000.** *Fax: 01224-868-860.* www.marcliffe.com. *Rack rates: £215–£245 double. AE, DC, MC, V.*

Parklands Hotel
$$–$$$ Perth

This four-star small hotel occupies a stylish Georgian town house once owned by Perth's lord provost (similar to an honorary mayor). Overlooking the woods of South Inch Park and near the railroad station, the Parklands is a peaceful oasis in a bustling little town. The 14 rooms are nicely decorated with flatscreen TVs. There are two restaurants, the **Acanthus** and the less formal **No. 1 the Bank Bistro.**

See map p. 333. 2 St. Leonard's Bank. ☎ **01738-622-451.** *Fax: 01738-622-046.* www. theparklandshotel.com. *Rack rates: £100–£130 double. AE, DC, MC, V.*

Salutation Hotel
$$ Perth

It's right on the main street of Perth, so the 84-bed Salutation benefits from a central location. After you've walked all over town and had your dinner, relax with a nightcap in the huge overstuffed couches by the fire in the lobby. It's no wonder the staff has its act together — a hotel has been on this site and welcoming guests since 1699.

See map p. 333. 34 South St., near the River Tay. ☎ **01738-630-066.** www. strathmorehotels.com. *Rack rates: £150 double. AE, MC, V.*

Dining Locally

Your best option in the area could be right in your own hotel, but here are a few other places to consider.

Jute Cafe Bar
$–$$ Dundee   INTERNATIONAL

This pleasant, airy cafe/bar is part of the Dundee Contemporary Arts complex in the so-called cultural quarter of the city, and it's one of Dundee's highlights. After the kitchen closes for the night (normally around 9:30 p.m.), it's a lively bar and one of the places to be seen in Dundee.

See map p. 333. 152 Nethergate. ☎ **01382-909-246.** www.dca.org.uk. *Main courses: £8–£15. MC, V. Open: daily noon to 4 p.m. and 5–9:30 p.m. (bar open all day to midnight).*

Deans @ Let's Eat
$$–$$$ Perth   SCOTTISH/FRENCH

In 2005, Willie Deans and his wife, Margo, took over ownership of this already well-regarded restaurant and put their stamp on the place, formerly known as Let's Eat. Chef Deans is a member of the Master Chefs of Great Britain, and his cooking usually has its share of flourishes. A typical menu will have dishes such as seared scallops with Stornoway black pudding, apple salad, and spiced cider vinaigrette.

See map p. 333. 77–79 Kinnoull St. ☎ **01738-643-377.** www.letseatperth. co.uk. *Reservations required. Main courses: £16–£25. MC, V. Open: Tues–Sat noon to 2 p.m. and 6:30–9:30 p.m. Closed Sun–Mon.*

Port-na-Craig
$$–$$$ Pitlochry   SCOTTISH/SEAFOOD

This restaurant once captured the attention of the Michelin inspectors, who bestowed their award for good food at reasonable prices. Since then, however, those proprietors moved on and the reputation of the restaurant has diminished (at least in the eyes of the Red Guide) — though the setting near the River Tummel remains very nice indeed.

See map p. 333. Off Foss Road. ☎ **01796-472-777.** *www.portnacraig.com. Reservations recommended. Main courses: £11–£16. MC, V. Open: Daily 11 a.m. to late.*

Silver Darling
$$$–$$$$ Aberdeen   SEAFOOD

Getting to this restaurant at the water's edge is a wee bit of an odyssey, but it's worth it. In the dining room, overlooking the entrance to the harbor, you find succulent French-influenced dishes using local produce, such as pan-fried halibut with crab gnocchi, ratatouille, and salad. The menu is pricey, but from the sea views to some of the highest-quality food in the area, Silver Darling is generally worth the extra dough.

See map p. 333. Pocra Quay, North Pier. Follow the road from Aberdeen harbor along the water until you reach the beach, and then turn right. ☎ **01224-576-229.** *www. silverdarling.co.uk. Reservations required. Main courses: £20–£25. AE, MC, V. Open: Mon–Sat noon to 1:30 p.m. (no lunch Sat) and 6:30–9:30 p.m.*

63 Tay Street
$$$ Perth   MODERN SCOTTISH

This restaurant is run by a local Perthshire boy, Chef Graeme Pallister, who, like his town rival at Deans @ Let's Eat (see above), is a Master Chef of Great Britain. The contemporary dining space overlooks the River Tay, and the menu includes main courses such as whole roast petit chicken with Swiss cheese gratin and fresh peas or sautéed local beef rib with crumbed oxtail. Fixed-price five-course dinners are offered on Saturday.

See map p. 333. 63 Tay St. ☎ **01738-441-451.** *www.63taystreet.com. Reservations recommended. Main courses: £20. AE, MC, V. Open: Tues–Sat noon to 2 p.m. and 6:30–9 p.m.*

Exploring Tayside and the Northeast

The territory covered in this chapter offers a host of scenic drives, historical castles, and whisky distilleries — as well as forested glens and mountains. Tayside, carved out of the old counties of Perth and Angus, is named for its major river, the 192km-long (119-mile) Tay. The river's waters offer some of Europe's best salmon and trout fishing, although many say it's not as good as it used to be. As you journey into Scotland's Northeast, you pass moorland and peaty lochs, wooded valleys and rushing rivers, granite-stone villages and ancient edifices.

A "Scotland's Treasures" ticket (£24 for one adult; £60 family) offers admission to Blair Castle, Scone Palace, Glamis Castle, and more. Tickets are sold at Blair, Glamis, and Scone visitor centers.

Braemar Highland gathering

The typical population of the village of Braemar is around 500 people. But when the village holds the Braemar Highland Games (every Sept) the population jumps by 20,000 or more. The throngs usually include dignitaries, not to mention Queen Elizabeth and other members of the royal family. There are Highland Games all over the Highlands and Islands, but this is perhaps the best of them all. A purely Scottish Highland experience, the games include feats of strength, such as the caber toss, as well as Celtic music traditional dance. For information, visit www.braemargathering.org.

The top attractions

Balmoral
Ballater

I would say this top attraction is just for royal worshipers. Because Balmoral Castle and Estate is a working residence for the queen and her entourage, visitor access is limited to a few months of the year and only to the ballroom, garden, and grounds. On display are pictures of other rooms as well as clothing and gifts belonging to royalty. You're free to walk the extensive grounds and gardens. Because the castle is closed to tourists when the queen is in town, it's a good idea to call in advance of your visit. In addition to the general opening times, guided tours are sometime offered one day a week in November and December. Last admission is approximately one hour before closing. Allow about one and a half hours.

See map p. 333. Balmoral, Ballater, off the A93 (13km/8 miles from Banchory). ☎ **01339-742-334.** *www.balmoralcastle.com. Admission: £8.70 adults, £7.70 seniors and students, £4.60 children 5–16, £23 family. Open: Apr–July daily 10 a.m.–5 p.m. Closed Aug–Mar.*

Blair Castle
Blair Atholl

This fine, fairy-tale castle up the road from Pitlochry has much to see. It's chock-full o' stuff: art, armor, flags, stag horns, and more items not typically found on the standard furniture-and-portrait castle tour. Between the 30 rooms and the grounds (including a walled garden), the castle has something (such as pony rides) for just about everyone. The most common theme in the Duke of Atholl's decoration scheme is hunting. Deer antlers decorate the long hallway and ballroom, and the weaponry collection spans hundreds of years. Blair Castle's long history includes a couple of Jacobite sieges and a sleepover by Queen Victoria. But while the castle is the ancient seat of the dukes and earls of Atholl, and although Duncan Atholl was the king murdered in Shakespeare's *Macbeth,* the real Duncan didn't live here. Last castle tour one hour before closing. Allow about two hours.

See map p. 333. Blair Atholl, off the A9 (10km/6 miles west of Pitlochry). ☎ **01796-481-207.** www.blair-castle.co.uk. *Admission to house and garden: £8.75 adults, £7.50 seniors and students, £5.25 children, £24 family. Open: Apr–Oct daily 9:30 a.m.–5:30 p.m.; Nov–Mar Tues and Sat 9:30 a.m.–2:30 p.m.*

Drum Castle and Gardens
Banchory

The family seat of the Irwins of Drum since the times of Robert the Bruce in the 14th century, this is the oldest intact building in the care of the National Trust for Scotland. Built at different times, it has a medieval tower, Jacobean mansion, and Victorian additions. Nothing in particular in the Irvine family collection is remarkable, but you're likely to enjoy the walk through the house, which includes an impressive vaulted library in the oldest section of the castle. Don't miss the grounds and gardens, a highlight of which is a collection of historic roses. Please note the peculiar opening days and hours: Call to confirm. Last admission to castle one hour before closing. Allow about two hours.

See map p. 333. Drumoak, off the A93 near Peterculter (16km/10 miles west of Aberdeen). ☎ **0844-493-2161.** www.nts.org.uk. *Admission: £8.50 adults; £5.50 seniors, students, and children younger than 16; £21 family. Open: May–June and Sept Thurs–Mon 11a.m.–5 p.m.; July–Aug daily 11 a.m.–5 p.m. Castle closed Oct–Apr. Grounds open: All year. Rose garden open: Apr–Oct daily 10 a.m.–6 p.m.*

Edradour Distillery
Pitlochry

You get a good primer on the whisky-making process at this distillery, pitched as Scotland's smallest, which produces only 12 casks of whisky a week that are matured for ten years before bottling. It's a cute site, too, with little whitewashed buildings with red doors and friendly staff using the smallest spirit stills that the law allows. Of course, it's quality — not quantity — that counts. Allow about one and a half hours.

See map p. 333. Off the A924, just outside Pitlochry. ☎ **01796-472-095.** www.edradour.co.uk. *Admission: £5. Open: June–Sept Mon–Sat 9:30a.m.–5 p.m. and Sun noon to 5 p.m.; May and Oct Mon–Sat 10 a.m.–5 p.m. and Sun noon to 5 p.m.; Mar–Apr and Nov–Dec Mon–Sat 10 a.m.–4 p.m. and Sun noon to 4 p.m.; Jan–Feb Mon–Sat 10 a.m.–4 p.m., closed Sun.*

Glenfiddich Distillery
Near Dufftown

In contrast to Edradour, Glenfiddich makes hundreds and hundreds of casks of Scotland's national spirit. It is one of the largest distilleries in the country, owned by William Grant & Sons, a family that has been making whisky since 1887. The tour starts with a video explaining the ins and outs of whisky making; then you see the mash-tuns and huge 5m-tall (17-ft.) wash-backs made of Douglas fir, the expansive bonded warehouses, and finally the bottling factory. In addition to the standard tour, there is also the "Connoisseur's Tour": a two-and-a-half-hour exploration of the distillery that concludes with a tutored nosing and tasting session (£20 and over

18 only). The shop sells a host of popular and extremely rare vintage single malts. Allow an hour and a half (more for the longer tour).

See map p. 333. Off the A941 (88km/55miles northeast of Aberdeen). ☎ **01340-820-373.** *www.glenfiddich.com. Admission: Free tours. Open: Mon–Sat 9:30 a.m.–4:30 p.m.; Sun noon to 4:30 p.m.*

If you truly love whisky, you can follow **Scotland's Malt Whisky Trail** throughout this region, visiting several distilleries, just as you might tour the châteaux of Bordeaux or wineries in the Napa Valley. For more information on itineraries, log on to www.maltwhiskytrail.com.

Pitlochry Festival Theatre
Pitlochry

This arts center on the south side of the River Tummel is the jewel of Pitlochry. People come here from throughout the region for a bit of culture. In addition to new and classic dramatic performances and exhibitions at the center's art gallery, the venue also offers a busy schedule of folk concerts, literary talks, and even culinary events. It's best to book tickets in advance.

See map p. 333. Port-Na-Craig (across the river from Main Street). ☎ **01796-484-626.** *www.pitlochry.org.uk. Theater tickets: From £15.*

Scone Palace
Near Perth

Scone (pronounced *scune*) was the first established capital of a unified Scotland, the hallowed ground where most of the country's early kings were enthroned and latter ones, up to Charles II, were crowned. For years it held the infamous Stone of Destiny, or Stone of Scone (see "The Stone of Scone: A long strange trip"). The castellated palace you will find today, however, dates only from the early 1800s, though parts of earlier buildings have been incorporated. Home to the earls of Mansfield, it is full of fine furniture, ivories, clocks, and needlework, and of particular note is the renowned porcelain collection. There is also a hall dedicated to the coronation of kings. The grounds are also quite nice. A replica Stone of Scone marks the location of its historical spot on Moot Hill, by a little chapel. Allow two hours.

See map p. 333. Braemar Road, on the A93. ☎ **01738-552-300.** *www.scone-palace.co.uk. Admission: Palace and grounds £9 adults, £7.90 seniors and students, £6 children, £26 family. Open: Apr–Oct daily 9:30 a.m.–5:30 p.m. (Sat until 4:30 p.m.). Closed Nov to mid-Mar.*

Treasure Tickets

If you're planning to visit Blair Castle, Glamis Castle, and Scone Palace, then consider buying a Treasure Ticket that provide joint admission to each. Prices are £24 for adults, £21 for seniors and students, £14 for children, and £60 for a family of up to three children and two adults.

Other cool things to see and do

✔ **Auchingarrich Wildlife Centre,** on the B827 near Comrie (☎ **01764-679-469;** www.auchingarrich.co.uk), offers a host of wild and domesticated animals (from lambs to emus), a wild-bird hatchery, and hiking trails. Younger children can burn off some steam at the facilities' "adventure" playground.

✔ **Discovery Point,** Discovery Quay, Dundee (☎ **01382-309-060;** www.rrsdiscovery.com), is home to the famous RRS *Discovery,* the ship sailed by Captain Robert Scott to Antarctica. You can tour the vessel and get all the details of Scott's historic trip. By the way, RRS stands for "royal research ship."

✔ **Dunnottar Castle,** near Stonehaven (☎ **01569-762-173;** www.dunnottarcastle.co.uk), is best known for its breathtaking views. Much of the red sandstone ruins, pitched above the cliffs and the North Sea, stand tall. Often the object of sieges, in the 17th century it was used as a prison for nearly 200 recalcitrant Presbyterian Covenanters, and visitors can see the cellar where they were held.

✔ **Glamis Castle,** near Forfar (☎ **01307-840-393;** www.glamis-castle.co.uk), is notable for being the family home of the late queen mother, born Elizabeth Bowes Lyon, wife of King George VI and mother of Queen Elizabeth. A royal residence since 1372, it's also famous for being the (historically inaccurate) setting for Shakespeare's *Macbeth.*

If you want to visit more castles than I have given details for, then follow the official **Castle Trail** linking about a dozen historic piles in the Northeast. Log on to the Aberdeen and Grampian tourist board Web site (www.aberdeen-grampian.com) for more information.

✔ **J. M. Barrie's Birthplace,** Brechin Road, Kirriemuir (☎ **01575-572-646;** www.nts.org.uk), is devoted to the creator of *Peter Pan,* who was born here in 1860. Watch for the little fast-moving light that represents everyone's favorite fairy, Tinkerbell. The displays contain manuscripts and artifacts from the writer's life.

✔ **Museum of Scottish Lighthouses,** Kinnaird Head, Fraserburgh (☎ **01346-511-022;** www.lighthousemuseum.org.uk), is a must-see for lighthouse buffs and is recommended if you have any interest in the towers of all shapes and sizes that have kept sailors safe at sea for more than 200 years.

The Stone of Scone: A long strange trip

Until the late 13th century, Scone Palace was the home of the Stone of Destiny, aka the Stone of Scone, on which important early rulers such as David I, Macbeth, and Robert the Bruce were enthroned. According to myth, the hunk of sandstone dates from biblical times, serving as Jacob's pillow. It reputedly traveled through Egypt, Spain, and Italy before coming to Scotland with Celtic pilgrims in the 9th century. It was then deployed for the enthronement of Dalriadic kings in Argyll before being used by Scottish royalty at Scone. So powerful was the lure of the stone that in 1296 English King Edward I stole and then lodged it in Westminster Abbey, where English kings and queens hoped to get some of its magic during coronations. On Christmas Day 1950, the stone was purloined by Scottish nationalists, who put it in Arbroath Abbey, where the 1320 Scottish declaration of sovereignty was signed. However, it was soon returned to London. In 1996, it was finally returned officially to Scotland with plenty of manufactured fanfare and is now on display in Edinburgh Castle. Presumably, this is where it stays.

Shopping for Local Treasures

With its cluster of tartan and woolens shops, such as Macnaughtons, Pitlochry offers the classic Highland gateway shopping experience, where you may just find the perfect wool sweater to keep you warm. Both Dundee and Aberdeen offer a full range of shops these days, with many of the stores you would expect to find in provincial cities. As ever, tourist attractions invariably have visitor centers with gifts and souvenirs. Also consider visiting the shops below.

- ✔ **Baxter's Highland Village,** Fochabers (☎ **01343-820-666;** www. baxters.com), is headquarters and retail outlet for Baxter's food products, which are primarily jams and soups. Besides the food shop, you can also stop in the store Coat & Swagger for clothing and gifts. Call to confirm seasonal opening hours.

- ✔ **Le Chocolatier,** 29 Scott St., Perth (☎ **01738-620-039**), is a heavenly shop that offers lots of tasty handmade sweets, from butter fudges to chocolates for diabetics. Open Monday through Saturday from 9 a.m. to 5 p.m.

- ✔ **McEwan Gallery,** on A939, near Ballater (☎ **01339-755429;** www. mcewangallery.com), is a trove of 19th- and 20th-century Scottish artworks. They are nice high-end souvenirs. Call to confirm seasonal hours.

Doing the Pub Crawl

While you might happily settle for your hotel's bar — especially if you're at the Craigellachie or Darroch Learg (p. 333) — or for one of the many rural taverns dotted about the region, for a serious crawl Aberdeen has a range of classic pubs, stylish bars, and nightlife options. Here are a couple of the better traditional options.

- ✔ **Old Blackfriars,** 52 Castle St. (☎ **01224-581-922**), features cask-conditioned real Scottish ales and a host of honest pub grub served all day until about 7:30 p.m. Open Monday through Saturday from 11 a.m. to midnight and Sunday 12:30 to 11 p.m.

✔ **The Prince of Wales,** 7 St. Nicholas Lane (☎ **01224-640-597**), dates from 1850, and is possibly the best place to grab a pint in Aberdeen. The Prince of Wales is an old-fashioned pub with cozy booths and an excellent spectrum of ales. The only problem is that it can get crowded, but that's the price of popularity. Open Monday through Saturday 11 a.m. to midnight, and Sunday noon to midnight.

Fast Facts: Tayside to the Northeast

Area Code

The area codes for this region are: Perth **01738,** Aberfeldy **01887,** Pitlochry **01796,** Dundee **01382,** Aberdeen **01224,** Elgin **01343,** and finally the royally confusing situation in the Royal Deeside region and Braemar, where the telephone company gives both five- and six-digit prefixes: **01339** or **013397.** You need to dial the area code only if you're calling from outside the city or area you want to reach.

ATMs

Your best bets for banks with ATMs are in Aberdeen, Dundee, and Perth.

Emergencies

Dial ☎ **999** for police, fire, or ambulance.

Hospitals

Hospitals in the area are Aberdeen Royal Infirmary, Foresterhill, on the west end of Union Street (☎ 01224-681-818), and Perth Royal Infirmary, Taymount Terrace, on the west side of town (☎ 01738-623-311). Aberfeldy's cottage hospital (☎ 01887-820-3140) is on Old Crieff Road. Dundee Royal Infirmary (☎ 01382-434-664) is on Barrack Road.

Information

Tourist offices are located at: The Square, Aberfeldy (☎ 01887-820-276); 22 Atholl Rd., Pitlochry (☎ 01796-472-215); 4 City Sq., Dundee (☎ 01382-434-664; www.angusanddundee.co.uk); The Mews, Mars Road, Braemar (☎ 01339-741-600); Lower City Mills, West Mill Street, Perth (☎ 01738-627-958; www.perthshire.co.uk); Elgin (☎ 01343-542-666); and St. Nicholas House, Aberdeen (☎ 01224-288-828).

Internet Access

The best place for Internet access in the region is CommsPort, 31–33 Loch St., Aberdeen (☎ 01224-626-468; www.commsport.com). The shop is open Monday through Wednesday and Friday through Saturday from 8 a.m. to 6 p.m., Thursday from 8 a.m. to 7 p.m., and Sunday from 10 a.m. to 5 p.m. Access to the Web costs £3 per hour.

Mail

Post offices are located at 371 George St., Aberdeen (☎ 01224-632-904); 3 Main St., Perth (☎ 01738-624-637); and 92 Atholl Rd., Pitlochry (☎ 01796-472-965).

Chapter 18

The Highlands

After Edinburgh and Glasgow, the Highlands region is the most popular draw for visitors to Scotland — and for good reason. Although it takes some effort getting there, the tourist trail through the Highlands can include breathtaking **Glen Coe** and the beautifully desolate Rannoch Moor; the scenic **"Road to the Isles"** west of Fort William into Lochaber, where mountains meet the sea; isolated western peninsulas such as Morvern, **Ardnamurchan**, or Knoydart; the Great Glen and, of course, the most famous body of water in Scotland, **Loch Ness.** But, honestly, that's only the beginning.

It's easy to be overwhelmed when you're trying to visit an area this remote, divided by lochs and mountain ranges, connected only by the sea, winding highways, and one-lane roads. Use a map to plot your course and mark off the things you want to see. Then figure out the best order in which to see them, whether coming or going.

The capital of the Highlands is **Inverness** and it is the region's only bona fide city. The pretty River Ness runs through the town center, which has plenty of shops, a first-rate regional arts center, a few excellent restaurants, transportation links to the south, and accommodations (as well as a nice castle and museum, but few other attractions). I suggest that Inverness is best as a one-day stop or a comfortable base from which to explore parts of the Highlands.

Southwest of Inverness, **Fort William** lies at the foot of Ben Nevis (the highest mountain in Great Britain), near the head of Loch Linnhe. This location, on the roads leading north through the Great Glen to Loch Ness and going west toward Glenfinnan, means that tourists regularly pass through Fort William, which has shops, bars, and restaurants to please visitors (but not much else to recommend it).

I don't really consider either Inverness or Fort William as particular highlights. **West Coast villages** and towns worth trying to see include Arisaig, Mallaig, Plockton, and Ullapool. **Durness,** in the far north, features a small memorial to the late Beatle John Lennon, who went there on vacations. If you're looking for truly wild and sparsely populated territory, I would suggest traveling north of the fishing port Ullapool, into the Assynt and Sutherland regions of the northwest Highlands.

Getting There

Inverness is well served by buses, trains, and planes. If you're making the big leap north from Glasgow or Edinburgh, you may want to consider taking public transportation — rather than driving — to reach the capital of the Highlands. Then, after you arrive, you can rent a car. You can also take the train from Glasgow to Fort William and transfer there for another train up to Mallaig — possibly the most scenic train ride in the entire U.K. Local bus services crisscross the Highlands, but, for optimal mobility, a car is quite useful.

- ✔ **By car:** The A82 runs through a good portion of the Highlands from Loch Lomond and Crianlarich north to Fort William and then into Inverness. From the east, the A9 from Perth heads north to Inverness and then on to Tain as well. Other key roads in the region include the A830 (the so-called Road to the Isles) from Fort William to Mallaig; the A87 from Invergarry to the Kyle of Lochalsh; the A835 from Inverness to Ullapool; and the A836 from Tain to Tongue and the far north coast.

- ✔ **By bus: Scottish Citylink** (☎ **0870-550-5050;** www.citylink.co.uk) routes hit all the major Highlands towns. Contact Traveline Scotland ☎ **0871-200-2233;** www.travelinescotland.com) for schedules and more information.

- ✔ **By train: First ScotRail** (☎ **0845-748-4950;** www.firstscotrail.com) travels to major towns in the region, including Fort William and Mallaig, on the West Highland Lines, as well as Inverness, Tain, Kyle of Lochalsh, and even Thurso. You have to rely on buses or local taxis after you arrive by train, however. ScotRail service to Inverness dovetails with long-distance trains from England. Contact Traveline Scotland ☎ **0871-200-2233;** www.travelinescotland.com) for schedules and more information.

- ✔ **By plane: Inverness/Dalcross Airport** (☎ **01463-23-2471;** www.hial.co.uk) is at Dalcross, 13km (8 miles) east of Inverness. The airport handles flights to and from Glasgow and Edinburgh, as well as the Western and Northern Islands.

- ✔ **By ferry: Caledonian MacBrayne** (☎ **01475-650-100;** www.calmac.co.uk) — or CalMac, as it's more colloquially known — serves 22 islands and four peninsulas over the West Coast of Scotland. In the Highlands, this includes service from Mallaig to Skye and Ullapool to the Outer Hebrides.

The Highlands

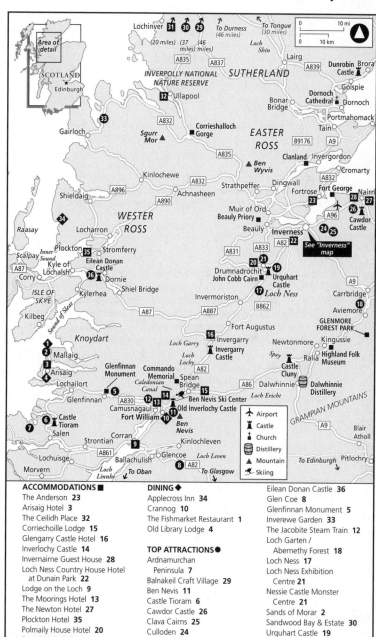

ACCOMMODATIONS ■

The Anderson **23**
Arisaig Hotel **3**
The Ceilidh Place **32**
Corriechoille Lodge **15**
Glengarry Castle Hotel **16**
Inverlochy Castle **14**
Invernairne Guest House **28**
Loch Ness Country House Hotel
  at Dunain Park **22**
Lodge on the Loch **9**
The Moorings Hotel **13**
The Newton Hotel **27**
Plockton Hotel **35**
Polmaily House Hotel **20**
Scourie Hotel **31**

DINING ◆

Applecross Inn **34**
Crannog **10**
The Fishmarket Restaurant **1**
Old Library Lodge **4**

TOP ATTRACTIONS ●

Ardnamurchan
  Peninsula **7**
Balnakeil Craft Village **29**
Ben Nevis **11**
Castle Tioram **6**
Cawdor Castle **26**
Clava Cairns **25**
Culloden **24**

Eilean Donan Castle **36**
Glen Coe **8**
Glenfinnan Monument **5**
Inverewe Garden **33**
The Jacobite Steam Train **12**
Loch Garten /
  Abernethy Forest **18**
Loch Ness **17**
Loch Ness Exhibition
  Centre **21**
Nessie Castle Monster
  Centre **21**
Sands of Morar **2**
Sandwood Bay & Estate **30**
Urquhart Castle **19**

Spending the Night

You may want to stay in tourist-friendly Inverness or Fort William, but the rest of the Highlands towns and villages have some real treats, too. Some accommodations have earned star ratings from the tourist board; see Chapter 8 for a description of the rating system and information on self-catering accommodations, of which there are quite a few in the Highlands. Rates listed here include full breakfast, unless otherwise stated. You may well get a better deal than the advertised rack rates.

Some of the hotels and guesthouses listed here may close for part of the winter (a good time to make repairs). Reserve ahead to ensure you have a room waiting for you.

In addition to the options listed below, be sure to read through the "Dining Locally" section that follows. I highlight a few of the restaurants listed there that also have limited overnight accommodations.

The Anderson
$$ The Black Isle

Formerly known as the Royal Hotel, and located in the handsome seaside village of Fortrose, the Anderson prides itself as a gastronomic oasis in the Highlands. Scottish ingredients get the international treatment, whether it's a bowl of Shetland mussels steamed in a red curry and coconut broth or a plate of wild Scotch venison goulash. The pub is no slouch either, boasting 160 single malt whiskies, real ales from Scotland and England, and some 60 Belgian beers. The nine overnight rooms combine antiques with modern conveniences in this historic building, while the welcome from owners Jim and Anne Anderson is always warm and accommodating.

See map p. 345. Union Street, Fortrose. ☎ 01381-620-236. www.theanderson. co.uk. Rack rates: £80 double. MC, V.

Arisaig Hotel
$$–$$$ Arisaig

In addition to views of the lovely bay at Arisaig, its small harbor, and the isles beyond, this hotel has two dedicated family rooms. The units are tidy and well appointed, if not exceptionally large. The best ones face onto the sea. A restaurant and popular local pub (renovated in early 2007), as well as a playroom for children, are on the premises.

See map p. 345. A830 at Arisaig harbor. ☎ 01687-450-210. Fax: 01687-450-310. www. arisaighotel.co.uk. Rack rates: £110 double. MC, V.

Avalon Guest House
$$ Inverness

On the road into Inverness from Loch Ness, the four-star Avalon is a bit of luxury on the edge of the town near the Eden Court Theatre. While the exterior is unassuming, the six bedrooms — all done in handsome, sumptuous earthy hues — are quite plush with leather easy chairs, plump pillows, quality linens, and MP3 docking stations. The owners have spruced up the en-suite bathrooms, as well the guest lounge (which were both fine before but are even better now). This is a great spot for couples.

See map p. 355. 79 Glenurquhart Rd. (A82). ☎ **01463-239-075.** *Fax: 01463-709-827.* www.inverness-loch-ness.co.uk. *Rack rates: £60 double. MC, V.*

Ballifeary Guest House
$$ Inverness

In the same neighborhood as the Avalon (see above), this four-star B&B is in a quiet residential area along the River Ness and within easy walking distance of the Inverness city center. The Edwardian villa has lovely sitting rooms and six well-kept overnight units that exude comfort with en-suite bathrooms. Families take note, however: The minimum age for guests is 15.

See map p. 355. 10 Ballifeary Rd. ☎ **01463-235-572.** *Fax: 01463-717-583.* www. ballifearyhousehotel.co.uk. *Rack rates: £70–£76 double. MC, V.*

The Ceilidh Place
$$–$$$ Ullapool

How many hotels organize their rooms on the basis of the mini-library that each unit contains? Fair to say, not many. But here at the Ceilidh Place, which has its own acclaimed bookshop on the premises, each overnight room features a set of books selected by a Scottish writer or luminary. This charming, if rather idiosyncratic, hotel often hosts live traditional- and folk-music performances, as well as other cultural events.

See map p. 345. 14 W. Argyle St. ☎ **01854-612-103.** *Fax: 01854-613-773.* www.the ceilidhplace.com. *Rack rates: £90–£130 double. MC, V.*

Corriechoille Lodge
$$ Near Spean Bridge

The sitting room of this stone guesthouse offers views of the nearby Nevis Range Mountains. An 18th-century stone fishing lodge, about 19km (12 miles) northeast of Fort William, was converted into this luxurious hideaway with all the trimmings. No children younger than seven are permitted, and the lodge is closed Monday and Tuesday nights. In addition to the guesthouse, there are two one-bedroom log cabins on the property.

See map p. 345. Just off the A82 (3km/2 miles east of Spean Bridge). ☎ **01397-712-002.** www.corriechoille.com. *Rack rates: £76 double. MC, V. Closed Nov to mid-Apr.*

Glengarry Castle Hotel
$$–$$$ Invergarry

You'd be hard pressed to find a prettier spot for such highly regarded country-inn lodgings. This 26-room Victorian mansion is on extensive wooded grounds with its own castle ruins (the real Glengarry Castle) and nice views of Loch Oich. Some of the warmly decorated rooms have four-poster beds and exposed ceiling beams; there are two family size units. The four-star hotel also has rowboats for guest use, while afternoon high tea is served for those in the mood for less robust activities.

See map p. 345. Off the A82 (1.5km/1 mile south of the intersection with the A87 in Invergarry). ☎ **01809-501-254**. *Fax: 01809-501-207.* www.glengarry.net. *Rack rates: £90–£110 standard double. MC, V. Closed mid-Nov to mid-Mar.*

Glen Mhor Hotel
$$–$$$ Inverness

This 50-bedroom Victorian hotel (nicely remodeled) overlooks the east banks of the River Ness, not far from the bluff with Inverness Castle. The lobbies and dining spaces, including **Nico's** (p. 352), are quite lovely with overstuffed chairs and oak paneling. The bedrooms tend to be large and prices vary widely depending on the season and whether or not you get a river view.

See map p. 355. 9–12 Ness Bank. ☎ **01463-234-308**. *Fax: 01463-713-170.* www.the invernesshotel.com. *Rack rates: £90–£145 double. AE, MC, V.*

Inverlochy Castle
$$$$ Fort William

Offering Fort William's most highly rated accommodations, Inverlochy Castle hotel is beautifully situated in the foothills of Ben Nevis. Staying here can be literally an experience fit for royalty: Queen Victoria visited for a week in 1873 and wrote in her diary, "I never saw a lovelier or more romantic spot." That sentiment still rings true today. The sitting rooms and dining area are flawlessly decorated and illuminated by chandeliers. The attention to fine detail and maximum comfort extends to the guest rooms as well, which have great views. The food is gourmet (and Michelin-starred), and after you've had your fill of rich food and posh interiors, you can tour the 200-hectare (500-acre) grounds.

See map p. 345. Torlundy (5km/3 miles north of Fort William on the A82). ☎ **01397-702-177**. *Fax: 01397-702-953.* www.inverlochycastlehotel.com. *Rack rates: £300–£510 double. AE, MC, V.*

Invernairne Guest House
$$–$$$ Nairn

Originally a 19th-century Italianate mansion and trading as a hotel since 1948, the Invernairne became a guesthouse when it ceased serving evening meals in the new millennium. Still, it's a cozy place with good access to Nairn's many beaches. From the inn you can see the sea and probably the dolphins that regularly swim up and down the Moray Firth. The baronial-style bar and lounge usually has a roaring fire going when the days are cool.

See map p. 345. Thurlow Road. ☎ **01667-452-039**. www.invernairne.com. *Rack rates: £80–£110. AE, MC, V.*

Loch Ness Country House Hotel at Dunain Park
$$$–$$$$ Dunain near Inverness

In a tourist-strategic position between Loch Ness and Inverness, the Dunain is a wonderful, old Georgian country-house hotel (recently refurbished) that's surrounded by gardens, with woods beyond. Some of the well-dressed bedrooms and suites in the main house have four-poster beds, while more chic accommodations are found in separate quaint cottages.

See map p. 345. Fort William Road, on the A82 (3km/2 miles south of Inverness). ☎ **01463-230-512.** *Fax: 01463-224-532. www.lochnesscountryhousehotel. co.uk. Rack rates: £165 double. MC, V.*

Lodge on the Loch
$$$–$$$$ Onich

The Lodge on the Loch hotel — scheduled to be closed for substantial renovations until April 2011 — offers some of the finest vistas in the Highlands: The serene family run retreat overlooks Loch Linnhe, 8km (5 miles) or so west of Glencoe. The house was built in 1870 as a country home and today the bedrooms are individually decorated. In the past, children under 16 were not admitted, but you may wish to call post-renovation to confirm that this is still the case.

See map p. 345. On A82 (16km/10 miles south of Fort William). ☎ **01855-821-238.** *Fax: 01855-821-190. www.lodgeontheloch.com. Rack rates: £100–£200 double. MC, V.*

The Moorings Hotel
$$–$$$ Near Fort William

On a quiet residential stretch outside Fort William's town center, this labyrinthine hotel is bigger than it looks. The large, comfortable rooms stretch back to the Caledonian Canal; some units have views of the locks (aka Neptune's Staircase) and the boats going through. The more costly superior rooms have better views, living areas, and king-size beds.

See map p. 345. Banavie, just off the A830 toward Mallaig, next to Caledonian Canal. ☎ **01397-772-797.** *Fax: 01397-772-441. www.moorings-fortwilliam.co.uk. Rack rates: £98–£148 double. AE, DC, MC, V.*

Moyness House
$$ Inverness

Moyness House may be the finest guesthouse in Inverness. This quaint, whitewashed Victorian villa was once home to 20th-century author Neil Gunn and the names of the six homey bedrooms are inspired by him, such as Silver Darlings or Lost Glen. Each unit is individually decorated and comfortably furnished, with modern en-suite bathrooms. Discounts offered on stays over three nights.

See map p. 355. 6 Bruce Gardens, just off A82. ☎ **01463-233-836.** *Fax: 01463-233-836. www.moyness.co.uk. Rack rates: £76–£90 double. MC, V.*

The Newton Hotel
$$$ Nairn

Just before you enter the coastal town of Nairn from the west, you should spot this castlelike hotel and conference center set amid 8.4 hectares (21 acres) of mature parkland and gardens. It could be just the thing you need after a busy day of sightseeing. In addition to the usual room facilities, nice touches include heated bathroom floors.

See map p. 345. Inverness Road, on A96. ☎ **01667-453-144.** *Fax: 01667-454-026. www. oxfordhotelsandinns.com. Rack rates: £45–£110 double. AE, DC, MC, V.*

Plockton Hotel
$$ Plockton

The village of Plockton (see "The top attractions," below) is one of the prettiest you find in the Highlands and this is the only hotel on the water-front, looking onto a sheltered bay in Loch Carron. The 11 overnight accommodations include two that work as family rooms, and there's a four-bedroom cottage annex nearby. All the units have en-suite bath-rooms, and a half-dozen offer sea views. The hotel's **dining room** and **award-garnering pub** are well known for fresh fish and seafood dishes.

See map p. 345. Harbour Street. ☎ **01599-544-274.** *Fax: 01599-544-475. www. plocktonhotel.co.uk. Rack rates: £120 double. AE, MC, V.*

Polmaily House Hotel
$$–$$$ Near Drumnadrochit

Polmaily knows how to provide family-friendly accommodations during the high season. The 14-room hotel features a heated indoor pool, video games, tennis courts, mountain bikes, and fishing. In the summer, parents will appreciate the supervised fun room, organized children's activities, outdoor play areas, and large suites.

See map p. 345. On the A831 toward Cannish. ☎ **01456-450-343.** *Fax: 01456-450-813. www.polmaily.co.uk. Rack rates: £110 double. MC, V. Closed Jan.*

Scourie Hotel
$$ Scourie

This one-time coaching inn way up north in Sutherland is one those hotels that believes guests have better things to do than sit in their rooms and watch television. (There are no TVs here, although they provide you with a radio if asked.) Rooms are quite homey and spacious. Some of them overlook Scourie Bay, while others have vistas toward the inland moun-tains, such as Ben Stack. It's a top spot for fishing enthusiasts, too, with hotel boats available.

See map p. 345. Scourie is about 69km (43 miles) north of Ullapool on the A894. ☎ **01971-502-396.** *Fax: 01971-502-423. www.scourie-hotel.co.uk. Rack rates: £76–£90 double. MC, V.*

Dining Locally

Your hotel (though probably not your B&B) is likely to have a restaurant, and most of those listed above also will serve meals to nonresidents who reserve a table in advance. But there are more options in the Highlands, and I list some of the better ones below.

Applecross Inn
$$ Applecross   FISH/SEAFOOD

This may not be the easiest place to reach, but many visitors feel the twists and turns of the road to Applecross are well worth the meal at the inn. This one-time fisherman's cottage sits right on the shores of the Inner Sound of Raasay, looking out toward the mountains on the Isle of Skye. Naturally, seafood dishes make up the majority of the menu, but you can expect local venison or sausages, too. The Applecross, with an excellent selection of real ale, is also rated one of Scotland's best country pubs. (It also has **overnight rooms** from £50 per person.)

See map p. 345. From the village of Lochcarron, take the A896 west, turning left on the country road to Applecross. ☎ **01520-744-262.** *Fax: 01520-744-440.* `www.applecross.uk.com.` *Reservations recommended. Main courses: £8–£16. MC, V. Open: Daily noon to 9 p.m.*

Café 1
$$–$$$ Inverness   INTERNATIONAL

The small, well-chosen menu may include items such as Angus rump steak, sticky pork belly, or halibut filet. It always has something for vegetarians, as well. The décor behind the stone exterior is simple and modern, and you find the service polite and professional.

See map p. 355. 75 Castle St. ☎ **01463-226-200.** `www.cafe1.net.` *Reservations recommended. Main courses: £8–£15. MC, V. Open: Mon–Sat noon to 2 p.m. and 5:30–9:30 p.m.*

Crannog
$$$ Fort William   FISH/SEAFOOD

Offering fine views, this restaurant sits on stilts out over the waters of Loch Linnhe — a location that led to severe storm damage a few years back. After repairs, the restaurant returned to its town pier location. The owners deploy their own fleet of boats (and run a smokehouse, too), so expect the freshest of fish. A plate of langoustines with hot garlic butter is highly touted. By the way, *crannog* is the Gaelic word for an artificial island on the banks of a loch — how appropriate.

See map p. 345. The Pier. ☎ **01397-705-589.** `www.crannog.net.` *Reservations recommended for dinner. Main courses: £12–£16. MC, V. Open: Daily noon to 2:30 p.m. and 6–9 p.m.*

The Fishmarket Restaurant
$$ **Mallaig FISH/SEAFOOD**

Situated right on the harbor and serving dishes that incorporate freshly caught fish, this restaurant is a casual place for a meal. Main courses might include poached haddock with mussels, roasted whole sea bass with fennel and ginger, or traditional fish and chips. Prawns come in by the ton here at Mallaig and, thus, are one of the restaurant's specialties.

See map p. 345. Station Road. ☎ 01687-462-299. Fax: 01687-460-040. Reservations recommended. Main courses: £10–£15. MC, V. Open: Daily noon to 2:30 p.m. and 6–9 p.m. (Coffee shop open: 11 a.m.– 5 p.m.)

The Kitchen
$$ **Inverness MODERN SCOTTISH**

One of the more exciting additions to the city of Inverness, the Kitchen occupies a purpose-built, multifloor glass-fronted edifice on the left bank of the River Ness. The setting is impressive while the cooking is modern and fresh. The fixed-price lunch for about £7 is good value. Similar cuisine, in slightly less stirring surroundings, is offered by a sister restaurant across the river, the **Mustard Seed** (16 Fraser St., ☎ 01463-220-220).

See map p. 355. 15 Huntly St. ☎ 01463-259-119. www.kitchenrestaurant. co.uk. Reservations recommended. Main courses: £10–£15. MC, V. Open: Daily noon to 3 p.m. and 5–9:30 p.m.

Nico's Bistro
$$–$$$ **Inverness SCOTTISH**

This upscale diner in the Glen Mhor hotel offers a relaxed place to dine. You can't really go wrong with a catch of the day, such as sea scallops or langoustines. The lounge is perfect for a predinner beer or an after-dinner cocktail, and outdoor seating is available.

See map p. 355. 9–12 Ness Bank. ☎ 01463-234-308. Main courses: £14–£23. AE, DC, MC, V. Open: Daily 11:30 a.m.–10 p.m.

Old Library Lodge & Restaurant
$$$ **Arisaig MODERN SCOTTISH**

Located in a 200-year-old stone building (formerly the village stables) down the street from the Arisaig Hotel (p. 346), this restaurant (which also has six **overnight rooms**) garners three stars from the Scottish tourist board. The evening menu might include pan-fried scallops with lime and dill, double loin lamb chops, or monkfish with tarragon and Pernod.

See map p. 345. ☎ 01687-450-651. Fax: 01687-450-219. www.oldlibrary.co.uk. Fixed-price 3-course dinner: £26. MC, V. Open: Daily 6–9 p.m. Closed Nov–Jan.

Riva
$$–$$$ **Inverness** **ITALIAN**

This bistro can be a lively spot for a meal, with fine wine, inventive Italian cuisine, and a location on the River Ness. The subtly flavored dishes can include braised loin of pork with cannellini beans or mixed seafood and shellfish tossed with linguine.

See map p. 355. 4–6 Ness Walk, by the Ness Bridge. ☎ **01463-237-377.** *www.riva restaurant.co.uk. Reservations recommended. Main courses: £9–£19. MC, V. Open: Daily 5–10 p.m.; Mon–Sat noon to 2:30 p.m. and daily 5–9:30 p.m.*

The River Café and Restaurant
$$ **Inverness** **SCOTTISH**

This small, simple venture by the water is a favorite among locals because of its good eats at even better prices. During the day, it acts very much like a cafe with croissant sandwiches or stuffed baked potatoes — as well as serving high teas. In the evening, the candles come out and the cuisine is more formal, with specialties such as filet of Scottish salmon or duck breast.

See map p. 355. 10 Bank St. ☎ **01463-714-884.** *www.rivercafeandrestaurant. co.uk. Main courses: £13–£26. MC, V. Open: Mon–Sat 10 a.m.–9:30 p.m.*

Rocpool
$$$ **Inverness** **MODERN SCOTTISH**

This is the original Rocpool, and it remains among the more ambitious modern restaurants in the city of Inverness. The menu may range from crispy polenta cake topped with fresh crab to pistachio-crusted goat-cheese soufflé. A pretheater menu offers good value. In addition to this centrally located restaurant, **Rocpool Reserve,** a small distance across town, is a boutique hotel with Chez Roux Restaurant.

See map p. 355. 1 Ness Walk. ☎ **01463-717-274.** *www.rocpoolrestaurant. com. Main courses: £12–£20. MC, V. Open: Mon–Sat noon to 10:30 p.m. (also Sun 6–10 p.m. in summer).*

Exploring the Highlands

You can find plenty of tourist attractions between Inverness and Fort William, but please don't confine yourself to the well-known Loch Ness hot spots. In addition to those heavily touristed sites, you have a wide choice of things to see throughout the Highlands: ancient monuments, lovely lochs, picturesque villages, natural areas for hiking, sandy and unspoiled beaches, and a good number of excellent castles.

Guided tours

The Highlands lends itself to smartly operated theme tours, whether relating to the area's rich historic heritage or unique natural history. Refer to my suggestions in "Seeing Scotland by Bus," in Chapter 7, for a list of reputable guided tours setting off from Edinburgh or Glasgow. Here are a couple of the more interesting specialized tours to take, too.

- ✔ **Ecoventure** (☎ **01381-600-323;** www.ecoventures.co.uk): This company takes you to see a resident colony of bottlenose dolphins living in the Moray Firth. As many as 130 live in one area, and they're generally friendly and unafraid to approach the boat. The tour also covers other sea life such as seals, porpoises, and even the occasional minke whale. Tours depart from Cromarty Harbor at the tip of the Black Isle, off the A832 at the junction of Bank Street and High Street in Cromarty. Reservations are highly recommended. Tickets cost £22 per adult, £16 for children. The tour lasts about two hours.

- ✔ **Jacobite Cruises** (☎ **01463-233-999;** www.jacobite.co.uk): Jacobite Cruises, which take visitors out on Loch Ness, are perhaps the most efficient and best organized tours of the loch. You can choose from a number of different excursions, such as the "Passion" cruise and tour, a six-hour-plus trip by boat and bus down the loch, through the Caledonian Canal, stopping at Urquhart (*irk*-ett) Castle and the Corrimony Cairns. Alternatively, the "Inspiration" cruise takes only one hour on the loch. The company runs minibuses to the launch site from the Inverness Tourist Information Centre on Bridge Street. Or you can drive to the Clansman Harbour, 13km (8 miles) southwest of the city outskirts, off the A82. Tours operate year round, and fares start at £12 per adult for the one-hour trip.

The top attractions

Ardnamurchan Peninsula
West of Fort William

One of the more remote areas of the Highlands, the Ardnamurchan Peninsula is the most westerly point in the entire British mainland. One highlight is the ruins of Castle Tioram (see the listing later in this section), but the peninsula also has pretty beaches (such as the one at Sanna Bay), tide pools, natural history, a nature visitor center near Glenbeg, and lots of hiking trails. The lighthouse at the craggy Point of Ardnamurchan can feel like the end of the earth on a windy day. From Kilchoan on the peninsula, you can take a ferry to and from Tobermory on the Isle of Mull in the summer. Allow one day.

See map p. 345. West of Fort William. Take the A861 from the Road to the Isles (A830) at Lochailort, or use the small ferry service to Corran, a few miles north of Ballachulish (A82). www.ardnamurchan.com. *Admission: Free. Open: Year-round.*

Inverness

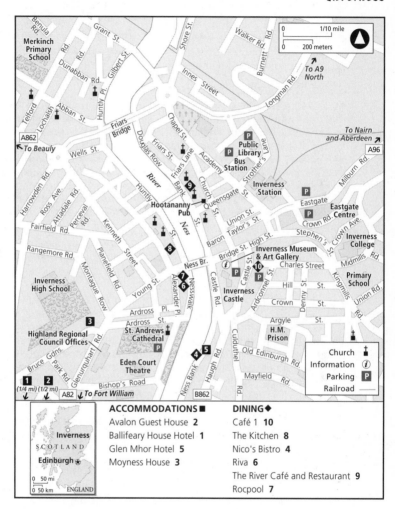

ACCOMMODATIONS ■
Avalon Guest House **2**
Ballifeary House Hotel **1**
Glen Mhor Hotel **5**
Moyness House **3**

DINING ◆
Café 1 **10**
The Kitchen **8**
Nico's Bistro **4**
Riva **6**
The River Café and Restaurant **9**
Rocpool **7**

Balnakeil Craft Village
Near Durness

This artist community, on the outskirts of Durness near Cape Wrath, has plenty of galleries selling local artwork. The craft village is housed in a former military communications installation with lots of flat-roofed institutional-looking buildings. Still the place is friendly, communal, and, yes, vaguely hippy-esque. The cafe serves tasty natural foods, and the bookshop is well stocked with local titles. If you've come this far, you may as well continue to the end of the road to see the old ruins of a 17th-century church and the lovely Balnakeil beach. Allow about two hours.

See map p. 345. Off the A838 (1km/one-half mile west of Durness; 108km/67 miles north of Ullapool). www.durness.org. *Admission: Free. Open: Year-round.*

Ben Nevis
Near Fort William

At 1,344m (4,410 ft.), Ben Nevis is the tallest mountain in the United Kingdom, although it's difficult to see just how tall it is from the usual vantage points around Fort William. The round-trip hike to the summit is about 16km (10 miles) and can take around seven hours (four hours up and three down). You will need to wear good boots and have both warm- and cold-weather gear, because the temperature and weather can fluctuate unpredictably at certain heights. Don't attempt to transverse the summit without a proper map and compass, and also don't start your ascent of Ben Nevis too late in the day. The tourist office in Fort William has trail maps if you're planning to make the big climb. Allow about seven hours.

See map p. 345. Path leaves from Glen Nevis Road, just outside Fort William. ☎ **01397-703-781**. www.visit-fortwilliam.co.uk. *Admission: Free. Open: Year-round.*

Castle Tioram
Near Blain on Loch Moidart

The impressive ruins of this classic medieval fortress (pronounced, roughly, *cheer*-rum) sit on a rocky spit of land extending into the picturesque waters of Loch Moidart. A key outpost for clan MacDonald for hundreds of years, Castle Tioram is one of my favorite ruined castles: a romantic site that is best accessed at low tide. Like so many castles in Scotland, Tioram was sacked and burned during Jacobite uprisings — in this instance apparently by its own owners in order to keep it from falling into the hands of forces loyal to the Hanovers in London. There are good hiking trails near the castle, too. Allow one to two hours.

See map p. 345. Off the A861 from Blain. Admission: Free. Open: Year-round.

Cawdor Castle
Near Nairn

Cawdor, with its dramatic drawbridge and medieval tower, is full of treasures, and particularly tapestries, from around the world. The gardens are pretty wonderful, too, with wildflowers, fountains, and a maze of holly bushes. Legend has it that the Thane of Cawdor (then spelled Calder) determined the location of the castle by giving instructions to build wherever his donkey decided to rest (as he had dreamed). The animal stopped in the shade of a mature holly, and deep within the castle, its stump (carbon dated to about 1370) still stands today. Although Macbeth was Shakespeare's Thane of Cawdor, neither he nor his good lady could have resided here: The castle wasn't built yet. Last admission 30 minutes before closing. Allow about two hours.

See map p. 345. On the B9090, off the A96 between Inverness and Nairn. ☎ **01667-404-401.** www.cawdorcastle.com. *Admission: £9 adults, £8 seniors, £5.50 children 5–15, £27 family. Open: May to early Oct daily 10 a.m.–5:30 p.m. Closed mid-Oct to Apr.*

Clava Cairns
Culloden

If you're visiting the nearby Culloden Moor Battlefield (see the next listing), Clava Cairns — also known as the Balnuaran of Clava — is worth a brief visit. Basically a 4,000-year-old graveyard, the cairns are part of best-preserved Bronze Age cemetery in Scotland. The large circular pits of rock and rubble, two of which are aligned on the winter solstice, are slightly eerie. Nearby are standing stones in a grove of trees and ruins of an ancient chapel. Allow about one hour.

See map p. 345. Off the B9091, just east of Culloden Battlefield. www.historic-scotland.gov.uk. ☎ **01667-460-232.** *Admission: Free. Open: Year-round.*

Culloden
Culloden Moor

This marshy field is where the hopes of Bonnie Prince Charlie's Jacobite uprising of 1745 (begun at Glenfinnan; see "Glenfinnan Monument," later in this section) ended in complete defeat on April 16, 1746. The bloody battle (the last significant one fought on the British mainland) was over in about an hour, and Charlie was among the few Jacobites who escaped unharmed. After their defeat, Highland life was censored and restricted by a London administration tired of rebellion. An impressive new visitor center provides all the background and key details about the events. Take the time to walk through the battlefield (with hand-held audio kit): It has clan stones and cairns in memory of those who lost their lives. The terrain is kept the same as 260 years ago, when boggy conditions contributed to the Jacobites' defeat. Allow about two and a half hours.

See map p. 345. Off the B9006 (8km/5 miles east of Inverness). ☎ **01463-790-607.** www.nts.org.uk/culloden. *Admission: £10 adults, £7.50 children and seniors, £24 family. Open: Site daily year-round; visitor center, restaurant, and shop Apr–Oct daily 9 a.m.–6 p.m., Nov–Mar daily 10 a.m.–4 p.m.*

Eilean Donan Castle
Dornie, Lochalsh

Grab your camera: Eilean Donan Castle could be the most photographed stone pile in the Highlands. On an islet in Loch Duich, this quintessential castle (which lay in utter ruins for two centuries) is accessible by an arched bridge. Originally built in the early 1200s by Alexander II to deter Viking invaders, the castle was demolished at the hands of Hanoverian troops during the Jacobite uprising of 1719. In the early decades of the 20th century, it was essentially rebuilt. Highlights include the ramparts, the banqueting hall, and the billeting room, as well as Jacobite relics. B-movie fans will be excited by the fact that *Highlander* was filmed here. Last admission is one hour before closing. Allow about two hours.

See map p. 345. Dornie, Kyle of Lochalsh, on the A87. ☎ **01599-555-202.** www. eileandonancastle.com. *Admission: £5.50 adults; £4.50 seniors, students, and children; £14 family. Open: Mar–Oct Nov daily 10 a.m.–6 p.m. (from 9 a.m. July–Aug). Closed Nov–Feb (except for gift shop).*

Glen Coe
Glencoe

It's hard to believe that such an unspeakably beautiful valley was the site of such a dreadfully bloody event. Glen Coe is where a historic massacre took place on February 6, 1692. On that fateful day, the Campbell Earl of Argyle's regiment — on orders approved by the king, William of Orange — slaughtered about 40 members of clan MacDonald, including some women and children. What makes their killings truly distressing is the fact that Campbell's troops had been staying as guests, albeit not especially welcomed ones. Thus, Glen Coe is right up there with Culloden when it comes to tragic bloodshed at the hands of troops loyal to the central government in England. Regardless of the area's grim history, this spectacular valley extends about 16km (10 miles) from the king's house in the east to the shores of Loch Leven and the village of Glencoe in the west. The National Trust for Scotland's ecofriendly visitor center has area trail maps and audiovisual presentations of local geography. Children receive a free fun guide with admission. Ranger-led walks take place throughout the summer. Allow about three hours.

See map p. 345. On the A82, just east of Ballachulish. ☎ **01855-811-307.** www. glencoe-nts.org.uk. *Admission to visitor center: £5.50 adults; £4.50 seniors, students, and children; £15 family. Open: Site daily year-round; visitor center daily Apr–Oct 9:30 a.m.–5:30 p.m., Oct 10 a.m.–5 p.m., Nov–Mar Thurs–Sun 10 a.m.–4 p.m.*

Plockton: The prettiest Highland village?

Not far from Eilean Donan, Plockton (www.plockton.com) is arguably the prettiest village in the Highlands. The crescent-shaped, harborside main street, on the shores of Loch Carron, is lined with cute cottages, while the sidewalks are punctuated with palm trees that defy the northern latitudes. Plockton gained fame in the U.K. as the location for a BBC TV series, *Hamish Macbeth,* starring a then little-known Robert Carlyle as a laid-back, pot-smoking policeman. Today, Plockton features some good pub grub at the Plockton Inn, on Innes Street, and the Plockton Hotel (see "Spending the Night," above). Plockton is about 10km (6 miles) northeast of Kyle of Lochalsh, off the A87.

Ullapool: Happenings at the harbor

Ullapool, on the shores of Loch Broom, is the busiest fishing port on the northwest coast of Scotland. Established reasonably recently, in 1788, as a planned village by the British Fisheries Society, the town has become a popular resort in its own right — the last outpost before the sparsely populated northwest. If you need to stock up at a supermarket, stop in Ullapool. It also has some good casual restaurants that feature freshly landed fish and seafood, like crabs, while the Ceilidh Place (see "Spending the Night," above) is a hub of cultural activity with frequent music and dance events through the summer season. The **Ullapool Museum,** West Argyle Street (☎ **01854-612-987;** www. ullapoolmuseum.co.uk), is open year-round; call for times.

Glenfinnan Monument
Glenfinnan

This monument marks the hopeful start of the 1745 Jacobite rebellion led by Bonnie Prince Charlie, who was trying to reclaim the English and Scottish crowns for his Stuart family lineage. Be sure to take your camera; this monument (and now slightly sacred historical ground) amid Highland scenery is a great spot for pictures, especially if you're lucky enough to see the steam train (see below) cross the arched viaduct behind the visitor center. (Fans of the *Harry Potter* films will recognize the setting.) The Jacobites allegedly left from this spot to successfully push all the way to Derby in England before turning back and being crushed at Culloden (see listing earlier in this section). The Jacobite cause has captured the Scots' collective imagination, and the small National Trust of Scotland visitor center provides a good primer on the Jacobites and Prince Charlie. The monument can be vaguely magical: On one of my visits, a lone piper broke the silence of twilight with mournful playing from a heather-filled hillside. Allow about two hours.

See map p. 345. On A830, next to Loch Shiel (29km/18 miles west of Fort William). ☎ *01397-722-250. www.nts.org.uk. Admission to visitor center: £3 adults; £2 seniors, students, and children; £8 family. Open: Site daily year-round; visitor center daily Apr–June and Sept–Oct 10 a.m.–5 p.m.; July–Aug 9:30 a.m.–5:30 p.m. Closed Nov–Mar.*

Inverewe Garden
Near Poolewe

The most impressive garden in the Highlands is on the south-facing shores of Loch Ewe, about 10km (6 miles) northeast of the village of Gairloch. Because the North Atlantic drift carries warmer waters up from the Caribbean, the climate here is surprisingly temperate. The plants are a testament to the ideal growing conditions. In late summer, you can see cabbages the size of basketballs in the large vegetable patch within the walled garden. The sprawling 20-hectare (50-acre) garden, however, encompasses much more than just vegetables, and includes rhododendron and pine walks, a "bambooselem," two ponds, and a rock garden. Diverse planting means something is in bloom all year-round, from azaleas in spring to Kaffir lilies in the autumn. Allow two hours.

See map p. 345. On A832. ☎ 01455-781-200. Fax: 01455-781-497. www.nts.org. uk. Admission: £8.50 adults; £5.50 seniors, students, and children; £21 family. Open: Daily Nov–Mar 10 a.m.–3 p.m., Apr–Oct 9:30 a.m. to sunset or 8 p.m.

The Jacobite Steam Train
Fort William and Mallaig railway stations

The 68km (42-mile) train ride between Fort William and the port town of Mallaig is one of the most picturesque rail journeys in Europe — perhaps the world. As you chug along past mountains, skirting lochs and glens, you pass the Glenfinnan Monument and miles and miles of dramatic, unspoiled scenery. It's hard to believe that the rail line wasn't built for the delight of visitors; rather, it was created to bring catches of fish inland. At the Glenfinnan station, a small train museum is worth a look, and you can take a break in the cafe located in an old train car. If you take the round-trip, the schedule allows you to have two and a half hours in Mallaig. Not every train on this route is the historic steam train, so confirm schedules if you want to ride the real thing. Allow about five and a half hours round-trip.

See map p. 345. Fort William and Mallaig railway stations. ☎ 01524-737-751. www. westcoastrailway.co.uk. Tickets: about £32 standard adult round-trip or £22 one-way. Open: Mid-May to Oct one round-trip Mon–Fri departing from Fort William at 10:20 a.m., returning from Mallaig at 2:10 p.m.; midsummer also departs Sat–Sun. No steam trains mid-Oct to late May.

Loch Garten/Abernethy Forest
Boat of Garten

Some 10km (6 miles) northeast of Aviemore in the Cairngorm Mountains, this aviary reserve on the shores of Loch Garten is operated by the Royal Society for the Protection of Birds (RSPB). It offers an observation center to spy on the osprey, once thought to be extinct in Scotland. They still, horribly, remain targets of assorted idiots, but since the mid-1950s, the ospreys have returned from Africa to nest here in the spring. The observation center deploys telescopes and video cameras to help visitors see the young birds of prey. Allow about two hours.

See map p. 345. Near Boat of Garten. ☎ 01479-831-476. www.rspb.org.uk. Admission: £3 adults, £2 seniors and children under 16, £6 family. Open: Apr–Aug daily 10 a.m.–6 p.m.

Loch Ness

Okay, this is it: The dark, deep (274m/900-ft.), mysterious, and legendary Loch Ness. In addition to looking for the elusive monster, you should seek out other local attractions, such as Urquhart Castle (see below) or the cairn of John Cobb, who died on the loch attempting to set a water speed record. Although the drive along the shore is good, the best way to experience the loch is by boat (see the listing under "Guided tours," earlier in this chapter). As for the monster, little is known for certain. Although no one can confirm that it exists, it's apparently against the law to kill it. Is it out there? I say no, but keep an eye out, just in case. Allow anywhere from one to four hours, depending on your interest level.

See map p. 345. On the A82 or the B852 on the eastern shore. Admission: Free. Open: Year-round.

Loch Ness Exhibition Centre
Drumnadrochit

Visiting this attraction is rather like reading *Loch Ness For Dummies* (if there were such a book). In other words, it covers the bases without burying you in details. Focusing mainly on monster myths and the technology of scientific monster-hunting, Loch Ness Exhibition Centre offers a reasonably entertaining exhibit using laser lights and digital projection displays. And while the kids may marvel at the smoke and mirrors, you actually learn a couple of things about the long history of sightings, research, and theories on the monster. Allow about one hour.

See map p. 345. Drumnadrochit, Loch Ness, off the A82. ☎ **01456-450-573.** www. lochness.com. *Admission: £6.50 adults, £5.50 students, £5 seniors, £4.50 children 6–16, £18 family; free for children under 6. Open: Daily Feb–May 9:30 a.m.–5 p.m.; June and Sept 9 a.m.–6 p.m.; July–Aug 9 a.m.–6:30 p.m.; Oct 9:30 a.m.–5 p.m.; Nov–Easter 10 a.m.–3:30 p.m.*

Nessie Castle Monster Centre
Drumnadrochit

Associated with the Loch Ness Lodge Hotel, this is the "other" Loch Ness exhibition: the older and slightly less expensive one, compared to the flashier competition in town. One focus of the exhibit is on the loch, which has an interesting history, while another is on the monster. A film covers the history of Nessie sightings and explains how many of those sightings are actually of something else, such as sea otters. The exhibition is full of pictures, including other freaks of beast lore. Allow about one hour.

See map p. 345. On the A82. ☎ **01456-450-342.** www.lochness-centre.com. *Admission: £5.50 adults, £4.50 students, £4.35 seniors, £4 children, £15 family. Open: Daily Mar–June and Sept–Oct 9:30 a.m.–5:30 p.m.; July–Aug 9 a.m.–7:30 p.m.; Nov–Feb 10 a.m.–3 p.m.*

Sands of Morar
Near Mallaig

Bonnie Prince Charlie apparently roamed these beautiful bleached beaches 250 years ago while fleeing his pursuers. Set against postcard-pretty seas, looking across at the islands Rhum and Eigg, Morar has been used by filmmakers intent on capturing the quintessential Scottish backdrop. *Highlander* and, to much better effect, *Local Hero* were filmed here. Unfortunately, the sands can get rather crowded — at least by local standards — with sun-seeking locals and tourists in the summer. But that is fine for the kids who can run free and meet new pals. Allow about one hour.

See map p. 345. Just off the A830, about 1.5km (1 mile) south of Morar. Admission: Free. Open: Year-round.

Sandwood Bay and Estate
Near Blairmore

Purchased in the early 1990s by the John Muir Trust, the Sandwood Estate has *the* beach that, by most accounts, is the most beautiful and unsullied on the entire mainland of Great Britain. Yes, getting there and back from the nearest road requires a 14km (9-mile) hike on a peat-and-stone trail. But then why do you think the dunes at Sandwood Bay are so pristine? The entire estate covers many thousands of acres and encompasses crofts and peat bogs as well as dunes and craggy coastline. From here, the ambitious can also hike to Cape Wrath. Allow about three hours.

See map p. 345. Take the B801 from the A838 to Blairmore (about 96km/60 miles north of Ullapool, via the A894). www.jmt.org. *Admission: Free. Open: Year-round.*

Urquhart Castle
Loch Ness

Despite the impressive ruins, this large and significant castle (pronounced *irk*-ett) has no strong clan association. Because its location on Loch Ness was important for trade routes through the Highlands, the castle changed hands many times since the 13th century. One of the last groups to occupy it (before the tourists invaded) was Cromwell's army in the 1650s; later it was blown up to prevent Jacobite occupation. A recent addition to the visitor center is an audiovisual display of views and history that plays before you see the real thing. Allow about two hours.

See map p. 345. Near Drumnadrochit, on the A82. ☎ **01456-450-551.** www.historic-scotland.gov.uk. *Admission: £7 adults, £5.60 seniors and students, £4.20 children. Open: Daily Apr–Sept 9:30 a.m.–6 p.m.; Oct–Mar 9:30 a.m.–4:30 p.m.*

Snow in the Highlands

Alas, it seems climate change has currently made snowfall increasingly rare in the Highlands, and some resorts have tottered on closure. In addition to the Nevis Range Gondola and Skiing (see "Other cool things to see and do"), the Highlands offers other legitimate ski resorts. **Glencoe** has moderately challenging slopes and some great views. The Glencoe Mountain Resort is near Kingshouse, off the A82 (☎ **0871-871-9929;** www.glencoemountain.com). The **Cairngorms** offers unpredictable weather, but when the snow base is good, the whole family can enjoy skiing or snowboarding, as well as other nonski activities. Cairngorm Mountain resort (☎ **01479-861-261;** www.cairngormmountain.com) is located 14km (9 miles) from the town of Aviemore and operates a controversial funicular railway to get you up the mountain.

Other cool things to see and do

✔ **Brodie Castle,** off the A96, about 11km (7 miles) east of Nairn (☎ **01309-641-371;** www.nts.org.uk), may look a bit austere, but this 16th-century tower house is a particularly good stop for art fans; the collection of paintings includes 17th-century Dutch works, as well as the Scottish Colourists.

✔ **Dornoch Cathedral,** on the main square of Dornoch, 13km (8 miles) south of Tain (☎ **01862-810-296**), dates from 1224 and was the site of one of the last witch burnings in the 18th century. But another reason you might wish to visit is because this is where Madonna married Guy Ritchie.

✔ **Eden Court Theatre,** Bishop's Road, Inverness (☎ **01463-234-234;** www.eden-court.co.uk), is much more than a place to see a play: It is a full-blown contemporary arts center with a range of drama, ballet, concerts, and art-house cinema. Redesigned and reopened in November 2007, it is the best thing in this vein for hundreds of miles.

✔ **Glenmore Forest Park,** off the B972 about 10km (6 miles) east of Aviemore (☎ **01479-861-220;** www.forestry.gov.uk), isn't simply a place of fine scenery. The attractions include Loch Morlich and its sandy beach as well as a grove of ancient Caledonian Pinewood, one of the few remaining in Scotland.

✔ **Highland Folk Museum,** Duke Street, on the A86, Kingussie (☎ **01540-673-551;** www.highlandfolk.com), describes 400 years of Highland life with collections of everyday objects, furniture, machines, and more. In addition to this site, with its re-created historic Blackhouse, in Newtonmore, the Folk Museum offers a reconstructed 18th-century township and 1940s working farm.

✔ **Inverness Museum and Art Gallery,** Castle Wynd, off Bridge Street, Inverness (☎ **01463-237-114;** www.invernessmuseum.com), reopened, with much improvement after renovations, in 2007. The permanent collection includes the story of the Highlands' geology, prehistory, traditional music, culture, and various inhabitants. There is space for contemporary art exhibitions and a section devoted to local wildlife, too.

✔ **John Cobb Cairn,** between Drumnadrochit and Invermoriston, is a place of pilgrimage for many wanting to honor Cobb, who lost his life on Loch Ness in 1952, while making a second attempt at the world water-speed record.

✔ **Nevis Range Mountain Experience,** 10km (6 miles) north of Fort William (☎ **01397-705-825;** www.nevisrange.co.uk), has a gondola that takes you up Aonach Mor Mountain, offering panoramic views. In summer, you can hike paths around the area. In winter, you can ski or snowboard if snow conditions are good.

Shopping in the Highlands

The major shopping center in the Highlands is the **Eastgate Shopping Centre,** 11 Eastgate, off High Street, in Inverness (www.eastgate-centre.co.uk). This American-style mall doesn't cater specifically to tourists, but it has major department stores. Eastgate is open from 9 a.m. until 5:30 p.m. most days, closing at 7 p.m. on Thursday and 5 p.m. on Sunday. **Balnakeil Craft Village** (see "The top attractions," earlier in this chapter) is a good place to find unique gifts, while Ullapool (see the sidebar "Ullapool: Happenings at the harbor") has some interesting small craft shops. Also consider

- ✔ **Edinburgh Woollen Mill,** 13 High St., Fort William (☎ **01397-703-064**), and 60 High St., at Monzie Square, Fort William (☎ **01397-704-737**), offering plenty of variety in finely crafted woolen and tweed apparel at its sister stores. The best part is their excellent bargains. Call for hours.

- ✔ **Highland Stoneware Pottery,** Mill Street, Ullapool (☎ **01854-612-980;** www.highlandstoneware.com), and Lochinver, north of Ullapool on the coast road (☎ **01571-844-376**), which has, since its inception in 1974, gained an international following. Visitors come to these two shops for the unique freehand-decorated pottery. Open Monday through Friday from 9 a.m. to 6 p.m. and Saturday in season only (Easter–Oct) from 9 a.m. to 5 p.m. They're closed two weeks around Christmas and New Year's.

- ✔ **Moniack Castle Wines,** Beauly Road, on the A862, 11km (7 miles) from Inverness (☎ **01463-831-283;** www.moniackcastle.co.uk), a popular winery and gourmet-food shop. They make six wines and three liqueurs from natural ingredients such as birch bark. You can also purchase top-quality marmalades, sauces, jams, and chutneys, all made here, like the wine, from local ingredients. Open Monday through Saturday from 10 a.m. to 5 p.m. in summer, and Monday through Saturday from 11 a.m. to 4 p.m. in winter.

- ✔ **Riverside Gallery,** 11 Bank St., Inverness (☎ **01463-224-781;** www.riverside-gallery.co.uk), a two-floor gallery near the banks of the River Ness with a wide range of traditional and contemporary pieces by Scottish artists. Open Monday through Friday from 9 a.m. to 5 p.m. and Saturday from 9 a.m. to 4 p.m.

- ✔ **Tea by the Sea (Dal-na-Mara),** 17 Shore St., Ullapool (no phone), a wonderfully petite boutique and tea shop, has a range of imported goods, whether wool caps, silk scarves, Panama hats, and other crafts/gifts. Open Monday to Saturday 11 a.m. to 5 p.m.

Doing the Pub Crawl

The Highlands have a good number of atmospheric, quintessentially Scottish pubs where you can relax and enjoy a bit of pub grub. Some of my favorites at country inns include the Arisaig, Plockton, and Scourie hotels. Listed below are a couple of additional pubs to consider.

✔ **Claichaig Inn,** Glencoe, follow the sign from the A82 or walk across the footbridge from the visitor center (☎ **01855-811-252**), has a pub with a rustic wood-burning stove that warms the lounge and bar. Climbers, tourists, and locals come here for a wee rest stop and excellent ales on tap. Open Sunday through Thursday from 11 a.m. to 11 p.m., Friday from 11 a.m. to midnight, and Saturday from 11 a.m. to 11:30 p.m.

✔ **Hootananny,** 61 Church St., Inverness (☎ **01463-233-651;** www. hootananny.co.uk), is a solid pub in the center of town with Scottish real ales from the excellent Black Isle brewery, live traditional and folk music at weekends, and some pretty popular Thai food, too. Open noon to midnight (to 1 a.m. Fri–Sat).

Fast Facts: The Highlands

Area Code

The area code for Aviemore is **01479;** Dornoch is **01862;** Drumnadrochit is **01456;** Fort William is **01397;** Glencoe is **01855;** Inverness is **01463;** Nairn is **01667;** and Ullapool is **01854.** You need to dial the area code only if you're calling from outside the city you want to reach.

ATMs

ATMs are definitely rare in the Highlands, with the exception of Inverness and Fort William, where the most convenient ATMs may be at the Safeway (Morrisons) supermarkets.

Emergencies

Dial ☎ **999** for police, fire, or ambulance.

Hospitals

The main hospital in the area is Raigmore Hospital, Inshes Road, Inverness (☎ 01463-704-000).

Information

For general information on the region, contact the Highlands Information Centre, Grampian Road, Aviemore (☎ 01479-810-363; www.visitaviemore.co.uk). Other tourist offices include: Castle Wynd, just off Bridge Street, Inverness (☎ 01463-234-353); and Cameron Square, about halfway down the High Street, Fort William (☎ 01397-703-781). Summer offices are located at 62 King St., Nairn (☎ 01667-452-763), and 6 Argyle St., Ullapool (☎ 01854-612-135).

Internet Access

The best place to jump on the Web is the Electric Post Office, 93 High St., Nairn (☎ 01667-451-617). It's open daily from 10 a.m. to 10 p.m., and the cost is £4 per hour.

Mail

A central post office is located at 2 Greig St., Inverness (☎ 01463-233-610).

Chapter 19

Hebridean Islands

. . . .

In This Chapter

▶ Using ferries to hop from island to island

▶ Finding the best sandy beaches and most picturesque ports

▶ Discovering historic standing stones, churches, and castles

▶ Getting to some of the smaller isles for just a day

. . . .

*T*he allure of Scotland's **Hebridean Islands** isn't difficult to under-stand: The history and culture of the Hebrides (heb-ri-*dees*) — com-bined with the beauty of the seascape — are captivating. Getting to the islands is half the fun, and when you arrive, you can be almost guaran-teed to have a peaceful retreat from the mainland, particularly at places such as Barra, Harris, Iona, or Eigg. If I had to pick my favorite region of Scotland — a hard choice, indeed — it would probably be the Hebrides.

Here are a few things you should know before you set out for these islands.

Similar to other remote regions of Scotland, on the islands, some busi-nesses — including hotels and attractions — close in winter. I have done my best to indicate when things are open, but if you're traveling between mid-October and mid-April, please check in advance.

Also, due to rather devout **Protestant** beliefs, some towns and villages become virtual ghost towns on Sunday, particularly in the northern parts of the Outer Hebrides. The **Western Islands,** home to the majority of Gaelic-speaking people in Scotland, may have road signs posted only in Gaelic. Finally, the Hebridean Islands get some of the most dramatic weather in Scotland — in summer, sunshine can be followed by rain fall-ing horizontally.

But none of this is reason not to include at least a stay on one of the many islands that you can visit, whether **Skye** and **Mull,** which hug the mainland coastline, or **Harris** or **Lewis,** which are more far-flung. There are no cities, per se, on any of the Herbridean Islands. The larger port towns are **Portree** on Skye, **Tobermory** on Mull, and biggest of all on the Isle of Lewis: **Stornoway** (not to be confused with Stromness on Orkney). The latter is the administrative center of the Outer Hebrides and the so-called capital of the Western Isles. All these towns all have banks, shops, grocery stores, and other helpful amenities.

Although the Inner and Outer Hebrides are made up of several islands, many of which are largely uninhabited, this chapter concentrates on the more notable ones. Also, remember that the southernmost Inner Hebridean island of Islay is included in Chapter 15, "Ayrshire and Argyll."

As long as you enjoy sailing on ferries, island hopping through the Hebrides can be a real blast, even if the trips are time consuming. Alternatively, you can fly to Lewis and Barra, or take one-day excursions from the mainland to isles close to the coast for a taste of island life.

Getting to the Islands

One of the best things about any visit to the Hebrides is the ferry ride. Indeed, unless you charter a boat yourself or fly in, there is no other way (with the exception of Skye, to which there is a bridge) to get to the islands. A network of boats links the Outer and Inner Hebrides to the mainland and, in some cases, to one another.

You probably will need a car to fully explore the islands, but you can get around without one, by bus or bike.

✔ **By ferry:** The principal provider of ferry services is **Caledonian MacBrayne,** or CalMac (☎ **08705-650-000** or 01475-650-100; www. calmac.co.uk). Travel times vary. The ferry from Mallaig to Armadale, Skye, takes only about 30 minutes. From Oban to Craignure on Mull means about 45 minutes on the ferry. The trip from Ullapool to Stornoway, Lewis, clocks in at slightly more than two and a half hours. The larger ferries all have cafes and bars with lounges.

In late 2008, the prices of ferry trips from the mainland were reduced significantly thanks to the Scottish Government and a trial scheme called the Road Equivalent Tariff (RET). This was a trial but it appears that an extension of RET until 2012 has been approved.

For additional savings on a trip through the Hebrides, you can take advantage of CalMac's "Island Hopscotch" tickets. For example, you may jump between Skye, Uist, Harris, and Lewis, using the mainland ports of Mallaig and Ullapool. Tickets for that hopscotch can be as low as £20 per passenger and around £75 for a car.

CalMac offices in the region include Armadale, Skye (☎ **01471-844-248**); Craignure, Mull (☎ **01680-812-343**); and Stornoway, Lewis (☎ **01851-702-361**). You can find contact information for other local offices on the Web site.

You are not allowed to take a vehicle onto some of the smaller islands, such as Iona or Eigg, for example. Also be warned that winter timetables offer fewer crossings that the summer service, which runs from about the end of March to the end of October (that is, when the clocks are set for British summertime).

✔ **By train: First ScotRail** (☎ **0845-748-4950;** www.firstscotrail. com) runs trains to the Kyle of Lochalsh (terminating near the Skye Bridge), Mallaig, and Oban. From the latter two, you can get connecting ferries to the islands. Regular passenger trains don't run on the islands. On Mull, however, a narrow gauge train runs the short trip from Craignure to Torosay Castle (☎ **01680-812-494;** www. mullrail.co.uk).

✔ **By bus:** From Glasgow, **Scottish Citylink** (☎ **0141-332-9644** or 0870-550-5050; www.citylink.co.uk) runs buses to ferry ports such as Oban and Ullapool. After you reach the islands, buses are controlled by local authorities and by private companies. The service is not as good as it perhaps should be, but pick up a local timetable and you get by just fine by leaving the driving to someone else.

✔ **By car:** You can drive onto Skye over the bridge at the Kyle of Lochalsh, on the A87, which is also the main road on the Isle of Skye. On Mull, the main road is the A849, which links Tobermory to Fionnophort via the ferry port at Craignure. Otherwise, it is mostly one-lane (single-track) roads, many of which are twisting and turning. Take your time and exercise caution, especially as the locals will know the roads like their palms and will travel at speeds that you should not consider imitating. The smallest of the islands don't allow tourists in cars at all, making them all the more tranquil.

✔ **By plane:** The main airport is on Lewis (☎ **01851-702-256;** www. hial.co.uk), about 6.4km (4 miles) east of Stornoway. You can arrange to fly there from Inverness, Edinburgh, or Glasgow. A nonstop flight from Glasgow is less than one hour long. There are some interisland flight services connecting Barra, Benbecula (part of North Uist), and Stornoway — but it's not necessary to fly. Taking a ferry is part of the enjoyment of travel on the Hebrides.

Spending the Night

Because the islands have limited dining and drinking options, the accommodations listed in this section are also places to grab some food and drink. The larger islands offer more accommodations options; you should contact local tourist offices if you want to spend the night on a smaller island. Breakfast is included except where otherwise noted. See Chapter 8 for an explanation of the star ratings given by VisitScotland. com and for suggestions on renting self-catering cottages, which is a possible option on any island tour.

Remember that hotels, large and small, may open seasonally on the Hebrides, so always phone in advance if you're traveling between October and Easter. Better to confirm a booking rather than show up unannounced.

Rates include breakfast, unless otherwise stated, and better prices may be obtained with internet or advance reservations. Finally, have a look

Hebridean Islands

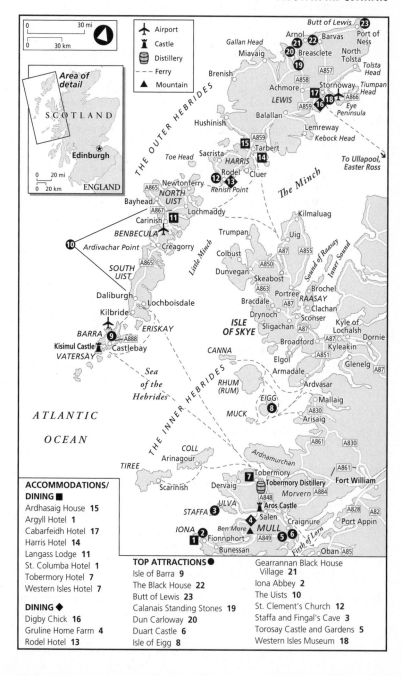

Legend:
- ✈ Airport
- 🏰 Castle
- Distillery
- - - - Ferry
- ▲ Mountain

0 — 30 mi
0 — 30 km

Area of detail

SCOTLAND

Edinburgh

0 — 20 mi
0 — 20 km

ENGLAND

THE OUTER HEBRIDES

Butt of Lewis **23**
Port of Ness
Gallan Head
Arnol **21** **22** Barvas
Miavaig **20** Breasclete North Tolsta
19 A857 Tolsta Head
Brenish A858
Achmore Stornoway Tiumpan Head
A859 **17** **18** A866
LEWIS **16** Eye Peninsula
Balallan
Hushinish Lemreway
Kebock Head
15 A859 Tarbert
Toe Head Sacrista **14**
HARRIS
Rodel Cluer
12 **13** Renish Point
Newtonferry
A865 NORTH UIST
Bayhead A867 Lochmaddy
Carinish **11**
BENBECULA
Trumpan
10 Ardivachar Point Creagorry
SOUTH UIST A865
Daliburgh Colbust
Kilbride Lochboisdale
BARRA A888
Kisimul Castle **9** Castlebay
VATERSAY

The Minch
To Ullapool, Easter Ross

Kilmaluag
Uig
A87 A855
Dunvegan
Skeabost A850
A863 Portree Brochel
Bracdale A87 RAASAY
Drynoch Sconser Clachan
ISLE Sligachan A87 Kyle of Lochalsh
OF SKYE Broadford A87 Dornie
CANNA Kyleakin
Elgol A851 Glenelg
Armadale A87
RHUM (RUM) Ardvasar
EIGG **8** Mallaig
MUCK A830 Arisaig

Sea of the Hebrides

ATLANTIC OCEAN

THE INNER HEBRIDES
A861 A830

COLL
TIREE Arinagour
Scarinish Dervaig Ardnamurchan A861
7 Tobermory Fort William
ULVA Tobermory Distillery
STAFFA **3** Aros Castle Morvern A884
IONA **2** Salen A828 A82
1 Ben More ▲ Craignure Port Appin
Fionnphort **4** MULL **5** **6**
Bunessan A849 Firth of Lorn
Oban A85

ACCOMMODATIONS/ DINING ■

Ardhasaig House **15**
Argyll Hotel **1**
Cabarfeidh Hotel **17**
Harris Hotel **14**
Langass Lodge **11**
St. Columba Hotel **1**
Tobermory Hotel **7**
Western Isles Hotel **7**

DINING ◆

Digby Chick **16**
Gruline Home Farm **4**
Rodel Hotel **13**

TOP ATTRACTIONS ●

Isle of Barra **9**
The Black House **22**
Butt of Lewis **23**
Calanais Standing Stones **19**
Dun Carloway **20**
Duart Castle **6**
Isle of Eigg **8**

Gearrannan Black House Village **21**
Iona Abbey **2**
The Uists **10**
St. Clement's Church **12**
Staffa and Fingal's Cave **3**
Torosay Castle and Gardens **5**
Western Isles Museum **18**

at "Dining Locally," where I have also highlighted those restaurants that have overnight rooms.

Ardhasaig House
$$–$$$ Ardhasaig near Tarbert, Harris

One reward of this small four-star hotel is the view of the nearby bay and mountains. The building dates from 1904, but the bar lounge is modern. Dining at Ardhasaig is often a treat; the menu changes pretty much daily, emphasizing what is fresh and locally available, such as pan-fried Harris scallops or fillet of venison. The five overnight rooms are comfortably if basically furnished (no TVs), and some include antique furniture, while all have views either of the hills or of the sea. In 2004, the old stone barn was converted into a self-contained suite with a king-size sleigh bed and sheepskin rugs.

See map p. 369. Off the A859, 5km (3 miles) northwest of Tarbert, Harris. ☎ **01859-502-066.** *Fax: 01859-502-077.* www.ardhasaig.co.uk. *Rack rates: From £110 double. MC, V.*

Ardvasar Hotel
$$–$$$ Ardvasar, Skye (near Armadale)

This lovely hotel (one of the oldest on Skye) is a good bet for a stay in the southern part of the island. Near the Armadale ferry terminal (sailings to/from Mallaig), the lodge, pub, and restaurant sit on the edge of the Sound of Sleat. Ten comfortable bedrooms (three are spacious "superior" class) have lovely views of the water or the rugged landscape of the island's interior. All have been individually decorated by a Highland interiors design specialist. The food is about as good as it gets in the area, and the pub bustles with grinning locals: It has been described as the hub of the local community.

See map p. 371. Off the A851, Skye. ☎ **01471-844-223.** *Fax: 01471-844-495.* www.ardvasarhotel.com. *Rack rates: £126–£136 double. MC, V.*

Argyll Hotel
$$ Iona

This environmentally aware hotel, dedicated to minimizing its impact on the fragile island ecology, was originally built in 1868. The outstanding and obliging hospitality more than compensates for some smallish overnight rooms. But why hang out in your bedroom when you can spend time exploring Iona or relaxing in the Argyll's lounges, which face the water? Dinner is recommended — not least because the ingredients in your meal are actually grown in the hotel's own organic garden. Bargain hunters can opt for a small double room with no en-suite bathroom. For environmentally conscious tourists, the Argyll is a must, but even those who are not will enjoy it.

The Isle of Skye

ACCOMMODATIONS ■	DINING ◆	TOP ATTRACTIONS ●
Ardvasar Hotel **12**	The Chandley	Armadale Castle Gardens
Cuillin Hills Hotel **4**	Restaurant **5**	& Museum of the Isles **13**
Dunollie Hotel **8**	Creelers of Skye **9**	Cuillin Hills **6**
Hotel Eilean Iarmain **11**	Kinloch Lodge **10**	Dunvegan Castle **2**
The Rosedale **4**	Three Chimneys	Skye Museum of Island Life
The Royal Hotel **4**	Restaurant **1**	and Flora MacDonald's Grave **3**
Sligachan Hotel **7**		

See map p. 369. Near the pier. ☎ **01681-700-334.** *Fax: 01681-700-510.* www.argyll hoteliona.co.uk. *Rack rates: £45–£131 double with continental breakfast. MC, V. Closed Dec to mid-Mar.*

Cabarfeidh Hotel
$$–$$$ Stornoway, Lewis

On Lewis, this modern hotel (built in the 1970s) is located on the edge of the Isle of Lewis's main town, Stornoway. Despite its recent vintage, there have been several refurbs to the Cabarfeidh, the latest in spring 2007. The rooms are large and well upholstered, and the service usually comes up trumps, too. The hotel's **Solas Restaurant** specializes in local seafood.

See map p. 369. Manor Park, Perceval Road South, north of the town center, Lewis. ☎ **01851-702-604.** *Fax: 01851-705-572.* www.cabarfeidh-hotel.co.uk. *Rack rates: £165 double. AE, DC, MC, V.*

Cuillin Hills Hotel
$$$–$$$$ Portree, Skye

Just outside Portree, this 19th-century hunting lodge features excellent views of the bay below and Cuillin crags in the distance. The four-star hotel has about two dozen rooms and is equally popular with hikers, birders, and sportsmen. The conservatory is the place to relax, while the rooms are full of quality furniture and generally have large bathrooms. The hotel's restaurant earns praise for its seafood and Highland game dishes.

See map p. 371. Off the A855, just north of town, Skye. ☎ **01478-612-003.** *Fax: 01478-613-092.* www.cuillinhills-hotel-skye.co.uk. *Rack rates: £210 double. AE, MC, V.*

Dunollie Hotel
$$ Broadford, Skye

The Dunollie sits on the old harbor wall in Broadford, with views across the Inner Sound of Raasay toward the Applecross hills of mainland Scotland. The 84-unit hotel is not the best example of modern architecture, but all rooms have en-suite bathrooms and TVs. It serves as a good vacation base from which to explore the Isle of Skye. It's popular with organized bus tours, too, which may affect your decision.

See map p. 371. On the A87 (about 8km/5 miles east of the Skye Bridge), Skye. ☎ **01471-822-253.** *Fax: 01471-822-060.* www.oxfordhotelsandinns.com. *Rack rates: £115 double. MC, V.*

Harris Hotel
$$ Tarbert, Harris

This 24-room hotel is just up the hill from the ferry terminal in the quaint harbor town of Tarbert. The pretty, whitewashed building, built in 1865, has modern décor, a comfortable selection of accommodations (including a pair of family rooms), a large garden, and a spacious resident's lounge. One guest, *Peter Pan* author J. M. Barrie, mischievously etched his initials in a dining room window.

See map p. 369. Near the Tarbert ferry terminal, Harris. ☎ **01859-502-154.** *Fax: 01859-502-281.* www.harrishotel.com. *Rack rates: £80–£98 double. MC, V.*

Hotel Eilean larmain
$$$–$$$$ Isleornsay, Skye

The Eilean Iarmain combines island hospitality with tranquillity and beautiful surroundings. Many of the century-old building's original antiques remain in place, and the 12 rooms in the main building contain period furniture. The views of the Sound of Sleat and the mainland beyond from the lodge are picture-postcard perfect. Four suites have been added to the converted 19th-century stable blocks.

See map p. 371. Off the A8561, Skye. ☎ **01471-833-332.** *Fax: 01471-833-275.* www. eileaniarmain.co.uk. *Rack rates: £100–£250 double. AE, MC, V.*

Langass Lodge
$$–$$$ Locheport, North Uist

Up a glen off the main road traversing the Isle of North Uist, the Langass is a traditional hunting lodge with a few modern additions such as the bright lounge off the bar, new dining room, and a wing of contemporary overnight units: the "Hillside Rooms," which are larger than those in the main building. There is a small garden and walking trails to the nearby loch and a prehistoric stone burial mound. The owner also specializes in fishing or hunting excursions. Meals can be quite tasty, with dishes favoring local ingredients, such as clams or venison.

See map p. 369. Off the A867, North Uist. ☎ **01876-580-285.** *Fax: 01876-580-385.* www. langasslodge.co.uk. *Rack rates: £90–£99 double. MC, V.*

The Rosedale
$$–$$$ Portree, Skye

This set of former fishermen's houses near the water's edge in Skye's largest harbor is warmly decorated, giving the place a snug B&B feel. An eccentric layout of stairs and corridors connects lounges to the bar and restaurant. The main building has cozy rooms that are simply decorated, while those in another wing are more individually decorated. Most of the units in either wing, however, overlook the harbor. Dinners normally reflect seasonal produce, and a cooked breakfast can be ordered for an extra charge.

See map p. 371. On the harbor, Beaumont Crescent, Quay Brae, Portree, Skye. ☎ **01478-613-131.** *Fax: 01478-612-531.* www.rosedalehotelskye.co.uk. *Rack rates: £70–£140 double. Rates include continental breakfast. AE, MC, V.*

The Royal Hotel
$$ Portree, Skye

If only I had a £5 note for every hotel named "The Royal" in Scotland. This one occupies an enviable spot just up the road from the Portree pier. The 25 overnight rooms — recently upgraded — are comfortable. Many overlook the harbor, some have been specifically designed for families, and room service is provided. Another treat in this part of the world is the adjacent gym and sauna that's available to guests.

See map p. 371. Bank Street, Skye. ☎ **01478-612-525.** *Fax: 01478-613-198.* www. royal-hotel-skye.com. *Rack rates: From £99 double. MC, V.*

St. Columba Hotel
$$–$$$ **Iona**

Although it doesn't have the character of the Argyll (see above), St. Columba's setting near Iona Abbey (p. 382) never leaves you at a loss for pretty views of the sea. A converted and expanded church manse dating from 1846, the community-owned hotel has some large and well-furnished rooms, including four for families (and, unusually, nine singles). Like the Argyll, it too has an organic vegetable and herb garden. Let them know when your ferry gets in and someone can come down and pick up your luggage.

See map p. 369. .5km (¼ mile) north of the pier, Iona. ☎ **01681-700-304.** *Fax: 01681-700-688.* www.stcolumba-hotel.co.uk. *Rack rates: £90–£130 double. Rates include dinner. MC, V.*

Sligachan Hotel
$$ **Sligachan, Skye**

This 21-room hotel was built in the 1830s and retains much of its original stonework, a classic look that complements the impressive location near the feet of the Cuillin Hills. Located in the middle of Skye, the Sligachan is convenient for visiting most parts of the island. Its **Seumas' Bar** is a fine place to enjoy Skye or Eagle ales, made at the microbrewery here.

See map p. 371. Off the A87 (14km/9 miles south of Portree), Skye. ☎ **01478-650-204.** *Fax: 01478-650-207.* www.sligachan.co.uk. *Rack rates: £90–£108 double. MC, V.*

Tobermory Hotel
$$–$$$ **Tobermory, Mull**

All the buildings at the harbor in Tobermory are brightly painted in pastel colors, and the soft pink Tobermory Hotel is no exception. These converted fishermen's cottages on the waterfront contain 15 overnight rooms (all en suite) and one double room with a separate bathroom. The hotel's "superior" double rooms overlook Tobermory Bay and feature king-size beds. Its **Water's Edge** restaurant is gaining a reputation for highlighting excellent local produce, whether Isle of Mull cheese made just outside town (see "Shopping," later in this chapter), Glengorm lamb, or shellfish landed at the pier.

See map p. 369. 53 Main St., Mull. ☎ **01688-302-091.** *Fax: 01688-302-254.* www.the tobermoryhotel.com. *Rack rates: £75–£120 double. MC, V.*

Western Isles Hotel
$$–$$$ Tobermory, Mull

Fans of the great movie *I Know Where I'm Going!* (see "Recommended movies," in Chapter 2) should recognize this hotel on the hill above Tobermory. A Victorian stone-front building overlooking the bay, it offers old-world charm — and after a few years of mixed reviews from guests, new owners appear to have given the place the upgrading that it needed (and held room rates down, too). The hotel occupies a desirable spot, and several rooms have vistas of the harbor below, though the best views are from the conservatory or summer veranda.

See map p. 369. Off Western Road, above Tobermory Harbour. ☎ **01688-302-012.** *Fax: 01688-302-297.* www.westernisleshotel.co.uk. *Rack rates: £83–£125 double. MC, V.*

Dining Locally

Few restaurants on the Hebridean Islands can thrive independently of a hotel (there often are not enough locals to keep them in business), so most of your dining options are likely to come from the previous section, such as at the Argyll Hotel on Iona or the Water's Edge in the Tobermory Hotel. However, a few other restaurants stand out — and I have also noted where they have overnight accommodations, too.

Although it isn't listed below, you might try the fish-and-chips van at Tobermory Harbour — it produces possibly the best "fish suppers" in all of Scotland.

The Chandlery Restaurant
$$$ Portree, Skye   FISH/MODERN SCOTTISH/FRENCH

One-time Scottish restaurant of the year, the Chandlery (in the Bosville Hotel) specializes in seafood and game dishes. It has been described as reason enough to make the journey to Skye. Occupying a lovely spot overlooking Portree Harbour, the place has an airy feel. Service is efficient and professional, serving up treats from Chef John Kelly such as hand-dived scallops from Loch Silgachan or fresh langoustines landed at the harbor. Signature dishes include a smoked ham hock and Mallaig monkfish terrine or seared loin of Highland lamb.

See map p. 371. Bosville Terrace, Skye. ☎ **01478-612-846.** www.bosville hotel.co.uk. *Reservations required. Fixed-price dinner: £40. AE, MC, V. Open: Daily 6:30–9:30 p.m.*

Creelers of Skye
$$ Broadford, Skye   SEAFOOD/MEDITERRANEAN

This simply decorated bistro on the edge of the village of Broadford, not far from the Skye Bridge, isn't interested in snobbery. However informal the restaurant may appear, its food can be outstanding. In addition to the house specialty, Cajun seafood gumbo, there are Mediterranean-influenced meals and more familiar Scottish dishes such as prawn cock-tail, fried haddock, pan-roasted sea bass, or wild venison.

See map p. 371. Off the A87 (next to the Skye Serpentarium), Skye. ☎ **01471-822-281.** *www.skye-seafood-restaurant.co.uk. Reservations recommended. Main courses: £12–£17. MC, V. Open: Early Mar to Oct daily 1–9:30 p.m.*

Digby Chick
$$–$$$ Stornoway, Lewis   MODERN SCOTTISH

A slightly surprising name, but this modern restaurant in the heart of Stornoway, the capital of the Outer Hebrides, offers tasty meals with some interesting flavor combinations. Dishes almost always highlight fresh local ingredients whether famous Stornoway black pudding or seafood and fish, such as halibut and haddock, landed only steps away from the dining room. The lunch and early dining menus offer good value.

See map p. 369. 5 Bank St., Stornoway, Lewis. ☎ **01851-700-026.** *www.digby chick.co.uk. Reservations suggested. Main courses: £18–£24. MC, V. Open: Mon–Sat noon to 2 p.m. and 5:30–9 p.m.*

Gruline Home Farm
$$–$$$ Gruline, Mull   SCOTTISH

Dinners at this small five-star B&B in the middle of Mull have an excellent reputation. They're generally only served by prior arrangement if you're not staying here, so don't consider dropping in for a bite as I once fool-ishly did. Dishes, such as pan-fried scallop of venison or prawn tails in garlic cream sauce, are made from mostly local produce. If you want wine, you must bring your own. No children younger than 16, either.

See map p. 369. Off the BB8035 (5km/3 miles southwest of Salen), Mull. ☎ **01680-300-581.** *www.gruline.com. Reservations required. Fixed-price dinner: £38. MC, V. Open: Call ahead for times during your visit.*

Kinloch Lodge
$$$ Sleat, Syke   SCOTTISH

Kinloch is the home of the Macdonalds, and the matriarch of the house, Lady Claire Macdonald, has become famous in the Scottish culinary cir-cles. Expect dishes such as halibut with spinach gnocchi or Scotch beef fillet steak with port peppercorn sauce. The lodge regularly hosts special cooking weekends when guests see demonstrations, do some cooking, and, of course, eat themselves silly. In addition to the restaurant, Kinloch has **overnight rooms** in the 17th-century hunting lodge.

See map p. 371. By the A851 (5km/3 miles north of Isleornsay), Skye. ☎ **01471-833-333.** *www.kinloch-lodge.co.uk. Reservations required. Fixed-price four-course lunch: £28. Fixed-price four-course dinner: £55. AE, MC, V. Open: Daily noon to 2:30 p.m. and 6:30–9 p.m.*

Rodel Hotel
$$–$$$ Rodel, Harris   MODERN BRITISH

The dining room at the small Rodel Hotel combines some excellent local produce (whether Hebridean lamb or shellfish) with a contemporary touch, which extends to the art on the walls. Near St. Clement's Church (see "The top attractions," later in this chapter) at the southern end of the Isle of Harris, the restaurant features dishes such as a salad of local prawns and crabmeat, Lewis mussels steamed in white wine, pave of Minch cod, or pan-fried sirloin steak with red-wine jus. The Rodel has basic **overnight rooms.**

See map p. 369. Harris (southern tip of the island). ☎ **01859-520-210.** *www.rodel hotel.co.uk. Reservations suggested. Main courses: £14–£17. MC, V. Open: Daily noon to 2:30 p.m. and 6–8:30 p.m.*

Three Chimneys Restaurant
$$$–$$$$ Colbost, Skye   SCOTTISH

This whitewashed shore-side restaurant (with luxury overnight rooms) is arguably the most popular on Skye — and probably the most famous in the Hebrides. Using superb Scottish produce, owners Eddie and Shirley Spear offer top-quality seafood and Highland game dishes from menus that change seasonally. Dishes might include brochette of scallops and monkfish wrapped in Ayrshire bacon or whole roast Skye lobster with lemon-thyme butter.

See map p. 371. On the B884 (about 8km/5 miles west of Dunvegan Castle), Skye. ☎ **01470-511-258.** *www.threechimneys.co.uk. Reservations required. Fixed-price three-course lunch: £35. Dinner: £55 for three courses. MC, V. Open: Daily 6:15–9:45 p.m. (also lunch Apr–Oct Mon–Sat 12:15 p.m.)*

Exploring the Hebrides

From the spiritual mecca of Iona to the sandy beaches of Harris, not to mention the many ancient and royal attractions in between, the Hebridean Islands offer a lot, with no shortage of natural beauty. Indeed, the islands are main attraction in themselves, but you will find plenty to see in addition to the scenery.

The biggest island of the **Inner Hebrides,** those islands that hug the coastline, is the **Isle of Skye.** Thanks to a controversial bridge (well, the toll was controversial at least), visitors can drive onto it at Kyle of Lochalsh. Your other option is to take a ferry from the mainland harbor of Mallaig. Eighty-one kilometers (50 miles) long and 37km (23 miles) wide, Skye offers memorable landscapes, historic attractions, and a good deal of accommodations and dining options. Portree is the main town on Skye.

Closer to central Scotland, and thus perhaps more accessible, is the Isle of **Mull,** home to the picturesque port of Tobermory, a few castles, plenty of scenery, and the added value of little sister island Iona. Mull has a reputation for being the rainiest of the Hebridean Islands, but on my visits, I have not found it noticeably wetter. After you arrive in Craignure (which has little to offer other than the nearby castles of Duart and Torosay), you can head north to Tobermory or west toward Fionnphort to catch a ferry to the Isle of Iona. Give yourself an hour no matter which way you decide to go — the highway turns into a single-lane road in either direction. Tobermory, the largest town on Mull, is worth a visit. Brightly painted houses and storefronts in pastel shades of blue, red, and yellow give Tobermory the look of a little Copenhagen and the feel of an Italian fishing village.

To see Mull and Iona in a single (if long) day, **Bowman's Tours** (ferry and coach) run from Oban from April through October. Fares are around £30. Call ☎ **01631-566-809,** or log on to www.bowmanstours.co.uk for more information. From Ullapool, the **MV *Summer Queen*** offers two- to four-hour cruises around some of the Summer Isles just off the north-west coastline (☎ **01851-612-472;** www.summerqueen.co.uk).

Beyond Skye are the **Outer Hebrides** or Western Isles. The combined island of **Lewis** and **Harris** (famous for its tweed) forms the largest island of the group — indeed the third largest isle in these seas after Great Britain and Ireland. You'll likely arrive either at the ferry terminals in Tarbert (a common name in western Scotland that essentially means isthmus) or farther north in Stornoway, the administrative capital of the Western Isles. The southern coastal drive on Harris is an attraction in itself — a rocky and barren landscape transforms into a Gulf Stream miracle of bleached beaches and blue waters.

Some of the other islands — Barra, Coll, Eigg, Rhum (Inner Hebrides) and North and South Uist or Barra (Outer Hebrides) — are smaller and sparsely populated, though a few can provide visitors with easy day-trip opportunities for a wee taste of island life.

The top attractions

Armadale Castle Gardens & Museum of the Isles
Armadale, Skye

The Armadale estate, on the sound of Sleat in southern Skye, covers more than 8,000 hectares (20,000 acres). It traditionally belonged to the clan Donald or Macdonald, known as the Lords of Isles, but now held in trust. The old castle is in ruins but it still occupies a magnificent spot with 19th-century woodland gardens, nature trails, and sea views. It isn't difficult to understand the allure of this place. The museum, opened in 2002, is full of information about the historically significant clan, at one time as powerful as Scottish royalty. The castle grounds are home to a large variety of different trees and plants, all flourishing thanks to the Gulf Stream's warming effects. Allow about two hours.

See map p. 371. Off the A851, just north of the ferry terminal, Skye. ☎ **01471-844-305.** `www.clandonald.com.` *Admission: Summer £6 adults, £4.40 seniors, students, and children, £20 family; winter £3.50. Open: Apr–Oct daily 9:30 a.m.–5:30 p.m.; Nov–Mar Fri 11 a.m.–3 p.m. Closed Nov–Mar, except gift shop 11 a.m.–3 p.m.*

Barra
Outer Hebrides

Fancy a flight that alights on a beach? That's one way to get to this compact but beautifully formed isle at the southern end of the Outer Hebridean archipelago. Castlebay is the main village and port, a location not much changed since providing the backdrop for the classic Ealing film comedy, *Whisky Galore* (p. 33). Barra, despite its compact dimensions, actually contains all the elements of the Western Isles topography: gorgeous shell sand beaches, rocky hills descending into deep sea bays, grassy dunes, and heather filled moorland. Lovely wee place, all in all.

See map p. 369.

The Black House
Arnol, Lewis

A Historic Scotland property, this attraction steps back 100 years or so to depict traditional island living. Built in 1885 and occupied (remarkably) until 1964, this "black house" is a traditional Hebridean stone, turf, and thatched-roof structure, which served as both home and byre. In the middle of the main room, an open peat fire glows and smolders on the dirt floor with the smoke drifting up through the thatch roof. Visitors are free to poke around and the information center gives more background on a lost way of life; the displays don't paint a particularly pretty picture of what was rather rough living. Across the road is the "white house," the more modern cottage built of stone and proper mortar which replaced black houses across Lewis and the Hebrides.

The peat fire has been known in the past to sometimes fill the black house with smoke, but that's the cost of authenticity. Allow about one hour.

See map p. 369. Off the A858, on the west side of Lewis. ☎ **01851-710-395.** `www.historic-scotland.gov.uk.` *Admission: £2.50 adults, £2 seniors and students, £1.50 children. Open: Daily Apr–Sept 9:30 a.m.–6:30 p.m.; Oct–Mar 9:30 a.m.–4:30 p.m.*

Butt of Lewis
Ness, Lewis

High cliffs overlooking the ocean are the principal reward for making it to the northern tip of Lewis. Another edge of the earth experience. You should see seabirds, seals, and spectacular windblown waves crashing against the rocks. The proud lighthouse, constructed by the Stevenson family, adds to the scenery. Look for the large hole in the ground near the parking area; legend has it that the Vikings dug the hole in an attempt to drag the island back to Norway with them. Also note the sigmoid waves of lazy beds on the hills leading to the sea: they used to be cultivated. If you're a hill walker, a trail takes one down the northeastern coast of Lewis passing old sheillings — summer settlements for crofters in times gone by. Allow about one hour.

See map p. 369. Follow the A857 to the end of the line, Lewis.

Calanais Standing Stones
Callanish, Lewis

Sometimes called the "Scottish Stonehenge," this ancient circle- and cross-shaped formation of large standing stones a top a flat hill by the sea is the most significant archaeological find of its kind in the region — and among the most important in Europe. There's no charge to see the impressive and ragged stones, which were erected sometime between 3000 and 2500 B.C. and were — until the mid-1800s — buried much deeper in the bog on top of the hill. In fact, they are much taller than they appear today but are still quite deep in peat. If you're here during the summer solstice, you may find tents pitched near the monoliths — Calanais has become a popular spot for New Agers to celebrate the longest day of the year. There are bunch of other sets of standing stones in all directions from Calanais: all part of some ancient, prehistoric community. Allow about one hour.

See map p. 369. Off the A858 (19km/12 miles west of Stornoway), Lewis. ☎ **01851-621-422.** www.historic-scotland.gov.uk. *Admission: Free. Open: Stones year-round; visitor center Apr–Sept Mon–Sat 10 a.m.–6 p.m., Oct–Mar Wed–Sat 10 a.m.–4 p.m.*

Cuillin Hills
Near Broadford, Skye

These brooding, massive hills — craggy enough to pass for mountains — are a point of pride for the residents of Skye. Considered some of the best climbing and hiking in Scotland, the 900m (3,000-ft.) peaks rise in the center of the island.

You might consider spending an afternoon walking amid the spectacular scenery, but if you're inexperienced, inquire about professional guides at the tourist office in Portree. A private company called **Walkabout Scotland** organizes multiday guided hiking tours (☎ **0845-686-1344;** www.walkaboutscotland.com). Allow three to six hours.

See map p. 371. South of the A87, between Broadford and Sligachan, Skye. Trails from Glen Brittle, south of Merkadale off the A863.

Doune Broch (Dun Carloway)
Carloway, Skye

Up the road from the Calanais Standing Stones (see above), this intriguing Iron Age stone ruin (a "broch" was a tower used for defensive purposes and/or as a home) is in remarkably sound condition — good enough for you to walk into, at least. Properly called Dun Carloway, the broch provides some insight into prehistory and was likely a Norse-built structure. It wasn't all bad back then, either: Regardless of the weather outside, stepping into the broch provides surprisingly effective protection from the elements. Allow about one hour.

See map p. 369. On the A858 (9km/6 miles north of Callanish), Lewis. ☎ **01851-643-338**. *Admission: Free. Open: Broch year-round; visitor center Apr–Sept Mon–Sat 10 a.m.–6 p.m.*

Duart Castle
Near Craignure, Mull

Fans of the entertaining 1945 film *I Know Where I'm Going!* (see "Recommended movies," in Chapter 2) should recognize the drawing room in this fine castle. With a commanding position overlooking the Sound of Mull and clearly seen from the Oban ferry, Duart was abandoned in 1751. Thanks to the efforts of Fitzroy Maclean, it was completely restored from ruins in 1911. When you're inside, make your way up the narrow, twisting stairs and you can walk outside on the parapet at the top of the castle. As the ancestral home of the clan Maclean, one floor is devoted to clan history, with various references to the 17th-century battle cry: "Another for Hector!" Today, Duart Castle remains the home for the clan chief. There are no special gardens to tour, but visiting the grounds is free. Allow about one and a half hours.

See map p. 369. Off the A849 (5km/3 miles southeast of Craignure), Mull. ☎ **01680-812-309**. *www.duartcastle.com. Admission: £5.50 adults, £4.90 seniors and students, £2.75 children, £14 family. Open: May to mid-Oct daily 10:30 a.m.–5:30 p.m. Closed mid-Oct to Mar.*

Dunvegan Castle
Dunvegan, Skye

The seat of the Macleod of Macleod chiefs, this is said to be Scotland's oldest castle that has been continually owned and occupied by the same family, going on 800 years now. In addition to antiques, oil paintings, rare books, and clan heirlooms — some dating to the Middle Ages — have a look at the legendary Fairy Flag, a relic thought to bring "miraculous powers" to the clan. Also displayed are personal items belonging to Bonnie Prince Charlie, plus there's a reasonably creepy dungeon. Last admissions 30 minutes before closing. Allow about two hours.

See map p. 371. Off the A850, northwest Skye. ☎ **01470-521-206**. *www.dunvegancastle.com. Admission: Castle and gardens £8 adults, £6.50 seniors and students, £4 children, £23 family. Open: Daily Apr to mid-Oct 10 a.m.–5:30 p.m.; groups by reservation only in winter.*

Eigg
Inner Hebrides

The Isle of Eigg lies not far off the west coast of Scotland and can be reached from either Mallaig or Arisaig. The latter offers summer cruises (on the *Sheerwater*), which often have the bonus of whale sightings on the hour-long ride. In 1997, the inhabitants made history and set up a trust to buy the island. Visitors can take a variety of walks on the island, including the slightly strenuous hike up An Sgurr (the notch), the largest exposed piece of pitchstone in the U.K. The hike takes about two hours. An easier trek is to see chapel ruins on Kildonan Bay. A small tea room and place to rent bicycles are located at the small pier. Eigg is close enough to Arisaig that you can easily make a day trip of it and get a small dose of island life. For information on sailings from Arisaig, log on to www.arisaig.co.uk or call ☎ **01687-450-224.** Allow six and a half hours.

See map p. 369. West of Arisaig. www.isleofeigg.org.

Gearrannan Blackhouse Village
Carloway, Lewis

This set of stone houses dates from about 1800, although Gearrannan was probably first settled around the time that Christ was born. The focus of the attraction is the working black house, which provides an interesting contrast with the Arnol Blackhouse (see above). It shows what happened once electricity was introduced. There are a proper fireplace, wood floors, tongue-and-groove wall paneling, more windows, and electric lamps. But the home is still at a tremendous tilt due to the slope of the hill. In the byre, there is a working loom and someone on duty to show how it operates. The other black houses have been turned into vacation accommodations and a youth hostel. Allow about one hour.

See map p. 369. Off the A858 (40km/25 miles west of Stornoway). ☎ **01851-643-416.** www.gearrannan.com. *Admission: £2.50 adults, £2 children. Open: Apr–Sept Mon–Sat 9:30 a.m.–5:30 p.m. Closed Oct–Mar.*

Iona Abbey
Iona

This spiritual landmark is a significant shrine to the early days of Christianity in Scotland. The settlement (of both historic and sacred value) was first established by St. Columba, a Celtic pilgrim from Ireland. Columba almost single-handedly brought religion to a pagan land in the sixth century. The large abbey standing here today is in very good shape, having undergone several restorations since the 13th century. Crosses laid into the abbey floor mark the graves of several monks, while there are impressive medieval crosses on the grounds. The cemetery has graves of early Scottish royals and chiefs. Allow about one and a half hours.

You can see Iona in one day, although overnight stays are quite relaxing on this tiny island.

See map p. 369. 1km (one-half mile) from ferry pier. ☎ **01681-700-512.** www.historic-scotland.gov.uk. *Admission: £4.70 adults, £3.80 seniors and students, £2.80 children. Open: Apr–Sept daily 9:30 a.m.–5:30 p.m.; Oct–Mar daily 9:30 a.m.–4:30 p.m.*

North and South Uist
Outer Hebrides

Although no single attraction on North and South Uist (pronounced *yewst*) necessarily stands out, these two islands (connected by causeways and the isle of Benbecula) are worth a visit. Certainly consider it if you're on Lewis and Harris or even in northwest Skye (from where the ferry crossing out of Uig takes just under two hours). Devote at least a full day to cross the rural landscape and take in the scenery, landmarks, and fresh air. Be sure to get off the main road, too, at least occasionally, to explore the rural lanes that get closer to the sea. At the Balranald Nature Reserve, you can spot many types of wading birds and other sea life. It is only about 82km (51 miles) from Lochmaddy south to Lochboisdale. Allow at least eight hours.

See map p. 369.

St. Clement's Church
Rodel, Harris

Is it worth traveling to the southern tip of Harris to see this far-flung attraction? Aye, it pretty much is. At the end of an amazing coastal route full of white beaches and aqua-blue waters, you arrive at this small but well-preserved early-16th-century pre-Reformation church. It is certainly the best of its type in the Western Isles, following a cruciform plan with a square tower at one end. The most impressive feature, aside from the intact stone edifice itself, is the carved tomb of Alexander Macleod of Dunvegan (aka Alasdair Crotach), who had it done well before he died in the late 1540s. Protected from the elements and literally built into the church, it is a remarkably well-preserved bit of medieval craftsmanship. There are other startling details elsewhere, including a carving of St. Clement and, curiously, a naked woman. Allow one hour.

See map p. 369. On the A859, Rodel. Admission: Free. Open: Daily dawn to dusk.

Skye Museum of Island Life and Flora MacDonald's Grave
Kilmuir, Skye

The place where Flora MacDonald was born is marked on South Uist. On northern Skye, if you follow a path from the Museum of Island Life to Kilmuir Cemetery, you can see the Victorian-era memorial marking the grave of the legendary Flora. She is credited with saving Bonnie Prince Charlie in 1746. The Young Pretender hid on Skye with her help after the battle of Culloden and escaped disguised as MacDonald's maid. Poor Flora was later arrested as an accessory and held in the Tower of London. Later, she moved to North Carolina and finally back to Skye before she died. The locally run "museum" actually consists of a set of thatched croft (smallholding) houses, showing how people lived on Skye a century or more ago. The re-created crofts contain antique domestic items, agricultural tools, and photographs of island life. Allow one hour.

See map p. 371. On the A855, take the A87 north from Portree towards Uig. ☎ **01470-552-206.** www.skyemuseum.co.uk. *Admission: £2.50 adults, £2 seniors and* *students, 50p children (school age). Open: Easter to Oct generally Mon–Sat 9:30 a.m.–5 p.m.*

Staffa and Fingal's Cave
Inner Hebrides

Just a short boat trip from Mull, the uninhabited Isle of Staffa is an attraction worth seeing if you're spending some time in the Mull-Iona area. Visitors enjoy watching the sea crash against the dramatic, vertical rock formations, especially the cathedral-like columns of Fingal's Cave. The cave is one of the natural wonders of the world and is famous for being the inspiration for Mendelssohn's *Hebridean Overture*. Birders, take note: Staffa is home to a large puffin colony. Unfortunately, in the midseason, some of the boats won't sail if they don't get enough reservations. Allow two to four hours.

*See map p. 369. The MB Iolaire (☎ **01681-700-358;** www.staffatrips.co.uk) departs daily from both Fionnphort and Iona. Tickets: £25 adults, £10 children. Turus Mara (☎ **0800-858-786** or 01688-400-242; www.turusmara.com) departs from Ulva Ferry, on the west coast of central Mull. Tickets: £25 adults, £23 children. Excursions are generally available Easter to Sept.*

Torosay Castle and Gardens
Near Craignure, Mull

Compared to nearby Duart Castle, Torosay is a relatively modern house, built in the Victorian era. Access to the interiors here is more limited, too, because most of the building is still used as a private home. But whatever the restrictions indoors, the surrounding gardens are the real attraction for many visitors. The 4.8 hectares (12 acres) of well-manicured grounds abound with fine and unique flora, Romanesque statues, and ivy-covered walls. You're welcome to explore the greenhouse and are encouraged to stop and smell the roses; this stop is a treat for anyone with a green thumb. Kids usually enjoy the small-scale train (£4.50 adults, £3 children) that runs to Torosay from Craignure. Allow one and a half hours.

See map p. 369. Off the A849 (about 1.5km/1 mile south of Craignure ferry terminal). ☎ 01680-812-421. www.torosay.com. Admission: Castle and gardens £7 adults, £4.50 seniors, £3.25 children, £15 family. Open: Daily Apr to early Oct 10:30 a.m.–5 p.m. (castle closed rest of year); gardens daily year-round 9 a.m. to dusk.

Western Isles Museum (Museum nan Eilean)
Stornoway, Lewis

This small museum is home to exhibits on various aspects of Hebridean life, history, and archaeology; it displays artifacts, photographs, prints, and paintings. The temporary shows, sometimes borrowed from other museums and collections around the islands and from the Scottish mainland, can be excellent. If you're in Stornoway, this museum is worth a visit — and you can't beat the price. Allow one hour.

Harris Tweed: New fashion icon

The Outer Hebrides doesn't produce much whisky these days (although watch out for a new distillery's whisky coming soon from Uig, Lewis), but it does boast one of the more famous textiles in the world. Harris Tweed is made from local lamb's wool, spun on either Harris or Lewis, and woven by hand looms on either Lewis or Harris. Finally, there are three mills on the Outer Hebrides producing authentic finished cloth. The fabric's fortunes had waned until recently. Now instead of old-fashioned it is fashionable among lots of groovy designers in London and cool clothes makers as far away as Japan (check the Web site www.thecroft.wordpress.com for examples). There are many outlets for Harris Tweed. One of my favorites for pieces of material is in the tiny seaside hamlet of Plocrapool, Harris (www.harristweedandknitware.co.uk). For bona fide Harris Tweed, the label must have the trademark orb. For information on Harris Tweed, contact the Harris Tweed Authority in Stornoway, 6 Garden Rd., ☎ 01851-702-269 (www.harristweed.org).

See map p. 369. Francis Street, Stornoway. ☎ 01851-709-266. Admission: Free. Open: Apr–Sept Mon–Sat 10 a.m.–5:30 p.m.; Oct–Mar Tues–Fri 10 a.m.–5 p.m., Sat 10 a.m.–1 p.m.

Other cool things to see and do

✔ **An Lanntair,** Kenneth St., Stornoway, Lewis (☎ 01851-703-307; www.lanntair.com), is an excellent arts and culture center, with exhibition space for art and an auditorium for drama, music, and films. The gift shop is good and so is the cafe/bar/bistro upstairs. Open Monday to Saturday from 10 a.m.

✔ **Ardalanish Farm & Isle of Mull Weavers,** off the A849 near Bunessan, Mull (☎ 01681-700-265; www.isleofmullweavers.co.uk), is an organic farm on the Ross of Mull that doesn't mind visitors. In fact, you're welcome to see how a demonstration organic farm works. In addition to self-guided walks, the weavers offer bundled yarn and tweed by the yard.

✔ **Aros** (the Home of Culture and Hospitality), just south of Portree on the A87 (☎ 01478-613-649; www.aros.co.uk), is a cultural center on the Isle of Skye that has an art gallery, shops, and cafe, and is a venue for music, drama, and films.

✔ **Aros Castle,** off the A848 (about 3km/2 miles north of Salen), Isle of Mull, is a monumental pile of rocks in the shape of a ruined tower house, on a hill overlooking Salen Bay. But it was once a stronghold of the MacDougalls and the Lords of the Isles. The ruins, at least during my last visit, were not fenced off.

Cruising the Inner Hebrides

The MV *Glen Tarsan* is a converted 26m (85-ft.) fishing boat that can take groups (Apr–Oct) to explore the Inner Hebrides. From Oban, typical cruises dot about the isles, such as Mull or Staffa, as well as sailing into West Coast inlets, looking for dolphins or eagles, fishing for lobster, mooring to allow onshore hikes, and sheltering at night in picturesque bays, when hearty meals are shared in the deck saloon. Cabins are spartan (as you would expect for a vessel) but comfortable, with en-suite heads and showers. A six-night cruise costs about £1,400 per person, including meals and house wines with dinner. Only drinks from the bar are charged extra. Call the **Majestic Line** at ☎ **0131-623-5012,** or log on to www.themajesticline.co.uk.

✔ **Mull Theatre,** Tobermory, Mull (☎ **01688-302-828;** www.mull theatre.com), is home to a surprisingly accomplished dramatic company that tours Scotland. This new facility opened in early 2007 outside Tobermory.

✔ **Skye Serpentarium,** on the A850 near Broadford, Skye (☎ **01471-822-209;** www.skyeserpentarium.org.uk), is crazy about its collection of reptiles and amphibians, many of which were seized (while being smuggled into the country) by Customs officials and sent to this serpentarium for the good life.

✔ **Talisker Distillery,** off the A863, Carbost, Skye (☎ **01478-614-308**), offers a tour that's among the best. Enthusiastic guides expound on the virtues of their single-malt whisky (the only one produced on Skye) and its production process.

✔ **Tobermory Distillery,** Tobermory, Mull (☎ **01688-302-645**), the only distillery on Mull, produces five different single malts with unpeated malted barley (not typical of island whisky). A visitor center is located on the premises.

✔ **Ulva** is the small isle located just across a narrow straight from the settlement of Ulva Ferry (off the B8073) in west-central Mull. During the Clearances, from about 1840 to 1882, when thousands of Scots were evicted from their homes, Ulva's population went from about 850 to less than 60 — and the remaining residents were forced to live in one small corner near the ferry slip called Desolation Point. A cafe, serving fresh oysters, is almost reason enough for you to hop the ferry to Ulva, but the isle is excellent for walking, too.

Shopping the Hebridean Islands

Despite their remoteness, the Hebridean Islands are home to a fair number of excellent craft and specialty shops. Some of the best gifts can be found at shops within the various attractions listed earlier in this chapter. In the Outer Hebrides, Harris Tweed is sold at a lot of stores, as well as at small home shops where the product is woven on site.

✔ **Baltic Books,** Cromwell St., Stornoway (☎ **01851-702-082**), has a good selection of books on the Outer Hebrides, from historical accounts of crofting life to current guides and lovely photograph books of scenery. Open Monday to Saturday 10 a.m. to 5 p.m.

✔ **Edinbane Pottery,** off the A850, between Portree and Dunvegan, Skye (☎ **01470-582-234**; www.edinbane-pottery.co.uk), is a workshop and gallery that produces some unique and mostly hand-thrown salt-glazed ceramics. Open April to October daily from 10 a.m. to 5 p.m.

✔ **Isle of Mull Cheese,** Sgriob-Ruadh Farm, near Tobermory, Mull (☎ **01688-302-235**; www.isleofmullcheese.co.uk), is a farm producing award-winning, artisan cheeses using only cow's and ewe's milk from the premises. Delicious. Open May to September daily from 10 a.m. to 4 p.m.

✔ **Isle of Mull Silver & Goldsmiths,** Main Street, Tobermory, Mull (☎ **01688-302-345**; www.mullsilver.co.uk), is part manufacturer, part retail shop. They make pieces in-house and have an impressive selection from across Scotland. The shop is open Monday through Saturday from 9:30 a.m. to 1 p.m. and 2 to 5 p.m. Hours may be extended in the summer.

✔ **Over the Rainbow,** Portree, Skye (☎ **01478-612-555**; www.skye knitwear.com), is stocked with colorful knits of first-rate quality, whether sweaters, scarves, or blankets. The shop also sells designer jewelry and accessories. Open Monday to Saturday from 9 a.m. to 5:30 p.m.

✔ **Tobermory Handmade Chocolate,** Main Street, Tobermory, Mull (☎ **01688-302-526**; www.tobchoc.co.uk), makes unique hand-made confections locally, whether 71 percent pure dark-chocolate treats (such as a rum truffle) or after-dinner mints. Open March to October Monday through Saturday from 9:30 a.m. to 5 p.m., Sunday from 11 a.m. to 4 p.m. in July and August.

Doing the Pub Crawl

Many of the inns and restaurants listed at the beginning of this chapter offer pub life, too. Below are a few more to consider. Call for the latest opening and closing times.

✔ **Isles Inn,** Somerled Square, Portree, Skye (☎ **01478-612-129**), is a cozy, friendly pub (with **overnight rooms**) in the center of Portree. It's a popular joint featuring traditional music most nights, especially in the summer.

✔ **Martyr's Bay,** near the pier, Iona (☎ **01681-700-382**), is a bar (and restaurant) with sea views, and is named for the nearby inlet where some 68 monks were killed by Vikings in the 9th century.

✔ **Mishnish,** Main Street, Tobermory, Mull (☎ **01688-302-009**), is a quayside pub (with overnight rooms) that's rather big for such a diminutive town. There are two main areas, with a warming fireplace, as well as "snugs" (small rooms) for a little more privacy.

✔ **Star Bar,** South Beach Street, Stornoway, Lewis (☎ **01851-702-289**), is right on the sea front and while compact, it is linked to the **Era** nightclub, which often features live bands in the so-called Jager Room at the weekend.

Fast Facts: The Hebridean Islands

Area Code

The area codes for the main towns and islands in the Hebrides are: Portree, Skye **01478**; Tobermory, Mull **01688**; Iona **01681**; Stornoway, Lewis **01851**; Tarbert, Harris **01859**. You need to dial the area code only if you're calling from outside the city you want to reach.

Emergencies

Dial ☎ **999** for police, fire, or ambulance.

Hospitals

The main hospitals in the Hebrides are Gesto Hospital, Lower Edinbane, Portree, Skye (☎ 01470-582-262); and the Western Isles Hospital in Stornoway, Lewis (☎ 01851-704-704).

Information

The main tourist office is Western Isles Tourist Board, 26 Cromwell St., Stornoway,

Lewis (☎ 01851-703-088; fax: 01851-705-244; www.visithebrides.com). Other tourist offices include: Bayfield House, just off Somerled Square, Portree, Skye (☎ 01478-612-137); Pier Road, Tarbert, Harris (☎ 01859-502-011); Pier Road, Lochmaddy, North Uist (☎ 01876-500-321); Pier Road, Lochboisdale, South Uist (☎ 01878-700-286); Main Street, Castlebay, Harris (☎ 01871-810-336); in the Caledonian MacBrayne ticket office at the far northern end of the harbor, Tobermory, Mull (☎ 01648-302-182); and opposite the quay, Craignure, Mull (☎ 01680-812-377).

Mail

You can find post offices at Gladstone Buildings, Quay Brae, Portree, Skye (☎ 01478-612-533); 16 Francis St., Stornoway, Lewis (☎ 0845-722-3344); and 36 Main St., Tobermory, Mull (☎ 01688-302-058).

Chapter 20

Orkney and Shetland Islands

. . . .

In This Chapter

▶ Uncovering accommodations and restaurants on the islands
▶ Discovering prehistoric sites and settlements

. . . .

*M*aking the trip to the northern isles of Orkney and Shetland can be rewarding, but if you plan to visit either island archipelago, you should know that getting there does take extra effort.

When you reach these islands, you will discover that they abound with grand views, old ruins, and a heritage unlike the rest of Scotland—given the long ribbon of history, they have as much in common with Scandinavia as with Scotland. Both island groups are quite prosperous: Orkney is fertile and Shetland benefits from oil industry wealth.

Visitors will find that accommodations, dining, shopping, and drinking options are more limited in such northern latitudes. In the off season, the quiet gets even quieter. Remember that although the Orkney and Shetland islands offer an escape from the crowds, in many ways you're escaping conveniences, too.

Kirkwall is the main town in Orkney, where the ferries from Aberdeen arrive. To the west, **Stromness** (not to be confused with Stornoway on the Isle of Lewis) is another key port village, where ferries arrive from the northern Scottish mainland city of Scrabster (near Thurso). In Shetland, **Lerwick** is the administrative capital and largest port town, receiving ferries from Aberdeen, Kirkwall, and in summer from Bergen, Norway, too.

Because of space constraints, this chapter is short and succinct, combing the accommodations and dining options into one section. For greater details, contact the local tourist information centers. For Orkney, call the Kirkwall center (☎ **01856-872-856**) or log on to www.visitorkney. com. For Shetland, call the Lerwick center (☎ **08701-999-440**), or go to the Web site, www.visitshetland.com.

Getting There

For many travelers, the simplest way to see the islands is to join a tour that covers the major sights in the area. If you're not on a tour, you can get to both Orkney and Shetland by ferry or by airplane. The major islands of the groups have ferry services that connect them to one another.

✔ **By ferry: NorthLink Ferries** (☎ 0845-600-0449; www.northlink ferries.co.uk) operates services from the mainland to Orkney and Shetland, either from Scrabster to Stromness, Orkney; Aberdeen to Kirkwall, Orkney; or Aberdeen to Lerwick, Shetland. Typical fares range from around £15 to £36 per adult (plus vehicle fee), depending on the route and the time of year. The trip from Scrabster to Stromness takes about 90 minutes; the overnight journey from Aberdeen to Lerwick takes 12½ hours.

Smaller companies also run boats to Orkney. Summer passenger-only ferries, run by **John O'Groats Ferries** (☎ 01955-611-353; www.jogferry.co.uk), go from John O'Groats to Burwick (May–Sept, 40 min.) and also runs day tours. **Pentland Ferries** (☎ 01856-831-226; www.pentlandferries.co.uk) travel from Gills Bay to St. Margaret's Hope (one hour).

✔ **By car:** If you've rented a car for your time in Scotland, you can take it with you when you visit Orkney by booking passage on one of the **NorthLink Ferries** (see above). You can make arrangements with many car-rental agencies for free vehicle pickup and delivery at ferry landings and airports in Scotland.

✔ **By plane: Kirkwall Airport** (☎ 01856-886-210) is about 5km (3 miles) from the center of Kirkwall, Orkney. **Sumburgh Airport** (☎ 01950-461-000) is 40km (25 miles) south of Lerwick on Shetland. Both airports are operated by Highlands and Islands Airports (☎ 01667-462-445; www.hial.co.uk). There is regular, if not necessarily frequent, nonstop service to Aberdeen, Glasgow, Edinburgh, and Inverness. For example, a flight from Inverness to Sumburgh takes about one hour and 45 minutes and costs around £150.

Spending the Night and Dining Locally

Your choices of accommodations and restaurants are more limited on Orkney and Shetland. I've tried to give you some of the better options in this section. Hotel-room prices include full breakfast unless otherwise stated. You may well get a better deal than the advertised rack rates.

I have also tried to indicate when ventures are closed throughout or during a part of the off season, but call in advance to confirm. Also, expect higher costs on the northern islands, despite some of the more established inns having a reputation for outdated accommodations.

The Orkney Islands

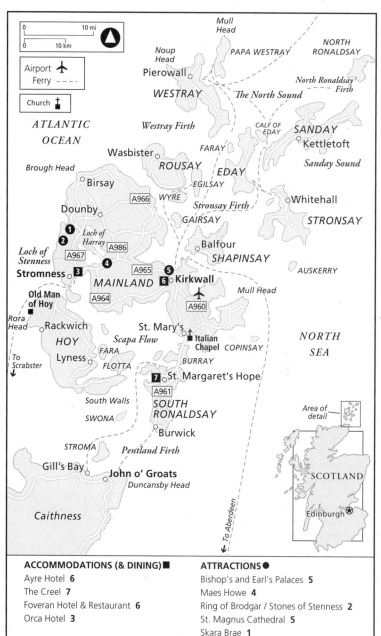

0 ——— 10 mi
0 ——— 10 km

Airport ✈
Ferry - - - -

Church ✝

ATLANTIC
OCEAN

Mull Head

NORTH RONALDSAY

Noup Head
PAPA WESTRAY

Pierowall o
WESTRAY
North Ronaldsay Firth

Westray Firth
The North Sound

CALF OF EDAY
SANDAY
o Kettletoft

FARAY
Sanday Sound

Wasbister o
ROUSAY
EDAY

Brough Head
EGILSAY

o Birsay
A966 WYRE

Dounby o
GAIRSAY
Stronsay Firth

o Whitehall
STRONSAY

①
Loch of Harray A986

②
A967

Loch of Stenness

④
A965

Balfour
SHAPINSAY

o AUSKERRY

Stromness **③**
MAINLAND
⑤
⑥ o **Kirkwall**

Old Man of Hoy ■
A964
Mull Head
A960

Rora Head
o Rackwich
St. Mary's
NORTH
SEA

HOY
Scapa Flow
■ Italian Chapel COPINSAY

To Scrabster ↓
Lyness o
FARA
FLOTTA
BURRAY

⑦ o **St. Margaret's Hope**
A961

South Walls
SOUTH RONALDSAY

SWONA

o Burwick

STROMA
Pentland Firth

Gill's Bay o
John o' Groats
Duncansby Head

Caithness

Area of detail

SCOTLAND

Edinburgh ⊛

To Aberdeen ↓

ACCOMMODATIONS (& DINING) ■
Ayre Hotel **6**
The Creel **7**
Foveran Hotel & Restaurant **6**
Orca Hotel **3**

ATTRACTIONS ●
Bishop's and Earl's Palaces **5**
Maes Howe **4**
Ring of Brodgar / Stones of Stenness **2**
St. Magnus Cathedral **5**
Skara Brae **1**

Ayre Hotel
$$ Kirkwall, Orkney

A renovated 18th-century hotel, the Ayre overlooks Kirkwall harbor — perhaps its strongest point. Rooms are simply decorated, but they do have en-suite bathrooms, TVs, and coffeemakers. The whitewashed building is conveniently located near the town center and by the water. Rooms with a sea view cost more.

See map p. 391. Ayre Road, Kirkwall, Orkney. ☎ *01856-873-001. Fax: 01856-876-289.* www.ayrehotel.co.uk. *Rack rates: £110 double. AE, DC, MC, V.*

Burrastow House
$$–$$$$ Near Walls, Shetland   SCOTTISH

Talk about getting away from it all. Still, if you're planning to spend some time on Shetland, a weekend dinner reservation at Burrastow House might be in order. The menus feature local fish, lamb, beef, and pork — even the cucumbers and tomatoes in your salad are likely to be grown locally. While sheep graze on the grass outside, you graze on mussel stew, monkfish, and homemade soups. If you're looking to spend the night, Burrastow is a **four-star guesthouse** with five en-suite rooms.

See map p. 393. Off the A971 (5km/3 miles from Walls, 43km/27 miles west of Lerwick), Shetland. ☎ *01595-809-307.* www.burrastowhouse.co.uk. *Reservations required for meals. Main courses: £10–£20. Open: 7:30–9 p.m.; weekends only for nonguests. Rack rates: £90–£100 double. AE, MC, V. Closed Nov–Mar.*

The Creel Restaurant with Rooms
$$$ South Ronaldsay, Orkney   FISH/SEAFOOD

This inn in St. Margaret's Hope is run by Joyce Craigie and husband Alan, who was named Scottish Restaurant Chef of the Year in 2006 by the country's Independent Chef's Association. For over 21 years, he and his staff have treated guests to dishes made almost exclusively with locally landed fish and shellfish — including some lesser-seen varieties such as torsk. There is also grass-fed Ornkey beef and lamb, which itself has dined on seaweed. There are three **overnight rooms,** all with sea views, and guests gush about the breakfasts.

See map p. 391. Off the A961, Front Road, St. Margaret's Hope (21km/13 miles south of Kirkwall), Orkney. ☎ *01856-831-311.* www.thecreel.co.uk. *Reservations recommended. Main courses: £15–£20. Open: Daily Apr–Oct; some weekends in winter (call first). Rack rates: About £110 double. MC. V.*

Foveran Hotel & Restaurant
$$ Near Kirkwall, Orkney   SCOTTISH

Overlooking the waters of Scapa Flow, this popular and highly regarded small three-star hotel is just a short trip from Kirkwall. Most rooms have sea views. If you decide to eat in-house, you should get a fine Scottish meal with locally grown produce, Orkney beef and lamb, fresh seafood, and excellent desserts.

The Shetland Islands

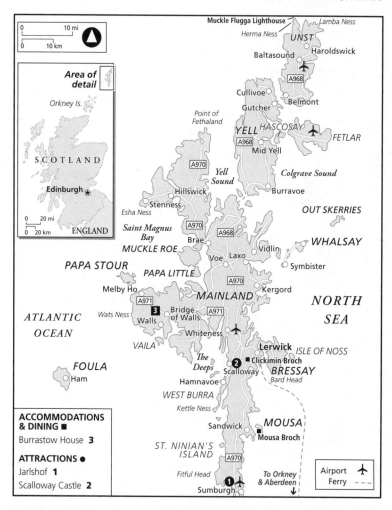

0 10 mi
0 10 km

Area of detail

Orkney Is.

SCOTLAND

Edinburgh ✵

0 20 mi
0 20 km

ENGLAND

Muckle Flugga Lighthouse
Lamba Ness
Herma Ness
UNST
Baltasound
Haroldswick
A968
Cullivoe
Gutcher
Belmont
Point of Fethaland
YELL HASCOSAY
A968
FETLAR
Mid Yell
A970
Yell Sound
Hillswick
Stenness
Esha Ness
Colgrave Sound
Burravoe
Saint Magnus Bay
A970
A968
OUT SKERRIES
MUCKLE ROE
Brae
Voe Laxo
Vidlin
WHALSAY
PAPA STOUR
PAPA LITTLE
Symbister
Melby Ho
A970
Kergord
A971
MAINLAND
NORTH SEA
ATLANTIC OCEAN
Wats Ness
3 Bridge of Walls
A971
Walls
Whiteness
VAILA
The Deeps
Lerwick *ISLE OF NOSS*
■ Clickimin Broch
2 ■
Scalloway *BRESSAY*
FOULA
Ham
Hamnavoe
Bard Head
WEST BURRA
Kettle Ness
Sandwick
MOUSA
■ Mousa Broch
ST. NINIAN'S ISLAND
A970
Fitful Head
To Orkney & Aberdeen
1 ✈
Sumburgh

ACCOMMODATIONS & DINING ■
Burrastow House **3**

ATTRACTIONS ●
Jarlshof **1**
Scalloway Castle **2**

Airport ✈
Ferry - - -

See map p. 391. Off the A964 (5km/3 miles southwest of Kirkwall), Orkney. ☎ **01856-872-389**. Fax: 01856-876-430. www.foveranhotel.co.uk. Main courses: £10–£20. Open: Daily 7–9 p.m. Rack rates: Around £110 double. MC, V. Closed Jan.

Orca Hotel
$ Stromness, Orkney

This small guesthouse seems to be getting the most positive feedback from recent visitors to Stromness, who generally praise its cleanliness and price. Family run with only a clutch of six rooms (all with en-suite bathrooms), the Orca is located right near the harbor and a five-minute walk from the ferry terminal.

76 Victoria St., Orkney. ☎ **01856-850-447.** *www.orcahotel.moonfruit.com. Rack rates: £46 double. MC, V.*

Stromness Hotel
$$ Stromness, Orkney

Established in 1901, the traditional 42-unit Stromness Hotel appears to be showing its age. Still, some of the overnight rooms in this traditional stone building have bay windows that overlook the harbor and Scapa Flow. The hotel hosts live music and a few annual festivals, too, while children younger than 14 stay free in parent's room.

The Pierhead, Victoria Terrace, Stromness, Orkney. ☎ **01856-850-298.** *Fax: 01856-850-610. www.stromnesshotel.com. Rack rates: £80–£100 double. MC, V. Closed Jan–Feb.*

Exploring Orkney and Shetland

Attraction for attraction, Orkney's ancient landmarks with World Heritage Site status gives it the edge for visitors over Shetland. It's been said that no other northern European location can equal Orkney's concentration of visible prehistoric monuments. The top sights are on the largest island in the group, what Orcadians call the Mainland. Orkney also offers spectacular seascapes and plenty of unspoiled nature. The town of **Stromness** (not to be confused with Stornoway, which is on Lewis) has been a natural harbor since Viking times, and **Kirkwall** is the lovely capital of the island chain.

To see some of the smaller islands of Orkney, such as Hoy or Shapinsay, **Orkney Ferries** (☎ **01856-872-044;** www.orkneyferries.co.uk) offers sailings and minicruises.

Of the more than 100 islands that make up the **Shetlands,** only about 15 are inhabited. Similar to Orkney, the principal island is called the Mainland. The Norse gave the island chain to Scotland through a marriage dowry in 1469, but the legacy of its Scandinavian origins shows in the faces of the locals, the names of villages, and the architecture of the main town, **Lerwick.** Nature abounds in the beautiful scenery, from Shetland ponies that roam freely to seals and porpoises that live along the coasts. Like the people of Orkney, Shetland residents' identities are probably more strongly tied to their islands than to Scotland.

Be sure to stop at the tourist offices in Kirkwell (Orkney) and Lerwick (Shetland) and pick up the handy maps showing both large and small attractions.

Joining a guided tour

A guided tour can be a smart, convenient way to get around and see specific sights. Here are two to consider.

- ✔ **Wildabout Orkney Tours** (☎ **01856-877-737;** www.wildabout orkney.com) offers excursions covering the island's prehistoric highlights, with guides also discussing the history, archaeology, and ecology of Orkney.

- ✔ **Shetland Wildlife** (☎ **01950-422-483;** www.shetlandwildlife. co.uk) specializes in guided tours that show off Shetland's diverse wildlife. It offers a selection of multiday tours, such as the "Shetland experience," which combines sea cruises and overland journeys in search of puffins, whales, otters, and more.

The top attractions

Get an "Explorer's Pass" from Historic Scotland (☎ **0131-668-8797**) for reduced admission prices to several attractions on Orkney.

Bishop's and Earl's Palaces
Kirkwall, Orkney

The impressive ruins of the Bishop's Palace date from the 12th century, although most of what's standing today — the Earl's Palace — was constructed in the 1600s. History says that King Haakon of Norway returned here to die after losing the battle of Largs (southwest of Glasgow) in 1263. The despotic Earl Patrick Stuart built the Earl's Palace next door in about 1606. Stuart, son of a bastard stepbrother to Mary, Queen of Scots, treated the local subjects rottenly, though he was ultimately executed for treason. In its day, his palace (completed after his death) was among the finest examples of French Renaissance architecture in Scotland. Last admission 30 minutes before closing. Allow about two hours.

See map p. 391. Across Palace Road from St. Magnus Cathedral, Orkney. ☎ **01856-871-918.** *www.historic-scotland.gov.uk. Admission: £3.70 adults, £3 seniors and students, £2.20 children. Open: Daily Apr–Oct 9:30 a.m.–5:30 p.m. Closed Nov–Mar.*

Jarlshof
Near Sumburgh, Shetland

This fascinating prehistoric and Norse settlement was discovered after a particularly violent storm in 1897 washed away the sand that had covered it for millennia. Subsequent archaeological digs have further revealed settlements and remarkable artifacts from different civilizations, from the Stone Age to the Viking era. Highlights include an oval Bronze Age house, an Iron Age broch (stone house and fortification), wheelhouses, a medieval farmstead, and the relatively modern 16th-century laird's house. As for the Scandinavian-sounding name meaning "earl's house," it comes from Sir Walter Scott's novel *The Pirate*. The correct name for the site is

Sumburgh, derived from the Old Norse *borg,* or "fort." Last admission 30 minutes before closing. Allow about two hours.

See map p. 393. Off the A97, at Sumburgh Head (35km/22 miles south of Lerwick), Shetland. ☎ **01950-460-112.** *www.historic-scotland.gov.uk. Admission: £4.70 adults, £3.80 seniors and students, £2.80 children. Open: Daily Apr–Sept 9:30 a.m.–5:30 p.m.; Oct 9:30 a.m.–4:30 p.m. Closed Nov–Mar.*

Maeshowe Chambers Cairn
West Mainland, Orkney

More remarkable sights. This strange turf-covered mound dates from about 3000 B.C., and contains a burial cairn that is probably the finest bit of Neolithic construction in northern Europe. By some estimates, as a prehistoric feat of engineering, it is only surpassed by the far more famous Stonehenge in England. You find a stone-built passage, a burial chamber, and smaller cells. Look for the inscriptions along the walls written by Vikings who pillaged the tomb's treasures in the 12th century, a bit of ancient Norse graffiti, if you like. During the shortest days of the year, in December and early January, the sun shines precisely down the entrance passage and illuminates the rear of the central chamber. Note that advance bookings are required to tour Maeshowe. Allow about one and a half hours.

See map p. 391. Off the A965 (14km/9 miles west of Kirkwall), Orkney. ☎ **01856-761-606.** *www.historic-scotland.gov.uk. Advance reservations required. Admission: £5.20 adults, £4.20 seniors and students, £3.10 children. Open: Daily Apr–Sept 9:30 a.m.–5 p.m.; Oct–Mar 9:30 a.m.–4 p.m.*

Ring of Brodgar and the Stones of Stenness
West Mainland, Orkney

Not far from Maes Howe, these two sets of standing stones are certainly impressive: The tallest stone of the Stenness henge is about 6m (19 ft.) high, a bit more imposing than those in the Brodgar group, which is saying something. The circles, part of the Neolithic Orkney World Heritage Site, are within walking distance of each other. Thirty-six of the 60 original stones in the Ring of Brodgar (probably erected between 2500–2000 B.C.) remain standing, while only 4 of 12 at Stenness (maybe as old as 3400 B.C.) are still upright. When the fog rolls in, the rings are quite a sight, but on any day most visitors are moved by these monuments. Allow about one and a half hours.

See map p. 391. Off the A965 (18km/11 miles west of Kirkwall), Orkney. ☎ **01856-841-815.** *Admission: Free. Open: Year-round.*

St. Magnus Cathedral
Kirkwall, Orkney

Dominating the town of Kirkwall, this sandstone cathedral honors Magnus, a Norse earl killed in the 12th century by cousin Haakon, who then went on to become king. After Magnus was buried in Birsay, however, miracles began occurring and he was made a saint in 1135. Magnus's nephew, Earl Rognvald, after a bit of crusading (and perhaps some slave-trading, too) then initiated construction of this cathedral in 1137. Along with Glasgow's St. Mungo's, it is Scotland's only pre-Reformation cathedral that remains substantially intact. It retains grand features, from huge sandstone columns to beautiful stained glass. Allow one hour.

See map p. 391. Broad Street, Orkney. ☎ **01856-874-894.** www.stmagnus.org. *Admission: Free. Open: Apr–Sept Mon–Sat 9 a.m.–5 p.m., Sun 2–6 p.m.; Oct–Mar Mon–Fri 9 a.m.–5 p.m. (closed for lunch 1–2 p.m.).*

Scalloway Castle
Scalloway, Shetland

These ruins date from the time of Earl Patrick Stuart — not a popular figure in these parts thanks to his corruption and brutality — who built this castellated mansion in 1600. In fact, he used forced labor to do it. After he was executed, the building fell into disrepair, but it still makes for good photographs. To gain access Monday to Saturday from 9:30 a.m. to 5 p.m., get the key from Shetland Woolen Company next door. On Sunday, get it from the nearby hotel. Allow about one hour.

See map p. 393. Off the A970 (about 10km/6 miles west of Lerwick), Shetland. ☎ **01856-841-815.** www.historic-scotland.gov.uk. *Admission: Free.*

Skara Brae
West Mainland, Orkney

While this list is alphabetical, the best is also saved for last. The turf-covered stone walls of this prehistoric beachside village — the best of its type in northern Europe — completes the Stone Age extravaganza of Orkney. It was exposed to modern humans only after a storm in 1850. Stone passages connect about a half-dozen now roofless rooms, where you can see beds, fireplaces, dressers, seats, and boxes for possessions, all carved of stone. A replica adjacent to the site re-creates what life may have been like when Skara Brae was inhabited (about 5,000 years ago), while nearby Skaill House (summers only) offers a 17th century version of bourgeois island accommodations. Last admission is 45 minutes before closing. Allow about two hours.

See map p. 391. B9056 off the A967 (about 31km/19 miles northwest of Kirkwall), Orkney. ☎ **01856-841-815.** www.historic-scotland.gov.uk. *Admission: £6.70 adults, £5.40 seniors and students, £4 children (reduced over winter). Open: Daily Apr–Sept 9:30 a.m.–5:30 p.m.; Oct–Mar 9:30 a.m.–4:30 p.m. (except Skaill House).*

Other cool things to see and do

- ✔ **Clickimin Broch,** near Lerwick, Stromness, was first inhabited from perhaps 700 to 500 B.C. This stone settlement includes the 2nd-century oval house, as well as the ruins of earlier prehistoric buildings and walls, which would have enclosed livestock.

- ✔ **Italian Chapel,** off the A961, Isle of Lambholm, Orkney, is where World War II Italian prisoners of war were brought. On this tiny island between East Mainland and Burray, they converted one of the corrugated steel Quonset (or Nissen) huts into a place of worship with an elaborately painted interior. Today it is one of the most visited landmarks in Orkney.

✔ **The Longship,** 7–15 Broad St., Kirkwall, Orkney (☎ **01856-888-790**), is a wine shop, founded over 150 years ago, that also sells the jewelry designs of Ola Gorie, as well as showing off the talents of other Orcadian craftspeople, whether with fashion accessories, clothing, or food.

✔ **Mousa Broch,** Mousa Island, Shetland, is considered the best surviving Iron Age broch, a tower of stone standing at over 13m (40 ft.) tall. Once there were some 120 of these dotted about Shetland. To get there, boats (☎ **01950 431-367**) leave from Sandwick on the A970, about 22km (14 miles) south of Lerwick.

✔ **The Old Man of Hoy,** Hoy, Orkney, is a 137m-tall (450-ft.) stack of sandstone that rises amid the cliffs along the western shores of Hoy. It's a real challenge to rock climbers; my advice is to see it from the cliff tops, from a touring cruise ship, or possibly from the ferry to Stromness.

✔ **Orkney Museum,** Tankerness House, Broad Street, Kirkwall, Orkney (☎ **01856-873-535**), covers aspects of Orcadian life during the last 5,000 years. The building dates from 1574, when it was a residence for church officials. Admission is free.

✔ **Stromness Museum,** 52 Alfred St., Stromness, Orkney (☎ **01856-850-025**), focuses on maritime history, including details about the World War I German fleet that roamed the Scapa Flow before being scuttled, and the ships of the Hudson Bay Company, which took Orcadians to Canada.

Fast Facts: Orkney and Shetland

Area Code

The area code for Kirkwall and Stromness is **01856**; Lerwick is **01595**. You need to dial the area code only if you're calling from outside the city you want to reach.

Emergencies

Dial ☎ **999** for police, fire, or ambulance.

Hospitals

The main hospitals on the islands are Balfour Hospital (☎ 01856-873-166), New Scapa Road, Kirkwall, Orkney, and Gilbert Bain Hospital (☎ 01595-743-300), Scalloway Road, Lerwick, Shetland.

Information

You can get information on visiting the islands from Orkney Islands Tourist Board, 6 Broad St., Kirkwall, Orkney (☎ 01856-872-856; www.visitorkney.com); or Shetland Islands Tourist Board, Market Cross, Lerwick, Shetland (☎ 01595-693-434; www.shetlandtourism.co.uk).

Mail

Post offices are at 15 Junction Rd., Kirkwall, Orkney (☎ 01856-872-974), and 46 Commercial St., Lerwick, Shetland (☎ 01595-693-201).

Part V
The Part of Tens

"Okay, we got one cherry lager with bitters and a pineapple slice, and one honey malt ale with cinnamon and an orange twist. You want these in pints or parfait glasses?"

In this part . . .

If you just want some quick listings of some of the best and most interesting spots in Scotland, you've come to the right place. Part V gives you the scoop on great Scottish golf courses, from the world-famous St. Andrews to some notable ones with which you may be less familiar. You can also find lists of the most evocative castles, engaging historic sites, and natural attractions that are likely to knock your socks off. If Scotland's famous and unique single-malt whiskies interest you, check out the rundown of distinctive distilleries that you can tour. You might find that after you've visited these locales, they become your favorites, too.

Chapter 21

Ten Outstanding Golf Courses

*I*t would be unfair to say *definitively* that the golf courses listed in this chapter are the ten best in Scotland. The country just has too many great courses. You would need to golf every day for nearly a year to hit all the courses. Each one in this chapter has its own special attraction. Some are more famous than others; some are more difficult than others. Remember, to play the championship courses, you need a bona fide and acceptable handicap. So here we go, in alphabetical order.

For every course, call ahead for information about tee times and requirements to play (if any exist).

Carnoustie

Although golfers have been playing here since 1560, somehow Carnoustie has remained one of Scotland's lesser-known championship courses. It's increasingly popular, in part because it has been the site of recent British Open tournaments (which people here just call the "Open"). The course has one of the toughest and longest finishes in the country.

Carnoustie, east of Dundee. Par 72. ☎ **01241-853-789.** www. carnoustiegolflinks.co.uk.

Gairloch Golf Club

It may be only 9 holes, but this course is still very much a tricky one. Combine that challenge to your driving and putting skills with a location along a golden beach and overlooking Skye and the Hebrides and you have a great course.

Gairloch. Par 35. ☎ **01445-712-407.** www.gairlochgolfclub.com.

Muirfield

Muirfield is the best championship course near Edinburgh, and it's regularly a location for qualifying play before the Open. If you're not an expert, you'll be more comfortable playing on one of the other courses near Gullane.

Muirfield. Par 71. ☎ **01620-842-123.** www.muirfield.org.uk.

Prestwick

The original home of the Open, this course remains a monument to the early days of golf. It has bumpy fairways, deep bunkers, and many blind shots, but this old-school course is well worth the time and the challenge.

Prestwick. Par 71. ☎ **01292-477-404.** www.prestwickgc.co.uk.

Royal Dornoch Course

This course's only downside is its location in the far north. You have plenty of room off the tee, but placing your drive depends greatly upon the winds. The course is challenging but accessible to nearly everyone.

Dornoch. Par 70. ☎ **01862-810-219.** www.royaldornoch.com.

Royal Troon

Despite popular belief, nonmembers (and women) aren't prohibited from playing this famous and fabulous course in Ayrshire on the Clyde Coast. The course has frequently hosted the Open, and each hole provides a challenge. The 8th hole, or "postage stamp," is the shortest in Open history. If you don't have the chops for Royal Troon, go to one of the excellent municipal courses nearby.

Troon. Par 71. ☎ **01292-311-555.** www.royaltroon.co.uk.

St. Andrews

 The Old Course at St. Andrews is arguably the most famous golf course in the world. All the "greats" of the sport have played here, apparently even Mary, Queen of Scots. This always-challenging seaside links golf course is the one in Scotland that most frequently hosts the Open. It's definitely the mecca of golf, if ever there was one.

St. Andrews. Par 72. ☎ **01334-466-666.** www.standrews.org.uk.

Traigh

This is perhaps the most picturesque 9-hole course in Scotland, and possibly in all of Europe. Just 3.2km (2 miles) up the road from Arisaig on the old highway, and set right along the country's most attractive shoreline, Traigh offers not only challenging golf (for a short course) but brilliant views, too.

Arisaig. Par 34. ☎ **01687-450-337.** www.traighgolf.co.uk.

Turnberry

The Ailsa Course at Turnberry is home to a fair amount of Open drama; golf heroes such as Jack Nicklaus, Tom Watson, and Greg Norman have all competed for the top prize here. The links-style course that runs along the Ayrshire seashore, against the backdrop of the grand Turnberry hotel (the Westin Turnberry Resort), is one of the most picturesque in Scotland. Book a room at the hotel to be guaranteed a tee time.

Turnberry. Par 72. ☎ **01655-331-000.** www.turnberry.co.uk.

Western Gailes

With its greens often tucked away in hollows, the course here requires finesse, accuracy, and precision. This natural links-style course (another qualifying venue for the Open) hugs the coastline less than an hour's drive from Glasgow and can be played practically year-round, because its sandy fairways and wind-swept greens drain quickly and the weather is generally moderate (if typically breezy).

Irvine. Par 72. ☎ **01294-311-649.** www.westerngailes.com.

Chapter 22

Ten Can't-Miss Castles and Historic Sites

● ●

In This Chapter

▶ Visiting the most impressive ancient monuments and medieval abbeys

▶ Discovering the most fascinating castles and historic ruins

● ●

*I*n a country with hundreds of ancient castles and ruins, choosing just ten of the best is certainly difficult. If you're a history buff or get a special charge out of walking in the footsteps of some of history's giants, put the attractions and locations in this chapter on your must-see list. But for each of these, you may prefer two others; remember, these are simply my own favorites.

Calanais Standing Stones

What some have called the "Stonehenge of Scotland," this impressive stone circle is one of the most significant archaeological finds of its kind in the entire U.K. (see Chapter 19). Much mystery surrounds the purpose and origin of these craggy stones (whose arrangement dates back to perhaps 3000 b.c.), but unlike their English cousins, here you can walk right up and touch them.

Callanish, Isle of Lewis, Outer Hebrides. ☎ **01851-621-422.** www. historic-scotland.gov.uk.

Castle Tioram

This ancient castle (pronounced *cheer*-rum) on a tide-swept island in Loch Moidart (see Chapter 18) has one of the most romantic — and isolated — settings in the Western Highlands. At lower tides you can walk across the sands to the castle. Although interior access to the ruins is not allowed, you can scale the small hill upon which the castle sits and let your imagination do the rest.

Near Blain, Ardnamurchan Peninsula, Highlands.

Culloden Moor Battlefield

British forces loyal to the Hanoverian king in London defeated Bonnie Prince Charlie's Jacobite rebellion here in 1746, ending an impressive but ultimately unsuccessful rebellion in an attempt to restore the Stuart crown. An impressive new visitor center with museum provides the complete history of the battle and its consequences. Flip to Chapter 18 for more on this historical site.

Near Inverness, Highlands. ☎ **01463-790-607.** www.nts.org.uk.

Culzean Castle

A mansion more than a castle, Culzean remains a classic example of the work of Robert Adam, Scotland's preeminent architect in the Georgian era. In addition to the castle, Culzean offers lots of parkland and gardens to explore. You can find details on Culzean and its surroundings in Chapter 15.

South of Ayr, South Ayrshire. ☎ **01655-884-455.** www.culzean experience.org.

Doune Castle

Made famous thanks to the film *Monty Python and the Holy Grail,* Doune Castle is one of the best because it has been modestly restored, giving visitors a feel for what life in a medieval castle truly was like during the heyday of this classic keep. See Chapter 16 for more details on Doune.

Doune, near Stirling. ☎ **01786-841-742.** www.historic-scotland. gov.uk.

Eilean Donan Castle

After Edinburgh Castle, Eilean Donan is probably the most photographed castle in Scotland. It has been restored and offers some interesting exhibits as well as a good bit of history, including defense of the area from Vikings and serving as a Jacobite stronghold. See Chapter 18 for more information on this castle.

Dornie, Kyle of Lochalsh, Highlands. ☎ **01599-555-202.** www.eilean donancastle.com.

Glasgow Cathedral

Glasgow Cathedral is the oldest pre-Reformation cathedral still standing soundly on the Scottish mainland. (The northern island of Orkney has another from the same era.) It marks the place where the earliest settlements of this industrial powerhouse were established. Flip to Chapter 12 for details.

Townhead, Glasgow. ☎ 0141-552-6891. www.historic-scotland.gov.uk.

Melrose Abbey

Of all the historic abbeys in the Borders region (see Chapter 14), the one in Melrose may be the most interesting. Built in the 12th century, it inspired Sir Walter Scott (who made sure it was secured), and it's also the place where the heart of King Robert the Bruce was buried.

Melrose, the Borders. ☎ 01896-822-562. www.historic-scotland.gov.uk.

Skara Brae

This prehistoric beachside village in West Mainland, Orkney, is the best of its type in northern Europe. Stone passages link several rooms, all furnished in stone, from the beds (upon which its Stone Age residents would lay straw) to fireplaces and even storage boxes. Go to Chapter 20 for details.

West Mainland, Orkney. ☎ 01856-841-815. www.historic-scotland.gov.uk.

Stirling Castle

In the central belt, Edinburgh Castle gets most of the attention, but the castle at Stirling is the best one to visit. There is a lot of work going on to restore all the various bits of this ancient seat of royalty — as historically essential as any castle in Scotland, in many ways the most important one in the country. Go to Chapter 16 for details.

Old Town, Stirling. ☎ 01786-450-000. www.historic-scotland.gov.uk.

Chapter 23

Ten Distinctive Distilleries

In This Chapter

▶ "Nosing" about for the good stuff

▶ Taking tours of distilleries large and small

*W*hisky is undoubtedly Scotland's best-known export. A good deal of the distilleries across the country are open to the public, many with tours of their facilities that explain exactly how whisky is made (and how it's different from American or Canadian whiskeys) and teach visitors how to "nose" Scotch properly. This chapter lists some of the best to visit.

Caol Ila

On Scotland's so-called Whisky Island, Islay (*eye*-la), Caol Ila (cull-*ee*-la) has to have one of the best settings for a distillery, nestled at the base of a hill at the shore just across from the isle of Jura. While it produces single malts, it also distills spirits for Johnnie Walker's premium blends.

Near Pork Askaig, Isle of Islay, Argyll. ☎ **01496-302-760.**

Dalwhinnie

Originally called Strathspey distillery, Dalwhinnie has the distinction of being Scotland's highest distillery, in elevation, at about 326m (1,073 ft.) above sea level. The tour of this distillery is good, too, but perhaps not on par with either the dramatic setting, where you may see snow on surrounding hills in early summer, or the sparkling white buildings with their pagoda-type roofs.

Dalwhinnie, South of Inverness, Highlands. ☎ **01540-672-219.**

Edradour

Edradour is among the smallest distilleries in Scotland, putting out only 12 casks a week, and one of the last remaining so-called farm distilleries that used to be commonplace in Perthshire. Edradour is produced by a small staff, using traditional methods and seemingly antique equipment.

Near Pitlochry, Perthshire. ☎ 01796-472-095.

Glenfiddich

Readers who haven't heard of Glenfiddich probably have little interest in this chapter. Glenfiddich is one of the three biggest selling whiskies in the world, which explains why some 125,000 visitors come here annually. It was the first distillery to recognize the potential of tourism and open a visitor center, and it's a good choice for those who want a well-organized tour of a large, modern distillery.

Near Dufftown, Speyside, Northeast. ☎ 01340-820-373.

Glen Grant

Beautiful gardens are a highlight of a visit to this fine Morayshire distillery. After the tour, take your dram of whisky (apparently a favorite of Italians) outside and taste it cut with a drop or two of water from the burbling Glen Grant burn.

Rothes, near Elgin, Speyside, Northeast. ☎ 01542-783-318.

Glenlivet

The Glenlivet is among the most popular single malts sold. The tours here have a reputation for being the most entertaining and informative of any in Scotland. Thus, if you're in the area and can visit only one distillery, you may want to make it Glenlivet.

Near Tomintoul, Northeast. ☎ 01542-783-220.

The Glenturret

By most accounts, this is the oldest distillery in Scotland. Illegal distilling at this site began as early as 1717. Because visitors can quite easily get here and back in an afternoon drive from either Glasgow or Edinburgh, Glenturret is very popular, but the staff manages to handle the crowds adeptly.

Near Crieff, Tayside. ☎ 01764-656-565.

Laphroaig

For fans of peaty flavors, Laphroaig from the isle of Islay — Scotland's whisky island — is often a preference and is perhaps the best known of all island single malts. The taste of this whisky carries hints not only of the local peat but of the sea air as well.

Near Port Ellen, Islay, Argyll. ☎ **01496-302-418.**

Strathisla

This fine single malt is better known for being the main ingredient in Chivas Regal, one of the most popular blends in the world. The distillery tour here usually ends with an informative and unique "nosing" of different whiskies from the various regions of Scotland.

Keith, Speyside, Northeast. ☎ **01542-783-044.**

Talisker

The only distillery on the rather large island of Skye, the Talisker tour is among the best in the country. Talisker produces whisky with the peaty flavor of the island. In addition to producing its own distinctive brand, Talisker produces whisky used in popular blends such as Johnnie Walker.

Carbost, Skye, Inner Hebrides. ☎ **01478-614-308.**

Chapter 24

Ten Stunning Natural Attractions

*Y*es, Scotland has a pair of vibrant cities, loads of historic monuments, numerous castles, dozens of distilleries, and gobs of golf courses. But the country is also home to some of the prettiest countryside you could ever imagine. Whether you like to hike, watch birds, or just hunt for perfect photographic backdrops, take in as many of these top nature spots as you can.

Ardnamurchan Peninsula

Isolated but reasonably easy to reach (in contrast to Knoydart, farther north), this picturesque western Highland peninsula forms the most westerly region of the entire British mainland. There are wind-swept bays and beaches with plenty of opportunities for hiking. Go to Chapter 18 for details.

West of Fort William, Highlands.

Arthur's Seat and Holyrood Park

It's rare to find a hike of such natural beauty in any city. But Edinburgh is no ordinary metropolis. You can walk to the top of Arthur's Seat or cheat and drive to the park — either way, you find plenty to take in, especially the views. Chapter 11 contains more information on this Edinburgh landmark.

At the foot of the Royal Mile, Edinburgh.

Cuillin Hills

These dark, brooding hills make a stunning backdrop on the Isle of Skye. However, you might want to also get out and hike around in a bit of the region, too. Some of the trails are easy, but don't attempt to climb the peaks unless you're an experienced hiker. You can find details on this area in Chapter 19.

Isle of Skye, the Hebrides.

Glen Coe

This lovely Highland valley runs some 16km (10 miles) and is fairly breathtaking every bit of the way — even though it's best known as the site of a 17th-century massacre. You can climb Ossian's Ladder, a trail up the hillside, or other equally strenuous paths on your own — or opt for a more moderate ranger-led hike. See Chapter 18 for additional information on the valley.

Between King's House and Ballchulish, Highlands.

Inverewe Garden

I'm cheating a bit with this recommendation, because Scotland's many marvelous gardens aren't exactly natural attractions as much as man-made wonders. But no matter how it came to be, Inverewe Garden is one of the loveliest gardens in the country, showing off some glories of nature: towering trees, flowering shrubs, and almost-tropical species that survive thanks to the warming North Atlantic flow from the Gulf of Mexico. For a more complete description of this garden and for visitor information, check out Chapter 18.

Near Poolewe, Wester Ross, Highlands.

Loch Lomond

I list it largely because it is so accessible. Only a 45-minute drive north from Glasgow puts you at this excellent body of fresh water. The pretty scenery is best seen by a boat tour, but plenty of spots along its shores make for good picnic stops, as well. Coming here allows you to get a taste of the Highlands without straying too far from the big city. Flip to Chapter 16 for details.

Northwest of Glasgow, West Dunbartonshire.

Loch Ness

Monster hunting aside, this huge loch in the middle of Scotland is a lovely natural wonder. Deep, dark, and brooding, it's little wonder that people believe Loch Ness hides a legendary beast. The best way to see it is by boat. Find out more about it in Chapter 18.

Between Fort George and Inverness, Highlands.

Sands of Morar

Between Arisaig and Mallaig on Scotland's beautiful west coast, the beaches of Morar are so spectacular that they've been used in several movies, most notably Bill Forsyth's *Local Hero*. The light is magical in the evenings, especially during summer when the sun slowly sets in the northwestern skies. Find out more about the Sands of Morar in Chapter 18.

Near Mallaig, Road to the Isles, Highlands.

Sandwood Bay

Within the nature conservation area of the Sandwood Estate, this beach is the most pristine on the Scottish mainland. In part that's because you need to walk for about 90 minutes from the nearest road to reach it. See Chapter 18 for more details.

Near Blairmore, Sutherland, Highlands.

Staffa and Fingal's Cave

Near Mull, the rock formations and cathedral-like columns of Fingal's Cave on the Isle of Staffa were enough to inspire Mendelssohn's *Hebridean Overture*. In addition to the geological beauty, the puffin colony here is a bonus. Go to Chapter 19 for details on boat tours of Fingal's Cave.

Staffa, the Hebrides.

Appendix

Quick Concierge

Fast Facts

American Express

The Edinburgh office is at 69 George St., at Frederick Street (☎ 0131-718-2505). It's open Monday through Friday from 9 a.m. to 5:30 p.m. and Saturday from 9 a.m. to 4 p.m. In Glasgow, the American Express Travel Service office is at 66 Gordon St. (☎ 0141-225-2905). It's open Monday through Friday from 8:30 a.m. to 5:30 p.m. and Saturday 9 a.m. to noon.

ATMs

In Scotland, ATMs (automated teller machines) are called *cash points* or *cash machines*. In the cities, as well as in many of the larger towns, ATMs now often connect to international systems such as Cirrus or PLUS. Many will give cash advances on major credit cards as well.

Business Hours

Most businesses are open Monday through Saturday from 9 or 9:30 a.m. to 5 or 5:30 p.m., with some exceptions. Many businesses and shops are closed Sunday, although many shops in the cities open on Sunday afternoons. Most cities also have extended shopping hours on Thursday until 8 p.m. Outside of Edinburgh and Glasgow, businesses may close for lunch, generally from 12:30 to 1:30 p.m.

Banks are normally open from 9 or 10 a.m. until about 5 p.m. on weekdays. Banks are good places to exchange currency and get credit card cash advances.

Restaurants and pubs have different restrictions on hours of operation depending upon their licensing, which is controlled by local councils. Although some bars may not open until late afternoon, most serve drinks from noon to midnight and maybe later on weekends. Some pubs in residential and rural areas, however, close at 11 p.m. Many restaurants stop serving food at 2:30 p.m. and resume at 5:30 or 6 p.m. Nightclubs in cities and larger towns have late-night hours, staying open until between 1 and 3 a.m. — but doors may not open until 10 p.m.

Cameras and Film

Most pharmacies sell photo supplies and many have photo-developing services, as well. One-hour film processing is available in larger cities. These services and products are more expensive abroad than in the U.S. If you have to buy photo supplies or film while you're in Scotland, go to a camera shop or department store. Never buy film from a souvenir stand near a tourist attraction, where the markup is high.

Credit Cards

The toll-free emergency numbers for major credit cards are: Visa ☎ 0800-891-725; MasterCard ☎ 0800-964-767; American Express ☎ 0800-700-700; and Diner's Club ☎ 702-797-5532 (members can call collect).

Currency Exchange

You can change money at any place with the sign bureau de change. You find these signs at banks, which give you the best rates; major post office branches; and many hotels and travel agencies. (See Chapter 5 for more information on dealing with money in Scotland.)

Customs

U.K. Customs restricts the value of goods you can bring into Scotland to about £150. U.S. citizens returning to Scotland after an absence of at least 48 hours are allowed to bring back, once every 30 days, $800 worth of merchandise duty-free.

Driving

In Scotland, cars travel on the left side of the road. (See Chapter 7 for more details on driving in Scotland.)

Drugstores

Drugstores are called *pharmacies* or *chemists* in Scotland. The regulations for over-the-counter and prescription drugs differ from those in the U.S., so you may not find commercial pharmaceuticals or your preferred medicine. Consider bringing your own products from the U.S.

Electricity

The electric current in Scotland is 240 volts AC, which is different from the U.S. current, so most small appliances brought from the U.S., such as hair dryers and razors, don't work (and the current could damage the appliance). If you're considering bringing your laptop or iron from home, check the voltage first to see if it has a range between 110v and 240v. If the voltage doesn't have a range, the only option is to purchase an expensive converter. If the voltage does have a higher range, then you still need to buy an outlet adapter because your prongs won't fit in the Scottish sockets. You can buy an adapter

for about $10 at an appliance store or even at the airport.

Embassies and Consulates

Embassies are located in London, the capital of Great Britain. Edinburgh has consulates for Australia (69 George St.; ☎ 0131-624-3700), Canada (30 Lothian Rd.; ☎ 0131-245-6013), and the United States (3 Regents Terrace; ☎ 0131-556-8315).

Emergencies

For any emergency, contact the police or an ambulance by calling ☎ **999** from any phone. You can also call the National Health Service Helpline, ☎ 0800-22-4488, which offers health-related advice and assistance from 8 a.m. to 10 p.m. daily. (See Chapter 9 for details on accessing health care in Scotland.) Every city and regional chapter lists local hospitals. For emergencies, treatment is free, although you will be billed for long stays.

Internet Access

Many hotels offer Internet access (though it's usually rather expensive), and Internet cafes are popular, especially near central railway stations. See the major city and regional chapters for more information.

Language

English is the principal language spoken in Scotland, although heavy accents and local vernacular (especially words used by lowland Scots) can make it difficult to comprehend. Ask the natives to speak more slowly if you can't understand them. Gaelic is spoken in the Highlands and islands, where signs are frequently in both Gaelic and English.

Liquor Laws

The minimum drinking age in Scotland is 18. Liquor stores, called *off-licenses* (or *off-sales*) sell spirits, beer, and wine and generally operate from 11 a.m. to 10 p.m.

Maps

Decent street maps and city plans are sold at most tourist information centers and major newsstands. For detailed *ordinance survey* maps, try the major booksellers such as Waterstone's or Borders.

Police

For emergencies, dial ☎ **999**.

Post Office

Most branches of the post office are open Monday through Friday from 9 a.m. to 5 p.m. and Saturday from 9 a.m. to noon. Smaller, rural branches may be open weekdays from 9 a.m. to 1 p.m. and 2:15 to 5:30 p.m., as well as Saturday from 9 a.m. to 1 p.m. Many post offices close early on one day of the week, but how early and what day depends on the office.

For information on mail services in Scotland and the U.K., call ☎ 08457-740-740 or visit www.royalmail.com. See the major city and regional chapters for more post office information.

Safety

Violent-crime rates are low in Scotland. There are few guns in the country, and most police officers don't carry them, either. As a tourist, the most important thing you can do is guard yourself against theft. Pickpockets look for people who seem to have the most money on them and who appear to know the least about where they are. Be extra careful on crowded trains in the big cities and when taking money from ATMs.

Smoking

In April 2006, a ban on smoking in all enclosed public spaces, including business offices, restaurants, and pubs, went into effect. Smoking was already prohibited on all trains and buses.

Taxes

A consumption tax of 20 percent is put on pretty much all goods and services. It's called VAT (value-added tax), and it works like local sales taxes do in the United States. But tourists are entitled to a partial refund (see Chapter 5 for more information). VAT is nonrefundable for services such as hotels, meals, and car rentals.

Telephones

The country code for Scotland is 44. To make international calls from Scotland, dial **00** and then the country code, local code, and telephone number. The U.S. and Canadian country code is **1**, Australia is **61**, and New Zealand is **63**. If you can't find a number, a directory is available by dialing a variety of numbers (thanks to privatization of the service), including ☎ 118-811 or ☎ 118-800 for domestic numbers and ☎ 118-505 for international numbers.

Scotland has pay phones that accept coins and credit cards, although the use of cellphones (called *mobiles*) means you see fewer pay phones. If you're interested in renting a cellphone to use during your visit, check out Chapter 10 for more information.

Time Zone

Scotland follows Greenwich Mean Time, which is five hours ahead of Eastern Standard Time in the United States (eight hours ahead of Pacific Standard Time). So, when it's noon in New York, it's 5 p.m. in Glasgow. The clocks are set forward by one hour for British *summertime* in late March, which expires at the end of October. The high latitude blesses the country with long days in the summer, with sunset as late as 10 or even 11 p.m. But the opposite is true in winter, when the sun sets as early as 3:30 or 4 p.m.

Weather Updates

For weather forecasts of the day and 24 hours in advance, and for severe road-condition warnings, call the Met Office at ☎ 0870-900-0100. An advisor offers forecasts for the entire region and beyond at your request.

Toll-Free Numbers and Web Sites

U.S. airlines

American Airlines
☎ 800-433-7300 (in U.S. and Canada)
☎ 020-7365-0777 (in U.K.)
www.aa.com

Continental Airlines
☎ 800-523-3273 (in U.S. and Canada)
☎ 0845-607-6760 (in U.K.)
www.continental.com

Delta Air Lines
☎ 800-221-1212 (in U.S. or Canada)
☎ 0845-600-0950 (in U.K.)
www.delta.com

Northwest Airlines
☎ 800-225-2525 (in U.S.)
☎ 870-0507-4074 (in U.K.)
www.nwa.com

United Airlines
☎ 800-864-8331 (in U.S. and Canada)
☎ 0845-844-4777 (in U.K.)
www.united.com

US Airways
☎ 800-428-4322 (in U.S. and Canada)
☎ 0845-600-3300 (in U.K.)
www.usairways.com

Major international airlines

Air France
☎ 800-237-2747 (in U.S.)
☎ 800-375-8723 (in U.S. and Canada)
☎ 0870-142-4343 (in U.K.)
www.airfrance.com

Air New Zealand
☎ 800-262-1234 (in U.S.)
☎ 800-663-5494 (in Canada)
☎ 0800-028-4149 (in U.K.)
www.airnewzealand.com

Alitalia
☎ 800-223-5730 (in U.S.)
☎ 800-361-8336 (in Canada)
☎ 0870-608-6003 (in U.K.)
www.alitalia.com

British Airways
☎ 800-247-9297 (in U.S. and Canada)
☎ 0870-850-9850 (in U.K.)
www.british-airways.com

Icelandair
☎ 800-223-5500, ext. 2, prompt 1 (in U.S. and Canada)
☎ 0845-758-1111 (in U.K.)
www.icelandair.com
www.icelandair.co.uk (in U.K.)

Lufthansa
☎ 800-399-5838 (in U.S.)
☎ 800-563-5954 (in Canada)
☎ 0870-837-7747 (in U.K.)
www.lufthansa.com

Qantas Airways
☎ 800-227-4500 (in U.S.)
☎ 084-5774-7767 (in U.K. and Canada)
☎ 13-13-13 (in Australia)
www.qantas.com

Budget airlines

Aer Lingus
☎ 800-474-7424 (in U.S. and Canada)
☎ 0870-876-5000 (in U.K.)
www.aerlingus.com

BMI Baby
☎ 0871-224-0224 (in U.K.)
☎ 870-126-6726 (in U.S.)
www.bmibaby.com

easyJet
☎ 870-600-0000 (in U.S.)
☎ 0905-560-7777 (in U.K.)
www.easyjet.com

Ryanair
☎ 081-830-3030 (in Ireland)
☎ 0871-246-0000 (in U.K.)
www.ryanair.com

Car-rental agencies

Alamo
☎ 800-GO-ALAMO (800-462-5266)
www.alamo.com

Auto Europe
☎ 888-223-5555 (in U.S. and Canada)
☎ 0800-2235-5555 (in U.K.)
www.autoeurope.com

Avis
☎ 800-331-1212 (in U.S. and Canada)
☎ 0844-581-8181 (in U.K.)
www.avis.com

Budget
☎ 800-527-0700 (in U.S.)
☎ 800-268-8900 (in Canada)
☎ 0870-156-5656 (in U.K.)
www.budget.com

Dollar
☎ 800-800-4000 (in U.S.)
☎ 800-848-8268 (in Canada)
☎ 0808-234-7524 (in U.K.)
www.dollar.com

Enterprise
☎ 800-261-7331 (in U.S.)
☎ 514-355-4028 (in Canada)
☎ 0129-360-9090 (in U.K.)
www.enterprise.com

Hertz
☎ 800-645-3131 (North America)
☎ 800-654-3001 (international reservations)
www.hertz.com

National
☎ 877-222-9058
www.nationalcar.com

Thrifty
☎ 800-367-2277
☎ 918-669-2168 (international reservations)
www.thrifty.com

Major hotel & motel chains

Best Western International
☎ 800-780-7234 (in U.S. and Canada)
☎ 0800-393-130 (in U.K.)
www.bestwestern.com

Clarion Hotels
☎ 800-CLARION (252-7466) or 877-424-6423 (in U.S. and Canada)
☎ 0800-444-444 (in U.K.)
www.choicehotels.com

Comfort Inns
☎ 800-228-5150 (in U.S.)
☎ 0800-444-444 (in U.K.)
www.ComfortInn.com

Courtyard by Marriott
☎ 888-236-2427 (in U.S.)
☎ 0800-221-222 (in U.K.)
www.marriott.com/courtyard

Crowne Plaza Hotels
☎ 888-303-1746
www.ichotelsgroup.com/crowneplaza

Days Inn
☎ 800-329-7466 (in U.S.)
☎ 0800-280-400 (in U.K.)
www.daysinn.com

Four Seasons
☎ 800-819-5053 (in U.S. and Canada)
☎ 0800-6488-6488 (in U.K.)
www.fourseasons.com

Hilton Hotels
☎ 800-HILTONS (800-445-8667)
(in U.S. and Canada)
☎ 0870-590-9090 (in U.K.)
www.hilton.com

Holiday Inn
☎ 800-315-2621 (in U.S. and Canada)
☎ 0800-405-060 (in U.K.)
www.holidayinn.com

InterContinental Hotels & Resorts
☎ 800-424-6835 (in U.S. and Canada)
☎ 0800-1800-1800 (in U.K.)
www.ichotelsgroup.com

Marriott
☎ 877-236-2427 (in U.S. and Canada)
☎ 0800-221-222 (in U.K.)
www.marriott.com

Omni Hotels
☎ 888-444-OMNI (6664)
www.omnihotels.com

Quality
☎ 877-424-6423 (in U.S. and Canada)
☎ 0800-444-444 (in U.K.)
www.QualityInn.com

Radisson Hotels & Resorts
☎ 888-201-1718 (in U.S. and Canada)
☎ 0800-374-411 (in U.K.)
www.radisson.com

Ramada Worldwide
☎ 888-2-RAMADA (272-6232; in U.S. and Canada)
☎ 0808-100-0783 (in U.K.)
www.ramada.com

Sheraton Hotels & Resorts
☎ 800-325-3535 (in U.S.)
☎ 800-543-4300 (in Canada)
☎ 0800-3253-5353 (in U.K.)
www.starwoodhotels.com/sheraton

Travelodge
☎ 800-578-7878
www.travelodge.com

Westin Hotels & Resorts
☎ 800-937-8461 (in U.S. and Canada)
☎ 0800-3259-5959 (in U.K.)
www.starwoodhotels.com/westin

Where to Get More Information

If you're looking for more information on Scotland, do not go to the tourist board for Great Britain. Start with the **Scottish Tourist Board** or, as it prefers to be called these days, **VisitScotland** (☎ 0845–225-5121; www.visitscotland.com). The Web site has information on accommodations, attractions, and general topics; and you can get details on special offers and promotions. You can also find recommended attractions as well as listings for hotels, guesthouses, B&Bs, self-catering lodging, RV and camping sites, serviced apartments, and hostels. Keep in mind, though, that hotels, restaurants, and attractions generally pay to be included in these listings.

Plenty of Web sites offer helpful and interesting information on Scotland; listed below are a few of the better ones. (Remember that things can change quickly in cyberspace, so a site may have been transformed by the time you read this.)

✔ www.geo.ed.ac.uk/scotgaz/scotland.html: A one-stop shop for info on Scotland's shopping, recreation, attractions, weather, tours, and more. This site also has good interactive maps.

✔ www.scotland.org.uk: An all-purpose site for travel in Scotland.

✔ www.geo.ed.ac.uk/home/scotland/scotland.html: A great place to get Scottish history, maps, and demographics. You can also search the encyclopedic reference guide on this Web site. *Warning:* Turn the sound off (or at least turn the volume down) on your computer before opening this site — a headache-inducing soundtrack of Scottish Muzak plays nonstop while the site is open.

Index

BUSINESS, CAREERS & PERSONAL FINANCE

**Accounting For Dummies,
4th Edition***
978-0-470-24600-9

**Bookkeeping Workbook
For Dummies**†
978-0-470-16983-4

Commodities For Dummies
978-0-470-04928-0

Doing Business in China For Dummies
978-0-470-04929-7

E-Mail Marketing For Dummies
978-0-470-19087-6

**Job Interviews For Dummies,
3rd Edition***†
978-0-470-17748-8

**Personal Finance Workbook
For Dummies***†
978-0-470-09933-9

Real Estate License Exams For Dummies
978-0-7645-7623-2

Six Sigma For Dummies
978-0-7645-6798-8

**Small Business Kit For Dummies,
2nd Edition***†
978-0-7645-5984-6

Telephone Sales For Dummies
978-0-470-16836-3

BUSINESS PRODUCTIVITY & MICROSOFT OFFICE

Access 2007 For Dummies
978-0-470-03649-5

Excel 2007 For Dummies
978-0-470-03737-9

Office 2007 For Dummies
978-0-470-00923-9

Outlook 2007 For Dummies
978-0-470-03830-7

PowerPoint 2007 For Dummies
978-0-470-04059-1

Project 2007 For Dummies
978-0-470-03651-8

QuickBooks 2008 For Dummies
978-0-470-18470-7

Quicken 2008 For Dummies
978-0-470-17473-9

**Salesforce.com For Dummies,
2nd Edition**
978-0-470-04893-1

Word 2007 For Dummies
978-0-470-03658-7

EDUCATION, HISTORY, REFERENCE & TEST PREPARATION

**African American History
For Dummies**
978-0-7645-5469-8

Algebra For Dummies
978-0-7645-5325-7

Algebra Workbook For Dummies
978-0-7645-8467-1

Art History For Dummies
978-0-470-09910-0

ASVAB For Dummies, 2nd Edition
978-0-470-10671-6

British Military History For Dummies
978-0-470-03213-8

Calculus For Dummies
978-0-7645-2498-1

**Canadian History For Dummies,
2nd Edition**
978-0-470-83656-9

Geometry Workbook For Dummies
978-0-471-79940-5

**The SAT I For Dummies,
6th Edition**
978-0-7645-7193-0

Series 7 Exam For Dummies
978-0-470-09932-2

World History For Dummies
978-0-7645-5242-7

FOOD, HOME, GARDEN, HOBBIES & HOME

Bridge For Dummies, 2nd Edition
978-0-471-92426-5

**Coin Collecting For Dummies,
2nd Edition**
978-0-470-22275-1

**Cooking Basics For Dummies,
3rd Edition**
978-0-7645-7206-7

Drawing For Dummies
978-0-7645-5476-6

**Etiquette For Dummies,
2nd Edition**
978-0-470-10672-3

Gardening Basics For Dummies*†
978-0-470-03749-2

Knitting Patterns For Dummies
978-0-470-04556-5

Living Gluten-Free For Dummies†
978-0-471-77383-2

**Painting Do-It-Yourself
For Dummies**
978-0-470-17533-0

HEALTH, SELF HELP, PARENTING & PETS

Anger Management For Dummies
978-0-470-03715-7

**Anxiety & Depression Workbook
For Dummies**
978-0-7645-9793-0

Dieting For Dummies, 2nd Edition
978-0-7645-4149-0

**Dog Training For Dummies,
2nd Edition**
978-0-7645-8418-3

Horseback Riding For Dummies
978-0-470-09719-9

Infertility For Dummies†
978-0-470-11518-3

**Meditation For Dummies
with CD-ROM, 2nd Edition**
978-0-471-77774-8

**Post-Traumatic Stress Disorder
For Dummies**
978-0-470-04922-8

**Puppies For Dummies,
2nd Edition**
978-0-470-03717-1

**Thyroid For Dummies,
2nd Edition**†
978-0-471-78755-6

Type 1 Diabetes For Dummies*†
978-0-470-17811-9

* Separate Canadian edition also available
† Separate U.K. edition also available

 **WILEY**

INTERNET & DIGITAL MEDIA

AdWords For Dummies
978-0-470-15252-2

Blogging For Dummies,
2nd Edition
978-0-470-23017-6

Digital Photography All-in-One
Desk Reference For Dummies,
3rd Edition
978-0-470-03743-0

Digital Photography For Dummies,
5th Edition
978-0-7645-9802-9

Digital SLR Cameras & Photography
For Dummies, 2nd Edition
978-0-470-14927-0

eBay Business All-in-One Desk
Reference For Dummies
978-0-7645-8438-1

eBay For Dummies, 5th Edition*
978-0-470-04529-9

eBay Listings That Sell For Dummies
978-0-471-78912-3

Facebook For Dummies
978-0-470-26273-3

The Internet For Dummies,
11th Edition
978-0-470-12174-0

Investing Online For Dummies,
5th Edition
978-0-7645-8456-5

iPod & iTunes For Dummies,
5th Edition
978-0-470-17474-6

MySpace For Dummies
978-0-470-09529-4

Podcasting For Dummies
978-0-471-74898-4

Search Engine Optimization
For Dummies, 2nd Edition
978-0-471-97998-2

Second Life For Dummies
978-0-470-18025-9

Starting an eBay Business
For Dummies,3rd Edition†
978-0-470-14924-9

GRAPHICS, DESIGN & WEB DEVELOPMENT

Adobe Creative Suite 3 Design
Premium All-in-One Desk Reference
For Dummies
978-0-470-11724-8

Adobe Web Suite CS3 All-in-One
Desk Reference For Dummies
978-0-470-12099-6

AutoCAD 2008 For Dummies
978-0-470-11650-0

Building a Web Site For Dummies,
3rd Edition
978-0-470-14928-7

Creating Web Pages All-in-One Desk
Reference For Dummies,
3rd Edition
978-0-470-09629-1

Creating Web Pages For Dummies,
8th Edition
978-0-470-08030-6

Dreamweaver CS3 For Dummies
978-0-470-11490-2

Flash CS3 For Dummies
978-0-470-12100-9

Google SketchUp For Dummies
978-0-470-13744-4

InDesign CS3 For Dummies
978-0-470-11865-8

Photoshop CS3 All-in-One
Desk Reference For Dummies
978-0-470-11195-6

Photoshop CS3 For Dummies
978-0-470-11193-2

Photoshop Elements 5
For Dummies
978-0-470-09810-3

SolidWorks For Dummies
978-0-7645-9555-4

Visio 2007 For Dummies
978-0-470-08983-5

Web Design For Dummies,
2nd Edition
978-0-471-78117-2

Web Sites Do-It-Yourself
For Dummies
978-0-470-16903-2

Web Stores Do-It-Yourself
For Dummies
978-0-470-17443-2

LANGUAGES, RELIGION & SPIRITUALITY

Arabic For Dummies
978-0-471-77270-5

Chinese For Dummies, Audio Set
978-0-470-12766-7

French For Dummies
978-0-7645-5193-2

German For Dummies
978-0-7645-5195-6

Hebrew For Dummies
978-0-7645-5489-6

Ingles Para Dummies
978-0-7645-5427-8

Italian For Dummies, Audio Set
978-0-470-09586-7

Italian Verbs For Dummies
978-0-471-77389-4

Japanese For Dummies
978-0-7645-5429-2

Latin For Dummies
978-0-7645-5431-5

Portuguese For Dummies
978-0-471-78738-9

Russian For Dummies
978-0-471-78001-4

Spanish Phrases For Dummies
978-0-7645-7204-3

Spanish For Dummies
978-0-7645-5194-9

Spanish For Dummies,
Audio Set
978-0-470-09585-0

The Bible For Dummies
978-0-7645-5296-0

Catholicism For Dummies
978-0-7645-5391-2

The Historical Jesus
For Dummies
978-0-470-16785-4

Islam For Dummies
978-0-7645-5503-9

Spirituality For Dummies,
2nd Edition
978-0-470-19142-2

NETWORKING AND PROGRAMMING

ASP.NET 3.5 For Dummies
978-0-470-19592-5

C# 2008 For Dummies
978-0-470-19109-5

Hacking For Dummies, 2nd Edition
978-0-470-05235-8

Home Networking
For Dummies, 4th Edition
978-0-470-11806-1

Java For Dummies, 4th Edition
978-0-470-08716-9

Microsoft® SQL Server™ 2008
All-in-One Desk Reference For Dummies
978-0-470-17954-3

Networking All-in-One Desk Reference
For Dummies, 2nd Edition
978-0-7645-9939-2

Networking For Dummies,
8th Edition
978-0-470-05620-2

SharePoint 2007
For Dummies
978-0-470-09941-4

Wireless Home Networking
For Dummies, 2nd Edition
978-0-471-74940-0